# INFORMATION SYSTEMS CONCEPTS FOR MANAGEMENT

# McGraw-Hill Series in Management Information Systems

Gordon B. Davis, *Consulting Editor*

# INFORMATION SYSTEMS CONCEPTS FOR MANAGEMENT

**THIRD EDITION**

## Henry C. Lucas, Jr.

Graduate School of Business Administration
New York University

**McGRAW-HILL BOOK COMPANY**

New York   St. Louis   San Francisco   Auckland   Bogotá
Hamburg   London   Madrid   Mexico   Montreal   New Delhi
Panama   Paris   São Paulo   Singapore   Sydney   Tokyo   Toronto

# INFORMATION SYSTEMS CONCEPTS FOR MANAGEMENT
## INTERNATIONAL EDITION

Copyright © 1986
Exclusive rights by McGraw-Hill Book Co—Singapore for
manufacture and export. This book cannot be re-exported
from the country to which it is consigned by McGraw-Hill.
2nd Printing 1987

This book was set in Times Roman by Black Dot, Inc. (ECU).
The editor was Christina Mediate;
The production supervisor was Diane Renda.
Project supervision was done by The Total Book.

**Library of Congress Cataloging in Publication Data**


Lucas, Henry C.
Information systems concepts for management.

(McGraw-Hill series in management information systems)
Bibliography: p.
Includes index
1. Management information systems. I. Title. II. Series
T58.6.L815    1986        658.4'0388    85-12831
ISBN 0-07-038931-4


**When ordering this title use ISBN 0-07-Y66506-0**


Printed in Singapore by
Chong Moh Offset Printing Pte Ltd

To Jonathan

# CONTENTS

# PREFACE

The purpose of this book is to help students of management learn the concepts of computer-based information systems. Managers allocate resources to the development and operation of computer-based systems and often use systems themselves. Managers make critical decisions about information systems: How can we use information processing strategically? What applications areas are to be emphasized? What should a plan for information processing in the organization contain? Which specific alternative for a proposed system will be implemented? What equipment should the organization acquire? How should one charge for and monitor information processing?

Many managers are users of information systems and work directly with computer input and output: they may also supervise people who work with microcomputers and information systems. These individuals come in contact with colleagues in the computer department, and the information services department reports to a manager in the organization.

Thus, the modern manager is confronted with many information-systems-related decisions and must understand issues in the management of information systems. This text is written from the perspective of the student who will be a user of information systems: It is not intended for the student who specializes in computer-based systems.

The text has been developed from M.B.A. and executive courses at Stanford and New York University. The students viewed these courses as their only exposure to computer-based information systems. One of the main goals of the book, therefore, is to help students majoring in such functional areas as finance, accounting, or marketing learn to make intelligent decisions about information systems and computers. No background on the part of the student is assumed, though it is helpful to provide some hands on computing experience with the course. For example, at NYU students have completed a proficiency course prior to taking the course using this text. The proficiency exercise shows how to use a time-sharing terminal and editor and run several packages.

We have had great success including work on a microcomputer in the course using this text. Students find the hands on work with the computer compensates for the abstract nature of discussions about information systems. They also learn something concrete and immediately applicable through exposure to a microcomputer and spreadsheet package. It appears that actually using a computer helps motivate the students for discussions like those about hardware and software.

To facilitate instruction in this course, NYU has installed several classrooms which feature personal computers, terminals and videotape players in a console that is connected to a large-screen projector. It is possible to play videotapes and to demonstrate some of the hardware and software in class. For example, in the classes on files and database management systems, the instructor in class can use a microcomputer database system to create an application in class and to process retrievals, all in about ten minutes of time.

Specific questions and problems may be found at the end of each chapter along with key words and recommended readings. Throughout the chapters themselves there is a series of management problems. These problems describe a situation in brief and ask the reader to suggest a solution. The management problems attempt to illustrate how the material in each chapter relates to a managerially oriented decision. The problems should help the student appreciate that a manager needs to have some grasp of technical issues in order to make decisions about information systems.

This edition also contains a series of brief applications descriptions. These examples show the variety of ways computer-based systems have been used to support decision, control the organization, and process transactions. The applications are intended to help the student become more creative in using information systems for problem solving.

The ultimate goal of the book, then, is to help the reader use information technology to become a more effective manager and decisionmaker.

I am indebted to my students and colleagues whose suggestions have helped shape the contents of the book, in particular to Nicholas Markoff and Jack Baroudi who conducted some of the research required to revise the original edition. Professor Jon Turner provided a number of useful suggestions from his experience using the text. I also wish to thank the following reviewers for their constructive comments: Alan Humphrey, University of Rhode Island; Dr. Ernest Kallman, Bentley College; Dr. James Kraushaur, University of Vermont; Stuart Miller, Vanderbilt University; and Roger Alan Pick, University of Wisconsin. Most important, I acknowledge the invaluable support of my wife, Ellen. She continues to provide insightful editorial advice on the manuscript while creating an environment which makes the development of the text possible.

*Henry C. Lucas, Jr.*

# ACKNOWLEDGMENTS

I acknowledge the permission of the following publishers to include the material described below in the text:

Columbia University Press for Figure 2-1 from H. C. Lucas, Jr., *Why Information Systems Fail,* 1975.

The editors of *INFOR* for Tables 1, 2, an 3 from H. C. Lucas, Jr. and J. R. Moore, "A Multiple-Criterion Scoring Approach to Information System Project Selection," February 1976.

The editors of the *IBM Systems Journal* for Figure 3 and Table 1 from J. H. Wimbrow, "A Large-Scale Interactive Administrative System," 1971.

Osborne/McGraw-Hill for Figure 7-6 from An Introduction to *Micro Computers* vol. 1, 2d. ed., A. Osborne.

*Scientific American* for Figure 7-3 from "Microelectronic Memories" by O. Hodges, September, 1977.

McGraw-Hill for Figure 7-7 from T. C. Bartee, *Digital Computer Fundamentals,* 4th e., 1977; Figure 11-5 from G. Davis, *Computer Data Processing,* 2d ed., 1973; Figure 18-12 from G. Davis, *Introduction to Computers,* 3d ed., 1977; Figures 20-1 and 20-4 from N. Nie et al., *Statistical Package for the Social Sciences,* 2d ed., 1975; Figure 8.3-1 from W. Cole, *Introduction to Computing,* 1969; Figure 2-11.1 from H. Hellerman and I. Smith, *APL 360: Programming and Applications,* 1976; and Figure 9-1 from D. Sanders, *Computers Today,* 1983.

*MIS Quarterly* for Figures 21-2 and 21-3 from Doyle, et al., "Computer Assisted Planning," vol. 7 no. 3.

Ablex Publishing for the dialog from INTERNIST by H. Pople in W. Reitman (ed), *Artificial Intelligence Applications for Business*, 1984.

Prentice-Hall for Figures 1-15 and 1-16 from R. Sprague and E. Carlson, *Building Effective Decision Support Systems*, 1982.

American Association for Artificial Intelligence for "R1: the Formative Years", by J. McDermott in *AI Magazine*, vol 2, no. 2.

Some of the material on managerial activities, computer files, vendor selection, systems analysis and design, project management, conversion and installation of systems, social issues, and the Hardserve example is taken from my earlier McGraw-Hill book, *The Analysis, Design, and Implementation of Information Systems* (3d ed.). Interested readers should consult this text for more details.

# ONE

# MANAGERS AND INFORMATION

In the first part of the text, we introduce the concept of information and define an information system. What is the nature of information? How are data interpreted by each individual and organization to become information? We examine decision making in some detail because one objective of an information system is to provide information to support decision making. Emphasis is placed on distinguishing among different types of decisions and their information requirements. With this background, we can examine frameworks for information systems—frameworks that provide a conceptual model to aid in the design of systems. Part One concludes with a scenario showing the wide variety of computer-based information systems existing today.

OVERVIEW

THREE MAJOR TRENDS

THE HISTORICAL EVOLUTION OF COMPUTERS

INFORMATION SYSTEMS

PERSONAL COMPUTING

THE ORGANIZATION AS AN INFORMATION PROCESSING
ENTITY

THE INTERDISCIPLINARY NATURE OF THE FIELD

PREVIEW

KEY WORDS

RECOMMENDED READINGS

DISCUSSION QUESTIONS

## CHAPTER 1

# THE INFORMATION SYSTEMS FIELD

## CHAPTER ISSUES

- What information is critical for the organization?
- What are the key decision areas for users and management involvement in information systems activities?

Let us join American Airlines flight 98 as plane #308 taxis into takeoff position on the runway at San Francisco International Airport. The pilot receives clearance from the control tower and advances the throttles. The jet roars down the runway and becomes airborne. Soon the flight attendants are serving breakfast.

Friends meeting us at the flight's destination in Dallas phone a toll-free number to see if the plane will be on time. They are informed of the estimated arrival time for Flight 98 at the gate in Dallas; the same information is visible to anyone in the airport on television monitors.

The plane lands at the posted time, we meet friends and continue into Dallas for a meeting. It is another uneventful flight like thousands of others every day. It all sounds routine, but this flight could not have taken place without a vast array of computer systems that support airline operations.

To start with, a computer system contains the entire history, maintenance record, flight times, and destinations of every plane in the American fleet. Every two weeks, the system adjusts American's flight schedules and matches the available planes to the most appropriate routes.

Several weeks before the flight, when we called to make a reservation, the Sabre reservations system showed the agent on the telephone what seats were available on flight 98. The computer system kept a record of our reservation, home phone number, method of payment, and itinerary for continuing or return flights.

Before the nose wheel was retracted after takeoff, a computer on plane 308 sent a cryptic departure message to a computer in Tulsa. The Tulsa computer looked up the plane's flight plan and the weather in route, and sent commands to the terminal television monitors in Dallas and Boston (the second stop on flight 98) to display the arrival time. The Tulsa computer also acknowledged that it had received the plane's message by sending a return message to flight 98's onboard computer.

To increase operational efficiencies, a computer keeps track of fuel prices at various locations and computes the cost of taking on extra fuel at cheaper cities to avoid buying fuel at more expensive locations. The computer also tracks the amount of fuel used by each of the airline's 4000 pilots. In the case of flight 98, a computer told the captain that he would need only 95 percent of his engines' total 96,000 pounds of thrust to take off in the 51°F weather. The computer also suggested that the flight would make better time at 41,000 feet instead of the planned 37,000 feet.

Back in the office a few days later, you turn to your workstation, a personal computer connected to a corporate computer network. The first action of the day is to check the mail. You turn on the computer and sign on to the mail system over the network; the mail system happens to reside on a large, mainframe computer in a nearby city. Using the system you are able to read messages, reply to them, and forward messages to another individual.

Next, you run a word processing program using only the local workstation to revise a report that needs a little more work before publication. Using the capabilities of the package, it is possible to move sentences and paragraphs, insert and delete words and lines, and add entire sections to the document. When it is completed, you run the spelling checker program to make a last check for typographical errors. Finally, you send the document over the network to a colleague 1500 miles away in a matter of seconds.

Before heading for the cafeteria and morning coffee, you run a spreadsheet program to check once again the budget for your department. The program makes it easy for you to compare budgets from the past year and to look for variances. You can make changes in budget categories and quickly see their impact on the total budget figure for the department.

With these and the other functions provided by your workstation, you are able to be far more productive than your predecessor "knowledge workers" of a decade or two ago. The local processing power of the workstation combined with the power of the computers in the communications network represents a capital investment to improve the productivity of individuals whose jobs primarily involve processing information, a group that constitutes more than 50 percent of the United States work force.

Airlines and workstations are only two examples. During the past three decades, the number of computer-based information systems in private- and public-sector organizations has grown exponentially. A new computer products and services industry has developed to supply the tools necessary to build computer-based information systems. A substantial number of individuals who design, build, and operate computer-based information systems now classify themselves as computer professionals.

Although a large number of people are employed to design and operate information systems, many more individuals are involved as users or "consumers" of information systems. Users include individuals from a broad spectrum of occupations, ranging from workers in a factory to the top management of a corporation. Use of an information system includes the receipt of a report, the submission of input for a system, and the operation of a terminal, personal computer, or a similar activity. In addition to work experiences with computer-based information systems, most individuals encounter these systems in other activities. Credit card users, travelers making reservations, social security recipients, and many others confront computer-based systems directly or indirectly.

In today's complex society, a knowledge of computer-based information systems is vital for an educated individual, particularly for the professional manager. It has been estimated that one-third to one-half of the current gross national product of the United States is currently attributable to the production and distribution of information. The computer industry itself is forecast to reach a trillion dollars a year in sales by the end of the century. This trend is a departure from a traditional economy based on the production and distribution of tangible goods; the United States is in an "information age." For most organizations—in the future, if not already—the determining factor in competition will be the processing and analysis of information.

## OVERVIEW

The purpose of this book is to present the concepts and issues necessary for the reader to understand and work successfully with computer-based information systems. The goal of the text is to help the reader develop sufficient knowledge to make intelligent decisions about these systems. Our perspective is that of the manager and user of information systems, not that of the computer professional. However, we shall discuss some topics of interest to computer professionals to gain an understanding of crucial issues in the field.

Table 1-1 contains the key areas for management attention to information processing activities in an organization. There are three main groups to consider in reviewing these activities: managers, users, and the staff of the information services department. It is difficult to distinguish between managers and users since the groups overlap. For our purposes, managers are those executives in the firm who make key decisions and allocate resources. Users, on the other hand, have daily contact with information systems and work with input, output, and/or

**TABLE 1-1**
AREAS AND ROLES IN MANAGING INFORMATION PROCESSING

| Management area | Chapters | Management | Users | Information services department |
|---|---|---|---|---|
| Policy | 6 | Establish, monitor | Influence, execute | Participate, execute |
| Planning | 5, 6 | Formulate, influence | Recommend, influence, execute | Formulate alternatives, evaluate, consult on technology |
| Organizational structure (pattern of processing) | 7-13 | Specify, select, provide resources | Delineate alternatives, develop criteria, evaluate, recommend, implement | Delineate alternatives, influence criteria, evaluate, implement |
| Applications | 1-4, 20, 21 | Select areas, set objectives, participate in development | Recommend areas, establish criteria, delineate and evaluate alternatives | Influence areas, criteria, evaluate |
| Systems analysis and design | 14-19 | Set objectives, provide resources, participate in design | Choose alternatives, control and influence design, implement | Evaluate alternatives, serve as expert consultant, furnish technological leadership, work on joint design/implementation effort |
| End user computing | 19 | Encourage, provide resources | Learn technology, use systems | Provide support, technology, access to data |
| Operations | 22 | Provide resources, evaluate | Establish performance criteria, evaluate | Influence criteria, monitor, report |
| Selection of equipment/services | 13 | Choose | Establish criteria, evaluate, recommend | Influence criteria, evaluate, recommend, execute decision |
| Charging | 22 | Establish policy, monitor | Recommend policy, monitor | Recommend, implement, execute |
| Control | 6, 22 | Evaluate, monitor | Report, monitor | Report |

the design of systems. Managers may also be users of systems. However, it will be helpful in a number of later discussions to distinguish between managers when they make decisions about information processing activities and when they act as users in the firm. Users work with systems but have more limited responsibilities for key decisions about information processing in general.

The third relevant group is the information services department staff. These individuals are charged with the responsibility for the design and operation of computer-based information systems. The staff consists of computer professionals who possess a number of technological skills. In later chapters, we shall discuss further the typical activities involved in operating the information services department. For now, these individuals represent some of the resources available to us in developing and operating computer-based systems.

Table 1-1 summarizes how the three groups are involved in the key management areas for information processing. One role of top management is to establish and monitor *policy* for information systems. Users try to influence the formation of policy and must execute policy once it is established. The information services staff desires to participate in the development of policy and its execution. All three groups are involved in *planning* for information systems. Top management must lead the planning effort, formulate plans, and influence others in the organization. Users make recommendations to influence the planning process and execute the plan. The information services staff must help formulate various alternatives and evaluate them, particularly where questions about technology are involved.

As we shall see in Chapter 6, a number of activities are subsumed under the planning process. The first of these is determining the *organizational structure* for information processing. Top management specifies the structure desired, selects alternatives, and provides resources to produce the agreed-upon information processing environment. Users help delineate alternatives and develop the criteria to evaluate them. They make recommendations and assist in implementing the organizational structure chosen. The information services staff helps develop alternatives and decision criteria and evaluates the alternatives. The staff also implements the chosen structure for processing.

The selection of *applications* areas and specific alternatives for applications is a critical task. Top management through the planning process selects areas for applications, sets the objectives of each application, and ideally participates in design activities. Users recommend areas for applications, establish criteria for selecting alternatives, and delineate various alternatives for a particular application. The information services staff serves as a resource to help establish criteria and evaluate alternatives.

During *systems analysis and design* top management must set the overall objectives, provide resources, and participate in key design decisions. Users choose the processing alternative and should have a major role in controlling the design and implementation of a new application. The information services department serves among other things as an expert consultant to evaluate alternatives, guide the project, and suggest tradeoffs and how to evaluate them during design.

To help reduce the backlog of systems, more organizations are addressing *end user computing*. Instead of relying on a professional computer staff member, users work with special languages and microcomputers or terminals to retrieve data of interest to them. Users may manipulate these data more with packages or routines they have written themselves.

The *operations* function is responsible for providing service to users of already developed information systems. After applications have been installed, they become operational; systems are executed on a routine basis. The interface among managers, users, and the information services department is often centered on the type of operational service provided. Top management must provide adequate resources for achieving satisfactory levels of operations and must evaluate the success of the information services staff in providing service to users. Users also want to help establish performance criteria and evaluate the quality of service. Finally, the information services staff must monitor service levels and report to management and users.

The development of a plan for information systems often results in the need to *select equipment or services*. Top management ultimately must approve the acquisition and help choose an alternative. Users establish criteria and evaluate alternatives before making a recommendation to management. The information services staff wants to influence evaluation criteria and also participate in the evaluation. Of course, the staff is also responsible for working with the results of the decision.

A critical decision for top management is whether and how to *charge* for information processing services, a topic we shall discuss in more detail later in the text. This topic is also important to users who want to be involved in setting a charging policy and monitoring its execution. The implementation and execution of a charging policy and plan require action by the information services staff.

Given a plan for information processing activities in the organization, one must see that these activities are under control. Top management must evaluate and monitor the activities involved in information processing. Users also should be involved in this process. The information services staff must report to users and management about their progress in executing the plan and on the level of service they provide for users.

We shall explore all these topics further. Our primary focus will be that of the manager and/or the user, though occasionally we shall also discuss the role of the information services staff.

## THREE MAJOR TRENDS

In the past few years, three major trends have drastically altered the nature of the information systems field. These trends make it imperative for the student of management to become familiar with both the use of computers and how to control them in the organization. These trends are:

**1** *The use of information processing technology as a part of corporate strategy.* Firms are implementing computer systems that give them an edge on the competition. In Chapter 6 we shall look at this phenomenon and see examples like the Merrill Lynch Cash Management Account. Firms that prosper in the coming years will be managed by individuals who are able to develop creative, strategic computer applications.

**2** *End user computing.* Due to the tremendous demand for computer systems, there are not enough systems analysts, programmers, and other computer professionals to develop all of the applications users would like to have. As a result, very high level computer languages are being employed so that users can extract the data they want themselves, without having to wait for a computer staff member to write a program.

**3** *The use of personal computers as managerial workstations.* The micro or personal computer has tremendous appeal; it belongs to the user, is easy to use, and has a variety of powerful programs which can dramatically increase the productivity of the user.

What do these trends mean for the management student? Unfortunately, it means that one must become more than just "computer literate," understanding how to run a time-sharing program will not be enough for a manager to compete effectively in the future. It is important for the student to have two kinds of knowledge about computers and information systems.

First, the student must be a competent user of computers; the personal computer, terminal, or other device connected to a network of computers is becoming as commonplace in the office as the telephone has been for the last seventy-five years. Managers today are expected to make the computer an integral part of their jobs.

Second, the manager must learn to control information processing technology. It is the manager, not the technical staff member, who will come up with the idea for a system that will provide the firm with a competitive edge. It is the manager who has to allocate resources to information systems and see that systems are designed well. The success of information processing in the firm lies more with top and middle management than it does with the information services department.

## THE HISTORICAL EVOLUTION OF COMPUTERS

In the late 1800s, Herman Hollerith invented the punched card for processing the 1890 census data. Gradually, the use of mechanical tabulating equipment for processing data spread to a number of different organizations. Tabulating operations include sorting, listing, summarizing, and performing limited mathematical computations on data in punched card form. These operations were performed with electronic accounting machines (EAM) through the end of World War II. However, EAM equipment is limited to the execution of a series of fixed instructions wired into control panels. Wires are plugged into holes in

## MANAGEMENT PROBLEM 1-1

Marsha Jackson is a recent MBA graduate with a degree in marketing. She accepted a position with General America, a large firm selling a number of consumer products. Because she had learned to use a microcomputer in her degree program, Marsha's first assignment was to survey the use of micros in the division where she works.

This division is responsible for sales of over-the-counter drugs like headache remedies, indigestion cures, and similar products. In business school, Marsha had worked with one make of personal computer. Much to her surprise, on taking a census of equipment, she found eleven different manufacturers represented! In addition, there were a variety of devices from different vendors for things like printers and plotters. Not only is there a lot of equipment, there are at least three different spreadsheet packages in use in the company.

Marsha is uneasy about this proliferation of equipment. She is not sure why, but feels somehow that it is probably not a good idea to have so many different kinds of computers. How do you think General America found itself in this position? What should it do? What should a policy about microcomputers cover? How can the firm support these devices?

---

the panels or "boards," and by changing the plugs, new instruction sequences are created.

In the 1940s, Howard Aiken at Harvard developed an electromechanical computer. John Mauchly and J. P. Eckert at the Moore School of Electrical Engineering at the University of Pennsylvania constructed the first all-electronic computer, the ENIAC, in 1945. The exclusive use of electronic components made the ENIAC much faster than its predecessor EAM equipment. The electronic computer also features a stored program that can be modified dynamically according to the data being processed. (John von Neumann, a Princeton mathematician, developed many of the concepts used in the invention of electronic computers.)

In 1954, the first computer for business applications was installed. Now, only three decades later, there are millions of computers in the United States, plus many more in other parts of the world. We have progressed through several generations of computers and their associated programs since the early days of the computer industry. In Part Three, we discuss computers and programs in much greater detail. Particular attention will be given in these chapters to the evolution of computers and to the major changes in each generation of equipment.

## INFORMATION SYSTEMS

What is an information system? Of the many definitions, we shall adopt one for discussion purposes. An information system is a set of organized procedures that, when executed, provides information to support decision making and

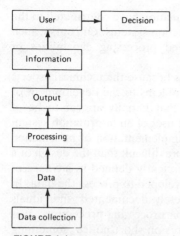

**FIGURE 1-1**
A schematic representation of an information system.

control in the organization. We define information as a tangible or intangible entity that serves to reduce uncertainty about some state or event.

The basic functions of an information system are diagramed in Figure 1-1. One of the most important parts of this figure is the user who interprets information. We shall explore the role of the user and the nature of information further in the next chapter. We should note that information is not just raw data. Rather, data are processed in some way, for example, collated and summarized, to produce output that is interpreted as information by the user–decision maker.

Since people first inhabited the earth, there have been information systems. Early systems were, of course, quite rudimentary and subject to extensive distortion and delays. Individuals, organizations, and nations have always collected and processed "intelligence." Early information systems were highly informal and involved the exchange of news, stories, and anecdotes with neighbors. As economies progressed beyond the subsistence level, information on the changing value of goods and services for barter and trade became important.

Formal organizations, from their inception, have required information systems to operate successfully. Production, accounting, financial, and external data on consumers and markets are vital to the operation of most modern businesses. As governmental bodies provide more services, they too develop greater needs for information. In fact, the overwhelming task of tabulating the 1890 census stimulated the invention of equipment to process data represented by different patterns of holes punched in cards.

What is the role of computers in information systems? Why are we concerned with computer-based information systems? Clearly, from the discussion above, information systems existed long before the development of electronic computers. However, the explosion of information and the need to process large amounts of data to extract small amounts of information have contributed to the increasing importance of computer-based information systems. Of course, such systems are possible because of the high-speed processing capabilities of computers.

We also need to study computer-based systems because the technical aspects of computers have added a whole new set of problems to the development of information systems. Computers are machines that initially appear to be of arbitrary design; they are difficult for the average user of an information system to understand. This means that the design and implementation of information systems featuring computer processing will be more difficult than the design of a manual system. An automated system has to be clearly defined in advance of conversion so that computer programs can be developed to process the data. In contrast, manual systems may never be completely documented; individuals simply make changes in their current information processing procedures. It is also usually easy to alter these manual procedures on short notice, something very difficult with a computer system.

The implementation of a manual information system is usually a part of its design; that is, individuals simply change or add to their present duties. Computer systems, however, involve major training and often require substantial changes for users. The organizational impact of manual information systems is usually minimal; workers are involved in making easily understood changes in procedures. Computer-based information systems may require major changes in thinking and work patterns on the part of the users.

Nearly all computer systems result in new input techniques such as the use of new forms or terminals and new output such as paper reports or displays. Some computer systems are even significant enough to create changes in the structure of an organization. For example, the development of a computer system in one manufacturing firm stimulated management to create a production control department. The process of developing the system showed that a department was needed to monitor and schedule production; furthermore, the new system provided information that could be used for these activities.

The flexibility of manual information systems is high; it is easy to change simple manual procedures. For computer-based information systems, many months and great expense may be required to make an alteration. As a result, these systems tend to be much less flexible than their manual counterparts.

For the above reasons, we need to consider the special requirements of computer-based information systems and the problems they create. Because these computer-based systems are usually very expensive to develop, their failure can be quite costly to the organization. In addition to direct costs, the failure of a computer-based information system will have an adverse impact on the organization's human resources. Information system failures have created dissention in organizations and led to conflict among individuals and departments. If one system fails or is not well-received by users, it will be very difficult to develop new systems in the future. As a result, the organization misses the significant benefits possible from a well-designed and operated computer-based information system.

## MICROS IN THE VINEYARDS

*Franciscan Vineyards in the Napa Valley of California uses a personal computer with a hard disk and a portable personal computer for processing. The vineyard is running a package that helps it record and compute information the government requires and that the winery needs.*

*The system keeps track of the weight tag number for a particular batch of grapes, the weight of the grapes, how many gallons the batch produced, the sugar content and the acidity and pH of the batch. The system can report on when certain grapes were crushed, when sulfur was added, and when the wine was transferred to a new tank. (Wine moving is very important in making wine.) The program also helps keep track of when the wine was racked and when the next racking is due.*

*By entering the whole "crush" over a weekend, the user can do an inventory in 45 minutes instead of a day. Once the wine is produced, the traffic manager uses the computer to prepare invoices. The system also produces an inventory of wine for sale and produces distributor and sales reports by variety of wine.*

*The president of the winery uses an electronic spreadsheet to keep track of the budget in each of the vineyard's cost centers. The budget is maintained for the last four years and for the future. The president can keep track of the cost of goods sold, the number of cases and the cost of production. He also uses the spreadsheet to derive a crop estimate for the five or six varieties of grapes that are planted in the 430 acres of the vineyard. The system helps plan for the future since many wines are sold five years after harvest.*

*P C Week*, Nov. 13, 1984.

## PERSONAL COMPUTING

Since the first microcomputers were marketed to the public, a whole new type of computing has developed. Micro or personal computers have exploded in business, doubling the total number of computers in the world in a short period of time.

The types of systems described above are very traditional; they involve data flows in the organization and multiple users who supply input and review the output of the system. Personal computing is very different. One important goal of this text will be to clearly distinguish between multiuser systems and the kind of computing we do as individuals with our own machines.

Microcomputers can be used for a number of tasks in the organization including:

1 Document preparation (word processing).
2 Financial analysis (electronic spreadsheets).
3 Personal filing and database systems.
4 Serving as a terminal connected to larger computers.
5 Presentation of graphics.
6 Giving access to external data bases.

Because the personal computer "belongs" to the user, the design of applications and the way in which it is used differ dramatically from the traditional system.

The microcomputer has had a very beneficial impact on the organization, extending computing to many individuals in the firm. However, it is necessary to recognize the differences that exist between doing something for oneself on a micro and developing a large system that must serve many different users on a larger, shared computer.

## THE ORGANIZATION AS AN INFORMATION PROCESSING ENTITY

- Product managers at Connoisseur Foods, a company discussed in Chapter 21, require reports on the sales of their products by region. If a product is not selling well, the manager can take immediate action.
- Supermarket buyers need to know how a new brand of a product is selling so that they can order supplies to replenish stocks. If the product is not selling

---

### MANAGEMENT PROBLEM 1-2

The president of Amalgamated Mills has recently become concerned over the firm's difficulties in processing transactions such as the receipt of orders and the preparation of invoices. Amalgamated Mills was founded shortly after World War II to manufacture women's and girls' sports clothing. The company has grown steadily; yearly sales currently exceed $15 million.

The office staff expanded to process the increasing volume of paperwork necessary to enter orders and process shipments and payments. Last year, over 40,000 invoices were written manually in the shipping department! Existing procedures have been modified only slightly to deal with the higher volume of processing necessary to support current sales levels.

The president is considering the development of a computer-based system to handle some of the processing associated with order entry and projections of raw materials requirements. The firm currently uses a service bureau for accounts-receivable processing on a monthly basis.

At one time, the president felt he understood all the office procedures. However, in recent years the president has grown uneasy since he is no longer familiar with all the procedures used in the office. There is one office manager who knows everything about operations; unfortunately no one else in the firm fully understands these procedures.

In contemplating a computer system, the president is worried that it might result in less control over operations. On the other hand, he feels that he personally has little control or understanding of present procedures. The president is also worried about becoming dependent on a small computer "elite" to process crucial information.

What advice would you offer the president to help in making his decision on whether to pursue computer processing?

---

well, then it is a candidate for removal from store shelves where space is highly competitive.

• Managers at an airline need to know load factors on various flights to plan schedules and marketing campaigns. This information is produced as a by-product of computer-based airline reservations systems.

From these examples, we can see one feature that almost all organizations have in common: they must acquire and analyze information and take action based on their interpretation of that information. Whether an organization manufactures a product or sells a service, it needs to process information. Most businesses need to know information on markets, sales, and costs. Manufacturing firms need the above information plus information on the manufacturing process itself. For example, a firm needs information about the status of inventories, orders, and basic manufacturing data for production control. Government agencies are also confronted with substantial information processing requirements. Who are the recipients of the agency's services? What is the cost of these services?

A view of the organization as an information processing entity is presented in Figure 1-2. The organization collects data from a number of sources, including its own internal operations and customers. Most organizations also attempt to

**FIGURE 1-2**
The organization as an information processing entity.

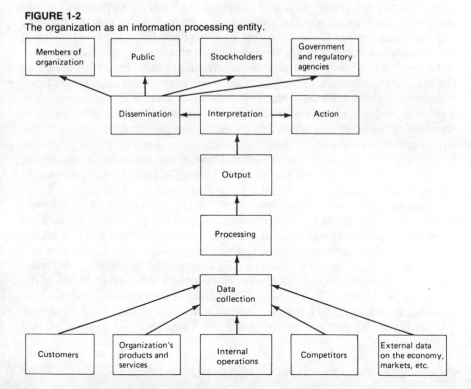

gather data on their competition and on other phenomena external to the organization, such as the economy. In fact, a number of firms exist to gather and sell data such as economic forecasts. Many government statistics are also used by organizations, and we classify these data as externally derived too. For example, the United States Department of Agriculture publishes detailed crop forecasts, which are very important to the food industry.

The organization must process all these data, and frequently some type of computer-based information system is used for this purpose. The output from processing may take many forms, such as tabular reports or graphic displays. It is likely that the output is interpreted and action taken on the basis of the information. For example, a firm might offer a new product or enter a new market because of the information derived from a market research study. Once the decision has been made to enter a new market, the product will be closely monitored. The firm may conduct research on how to best promote the product through advertising or free samples. The data collected on the experiment are then analyzed, and the product manager derives information from them to help in devising a marketing plan.

A great deal of interpreted information is disseminated within an organization for use by its members. The orders processed by a manufacturing firm using a computer provide important information for several groups in the firm. For example, the file of open orders is of interest to the sales force because it shows what products are selling well. The production scheduling department would like to see what goods must be shipped by certain dates to plan production. Customer services would like to be able to inquire about the status of individual orders when customers or sales representatives phone with a question.

Many organizations must also make information available to the public, for example, to stockholders. Publicly held firms and government agencies are faced with reporting requirements by the Securities and Exchange Commission and by legislation, respectively. Many private organizations also provide information to government agencies and regulatory bodies. Automobile firms must provide large amounts of data about tests conducted on vehicle safety and pollution. Drug companies submit extensive information to the government concerning tests of new medicines. Most firms and individuals also furnish a large amount of data to the Internal Revenue Service.

Although processing information clearly is not the ultimate goal of most organizations, we can see that it is one vital component of their operations. Individuals who are or will become members of organizations need to understand the role of information: How is it produced and analyzed, and how is it processed to contribute to the goals of the organization? In a modern organization, the processing of information contributes significantly to the success of the enterprise, and managers should be knowledgeable about information processing tools, techniques, and concepts. This book has been written for the manager who wishes to become an intelligent user or "consumer" of computer-based information systems.

**THE INTERDISCIPLINARY NATURE OF THE FIELD**

It is not really possible to present a theory of information systems; as in many other fields, there is no one central theory on which we can rely. This lack of unifying theory should not be alarming; there is no one theory of marketing, just as there is no one theory of accounting. Accounting is a field created by humans, and accounting theory is arbitrary when compared with the scientific theories of a field like physics.

The information systems field in general is concerned with the effective use of information technology in an organization. Figure 1-3 places the information systems field in perspective on a continuum ranging from computer science on one extreme to psychology on the other. Computer science contributes the mathematical foundation of computer systems. These results help electrical engineers develop computer devices and programs. Operations research provides a number of approaches to improve decision making and to develop solutions to complex problems. The functional areas of management, such as accounting, finance, production, and marketing furnish the specific decision setting and context for information systems.

Organizational studies help us understand how information systems affect the organization. How can we design systems to ensure successful implementation? The field of psychology also aids in understanding the decision processes of individuals and the nature of information necessary for decision making. Individual psychology is also important in planning the successful implementation of a new system.

Those who study the information systems field must extract relevant components from these many different contributing fields and combine them into a meaningful set of concepts dealing with information processing in organizations. The interdisciplinary nature of the field contributes richness but also increases the complexity of information systems. It is hoped that the student of information systems will find the lack of precise boundaries challenging and intellectually stimulating.

**PREVIEW**

With this introduction to the information systems field, we are prepared to explore the nature of information in greater detail. In Chapter 2 we examine the nature of decision making and managerial activities, and Chapter 3 introduces several frameworks for systems. Before concluding Part One, we survey a number of computer-based information systems to demonstrate the pervasive nature of these systems.

The second part of the book deals with the interaction of the organization and information systems. Part Three discusses computer technology: users need a basic understanding of computers, especially computer files, to make many decisions about information systems.

| | | | Continuum | | | |
|---|---|---|---|---|---|---|
| Psychology | Organizational studies | Functional areas of business | Information systems | Operations research | Electrical engineering | Computer science |
| | | | Contribution | | | |
| Decision making | Impact of information on the organization | Accounting, marketing, finance, production | Combination and synthesis of fields; effective use of information technology in organization | Problem-solving techniques | Machine design | Hardware theory |
| Use of information Impact of systems | | | | | Software design Management techniques File design | Software theory File structures |

**FIGURE 1-3**
The nature of the information systems field.

---

**MANAGEMENT PROBLEM 1-3**

Assume that you have just been appointed to chair the board of a medium-sized manufacturing firm that makes small consumer appliances. The company has experienced stagnant growth over the last five years, and a new board of directors was just elected by dissident stockholders.

One of your first tasks is to help top management discover why sales are constant and profits have been declining. Currently, the firm is faced with excessive inventories and problems in the acquisition of raw materials. Prices for these materials have been fluctuating widely in recent months, and the previous management seems to have been unable to cope with this problem.

How would you approach this task? What sources of information would you seek to help understand and solve problems in the company?

---

In Part Four, we present systems analysis and design techniques, topics of vital importance for a user. We shall advocate that users form a significant part of a design team and that a user be in charge of the design of a new system. Part Five presents detailed examples of several different information systems to illustrate the material covered to this point. Finally, the last part of the book presents issues of special management concern: the relationship between user departments and the information services department and the social consequences of information systems.

**KEY WORDS**

| | | |
|---|---|---|
| Computer science | Implementation | Organizational studies |
| Data | Information | Output |
| Data collection | Intelligence | Processing |
| Decision making | Interdisciplinary field | Psychology |
| EAM | Internal information | Program |
| External information | Interpretation | System |
| Electronic computer | Operations research | Users |

**RECOMMENDED READINGS**

Ackoff, R. L.: "Management Misinformation Systems," *Management Science*, vol. 14, No. 4, December 1967, pp. B140–B156. (This article should be read by all students of information systems; it points out some common fallacies in the assumptions underlying many approaches to information systems.)

Dearden, J.: "MIS is a Mirage," *Harvard Business Review*, January–February 1972, pp. 90–99. (Dearden is a consistent critic of information systems; do you agree with his contentions? Why or why not?)

Mason, R., and I. Mitroff: "A Program for Research in Management Information Systems," *Management Science*, vol. 19, no. 5, January 1973, pp. 475–487. (This article describes an information system from the perspective of an individual decision maker. While delving into the philosophical concepts underlying information systems, it presents a very appealing framework for the study of systems.)

## DISCUSSION QUESTIONS

1 What is responsible for the explosion of information processing that has occurred over the past several decades?

2 What role does the manager play in the development of information systems? Does this role change in the operation of a system after it has been implemented?

3 Why does the addition of a computer to a manual information system result in complications?

4 What is the similarity between the fields of accounting and the interdisciplinary field of information systems? What are the major differences between these two fields?

5 Manufacturers of early computer devices forecasted far fewer sales than actually occurred. Why do you suspect that the sales estimates were so incorrect?

6 Can you think of other definitions of information systems than the one presented in this chapter? What are their advantages and disadvantages compared with the one we adopted?

7 How can there be more than one interpretation of information? Can you think of examples where the same information is interpreted in different ways by different individuals?

8 What is the value of information? How would you try to assess the value of information to a decision maker?

9 What different types of information exist? Develop categories for describing or classifying information, for example, timeliness and accuracy. Develop an example or two of information in each category.

10 What do you think the crucial factors are in the success of an information system from the standpoint of a manager?

11 How would you define successful implementation? How would you measure it?

12 Can you think of an example where the failure of an information system led to a major disaster? What can we learn from such a catastrophe?

13 What types of organizations are likely to have the most severe information processing problems?

14 What is the relationship between information systems and marketing?

15 How would you characterize the training of a computer scientist compared with the training of a specialist in information systems?

16 What is the role of operations research in information systems? Is an operations research model an information system?

17 How can operations research be used to design information systems? Can operations research be used in the operation of information systems?

18 Develop a list of the different information systems that you encounter during a typical week. How many of these systems are computer-based?

19 What factors would you consider if you were placed on a design team developing a new information system? What would be your major concern about the project?

20 Do you think the information systems field, while lacking a theory, will ever develop principles similar to those of accounting? Would this in your opinion be desirable? Why or why not?

# THE NATURE OF INFORMATION AND DECISION MAKING

# THE NATURE OF INFORMATION AND DECISION MAKING

## CHAPTER ISSUES

- What kind of decisions are made in the organization?
- What information should be provided for decision makers?
- What decisions are amenable to computer support?

The user of a system receives information in the form of output. In this chapter, we explore the nature of information and how it is interpreted. Too frequently the designers of an information system have considered output to be information while users have not. The decision maker, not the systems designer, defines and uses information. It is extremely important for users of information systems to be aware of different types of information and to think about how they interpret that information.

## DEFINITION

In the last chapter, we defined information as some tangible or intangible entity that reduces our uncertainty about some state or event. As an example, consider a weather forecast for clear and sunny weather tomorrow; this information reduces our uncertainty about whether an event such as a baseball game will be held. Information that a bank has just made our firm a loan reduces uncertainty about whether we shall be in a state of solvency or bankruptcy next month.

Another definition for information has been suggested by Davis and Olson (1985): "Information is data that has been processed into a form that is meaningful to the recipient, and is of real perceived value in current or prospective decisions." This definition of information systems stresses the fact that data have to be processed in some way to produce information; information is more than raw data. In later chapters we shall discuss information systems that process data to produce information. In this chapter, however, we focus on information and its interpretation.

## THE INTERPRETATION OF INFORMATION

### The Context of the User

In a discussion of research programs for information systems, Mason and Mitroff (1973) suggested in part that an information system serves an *individual* with a certain *cognitive style* faced with a particular *decision* problem in some *organizational setting*. In addition to these variables, we suggest the importance of *personal and situational* factors in the interpretation of information. We shall examine each of these factors to see how they influence the interpretation of information. (See Figure 2-1.)

Clearly, the nature of the problem influences the interpretation of information. How serious is the decision? What are the consequences of an incorrect decision versus the gains from a correct one? A more important decision may require extra care in analyzing data compared with a minor decision. The decision by an oil company to enter the information processing field is more important than the decision to lease additional office space. In such a strategic decision to diversify, the consequences and costs involved plus the impact on the organization mean that information will be scrutinized much more closely.

The organization itself affects the interpretation of information. Studies have shown that an individual becomes socialized by the organization; that is, over time we are influenced by the organization in the way we approach problems. The attitudes of a new employee at an automobile company differ substantially in most instances from those of the chairman of the board. As the new employee

**FIGURE 2-1**
Influences on the interpretation and use of information.

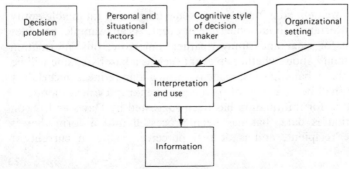

associates over the years with other employees of the firm, he or she is influenced by their attitudes and the environment of the workplace. Gradually new employees begin to change their attitudes to ones more consistent with those with whom they associate—a process known as socialization.

People who have different ideas interpret information differently; many of the ideas will have been influenced by peers and by the socialization process in the particular organization for whom the individual works. Several individuals trying to influence a decision by the government to regulate prices in an industry may use the same information. However, the head of a corporation in the industry, the leader of a consumer group, and a government decision maker in a regulatory agency will probably all interpret the information differently.

Personal and situational factors also influence the interpretation of information. One study showed that given comparable information, decision makers interpreted a problem differently, depending on their position. In this exercise, finance executives saw financial problems, sales executives recognized sales problems, and so forth. In all these scenarios, the information was the same—it was just interpreted differently (Dearborn and Simon, 1958).

Psychologists studying the thought patterns of individuals have developed the concept of "cognitive style." Although there is no agreement on exactly how to describe or measure different cognitive styles, the concept is appealing since people do seem to have different ways of approaching problems. One of the simplest distinctions is between analytic and heuristic decision makers. The analytic decision maker looks at quantitative information; engineering is a profession attractive to an analytic decision maker. The heuristic decision maker, on the other hand, is interested in broader concepts and is more intuitive. Most researchers believe that we are not analytic or heuristic in every problem, but that we do have preferences and tend to approach the same type of problem with a consistent cognitive style.

The phenomenon of cognitive style can create considerable problems in the interpretation of information. Consider the staff member who brings a report laden with data to a heuristic decision maker. The recipient of the report says, "Don't give me all these numbers; I want to know your conclusions and recommendations." The analyst, sadder but wiser, prepares the next report without any data; instead only interpretations and conclusions are presented. Unfortunately, the recipient of this report is an analytic decision maker who rejects it: "You haven't given me the data so that I can draw my own conclusions and compare them with yours."

### An Interpretational Model

We have suggested a number of factors that influence the interpretation of information. How are all these factors combined; what is their net impact on the interpretation of information? Figure 2-2 summarizes all the variables described above. The figure portrays one representation of how a user of information systems develops a model to interpret information and how this model is constantly executed and revised.

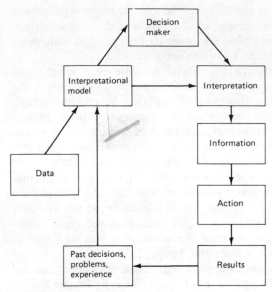

**FIGURE 2-2**
Model for interpreting information.

We expect the model to be formed inductively by the decision maker and to be heavily influenced by beliefs. For example, a decision maker may observe data on sales and production over time and find that these data seem to predict customer reaction to a product. The decision maker is building an interpretational model based on his or her beliefs and analysis of historical data and observations.

---

**MANAGEMENT PROBLEM 2-1**

A group of information systems designers was discussing problems in the bank where they work. One of the designers said, "No matter what I do, there seem to be some people who just will not use the branch market potential report. This report should be very valuable since it shows the potential for various types of loans and deposits, in the area served by the branch."

Another analyst commented, "I have had the same problem with some of the systems I have developed. We recently installed a system that would allow managers to inquire on a terminal about the status of the bank's commercial loan portfolio. The other day I looked at the results of a monitor which keeps track of who makes an inquiry and the nature of the request. It turns out that a group of four or five managers is using the system a lot while some fifteen people we thought would use it are not."

As a manager interested in the effective utilization of information systems, what do you think is the cause of these problems? How could they be solved?

---

### AN ELECTRONIC HOSPITAL

*At the LDS Hospital of the University of Utah in Salt Lake City, doctors use a terminal to retrieve patient records. If a patient enters the emergency room, the staff attaches him or her to microcomputer-based equipment to monitor vital signs. The patient's name is also logged into the hospital's central system. If the patient has been in the hospital within the last 15 years, a history will be immediately displayed to the staff.*

*The hospital has 24 computers, 250 terminals and 70 printers which support all aspects of health care. Orders for tests are sent to the laboratory; the staff there inputs the results through the laboratory computer to the central hospital system. In radiology, the doctor uses the computer to enter findings from X-rays. The system suggests possible interpretations to aid the analysis by the physician.*

*The staff also enters any drug orders into the computer. The drug order is then posted to the patient's data file. The system sets up a drug schedule and is reviewed by an expert system to determine if the order is safe given what the system knows about the patient's history and other drug orders.*

*Computers have been used in hospitals for many years; this system integrates all of the different components of hospital systems into a network supporting all aspects of the patient's interaction with the hospital.*

*IEEE Spectrum,* June 1984.

---

After testing the interpretational model and developing confidence in it, the decision maker uses the model deductively. Data are observed and the decision maker uses the model to interpret them. Now, the decision maker perceives data on sales and production as constituting information on product acceptance; he or she may even ignore other information conveyed by these data.

After an interpretational model has been formed, further experiences are fed back to modify the model; past decisions, problems, and experiences all influence the future interpretations of information. These experiences are based on actions taken on the basis of information and the results of those actions. If changes in a new product based on sales and production data increase sales, then the interpretational model described above will be reinforced.

### Implications for Information Systems

What does the existence of a model for interpreting information imply for information systems? The presence of different interpretational models creates many serious problems for the designer and user of information systems. First, the meaning of information is clearly in the mind of the recipient. What one party perceives as useful and relevant information may be meaningless to another person. Even more serious is a situation where two individuals agree on the importance of information but develop completely opposite interpretations of what the information means.

An example will help show the difficulty of designing an information system, given the diversity of interpretational models. Suppose that we have received the following information. An unfriendly country within the last 48 hours has

1 Called the U.S. ambassador for an urgent meeting tomorrow
2 Nationalized the subsidiaries of two United States firms
3 Held joint maneuvers of its Air Force and Army along its borders

A "hard liner" might interpret this information to mean that the unfriendly country is planning to expropriate all U.S. investments, and call for U.S. troops to evacuate American citizens. This analyst might suggest economic sanctions against the country.

A "moderate," on the other hand, might interpret the above information to mean that the country wishes to negotiate compensation with the United States for expropriating U.S.-owned companies. The unfriendly country may also want to arrange for technicians from the United States to assist in running these firms.

A cynic might suggest that all the information is unrelated and has no significance whatsoever. The unfriendly country is so bureaucratic and has such poor communications that none of the events is really connected. The action of the United States should be to do nothing.

All three individuals agree on the information; only the interpretational models differ. In each instance, however, the differing interpretations based on different backgrounds and beliefs lead to widely varying recommendations for action. The point is that we must carefully consider how information is interpreted in thinking about information systems.

## DECISION MAKING

We have suggested that, in general, information systems exist to support decision making. Before we can continue our discussion of the nature of information, we need to examine the decision-making process in more detail to see how information is used.

### Problem Finding and Solving

A manager must be aware of a problem before a decision can be made. A problem exists when the decision maker's ideal situation differs from reality, for example, when sales are below expectations. This example corresponds to something we call "disturbance handling"; the manager discovers the discrepancy between an ideal model and reality and attempts to find some way to eliminate the discrepancy.

After noting the existence of a problem, the decision maker must decide what caused it. Are inventories up? Is the advertising budget too low? After determining the cause or causes, the decision maker tries to solve the problem by developing some program to remedy the situation. There is also another type of problem-finding activity undertaken by the manager who is looking for improve-

---

**MANAGEMENT PROBLEM 2-2**

The governor of a state is confronted with a series of conflicting recommendations from his staff. All the reports he read on current welfare problems indicated that projected payments would rise well beyond budgeted levels for the rest of the year.

The director of welfare suggested in her report that the new higher amounts for payment passed by the legislature were to blame for the problem.

The governor's advisor for economic affairs indicated that the recent decline in the state's economy had resulted in a large increase in unemployment. As unemployment benefits ran out, he said, many of the unemployed became eligible for welfare, thus accounting for the increase in expenditures.

A state senate leader felt that most of the increase resulted from cheating by many people on welfare, which resulted in abnormally high expenditures in the early part of the year. This high rate of expenditures was the basis for the projections for the rest of the year. The obvious solution was to increase the standards for obtaining welfare and investigate applicants and present recipients more closely.

Who is right? What is responsible for so many different positions? How can the governor solve these conflicting viewpoints and arrive at the cause of the problem?

---

ment projects. In this sense, the problem can be defined as "what else could we be doing at the present time?" The manager is trying to anticipate problems and plan for them.

### Stages in Decision Making

In finding and solving a problem, the decision maker faces a myriad of decision cycles. What is the problem and what is the cause of the problem? What additional data are needed, and how should the solution be implemented? Each of these major steps in solving a problem involves the solution of subproblems, and many decisions have to be made.

Simon (1965) suggests a series of descriptive stages for decision making that help in understanding the decision process. The first stage is defined as Intelligence, which consists in determining that a problem exists. The decision maker must become aware of a problem and gather data about it. We described this stage as problem finding or identification.

During the Design stage, the problem solver tries to develop a set of alternative solutions. The problem solver asks what approaches are available to solve the problem and evaluates each one. In the Choice stage, the decision maker selects one of the solutions. If all the alternatives have been evaluated well, the Choice stage is usually the simplest one to execute. We should also add a stage to Simon's model called Implementation, in which we ensure that the solution is carried out.

## Types of Decisions

To complete our discussion of problem solving and decision making, we relate different types of solutions to the type of problem involved. Anthony (1965) offers one view of three different types of decisions made in organizations. Clearly, these are not discrete categories, but instead they form a continuum for classifying decisions.

The first decision area is strategic planning in which the decision maker develops objectives and allocates resources to obtain these objectives. Decisions in this category are characterized by long time periods and usually involve a substantial investment and effort. The development and introduction of a new product is an example of a strategic decision.

Decisions that are classified as managerial control in nature deal with the use of resources in the organization and often involve personnel or financial problems. For example, an accountant may try to determine the reason for a difference between actual and budgeted costs. In this case, the accountant is solving a managerial control problem.

---

### DECISION SUPPORT SYSTEMS

*At Florida Power and Light Company a decision support system showed that centralizing the inventory distribution system could bring added efficiencies. The utilities saved $13.5 million last year in inventory carrying costs. Shaklee Corporation should be able to cut its delivery time to customers by one-third and save $850,000 through a computer system. An airline is saving as much as $500,000 a month in fuel costs as a result of a new system.*

*These companies are taking advantage of decision support systems which differ from conventional computer applications like inventory control; the primary use of the systems above is in operational planning such as helping develop complex production schedules. Other firms use decision support systems to aid strategic planning and to guide decisions, for example, on whether to enter a new market.*

*The heart of these systems is a computer software model describing the decision. The computer simulates a number of "what if" scenarios given different assumptions by the firm.*

*A good example of one of these systems is a fuel management allocation application developed at an airline. During the first month of operation fuel cost was cut by two cents a gallon. Since the airline used 25 million gallons that month it saved $500,000. The Airline stores data on fuel prices and availability along with storage costs and capacities at the 30 cities it serves. For each of its 56 aircraft, performance and a tentative monthly schedule are included. The computer requires only fifteen minutes to produce a list of the best fueling stations and vendors for each flight, a task that required over a month to perform manually. Now the schedule can be run two or three times a week.*

*Decision support systems offer the opportunity for direct cost savings in operational applications and for improving the decision-making process in general.*

*Business Week,* January 21, 1980.

---

Operational control decisions deal with the day-to-day problems that affect the operation of the firm. What should be produced today in the factory? What items should be ordered for inventory?

Who makes the preponderance of each of the three types of decisions? Anthony does not really specify what types of decisions are handled by different managers. However, from the nature of the problems, we suspect that top managers in the organization spend more time on strategic decision making than supervisors, while the reverse is probably true for operational decisions.

## CHARACTERISTICS OF INFORMATION

Information can be characterized in a number of ways; some kinds of information are more suitable for a decision problem than others. We must be certain that the characteristics of information fit the decision situation and the interpretational model of the decision maker.

The time frame for information can be historical or predictive. Historical information can be used to design alternative problem solutions and to monitor performance. Information may be expected or it may be unanticipated. Some information systems experts feel that information is worthless unless it is a surprise to the recipient. However, information that confirms something also reduces uncertainty. Surprise information often alerts us to the existence of a problem; it is also important in developing and evaluating different decision alternatives. Information may come from sources internal to the organization or from external sources such as government agencies.

Information may be presented in summary form or in detail. Summary information is often sufficient for problem finding; however, both summary and detailed information may be needed for other uses. Information can be frequently updated or relatively old. Information can also be loosely or highly structured. An example of highly structured information is a report with clear categories to classify all the information it contains. Loosely organized information might be different forms of information from multiple sources. Information also varies in its accuracy.

**TABLE 2-1**
INFORMATION CHARACTERISTICS VERSUS DECISION TYPES

| Characteristics | Decision type | | |
| --- | --- | --- | --- |
| | Operational control | Managerial control | Strategic planning |
| Time frame | Historical | ⟶ | Predictive |
| Expectation | Anticipated | ⟶ | Surprise |
| Source | Largely internal | ⟶ | Largely external |
| Scope | Detailed | ⟶ | Summary |
| Frequency | Real time | ⟶ | Periodic |
| Organization | Highly structured | ⟶ | Loosely structured |
| Accuracy | Highly accurate | ⟶ | Not overly accurate |

**RAILROAD APPLICATIONS**

*The Association of American Railroads is planning to expand a nationwide computer system that provides data on the location of over two million freight cars, trailers, and containers for some 27 railroads in North America. The Missouri Pacific Railroad is also expanding a computer-based car scheduling system; it will soon cover its entire 12,000 mile network.*

*The American Association of Railroads is using its system to send out car service directives advising railroads on how to move rolling stock from one region to another to respond to various shortages. Computer systems are paying off in the more efficient use of rolling stock and locomotives. Another benefit is less costly maintenance and better long range planning.*

*The trade group is studying whether new computer applications could be developed to eliminate waybill and other paper bottlenecks. These efforts are expected to become more important to rail operations, as the railroad industry is deregulated. The computer is the only way that the railroads will be able to analyze information and react to fare changes under deregulation.*

*The Santa Fe Railroad has a system that keeps track of every freight car and locomotive on the line. Every time a car enters a rail yard, a Santa Fe clerk enters an identification number into a central computer file. When a shipper requests a freight car, the system locates the nearest suitable one and sends dispatching instructions to the yard. A similar system, in use at the Southern Pacific Railroad resulted in a savings of $5 million per year.*

*The Missouri Pacific computerized its di. patching operation as well. Prior to the computer, a shipper had to call one of the company's 300 freight stations and wait while an agent searched for cars that might be available. The application that keeps track of rolling stock has resulted in a 10 percent average improvement in car utilization, savings which have exceeded the original expectation of an $8 million return from the $45 million system.*

*In 1978 the railroad began to schedule car movements along a 546 mile portion of the track, from Dallas to Memphis. If a freight car unexpectedly misses its train, the computer assigns it to the next one. Another 3,000 miles of track has been added to the computer system. Customers can also use the results of the computer system to help keep shipments on track; a computer at Ford Motor Company receives 50,000 reports a day on the location of its 31 railroad cars.*

*To speed up shipments railroads share information among themselves. The computers of the Missouri Pacific, Southern Pacific, Conrail and Burlington Northern often exchange information to obtain shipping data.*

*These applications are helping the railroads become far more efficient and compete with alternate modes of transportation. The investments are large, but the return on such operational systems can be extremely high.*

*Business Week, February 4, 1980.*

In general, different types of decisions require different kinds of information; providing inappropriate information is one common failing of computer-based systems. (See Table 2-1.) In one organization, the vice president of finance receives detailed reports on the status of an inventory with 52,000 items at a remote location. The report is not used, and this executive is frustrated over receiving so much unneeded information.

Operational control decisions are characterized by historical information. Usually the results are expected, and the source of the information is the internal operations of the organization. The data—for example, production-control data, inventory status, or accounts-receivable balances—must be detailed. Because we are working with the day-to-day operations of the firm, operational control information is often required in close to real time. This information tends to be highly structured and accurate.

Information for strategic decisions, on the other hand, tends to be more predictive and long range in nature. Strategic planning may uncover many surprises. Often, external data on the economy, competition, and so forth are involved in strategic decision making. Summary information on a periodic basis is adequate; there is usually no need for highly detailed or excessively accurate information. Strategic planning decisions are usually characterized by loosely structured information. The requirements for managerial control decisions fall in between those of operational control and strategic planning.

Obviously, there are many ways to classify information, and this complicates the decision maker's problem in expressing what is desired as output from an information system. The most important thing for the user of information systems is to be aware of the intended use of information and the type of decision problem. Then the user should try to decide on the general characteristics of the information needed, using categories such as these as guidelines to develop more detailed information requirements. Consideration of characteristics similar to the ones described here should make it possible to avoid requesting grossly inappropriate information from an information system.

## KEY WORDS

| | | |
|---|---|---|
| Accuracy | Historical | Problem solving |
| Anticipated | Internal | Real time |
| Binary | Interpretive model | Strategic planning |
| Choice | Managerial control | Structured |
| Design | Operational control | Summary |
| Detail | Prediction | Surprise |
| External | Probability | Value of information |
| Frequency | Problem finding | |

## RECOMMENDED READINGS

Anthony, R.:*Planning and Control Systems: A Framework for Analysis,* Division of Research, Graduate School of Business Administration, Harvard University, Boston, 1965. (This short book explains Anthony's framework for decision making more fully and is well worth reading.)

Davis, G. B., and Olson, M.: *Management Information Systems: Conceptual Founda-*

*tions, Structure, and Development,* 2d ed., McGraw-Hill, New York, 1985. (See especially the first several chapters on the nature of information.)

Masterman, J.: *The Double-Cross System,* Avon, New York, 1972. (A most enjoyable book describing a system used by Allied intelligence, primarily the British, to feed false intelligence to the German high command during World War II. The book provides an excellent example of an analysis of a user's interpretational model and the development of information to suit that model.)

Pounds, W. F.: "The Process of Problem Finding," *The Industrial Management Review,* vol. 11, no. 1, 1969, pp. 1–20. (An insightful paper describing the nature of problem finding; the author gives several examples of different kinds of problems that managers in one company faced.)

## DISCUSSION QUESTIONS

1 What alternative definitions for information can you propose?

2 What do you think selective perception is? How does it affect the design and use of information systems?

3 Why is information more than just data?

4 How would you measure cognitive style? How does this concept help in the interpretation of information and the design of information systems?

5 Can an organization bias the information it develops and uses?

6 How can different interpretations of information lead to conflict? How can this conflict be resolved?

7 Develop procedures for eliciting and defining information needs for a decision. How could you implement your plan? What are the problems?

8 How does the importance of a decision reflect itself in the users' interpretation of information?

9 Would you expect an analytical decision maker to be more favorably disposed toward computer-based reports than a heuristic one? Why or why not?

10 Pounds suggests that a problem exists when the decision maker's normative model of what should be conflicts with reality. How does this normative model relate to our information interpretation model? Are they completely independent?

11 Can the same information system be used by more than one decision maker?

12 How can we custom-tailor information systems to suit different decision makers at a reasonable cost?

13 Examine one particular indicator with which you are familiar for bias, reliability, etc. For example, how valid is a grade point average?

14 What other characteristics of information can you define beyond the ones listed in this chapter?

15 Are there information systems that deal with decisions or processes outside Anthony's categories for decisions? What types of systems are these?

16 What are the most frequent indicators for evaluating the performance of lower, middle, and top managers?

17 Is there any way to "beat" an indicator like a standardized aptitude test for college admissions? What kind of behavior does this indicator motivate?

18 Of what value are formal theories of information to a decision maker?

19 Why is there no formal theory of information systems?

# FRAMEWORKS FOR INFORMATION SYSTEMS

# FRAMEWORKS FOR INFORMATION SYSTEMS

## CHAPTER ISSUES

- What kind of information systems should be developed in the organization?
- What information should be provided by computer-based systems?

A "framework" is a conceptual model that helps us understand and communicate about information systems. The framework developed in this chapter will facilitate future discussions about different types of decisions, their information requirements, and different kinds of computer-based information systems.

We review the nature of managerial activities in the first part of the chapter. Many computer-based systems purport to be "management information systems," and an understanding of managerial activities aids in the analysis and design of such systems. Managers also allocate resources to information systems activities, so it is essential to understand the different roles of management within an organization.

## MANAGERIAL ROLES

### The Research

Mintzberg (1973) reviewed the small amount of literature available about managerial work and presented his own observational study of the activities of five top managers. Mintzberg spent a week recording the activities of each manager in detailed categories. This work identified 10 roles played by managers and divided them into three basic categories. A role is a position occupied by a manager; it can be identified by a set of activities. For example, a television actor may portray a detective in one show and a Western cowboy in another. The actor's activities and style, along with the dress and set, inform the audience which role is being played.

Roles are defined by grouping activities together and assigning descriptive labels. The most support for these roles comes from Mintzberg's own study, and therefore our discussion may be biased toward top managers since they were the subjects involved in the research. However, Mintzberg feels that the results are applicable to all managers and that only the proportion of the time spent in the different roles varies between a supervisor and a president. Additional studies are cited to support the author's observations.

## Interpersonal Roles

There are three interpersonal roles characterized by their involvement with people both inside and outside an organization. The first is a figurehead role where the manager performs social or symbolic duties such as visiting a sick employee or working on a charity drive. A second interpersonal role is as leader: the manager must motivate workers and see that the organization is staffed and the work force well trained. The last interpersonal role finds a manager as a liaison: the manager makes contacts both inside and outside the organization to exchange information, problems, and ideas.

## Informational Roles

Managers have two informational roles that are clearly important in considering information systems. The manager in the first informational role acts as a monitor, observing and processing different types of information. Most of the information is current and has been developed from the organization and/or its surrounding environment. The manager is a nerve center for organizational information.

The next information-handling role finds the manager disseminating data. Information is transmitted to relevant colleagues, such as subordinates, superiors, and individuals outside the organization. Finally, a manager plays a minor role as spokesperson: the manager makes comments directed to individuals outside the organization to explain company policies and actions.

## Decisional Roles

The manager's set of four decisional roles also has important bearing on information systems. First, the manager functions as an entrepreneur, searching for an initiating improvement project to bring about positive changes in the organization. The manager is also a disturbance handler, taking action when the organization faces some unanticipated consequences. The resource allocation role involves decisions on the allocation of resources in the manager's area of responsibility. The final decisional role for the manager is as negotiator, trying to adjudicate disputes in the organization.

## Managerial Activities

It is interesting to see how managers spend their time in the various activities constituting the roles described above. First, the manager's work consists primarily of verbal and written contacts. Many activities are fragmented, and frequent interruptions are the rule. The manager's work frequently seems never to be completed because of an awareness that something overlooked could improve the situation. Thus, the manager appears to be much like the student preparing for an examination: the student is never confident that an additional hour of study would be wasted because that hour could uncover the answer to a key question on a test. Since the work is never done, managers seem to work at a vigorous pace.

There are five main tools used by managers in their work, including the mail, telephone, scheduled meetings, unscheduled meetings, and observational tours. The managers observed appeared to favor verbal media; they spent much time in contact with people. Scheduled meetings consumed the greatest percentage of managerial time, and external contacts one-third to one-half of the time spent on interpersonal activities.

## Applicability of the Findings

How applicable are these findings, which are based primarily on the activities of top managers? Even though little data exist, the results seem intuitively appealing. Is it possible to generalize the results above to supervisors and clerical workers in the organization? It does appear that various roles are descriptive of activities of individuals at different levels of management. We might, however, find that activities differ in importance between, say, a supervisor and the president of the company. The figurehead role is played far more often by the president than by the supervisor.

One might also expect the situations surrounding different roles to differ. The president of the company acting as a figurehead may talk to comparable leaders in the government or in other organizations. A first-line supervisor, on the other hand, may be a figurehead for a company baseball team or may preside over a retirement dinner for a subordinate in the department. One would also expect the tools used by management to differ among levels of managers. A supervisor spends more time on observational tours and less time answering mail than the president of the company.

## FRAMEWORKS FOR INFORMATION SYSTEMS

Now that we have completed a review of managerial roles and examined information and decision making in the last chapter, we can construct a framework for viewing information systems. A framework, as we have seen, is a conceptual model for organizing thought and discussion about information systems.

We have stated that there is no one theory of information systems. However, a user or designer of a system needs some conceptual model of an information system. Unfortunately, there is no one clearly accepted framework for information systems. Because of the ill-structured nature of the field and its interdisciplinary origins, we can at best expect to develop an intuitive or a verbal model of information systems. We present several different approaches to frameworks, and adopt one for purposes of communicating in this text. It is not essential that everyone adopt the framework we use here. However, it is important for each individual dealing with information systems to have some conceptual model behind the decisions pertaining to these systems.

### Anthony

Our first framework was actually presented in Chapter 2 when we discussed different types of information used for various kinds of decisions. These categories of decision types suggested by Anthony can be considered one framework for information systems. To review, Anthony proposed three types of decisions:

---

**DON'T LEAVE HOME WITHOUT IT**

*American Express Travel Services views itself as being in the communications and information-processing business. The company spends $300 to $400 million annually, some 4 to 5 percent of its $8.1 billion revenue, on information processing. From its Phoenix computer center, the company approves 250,000 credit card purchases world-wide, averaging a five second or less response time.*

*The network also helps to control operating costs; the number of card-holders has increased by more than 50 percent over the last five years. However, AmEx has been able to hold losses from fraudulent use of cards almost constant and less than losses by its competitors.*

*The firm is now using its network as a vehicle for delivering new services. AmEx has added a service for customers to obtain refunds for lost or stolen traveler's checks by phone from any of its 800 automatic check dispensers.*

(*Business Week*, October 24, 1983).

---

1 Strategic planning is the process of deciding on organizational objectives and the means for achieving them; the planner focuses on the relationship between the environment and the organization.

2 Managerial control decisions involve a manager ensuring that resources are used efficiently and effectively to achieve the objectives stated during strategic planning. Managerial control decisions are often subjective in their interpretation of information; interpersonal interaction is important in these decisions.

3 Operational control decisions involve ensuring that specific tasks are completed efficiently and effectively.

In Chapter 2, we stressed that different types of decisions require different types of information; for example, strategic planning decisions require infrequently updated, predictive, aggregated data from external sources. The major contribution of Anthony is this distinction among types of decisions and their information requirements.

### Simon

Earlier we discussed the decision-making stages proposed by Simon, including Intelligence, Design, and Choice. Anthony is concerned with the purpose of decision-making activities, and Simon is concerned with methods and techniques of problem solving. In addition to the stages described above, Simon proposes that there are two types of decisions: programmed and nonprogrammed. Programmed decisions are routine and repetitive; some specified procedure may be applied to reach a decision each time the situation arises. Programmed decisions require little time spent in the Design stage.

On the other hand, decisions that are nonprogrammed are novel and unstructured. For these decisions, much time has to be spent in Design. There is no one solution to these nonprogrammed decisions, since the problem has probably not appeared before. Clearly, few decisions are at one polar extreme or the other. Just as with Anthony's decision types, decisions are expected to fall someplace along a continuum between programmed and nonprogrammed.

Different types of decision-making technology are suitable for attacking each type of problem. Programmed decisions have traditionally been made through habit, by clerical procedures, or with other accepted tools. More modern techniques for solving programmed decisions involve operations research, mathematical analysis, modeling, and simulation.

Nonprogrammed decisions tend to be solved through judgment, intuition, and rules of thumb. Modern approaches to nonprogrammed decisions include special data analysis programs on computers, training for decision makers in heuristic techniques, and heuristic computer programs. Over time we expect to see new technology providing more programming to nonprogrammed decisions; that is, decisions will tend to move toward the more programmed pole of the continuum.

**TABLE 3-1**
THE GORRY AND SCOTT MORTON FRAMEWORK

| Classification | Operational control | Management control | Strategic planning |
|---|---|---|---|
| Structured | Order processing<br>Accounts payable | Budgets<br>Personnel reports | Warehouse location<br>Transportation mode mix |
| Semistructured | Inventory control<br>Production planning | Analysis of variance | Introduction of new product |
| Unstructured | Cash management | Management of personnel | Planning for R&D |

## Gorry-Scott Morton

Gorry and Scott Morton (1971) have synthesized the work of Anthony and Simon to develop a very appealing framework for information systems. The results of their efforts are shown in Table 3-1. This matrix classifies Anthony's decision types from operational control to strategic planning on a structured to unstructured scale. (Gorry and Scott Morton feel that "structured" and "unstructured" are better terms than "programmed" and "nonprogrammed.")

The three decision phases of Intelligence, Design, and Choice are structured for a fully structured decision. An unstructured problem means that all three

---

## MANAGEMENT PROBLEM 3-1

David Masters, vice president of finance for the Major Metals Company, is responsible for overall inventory levels in the firm. Major Metals is an integrated mining and metals-producing company with locations throughout the United States. The firm has several computer centers, all reporting to Masters at corporate headquarters in Chicago.

One of the major inventories in the company consists of spare parts for mining and metal-production operations. At one of the divisions, this inventory has a value of over $30 million and consists of around 60,000 items. Analysts at the computer center serving this division are developing a new inventory control system to replace the existing one. A number of new features are being added to this more advanced computer application, including an operations research model for determining reorder points and quantities.

Masters feels that the design of such a system should be under the control of the local design staff who know conditions best. However, he is disturbed about a report he received from the present system, which he does not find useful. Masters fears that this report will be continued in the new system.

Every month, Masters receives an inventory status report showing the quantity of each item in inventory, its usage during the month, the receipt of new merchandise, and the value of the item. Since there are 60,000 items in inventory, this report is voluminous.

Why do you suppose the analysts ever sent this report to the vice president? How does the material discussed in this chapter apply to the distribution of the inventory status report? What should Masters do?

phases are unstructured, and any decision between is semistructured. As in Simon's framework, the line between structured and unstructured decisions shifts over time as new decision techniques are developed and applied to unstructured problems.

From Table 3-1 it appears that most existing information systems have attacked problems in the structured, operational control cell. These problems are similar in many organizations and are among the most easily understood. It is easier to mechanize these decisions and to predict and achieve cost savings than it is for less structured decisions or for strategic planning decisions. Since operational systems are important to the daily functioning of the firm, they are high-priority applications.

Many individuals in the information systems field believe that decisions with the greatest payoff for the organization are unstructured in nature. The development of systems for unstructured problems is a major challenge and is undoubtedly more risky than the development of comparable systems for structured problems. The goals and design techniques for unstructured decisions differ from those for structured ones. In the structured case, the goal of an information system is usually to improve the processing of information. In an unstructured situation, the goal of the information system is more likely to be one of improving the organization and presentation of information inputs to the decision maker.

We shall see a large number of computer applications in this text. Organizations and individuals have been extremely creative in developing new uses of computers. Huge computer complexes support the kind of airline systems described in the first chapter; microcomputers are used by professionals in a variety of fields for personal decision support and analysis.

A framework such as the Gorry-Scott Morton model can aid our thinking in studying different kinds of systems. What kind of management support does the

---

## MANAGEMENT PROBLEM 3-2

The recently hired director of information systems for a major manufacturing firm was contemplating his new position. After surveying existing applications in the firm, he found that most computer systems were mundane and primarily processed transactions. Users were happy with the service received from the information services department but had low expectations about the potential of computers.

The new director wanted to continue existing good service levels but also thought that computers could do a lot more for the firm. The director had the support of top management, but because of little user understanding of the potential for new systems, he knew that any innovative ideas would have to be his own.

How should the director proceed to bring more benefits from computer-based systems to the firm? How will the frameworks described in this chapter help him in this task? What problems do you expect the director will encounter?

---

system provide? What is the nature of the problem? A manager should not be terribly surprised when a structured operational control or transactions processing system fails to provide much information that is of interest for decision making.

Depending on the type of system, we may also find that our implementation strategies will differ. The task of designing a structured transactions processing system is different than the task of building a model for a manager to use in making plans for the corporation.

Tremendous advances in hardware and software have brought us a variety of ways to apply computer support to a problem area. We are limited only by our imagination and knowledge of the technology and the organization in applying

---

## A STRATEGY FOR SERVICE

*It has been estimated that ordering, inventory and supply functions consume 40 percent of a hospital's operating budget. Hospitals have done almost everything possible to hold down labor costs; in order to stay within government guidelines the materials handling function is now being examined.*

*Capitalizing on this need American Hospital Supply Corporation, the largest company in the hospital supply business with some $2 billion in sales, is assisting hospitals in better managing their materials.*

*American Hospital Supply is the only company currently offering automated order entry and inventory control systems to hospitals. It costs about $1,400 a month for most of the company's customers and the firm has signed up 3,000 of the 7,000 hospitals in the country.*

*These hospitals use computer terminals to communicate directly on-line with American's central computer in Illinois. Incoming orders are immediately routed by the computer to the company's regional distribution center located nearest the customer. There are some 90 of these regional centers around the United States. Within minutes of typing the purchase order on its terminal the hospital receives back a printed confirmation from the firm giving the price of the items and their delivery date. American claims that the system cuts the cost of a typical purchase by 20 percent. Hospitals can also save money by reducing inventories since American says that it ships 95 percent of all orders on the same day they are received.*

*The hospital is encouraged to combine the order entry system with an inventory control system to track incoming supplies, disbursements and stock levels and compare projected inventory with actual supplies on hand.*

*In addition to providing a service that generates revenue in its own right, hospitals are more likely to purchase supplies from American if they are using part of its systems. The average hospital order on the American system is for 5.8 items while the industry average is only 1.7 items per order. American supplies some 133,000 different items to hospitals.*

*Business Week, September 8, 1980.*

information systems to solve problems or improve the competitive position of the firm.

## KEY WORDS

| | | |
|---|---|---|
| Decision | Liaison | Resource allocator |
| Disseminator | Managerial control | Spokesperson |
| Disturbance handler | Management informa- | Semistructured |
| Entrepreneur | tion systems | Strategic planning |
| Exception reports | Monitor | Structured |
| Figurehead role | Negotiator | Transactions processing |
| Informational roles | Nonprogrammed | Unstructured |
| Interpersonal roles | Operational control | |
| Leader | Programmed | |

## RECOMMENDED READINGS

Anthony, R.: *Planning and Control Systems: A Framework for Analysis,* Division of Research, Graduate School of Business Administration, Harvard University, Boston, 1965. (A complete and readable exposition of Anthony's framework for decision making; it is highly recommended.)

Gorry, G. A., and M. S. Scott Morton: "A Framework for Management Information Systems," *Sloan Management Review,* vol. 13, no. 1, 1971, pp. 55–70. (Consult this reference for more details on the framework adopted in this chapter.)

Lucas, H. C., Jr., K. W. Clowes, R. B. Kaplan: "Framework for Information Systems," *INFOR,* vol. 12, no. 3, October 1974*b*, pp. 245–260. (A review comparing and contrasting a number of frameworks for information systems. Each of the frameworks is evaluated, and the authors recommend the Gorry–Scott Morton framework.)

Mintzberg, H.: *The Nature of Managerial Work,* Harper & Row, New York, 1973. (Mintzberg's book is recommended reading for any student of information systems. The details of the study referenced in this chapter are presented along with the findings of other studies.)

Simon, H.: *The Shape of Automation for Men and Management,* Harper & Row, New York, 1965. (Essays by Simon describing some of his ideas on problem solving.)

## DISCUSSION QUESTIONS

1 Why have so many transactions-processing computer systems been developed?

2 Keep a diary categorizing your daily activities according to the classifications used by Mintzberg. How do your activities compare with those of the managers in his study?

3 How could Mintzberg's technique of structured observation be used in designing an information system?

4 Describe the purposes of a framework. What kinds of problems are encountered when individuals with different backgrounds try to communicate without some common conceptual model?

5 Why is the line between structured and unstructured decisions shifting more toward structured? Are unstructured decisions being eliminated, or will we continue to be faced with this type of decision problem?

6 How would you define and recognize the characteristics of a management information system?

7 Sketch a framework for information systems of your own. How does it compare with the ones discussed in the chapter?

8 Several authors have suggested functional frameworks for information systems, for example, information systems to serve logistics, finance, and marketing functions. What are the advantages and disadvantages of this approach to frameworks?

9 What are the problems in developing an information system to support unstructured decision making?

10 What are the characteristics of an information system to support strategic planning activities in an organization?

11 What aspects of management are like a science? What aspects of management defy a scientific approach?

12 Compare and contrast an information system for processing orders with one for planning a corporate acquisition. On what technological characteristics would you expect these systems to differ? What types of information and to whom should the information be provided by each of these systems?

13 What type of technology would you expect to see used for operational control, managerial control, and strategic planning systems? For example, where would an on-line system be used versus a batch system?

14 What role can information serve for a decision maker acting as a disturbance handler? What role can information serve for a decision maker acting in the information, interpersonal, and decisional roles?

15 Can an information system be of any assistance to a manager acting as a negotiator?

16 What is wrong with the classic views of management activities?

17 What problems are created by providing the wrong type of information for a particular decision setting? What do the Simon, Anthony, and Gorry–Scott Morton frameworks suggest is likely to happen?

18 What level of management would you expect to be associated with different decision types; for example, who makes the preponderance of planning decisions in an organization?

19 Think of an example of a structured versus an unstructured decision problem and compare the two on the information differences presented by Anthony.

20 What top management functions and activities can be supported by a computer-based information system?

# AN OVERVIEW OF COMPUTER APPLICATIONS

# AN OVERVIEW OF COMPUTER APPLICATIONS

## CHAPTER ISSUES

- What are the major components of a system?
- How can computers be applied in an organization?

In this chapter, we discuss the general structure of information systems and look at examples of different kinds of systems. Our purpose is to gain an appreciation for the many different applications employing computer-based information systems.

## TYPES OF SYSTEMS

Figure 4-1 is a simple illustration of the basic components of a computer-based information system. A system processes input that is provided by a user, for example, a list of hours worked by employees. The input is first edited for errors and corrected, if necessary, through manual intervention. An entry that indicates someone worked 120 hours in a week is probably incorrect and should be questioned. The input becomes immediate output (a check) or is used to modify the files (pay records) of the system. Input can also be used to request the retrieval of information stored in the system, such as the names of all employees who worked overtime last week.

Files containing data are a major component of the information system. The files correspond to the information kept in folders, file cabinets, or notebooks in a manual information system. Information may be retrieved from a file, or the

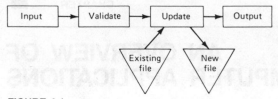

**FIGURE 4-1**
Components of a computer-based information system.

file contents may be altered by modifying, adding, or deleting data in the file. We are also interested in some type of output from a system that may be a short response to an inquiry request for information from a file or the result of elaborate computations. Output is produced in many different formats and modes of presentation such as printed report, a display on a televisionlike screen, or a verbal response.

It is helpful to distinguish among the types of information systems according to the technology employed. In a simple batch system, all input is processed at one point in time to produce the desired output. The input data are collected and used to update the files periodically, for example, daily, weekly, or monthly. The data are frequently out of date in this type of system because updating is periodic, but batch processing is very economical. A payroll system is an example of an application that is usually operated in batch mode because pay checks are issued periodically.

A simple inquiry system features on-line retrieval of information from files that are updated in batch mode. A system for production control might be updated overnight and have its files available for inquiry using a terminal during the day.

An inquiry and post system is similar to a simple inquiry system in processing retrieval requests for information. However, it also accepts and edits input on-line for later updating in batch mode. This input is saved on a file and is used to update the system later. The production control system above could be operated in this manner to accept input from factory-floor data terminals during the day. Then in the evening, when the computer schedule is less heavy, the files could be updated in a batch processing run.

An inquiry and on-line updating system actually makes modifications to files as the information is entered from terminals. These systems require more complicated technology and are exemplified by on-line reservations systems.

A command and control system or real-time system is one in which information has to be fed back instantaneously to control an operation. For example, sensors on a missile feed information to a computer that must process the data in time to provide guidance control for the missile.

The applications above run on mainframe or minicomputers, computers which feature multiple users accessing shared data and programs. The fastest growing area of the computer industry, however, is the microcomputer sector.

TABLE 4-1
CHARACTERISTICS AND APPLICATIONS OF VARIOUS TECHNOLOGIES

| Type of system | Characteristics | Example |
|---|---|---|
| **Mainframe and Minicomputers** | | |
| Simple batch system | Updating at one point in time | Payroll |
| Simple inquiry | Update in batch, retrieve on-line | Inventory status |
| Inquiry and post | Update in batch, retrieve on-line, enter and edit data on-line | Production control with factory-floor input |
| Fully on-line | All input, output, and updating done on-line through terminals | Reservations system |
| Command and control | Fully on-line and instantaneous feedback to control some process | Missile launching and guidance |
| **Personal computers** | | |
| local | No shared data, private analysis | Spreadsheet analysis |
| on-line | Access to corporate data | Extracting sales data |

These computers can be used for entirely personal work, for example, financial analysis or word processing. Most personal computers can also be turned into terminals to connect with mainframe or minicomputers; the user extracts data from the larger system and downloads it (mainframe transfer to the PC) to the personal computer for processing.

Table 4-1 summarizes the types of systems and their characteristics, and provides an example of a typical application employing each type of technology.

## APPLICATIONS

In the rest of this chapter, we present a survey of various computer-based information systems to illustrate the diversity of situations in which these systems have been used. Our vehicle for presentation will be to follow a hypothetical user through a day's activities. We shall discuss the information systems encountered and briefly describe their characteristics. These information systems do not necessarily exist in exactly the form described here. However, all the applications areas suggested have been supported by computer-based information systems similar to the ones encountered below.

### The Manager

Our hypothetical user is Martha Johnson, the executive vice president of Diversified Products, Inc. Diversified is a medium-sized conglomerate whose major operation is the production of automobile parts for new car and replacement markets. Several smaller subsidiaries manufacture parts for other consumer durable products.

Martha has an M.B.A. from a leading business school and has been working for Diversified for about 5 years. She began as controller, having majored in accounting and finance. Martha was recently promoted to executive vice president, a position with major operating and financial responsibilities.

### The Morning

We join Martha on her way to work in the morning. She lives in a townhouse near a rail line serving the central city where Diversified's headquarters and main production facilities are located. This morning she listens to a weather forecast and decides to drive to the railroad station because showers are predicted.

**A Weather System**  Behind the forecast is a huge system of reporting stations and computer equipment; data from all over the world are collected and processed to study and predict the weather. Some of the largest computational programs for modern computers were developed for the task of weather forecasting. However, the general public rarely glimpses the people or machines monitoring the weather and generating these forecasts.

**A Police System**  While driving to the station, Martha encounters the well-known phenomenon of a radar speed trap, though fortunately she is heading in the opposite direction! She notices that immediately after stopping the offending motorist, the police officer does not leave the patrol car but instead speaks on the car radio. Had she been able to overhear the conversation, Martha would have heard the officer checking with the dispatcher to get information about the automobile to be cited. What kind of data would the officer receive and how?

At the heart of this police information system is a computer-based file containing information on wants and warrants, and these data can be retrieved from the file on-line for an inquiring officer. The police officer in the field radios the command center and requests information on a given license number. At the center, an operator using a terminal connected to an on-line system enters the license number. The computer is programmed to search for any information on the file about a car with that license plate or the person to whom it is registered.

Typical questions would be, "Are there any outstanding tickets or warrants for the car or driver? Is the automobile stolen?" Information is retrieved and radioed back to the police officer. If the driver is wanted, the officer takes special precautions or calls for assistance in approaching the automobile. Such information has greatly increased the safety of the police officer.

However, as with any benefit, there are costs connected with such a system. Police systems have raised issues of invasion of privacy over the records of data

---

**MANAGEMENT PROBLEM 4-1**

The chief executive of a small firm specializing in the acquisition of cable TV companies feels that the major reason for the firm's success is its ability to perform an economic evaluation of a proposed acquisition in 2 or 3 days. Larger competitors, because of standards and bureaucratic procedures, are not able to move as rapidly.

However, there are several problems with the analysis conducted by the firm. Because of the computational complexity of financing arrangements and depreciation schemes, very few possibilities are computed. The controller of the firm uses a pocket calculator for the computations; there is not sufficient time for a complete analysis of the myriad possibilities available.

The chief executive thought that a computer might be able to help, but he is unsure of how to proceed. Clearly a number of alternatives are available beyond the simple hand calculator used now. The choices appear to be either a microcomputer for the firm or the use of a time-sharing system.

Although the chief executive and the controller have narrowed the choices to the two above, they would like some help in making a final decision. What criteria should they use? Having chosen a processing alternative, how do they develop a system to assist in making decisions about acquisitions? (What type of information system is this?)

---

maintained on them. These systems also can result in abuses to citizens if not updated properly. For example, in one city, some stolen cars were recovered, but the computer system was not updated. Several rightful owners of the returned automobiles were arrested later because the information system was not kept up to date!

**A Sales Application**   After arriving at work, Martha receives a summary management report on sales in Diversified's major division. Diversified employs about 150 sales representatives nationwide. Twenty-five of these representatives call on Detroit manufacturers to sell new car parts while the others concentrate on sales of auto replacement parts through chain stores and other retail outlets.

The company has developed a fairly elaborate batch sales-information system as an outgrowth of its order-entry computer system. Sales force members complete orders and send them to the data processing center where they are transcribed into a machine-readable medium. The orders are summarized by type and product and printed by due date for production control scheduling purposes. The orders are also analyzed to extract sales information; past sales history is kept on a computer file. Each sales representative receives a monthly report showing his or her accounts and 12 months of historical sales data. The reports also contain this-year-to-date and last-year-to-date figures on sales by unit and dollar volume.

There is a goal or quota for each sales representative that is also shown on the report. This system has eliminated much of the sales representatives' bookkeeping and allowed them to concentrate on sales. The sales information system also produces a summary report by territory and by product for management. A batch retrieval program allows managers to select different types of information based on their needs. Martha Johnson, for example, likes to receive a report of sales by product and sales by product within each geographical region. She uses this information to obtain a feeling for how different product groups are doing and to compare sales with inventories in different parts of the country.

**The Production System**   A 10 A.M. meeting is scheduled to discuss a request for a new production control system. Most of the operations of Diversified are classified as job shop as opposed to assembly-line production. There is a series of manufacturing operations on each product, and a number of different machines can be used for these operations; there is no one sequence of steps. Scheduling job shops is difficult because of the combinatorial number of paths through the shop for a given product.

Early in the days of computer use, Diversified developed a time-sharing simulation model to help in the scheduling process. A production control scheduler inputs the jobs to be completed to a terminal connected to a commercial firm selling time-sharing services. A model developed by a consulting firm simulates the flow of orders through the shop and prints the best schedule. The simulation program has a table showing all machinery requirements for different orders. Various scheduling rules are tried, and the best scheduling rule for time and cost is selected.

The purpose of the 10 A.M. meeting is to discuss a proposal for installing factory-floor data-collection terminals to record the status of production. Several managers in the company have questioned the advisability and need for such data, and the meeting continues until 11:30.

**Microcomputers**   Before lunch, Martha returns to her office and has a chance to meet with her secretary. The secretary has just finished making the corrections to a report Martha has written. The secretary uses a microcomputer with a word processing package for this type of report.

Martha dictates the report based on an outline, and the secretary types from the dictation on the microcomputer keyboard. The system features a CRT display and a letter-quality printer to run off the final document. The secretary enters the report and then uses an editing program to make changes and corrections. The secretary also types in special commands to the word processing program so that different headings are centered and/or printed in a different type font than the rest of the paper. There are a variety of these special commands to allow for underlining, boldface print, and so on.

Martha also has a microcomputer in her office which she uses for various tasks. She can connect her microcomputer to the company's mainframe system and extract data from its massive files. Her extracted data are stored on small, floppy diskettes or on a small hard disk drive in her microcomputer. Then, disconnected from the mainframe, the microcomputer is used to process the extracted data using special, powerful software packages.

Of course, the microcomputer can also be used to "stand alone" for data that Martha enters herself. An example is an analysis she just performed of budget variances for two departments. Her secretary entered some of the data in an electronic spreadsheet program. This program provides the user with a spreadsheet with addressable rows and columns on the screen. Algebraic relationships among the cells defined at the intersection of a row and column are defined. Then, if the user wants to change a number or an assumption, the entire spreadsheet is recalculated. This package makes it very easy to try a number of different assumptions or pieces of data; the results are recalculated automatically. This kind of application is a good example of a simple decision support system in which the user is interested in "what if" kinds of questions.

The word processing example is a part of a larger trend called "office automation." The idea is to use computers to support office workers. Martha has been investigating the possibility of buying an electronic mail system for Diversified. This application uses a computer to set up electronic mailboxes for each user of the system. Users work with terminals to access the mail in their mailbox whenever they wish to review it. The advantages of this type of system make it very attractive; individuals do not have to be interrupted by phone calls or play "telephone tag" (it is estimated that less than 30 percent of phone calls actually reach the other party the first time dialed).

The major problem with the system is that it requires discipline on the part of users. Each person must have easy access to a terminal and be willing to use the computer. While Martha knows that she and some of the other executives will work with it, she also believes that there are several who are quite opposed to computers. "This is a difficult implementation problem," she thought after reading the latest magazine article about electronic mail. "Maybe next year, but Diversified is just not ready today."

### Lunch

**Computer-Aided Design**  Martha lunches with the head of engineering for Diversified; they discuss a recent demonstration at a customer's location. The customer, one of the major automobile manufacturers, showed them its engineering research center. The manager of engineering was fascinated by the customer's computer-aided design system. Automobile designers sit in front of cathode-ray tube (CRT) terminals, which resemble a television set, and work interactively with the computer to design new products. An engineer uses a light pen to indicate changes on the screen and the computer system makes the changes on-line instantaneously. Several complete cars had been designed in this manner.

The system at the auto firm was custom designed by its own engineering and computer staff. Since that time, a number of vendors have developed special software packages for their computers; independent software firms have also put together computer-aided design systems on different kinds of hardware.

Based on the demonstration and what had been appearing in the trade press, Martha and the manager of engineering agree to begin a project to evaluate the various offerings. Within a year, they would like to have a computer-aided design system working at Diversified.

The engineering manager is particularly enthusiastic since not only does such a system help in design for new products, it stores all existing designs (once they have been entered) so that a minor change needed for a new customer does not require a complete redrafting of the part.

**Two Customer-Oriented Systems**   After lunch, Martha has a few minutes to conduct two items of personal business. First, she wishes to see if a check has been credited to her bank account. She stops at a branch of the bank and keys in her account number on a standard Touch-Tone phone. She receives a response giving the balance of her checking account: "four two oh one dollars and seven five cents."

This bank system is basically a batch on-line inquiry application. The telephone is an inexpensive terminal; computer output is produced by an audio-response unit. Numbers are prerecorded on this device and the computer program accepts the account number, locates the balance on file, and gives instructions to the audio response unit on what numbers to "play" for output.

Back at the office, Martha decides to try another letter to *Modern Living* magazine (earlier she had resolved to cancel her subscription). First, her subscription was not renewed as requested. Then two copies of the magazine started arriving each month. Several letters also came demanding payment even after Martha sent a copy of her cancelled check. This time Martha is writing to the publisher in hopes of obtaining satisfaction.

At the magazine, chaos had prevailed since a consultant had designed and programmed a new subscription system. For some reason, unknown to the magazine staff, the new system did not work. The computer cancelled subscriptions after the magazine sent two copies each month. Customers cancelled other subscriptions because they were not receiving copies. Circulation dropped and the magazine had to resort to costly overprinting to be sure enough copies were available. Because of the decline in circulation, advertising revenue also decreased. Finally, after the magazine hired some staff members with computer experience and turned to another consultant for help, the situation is improving. However, *Modern Living* was very close to bankruptcy at one point because the subscription system failed so badly.

**Afternoon**

**Marketing Research**   After lunch, Martha attends a meeting with the marketing department. This department is looking at marketing models to see how they could be used to assist the company. The department requested more funds in its budget to hire an operations research staff member and for time-sharing services. Several models were available to help in advertising decisions; there were also models to suggest strategies for new product selection and introduction. In addition to the models already available, a number of statistical techniques to answer different marketing questions could be applied to sales data already collected by the sales information system.

The marketing department also wants funds to use an existing information storage and retrieval system. Several vendors offer very large data bases of information useful for such research. For example, one company has much of the information for over 300,000 National Aeronautics and Space Administration (NASA) citations in a data base that can be accessed by customers for a fee. The user of these services dials a computer in California and employs a simple language to submit retrieval requests. A computer program searches for abstracts fitting the key words entered by the user. Abstracts can be printed at the computer center and mailed to the requester if a large number of citations is found.

**Planning Systems**    Later in the afternoon, Martha receives the output from the latest run of Diversified's planning model. Using a specially developed language for planning, a staff member constructed a model of the firm. Simple equations are used to express basic relationships among demand, production, sales, and inventory. The staff develops various scenarios and compares the output to predict the results of different courses of action.

Economic data obtained from a firm selling time-series data on the economy supplements the planning model. The vendor of economic data has a large computer model of the economy, constructed with sophisticated regression techniques. Information developed from this model is made available to customers; Diversified uses these data to provide information on general economic conditions for its own model.

Martha is particularly interested in a cash flow forecast for the next 4 or 5 years for a new subsidiary under consideration for acquisition. On the next run, she asks the analyst to show what would happen to cash flow projections if the new subsidiary is acquired this year and an existing, unprofitable subsidiary is sold in 3 years.

**Airplane Reservations**    Before leaving work Martha calls an airline to make a reservation for a trip the following week. The passenger agent who answers the phone converses with an on-line reservation system through an alphanumeric CRT terminal (unlike the graphics terminal for automated design, this TV-like terminal prints only letters and numbers). The agent obtains information on what flights are available from the computer system; a computer program checks the file of flights and times and displays them on the agent's screen.

Based on the schedules, Martha requests a round-trip flight. The agent enters her request; the computer system checks a file for the flight requested and indicates that space is available. The agent enters Martha's name, and the

**TABLE 4-2**
SUMMARY OF SYSTEMS

| System | Decision type | Technology |
|---|---|---|
| Weather | Operational | Batch, on-line |
| Police want/warrant | Operational | On-line |
| Sales, order entry | Transactional, operational, management | Batch |
| Production control | Operational | On-line (time-sharing) |
| Microcomputer | Decision support | Personal computer |
| Microcomputer | Word processing | Personal computer |
| Automobile design | Operational | On-line |
| Account inquiry | Transactional | On-line inquiry |
| Subscription | Transaction | Batch |
| Marketing models | Managerial and strategic | Time-sharing |
| Planning model | Strategic | Time-sharing |
| Reservations system | Transactional, operational | On-line |
| Supermarket system | Transactional, operational | On-line |

computer program places it on a file. Later, plans can be changed easily. Martha's record can be consulted by the agent when she appears for her ticket and proceeds to the gate to board the plane.

**A Supermarket System**   On the way home, Martha stops at a supermarket that has a new, automated checkout system. The system appears fast to Martha, but she wonders if it is economical. Each grocery item is coded with something called the Universal Product Code, and this code can be read by an optical scanner in the counter when the item and code are passed over the scanner. Price information is retrieved by a computer program, which also maintains a running total of the groceries purchased by the customer. The clerk no longer has to operate a cash register. By knowing every item sold, the store can keep track of inventory and place appropriate reorders. Experience has shown that store shelves can be replenished more quickly when scanners are used. Stores can also accommodate more customers and hence can make more sales, because scanners expedite the checkout process.

## IN CONCLUSION

In this brief sketch, we observed a number of different information systems. These systems employ different types of computer technology and support different kinds of decisions (see Table 4-2). Some of the systems have problems, while others appear to work well. In later chapters, we shall explain some of these problems and try to suggest how to design successful computer systems.

We should emphasize that the scenario described in this chapter is hypothetical; however, applications such as these do exist. It should be obvious that computer-based information systems have been applied to many diverse situations. While we always are constrained by cost and technology, to a great extent we are limited only by our imagination, creativity, and ability to deal successfully with the changes created by computer-based information systems.

## KEY WORDS

| | | |
|---|---|---|
| Alphanumeric | Graphics | Office automation |
| Audio response | Edit | On-line |
| Batch | Electronic mail | Output |
| Command and control | Inquire and post | Posting |
| Computer aided design | Inquiry | Simulation |
| CRT | Microcomputer | Update |
| Files | Models | Word processing |

## RECOMMENDED READINGS

*Business Week.* (See section on information systems for current applications.)
*Byte* and other popular computing magazines. (Frequent articles on microcomputer applications.)
*Computer World.* (A weekly newspaper with frequent briefs on applications.)
*Time* (See section on computers.)

## DISCUSSION QUESTIONS

1 What are the advantages and disadvantages of batch computer systems?
2 Do you expect input editing to be easier for a batch or for an on-line system?
3 Why do you suppose inquiry and post systems were developed instead of fully on-line applications?
4 What are the advantages and disadvantages of fully on-line computer systems?
5 How do backup requirements differ between batch and on-line systems?
6 What applications, if any, exist for command and control systems in business?
7 How does time sharing differ in its use from both batch and on-line systems?
8 What are the drawbacks to mathematical models applied to management problems?
9 What are the problems with simulation as a tool in business analysis?
10 Why do so many batch computer systems exist?
11 What factors inhibit the development of on-line systems? (Hint: think of the major components of such systems.)
12 What are the social issues involved in having massive files of personal data available on-line?
13 Computer-aided instruction has been suggested as one way to improve education. What do you think its limitations are?
14 Why are so many time-sharing applications developed in user departments rather than under the control of an internal information systems department?
15 One critic has suggested that management information can never be automated. What is your reaction to this statement?
16 Examine a computer application with which you are familiar. Describe its purpose, input, output, processing, and files.

**17** Inventory control is one of the most popular computer applications. Why? What has its impact been on the economy?

**18** An entire industry exists for selling information. Make a survey of some of the data for sale and classify it by functional area, for example, marketing, finance, economics.

**19** Why is it useful to have interaction capabilities when working with a computer-based model?

**20** What factors from a user's standpoint are different in the design of a batch versus an on-line system?

**21** What are the major advantages and disadvantages of inquiry and post systems where data are captured on-line but files are updated later, say, at night?

# PART TWO

# ORGANIZATIONAL ISSUES

In this part we review what is known about the impact of computer systems on the organization. Our emphasis is on the design of systems that have a positive impact on the organization and its members. The analysis is aided by two models: the first explains the development of power by different departments in an organization, and the second focuses specifically on information systems in the context of the organization.

The impact of computers on the organization is of key concern to management. Chapter 5 provides the preparation necessary to discuss the implementation of systems, in the section of the text on systems analysis and design.

Top management has a key role to play in the management of information processing activities in the organization. There is much emphasis today on using information technology as a part of corporate strategy, a topic which is addressed in depth in Chapter 6. In this part we also discuss information systems policy; what are the key areas for the involvement of top management? What policy should top management establish for the information systems effort in the organization? A successful information services function begins with strong and effective leadership at the top levels of the organization.

## CHAPTER 5

# THE IMPACT OF INFORMATION SYSTEMS ON THE ORGANIZATION

## CHAPTER ISSUES

- What benefits have come from computer systems?
- How should the organization prepare for the impact of computers?
- How should the organization approach the design and operation of information systems?

## IMPACT ON THE ORGANIZATION

A technology as pervasive as computers and information systems has a wide range of impacts on an organization. We shall examine some of these impacts and how they affect planning for the implementation of systems. Computers can affect the strategy of the firm, its revenues and expenses, the structure of the organization, and individuals working in the organization.

### Strategy

A number of organizations have used computers to gain a competitive edge; they have designed creative applications that allow them to compete more effectively. In Chapter 6 we shall examine some of these applications, including one at a brokerage firm and another at a hospital supply corporation.

One good example of strategic computer use comes in the drug supply industry. McKesson Corporation has developed a system called Economost which has increased and protected its share of the market. The first version of the system featured hand-held terminals used by McKesson customers, generally

63

drug stores. When a product was out of stock or the stock was low, an employee checking store shelves read a product code from the shelf label and keyed it into the terminal. Upon completion of the inventory, the terminal was used to transmit the order over phone lines to the McKesson central computer.

Over the next eight years, McKesson enhanced the system. Various terminal types have been included for different needs. There is also a bar code scanner for picking up a product code directly from a bar code on the shelf label, eliminating the keying operation. Since the system knows what products are stored in which aisles, the system creates packing lists ordered so that items for the same section of the store can be packed in the same container.

McKesson also offers a claims service for programs like Medicare. Individuals apply and receive plastic identification cards like a credit card. On paying a nominal amount, say $1 for the prescription, they use the credit card to prepare a claims form which is used by the drug store to obtain the remaining payment from the insurance company. A McKesson subsidiary processes the claims; the entire application tends to keep customers coming back to the same drug store.

### Revenues

Some firms have used computers to generate additional revenue. McDonnell Douglas is a large aerospace organization; it has a subsidiary offering computer services and consulting to various clients. McDonnell has also bought a major time-sharing company with a large, world-wide communication network for computer users.

Other firms make information products available through computer systems. There is an abundance of financial data bases and services to which one can subscribe. It is possible to obtain hundreds of types of data about companies and their financial conditions. One firm, Mead Data, offers a system called Lexis which contains citations for various court decisions. The system is used heavily in law offices where attornies and their assistants search for past decisions that may be relevant to the legal problems at hand.

### Savings

One traditional use of computers in organizations has been for cost savings. Companies have automated clerical tasks to reduce costs. Insurance companies and banks generate products that are really information: bills, notices, renewals, and so on represent output products that must be printed and distributed to customers. It is not clear that these systems have resulted in the elimination of existing positions, but they probably reduce the number of additional employees needed in the future.

Manufacturing firms have saved money by using computers to control their inventories. Computer programs calculate the best balance between the cost of carrying inventory and the cost of ordering or making items. Economic order quantity models have existed for years, but they were difficult to apply to an inventory with many different items without a computer to do the processing.

## Better Quality

One reason to use a computer is to improve the quality of output. Computer-aided-design is a good example. An engineer or draftsman uses a computer terminal to create engineering drawings. He or she stores the drawing on a computer file; it can be recalled later for easy modification. A system like this will also plot a drawing copy; changes are redrawn in minutes. The system reduces much of the drudgery of design work and will probably reduce the need for draftspeople.

Word processing is another example of using computers to improve quality. A typist enters the document using a computer terminal. Often the author actually composes the document on the computer. The user can make changes and then print the document. This process is far more efficient than retyping the document manually with each change. The output is always attractive; there will be no strikeouts or correction fluid on the finished product.

## The Only Way

There may be no other way to do some task than to use a computer. How else could an airline associate a passenger name with all of the legs of a trip and have the information accessible anyplace in the world in a few seconds without the use of a computer? The first American Airlines Sabre reservations system began working only a few months before the airline had estimated that its manual reservations procedure would break down because of overloading. There are many other applications where, because of the complexity of the procedures, the size of the database, or the necessity to have communications across a wide geographic area, a computer system is the only way to solve a problem.

## IMPACT ON ORGANIZATIONAL STRUCTURE

The discussion above relates to how computers have impacted the way the organization conducts business. This section examines how computers have impacted the internal structure of the organization. What kind of changes have been observed in the past? How should management plan for the introduction of computers?

## Early Predictions

Leavitt and Whisler (1958) presented one of the best-known sets of predictions for the impact of computers on organizations. These authors suggested that firms would recentralize as a result of new computer technology; the availability of more information than previously possible would allow management to centralize. The trend until the development of computer systems had been toward decentralization because centralized management could not cope with the amount of information and the number of decisions required in a large organization. Computers offer the power to make centralized management possible so the organization can be tightly controlled by a group of top managers.

Little evidence supports this early prediction. In a few cases, researchers have found examples of recentralization after computer systems were installed; however, there is no overall trend evident. Occasionally a system has replaced a level of management, for example, a military command and control system. Unfortunately, there have been too few studies, and research in this area is hard to conduct because so many variables besides computer systems affect the structure of an organization.

Another problem in validating predictions of computer impact occurs in defining variables such as centralization and decentralization. Moreover, early predictions assumed that decentralization is negatively motivated. However, there may be other reasons to decentralize—for example, to train managers or to provide more autonomy for supervisors.

There is no real reason why computer systems lead naturally to centralization. We can consider centralization and decentralization as variables in the systems design process. Certainly, centralization is not something that should be measured after a system has been implemented. Management should specify the goals of the organization and the degree of centralization desired. Given the sophisticated communications capabilities of on-line computer systems and large data-base systems, we can design a computer system that provides information for decision making at any level or geographical location in an organization.

### Distribution of Power

As mentioned earlier, some of the first studies of the impact of the computer on organizations are not helpful because they have not really provided a basis for designing successful systems. The real problem with the impact of information systems on organizations is a subject not covered in past studies: information systems affect the distribution of power in the organization. "Power" is the potential to influence others to act according to our wishes. Different departments in organizations have different levels of power, and a theory proposed by Hickson et al. (1971) offers some insight into these power relationships. These authors suggest a model with four major conditions, described below, that produce a department having a high level of power. As we shall see, the information services department meets all these conditions for high power, and by its activities, this department alters the distribution of power in an organization.

One hypothesized determinant of power is the extent to which the department copes with uncertainty for other departments. Uncertainty is defined as the lack of information about future events that make their outcomes less predictable. An information services department copes with a great deal of uncertainty for user departments. When a new system is designed, the user often yields control over an operation to the information services department.

For example, consider the department that used to prepare budget statements manually but that has just implemented a computer system to process budgets. Before the computer system, when a group of clerks and analysts prepared the budget, the manager of the department had complete control. If the department was behind schedule, the manager could arrange overtime or employ temporary help to see that the job was completed. A solution to most problems was within the manager's own department. Now, with the computer system, the manager has added uncertainties about whether the information services department will finish processing on time and with acceptable accuracy. The development of this computer system has created uncertainty for the manager where none existed before. Interestingly enough, only the information services department can cope with this new uncertainty.

Information systems are designed to provide information for decision making, and so the information services department is in the business of supplying information. We have defined information as some tangible or intangible entity that reduces uncertainty. Thus, the information services department supplies a product that reduces uncertainty by its very nature. Furthermore, in the operation of systems, there are many uncertainties, such as whether a job will be completed on time and whether the output will be satisfactory. This uncertainty also is controlled by the information services department.

A second hypothesized determinant of high power is whether or not a department can be replaced easily. These are a few alternatives to a mature information services department. Dissatisfied company management could hire an entirely new computer staff, but this would create chaos during the transition period. One can also turn to a service bureau for processing, but it would be difficult and expensive to convert all present applications. Another alternative to the information services department is a facilities management arrangement in which a consultant contracts to run an information services department. However, most facilities management contractors hire a proportion of the people currently working in the information services department. A facilities management agreement also meets resistance from management, which is often uneasy about having another organization responsible for the processing of vital information. Thus, for a mature information services department, there are not many possible substitutes.

A third proposed determinant of high power for a department is the number of links between other departments and the department in question. The greater the number of links to a department, the greater its power. Clearly, here is another situation where the information services department has the potential for becoming quite powerful. The information services department may accept input from a wide variety of departments in the organization and provide them all with some type of service. The importance of each link also must be considered in assessing departmental power. If a link were separated, how long would it take for the organization to stop? The building and grounds department has a large number of links to each department. However, the lack of janitorial services would be only an inconvenience; in most organizations the final output would not be affected drastically.

For the information services department, the number of links and the importance of output depend on the type of applications developed. Transactional and operational control systems are usually associated with greater power, since these systems have an immediate impact on workloads in the company. Most organizations, for example, are heavily dependent on on-line transactions processing systems.

The degree of interdependence between the department of interest and all other departments in the organization is a final condition for power. The greater the dependence of department A on department B, the greater is department B's power. The information services department tends to exhibit reciprocal interdependence with user departments. That is, the information services department and user departments are mutually dependent on each other to process work, and unfortunately, this type of mutual dependence is the most demanding. An information services department depends on users during systems design to supply information and to provide an understanding of what is needed. On the other hand, the user is dependent on the information services department for the technical aspects of design and for seeing that a system is implemented. During operations, the user must supply input and help maintain the data base. The user in turn is dependent on the information services department to provide processing services.

The information services department has a potentially high score on all the conditions for power discussed above, particularly on coping with uncertainty. Limited evidence suggests that coping with uncertainty is the most important condition for high power (Hennings et al., 1974). As an information services department develops systems for different departments, it becomes more powerful in the organization. However, this trend is often not realized because no one stops to look at the department as a whole and consider the total of all applications. When there are significant power shifts in an organization, users can become resentful of dependence on the information services department, possibly without knowing the real reasons for dissatisfaction. As a result, users may stop working with systems or not seek added computer help when it could be of great assistance.

One study in the manufacturing sector showed that managers and chief executives officers at plant locations generally rated information services departments as low on power. These managers did not perceive information processing, at least in their industry, as critical to the success of their operations. It is quite possible that computing in the companies in the sample was not really central to the task of making a product. Another explanation is that the managers in the plants did not realize the extent to which the firm really did depend on its information systems. It appears to one who studies computer applications that the technology is rather crucial to many organizations. The extent to which this dependence is recognized may be far less than theory would predict.

## IMPACT ON INDIVIDUALS

### Early Predictions

Many early studies of the impact of computer systems were concerned with user reactions. Some of these studies dealt with the psychological reaction of workers, and others concentrated on overall changes in levels of employment. Although isolated changes in employment have occurred, it is difficult to find an overall trend. It is safe to say that the impact of computers on unemployment levels has been no greater than that of any other technological change. The lack of an adverse impact is particularly significant in view of the short period of time that has elapsed since computers were introduced and the rapid development of computer systems.

Early writers were also interested in the impact of computer systems on jobs and job content. Turner (1980) presents an extensive review of the literature on the impact of computers on jobs and job content. He concludes from these studies that computer-based systems tend to make clerical jobs more demanding through increased workload and pace of work. Clerical jobs associated with computers tend to become more anxiety provoking as a result of greater strain and tension. Computers are also associated with job formalization at the clerical level since they generate more rules and procedures to follow. However, it does appear that computer use is associated with greater productivity as measured by output per worker. These studies do suffer from certain research problems and they are relatively few in number.

---

### MANAGEMENT PROBLEM 5-1

A major United States bank was dependent on its computer systems for processing many different kinds of financial transactions. For several months, the information services department warned that it needed additional computer capacity but was out of physical space.

Bank management was relatively unconcerned; they were spending enough on computers at present. The decision to expand and obtain a new computer was deferred several times.

One day, the bank's computers were unable to process all the transactions. The bank lost track of its deposits and failed to clear its accounts with other banks on time. Such an incident cost the bank a large amount of money in fines and in lost interest on funds.

Bank management became very aware of the computer problem because of this malfunction and the attendant crisis. Now how do you think computers are viewed in the bank? What types of computer systems do you think result in the most power for the information services department? How can managers cope with the problems of power transfers in the organization because of computer systems?

---

Turner's own study of clerical employees in banking found that high productivity, mental strain symptoms, and job dissatisfaction were associated with the use of computers. Stress on the job appeared to be the primary mechanism by which the use of computer systems affected clerical workers. In this study, systems with more structured processing were both more productive and more stressful than interactive systems.

Turner suggests creating jobs with more decision latitude and more opportunities for problem solving to mitigate the negative aspects of systems. This study and review of prior research are thought provoking. Although the results are still preliminary, management needs to consider carefully the impact of computer systems on users.

Other writers have speculated on the changes computers might bring to management. They have suggested that computers would assume more of top management's innovative activities and lead to a managerial elite. Computers would tend to accentuate differences among different levels of management (Leavitt and Whisler, 1958). Middle managers were expected to suffer the most from computer systems, and it was predicted that there would be fewer middle managers. Individuals holding middle management positions would need fewer skills and hence would receive lower pay. These workers would have less status in the organization and lower mobility. Early predictions also suggested that many nonmanagement employees would be replaced. For those remaining, jobs would become more boring, and the worker would have less self-control.

While only a few similar studies have been undertaken recently, they have all failed to confirm the predictions. First, it is hard to define middle management. Even still, the drastic changes forecasted do not appear to have occurred. Clerical personnel seem to have been replaced occasionally by a computer system, but the effect is not necessarily widespread. Often more work is done by the same number of workers than would have been possible before a computer system. In fact, middle managers are rapidly integrating microcomputers into their work!

Although the research results are not extensive, it will become evident as we discuss systems analysis and design later in the text that computer systems do have the potential to affect individuals and their jobs. The design techniques to be suggested will help reduce the negative impact of the changes created through the implementation of computer-based systems.

## A Conflict Model

A major impact of computers on an individual occurs when conflict arises between users and the information services department. Conflict can be caused by a number of conditions, one of which is the fact that power is transferred from users to an information services department. If a system does not fit users' needs or is not installed on schedule, there may also be conflict. Conflict is likely to result if the system is not operated according to specifications.

In addition to the problems listed above, there are a number of conditions that have the potential to create conflict in an organization (Walton and Dutton, 1969). We do not expect the relationships between each information services department and other departments to fulfill all conflict conditions, but the potential is there for such problems to arise.

Our first condition is mutual dependence, which increases the potential for conflict because the failure to perform by one party causes serious difficulties for the other. Dependence develops between an information services department and user departments as described earlier for the power model, so there is a high potential for conflict.

Task differences also create conflict. Computer work is highly specialized, and there are many differences between the tasks of a programmer and the average user. Uncertainty has also been known to lead to frustration and conflict, and we have seen that a large amount of uncertainty surrounds computer work. Conflict can also be fostered by ambiguities: In computer activities, who is responsible for a problem? Has the operations staff made an error, or is the system badly designed? There is also the possibility that the error is the responsibility of the user.

Occasionally, when people depend on common resources, conflict arises. Computers may be seen as taking limited funds from a fixed budget in user departments, or several departments may compete for limited computer resources. Job dissatisfaction is another condition that leads to conflict. Users of the information services department may be unhappy in their job or jealous of other workers in the organization. Computer jobs have been known to pay more highly than other positions, and if a user feels service is bad, the fact that the computer staff is more highly paid may be resented.

Communications obstacles have become a major problem between the computer staff and users. The computer field has developed its own jargon, and many computer professionals do not realize they are using strange and unfamiliar terminology. The user may feel that the information services department staff members are trying to demonstrate superior knowledge or avoid making an accurate explanation of a problem by using jargon. In certain situations an information services department staff member may also be confused by user jargon.

Performance rewards differ drastically among information services department staff members and users, and these differences have a potential for creating conflict. Reward structures are hard to assess, but a few companies appear to pay for harmonious relationships among users and the computer staff or for successfully designing and implementing systems. Personal characteristics and traits often differ among information systems staff members and users, which is also a condition leading to conflict. Technically, computer work can be very demanding, and the staff member is usually highly committed to a career. Computer professionals may not empathize with and understand user problems, which often creates conflict.

Certainly not all the conditions described above exist in any one organization; however, the relationship between the computer staff and users has a potential

---

## MANAGEMENT PROBLEM 5-2

A new payroll system is being implemented at the Old Shoe Company. While payroll is often considered to be a simple computer application, it often turns out to be very complex. At Old Shoe, the payroll system also collects data for the cost accounting system.

A single programmer-analyst has worked for several months to develop a new version of the system. The old version had to be replaced because Old Shoe had just acquired a new subsidiary. This new subsidiary increased the number of employees at the company beyond the number of digits in the employee identification number in the old system. Thus, there is intense time pressure to install the new system to run the total payroll for the company.

The head of the payroll section is very unhappy with the new system. She feels that the original system works well, despite examples that showed that it has errors in it.

The information services department is running a parallel test. That is, the old and new systems are being run simultaneously to check the results of one against the other. Of course, this type of test requires a lot of extra work. Duplicate input has to be prepared and the results of the two systems compared. Extensive overtime is required on the part of the payroll clerks.

The head of the payroll department refuses to accept the new system because the number of errors is "unreasonable." The programmer-analyst thinks that the payroll department head is unreasonable because the new system has actually shown some errors in the original one! He maintains that the few errors in the new system could easily be corrected after it is operational.

What type of information would you want to help you decide whether to install the new system? How would you resolve the dispute between the payroll department head and the programmer-analyst? What kind of problem is this?

---

for leading to disruptive conflict. As a result of this conflict, users may sabotage the information services department by withholding data or providing incorrect input. Because of the dependence of the information services department on users, it is easy for users to make the information services department appear in an unfavorable light.

On the other hand, the information services department can sabotage users through delays in processing or by withholding service. Controls can be relaxed, which will introduce more errors in the processing. In the case of heightened warfare, users may refuse to cooperate in the development of new systems, systems that could have a significant payoff for the organization. The computer staff then tends to become discouraged, and the department experiences high turnover. New systems are not designed at all or are not well designed. As conditions worsen, we face a continuing spiral of poor performance and increasing levels of conflict.

### TORNADO WARNING

*The 1984 tornado season began with 45 twisters in March killing 59 people and doing millions of dollars worth of damage. The outcome might have been worse if it had not been for a $2.2 million computerized system used by the U.S. Weather Service to sound an advance warning.*

*The Centralized Storm Information System relies on four minicomputers to compose satellite pictures of the U.S. and combine them with weather data from the earth including barometric pressure and air temperature. The system is able to translate the satellite view of the earth from radio signals into a picture in about six minutes, a half hour faster than previous equipment.*

*Using the system, Weather Service meterologists can determine whether the dangerous combination of low barometric pressure, high temperature and rain-swollen clouds is about to become a tornado. The Weather Service feels its accuracy in predicting tornados has risen from 40 to 45 percent to near 53 percent. In addition, the predictions of severe storms has increased from 60 percent to 80 percent.*

*One of the major advantages of the system is the fact that it combines in one place data that weather forecasters had to obtain by strolling past 30 ft weather maps each containing different information. The system processes all of these data and overlays it in color on the satellite picture of the U.S. on the screen.*

*Computerworld*, April 30, 1984.

---

## INFORMATION SYSTEMS IN THE CONTEXT OF THE ORGANIZATION

Earlier we suggested that organizational factors are equally as important as technical details in the design and operation of computer-based information systems. The problem with the studies described above is their lack of emphasis on how we can develop successful systems. The power and conflict models discussed earlier in the chapter have helped to develop the model of computer-based information systems in the context of the organization presented below. The purpose of this model is to help understand the organizational impact of systems and to predict the results of implementing a system.

### A Descriptive Model

Figure 5-1 presents a descriptive model of information systems in the context of the organization. Boxes represent important components of information systems activities, and arrows between the boxes indicate predicted relationships.

The numbers on the arrows in the figure correspond to relationships stated formally as propositions in Table 5-1. While some of these relationships may appear to be self-evident, they are included to make the model complete.

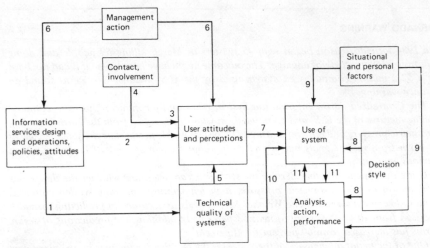

**FIGURE 5-1**
Information systems in the context of the organization. (Adapted from H. C. Lucas, Jr.: *Why Information Systems Fail*, 1975, courtesy Columbia University Press.)

Experience has shown that it is important to subject even the most obvious relationship to scrutiny. Several times we have been confronted with counterintuitive results that required the revision of an "obvious" relationship.

The first part of the model deals with user attitudes and perceptions of information systems. Attitudes and perceptions are important in determining user reactions to systems and in influencing the use of the system. Attitudes have an action or behavioral component, especially when the attitude is related to something as specific as a particular computer system. If attitudes are highly negative, we expect little cooperation with a system, low levels of use, and in some instances, even sabotage of the system.

We expect that the systems design and operations policies of the information services department will influence user attitudes and perceptions directly and indirectly. Direct influence comes from daily user contact with the department; if this contact is satisfactory, it should result in positive user attitudes. Indirect influence by the information services department on user attitudes comes primarily from the quality of service. Often contact between this department and users is initiated because of service problems. If systems are unreliable or if they are poorly designed and do not work properly, users will have contact with the information services department that is based in conflict, a condition leading to unfavorable attitudes.

User attitudes should also be influenced by management action and encouragement, for example, management support for the design of new systems and membership on steering committees. User attitudes and perceptions should also be influenced by contact and involvement in the design of systems.

Proposition 7 is based on the expectation that favorable user attitudes and

**TABLE 5-1**
THE FORMAL PROPOSITIONS OF THE MODEL AND THEIR SUPPORT

| Proposition | Evidence |
|---|---|
| 1  The systems design and operations policies of the information services department and the execution of these policies influence the technical quality of information systems | Some support |
| 2  The systems design and operations policies of the information services department influence user attitudes and perception of information systems and the information services staff. | Reasonable support |
| 3  User contact with information services staff members under adverse conditions leads to unfavorable user attitudes and perceptions of information systems and the information services staff. | Weak support |
| 4  User involvement in the design and operation of information systems results in favorable user attitudes and perceptions of information systems and the information services staff. | Some support |
| 5  Systems with higher technical quality result in more favorable user attitudes and perceptions of the information services staff. | Strong support |
| 6  High levels of management support for and participation in information systems activities result in favorable information services staff attitudes toward their jobs and users, and favorable user attitudes and perceptions of information systems and the information services staff. | Reasonable support |
| 7  Favorable user attitudes and perceptions of information systems and the information services staff lead to high levels of use of information systems. | Strong support |
| 8  Individuals with differing decision styles have differing levels of use of information systems, perform different analyses of data, take different actions based on information, and have differing levels of performance. | Reasonable support |
| 9  Different personal and situational factors lead to differing levels of use of an information system and different actions. | Reasonable support |
| 10  High levels of system use result from a system with high technical quality. | Strong support |
| 11  High levels of use of an information system make it more likely that a user will take action based on the information provided. Depending on the nature of the analysis, the problem, and the information, high levels of use may lead to high or low levels of performance or may be caused by low performance. | Some support |

perceptions lead to high levels of system use, especially if a system is of high technical quality. High technical quality should lead to more favorable attitudes and perceptions since a high-quality system is easier for a user to interact with and produces better output than a low-quality system.

The use of an information system is a very complex phenomenon. Different situational and personal factors should influence use; a supervisor with 20 years of experience operating a department one way would probably not use an inventory reorder report as extensively as one with six months on the job. Decision or cognitive style also can be expected to influence the use of the system. Quantitatively trained individuals may wish for different types of information than their counterparts who have a more intuitive decision style, as discussed earlier.

The relationship between an information system and performance by the decision maker is very complex. High levels of performance depend on analyzing the output of an information system and taking action consistent with that output. On the other hand, low performance may stimulate the use of the system to determine the nature and cause of problems. It appears that different types of data are needed to support these different aspects of managerial decision making.

A manager is frequently concerned with problem-finding activities, that is, determining that a problem exists. Most computer-based information systems address this aspect of decision making through exception reports, comparisons of this year versus last year, or comparisons of budgeted with actual performance. Under these conditions, low performance would be associated with high levels of use of an information system as a decision maker tries to determine the reasons for poor performance.

---

**THE CORNER DRUG STORE**

*Computers are being used by pharmacists to avoid dangerous interactions among prescription drugs, foods, allergies and over-the-counter medicines. One source estimates that $4.5 billion in hospital bills and over 100 deaths result each year from interactions such as those described above. While only about 20 percent of drug store chains are computerized now, by 1990 the total is expected to be over 90 percent.*

*Future enhancements include the ability to notify customers when a drug has been recalled. Systems will also be able to notify the pharmacist when a patient is refilling a prescription more or less often than prescribed.*

*The customer of a store featuring such a system completes a profile form describing their medications and any chronic illnesses. Before filling the prescription, the pharmacist calls up the profile to check for interactions; if there is a problem, he or she calls the prescribing physician.*

*In one chain, there is a database containing 17,000 possible interactions. In the stores using the system, 15 to 17 percent of all prescriptions were found to have a potential for interaction and 5 percent of these could have resulted in hospitalization or a fatality.*

*The New York Times, July 21, 1984.*

---

After problem definition, the decision maker enters the problem-solving stage. We expect the use of problem-solving output from a system to be associated with high performance if the decision maker takes action consistent with the information. A problem-solving information system may provide such features as computational facilities and the simulation of different alternatives.

## Implications for Systems Design

If we accept the model and results, what are some of the implications? From a systems design standpoint, the manager should consider the following action steps, which are intended to produce high levels of systems use and successful implementation.

**1** Urge the formation of a steering committee of users and information services department staff members to determine priorities for the development of new applications.

**2** Encourage training sessions for the information services department staff to help its members adopt a role as catalyst in the development process.

**3** Insist that a user be placed in charge of the design team for a new system.

---

## MANAGEMENT PROBLEM 5-3

A major bank has an information system designed to keep track of loan officer assignments to clients and calls made on clients. The system was intended for use by the commercial loan department.

The bank has a large number of loans, and one officer might have 50 or 60 clients. As a result, it is very difficult for officers to maintain their own records. The computer system is designed to solve this problem.

In theory, an officer simply fills out a form when establishing a relationship with a new client or after having visited an existing account. This form is used to update a computer file and a report is produced showing each officer's clients and the date of the most recent call on the client.

Unfortunately, the system has fallen into disuse. A number of clients are listed on the report but no longer do business with the bank. Some accounts are listed as belonging to retired or deceased loan officers!

An administrative assistant in the loan department sent corrections each month to the input/output control section of the information service department. For some unknown reason, only about half of these corrections were ever made, according to the next report. As a result, after several months of trying, the administrative assistant gave up and no longer submits input or corrections. However, the report continues to be produced on a regular basis, though it is never read by users.

Use the model of Figure 5-1 to analyze the situation described above. What are the key variables? What action is required to improve the situation?

---

**4** Provide sufficient resources so that the staff can spend time on systems design.

**5** Work personally with a design team to show interest and commitment.

**6** See that decisions and not just data flows are considered in systems design.

**7** Ask probing questions to see if designers have considered the multiple roles of information for the organization and different decision makers.

**8** Review all proposed output from a new system, be selective, and avoid information overload.

**9** Examine the user interface with the system; see that users have experimented with the input and output and find it acceptable.

**10** Plan for implementation for subordinates and colleagues, consider different personal and situational factors, and prepare for changes.

**11** Ensure that adequate resources have been devoted to training and user documentation.

### Implications for Operations

After systems are designed, they have to be operated. What can a user of information systems do to improve the operation of existing systems?

**1** Do not allow any new system to be developed until existing ones are operating satisfactorily.

**2** Request the name of a single user representative in the information services department to handle all questions from you or your subordinates.

**3** Urge the formation of a steering committee of users in the information services department staff to set priorities for the operation of information systems.

**4** As a member of the steering committee, see that sufficient resources are set aside for making changes to existing systems and that a committee of users sets priorities on these modifications.

**5** If an on-line system affects your activities, insist on adequate computer or manual backup in case of system failure.

**6** Insist on a schedule of input and output for all batch computer system runs affecting you or your staff.

**7** Conduct periodic surveys of your staff to solicit ideas for changes and to determine if service levels are satisfactory.

### IN CONCLUSION

In this chapter, we reviewed the impact of information systems on the organization and individuals and presented a model of systems in the context of the organization. Managers and users of information systems have a crucial role to play in the design process. We shall explore this role further in Part Four when we discuss the implementation of systems in more detail.

## KEY WORDS

| | | |
|---|---|---|
| Action | Design policies | Situational and personal |
| Ambiguities | Job dissatisfaction | factors |
| Analysis | Management action | Task differences |
| Attitude | Mutual dependence | Uncertainty |
| Centralization | Operations policies | Use |
| Common resources | Performance | |
| Communications | Performance rewards | |
| obstacles | Personal characteristics | |
| Decentralization | and traits | |
| Decision style | Power | |

## RECOMMENDED READINGS

Leavitt, H. J., and T. L. Whisler: "Management in the 1980's," *Harvard Business Review,* November–December, 1958, pp. 41–48. (A historic article presenting many of the early predictions of the impact of computers on the organization and individuals.)

Lucas, H. C., Jr.: *Why Information Systems fail,* Columbia, New York, 1975. (This book presents in detail the model of information systems in the context of the organization discussed in this chapter and describes the research findings that test the propositions of the model.)

Mumford, E., and D. Henshall: *A Participative Approach to Computer Systems Design.* London: Associated Business Press, 1976. (A good, in-depth case study.)

Walton, R. E., and J. M. Dutton: "The Management of Interdepartmental Conflict: A Model and Review," *Administrative Science Quarterly,* vol. 14, no. 1, March 1969, pp. 73–84. (This article contains, in much greater detail, the model of conflict discussed earlier in the chapter.)

## DISCUSSION QUESTIONS

1 Are the information services department staff members highly specialized? What other functional areas in the organization are highly specialized?

2 The information services department is often considered to provide a support function; can a support department really be powerful? Are there different kinds of power in the organization?

3 What kinds of management problems result from interdepartmental conflict?

4 Are there any organizations that are completely dependent on computers for their operations?

5 What kinds of employees are most likely to be replaced by a computer system? How does your answer depend on the type of computer system and the decision levels affected?

6 How would you measure the extent of unemployment created by the implementation of computer systems? What factors tend to mitigate the problem of increased unemployment if it actually occurs?

7 What signs might indicate the presence of conflict between two departments? How could this conflict be reduced?

8 Are computer systems creating more centralization in organizations? How do you define centralization? Why should computer systems have any impact at all on the degree of centralization?

9 How would you recognize a successful computer installation? What signs would you expect to find?

10 How can communications obstacles between users and the information services department be reduced?

11 How should users be involved in the allocation of scarce computer resources?

12 Two methods of charging for computer services, full charge-out to users and overhead charging, have been suggested. What are the advantages and disadvantages of each method?

13 Consider a typical manufacturing organization and describe the mutual dependence that exists among departments.

14 Why should users be involved in the design of systems? How much influence should they have?

15 What will happen to information systems if users have negative attitudes?

16 How are attitudes formed? How can they be changed?

17 After considering the model of information systems in the context of organizations discussed in this chapter, suggest what you think will be the result of an unresponsive information services department? What will happen if management fails to support computer-related activities?

18 How much does a manager have to understand about computer systems? What are the most important management decisions to be made about computer-based information systems?

19 What tools does the manager have available to influence computer activities in the organization?

20 As a user, where do you think the information services department should report? Should it be responsible to accounting?

21 Why do so many users turn to outside computer services, for example, to acquire time sharing or special packages?

22 Early forecasts suggested that middle managers would be reduced in number and stature as a result of the computer systems. Has this prediction been fulfilled? Why or why not?

23 Do computer systems have an impact beyond the organization, for example, on stockholders or customers? What kinds of impact and what problems are created for these groups?

CHAPTER **6**

# TOP MANAGEMENT AND INFORMATION SYSTEMS

# TOP MANAGEMENT AND INFORMATION SYSTEMS

## CHAPTER ISSUES

- How does information processing technology relate to corporate strategy?
- What are key management decisions about information systems?
- How much should the organization invest in information processing services?

Managers often experience difficulty taking advantage of information processing technology when formulating corporate strategy. Many top managers also seem unable to cope with the problems of controlling information processing activities in their organizations.

The president of a medium-sized manufacturing company remarked, "I receive about the same information today as was provided thirty years ago before our computers. Only now I spend millions to get it." The chairperson of a three-billion-dollar conglomerate has commented repeatedly, "I get nothing from our computers."

This chapter (1) suggests an approach to incorporating information processing technology in the strategy formulation process and (2) presents a framework for top management to direct the information processing resource so that they may achieve strategic objectives.

## BACKGROUND

### Symptoms

Following are some common problems related to information processing:

• Managers and other users are uncomfortable with the method by which new applications are chosen.
• There appear to be no priorities for selecting new computer applications.
• One or more new computer applications is experiencing significant cost/schedule overruns.
• There are many complaints about the quality of information processing service.
• Requests for computer staff and equipment are escalating.
• The firm's information systems are not congruent with the firm's goals.
• Top management feels that information processing is not under its control.

If an organization has a number of these symptoms, it may be depriving itself of the opportunity to gain a major competitive advantage through the creative use of information technology. From the service sector to manufacturing, information processing technology can play a major role in managing the firm.

### The Impact of Computing

When applying technology to a business problem, for instance, the introduction of a new manufacturing process, executives are usually concerned with the first-order effects of the technology; that is, they want to reduce manufacturing unit costs, improve product quality, etc. The impact of computing technology is different from the impact of many other types of technology in that the secondary effects of computing are often more important than their primary impact. As an example, consider a transactions processing system that is designed to automate the accounts receivable function. The primary objective of such a system might be to reduce errors in posting receivables and to maintain correct account balances. The secondary effect of this system in combination with a payments system is that the firm now knows its exact cash position at the end of each day. By reducing uncertainty in the firm's cash position, the treasurer may have a significant new source of funds for short-term investment.

Accurate cost data have permitted some firms to price products differentially in different parts of the country. In these cases the cost data collected for accounting purposes had a secondary effect on merchandising strategy. In addition the firm has the ability to reflect costs more accurately in setting prices, which should lead to higher revenue.

The firm should carefully manage and control information processing technology, because of its primary impact and because of its potential secondary effects.

## INFORMATION PROCESSING TECHNOLOGY AND CORPORATE STRATEGY

A key task of top management is formulating corporate strategy. What does the corporation do well? Can it continue this activity at a high level of performance? What opportunities for new directions are available? What are competitors doing? A firm can continue its present course, maintaining momentum where it is doing well. Alternatively, the corporation can change its strategy dramatically by making a decision among competing alternatives for new ventures.

As an example, a single-product single-market firm might try to diversify to reduce cyclical fluctuations in product demand and to reduce the impact of a major change in consumer buying patterns. A large energy company has decided to enter the market for information processing equipment by purchasing a number of high-technology firms and integrating them into a new subsidiary. This new business is expected to grow and to help the energy producer cope with the uncertainties in its primary petroleum market.

There are three levels of integration of information processing technology with corporate strategy as shown in Table 6-1. At the lowest level of integration, we find independent information systems that help the firm implement strategy by creating greater operational efficiencies. These systems are not directly linked to the strategy formulation process or integrated with a strategic plan. The need for such a system is usually perceived by an operational unit, and its primary objective is to improve efficiency. Most existing information systems fall into the independent category: they process routine transactions, produce output that goes to customers, provide exception reporting, etc.

The second level of integration is characterized by policy support systems designed to aid the strategic planning process. In this case the system helps in formulating the plan but is not a part of it. That is, the system is not part of an end product or service produced by the firm. A planning application is a good example of one of these policy support systems. The data needed for forecasting for a large conglomerate are contained in a common data base accessible

**TABLE 6-1**
LEVELS OF INTEGRATION OF INFORMATION PROCESSING TECHNOLOGY

| Level of integration with strategy formulation | Primary objective | Secondary effect |
|---|---|---|
| Independent | Operational efficiency | Managerial information |
| Policy support | Aid repetitive decision making | Better understanding of problem dynamics |
| Fully integrated | Offer new products, markets, directions | Change the decision-making process, alternatives considered, and evaluation criteria |

through the computer. A set of analytic tools in the system includes a bank of models with a large mathematical programming routine that helps select a course of action to maximize corporate performance over a multiyear planning horizon. In addition econometric and risk analysis models are available.

The majority of firms do not appear to have reached the third and most important level of integration between information processing and corporate strategy. At this level the technology itself becomes a part of the strategy; it expands the range of strategic alternatives considered by the firm. At this third level, technology bears an integral relation to a company's strategic thinking by helping to define the range of possibilities. At the same time, it provides a good portion of the means by which the strategy, once chosen, is to be implemented. Several examples may help to illustrate this level of integration between technology and strategy.

A university professor of economics developed and marketed a model of the national economy through a new firm. Although such models were theoretically possible before the advent of electronic computers, computational requirements made them infeasible to solve. The development of information technology made it possible to create the kind of model that forms the nucleus of the firm's business. Furthermore, the company offers a variety of services in which the customer accesses its computer, services made possible only because of the options provided by information processing technology.

Merrill Lynch is the largest stock brokerage firm in the United States and is planning to become one of the major financial institutions in the world. Several years ago, when a customer had funds in his or her brokerage account, they earned no interest. There could be cash in such an account because of the sale of stock or because of dividends on stock held by Merrill for the client.

The firm developed a new product. At the time the product was conceived, interest rates were extremely high and a number of small investors were keeping their funds in liquid assets accounts. These funds buy large securities with a value of $100,000 or more. Then the funds sell shares, usually with a par value of $1 and require a minimum deposit of some kind, possibly as low as a few thousand dollars. The funds keep the value of the ownership units at $1 by varying the dividends and buying short-term securities.

Now, the small investor, instead of being limited to bank or Savings and Loan passbook accounts, could take advantage of higher interest rates that were previously only available to those with a large amount to invest. (Today banks and S&L's are able to offer money market accounts, but they were not at the time Merrill developed its new account.)

Merrill Lynch decided that an account that automatically invested idle cash in Merrill's own Ready Assets (liquid assets) Fund would be appealing to its customers. In fact, this new account, called a CMA for Cash Management Account, is like a bank account and brokerage account combined. The customer is able to write checks against the account and even receives a bank charge card.

Has it been successful? At first the account was slow to win acceptance, but today Merrill Lynch has over 1,000,000 CMA customers. Other brokerage firms have hired Merrill employees to try and develop similar products. Merrill has patented the account and is asking for licensing fees. In an out of court settlement of a suit, another brokerage firm agreed to pay Merrill $1,000,000 for having hired a Merrill employee to set up a similar system. Merrill Lynch has gained a significant competitive advantage with its Cash Management Account System.

Could this system have been developed without confidence in information processing? With a million accounts to update, the magnitude of the catastrophe is hard to imagine if computer systems do not work. In fact, this product could never be offered unless a firm had computer technology and could manage it. The volume of updating and the short time requirements would be just too great for a manual system.

On a smaller scale, information processing technology made it possible for a new market research firm to offer a service that could not be obtained from its competitors. The company developed a strategy that is intertwined with information technology. The firm has purchased grocery store point-of-sale scanning equipment and given it free to 15 supermarkets in two towns selected on the basis of their demographic makeup. There are 2000 households in each of the two test markets using the scanning equipment; their purchases are recorded on the firm's computer in Chicago. Since each product is marked by the universal product code, researchers can pinpoint a family's purchases by price, brand, and size and then correlate the purchase information with any promotions such as coupons, free samples, price adjustments, advertising, and store displays.

This technology means that the company can conduct careful, scientific tests of marketing strategies to determine what is the most effective approach for its customers. For example, through cooperation with a cable TV network, the firm can target different TV spots to selected households and analyze the resulting purchases. The imaginative use of the technology has allowed the firm to gain a competitive lead over much larger, better established market research firms.

These examples illustrate how the integration of information processing technology with strategy formulation expanded the opportunities for each firm. The technology allowed the first firm to create an econometric model and then to use time-sharing services to market its product directly to the customer. Technology created the opportunity for a new form of business and expanded revenues. In the brokerage firm, the technology made it possible to offer a new service that probably expanded the market share of the firm and increased the size of its liquid assets fund. Technology helped the market research firm gain a competitive edge and set a new standard for service in the industry.

### A Range of Opportunities

Parsons (1983) has identified three levels of information systems opportunities for a firm: the industry, the firm, and the strategic level.

At the industry level, information technology may change the nature of the industry's products and services. As an example, Merrill Lynch's CMA is a radically new product that has influenced the entire brokerage industry. Another example is the use of technology to electronically edit manuscripts and news stories.

As customers become more computer literate, the market facing a firm changes. Banks and others offering financial services will find large numbers of customers with home computers capable of acting as a terminal to access the bank's computers directly. Because of communications networks, financial institutions no longer have a market restricted to local geographic areas; the world may become a large bank's market.

Parsons also argues that information processing may change the economics of production. He uses the example of computerized warehouses and inventory control. There will also be dramatic changes as computers are used to develop integrated manufacturing systems. Factory floor data collection devices will feed information on parts produced, yields, rejects, and worker hours to central computers charged with keeping track of in-process inventories, payroll hours, and cost-accounting data.

At the firm level information processing will have an impact on five forces that confront the business: suppliers, buyers, substitutes, new entrants, and rivals in the industry.

A firm may use information processing to change its relationship with its suppliers. Sophisticated quality control systems can force suppliers to change their own quality control efforts. The availability and price of information technology itself becomes an influence on the firm; computer hardware and software vendors are becoming major suppliers to the firm.

Buyers will have many more choices. The firm will have to continually innovate to keep its market share, as competitors figure out new ways to use the technology to gain an advantage with buyers.

Electronics may be substituted for certain products or practices. Seeing that the movement of paper documents can be reduced through electronics, an overnight carrier is developing its own electronics-based distribution business. Information processing can also affect entry by reducing barriers or creating new ones. A bank may find reduced barriers to entry since it can reach customers electronically; by the same token the technology creates a different barrier to entry which is the investment required in computer hardware and software to offer the bank's services.

Electronics can also be used to fuel rivalries. The brokerage product described earlier is an example. Airlines have fought battles with their computerized reservations systems by changing the order of flights; the carrier puts its own flights first on the output displays to increase the likelihood that their flight will be chosen. The situation became sufficiently competitive that the government is considering the regulation of reservations systems!

From the standpoint of overall strategy, Parsons suggests that a firm can use the technology to develop cost leadership. A financial institution that is able to use the technology to reduce its operating costs can be more profitable and agressive than a high-cost producer. Transactions processing costs represent a significant cost of doing business in the financial sector.

By using the technology to create a higher quality product, a manufacturer can differentiate itself from others in the market. Consider that initially Merrill Lynch had the only Cash Management Account; it effectively differentiated its brokerage accounts from those offered by competitors.

Finally, the technology may help a firm concentrate in a particular market or product niche. Computer-aided design may help a firm become a custom manufacturer of tools or semiconductors because it can respond quickly to requests from customers. An information system that tracks sales may lead to a different market strategy that concentrates specifically on one niche.

### A Framework

McFarlan and McKenney (1983) have suggested a framework for classifying the strategic use of information technology. See Table 6-2, which arrays a firm's existing applications against applications that are currently under development.

In the strategic cell, companies are critically dependent on the smooth functioning of the information systems activity. These firms need significant amounts of planning; the firm would be at a considerable disadvantage if information processing did not perform well. The authors found one bank that fit this cell well. Without computers the bank would be awash in a sea of paper; it could not possibly keep up with the volume. More than that, banks are offering new services based on home computers connected to their own computers. The bank must think of how to strategically use its computer systems to offer services that will let it capture a greater market share.

In a turnaround company, there is a need for planning, too. It is likely that

**TABLE 6-2**
INFORMATION SYSTEMS STRATEGIC GRID

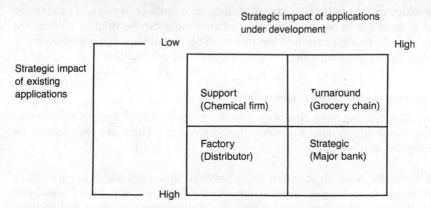

*From McFarlan and McKenney, 1983.

corporate performance is being inhibited by poor performance in the information processing department. McFarlan and McKenney found a firm in this cell which had adequate operating systems in production, but whose new applications were critical for keeping up with growth. The firm could not maintain control over its rapidly expanding operations without the new computer applications.

The authors argue that in the factory setting, there is not much to do but run existing applications. They maintain that strategic goal setting and linkage of information systems to the corporate plan are not too important here.

Finally, in a support environment, information processing is probably not critical to the firm so that strategic integration will not be key to success. The authors expect to find low levels of senior management involvement in this situation.

The McFarlan and McKenney framework is a useful one for diagnosing the state of an organization. We can look at the nature of the business, plans for the future, and existing and planned computer applications. In a turnaround situation, we may want to emphasize to management the importance of leading the information systems effort where in the strategic cell, management may already be aware of the importance of technology to the firm.

However, McFarlan and McKenney argue that in a situation in the support cell, it is quite appropriate for management to be relatively uninvolved in information processing. While this may be true for certain systems, the advice is bad in general because it encourages management to ignore information processing and new opportunities that it might provide. It is quite possible that a firm in the support cell will be able to come up with a strategic computer application that allows it to gain a competitive edge. In fact, if the support cell position is a characteristic of the industry, then the firm that first finds a strategic edge through information technology may in fact move far ahead of others.

Those authors concerned with the use of information technology as a part of corporate strategy have all taken a slightly different approach to classifying systems. One common thread seems to run throughout the discussions: that technology can contribute to a firm's strategy in a number of ways. It can reduce costs to help a firm compete by being efficient or it can be used to tie the firm more closely to suppliers and customers. The technology can also become a product itself, allowing a firm to gain a significant competitive edge.

### Capitalizing on Information Technology

How does the firm take advantage of information technology and achieve the highest level integration of technology and strategy? There are two steps to be followed by top management:

**1** Look for ways to incorporate technology in a product or service. Does information processing provide an opportunity for a new approach to business? Does the technology make it possible to differentiate a product and services from the competition? Technology can help open new markets or increase existing market share.

**2** To integrate technology with planning, the firm needs information about likely future technological developments. To conduct a technology assessment, the organization must invest resources in research and development. A small group of corporate researchers can collect information from a number of sources to estimate technological trends. The firm can invest selectively in university

---

### OPTICAL SCANNING FOR MARKET RESEARCH

*Early experiments with supermarket scanners for checkout have encouraged market researchers by their potential for collecting large amounts of data on purchases. However, supermarkets have been very slow to install laser scanning systems which identify purchases by optically reading Universal Product Codes printed on each grocery item. Market research firms, because of the relatively small number of scanner installations, still rely on relatively simple techniques such as asking shoppers to maintain diaries of their purchases.*

*A Chicago firm, Information Resources, Inc., purchased scanning equipment and provided it free to 15 supermarkets in two carefully selected towns, Marion, Indiana and Pittsfield, Massachusetts. These two cities have demographic makeups which makes them ideal as test markets. The company has enlisted 2,000 households in each of the two test markets. The householders have identification cards which are presented at the grocery store when they make a purchase. The card alerts the point of sale terminal to send an item by item list of the customer's purchases to the Information Resources computer in Chicago.*

*From the Universal Product Code, researchers at the company can determine purchases exactly according to price, brand and size. These data are related to any promotional experiments under way. As a result, Information Resources can monitor the grocery purchases of a representative sample of 4,000 households. The firm can determine how these consumers react to marketing strategies like television commercials, newspaper ads, displays in the store, coupons and free samples.*

*Through a cooperating cable television system, stations selectively broadcast commercials to target families on a house by house basis. The Chicago market research firm can experiment with different television commercials on selected households and compare the buying reactions in the store.*

*In one example, Information Resources attempted to determine the cost effectiveness of giving away a product sample. It divided household panelists into four groups of a 1,000 each and provided various combinations of samples and advertising. Sales doubled in all of the groups receiving samples during the period, but the group exposed to advertising was more loyal to the brand in subsequent weeks.*

*This innovative application demonstrates how computers can be used to offer a unique service and to collect data for market research.*

*Business Week,* May 5, 1980.

programs to keep up a research and can sponsor or subscribe to studies conducted by consulting firms.

One of the greatest impediments to using information technology for strategic purposes has been an inability on the part of top management to manage the information systems function successfully. If executives do not believe that they can control information processing services, they probably will be unwilling to rely on this technology to accomplish strategic goals.

## MANAGING INFORMATION PROCESSING

This section discusses the key variables and concerns for top management in managing information processing activities in the organization. Figure 6-1 presents a framework for viewing management decision areas involved in information processing; positive management action is needed in all areas illustrated in the figure. Without such action decisions will occur by default; management can and should control information processing. Table 6-3 summarizes the actions for management in each of the areas discussed below. Where possible, we offer recommendations for management policy. When the recommendations depend on circumstances unique to the firm, Table 6-3 lists some of the factors that should be taken into account in developing a policy.

**Figure 6-1**
A framework for managing information processing.

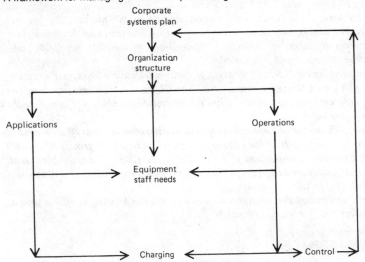

## A Corporate Plan

A plan for information processing should be coordinated with corporate strategy. The plan will serve as a road map to show the direction of the systems effort. It also furnishes the basis for later evaluation of the performance of the information processing function.

Many organizations agree that a plan is needed but do not develop one. A frequent reason is that the 3-to-5-year information-systems planning horizon is not compatible with the planning horizon of the organization. In other instances, the corporation does not have a plan at all. It is both possible and highly desirable to develop an information processing plan even without a formal corporate plan. The technology is too pervasive and important for planning to occur by default or solely through decisions made by personnel in the information services department.

A typical plan describes the breakdown in activities and resources required for the development of new applications and the operation of existing systems. A key task for the organization is to identify areas for new applications of technology. What are the applications areas with the highest return? What applications will most further the strategic goals of the corporation? What new opportunities does the technology provide?

Table 6-4 contains a possible table of contents for an information systems plan. The plan first begins with an executive summary containing the key points in the plan. The document should have a section on the goals of information processing in the organization, both general and specific. One general goal might

---

## MANAGEMENT PROBLEM 6-1

The president of Ready-to-Wear, a medium-sized clothing manufacturer, was upset with information processing in his firm. "We have a system that was designed in 1939 and run on tabulating equipment. For its day, this was a good system. Now, we are spending over $500,000 a year on a computer, and I receive exactly the same information as the 1939 system. Only now it costs more and there are more errors and complaints."

The president has tried a succession of consultants to advise him, and there has been a new manager of the information services department about every six months. Interviews with users show them to be upset by computer processing and unwilling even to suggest new applications. The controller would like to eliminate the entire computer area and turn to an outside service bureau. In fact, this course was attempted several years ago.

The president is willing to give the computer one last chance. He has retained you to help him develop a set of systems that will meet the basic needs of the firm for order entry, accounting, production control, work-in-process inventory, finished-goods inventory, and raw materials and purchasing. What is your plan for helping the firm?

**TABLE 6-3**
SUMMARY OF ISSUES AND RECOMMENDATIONS

| A corporate plan | |
|---|---|

See that a 3-to-5-year MIS plan is developed

Participate in the planning process

| Issues | Recommendations |
|---|---|
| Mechanism | Operational plan of 1 year |
| | Longer-term plan of 3 to 5 years |
| | Technology assessment |
| | Link to organization plan |
| | Separate information systems planning officer |
| Involvement | User and management input |
| Contents and format | Applications needs |
| | Operations needs |
| | Implications for staff and equipment |
| Priorities | Steering committees to choose applications |
| Reporting | Annual report of information services department tied to plan |

| Organization structure | |
|---|---|

Evaluate various patterns for providing computing to choose the most effective alternative

Develop a policy that balances coordination costs and local autonomy

| Issues | Alternatives |
|---|---|
| Type | Centralized distributed, decentralized for operations and analysis/design |
| Evaluation | Criteria: service levels, cost responsiveness, flexibility, history of organization |
| Control | Balance local autonomy with corporate needs |

| New applications | |
|---|---|

Convene a committee of users and managers to be affected by the system to choose an alternative for design

Be sure that a realistic number of alternatives are considered, including the status quo or the no-new-systems alternative

| Issues | Recommendations |
|---|---|
| Generate new ideas | Also from plan, procedures for submission of requests, new applications |
| Selection | Use of committees; use formal approaches for selection |
| Development | Extensive user input, management involvement setting goals, reviewing system |
| Tools | Acquisition and use of tools-structured approaches |

**TABLE 6-3**
(CONTINUED)

## Operations

Establish criteria for measuring the performance and service levels of computer operations

Measure and evaluate the operations function regularly

| Issues | Recommendations |
|---|---|
| Measurement | Develop user-oriented measures |
| Evaluation | Administer regular evaluations including a variety of measures |
| Control | Are there adequate controls? |

## Equipment/staff needs

Review equipment recommendations

Authorize adequate staffing levels; systems design is labor intensive!

| Issues | Recommendations |
|---|---|
| Evaluation and choice criteria | Develop evaluation methodology |
| Compatibility among vendors | Establish vendor compatibility policy |
| Technological assessment | Consider changes in technology in decisions |
| Staff increases | Examine alternatives such as adding to the staff, contract services, packaged programs, more user programming |

## Charging

Determine the objectives of a charging policy

Design and implement the policy

| Issues | Alternatives |
|---|---|
| To charge | Yes-or-no advantage and disadvantages |
| Charging mechanism | Full or partial charge-out; accounting techniques |

## Control

Evaluate the contribution of information systems to corporate goals and strategy

Evaluate information services performance with respect to the plan

Take the needed corrective action to achieve the plan, e.g., add resources, modify schedules, etc.

| Issues | Recommendations |
|---|---|
| Overall evaluation | Compare results to plan |
| Frequent feedback | Monitor progress on systems development projects, conduct user surveys as discussed under "Operations" |

**TABLE 6-4**
CONTENTS OF AN INFORMATION SYSTEMS PLAN

---

Executive summary
Goals
Assumptions
Scenario—information processing environment
Applications areas
   status, cost, time, schedule
Operations
Maintenance and enhancements
Organizational structure—pattern of computing
Impact of plan on the organization—financial impact
Implementation—risks, obstacles

---

be to provide unique customer services, and a specific goal could be to complete a major on-line system during the year.

Any plan is based on certain assumptions about the business. Will the firm continue to pursue its current business strategy? Are major new lines of business contemplated? Is the organization divesting itself of certain components? It is mandatory for this plan to be linked to the organization's strategic plan.

Sometimes it is helpful to provide a short scenario of the information processing environment that will result from the execution of the plan. For example, the plan might describe an environment of distributed processing with extensive local computer power tied in a large network to central machines.

A critical element of the plan is the new applications areas being planned. Some systems will be in the process of development, and they should be identified along with a report of their status. For major new applications areas, there should be a breakdown of costs and schedules. For an insurance firm a major applications area might be the development of systems to report losses for customers being insured against factory accidents. Such an application area might have several potential systems developed for it.

The plan should outline and set priorities for applications areas; for example, marketing promotions, production control, etc. Once the priorities for applications development are identified, during the development of the applications, specific alternatives should be chosen for implementation, as we shall discuss later.

To set priorities, a corporate steering committee containing high-level representation of concerned managers should be convened. This committee can make the tradeoffs among functional areas. A committee ensures that the decision on priorities is a management decision, rather than a choice left to the information services staff.

The operation of existing systems must continue; the plan should identify the existing systems and the costs of maintaining them. Estimates are that a

---

**KEEPING CATTLE TRIM**

*A California computer system helps a feedlot operator decide when cattle are putting on too much weight. Hartman and Williams, one of the oldest feedlot operators in the Imperial Valley, wants a certain amount of fat on the cattle to help produce tender beef. However, it takes more feed to produce a pound of fat than it does a pound of lean beef.*

*The computer keeps track of weight gain in proportion to feed. When the rate of gain drops, feed is being turned into excess fat instead of lean meat.*

*The computer monitors the feeding pattern of the cattle. It estimates weight gain from consumption to help the feedlot determine at which point the animal has reached a diminishing level of return.*

*The feedlot features Brahman cattle which tend to be leaner than other breeds. They arrive weighing about 300 pounds and in nine months gain 600 to 700 pounds. The computer also checks records maintained for each lot of cattle in the yard. There are up to 22,000 head of cattle in more than 100 lots. The computer helps assure that the right formula and feeding schedule are used for each lot.*

*Investors own some of the cattle and the computer prepares an itemized bill for them, and a profit and loss statement. Finally the computer is used to analyze commodity prices so the feedlot operator can determine which are the best buys at any one time.*

*Computerworld*, November 14, 1983.

---

minimum of 50 percent of the total development budget in most organizations goes to maintenance and enhancement of existing applications.

The plan should also describe the existing and any new organizational structure for computing. Where will computers be located and how are they to be managed? Where does one find systems-analysis resources?

Management is also interested in the impact of a plan on the organization, particularly its financial impact. Finally, the plan should identify implementation risks and obstacles. For many ambitious plans, the availability of adequate numbers of computer staff professionals may be the key obstacle to implementation.

The information services department should also be encouraged to develop an annual report that discusses progress made during the year. The report should be tied to the goals in that year's plans, and it becomes an input for the preparation of the next plan.

**Organization Structure**

Existing information technology offers considerable flexibility in developing patterns for the structure of the information services function. The firm must identify possible processing patterns, evaluate them, and choose an alternative

**TABLE 6-5**
ORGANIZATIONAL STRUCTURE FOR PROCESSING

**Patterns**

|  | Hardware | Systems development |
|---|---|---|
| Centralized | X | |
| Distributed | | |
| Decentralized | | X |

Example: multidivision firm with a central computer group and analysts employed by the divisions

**Evaluation Criteria**
Level of service
Responsiveness
Reliability
Cost
Management task

for implementation. Processing alternatives can be divided into three broad groups that represent points on a continuum. At one extreme is completely centralized processing; all systems analysis and design is performed by a central group and all equipment is operated centrally.

At the other extreme is complete decentralization; all equipment is resident at local sites, and these sites have their own staff for analysis and design work. Distributed processing occurs when local sites are tied together in some type of communications network.

Table 6-5 presents some of the evaluation criteria that can be used to select a particular structure for processing. These criteria, such as levels of service, system responsiveness, and reliability, are oriented toward the interests of the user. In general there is no rule as to what kinds of systems are most responsive or provide the highest level of service. It appears that local processing is associated with more favorable user perceptions of service levels and greater responsiveness. The availability of a network of computers or of several computers at a central site provides high reliability. The least potential reliability is associated with a single system having no backup. Costs must be computed for every alternative; the cost of a particular pattern of processing depends on the configuration, the location of data, etc. The task of managing either a centralized or decentralized configuration is complex and will depend on the existing information processing organization.

The challenge of a centralized system is to make it responsive; that of decentralized and distributed systems is to make them coordinated. Management must trade off the benefits perceived by users in having and controlling their own computer equipment against the need for overall coordination in the organization. Allowing a proliferation of small computers can lead to high costs if the organization decides to connect diverse equipment through a network.

Also, the firm must ask if there are opportunities to develop common systems that can be used in multiple locations to prevent the duplication of development efforts.

## New Applications

Rarely today are totally infeasible applications suggested by users. Instead, some type of system can be undertaken to improve information processing that will be feasible. The question is what is both feasible and desirable? A corporate steering committee should have chosen applications areas as a part of developing a plan for information processing. Now, the task is to choose what type of system, if any, will be developed. Management must consider the existing portfolio of applications and provide guidance on the amount of investment possible and the balance of the portfolio. For example, the firm will want to have some low-risk projects under way to offset projects with a high risk of failure.

In Chapter 14 we advocate a procedure in which the information services department and users form a committee to select alternatives for new applications. Many firms have tried such selection committees and eventually disbanded them claiming that they do not work. A committee given both a proper role and information can succeed in this task. The committees that have failed are ones that were treated as rubber stamps for decisions already made elsewhere in the firm: the committee should make real decisions.

First, the committee should agree with the information services department on the number of alternatives to be considered for each system. Examples of alternatives for a single application are the use of an applications package, an on-line system, a batch system, or maintaining the status quo. The selection committee and the information services department then agree on a series of criteria to be used to evaluate each of these alternatives. A scoring and weighting procedure is applied to help make the final selection.

Management must also see that a new application is implemented successfully after an alternative has been selected. It can take one to three years to develop a major new application, and we expect to use the new system for five to seven years. Thus a system may be around for the next decade, and the chances for making significant changes in it for the next five years are small.

Systems analysis and design is an area that requires a great deal of management attention. Managers must demonstrate that they are behind the development of a new system and see that there is adequate user input in the design process. Frequent group review meetings are important during the design process. Top management must participate in these meetings and make clear that it supports the changes that are likely to come from the system. Later in the text we discuss system analysis and design in more detail along with how the organization can implement systems so they are successful.

## Operations

The major concerns in the operation of existing systems are credibility and service levels. It is very difficult to gain enthusiasm or cooperation in the development of new systems if existing service levels are unsatisfactory. Management must be sure that the information services department is providing effective service as perceived by its customers. Often the measures used to evaluate service are created and evaluated in the information services department itself; they tend to have little meaning for users. However, management sees a report that describes the percentage of output reports processed on time, the availability of the computer, etc., and assumes that adequate measurement is taking place.

Table 6-6 lists some critical management concerns in the operation of existing information systems. Efficiency considerations include the utilization of equipment, the quality of scheduling, and smoothness of operations. As hardware becomes less expensive, having a machine that is fully utilized is less important than having adequate capacity for processing. A key task of operating management in the computer area is to schedule jobs on the computer so that all processing is done satisfactorily.

Efficiency is important, but most managers and users are more interested in effectiveness. One approach to measuring effectiveness is to conduct a user evaluation and survey at a detailed level. For example, one can ask about specific systems and reports. Measures of system "uptime" for an on-line system are also one good indicator of effectiveness. Adherence to schedules is important; so is the error experience of users. There will always be errors, but is their number reasonable and are there edit and error checks that catch errors?

The firm can conduct user surveys of service levels to supplement measures of on-time performance or computer uptime supplied by the computer operations group. These surveys can be treated statistically to extract key factors (combinations of items on the survey) that serve as a measure of performance. Over time

**TABLE 6-6**
OPERATIONS

| |
|---|
| **Efficiency** |
| Utilization of equipment |
| Scheduling |
| Smooth operations |
| **Effectiveness** |
| User evaluation and survey |
| Uptime |
| Meeting schedules |
| Error experience |
| **Control** |
| Exposure analysis |
| Backup |

---

**MANAGEMENT PROBLEM 6-2**

AgChem is a major chemicals firm. Their chairman is the one quoted in this chapter as saying "I get nothing from our computers." The vice president of finance has the responsibility for information processing activities in the firm. He has just succeeded in making the department a division, the highest-level organizational entity in the firm. In addition, a new manager of the division has been recruited to try to "turn the computer area around."

The new manager and the vice president of finance are trying to develop a strategy for the turnaround beginning at the top and working through the various levels of the organization.

The vice president is very capable but has had no formal experience with computers. He knows, however, that there are many problems. Users constantly complain about information services. The new director of information processing has conferred with his staff. He feels that some of the criticism is justified but that a lot of the users and top management just do not realize the extent to which they and the entire firm are dependent on the computer.

The vice president and the new manager of information services would like some help in trying to improve the situation at AgChem. Can you suggest ways they might go about creating both better service and a better image for information processing?

---

the survey is repeated, the factors computed, and the progress of the operations function evaluated. Such a technique provides a measurement and an evaluation that include criteria important to users as well as indicators from the operations group.

Management is responsible for control in the organization. Computer systems process vital transactions, and many applications are concerned with control. Thus, the computer area is one of extremely high exposure for most organizations. Management must assure itself that adequate controls exist within systems and that computers are applied effectively to the control of the organization. One major component of control is adequate backup. To determine the level of control, management can conduct an audit, a topic we shall discuss in Chapter 23.

### Equipment/Staff Needs

The requirements to operate existing systems and the resources to develop new applications determine staff and equipment needs. One of the by-products of the planning process is the identification of needed resources; requirements are compared with available resources to determine what incremental equipment and staff are necessary. Top management must make the decision of what action to take when there is a discrepancy between the resources needed to accomplish the plan and the resources available.

There are a large number of options for equipment, and management must help develop criteria for comparing alternatives. One important issue today is the extent to which compatibility among different vendors is stressed. If many incompatible systems are acquired, the organization will not be able to take advantage of common software.

For the staff, the obvious way to expand resources is to hire more individuals. However, there is a limit to the number of people that can be absorbed productively into the organization. Another alternative is to use more packaged programs to improve staff productivity. Outside contractors can be employed to develop systems or supply staff members.

All trends in the future point to the conclusion that hardware costs will continue to decline and that there will be an insufficient number of computer professionals to develop systems. These observations suggest that the organization will have to give more responsibility to users for systems. The firm should acquire higher-higher level languages such as report generators and encourage users to retrieve their own data and design reports. The firm should also invest in a database management system and in a query language to extend the computer to the end user. The organization can prepare to use the technology better by making it widely available and easily understood.

### Charging

Two basic types of cost are associated with computer activities: development and operations. Development costs are incurred during the design of a new system. They can be estimated in advance, but our history has not been one of conspicuous success in staying within the estimated cost. Investment cost can be highly variable, especially if a project is not completed on time.

The major costs of systems development are personnel expenses. For most systems, the cost of computer time for testing and debugging is small compared with the labor cost. The systems analyst has to estimate both the number of days and the average costs necessary for computer department employees to design the system. Management may also want to allocate the salary expenses of users to the project when they are heavily involved in systems design activities.

In contrast to development costs, operations costs are usually more predictable, at least by the time program testing has begun. These costs include charges for computer time, supplies, and labor. Sometimes all the various components of computer cost are combined into one hourly charge keyed to computer resource utilization; for example, X dollars per CPU minute, Y dollars per 1000 lines printed, etc. Other charging algorithms are based on the units of work processed by the department, such as the number of checks processed, bills printed, etc.

There are two polar approaches to accounting for computer expenses: overhead charge-out and full charge-out to users. Table 6-7 describes the advantages of each approach (Dearden and Nolan, 1973).

In one approach all expenses for computers are treated as company overhead. Accounting is cheaper, and it is not necessary to keep track of many individual

**TABLE 6-7**
COMPARISON OF CHARGING MECHANISM FOR OVERHEAD VERSUS CHARGE-OUT

**Overhead advantages**
Cheaper accounting
Responsibility for control remains with computer department
Makes all computer costs visible
Computer expenses reviewed by top management
Creates stability for computer department
**Charge-out advantages**
Users have to allocate resources to computer services and consider tradeoffs for other uses of funds
Shows how computer department is interacting with user departments
Provides data for comparison of external services with internal computer services
Provides information on relative costs of applications
User does not see computer as a free good

charges or go to the expense of developing and executing a charge-out procedure. Some advocates of this approach argue that it leaves decision making in the computer department where technical competence exists to make decisions. Because of the large expenditure charged against overhead for computer expenses, it is possible that top management will review computer expenses more under this charging system. Overhead charging does create stability for the computer department since it can count on the same processing load. For example, if user departments change their processing activities under a full charge-out scheme, there can be wide fluctuations in the computer department budget.

In a full charge-out scheme, all computer expenses are charged to users. Users have to make resource allocation decisions; this approach leads to the complete decentralization of computer decisions. By examining the accounting system and comparing charges, management can see where the computer department is providing the most service and has developed the most applications. The charges make it possible to compare an internal department with an outside computer service organization, which is always an alternative to internal processing. Charging also provides data on the relative cost of each application. Since the computer is not a free good, users may exercise more restraint in requesting systems.

A partial charge-out approach offers a flexible alternative to full overhead or full charge-out accounting. The exact nature of the partial charge-out scheme depends on the individual organization. One approach that has been used is to charge users for operations since the amount involved is more certain. New applications are treated as a research and development effort and are charged to overhead. This partial charge-out approach recognizes that a new computer application is a capital investment, just as is adding a new piece of machinery.

An approach to selecting a charging mechanism based primarily on user and organizational considerations has been suggested by Dearden and Nolan. If the

---

**MANAGEMENT PROBLEM 6-3**

Nelson Hayes is Vice President of Administration for Hawkins and Smith, a major drug manufacturer. The firm has a large, central computer installation that provides batch, on-line, and time-sharing services to users. Nelson maintains a corporate consulting group that specializes in APL services. His consultants are hired by divisions to assist in developing applications for the division.

Nelson is concerned about the rapid growth of microcomputers in the firm as a whole. "Micros can do a lot for us, but it is more cost effective to add a time-sharing user than to pay for a micro. With a big system in place, all we need is to add a terminal . . . even if we need more memory it is a lot cheaper per byte on a mainframe than on a PC."

Users, on the other hand, have taken quickly to the PC. They are not eager to have any kind of corporate direction. Senior management worries about incompatibility among different vendors. Management has asked your help in coming up with a policy for microcomputer acquisition and use that satisfies both Nelson and users.

---

user population is not too knowledgeable about computer systems, the opportunity for applications in the organization, and the cost and limitations of systems, then overhead accounting is favored. On the other hand, if users have widely diverse needs and are sophisticated and knowledgeable about computers, then full charge-out schemes are more appropriate.

We recommend a partial charge-out approach. For new systems development, at least a portion of the cost should be charged to overhead. Depending on organizational practices, management may insist on some matching investment funds from the user department or division. However, the user should not have to bear the full cost, especially given the uncertainty in cost and payoff in developing a new computer application.

For operations, develop a charge-out scheme for users. It may be desirable to set up some type of flexible rate to help in allocating resources; for example, charge less for jobs that can be run on the third shift and charge more for daytime use of the computer. The cost allocation method should assure users of roughly the same charges for the same job; otherwise it is very difficult for them to budget.

**Control**

Management control is concerned with the broad question of whether information technology is making a contribution to corporate strategy. From our earlier discussions, this contribution could be in the form of independent systems, policy support systems for planning, or through a close linkage between technology and strategy formulation. One reason top management may feel uneasy about information processing is its realization that often managers are not controlling the technology. One way to gain control over information processing is to participate in the decisions mentioned above and to be knowledgeable about information processing activities in the organization.

On an operational level, one control mechanism is to compare actual results with the information processing plan. On a more frequent basis, user reactions to service levels can be measured and reported and progress on individual systems development projects monitored. Management should establish performance criteria and the information services department should report on them.

One major management problem is what action to take when it appears that some part or all the information processing function is out of control. A common solution, though not necessarily the best, is to replace the manager of the information services department. Instead of that reflex response, top management should take a careful look at how it is contributing to controlling information processing. The framework in Figure 6-1 is one starting point for such an examination. Has management helped develop a plan for information processing? Does management get involved in the selection of applications and the determination of priorities? Do top managers set the objectives for new systems and participate in their design?

In some instances changes in personnel may be appropriate when the operation is out of control. However, in others the best action may be to provide additional resources. Possibly processing schedules are not being met because of a lack of manpower or computer power. The design of new systems is a research and development activity with high uncertainty. If a high-risk complex system causes delays and yet appears well managed, the appropriate action may be to add resources or extend the schedule.

In summary, the first step in exerting control is knowing what to measure. The second step is conducting the evaluation. The third step is determining what action is most likely to improve the situation if part of the operation is out of control.

## MANAGEMENT COMMITTEES

Because of the size of the investment involved and the importance of key systems to the organization, many firms are establishing committees to help manage information processing activities. A committee can bring to bear many different points of view on a problem, and it ensures widespread representation of functional areas and management levels in key decisions.

One large multinational firm has organized a series of committees to deal with planning for information systems and the review of proposals for new systems. An office of the president and of the chairperson are at the head of this firm. Each major line of business in this multinational is organized into a company with its own president and staff. There are also corporate vice presidents for various functional areas, such as a vice president of finance. Service units such as research and development and information processing are corporate divisions reporting to appropriate corporate vice presidents.

This firm has recently established a corporate level steering committee for information processing. Its objective is to review plans and determine the appropriate size of the firm's investment in information processing. The corporate committee reviews division plans, organizes and approves education about systems, and seeks areas for the development of common systems serving two or more suborganizations, such as two different companies with common information processing requirements. The purpose of a common system is to avoid the cost of developing a tailored application at each site.

Each division also has a local steering committee that is charged with the responsibility of developing and approving long-range plans for information processing in that suborganization. The local committee also reviews and approves short-term plans and the annual budget for information processing activities in the division. This committee serves to review proposals for new systems and to assign priorities to them. Finally, the local committee reviews and approves staffing requirements for information services.

The corporate and division committees could be supplemented by a separate committee to examine alternatives for a given application during the feasibility study for a new system. We shall discuss such a committee later in the section of the text on systems analysis and design. Another type of committee will also be recommended; a team composed of users, managers, and the information services department staff that works on the actual design of a computer-based system.

For the multinational firm discussed above, the corporate level and division level steering committees deal with policy. In a smaller firm, only a corporate level committee might be appropriate. However, the organization should develop a mechanism that involves users and the systems staff to (1) set policy and review plans, (2) select alternatives for a given application, and (3) participate in the actual design of a system.

## SUMMARY

This chapter has presented a framework for examining the relationship between information processing and corporate strategy. The approach identifies three levels of the relationship between information technology and strategy formulation.

Most organizations appear to be at the first or second levels. At the first level, systems that are independent of the firm's strategy help achieve some stated objective through greater efficiency or better management. Second-level policy support systems contribute to the planning process directly. At the third level, information technology is merged with strategy formulation; technology serves to expand the range and number of strategic opportunities considered by the firm. In addition to the strategy formulation role for information processing, the technology also helps to implement the adopted strategy.

The second part of the chapter presented a framework for top management use in managing information processing activities in the organization. If information technology is to make a contribution to strategy formulation and to the operation of the firm, management must become more adept at coping with information processing activities. The framework for management stresses the importance of the planning process, the development of organizational structures for processing, the identification and development of new applications, the operation of existing systems, the identification of equipment and staff needs, and charging for services and monitoring information processing in general. The purpose of the framework is to assist top management in determining the key issues for concern in managing the information processing resource.

By including considerations of information technology in the development of corporate strategy and by effectively managing information processing activities in the organization, this technology will make its maximum contribution to the organization. Managers will no longer have to ask, "What am I getting from information technology?" Instead they will be able to point out the nature and extent of the contribution technology makes to the organization.

## KEY WORDS

| | | |
|---|---|---|
| Acquisition | Equipment | Strategic |
| Alternative | Microcomputers | Structure |
| Application | Overhead | Tactical |
| Charge-out | Operations | Technology |
| Control | Plan | Technology assessment |
| Criteria | Processing pattern | |

## RECOMMENDED READINGS

Kantrow, A.: "The Strategy-Technology Connection," *Harvard Business Review*, July–August 1980, pp. 6–21. (A good paper on technology and strategy in general.)

Lucas, H. C., Jr., and J. Moore: "A Multiple-Criterion Scoring Approach to Information Project Selection," INFOR, February 1976, pp. 1–12. (A procedure for a more rational selection of alternatives for a computer application.)

McFarlan, W., and J. McKenney: *Corporate Information Systems Management,* Richard Irwin, Homewood, Ill., 1983. (A good book for managing information processing.)

Nolan, R. L.: "Managing the Computer Resource: A Stage Hypothesis," *Communications of the ACM,* July 1973, pp. 399–440. (A famous and controversial paper describing the growth pattern of information services departments over time.)

Nolan, R. L.: "Managing Information Systems by Committee," *Harvard Business Review,* July–August 1982, pp. 72–79. (A good article on executive steering committees.)

Parsons, G.: "Information Technology: A New Competitive Weapon," *Sloan Management Review,* Fall 1983, pp. 3–14. (An analysis of how computers affect strategy.)

## DISCUSSION QUESTIONS

1 Locate an article in the popular business press about the strategy of a corporation. Describe the interrelationship between technology and the strategy of the firm. Compare two firms and note the differences.

2 Why did most firms first develop systems to improve operational efficiency?

3 Should a manager actually use a decision support system, or should there be a technical staff member to isolate the manager from the system?

4 What is the advantage of full charge-out for information processing costs?

5 How can users evaluate the level of service quality from an information services department?

6 One bank information services department developed 69 quality indicators for information processing. Do you think this was a good idea? What do you predict was the reaction of users?

7 What structural patterns of the organization would influence the structure of information processing?

8 Why do you think preliminary evidence indicates that users are more satisfied when the computer is located at their site?

9 Examine the trend toward distributed processing according to the conflict model in the previous chapter.

10 How does strategic planning differ between a firm that offers services and one that manufactures a product? Is there a difference in the impact of technology on strategy in the two types of firms?

11 How would management go about assessing the probable information processing technology available over the next five years?

12 What criteria are the most important for an organization in choosing among competing alternatives for a particular computer application?

13 Why should the decision on what applications to undertake not be left to the manager of the information services department?

14 What do you think the role of top management should be in the design of a specific information system?

15 Is it likely that the president of a firm who feels that he or she receives nothing from computers knows the contribution of computers to the organization?

16 It has been said that problems with information processing start at the top of the organization. What does this mean? Do you agree or disagree? Why?

17 Why do priorities have to be set on new computer applications?

18 Why do you think managers seem to know more about other functional areas than information processing?

19 What options are open to the organization if equipment and staff needs exceed available resources?

20 What actions can management take if information processing activities seem to be out of control? What different actions are suitable when the problem is in operations rather than systems analysis and design?

21 What is the role of external expertise in the development of a strategy for information systems?

22 Why have information services departments historically been reluctant to develop plans?

# PART THREE

# COMPUTER TECHNOLOGY

This section of the text contains the most technical material we shall discuss. Users and managers are often involved in important decisions about computer technology, as shown in the accompanying table. To make these decisions intelligently, the decision maker must understand some of the technical issues involved. As we discussed in the last chapter, a basic knowledge of technology is necessary to manage information processing activities effectively.

In Chapters 7 and 8, we discuss computer hardware. Users and managers are often involved in the selection of the appropriate technology for a computer application. Should the system operate in batch mode or on-line? Should data be collected on-line but be processed in batch? For this application, what are the advantages and disadvantages of each alternative?

The user may be involved in the selection of the entire computer system; possibilities here range from a personal computer to a large, general-purpose computer system. It is also very likely that the user will have some say in the acquisition of specific devices, such as terminals for an on-line application. Finally, management must decide where computers will be located, and what applications each computer will execute.

There are also many important decisions concerning computer software, a topic discussed in Chapter 9. Should a user buy a particular program for a personal computer? What is a fourth generation language?

Computer files are the basic building block of a computer-based information system. Different types of file structures are necessary to support the requirements of different applications. The user who works on the design of a system must be conversant with the different options available with direct-access and sequential files. Decisions about response time also have implications for file design; if an application is to operate on-line, then direct-access files are

**MANAGEMENT DECISIONS ON TECHNOLOGY**

| Chapter | Decision area | Examples of alternatives |
| --- | --- | --- |
| 7,8 Hardware | Selection of technology Equipment selection for an entire system Selection of specific devices | Batch or on-line system General-purpose or minicomputer Terminals |
| 9 Software | Choice of languages Acquisition of packages | Personal computer programs Statistical analysis package Accounts receivable package |
| 10 Files | Capabilities of application | Direct-access or sequential file organization |
| 11 Database | Selection of data-base management system | On-line or batch processing Various data-management packages available |
| 12 Communications | Voice and data communications | Distributed processing Local area network vs. PBX |
| 13 Sources of services | Hardware Software | Service bureau, internal facility Consultant, internal staff, packages |

required. Many organizations are investigating the development of a comprehensive data base for a number of important reasons. Very complex software packages known as database management systems are available and managers must decide whether to acquire a package and, if so, which one. Computer files are discussed in Chapter 10 and databases in Chapter 11.

The topic of communications is of great interest to management. Deregulation by the government combined with the entry of new carriers creates many choices for communicating both voice and data. How should computers be configured? What kind of network, if any, do we want? What are the opportunities to communicate directly with the computers of suppliers and customers?

A manager is always concerned with the various sources available for products and services. In the computer field, there are options on suppliers for both hardware and software; we discuss some of the possibilities and their advantages and disadvantages in Chapter 13. There are hundreds of new software products announced each month for personal computers. Here the problem is not the source, but having enough information to decide what package to buy for a specific application.

The purpose of the material in this section is not to educate computer experts. Rather the objective is for the reader to gain enough understanding of computer hardware and software to make intelligent decisions about them. It is far more important to understand the concepts in this section than the specific details.

# FUNDAMENTALS OF COMPUTER EQUIPMENT

# FUNDAMENTALS OF COMPUTER EQUIPMENT

## CHAPTER ISSUES

- How does a personal computer work?
- What is the best technology for the organization?
- How does the organization select from the various options for computer equipment?

Why should one be interested in the way computer equipment works? After all, most people drive cars without understanding much about how they operate. Unfortunately, computers are more complex than automobiles, though possibly in a few years learning to use one will be as easy as learning to drive. Even for the apparently simple task of deciding what personal computer to buy and what options to purchase with it, we have to understand something about the technology.

In this chapter we shall discuss how computers work and in the next chapter we trace some of their historical evolution to provide background on how the industry has reached its present state.

People invented computers and their associated equipment, and one of the most difficult aspects of computers is a consequence of this human involvement. Of the engineering and design decisions made during computer development, many often appear arbitrary. Computer science is thus unlike a field such as mathematics, in which theorems are developed and proved rigorously. The reasons for a certain design feature may not be obvious, even to a computer expert. Designers make decisions by balancing performance, estimates of how the computer will be used, and costs. Because of the arbitrary nature of design decisions, we shall try to discuss general concepts that underlie the operation of most computer systems, although specific machines differ from any general discussion.

The equipment we discuss in this chapter and the next is often referred to as computer hardware—the parts of the computer that can be touched physically. Chapter 9 is about computer software, the instructions in the form of programs. that command the hardware to perform tasks. Physically, programs are entered in the computer by a keyboard or a terminal. However, once inside the computer, a program cannot be seen; it is represented electronically in computer memory.

## A BASIC PERSONAL COMPUTER

The computer you are most likely to have encountered first is a personal computer or microcomputer. There are millions of these devices in schools, homes, and offices; generally they feature a keyboard for entering data, a CRT or television-like output device for displaying data, and some form of storage.

A typical schematic for such a computer is shown in Figure 7-1. In this section we shall present an overview of the parts of the computer; in subsequent sections the text discusses the components in more detail.

The heart of the computer is the Central Processing Unit or CPU. It contains the logic which controls the calculations done by the computer. In most personal computers, the central processing unit is connected to a bus; the bus is a communications device, really a connection, among various parts of the computer. The bus carries (1) instructions from programs telling the computer what to do and (2) data. One of the most frequently used connections on the bus is between the CPU and random access memory or what is often called primary memory.

Primary memory of the computer holds two kinds of information. The first is data as one might expect. For example, if we wanted to add two numbers together like 178 and 256, these numbers would be stored in computer memory. Once added, their sum 434 would also be placed in memory.

Instructions in the form of programs are also stored in primary memory. The instructions or software tell the CPU what to do. One main feature of memory is its passive nature; memory is only a storage place for information. Instructions are actually executed in the CPU; data are moved between the CPU and memory when involved in a calculation. Another way to look at memory is to consider that primary memory has no logic capability. It stores data only since logic is required to process data.

The diskette drive or disk (or even a casette recorder on some home computers) is another form of storage. This secondary storage is usually larger than primary memory and is less costly. In Chapter 11 we will discuss secondary storage in much greater detail. Note, however, the disk controller in Figure 7-1. There is logic required to connect or interface the disk to the computer.

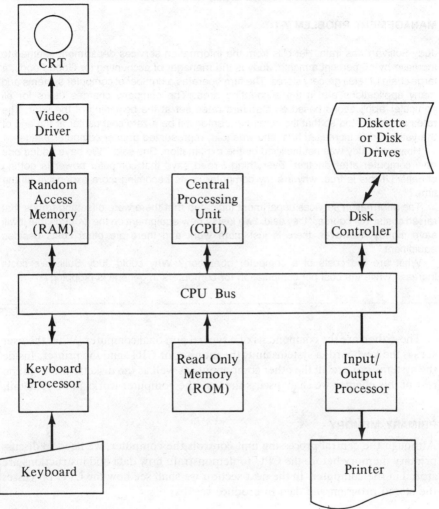

**FIGURE 7-1**
Schematic of a microcomputer.

While the CPU contains the most logic of the computer, we can see that there are other functions where the component must display some logic such as the disk controller. Similarly there is a keyboard processor to interface the keyboard with the computer and a video drive to control the CRT. Finally, we have an input/output processor which is dedicated to controlling devices like printers.

The last component in Figure 7-1 is called Read Only Memory or ROM. We need to defer discussion of ROM until the operations of the CPU are explained in a little more detail.

---

**MANAGEMENT PROBLEM 7-1**

Judy Sullivan was irate. Her bills from the information services department seemed to increase by 10 percent a month. Judy is the manager of accounting for Good Foods, a large chain of retail grocery stores. The firm operates a number of computer systems and many applications are in the accounting area. The company charges users for all computer applications based on standard rates set at the beginning of the year. The rates are estimated so that the computer center will be a zero cost center at the end of the year. Judy's increased bills, she was told, represented greater computer usage.

However, Judy was not mollified by the explanation. She said, "We have added one new computer after another. Everything I read says that computer power is getting cheaper. If this is true, why are my computer costs becoming more expensive all the time?"

The information services department indicated that there were offsetting trends that raised costs. "Of course," they said, "we justify new equipment on the grounds that it will save money. However, there is just more work and there are other costs besides equipment."

What are the costs of a computer operation? Why could Judy Sullivan's costs increase while the cost per computation for computers in general is dropping?

---

These then are the components of a typical personal computer. What the user sees is the keyboard, a systems unit, the monitor or CRT, and the printer. Inside the systems box are all the other components as well as the diskette drive. In the rest of this chapter we shall discuss the way the computer works in more detail.

## PRIMARY MEMORY

Although the central processing unit controls the computer, we need to discuss primary memory before the CPU to demonstrate how data and instructions are stored in the computer. In the next section we shall see how the CPU processes the stored program and data to produce results.

### The Arithmetic Basis of Computers

A computer can perform computations through an electronic counterpart to the arithmetic operations we perform on a routine basis. However, computer systems at their most fundamental level use a different number base than the common base 10 with which we are familiar.

The number 46 in base 10 can be represented as $4 \times 10 + 6 \times 1$. Furthermore, 10 is equal to $10^1$ and 1 is equal to $10^0$ (anything raised to the 0 power is 1 by definition). In our system of arithmetic, the position of a digit represents the power to which the base is raised before multiplication by the digit. For the number 46 above, 6 is in the "0 position," and 4 is in the 1 position. We can represent 46 then as $6 \times 10^0 + 4 \times 10^1$. This same procedure could be continued for more digits. For example, the number 346 can be represented as $6 \times 10^0 + 4 \times 10^1 + 3 \times 10^2$; now there is a 3 in the $10^2$ position that adds $3 \times 10^2$, or 300, to the number.

There is no reason why we must use the base 10 for arithmetic; it is convenient for human beings, but not for computers. A computer can be designed most easily to base 2, or the binary system. The two digits of the binary system (0 and 1) can be represented as "on-off," for example, through the presence or absence of an electrical signal.

A binary number is represented in the same positional notation as a base 10 number. The number 101110 in binary, starting with the right-most digit and working left, would be converted to base 10 as:

$$
\begin{array}{rcrcr}
0 \times 2^0 &=& 0 \times 1 &=& 0 \\
1 \times 2^1 &=& 1 \times 2 &=& 2 \\
1 \times 2^2 &=& 1 \times 4 &=& 4 \\
1 \times 2^3 &=& 1 \times 8 &=& 8 \\
0 \times 2^4 &=& 0 \times 16 &=& 0 \\
1 \times 2^5 &=& 1 \times 32 &=& \underline{32} \\
& & & & 46
\end{array}
$$

which adds to 46 in base 10.

---

**THE IRS CALLS**

*The IRS has added computers to its tax collection force. There are now at least 12 automated collection systems (ACS) at the 21 IRS collection centers. The software running on mainframe computers assists collectors in initiating dunning letters and phone calls to delinquent taxpayers. The system includes an automatic call distributor connected to a large database.*

*If a taxpayer disregards the first four collection notices sent by the IRS regional offices, his or her file will be shifted to an automated collection site. Shortly the system will include 2000 operators and terminals.*

*The IRS has one objective: collect the $27 billion it is owed in back taxes. Forecasts based on test samples suggest that the $100 million computer system will more than pay for itself.*

*The system updates its accounts weekly. The operator presses a Next Case function key on the terminal that displays taxpayer name, address, social security number, and tax liability. The display also ahows a history of collection steps and their outcome.*

*If a dunning letter or levy against wages is in order, the operator uses the system to notify the IRS regional office. If a phone call is in order, the operator presses a Dial function key which tells the system to call the taxpayer using the least expensive routing for the call. If busy, the computer schedules the call for later. The system is designed to take time zones into account and not to call before 8 A.M. or after 8 P.M. local time!*

*Computerworld,* April 23, 1984.

---

At the most basic level, computers store and process data in binary form: however, this is not an easy system for humans to use. Therefore, the binary digits in computer memory are grouped together to form other number bases for performing operations. For one series of machines, three binary digits are combined to produce an octal, or base-8, computer. Another popular line of computers groups four digits and is therefore a hexadecimal, or base-16, machine. Fortunately, even programmers rarely work at the binary level. For many applications, software or the design of the hardware makes the machine look as if it performs base-10 arithmetic from a programming standpoint.

All types of symbols can be coded and represented as binary numbers. For example, we could develop the following table to encode four alphabetic letters using two binary digits:

$$A = 00$$
$$B = 01$$
$$C = 10$$
$$D = 11$$

Thus, a series of binary digits can be coded to represent characters with which we are more familiar.

### Memory Organization

Now that we have a convenient way to represent numbers and symbols, we need a way to store them in memory. Different computer designers have adopted different schemes for memory organization. Generally, all computers combine groups of bits (binary digits) to form characters, sometimes called bytes. The number of bits determines the size of the character set. From the example above, it should be evident that we can code $2^n$ distinct characters with a binary number of n digits. For example, if there are 4 bits, then there can be $2^4$, or 16 symbols for alphanumeric data. Alphanumeric data are used for input and output display. Usually a different format for numbers is used for computation purposes. (See the section on arithmetic operations.) Many modern computers use an 8-bit character, or byte, giving a character set of $2^8$, or 256, symbols.

After a character size and a set of symbols have been developed, the next design issue is to decide how to organize the memory of the machine. One basic use of memory is to store and fetch data; therefore we need some way to reference storage. An everyday example will help to clarify the problem. Suppose that we are expecting an important piece of mail. The mail delivery will be made to the mailbox at our street address; we know that by looking in the mailbox at our address we shall find the mail if it is there.

Now consider computer memory to be a group of mailboxes. We need an address to define each piece of data stored in memory so that it may be placed in a particular location (mailbox) and retrieved from that location. It is possible to have an address for each character in memory, or sometimes groups of characters are combined to form words and the words are given an address. With IBM 370 architecture, four 8-bit bytes are combined to form a word, though each byte also has an address. A word structure is convenient because many numbers will fit within a single word as do many types of instructions.

Instructions, as well as data, must be stored in memory, and deciding on the instruction format is another design problem. At a minimum, the instruction must contain an operation code that specifies what operation is to be performed, for example, add or subtract. The operation code is combined with one or more addresses. For example, a single-address machine is designed with instructions that have one operation code and one address. For most instructions the single address specifies the memory location for one piece of data to be operated on by the instruction. In the case of an add instruction, the address specifies the memory location whose content is to be added to some data already contained in the central processing unit. A machine with a two-address instruction format can have an add instruction that refers to both addresses in memory of the addends.

## Memory Technology

From the standpoint of the programmer and the user, the technology used for primary memory is not important. However, a general understanding of memory technology helps in appreciating the characteristics of secondary storage and file structures, and these are topics of vital importance to users.

**Core Storage**  The earliest memory technology of interest to us is magnetic core storage. Most current computers do not use core storage for primary memory. Many computer professionals continue to refer to primary memory as "core storage" regardless of whether core technology is used or not!

Figure 7-2 is a diagram of a simple core memory. Remember that we are interested in representing 0 or 1 in memory. For core memory, these two states are determined by the direction of magnetization of the core. Each core in Figure 7-2 can be uniquely located by the two lines running through it. Each of these lines has one-half of the current necessary to reverse the direction of magnetization. When current is passed through a vertical line and a horizontal line, only the core at the intersection receives the full current necessary to reverse its direction of magnetization. Other cores—not at the intersection but on one of the two lines—receive one-half the current necessary to change their state, so they are not affected. Core memories contain two additional lines—one to sense the direction of magnetization and one to aid in writing.

To read information from memory, current is passed through the two appropriate grid wires. If the core is already magnetized in the same direction as the current, nothing happens. Otherwise, the core changes its direction of magnetization. The change induces a current in a sense wire, and this current is interpreted to determine the original state of the core. The presence or absence of current in the wire can be interpreted as a 0 or 1. For cores in which the direction of magnetization was changed, the data have been "reversed." For the

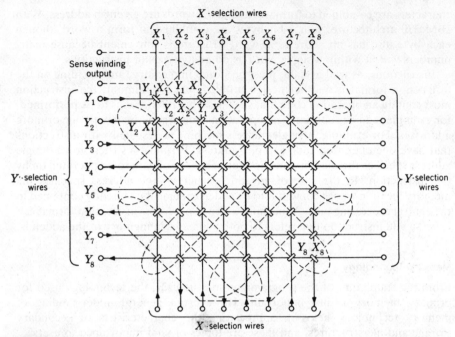

**FIGURE 7-2**
Core memory plane. (From T. C. Bartee: *Digital Computer Fundamentals,* 4th ed., McGraw-Hill, 1977.)

cores that were read, data have to be rewritten. An inhibit wire (omitted from Figure 7-2) blocks the rewrite current from the cores that did not change state during the read operation.

In summary, to read, we write into storage, sense any changes, and rewrite into storage to regenerate the original core state. Because of the need to rewrite data just read, core storage readout is referred to as "destructive" readout.

**Semiconductor Memory**   Modern computers have main memories of semiconductor devices. Semiconductor memories offer significant increases in speed over other memory technologies, are smaller, and are compatible with normal circuitry of the central processing unit. The major disadvantages of semiconductor memory is its volatility. Semiconductor memories must be constantly powered and lose their contents (are volatile) if the power fails.

Figure 7-3a shows schematically how a typical semiconductor memory works. The memory is organized in an array of rows and columns; the cell at the intersection of each column and row stores one bit so that the diagram in Figure 7-3a contains 64 bits. Three binary digits specify the row (1 to 8) and three the column (1 to 8).

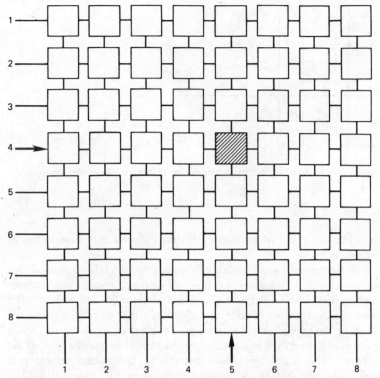

**FIGURE 7-3a**
Semiconductor memory.

Figure 7-3b shows one cell storing a single bit in detail. A zero charge on the capacitor might represent a binary 0 and a very small charge a binary 1. When the selection line or row of the array is activated (row 4 in Figure 7-3a), it turns on all the transistor switches in each of the cells connected to it. The transistor is an on-off switch connecting the storage capacitor to its data line, which is the column of the array. When both the row and column lines are activated, they determine the cell selected for reading or writing (cell 4, 5 in Figure 7-3a.) Every few milliseconds the capacitor must have its charge regenerated because the charge is lost from being read and through leakage (Hodges, 1977).

To produce integrated circuits containing many semiconductors, special equipment is utilized to develop first a picture of an electronic circuit on a drafting board or computer terminal screen. A reduced image of the circuit is made into something called a mask, which is like a photographic negative. When light rays are projected through such a mask onto thin films of a liquid plastic, exposed areas harden. Unexposed plastic is washed away leaving a microscopic structure corresponding to the original drawing of the circuit. Acids are then used to cut away the surface of areas that were not covered by the plastic,

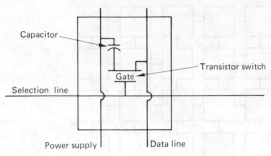

**FIGURE 7-3b**
Detail of cell. (*Adapted from "Microelectronic Memories," by O. Hodges,* Scientific American, *September 1977.*)

. producing an engraving of the original circuit. Chips are actually sandwiches of many of these layers.

To produce an integrated circuit a slice of semiconducting silicon is used as a base on which the circuit is engraved and built up with subsequent applications of the process described above. Parts of the semiconductor base must be turned into transistors. Foreign atoms (dopants) lodged in microscopic regions of a silicon crystal make the crystal either extra rich or extra poor in electrons. When such regions are placed together in a sandwich, they become transistors that act as on-off switches. The transistors allow current to flow when an external electrical field is applied but block current flow when the external field is removed. Today, small silicon chips hold more than 500,000 components like transistors.

## THE CENTRAL PROCESSING UNIT

As stated earlier, the CPU controls the operation of the computer; it contains most of the logic circuitry for the machine. Program instructions are stored in memory along with data. In a basic computer system the instructions are stored sequentially beginning at some location in memory. The CPU by convention always fetches the next instruction in sequence and executes it unless the program instructs it to do otherwise.

### Components of the CPU

Figure 7-4 shows the CPU and primary memory in more detail than Figure 7-1. A discussion of CPU operations helps in understanding programming languages in the next chapter. Note the presence of a storage address register (SAR) and storage buffer register (SBR) in primary memory. The SAR is connected to memory in such a way that when an address is placed in it and a read command is given, the contents of the memory at that address appear in the storage buffer

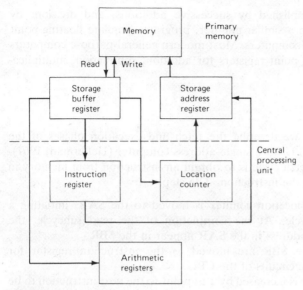

**FIGURE 7-4**
Central processing unit and memory.

register. Similarly, when a write command is issued, the contents of the SBR are written into memory at the address location contained in the SAR.

The CPU contains a number of registers. The purpose of the instruction register is to hold instructions that are decoded and executed by the circuits of the CPU. The location counter keeps track of the address from which the next instructions should be fetched.

The arithmetic unit contains registers that hold data during the execution of arithmetic operations by CPU circuits. Several types of numbers can be processed by computers. A fixed-point number is an integer; the decimal point is fixed and is assumed to be to the right of the right-most digit. Examples of fixed-point numbers are 2, 512, and 671. A floating point number corresponds to scientific exponential notation; the position of the decimal point is indicated by digits associated with the number. For example, we might have a floating point format of .1632E03 meaning that the number 0.1632 is to be multiplied by $10^3$. The number in conventional form, then, is 163.2. The number 16.32 would be presented by .1632E02. The exponent allows the decimal point to "float." It is also possible to have registers that perform decimal arithmetic.

Are arithmetic registers really necessary? One early computer had no registers; mathematical operations were performed by looking up information in tables in memory! The presence of arithmetic registers, however, speeds computations; if registers are not used, a program requiring memory and execution time must be written to stimulate desired arithmetic operations. Some early computers had only fixed point addition and subtraction capabilities.

Multiplication was accomplished by successive additions, and division, by successive subtractions. In a similar manner, programs simulate floating-point operations on many microcomputers. Most modern general-purpose computers feature fixed and floating-point registers for addition, subtraction, multiplication, and division.

### Operation of the CPU

Referring to Figure 7-4, we describe the fetch and execution phases of the instruction cycle of the CPU for a single-address computer (Hellerman, 1967).

The objective of the fetch cycle is to obtain an instruction from memory in preparation for executing the instruction. The steps are:

**1** The address of the location counter is moved to the SAR, initiating a read-from-memory subcycle. At the completion of the read subcycle, the contents of the memory address in the SAR appear in the SBR.

**2** The contents of the SBR are moved to the instruction register for interpretation by the logic circuits of the CPU.

**3** The location counter is increased by 1 to point to the next instruction to be fetched.

**4** The instruction is decoded to yield an address.

---

### MANAGEMENT PROBLEM 7-2

A major bank, Eastern National, centralized all its information processing activities when third-generation computers were first installed. The prevailing argument in the industry at the time was that "economies of scale" justified centralization. Each larger member of a computer manufacturer's family provided more processing power per dollar. That is, moving from one machine to the next more powerful in the line might increase costs by 30 percent while processing power increased by 1½ times. Thus, it made economic sense from the standpoint of hardware rentals to have a few large machines rather than many small machines located in different areas.

What do you think the disadvantages of centralization might be for Eastern National Bank? Are there other considerations beyond hardware cost that might enter into an analysis of centralization?

Currently, Eastern has reversed its trend toward centralization. A computer department spokesman said, "Now, with the availability of cheap minicomputers, the arguments for centralization are no longer valid. It is better to have each user develop applications for a dedicated minicomputer. Someday we will tie all the different minicomputers together. Right now, we can be more responsive to the user this way."

Are there management considerations that should be explored in Eastern's new approach, known in the industry as "distributed processing"? What technical problems might the proliferation of minicomputers in the bank create?

---

During the execution cycle, the instruction is interpreted and the operation it signifies is performed:

**1** The address of the data on which the operation is to take place is sent to the SAR. A read-access subcycle is started to fetch the datum that then appears in the SBR.

**2** The datum is routed to a machine register.

**3** The operation—for example, a subtract—is performed on the datum.

### An Instruction Set

What operations can be performed by a typical computer? Table 7-3 contains the instruction set for the Intel 8088 processor, the CPU of the popular IBM Personal Computer. Note the different classes of instructions in the table including data movement, arithmetic, logical comparison, and branching. Large computers have repertoires of well over 100 instructions along with 10 or more registers capable of performing arithmetic operations or serving as index registers. These machines contain more operations and support several data formats.

### MICROPROGRAMMING

#### Background

When computer manufacturers planned a new series of computers in the late 1950s (the "third generation"), they faced a number of serious marketing problems. Organizations had substantial investments in programs for their existing computers. These programs were frequently written in assembly language, a language that is generally unique for a given machine. That is, an assembly-language program cannot be executed on just any computer; it exhibits low compatibility among computers. How could a new machine be sold if it made obsolete a customer's program library so that all programs had to be replaced? How could customers convert? Would they have to keep a second-generation computer and a third-generation machine together while they translated their programs?

When a customer wanted to move up to a more powerful computer, it might have been necessary to switch to a new series of machines, requiring conversion. Computer manufacturers wanted to avoid major conversion problems in developing their new generation and also wanted to provide upward and downward compatibility. That is, there would be a family of machines, each capable of executing programs written for any "lower" member of that family. Of course, compatibility would only be possible within limits of memory and peripheral equipment.

To develop compatibility among computers in a family requires similar instruction sets. However, more powerful computers at the top of a product line

**TABLE 7-1**
EXAMPLES OF CLASSES OF INSTRUCTIONS AND INSTRUCTIONS FOR THE INTEL 8088,
A POPULAR CHIP FOR MICROCOMPUTERS

| Instruction | Meaning |
| --- | --- |
| **Data Transfer** | |
| MOV = Move | To move data from memory to a register, a register to memory, memory to the accumulator and vice versa |
| XCNG = Exchange | Exchange a register or memory with a register or a register with the accumulator |
| IN = Input from | Input from a fixed or variable port |
| OUT = Output | Ouput to a fixed or variable port |
| **Arithmetic** | |
| ADD = Add | Add contents of register or memory to accumulator |
| ADC = Add with carry | Add contents of register or memory to accumulator with carry |
| SUB = Subtract | Subtract contents of register or memory with accumulator |
| SUB = Subtract with borrow | Subtract contents of register or memory with accumulator |
| CMP = Compare | Compare registers and/or memory or compare with accumulator |
| **Logic** | |
| NOT = Not | Invert |
| AND = And | Register/memory logical and with register/memory or accumulator |
| OR = Or | Register/memory logical or with register/memory or accumulator |
| XOR = Exclusive Or | Register/memory logical exclusive or with register/memory or accumulator |
| **Control** | |
| CALL = Call | Call a routine |
| JMP = Jump | Jump to a new location to begin execution without conditions |
| NET = Return | Come back to code from a call. |
| J** = Jump on | ** become a series of letters indicating conditions like jump on less or equal, jump on equal, etc. |

usually have more extensive and capable repertoires of instructions than smaller members of the line. Thus, another major problem for computer manufacturers was how to develop identical instruction sets for small and large machines at a reasonable cost.

Several solutions can be suggested for the problem of conversion. For example, we could write a program to translate existing programs in assembly language to a higher-level language for the new series of computers. Theoretically, this approach is easy. However, it becomes difficult in practice, and it was several years after the introduction of new equipment before such a program was developed for one of the major manufacturers. (Even then, a customer and not a computer vendor wrote the program!)

Another possibility is a simulation program. Such a program would make the new series of computers look like earlier machines; the new computer would execute programs of the old computer. The only drawback here is speed; it takes several simulated instructions to execute each old series program instruction. The manufacturer could be in the position of trying to sell a new computer that took longer to execute programs than the computer being replaced! Moreover, neither of these solutions solves the instruction set compatibility problem.

### A Solution

Certain operations in the CPU of Figure 7-3 are required by almost all instructions, for example, adding 1 to the contents of the location counter. The process of executing an instruction is made up of two types of activities: register-to-register transfers and control commands such as for clearing a register or initiating a memory read (the reader should review the discussion on page 124 about the basic instruction fetch and execution cycles of the CPU). Each instruction in machine language can be thought of as a series of more primitive or fundamental instructions such as:

Move the contents of the arithmetic register to the SBR.
Move the contents of the SBR to the arithmetic register.
Add 1 to the location counter.
Read from main storage.
Write to main storage.
Clear the arithmetic registers.

As an example of how an instruction is formed, suppose we wanted to store the results of an arithmetic operation back in main memory. The instruction in machine language would be something like STO 250; that is, store the contents of an arithmetic register at location 250. A microprogram for a hypothetical computer to accomplish this might appear something like:

Move the contents of the arithmetic register to the SBR.
Move the address portion of the instruction (250) to the SAR.
Write into main memory.
Add 1 to the location counter.

Following this approach, we have broken a machine-language instruction into a series of more fundamental instructions, or microinstructions. These more primitive instructions are combined into a "program" to produce a machine-language instruction like STO. The technique described above is called "micro-programming," and it represents a major advance in the design of computer hardware.

## Applications of Microprogramming

How does microprogramming solve our marketing problems in selling third-generation computers? First, by combining different microinstructions, we can create a large variety of microprogrammed instructions at a reasonable cost. Microprogramming is cheaper than actually wiring the computer (called "hardwiring") to perform, say, the STO instruction using circuits directly. In a microprogrammed family of computers, small, less capable models use microprogramming extensively, and larger models are hardwired. The hardware costs more for a hardwired machine, but a wired instruction executes faster than several microprogrammed steps. Microprogramming thus solves the problem of creating compatible instruction sets at a reasonable cost for a family of computers.

How does microprogramming help in conversion? A microprogramming feature can be used to simulate, with both hardware and software, one computer's instruction set on another computer—a process known as emulation. Microprogramming features are used to make a new machine look like the one being replaced. Under emulation, a new computer executes computer instructions for a different computer through both software and microprogrammed steps. Emulation is considerably faster than simulation with a software program alone because the microprogrammed steps in the hardware execute faster than software instructions.

---

### BETTING ON A MICRO

*Resorts International operates a large gambling casino in Atlantic City, New Jersey. The slot machines in the casino have been specially modified to contain a microcomputer. The computer counts the number of coins droped in the slot, the number of times someone pulls the handle, the number of hits, and the amount paid out of the jackpot. The micro send this information back to minicomputers at a central computer room.*

*In addition to accounting, the system is used to help catch cheats. Some players try a little too hard to beat the house by soldering a wire to a quarter; then the player dips the quarter four times to convince the machine he is betting a dollar. The computer in the slot measures the amount of time each coin sits on its trigger; if the time is too great the computer dispatches a message to the mini which notifies the security department.*

*The casino also has a microcomputer in each pit on the floor; it is used to control complimentary services or comps. These comps are coupons for a free meal or show; they are distributed to players depending on how long they play or how much they bet. The system keeps a central record of the comps distributed by the casino so that it becomes difficult for freeloaders to move from one pit to another, collecting a comp at each one.*

PC Week, May 29, 1984.

---

## MANAGEMENT PROBLEM 7-3

Steve Harmon, the controller of Pension Management Associates, wants to buy a personal computer for his own use. A number of securities analysts and fund managers in the firm use a variety of different equipment. Steve feels, however, that their needs are quite specialized where he wants general-purpose equipment. The firm has tried to standardize as much as possible on one or two brands of microcomputer.

Steve would like to run spreadsheet analyses for his accounting work. He would also like to be able to perform word processing because he must prepare a number of reports for management. In fact his ultimate plans are to have a micro for his secretary as well as one in his own office. Steve has also read about personal filing programs that would let him set up files of data and retrieve information from them.

He is wondering now whether to petition management for an exception to the policy of a standard microcomputer. He has narrowed his choice to two different models, and would like some advice before approaching senior management with a request for one of the computers.

In addition to these original factors motivating the development of micro-programming, many other uses have developed for it. Manufacturers now use microprogramming to provide very complex instructions or to tailor a piece of equipment for a specific job. The extensive use of microprogramming for such special purposes has produced microprograms called "firmware." If some process has little chance of being changed, microprogramming offers greater speed than writing a software program. However, the cost is flexibility, since a software program is much easier to modify than a microprogram.

### Read Only Memory

Earlier we deferred a discussion of read only memory (ROM); now it is possible to explain what purpose a ROM serves in a computer. Read only memory is exactly what the name implies; the computer can read information from the memory, but it cannot write anything into memory; that is, the computer does not change the memory.

What good is it then? ROM holds the microcode or microinstructions for a processor. The ability to microprogram a processor means that quite specialized instructions or data are placed in the ROM to provide the processor with its logic. It is the computer manufacturer who "burns" the information into the ROM.

In the personal computer in Figure 7-1, there are actually several ROMs, one for the CPU, one for the keyboard, and one containing instructions to start the computer when it is turned on called the "boot" ROM.

## SUMMARY

In this chapter we have discovered how a computer works. The example is of a microcomputer, but the same principles apply to all modern digital computers. The important thing to remember is that a computer with a processing unit and memory is executing whatever piece of computer software that happens to be running on a computer. In the next chapter we shall look at how computers have developed historically and at the different types of computers available today.

## KEY WORDS

| | | |
|---|---|---|
| Base | Fetch cycle | Nondestructive readout |
| Binary | Firmware | Primary memory |
| CPU | Hardware | RAM |
| CRT | Input/output | Register |
| Capacitor | Instruction set | ROM |
| Core | Large scale integration | Secondary storage |
| Cycle time | (LSI) | Semiconductor memory |
| Digital | Location counter | Storage-address register |
| Disk | Microprogram | Storage-buffer register |
| Diskette | Microsecond | Volatile storage |
| Execution cycle | Nanosecond | |

## RECOMMENDED READINGS

*Byte,* McGraw-Hill, New York. (A monthly magazine devoted to microcomputers; contains feature articles and many ads for different products.)

Bartee, T. C.: *Digital Computer Fundamentals,* 4th ed., McGraw-Hill, New York, 1977 (Contains a great deal of information about computer hardware, especially input/ output devices).

Osborne, A.: *An Introduction to Microcomputers,* 2d ed., vol 1, Osborne/McGraw-Hill, New York, 1980. (A technical book on microcomputers and their programming.)

## DISCUSSION QUESTIONS

1 Why have electronic computers replaced electronic accounting machinery? What are the advantages of computers?
2 What is the function of primary memory in the computer? How does it interact with the CPU?
3 What is the advantage of semiconductor memory over core storage?
4 Why is the binary system suitable to computers?
5 What two major items are stored in primary memory? How can one distinguish between them?
6 What is the advantage of having floating point arithmetic registers?
7 Why would a designer use microprogramming to make one computer execute the programs of another computer?
8 What is firmware?

9 What is the difference between ROM and RAM?

10 What is stored in a ROM?

11 What is a bus?

12 Why is there a need for a diskette controller in Figure 7-1?

13 What are the key factors to consider in purchasing a personal computer?

14 What is the difference between the fetch and the execute cycle in executing an instruction?

15 Why does a computer need a lot of instructions?

16 What is the difference between microcomputer and a mainframe computer?

17 Explain the concept of emulation. How is it useful even if not trying to replace one's computer with a new model?

18 What changes in technology do you think are responsible for making personal computers possible?

19 What are the minimum features for home computer? How about a microcomputer to be used in an office?

20 The popular IBM PC does not have floating point arithmetic. However, one can buy a coprocessor that does floating point arithmetic in the hardware. What would its advantages be? Who should consider buying it?

21 What are the differences between secondary storage and primary memory?

22 What other input/output devices can be used with microcomputers in addition to the ones shown in Figure 7-1?

23 What major uses do you see for a personal computer in an organization?

24 What is the difference between hardware and software? Where do the lines blur?

25 What are the advantages of using hardware for processing as opposed to software? Where is software advantageous? (Hint: think of speed and then of ease of making changes to a process.)

THE GENERATIONS
  The Mainframe
  A Short History
SPECIAL FEATURES
SECONDARY STORAGE
  Motivation
  Devices
I/O DEVICES
  Input
  Output
  Terminals
ON-LINE VERSUS BATCH
  Hardware Requirements
IMPLICATIONS
SUMMARY
KEY WORDS
RECOMMENDED READINGS
DISCUSSION QUESTIONS

## CHAPTER 8

# A PROLIFERATION OF COMPUTERS

## CHAPTER ISSUES

- Why are there so many types of computers?
- What computer is best for each task?

In the early days of computing, things were relatively simple. About seven or eight manufacturers offered computers that were known as mainframes. The term originated when most computers were rented, but some customers bought all but the peripheral equipment like tape drives and printers. The CPU and main memory that were purchased were called the "mainframe."

Now, mainframe refers to a type of computer, generally one that is very large and quite powerful. To see how the range of computers has expanded, this chapter presents the historical evolution of computers over the three plus decades that commercial organizations have used these machines.

Table 8-1 and Figure 8-1 present an overview of the current environment, though it is shifting all the time! Mainframe computers are an important part of computing; these machines are the most powerful available. In fact, so called supercomputers are a type of mainframe. As shown in the figure, these computers are the most expensive today; they can execute certain types of programs at a rate of well over 500 million floating point instructions per second!

After mainframes, the next computers developed were minicomputers. These systems are smaller and less powerful than mainframes, and are considerably less expensive. They have been used heavily for time-sharing and feature software that makes them quite efficient for this purpose. Universities are heavy users of minicomputers.

**TABLE 8-1**
TYPES OF COMPUTER SYSTEMS

| Type | Speed (mips*) | Word size bits | Main memory K bytes | Secondary storage bytes | Software | Applications |
|---|---|---|---|---|---|---|
| Mainframes | 0.5–10 | 32 | 64,000 | $5 \times 10^8$ to $3 \times 10^9$ | Extensive operating systems, application packages | Batch, time sharing, on-line transactions processing simultaneously |
| Superminis | 0.1–2 | 32 | 5,000 Virtual | $10^8$ to $10^9$ | Time sharing | Specialized, scientific, engineering, transactions processing |
| Minis | 0.1–0.5 | 16–32 | 16–1,000 | $10^6$ to $10^8$ | Time sharing | General-purpose time sharing, small commercial applications on-line |
| Micros | 0.001–0.5 | 8 16 32 | 64–690 | $3 \times 10^5$ to $3 \times 10^7$ | Simple operating system User friendly software | Dedicated applications, intelligent terminals, word processors, small business systems, personal computers |

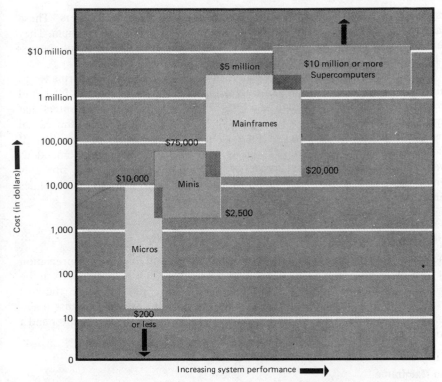

**FIGURE 8-1**
Computer systems may be classified into micro, mini, mainframe, and supercomputer categories depending on size, cost, and system performance. Any such classification is arbitrary since categories overlap, the most powerful systems in one category may exceed the capabilities (and cost) of the least powerful systems in another. (*Courtesy of Donald H. Sanders:* Computers Today, *McGraw-Hill, 1983.*)

As the minicomputer manufacturers improved the performance of their products, they created computers that became known as superminis. Notice in Table 8-1 that a supermini generally is faster than a minicomputer and that it has a 32 bit word size compared with the 16 bits of a minicomputer.

The most explosive growth in the industry has been in microcomputers. At first, these computers accessed only 4 bits at a time; they were developed for calculators. Soon engineers began designing logic into all kinds of products. A good example would be the computer chips that control the engines on many cars today. Sensors bring data to the computer about the load on the engine, spark timing, the position of the accelerator, and the condition of the exhaust gases. A relatively slow computer is fast enough to deal with these parameters and control the engine.

In 1977 Apple computer corporation introduced its first personal computer containing a microprocessor. Within six years, several vendors were selling well in excess of a million personal or microcomputers a year. What is a micro? At first it was easy to distinguish between micros and other computers. These machines had the ability to fetch 8 bits at a time and do arithmetic on them. They were dedicated to a single user at a time; they could not be shared simultaneously by more than one person with a terminal.

However, as with any product, the vendor tries to enhance performance to gain a competitive edge. Now personal computers are available that fetch and process 16 bits or 32 bits of data at a time. There are also microcomputers that support more than one user. As a result, it is very difficult for the casual observer to determine whether or not a computer is a big micro or a small mini!

This problem is shown rather clearly in Figure 8-1. There is tremendous overlap among the different types of computers. The figure is probably conservative and if anything, underestimates the degree to which the lines demarcating various types of computers are blurring.

## THE GENERATIONS

To see how we reached the situation described above and to gain an appreciation for the significant trends as the technology has evolved, it is helpful to look at the different generations through which computers have passed. Since the first twenty years of computers produced mainframes only, we shall discuss mainframes by introducing the differences between the micro in the last chapter and a modern mainframe computer.

### The Mainframe

Figure 8-2 presents a generic model of a mainframe computer. One of the major differences between this and the microcomputer in Figure 7-1 is the lack of a bus

**FIGURE 8-2**
A basic mainframe.

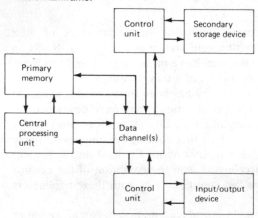

A basic computer system model.

architecture. Mainframes most often feature a direct connection between the CPU and memory; data are not passed back and forth on a bus.

A bus architecture is more modular in the sense that different devices can be connected to the bus easily. However in the early days of this architecture, buses were slow and mainframes needed a direct connection for speed.

Organizations using mainframe computers generally process large amounts of data. The computers may access databases with billions of characters of data and control networks of hundreds or thousands of terminals. As a result, the computers need to be very fast.

The mainframe usually has a data channel which is as powerful as the CPU on some smaller computers. The data channel accepts instructions from the CPU, for example, to retrieve data from a disk file. The CPU goes on to another job while the data channel is busy. When the data channel finishes, it interrupts the CPU to let it know the data are available. The CPU then restarts the program that was interrupted if its priority is higher than other programs that are waiting to run.

Just as with the microcomputer, control units on the mainframe serve to interface the computer, in this case the data channel, with different I/O and storage devices. This architecture has created mainframe computers that are extremely fast and which are used in database, transactions processing, and numerous other applications.

### A Short History

Computer professionals frequently speak of different computer generations, each generation generally corresponding to the introduction of new computers with radically different hardware technologies from their predecessors. Changes in generations also have been accompanied by dramatic changes in performance. Each new generation has provided greatly increased computing speeds and more storage at lower cost than the equipment of the prior generation. (See Table 8-2.) Computer generations also can be characterized by changes in software, and in Chapter 9 we shall complete Table 8-2 by adding the software characteristics of each generation.

The first computer generation is characterized by vacuum-tube components and rotating memory on one of the most popular models, the IBM 650. (Note that IBM is used as an example in the text because its machines are the most familiar to computer professionals and users.) Second-generation computers use transistorized components for the central processing unit and magnetic cores for memory. Data channels appeared in this generation along with special features to improve central processing unit speeds. Computers were first used for commercial on-line systems involving communications and for time-sharing systems where users are presented with interactive computational capability through a terminal.

The third generation of computer hardware is characterized by more miniaturization and monolithic circuits (many electronic components on a chip) for

**TABLE 8-2**
HARDWARE GENERATIONS

| Generation | Model | Monthly rental | Hardware characteristics | Organization | Cycle time microseconds (1) | Storage access (2) |
|---|---|---|---|---|---|---|
| First (1950s) | IBM 650 | $3200† | Vacuum tubes, Memory = 3000 bits (600 digits), 1–4 K‡ of drum memory | 5 bits/digit, 10 digits/word | 100 | 1 word (10 digits) |
| Second (1961) | IBM 1410 | $4000 | Transistorized CPU, data channel, memory = 10 K words | 6 bits/digit, 1 digit/word | 4.5 | 1 word (1 digit) |
| Third (1965) | IBM 360/40 | $5300 | Monolithic circuits, more CPU features, communications emphasis, memory = 65 K bytes | 4 bits/digit, 2 digits/byte, 4 bytes/word | 2.5 | 2 bytes (4 digits) |
| Third-and-a-half (1971) | IBM 370/135 | $6400 | Semiconductor primary memory, virtual memory, communications emphasis, memory = 98 K bytes | 4 bits/digit, 2 digits/byte, 4 bytes/word | 0.77 | 2 bytes (4 digits) |
| Fourth 1979 | IBM 4331 | $1900 | Uses 64 K bit chip, 0.5 million bytes main memory, large disk storage | 4 bits/digit, 2 digits/byte, 4 bytes/word | 0.90 | 4 bytes (8 digits) |
| 1984 | 4361 | $8500 | 64 K bit chip 2.048 million bytes main memory, large disk storage | 4 bits/digit, 2 digits/byte, 4 bytes/word | 0.10 | 8 bytes (16 digits) |

**TABLE 8-2 (continued)**

| Generation | Access time per digit (1) ÷ (2) microseconds (3) | Binary add time, microseconds (4) | Binary add size (5) | Add time per 2 digits (4) ÷ (5) microseconds (6) | 2-digit adds per hour [1 ÷ (6)] (3600) millions (7) | Rental hour (monthly rental ÷ 176 hours) (8) | Cost per million 2-digit adds (8) ÷ (7) (9)* |
|---|---|---|---|---|---|---|---|
| First (1950s) | 10 | 700 | 1 word (10 digits) | 70 | 51.4 | $18.18 | 35.00¢ |
| Second (1961) | 4.5 | 88 | 10 words (10 digits) | 8.8 | 409 | $22.73 | 5.56¢ |
| Third (1965) | 0.63 | 12 | 4 bytes (8 digits) | 1.5 | 2400 | $30.11 | 1.25¢ |
| Third-and-a-half (1971) | 0.19 | 4.2 | 4 bytes (8 digits) | 0.53 | 6792 | $36.36 | 0.54¢ |
| Fourth 1979 | 0.11 | 3.4 | 4 bytes (8 digits) | 0.43 | 8372 | $10.80 | 0.13¢ |

*These figures are for comparison among machines; because of the limited configurations, the absolute costs are not meaningful.

†Costs are for rental of CPU and main memory; no peripherals are included. No adjustment has been made for inflation.

‡K = 1024

central processing units. More CPU features to improve performance were added during this generation as well. Third-generation machines made it easier to develop on-line applications requiring telecommunication capabilities.

Third-generation computers evolved into the third-and-one-half generation through the use of semiconductor technology for main memory in some machines. A concept developed from time sharing called "virtual memory" has also been implemented through special hardware facilities. (See the section on virtual memory in the next chapter.)

The fourth generation of computers is characterized by very large, fast semiconductor memories, small size, and lower power requirements. Fourth-generation machines are designed to ease the development of on-line applications and facilitate the use of large databases.

## SPECIAL FEATURES

In the second-and third-generation computers, several special features were added to the central processing unit in some machines to improve speed. An example of such a feature is instruction look-ahead. The idea is to have the CPU accomplish several tasks in parallel; the look-ahead unit decodes program instructions in advance of their execution. While one part of the CPU is executing an instruction, another part of the CPU fetches instructions that follow the one being executed and decodes them. This concurrency of instruction fetch, decoding, and execution produces added speed.

Another feature that speeds processing is memory interleaving. Memory in this scheme is split into several modules, for example, four modules for four-way interleaving. Consecutive addresses are located in different modules so that four locations in sequence can be fetched at once. Interleaving can also be combined with look-ahead.

In multiprocessing, more than one central processing unit is present. Operations occur in parallel, similar to the parallel operations we discussed with the use of data channels.

Another innovation is the use of high-speed buffer memory to speed processing. A fast central processing unit is connected to a high-speed semiconductor memory. This memory may be smaller than regular storage (tens of thousands of characters versus hundreds of thousands or millions of characters of main memory). Main memory is also slower than the buffer. All computations are carried in buffer memory; the hardware automatically moves programs and data from main memory to the buffer cache memory when needed. Primary memory is assigned to a certain sector of cache memory. When a program or data are needed for main memory, hardware logic checks to see if they are in its buffer segment. If they are, computation proceeds; if not, the present contents of the buffer are written back to main memory (if the data in the sector have changed since it was loaded). The part of main memory required is now copied into the buffer sector. If there are few access references to main memory, execution will proceed at a speed near the cycle time of the high-speed buffer memory.

We shall postpone the discussion of another innovation, virtual memory, until the next chapter, since it involves software. All the features described here are invisible to a programmer; they are accomplished by hardware without explicit instructions from a program.

These approaches to hardware architecture have been designed to improve operations, that is, to gain speed at a reasonable cost. Many different approaches to the design of computers have been implemented, and the concepts discussed in this chapter should provide a good background for understanding specific design decisions.

## SECONDARY STORAGE

### Motivation

Secondary storage generally refers to storage devices that have to be accessed through a data channel; the CPU cannot fetch data or instructions directly from them. There are several reasons for the use of secondary storage devices. First, primary memory is very expensive; we often cannot afford to have sufficient primary memory to process large amounts of data. Some applications have files containing billions of characters of data, exceeding the capacity of the primary memory of any computer available today.

Even if we could afford enough primary memory and could physically attach it to our computer, we really would not want to fill it with data! Many programs use primary memory, each processing its own data. If we left all the data for one application in memory all the time, we would have to dedicate the entire computer or a significant part of it to just that application. Therefore, we do not want to store data in primary memory when they are not needed. Secondary storage devices provide a flexible storage capability for data and programs.

### Devices

Table 8-3 contains a list of some of the important secondary storage devices arranged by average access time (how long, on the average, it takes to retrieve data from the device). In general, the cost per character of storage drops with access time; that is, faster devices—as we might expect—cost more. Note that, while the CPU and memory might operate at speeds of less than 50 nanoseconds ($10^{-9}$ second), most secondary storage devices have access times in the millisecond ($10^{-3}$ second) range, or nearly a million times slower than primary memory. Below, we briefly mention different secondary storage devices; we shall discuss these devices in greater detail in Chapter 10 on files.

Direct-access storage refers to the device's capability to locate information stored anyplace on it in roughly the same length of time. Direct-access storage

**TABLE 8-3**
SECONDARY STORAGE DEVICES

| Device | Monthly rental | Average access time | Transfer rate bytes/sec | Capacity million bytes*† | Monthly rental/ million bytes | Type |
|---|---|---|---|---|---|---|
| Fixed-head disk | $ 5495<br>3245<br>$ 8740 | 2.5 milliseconds | 3000 K‡ | 5.4 | $1619.00 | Direct |
| Semiconductor (16K chip) system including control unit (volatile storage, information lost when power off) | $ 4305** | 0.4 millisecond | 1750 K | 12 | $ 359.00 | Direct |
| Movable-head disk and controller | $ 1450<br>2685<br>$ 4135 | 38.4 milliseconds (30.0 seek time, 8.4 rotational delay | 806 K | 200 | $ 21.00 | Direct |
| Movable and fixed-head disk and controller | $ 1915<br>2045<br>$ 3960 | 8.3 millisecond average rotational delay for 2.28 million characters, 25 millisecond seek, and 8.3 milli- second rotational delay for rest | 1198 K | 634 | $ 6.25 | Direct |
| Mass storage and controller | $12,937<br>3965<br>$16,902 | 15.5 seconds (5.5 to fetch cartridge; 10.0 to load, read to a disk, and unload) | 874 K | 35,300 | $ .48 | Direct |
| Magnetic tape and controller | $ 608<br>1101<br>$ 1709 | Contingent on record size and density | 470 K | 180 (6250 bpi at 2400 feet) | Not applicable | Sequential |

*Byte = 1 character or 2 digits.
†Ignoring interrecord gaps.
‡K =.1024.
**Based on 2-year lease contract.

**MANAGEMENT PROBLEM 8-1**

John Trout has just assumed a position as vice president for administration at Technical R&D, a diversified research and consulting firm. John's previous experience was in accounting and finance. At Technical, all information systems activities now report to him. Because of his lack of familiarity with computers, John has been reading widely in the field to prepare for his new assignment.

Mary Jackson is the director of information systems for Technical and reports to John. She has been supplying him with information about the use of computers at Technical and about computers in general. Technical employs computers for its own internal administrative work; in addition, large computers are used for scientific computations by the professional staff.

Mary explained the history of computers at Technical. In the second generation, Technical maintained complete separation between administrative and scientific processing. A separate, character-oriented business computer was used for all administrative work and a large, fixed-word-length scientific computer was utilized by the professional staff. Even though third-generation computers eliminated much of the distinction between business and scientific processing, Mary felt there were good management reasons for maintaining this separation at Technical R&D. Now, even with the latest equipment, Technical still has a separate computer for administrative processing and a larger machine in the same family for use by the professional staff.

John wondered what the "management considerations" were that convinced Mary that two computers were necessary. What would the advantages be of using a single, large computer for all kinds of Technical's processing?

---

contrasts with sequential storage, in which all the data are arranged in order and the device must be scanned in that order to find specific information. The fastest secondary storage device is constructed of semiconductors and has no moving parts. Rotating memories are slower and less reliable, because of their mechanical components.

One mass-storage device uses magnetic tape strips arranged in cartridges that are retrieved, read, and transferred to a disk storage device. A mass-storage device might replace an entire magnetic tape library. Mass-storage devices are slow in placing the data on the disk, but once there, the data can be processed at disk speeds.

Magnetic tape is one of the oldest storage media. Data are stored in sequence on a tape; to retrieve the information we have to search one-half the tape, on the average. Magnetic tape is cheap and provides convenient off-line storage and backup.

All these devices share two common characteristics. We have to access them through the data channel at speeds considerably slower than we can access primary memory. Second, all use a magnetic medium of some type to store data.

---

**OH, WHAT A FEELING!**

*With its tremendous growth in sales, Toyota needed an order processing system that was readily accessible to branches and dealers throughout the world. An example of how the system works is illustrated with the West German branch of Toyota which has some 300 employees.*

*A major function of the system is to provide a fast response to orders from 1000 Toyota dealers in West Germany for some 65,000 different spare parts. Large dealers have their own terminals for entering orders and spares are often shipped the same day as ordered.*

*The system was recently expanded to include ordering new cars, some 5000 of which arrive every month. The system allocates vehicles to specific orders and keeps local records.*

*The system operates on the General Electric Information Services Company worldwide teleprocessing network. Before the system was installed, it took about 12 weeks for orders to be acknowledged from Japan. Now orders are entered through terminals in Vienna and there is no need to transmit a physical document through the mail, speeding response time.*

*Computerworld,* April 9, 1984.

---

## I/O DEVICES

One of the largest bottlenecks in information systems is input/output. Devices to enter data generally have some mechanical component that requires human interaction. A computer may be capable of fetching over a million characters per second from primary memory. However, consider a standard 2000-line-per-minute printer. With 130 characters per line, the printer operates at $2000 \times 130 \div 60$, or 4333 characters per second. Below we discuss some of the common I/O devices in use today. (See Table 8-4.)

### Input

One of the earliest input media was punched paper tape, a narrow strip of tape punched with holes representing characters. A device reads the tape and transmits the characters to the computer. Paper tape is difficult to use and is not well suited to large volumes of input. Paper tape is essentially obsolete as an I/O medium for commercial computer applications.

The familiar punched card still is used for input, but is slowly being eliminated. An individual transcribes information to the cards using a keypunch. The information should be verified by another operator, who rekeys the original information and compares the holes in the cards and notes any discrepancies. An alternative is to have a computer punch cards, each containing information relevant to a particular user (for example, in a billing application). The card is sent to the customer, who returns it with payment. If the payment matches the amount billed, the card or "turnaround document" is entered directly into the computer.

**TABLE 8-4**
COMMON INPUT/OUTPUT DEVICES

Input devices
  Punched cards
  Key to tape
  Key to disk
  Magnetic-ink character recognition (MICR)
  Mark sense
  Bar code
  Optical character recognition (OCR)
  Terminals
  Voice
  Graphics mouse
  Touch screen
  Special devices (for example, analog to digital)

Output devices
  Card punch
  Line printer
    Impact
    Nonimpact
  Laser printer
  Computer output to microfilm (COM)
  Voice synthesis
  Terminals
  Special devices (for example, digital to analog)

Terminals
  Interactive
  Hard copy
    Serial impact
    Nonimpact
  CRT (single or multiple color)
    Alphanumeric
    Graphics
      Dynamic
      Storage tube

To speed data transcription, key-to-tape and key-to-disk units have been developed. These devices may offer formatting aids beyond the card keypunch; they are also faster and quieter than the card-oriented keypunch. Several operators may use the same tape or disk, and the results may be aggregated and placed on a computer-compatible tape or disk for final input.

Magnetic-ink character recognition (MICR) has found its greatest acceptance in banking. All checks are coded with an account number and code identifying the bank. A human operator enters the amount on the check when it is processed, using a special coding device. The magnetic ink characters are read and the checks sorted by area and account number. However, a few applications beyond banking have been suggested for MICR.

Mark sensing can be used for input where there are a few alternatives that can be represented by simple choices. Mark sensing is a technique used to read answers in most standardized "machine-scored" tests. A question with four answers requires four columns on the answer sheet. The student darkens a choice for each question and a mark-sensing device reads the marks. Unfortunately, when there are many choices, mark sense forms become large because a space is required for each option. For example, consider the amount of space required to enter one's name on the test form compared with the space to answer questions.

Bar coding is becoming increasingly popular, particularly for inventory and factory floor automation. A bar code is a series of lines which encode information; the lines are read by a scanner connected to a computer. Bar codes can be attached to products moving through an assembly process; a reader then inputs data to the computer on the location of the product. Similarly a retail store can encode its products with bar codes. The clerk at the cash register uses a wand to read the bar code; the data update computer files on sales and inventory.

Optical character recognition (OCR) is gaining increasing use as an input technique. OCR readers have a variety of capacities and costs and many employ laser technology to read data. The simplest OCR scanners are bar-code readers that optically scan information coded with bars. There are several OCR-type fonts that are easier for machines to read than standard printing such as the type in this book. These special OCR-type fonts can be read by equipment slightly more sophisticated than bar-code readers. A number of scanners can read documents typed using the OCR B-type element. More complex OCR devices also read hand-printed numbers and a few characters. The most advanced units read typed or hand-printed letters, although care must be taken preparing the data. With OCR, rejects may be high, but only rejected documents have to be keyed into the machine. Successfully read input reduces the transcription process and allows data to be captured closer to its source.

A variety of terminals is available for data input as well as output. The most general are described in the next section. There are also special input terminals that feature badge readers (to identify the individual entering data) and card readers for, say, a factory-floor production control application. Terminals make it possible to extend data collection to the original source of the data and reduce intermediate transcription.

Experiments are currently underway on voice-input devices. Voice input of numbers is being used in several instances where the individual providing information must have both hands free. One personal computer vender offers a speech recognition chip with its microcomputer. It is likely in a few years that at least limited commands to a computer will be given vocally.

Personal computers have also stimulated the use of several different types of input devices. There is great interest now in the mouse, a device connected to a computer which the user moves around a surface like a desk top. The motion of the mouse moves a cursor or spot of light on the display; this cursor identifies instructions or commands to the computer. For example, putting the cursor on a symbol of a wastebasket means that the current document is to be deleted. (This symbol is sometimes called an icon and the entire approach is known as a graphics or object-oriented interface.)

In addition to mice, there are joysticks and trackballs which move some kind of pointer or cross hairs around on the display. There are also graphics tablets where the user draws a picture that is reproduced on the screen.

There is also interest in touch screen input. One Hewlett Packard microcomputer features this mode of input. A user touches his or her choice for input, for example, a symbol on the screen. The system senses the position where the screen was touched and accepts it as the user's input. This approach to input can help someone who is uncomfortable with a keyboard use a computer more easily.

Finally, there are a number of special-purpose input devices. For example, for industrial process control, analog sensors (for continuous signals, as opposed to discrete or digital signals) may feed data to some device that converts them into digital signals for processing on a digital computer.

### Output

A number of output devices are available. The line printer is used heavily for output, especially in batch systems. An impact line printer has a print element that comes in physical contact with the paper; usually a type slug presses a ribbon against the paper when hit by a hammer device. Because of this physical impression, multiple copies can be created with carbon paper. Impact printers come in a variety of speeds, although the maximum currently available is in the neighborhood of 2000 lines per minute.

Nonimpact printers use other technologies to create an image. Some approaches are similar to commercial photocopying processes, and others employ charged particles of ink or print thermally. One printer uses special electrostatic paper and another uses a laser and a process similar to xerography to produce images. Nonimpact printers, with speeds in the range of 10,000 to 20,000 lines per minute, are considerably faster than impact printers. However, additional copies cannot be made with carbon paper; duplicate output must be printed or the original must be photocopied.

Laser printers work like conventional photocopiers. They produce a page at a time, which makes the printing very fast. In addition, because the technology does not rely on impact printing, a variety of type styles and fonts are available. A good text processing system and a laser printer can produce output of book quality.

Computer output to microfilm (COM) offers one approach to reducing the bulk of the information printed by computers. Usually, the microfilm device is off-line; that is, it is not directly connected to the computer. The computer system produces an output magnetic tape at high speed. The tape is mounted on a computer output microfilm device, which produces the microfilm. Some devices require a separate step to develop the film, though at least one COM unit produces film directly from computer input. One limitation of microfilm is that a

---

**WINDOWS FOR COMPUTING**

*Many personal computer software systems feature windows, the ability to have a split screen with each window containing a different application or part of an application. For example, in word processing, it might be useful in moving a paragraph to have a window containing the text to be moved and the target location of the text.*

*Ohio Medical Indemnity Mutual Corp., Ohio's Blue Cross/Blue Shield insurer, has improved productivity from 15 to 33% by applying the window concept to a mainframe system. The environment is complex because the company has its own computer, but also has to access four computers of the Ohio Blue Cross Plans which have membership files.*

*Prior to the installation of multiscreen terminals, clerks were continually switching between applications or between computers to answer questions. Since accessing each computer required a logoff from the current machine and a logon to a new one, delays mounted. With the multiscreen terminal the clerks are always on-line and can display a file from each of four machines at one time or four files from the same computer.*

*Computerworld,* July 30, 1984.

---

special viewing device is needed to read it; special equipment also is required to produce a paper copy.

Early audio response units actually featured syllables or complete words recorded on a magnetic medium. Such an approach, using bubble memory instead of magnetic media, is used to store some of the recorded messages we hear over the phone system. In addition to this type of playback, there are now chips that synthesize the human voice. Some of the words are hard to understand, but the ability to combine syllables into words and to provide different intonation is a remarkable achievement. There even exists a machine that reads a book and then produces an audio version for individuals who are blind.

There are a number of terminals that can be used for output, as described below. A myriad of special devices has been developed for output, especially for analog output for industrial process-control applications.

**Terminals**

Most terminals can be used for input or output. Interactive terminals are designed for a single user who is communicating with a computer on-line (we shall discuss different on-line systems later in this chapter). Some interactive terminals produce a hard copy, that is, a printed copy that can be removed from the terminal. However, cathode-ray tube (CRT) terminals and similar display devices produce output on a TV-like screen, and unless a special copying device is used, the next display will erase the current one.

Interactive hard-copy terminals usually have serial-print mechanisms. Such a

---

**MANAGEMENT PROBLEM 8-2**

Mastercraft Tool Company manufactures a variety of manual and power tools for professional workers and home workshops. The tools are sold through specialty and hardware stores throughout the United States and abroad. For a number of years, the firm has been concerned over production-control problems.

Manufacturing a tool involves a sequence of steps requiring different machines; it is a classical "job shop" production situation. There are some 10 manufacturing departments at Mastercraft, much work in process, and large finished-goods inventories. The firm manufactures for inventory and fills orders from its stock of tools. There is limited back ordering for popular items.

The top management of Mastercraft has reviewed several proposals for computer-based processing to provide better production-control information. Because of the rather low skill level of some workers, management is concerned over the impact of a computer system on production employees.

At the present time, the nature of the system, either batch or on-line, is being considered. The president said, "I can see advantages and disadvantages to either possibility. Clearly we have to obtain input from workers or the system will fail. I just don't know how to evaluate the potential impact of batch forms versus a terminal for factory workers."

As a consultant to Mastercraft, can you help the president with his decision problem? What factors should he consider in evaluating different input and output alternatives? Which alternatives should he consider?

---

terminal prints one character at a time, unlike a line printer, which produces an entire line of characters each time it prints. Hard-copy terminals are available in either impact or nonimpact form. Nonimpact devices may be thermal types in which a heated matrix of styli creates an impression on heat-sensitive paper. Other nonimpact terminals squirt an electronically controlled jet of ink at the paper to form characters. Nonimpact printers tend to be faster than impact terminals and are highly popular, since many interactive applications have no need for multiple copies.

Cathode-ray tube terminals are enjoying increasing popularity for input and output: they are quiet and very fast compared with printing terminals. Many CRTs feature one color, though multiple-color models are available. An alphanumeric CRT displays lines of characters and is a direct replacement for a printing terminal where no hard copy is required. Graphic CRTs make it possible to plot lines to form graphs or figures on the screen.

Many terminals have been developed with logic capabilities of their own. These terminals are referred to as "intelligent" because they can do more than respond to input from the user or output commands from the computer. Intelligent terminals may use their logic to perform editing functions before transmitting information to a main computer.

## ON-LINE VERSUS BATCH

Batch processing implies that all input is collected, a program edits the input, updates files, and produces reports. A batch system executes periodically, anyplace from several times a day (unusual) to once a month or even once a year. During the first generation of computers, all the processing had to be batch since no one had figured out a way to attach terminals to a computer.

During the second generation, the need for on-line access to a computer became evident. The first on-line systems represented a significant research and development effort. The companies adopting this technology had to create a terminal network, software to operate the terminals interactively, and finally applications software to actually do the processing desired by users.

The first on-line system for commercial use was developed as a joint project between IBM and American Airlines and was known as the Sabre reservations system. American had predicted that its reservations procedures would soon break down. IBM had gained experience connecting terminals to a computer in building an air defense radar system.

Reservations agents have a need to access a central database from different geographical locations in a system in close to "real time." A passenger agent in Atlanta must be sure that a New York flight has a seat left before making a reservation. The Atlanta agent must be certain that some other agent in Los Angeles is not selling the same seat at the same time. By maintaining a continually updated central file of flights and reservations and providing on-line access through terminals, both the Atlanta and Los Angeles agents can check on up-to-the-second seat availability before making the reservation.

Time sharing can be considered a special case of on-line systems. Time sharing was motivated by the slow turnaround time (time from submitting a run until receipt of output) characteristic of early batch systems. Researchers at MIT recognized that there is a severe mismatch between human information processing and computer speeds. In early batch systems, a programmer might have only two or three runs a day at most because of the large number of people using the machine. The MIT Project MAC group developed a special on-line system that gave each user an individual computational ability through a terminal. It appeared to each user that the central computer was available solely to that individual, even though many users in actuality were sharing the CPU. The name "time sharing" reflects the sharing of a computer resource by multiple users.

### Hardware Requirements

On-line systems were first created by adding special hardware to existing systems and by writing complex control programs, usually in assembly language. We shall explain more fully how these systems work in the next chapter, on software. In this section we discuss some of the hardware features, especially the communications necessary for on-line systems.

For the central computer, the major addition needed for on-line processing is a communications controller. An on-line system uses communications lines, such as those of the public phone system. Just as a printer or card reader needs a controller, so do communications lines.

The logic requirements for a transmission controller are very demanding. It must do the following:

1 Establish a circuit.

2 Recognize the line speed—for example, whether the speed is 120 or 960 characters per second.

3 Send a start-of-message signal.

4 Receive the message acknowledgement.

5 Translate from transmission code to computer code and vice versa.

6 Check for errors and for the completeness of the message.

7 Receive a retransmission if necessary.

8 Assemble the message.

9 Recognize the end of message.

10 Release the circuit.

11 Transmit the message to the CPU.

Many steps are necessary to perform these functions. Because of these requirements, on-line systems frequently feature a communications "front end," a device with considerable logic capability that handles the communications functions to remove some of the load from the CPU. On-line systems also require communications networks of some kind, even if it is a simple dial-up phone line from a terminal to the computer. Since the topic of communications is so important, Chapter 12 is devoted to it.

## IMPLICATIONS

These last two chapters contain a great deal of information about computer technology. What does all of this mean for management?

1 The price/performance ratio for computers continues to decline, that is, the price is continually dropping for increased levels of computing.

2 Logical functions are no longer the most expensive part of the computer. In the first generation, the CPU was the scarce and expensive resource. Today, large scale integration and very large scale integration (VLSI) using current technology can put half a million transistors on a small silicon chip. Processing logic is now readily available at a rather small cost.

3 Organizations are spending increasing amount of money on computers because they are becoming indispensible for many applications. While unit costs may go down, the total expenditure for information processing is increasing in most organizations.

4 The ease of use and the appeal of a personal computer is helping to give many more individuals access to computers. To compete in the coming years, a manager will have to be an intelligent user of computers.

A basic understanding of hardware and how it works will help the professional knowledge worker select and use appropriate computer equipment.

## SUMMARY

Electronic computers have evolved at a rapid rate. Today's desk-top computers have more power than first-generation computers that filled a room. The cost of computer hardware is continually being reduced as technological breakthroughs in the fabrication of components continue. Although fascinating in its own right, the technology becomes even more exciting when we apply it to problems in the organization.

## KEY WORDS

| | | |
|---|---|---|
| Batch | Graphics | Nanosecond |
| Bubble memory | Graphics input | Nonimpact |
| Buffer | Hardware | OCR |
| Cache | Impact printer | On-line |
| CPU | Input/output | Primary memory |
| CRT | Intelligence | Secondary storage |
| Communications | Large scale integration | Semiconductor memory |
| Controller | (LSI) | Software |
| Cycle time | Laser printer | Tape |
| Data channel | MICR | Time-division multi- |
| Database | Mark sense | plexing |
| Disk | Microfilm | VLSI |
| Direct access | Microsecond | Voice input |
| Generations of com- | Minicomputer | Voice synthesis |
| puters | Mouse | Volatile storage |

## RECOMMENDED READINGS

Bartee, T. C.: *Digital Computer Fundamentals,* 4th ed., McGraw-Hill, New York, 1977. (Contains a great deal of information about computer hardware, especially input/output devices.)

Bohl, M.: *Information Processing,* 4th ed., Palo Alto, SRA, 1984. (A good introduction with a clear explanation of the details of hardware.)

Osborne, A.: *An Introduction to Microcomputers,* 2d ed., vol. 1, Osborne/McGraw-Hill, New York, 1980. (A somewhat technical book on microcomputers and their programming.)

Sanders, D.: *Computers Today,* McGraw-Hill, New York, 1983. (A good introductory book.)

## DISCUSSION QUESTIONS

1 Distinguish between computer hardware and software. With which is a manager most concerned?

2 Many data channels steal cycles from the central processing unit to access primary memory. For what purpose does the data channel access memory?

3 What is the purpose of a control unit? Could the same control unit control more than one type of device?

4 Why was conversion from first- to second-generation computers not much of a problem?

5 Why is it difficult to convert machine language for one computer to machine language for another?

6 What is the advantage of a data channel? How much logic must it contain?

7 Buffers are locations in memory reserved for storing data, for example, a group of data being entered from a card reader. How could multiple buffers be used to speed input/output operations?

8 There are some very large storage devices using lasers to burn holes in a tape or disk, the holes representing 0s or 1s. What are the disadvantages of such a device? For what applications is it best suited?

9 What are the differences between a character orientation and a word orientation for a computer? Which would you expect to be the faster? For which types of processing is each better suited?

10 What is the advantage of having more than one address in an instruction?

11 Some computers have many register-to-register operations. What is the advantage of this capability?

12 The presence of floating-point hardware increases the cost of the machine because of the additional circuitry and registers. What else has to be added?

13 Why is a computer manufacturer interested in compatibility within its own line of machines? Does a manufacturer want to be compatible with the computers of other manufacturers? What are the advantages and disadvantages of such a strategy?

14 What is a purpose of the location counter in the CPU? How do you suppose a branch instruction (GO TO) in the program is executed?

15 What is firmware? What are its advantages and disadvantages compared with software?

16 Why is an interrupt facility preferable to testing for a channel being busy?

17 What are the reasons for having secondary storage? Why not just add more primary memory?

18 How would the development of direct-access memory technology as fast as primary memory, but as inexpensive as tape, change information system processing?

19 What are the disadvantages of secondary storage?

20 Why is there such a mismatch between input/output and internal computer speeds? How can this mismatch be reduced? What I/O units are helping to solve this problem?

21 Why should we not necessarily be overjoyed with the development of ultra-high-speed printers?

22 What is the advantage of OCR over mark sensing? What are its disadvantages?

23 What is the advantage of a nonimpact CRT terminal from a user's standpoint?

24 What factors underlie the trend toward on-line systems?

25 What would be the major use for voice input to computers if it were perfected?

26 Why have special design features been added to CPUs?

27 What is the advantage of a buffer cache memory? Under what conditions would its performance be best? Worst?

28 What applications do you have for a personal computer?

## CHAPTER 9

# COMPUTER SOFTWARE

## CHAPTER ISSUES

- What computer languages are available and which one should be used for a particular application?
- What is the role of a language in the development of systems?

Why do managers or users need to know anything about computer programs and software? Because users help design systems, it is important for them to understand which programming tasks are easy and which are difficult. Should a packaged program be used for a particular application? There has been considerable difficulty in turning system specifications into working programs, and we have encountered serious problems in writing and managing program development. A basic understanding of software helps a user make intelligent management decisions about programming and project management.

The dramatic penetration of businesses by microcomputers places the manager in the position of a direct, "hands on" user of computers. What software should the manager buy and use? How does one choose? What types of languages are there?

In this chapter, we explore computer programs and languages along with different types of operating systems and packaged programs. Table 9-1 shows that the different hardware generations discussed in the last chapter can also be characterized by differences in computer software. (Remember we defined software as the instructions that tell a computer what actions to take.) In this chapter, we shall discuss these different types of software.

**TABLE 9-1**
SOFTWARE GENERATIONS

| Generation | Software |
|---|---|
| First | Machine language |
| | Assembly language |
| Second | Assembly language |
| | Higher-level languages |
| | Batch operating systems |
| | Dedicated on-line systems |
| | Experimental time sharing |
| Third | Preponderance of higher-level languages |
| | Expansion of packaged systems |
| | Operating system mandatory |
| | Mixed on-line and batch applications |
| | Virtual-memory time-sharing systems |
| Third-and-one-half | Expanded operating systems |
| | Virtual-memory batch systems |
| | Batch, on-line, and time sharing mixed |
| | Data-base and communication packages |
| Fourth | More applications programs |
| | Higher-higher level or "fourth generation" languages |
| | Applications generators |

## PROGRAMMING LANGUAGES

### A Simple Computer

In the last chapter, we saw that binary representation is the fundamental language of computers; however, binary is difficult for people to use. Since the number base is not relevant to the concepts discussed below, we shall design a simple computer using base-10, or decimal, numbers.

In designing our computer, we must:

1 Select a character or word organization.
2 Define a character set.
3 Determine memory size.
4 Decide on the instruction set and data format.
5 Determine the type and number of arithmetic and other registers.
6 Define the instruction set.
7 Choose a machine base (we have already chosen decimal).

We shall design a fixed-word-length computer with six digits per word to simplify some of our other tasks. Since we are developing a very simple machine, we use only decimal numbers for our character set: there will be no alphabetic characters. Furthermore, the computer will perform arithmetic on numbers in the same code as the input/output representation of these numbers.

Remember that memory contains both data and instructions so we must also define the format for each. The numbers in our computer will be signed integers with up to six digits, for example +173426 or −421376. Again because our computer is very simple, we shall limit the size of primary memory to 99 locations, numbered 1 through 99.

An instruction consists of four digits; the first two are an operation code and the last two are the operand. The format is XXYY where XX is the two-digit instruction and YY the address of the operand. Since we are limiting the size of memory to 99 locations, we need only two decimal locations to address all memory.

Since the machine is simple, we shall have only one register that can be accessed by a program. Of course, there is an instruction register, a location counter, and so forth, but these registers are a part of the CPU and do not concern a programmer. The accessible register is for arithmetic, and we shall call it the A register. The A register will be capable of addition, subtraction, multiplication, and division, making it a general-purpose arithmetic register.

Instructions that call for arithmetic operations such as add and subtract have one address for an operand in memory. The other number needed for the computation is assumed to be in the A register; that is, the A register is the implied address for these instructions. This assumption and method of performing computations are necessary since we are designing a single-address machine. We also have a condition indicator that can be tested by several instructions to make a decision about transferring to some other part of a program.

The instruction set for this simple computer is shown in Table 9-2. There are instructions to perform arithmetic and to test for various conditions and then transfer to another part of the program, as well as simple input/output instructions.

**Machine-Language Programming**

Table 9-3 contains a short program written for our simple computer in machine language. The program is designed to add a series of numbers and print their sum. The bottom half of Table 9-3 is a map of memory. Because our computer is so simple we have no provisions in the instruction set for writing a constant in the program. Every number has to be input to the program during execution. In location 99 we input and store the constant, which will be used as a counter to see how many numbers we have added.

Location 98 contains another input from the user—the number of items to be added. Location 97 is a counter; that is, the program will use this location to total the number of items added so far, such as a 2 for two numbers, a 3 for three numbers, and so forth. In location 96 we keep the sum as it is accumulated. Finally, the next number to be added is stored in location 95.

The program begins in location 1 and requires 16 memory locations for all its instructions. The program first reads and stores the number 1. It then subtracts 1 from itself, giving zero, which is stored to initialize the counter. Next, the

**TABLE 9-2**
INSTRUCTION SET FOR A SIMPLE COMPUTER

| Operation code | Instruction |
| --- | --- |
| 01 | Subtract the contents of the memory location addressed from the contents of the A register. |
| 02 | Add the contents of the memory location addressed to the contents of the A register. |
| 03 | Multiply the contents of the A register by the contents of the memory location addressed. The product is in the A register. |
| 04 | Divide the contents of the A register by the contents of the memory location addressed. The quotient is in the A register. |
| 05 | Store the contents of the A register in the memory location addressed. (The contents of the memory location are replaced by the contents of the A register.) |
| 06 | Load the A register with the contents of the memory location addressed. (The contents of the A register are replaced by the contents of the memory location addressed.) |
| 07 | Print on the teletypewriter the contents of the memory location addressed. |
| 08 | Read a number entered from the teletypewriter and place it in the memory location addressed. (The user is prompted with the word "INPUT" before entering the data.) |
| 09 | The contents of the A register are compared with the contents of the memory location addressed, and a condition code indicator is set as follows: |

| Contents of A register | Contents of memory location | Condition code |
| --- | --- | --- |
| > | | + |
| = | | 0 |
| < | | − |

| | |
| --- | --- |
| 10 | Jump to the memory location addressed and execute that instruction next if the condition code is negative. If not, continue to execute the next instruction in sequence. |
| 11 | Jump to the memory location addressed and execute that instruction next if the condition code is zero. If not, continue to execute the next instruction in sequence. |
| 12 | Jump to the memory location addressed and execute that instruction next if the condition code is positive. If not, continue to execute the next instruction in sequence. |
| 13 | Jump to the memory location addressed and execute that instruction next unconditionally. |
| 14 | Stop executing the program. |

**TABLE 9-3**
A PROGRAM TO ADD A SERIES OF NUMBERS

| Instruction address | Operation code | Memory location | Comment |
|:---:|:---:|:---:|---|
| 1 | 08 | 99 | Read a number (must be 1) into memory location 99 |
| 2 | 08 | 98 | Read the number of items to be added into location 98 |
| 3 | 06 | 99 | Load the A register with the 1 in location 99 |
| 4 | 01 | 99 | Subtract the 1 from itself to get 0 |
| 5 | 05 | 97 | Store the 0 in location 97 to be a counter |
| 6 | 08 | 95 | Read a number to be added into location 95 |
| 7 | 02 | 95 | Add the new number to the A register |
| 8 | 05 | 96 | Store the sum in location 96 |
| 9 | 06 | 97 | Load the counter into the A register |
| 10 | 02 | 99 | Add 1 to the counter |
| 11 | 05 | 97 | Store the incremented counter back in location 97 |
| 12 | 09 | 98 | Compare the A register with location 98 |
| 13 | 06 | 96 | Load the A register with the sum so far from location 96 |
| 14 | 10 | 06 | Jump to location 06 if the A register is less than the number of items to be added |
| 15 | 07 | 96 | Write the sum from location 96 |
| 16 | 14 | 99 | Halt |

| Memory map | |
|---|---|
| **Location** | **Contents** |
| C 99 | 1 |
| N 98 | Number of items to be added |
| I 97 | Counter of numbers added so far |
| S 96 | Sum of numbers so far |
| A 95 | The next number to be added |

program reads the number of items to be added and stores it in location 98. The user of the program supplies this input.

Our strategy in the program is to add each number to the sum that has been accumulated so far, increase a counter by 1, and compare it with the number of items to be added. When the program has added this many numbers, it prints the results and stops. Until it has reached this total, the program loops back and picks up the next input item to be added. This loop is between the instructions stored at locations 6 and 14.

Each number to be added is read into location 95 and added to the A register. (The first time through, the A register is at zero because it has just been initialized. On subsequent passes through the program, the A register contains the total sum accumulated so far.) The counter is then incremented, stored, and compared with the number of items to be added from location 98. The comparison instruction is located at address 12, and this sets the condition code. Before testing the condition code, we use the instruction at location 13 to load the sum accumulated so far into the A register. The instruction in location 14 transfers control to the beginning of the loop, that is, the instruction located at location 6, if the counter does not equal the number of items to be added yet. If we loop back, the sum so far is ready in the A register for the next number. If we are done, the final sum is in the A register to be printed by the next-to-last instruction. Finally, the last instruction halts the program.

## Assembly Language

One problem with machine language is remembering the operation codes and their numbers. For example, an add instruction is the number 2 and a subtract the number 1 in our simple computer. The first improvement to be made in this machine language is to substitute mnemonics for the operation codes. We would like to be able to write instructions of the form ADD, SUBTRACT, etc. Table 9-4 contains three-letter mnemonics for our simple decimal computer machine language.

The next aid in writing programs is to use symbols instead of address locations for data. In other words, we would like to introduce algebraic variables such as X, Y, and PAY. This enhancement involves more than just replacing a number with a group of alphabetic characters as we did with the operation code. We also

**TABLE 9-4**
MNEMONIC INSTRUCTIONS FOR SIMPLE
COMPUTER EXAMPLE

| Operation code | Mnemonic |
| --- | --- |
| 01 | SUB |
| 02 | ADD |
| 03 | MLT |
| 04 | DIV |
| 05 | STA |
| 06 | LDA |
| 07 | WRT |
| 08 | RDD |
| 09 | CMP |
| 10 | JLT |
| 11 | JEQ |
| 12 | JGT |
| 13 | JMP |
| 14 | HLT |

want to give responsibility for memory management to the programming language. We would like to refer to a variable such as X without being concerned over where X is actually stored in memory. It is also desirable to have something called a statement label, a variable that labels the statement so that control can be transferred to the labeled instruction from some other place in a program.

The simple program of Table 9-3 is written in this new assembly language in Table 9-5. It is certainly much easier to write and understand the program in Table 9-5. What must be done to enable the computer to understand the assembly language? The computer is able to process machine language; it can execute the program of Table 9-3 directly. Unfortunately, the computer will not accept the program of Table 9-5.

The answer to our problem is to write a program in machine language, the language of Table 9-2, to translate the assembly language in Table 9-5 into machine language. The language of Table 9-5 is called assembly language, and the program to translate it into machine language is called an "assembler." In general, an assembler produces one machine language instruction for each assembly language instruction in the program. Figure 9-1 illustrates the assembly process. The input to the translator is known as the "source language," and the output is the "object program."

We write the assembler in machine language. The plan is to scan the source program in assembly language twice from beginning to end; that is, we shall

**TABLE 9-5**
THE PROGRAM OF TABLE 9-3 IN SIMPLE ASSEMBLY LANGUAGE

| Label | Operation code | Operand | Comment |
|-------|----------------|---------|---------|
| | RDD | C | Read a number (must be 1) as variable C |
| | RDD | N | Read the number of items to be added into variable N |
| | LDA | C | Load the A register with the 1 in variable C |
| | SUB | C | Subtract the 1 from itself to get 0 |
| | STA | I | Store the 0 in I, a counter |
| B | RDD | A | Read a number to be added into A |
| | ADD | A | Add the new number to the A register |
| | STA | S | Store the sum in S |
| | LDA | I | Load the counter I into the A register |
| | ADD | C | Add 1 to the counter |
| | STA | I | Store the incremented counter back in I |
| | CMP | N | Compare the A register with the number of items to be added, N |
| | LDA | S | Load the A register with the sum so far, S |
| | JLT | B | Go to instruction labeled B if the A register contents are less than the number of items to be added |
| | WRT | S | Write the sum, S |
| | HLT | C | Halt |

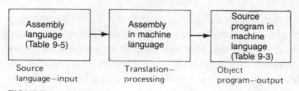

**FIGURE 9-1**
The assembly process.

write a "two-pass" assembler. For example, the input might be on tape that is read once, rewound, and read again. On the first pass, the assembler constructs a symbol table in memory of the symbols used, for example, X and Y. The assembler also places the location of statement labels in this table. The assembler looks up in a table in memory similar to Table 9-4 the mnemonics for subtract, add, etc., and substitutes the decimal operation codes of 1, 2, etc.

Before the second pass through the input, the assembler processes the symbol table and assigns memory locations to each symbol. It might place the symbols in order alphabetically or in the order encountered in the program, for example, C at location 99, N at location 98, etc. On the second pass through the input, the assembler substitutes the assigned locations for the symbols. It also places the address of the statement label wherever it encounters the label in the address field of the instruction.

The object program is complete at the end of the second pass of the assembler. During the assembly it is written on an output device, such as a tape. When ready to be run, the object program is loaded from the tape, and execution begins.

Unfortunately, we cannot actually write an assembler for our simple decimal computer because we have a limited character set: there are no alphabetic characters. However, we can add this capability with a slight redesign in the computer. (What changes would be needed?)

Assembly language is only used today by a computer professional, generally in building other software where speed is required. There is no reason for an end-user to write assembler code. However, it is important to understand its uses and limitations. The most popular electronic spreadsheet program for micros is written in assembly language for speed of execution.

### Higher-Level Languages

Higher-level languages make the computer easier to program and extend the use of computers to more individuals. The most significant of these languages appeared around 1957 and is called FORTRAN for FORmula TRANslation. This language is designed to facilitate the use of computers by scientists and engineers and is well suited to solving mathematically oriented problems on the computer. With FORTRAN we can write a complex formula in one statement, for example. $X = (A + B)*(C - D)/E$.

An assembly-language program to accomplish this computation is shown in Table 9-6. The assembly-language version requires eight instructions compared with a single line for the FORTRAN statement. For many problem solvers, particularly nonprofessional programmers, a higher-level language eases the conceptualization of program structure. A complete FORTRAN program is given in Table 9-7.

A number of other higher-level languages have been developed. BASIC is a language very similar to FORTRAN except that it was designed for time sharing. APL is a very powerful time-sharing language that closely resembles mathematical notation; see Table 9-8 for an example of an APL program and its execution at a terminal.

COBOL (COmmon Business-Oriented Language) was developed to facilitate programming for business applications. An example of a COBOL program may be found in Table 9-9. Most commercial programs in the United States are written in COBOL, whereas most scientific computing employs FORTRAN. COBOL has been standardized to a greater extent than other languages, which gives the user the potential ability to transport COBOL programs from one system to another without a massive conversion effort. The language also features English-like sentences, easy program maintenance, and comprehensive data-editing capabilities.

Many organizations, particularly small ones, use a language called Report Program Generator, or RPG. This language is suitable for business applications. RPG provides fixed program logic automatically; programmers work from special RPG coding forms. The user defines the file, the output files, extra space for the compiler, input record formats, calculations, output, and any telecommunications interface. Because much of RPG is structured already, the programmer does not spend time with complex control logic. The language also makes it easy to update files, and many versions support direct access files with indices.

The language PASCAL is becoming increasingly popular, especially on small computers. It features a simple yet powerful design and is oriented toward the preparation of clearly structured programs. Table 9-10 is an example of a PASCAL program.

How is a higher-level language translated into a machine language?* Early translators for higher-level languages—called compilers—first translated a source program into assembly language and then called on an existing assembler to produce machine language. Clearly this two-stage process is time-consuming. One of the major contributions of computer science is the development of a mathematical theory of languages and a structured approach to writing compilers. See Figure 9-2 for a schematic of the compilation process.

---

*The material in this section is advanced and may be omitted by the casual reader.

**TABLE 9-6**

AN ASSEMBLY-LANGUAGE PROGRAM FOR THE FORTRAN STATEMENT
X = (A + B)*(C − D)/E

| Program | Comment |
|---------|---------|
| LDA A | Load A into A register |
| ADD B | Add B to A register |
| STA T | Store the sum in a temporary location |
| LDA C | Load C into the A register |
| SUB D | Subtract D from the A register |
| DIV E | Divide the results by E |
| MLT T | Multiply the results by T |
| STA X | Store the final result in X |

**TABLE 9-7**

A FORTRAN PROGRAM TO COMPUTE
RATE OF RETURN

```
C***********************************************************************
C* RATE OF RETURN PROGRAM                                            **
C* CALCULATES THE RATE OF RETURN WHEN INITIAL INVESTMENT AND CASH    **
C* FLOWS ARE KNOWN. ASSUMPTIONS ARE:                                 **
C* -THE ENTIRE INVESTMENT IS MADE AT ONE TIME AT BEGINNING           **
C* -CASH FLOW IS NET CASH SAVINGS FOR A PERIOU(DAY,WEEK,MONTH,OR YEAR)**
C* -CASH FLOW FOR EACH PERIOD IS INPUT WITH LIMIT OF 100 CASH FLOWS  **
C* -ERROR IF RATE OF RETURN NEGATIVE OR GREATER THAN 80 PERCENT      **
C* CARD INPUT-                                                       **
C* -FIRST CARD--PROBLEM NO IN COLS 1-10 RIGHT JUSTIFIED              **
C*              --NUMBER OF CASH FLOWS IN COLS 18-20 RIGHT JUSTIFIED **
C*              --SUM INVESTED IN COLS 21-30 INPUT AS F10.2          **
C* -SUCEEDING CARDS--CASH FLOWS EIGHT PER CARD IN FIELDS OF F9.2     **
C* AUTHOR-ALISON DAVIS                                               **
C* DATE WRITTEN-2/17/76                                              **
C***********************************************************************
C
C
C***********************************************************************
C* DESCRIPTION OF VARIABLE NAMES                                     **
C* BRATE-LOWER VALUE IN TRIAL AND ERROR CALCULATIONS, INITIAL VALUE 0 **
C* CASH-CASH FLOWS AS AN ARRAY                                       **
C* NFLOWS-NUMBER OF PERIODS OF CASH FLOWS.                           **
C* NTRIAL NUMBER OF TRIALS BEFORE CLOSE-ENOUGH RESULT OBTAINED       **
C* NUMPRO-PROBLEM NUMBER                                             **
C* PVC-PRESENT VALUE OF CASH FLOWS USING TRIAL RATE                  **
C* RATE-RATE OF RETURN                                              **
C* URATE-UPPER RATE FOR TRIAL AND ERROR CALCULATIONS,INITIAL VALUE 80 **
C* VESTMT-INVESTMENT                                                 **
C* VSUM-CASH FLOW ACCUMULATOR FOR DATA VALIDATION                    **
C***********************************************************************
C
C
C***********************************************************************
C*DIMENSION-AND-INITIALIZE FOR INTIAL TRIAL                          **
C***********************************************************************
      DIMENSION CASH (100)
      URATE = .80
      BRATE = .0
      RATE = .40
```

*Source:* G. Davis, *Introduction to Computers,* 3d ed., McGraw-Hill, New York, 1977.

**TABLE 9-7**
(Continued)

```
C
C
C*************************************************************************
C* 100 INPUT AND INPUT VALIDATION. ERROR OUTPUT FOR NEGATIVE RETURN    **
C* OR RETURN GREATER THAN 80 PERCENT.                                  **
C*************************************************************************
  100 READ(1, 900) NUMPRO,NFLOWS,VESTMT
  900 FORMAT (2I10,F10.2)
      READ (1,910)(CASH(I),I=1,NFLOWS)
  910 FORMAT(8F9.2)
C                              *TEST FOR CASH FLOWS GR THAN INVESTMENT
      VSUM = 0
      DO 110 I=1,NFLOWS
         VSUM = VSUM + CASH(I)
  110 CONTINUE
      IF (VSUM .LE. VESTMT) WRITE (3,915) VSUM,VESTMT
  915 FORMAT (14H CASH FLOWS OF ,F10.2,18H AND INVESTMENT OF ,F10.2,
     -        21H MAKE NEGATIVE RETURN )
      IF (VSUM .LE. VESTMT) STOP
C                              *TEST FOR RETURN GREATER THAN 80 PERCENT
      PVC = 0
      DO 120 I=1,NFLOWS
         PVC = PVC + CASH(I)/(1.80**I)
```

```
  120 CONTINUE
      IF(PVC .GT. VESTMT) WRITE (3,920)
  920 FORMAT (39H RATE OF RETURN GREATER THAN 80 PERCENT)
      IF (PVC .GT. VESTMT) STOP
C                              *ELSE CONTINUE BECAUSE DATA IN VALID
C
C
C*************************************************************************
C* 200 PERFORM COMPUTATION TO OBTAIN RATE OF RETURN USING TRIAL RATE.  **
C* RATE ADJUSTED AND COMPUTATION REPEATED UNTIL RATE CLOSE ENOUGH.     **
C* CLOSE ENOUGH IS ABSOLUTE DIFFERENCE BETWEEN INVESTMENT AND PRESENT  **
C* VALUE OF CASH FLOWS NOT MORE THAN .001 AS FRACTION OF INVESTMENT.   **
C* IF CLOSE ENOUGH NOT OBTAINED BY 100 TRIALS, STOP PROCESSING AND     **
C* GIVE MESSAGE                                                        **
C*************************************************************************
  200 DO 220 ITRIAL=1,100
         NTRIAL = ITRIAL
         PVC = 0
         DO 210 I=1,NFLOWS
            PVC=PVC+CASH(I)/((1.0+RATE)**I)
  210    CONTINUE
         DIFFR = VESTMT - PVC
         IF((ABS(DIFFR/VESTMT).LE..001).OR.(DIFFR.EQ. 0)) GO TO 300
         IF (DIFFR.LT.0)BRATE = RATE
         IF (DIFFR.GT.0)URATE = RATE
         RATE = (URATE + BRATE)/ 2.0
  220 CONTINUE
C                              *NORMAL LOOP EXIT MEANS RATE NOT CLOSE
C                              *ENOUGH BY 100 TRIALS. WRITE MESSAGE
      WRITE (3,925) DIFFR
  925 FORMAT (41H TERMINATION AT 100 TRIALS. DIFFERENCE OF F10.3)
C
C
C*************************************************************************
C* 300 PRINT RESULTS AND STOP RUN                                      **
C*************************************************************************
  300 RATE = RATE * 100.0
      WRITE (3,930) NUMPRO,VESTMT,NFLOWS,NTRIAL,RATE
  930 FORMAT(15H PROBLEM NUMBER I16,/ 14H INVESTMENT OF F20.2,/
     -21H PERIODS OF CASH FLOW I10 / 14H NUMBER TRIALS I17 /
     -15H RATE OF RETURN F19.2, 8H PERCENT //)
      WRITE(3,935)(CASH(I),I=1,NFLOWS)
  935 FORMAT (11H CASH FLOWS  /, (6F10.2))
      STOP
      END
```

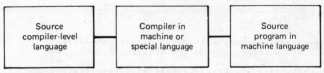

**FIGURE 9-2**
The compilation process.

**TABLE 9-8**
AN APL STATISTICAL PROGRAM

| | | |
|---|---|---|
| **Beginning** | ∇ | *STAT* |
| **of** | [1] | *'ENTER DATA X'* |
| **Program** | [2] | *X←,☐* |
| | [3] | *N←ρX* |
| | [4] | *MIN←⌊/X* |
| | [5] | *MAX←⌈/X* |
| | [6] | *M←(+/X)÷N* |
| | [7] | *SD←((+/(X-M)*2)÷N)*0.5* |
| | [8] | *MED←0.5×+/(X[⍋X])[⌈(N+0,1)÷2]* |
| | [9] | *'NO. NUMBERS= ';N;' MIN= ';MIN;' MAX= ';MAX* |
| | [10] | *'MEAN= ';M;' STD.DEV.= ';SD;' COEF.OF VAR.= ';SD÷M* |
| | [11] | *'MEDIAN= ';MED* |
| | ∇ | |

```
Beginning       STAT
        of ENTER DATA X
  Execution ☐:
              1
           NO. NUMBERS= 1 MIN= 1 MAX= 1
           MEAN= 1 STD.DEV.= 0 COEF.OF VAR.= 0
           MEDIAN= 1

                STAT
           ENTER DATA X
           ☐:
              1 2
           NO. NUMBERS= 2 MIN= 1 MAX= 2
           MEAN= 1.5 STD.DEV.= 0.5 COEF.OF VAR.= 0.3333333333
           MEDIAN= 1.5

                STAT
           ENTER DATA X
           ☐:
              3000 6000 5000 35000 8000 60000 7000
           NO. NUMBERS= 7 MIN= 3000 MAX= 60000
           MEAN= 17714.28571 STD.DEV.= 20040.77476 COEF.OF VAR.= 1.131334059
           MEDIAN= 7000
```

Source: H. Hellerman and I. Smith, *APL/360: Programming and Applications*, McGraw-Hill, New York, 1976.

**TABLE 9-9**
A COBOL PAYROLL PROGRAM AND SAMPLE OUTPUT

```
00001              IDENTIFICATION DIVISION.
00002              PROGRAM-ID. PAYROLL.
00003              AUTHOR. GORDON DAVIS.
00004              *SAMPLE SOLUTION TO PROBLEM 5 IN CHAPTER 19.
00005              *THIS PROGRAM READS HOURS-WORKED AND RATE-OF-PAY FOR EACH
00006              *EMPLOYEE AND COMPUTES GROSS-PAY.
00007              *
00008              *
00009              ENVIRONMENT DIVISION.
00010              CONFIGURATION SECTION.
00011              SOURCE-COMPUTER. CYBER-74.
00012              OBJECT-COMPUTER. CYBER-74.
00013              INPUT-OUTPUT SECTION.
00014              FILE-CONTROL.
00015                  SELECT PAYROLL-FILE ASSIGN TO INPUT.
00016                  SELECT PRINT-FILE ASSIGN TO OUTPUT.
00017              *
00018              *
00019              DATA DIVISION.
00020              FILE SECTION.
00021              FD  PAYROLL-FILE
00022                  LABEL RECORD IS OMITTED.
00023                  01  INPUT-RECORD              PICTURE X(80).
00024              *
00025              FD  PRINT-FILE
00026                  LABEL RECORD OMITTED.
00027                  01  PRINT-LINE               PICTURE X(132).
00028              *
00029              WORKING-STORAGE SECTION.
00030              77  OVERTIME-HOURS               PICTURE 99.
00031              77  REGULAR-HOURS                PICTURE 99.
00032              77  GROSS-PAY                     PICTURE 9999V99.
00033              77  REGULAR-PAY                   PICTURE 9999V99.
00034              77  OVERTIME-PAY                  PICTURE 9999V99.
00035              77  REGULAR-TOTAL                 PICTURE 99999V99.
00036              77  OVERTIME-TOTAL                PICTURE 99999V99.
00037              77  GROSS-TOTAL                   PICTURE 99999V99.
00038              77  MORE-CARDS                    PICTURE XXX.
00039              01  PAYROLL-DATA.
00040                  05  NAME                      PICTURE X(30).
00041                  05  RATE-OF-PAY               PICTURE 99V999.
00042                  05  HOURS-WORKED              PICTURE 999.
00043                  05  FILLER                    PICTURE X(42).
00044              01  DATE-RECORD.
00045                  05  DATE-IN                   PICTURE X(8).
00046                  05  FILLER                    PICTURE X(72).
00047              01  COMPANY-HEADER.
00048                  05  FILLER                    PICTURE X(58)    VALUE SPACES.
00049                  05  FILLER                    PICTURE X(17)    VALUE
00050                                         *THE SMALL COMPANY*.
00051                  05  FILLER                    PICTURE X(57)    VALUE SPACES.
00052              01  WEEK-HEADER.
00053                  05  FILLER                    PICTURE X(46)    VALUE SPACES.
00054                  05  FILLER                    PICTURE X(31)    VALUE
00055                                         *REPORT OF WAGES PAID WEEK OF *.
00056                  05  DATE-OUT                  PICTURE X(8).
00057                  05  FILLER                    PICTURE X(47)    VALUE SPACES.
00058              01  DETAIL-HEADER-1.
00059                  05  FILLER                    PICTURE X(56)    VALUE SPACES.
00060                  05  FILLER                    PICTURE X(14)    VALUE
00061                                         *HOURLY   HOURS*.
00062                  05  FILLER                    PICTURE X(13)    VALUE SPACES.
00063                  05  FILLER                    PICTURE X(27)    VALUE
00064                                         *REGULAR  OVERTIME  TOTAL*.
00065                  05  FILLER                    PICTURE X(22)    VALUE SPACES.
```

On the printer used, the card code for apostrophe (') printed as a not equal sign (=).

**TABLE 9-9**
(Continued)

```
00066        01  DETAIL-HEADER-2.
00067            05  FILLER              PICTURE X(20)    VALUE SPACES.
00068            05  FILLER              PICTURE X(13)    VALUE
00069                               #EMPLOYEE NAME#.
00070            05  FILLER              PICTURE X(24)    VALUE SPACES.
00071            05  FILLER              PICTURE X(14)    VALUE
00072                         #RATE    WORKED#.
00073            05  FILLER              PICTURE X(15)    VALUE SPACES.
00074            05  FILLER              PICTURE X(24)    VALUE
00075                         #PAY     PAY        PAY#.
00076            05  FILLER              PICTURE X(23)    VALUE SPACES.
00077        01  DETAIL-LINE.
00078            05  FILLER              PICTURE X(20)    VALUE SPACES.
00079            05  NAME-PRINT          PICTURE X(30) .
00080            05  FILLER              PICTURE X(6)     VALUE SPACES.
00081            05  RATE-PRINT          PICTURE Z9.999.
00082            05  FILLER              PICTURE X(5)     VALUE SPACES.
00083            05  HOURS-PRINT         PICTURE ZZ9.
00084            05  FILLER              PICTURE X(13)    VALUE SPACES.
00085            05  REGULAR-PAY-PRINT   PICTURE ZZZ9.99.
00086            05  FILLER              PICTURE X(3)     VALUE SPACES.
00087            05  OVER-PAY-PRINT      PICTURE ZZZ9.99.
00088            05  FILLER              PICTURE X(3)     VALUE SPACES.
00089            05  GROSS-PAY-PRINT     PICTURE ZZZ9.99.
00090            05  FILLER              PICTURE X(22)    VALUE SPACES.
00091        01  TOTAL-LINE.
00092            05  FILLER              PICTURE X(74)    VALUE SPACES.
00093            05  FILLER              PICTURE X(8)     VALUE #TOTALS
00094            05  REGULAR-TOTAL-PRINT PICTURE $ZZZ9.99.
00095            05  FILLER              PICTURE X(2)     VALUE SPACES.
00096            05  OVER-TOTAL-PRINT    PICTURE $ZZZ9.99.
00097            05  FILLER              PICTURE X(2)     VALUE SPACES.
00098            05  GROSS-TOTAL-PRINT   PICTURE $ZZZ9.99.
00099        *
00100        *
00101        PROCEDURE DIVISION.
00102        MAINLINE-CONTROL.
00103            PERFORM INITIALIZATION.
00104            PERFORM READ-AND-CHECK UNTIL MORE-CARDS = #NO#.
00105            PERFORM CLOSING.
00106            STOP RUN.
00107        *
00108        INITIALIZATION.
00109            OPEN INPUT PAYROLL-FILE.
00110            OPEN OUTPUT PRINT-FILE.
00111            MOVE #YES# TO MORE-CARDS.
00112            READ PAYROLL-FILE INTO DATE-RECORD AT END STOP RUN.
00113            WRITE PRINT-LINE FROM COMPANY-HEADER AFTER ADVANCING
00114                 2 LINES.
00115            MOVE DATE-IN TO DATE-OUT.
00116            WRITE PRINT-LINE FROM WEEK-HEADER AFTER ADVANCING 2 LINES.
00117            WRITE PRINT-LINE FROM DETAIL-HEADER-1 AFTER ADVANCING
00118                 2 LINES.
00119            WRITE PRINT-LINE FROM DETAIL-HEADER-2 AFTER ADVANCING
00120                 1 LINES.
00121            MOVE SPACES TO PRINT-LINE WRITE PRINT-LINE.
00122            MOVE ZEROES TO REGULAR-TOTAL, OVERTIME-TOTAL, GROSS-TOTAL.
00123        *
00124        READ-AND-CHECK.
00125            READ PAYROLL-FILE INTO PAYROLL-DATA AT END
00126                 MOVE #NO# TO MORE-CARDS.
00127            IF MORE-CARDS = #YES# PERFORM PROCESS-AND-PRINT.
00128        *
```

**TABLE 9-9**
(Continued)

```
00129          PROCESS-AND-PRINT.
00130              IF HOURS-WORKED IS GREATER THAN 40
00131                  MOVE 40 TO REGULAR-HOURS
00132                  SUBTRACT 40 FROM HOURS-WORKED GIVING OVERTIME-HOURS
00133                  PERFORM OVERTIME-CALCULATION
00134              ELSE
00135                  MOVE HOURS-WORKED TO REGULAR-HOURS
00136                  MOVE ZERO TO OVERTIME-PAY.
00137              MULTIPLY RATE-OF-PAY BY REGULAR-HOURS GIVING REGULAR-PAY
00138                      ROUNDED.
00139              ADD OVERTIME-PAY TO REGULAR-PAY GIVING GROSS-PAY.
00140              ADD REGULAR-PAY TO REGULAR-TOTAL.
00141              ADD OVERTIME-PAY TO OVERTIME-TOTAL.
00142              ADD GROSS-PAY TO GROSS-TOTAL.
00143              MOVE NAME TO NAME-PRINT.
00144              MOVE RATE-OF-PAY TO RATE-PRINT.
00145              MOVE HOURS-WORKED TO HOURS-PRINT.
00146              MOVE REGULAR-PAY TO REGULAR-PAY-PRINT.
00147              MOVE OVERTIME-PAY TO OVER-PAY-PRINT.
00148              MOVE GROSS-PAY TO GROSS-PAY-PRINT.
00149              WRITE PRINT-LINE FROM DETAIL-LINE.
00150          *
00151          OVERTIME-CALCULATION.
00152              MULTIPLY RATE-OF-PAY BY OVERTIME-HOURS GIVING OVERTIME-PAY
00153                      ROUNDED.
00154              MULTIPLY 1.5 BY OVERTIME-PAY ROUNDED.
00155          *
00156          CLOSING.
00157              MOVE REGULAR-TOTAL TO REGULAR-TOTAL-PRINT.
00158              MOVE OVERTIME-TOTAL TO OVER-TOTAL-PRINT.
00159              MOVE GROSS-TOTAL TO GROSS-TOTAL-PRINT.
00160              WRITE PRINT-LINE FROM TOTAL-LINE AFTER ADVANCING 2 LINES.
00161              CLOSE PAYROLL-FILE, PRINT-FILE.
```

```
                      THE SMALL COMPANY

             REPORT OF WAGES PAID  WEEK OF  75/07/25

                    HOURLY    HOURS              REGULAR   OVERTIME      TOTAL
EMPLOYEE NAME        RATE      WORKED              PAY        PAY         PAY

RONALD JENKINS       9.750     25                243.75      0.00      243.75
BARBARA CLSON        3.500     42                140.00     10.50      150.50
MARGARET JOHNSON     2.500     58                100.00     67.50      167.50
NANCY BATES          8.025     35                280.88      0.00      280.88
JOHN WEBER           6.500     25                162.50      0.00      162.50
STEVE MILLER        10.000     30                300.00      0.00      300.00

                                    TOTALS   $1227.13   $   78.00   $1305.13
```

*Source:* from Instructors Manual to accompany Gordon B. Davis, *Introduction to Computers,* 3d ed., 1977, by Davis, Davis, and DeGross. Copyright © 1977. Used with the permission of McGraw-Hill Book Company.

**TABLE 9-10**
A PASCAL PROGRAM TO REPORT SALES

```
00100      PROGRAM TAXCOM(INPUT,OUTPUT);
00200
00300      /* THIS PROGRAM READS A FILE OF LENGTH "N"
00400         CONTAINING SALES FIGURES.  BASED ON
00500         A CODE IT DETERMINES IF THE SALE WAS TAXABLE
00600         OR NOT. THE PROGRAM THEN CALCULATES
00700         THE TOTAL DOLLAR AMOUNT OF TAXABLE SALES,
00800         THE TOTAL DOLLAR AMOUNT OF NON-TAXABLE
00900         SALES AND THE APPROPRIATE TAX. */
01000
01100
01200      /* DECLARE VARIABLES AND CONSTANTS */
01300
01350      CONST TAXRATE =0.07;
01400      VAR I,N,CATEGORY: INTEGER;
01500          SALES1,SALES2,AMOUNT,TAX: REAL;
01600
01700    /* BEGIN PROCESSING */
01800
01900      BEGIN
02000
02100         SALES1 := 0.00;
02200         SALES2 := 0.00;
02300         AMOUNT := 0.00;
02400
02600         /* READ LENGTH OF FILE  */
02800         READLN(N);
02900
02902         /* ENTER LOOP */
03000         FOR I := 1 TO N DO
03100           BEGIN
03102
03104             /* READ FROM FILE TAX CATEGORY AND AMOUNT */
03200             READLN(CATEGORY,AMOUNT);
03201
03202               /* BASED ON CATEGORY CALCULATE */
03300               IF CATEGORY=1 THEN
03400                  SALES1 := SALES1+AMOUNT
03500               ELSE
03600                  SALES2 := SALES2+AMOUNT;
03700           END;
03750         /* END OF LOOP */
03775
03787      /* CALCULATE SALES TAX */
03800        TAX := SALES1 * TAXRATE;
03850
03875        /* PRINT RESULTS */
03900        WRITELN('TAXABLE SALES:   $', SALES1:5:2);
```

**TABLE 9-10**
(Continued)

```
04000          WRITELN('NON-TAXABLE SALES:   $', SALES2:5:2);
04100          WRITELN('TAX DUE ON SALES:   $', TAX:5:2);
04102
04104     /* END OF PROGRAM */
04200     END.
@
```

| Data | Results |
|------|---------|
| 10 | TAXABLE SALES:      $ 129.90 |
| 1 12.45 | NON-TAXABLE SALES:   $  84.15 |
| 1 30.00 | TAX DUE ON SALES:    $   9.09 |
| 2 11.10 | @ |
| 1 30.50 | |
| 1 09.95 | |
| 2 40.00 | |
| 2 23.05 | |
| 1 14.50 | |
| 1 32.50 | |
| 2 10.00 | |
| @ | |

The components of a modern compiler may be broken down into a series of modules or stages, although some of the stages interact with each other rather than follow each other in strict sequence.

The lexical analysis component of the compiler analyzes symbols in the source language statement and identifies them. For example, the FORTRAN statement $X = (A + B)*(C - D)/E$ contains three types of symbols. First, are the variables X, A, B, C, D, and E, and in some languages these variables could be composed of from 6 to 30 characters each. There are also operators, the $+$, $*$, $-$, and $/$. Finally, parentheses indicate the proper order of computations (some compilers classify parentheses with operators). Most languages have many other kinds of statements besides the computational one shown above, such as those for I/O, conditional tests (if a certain condition exists take the following action), looping, and others.

The next stage of the compiler is syntactic analysis, which examines the input program statements and tries to develop a syntactic representation of each statement (Cardenas et al., 1972). The set of rules specifying legal statements (symbol combinations) in a language is called the "syntax" of the language.

A typical compiler in the syntactic analysis stage uses a formal representation of the language to screen input classified by lexical analysis routines. The input language is matched against permissible language structures, much as we might diagram an English sentence to see if it exhibits acceptable grammar. The matching process frequently involves the construction of a tree that classifies the various parts of the source statement according to their type. For example, in an English language statement such a tree would identify the verbs, prepositions,

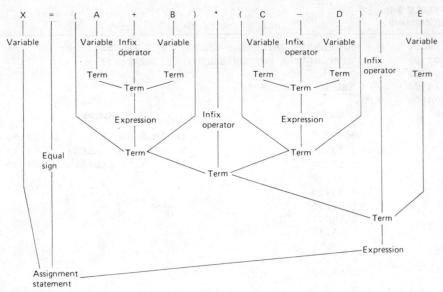

**FIGURE 9-3**
An example of a parse tree.

adjectives, and so on. Figure 9-3 is a possible parse tree for the FORTRAN expression discussed earlier. The syntactic analyzer routines call on the lexical analysis routine to classify each symbol (variable, operator, etc.) as the syntactic analyzer builds the tree. The entire process of lexical and syntactic analysis is referred to as "parsing" the input program.

Given a representation of the input in the form of a parse tree, the next step of the compiler is to interpret the parse tree. That is, the parse tree is used to generate a sequence of machine-language instructions: Figure 9-3 has to be converted into the machine language of Table 9-7. However, before machine-language instructions are generated, an intermediate linear language is produced called "pseudocode." Why bother with this step? Does it not just add time and complexity to compilation?

By accepting some inefficiency here we can produce a better program. Frequently, in interpreting the parse tree, the compiler generates a number of redundant instructions. For example, the same value might be moved from a register to memory in one instruction and in the next instruction be loaded back into the same register. To avoid such unnecessary steps, the optimization phase examines the pseudocode and attempts to recognize and eliminate redundant operations, such as inefficiencies in register allocation, excessive use of temporary locations, and removal of invariant calculations in loops.

After optimization, the pseudocode is used to generate machine language, or object code. However, before the computer executes this code, one additional step is necessary. In many languages it is possible to employ subroutines. A subroutine is used to avoid repeating coding steps or to modularize a program. Subroutines may be written by one programmer and saved in a library for use by others. Also, some languages are procedural; that is, a program consists of a series of modules called procedures. All these procedures and subroutines must be combined and the complete program loaded into memory for execution.

### Special-Purpose Languages

Special-purpose languages are designed with the same philosophy as higher-level languages: to extend the capabilities of the computer to end users. Frequently, special-purpose languages are translated into a higher-level language that is compiled to produce machine language.

An excellent example of a special-purpose language is the Statistical Package for the Social Sciences (SPSS) (Nie et al., 1975). This very complete statistical

---

**MANAGEMENT PROBLEM 9-1**

The manager of production for Homeware, Inc., had just finished reading an article about how a time-sharing system was used by a manufacturing company to simulate different production schedules. The company in the article resembled Homeware; both firms operate more of a job shop than an assembly line.

The manager wondered if a similar system could not be developed for Homeware to solve some of its production problems. He approached the information services department with a proposal for a system. The response from the computer staff was fairly positive.

The manager worked with the computer staff to define the input language he would like to use and the logic of the simulation. The input language must be unique for each company, and the computer staff indicated that they would have to write an input parser especially for this application.

The manager did not really know what an input parser was, but it sounded rather formidable. The computer department also said they would have to hire a systems programmer (a programmer who specializes in software systems as opposed to applications programs) to write this routine. "It is a lot like writing part of a compiler," said the main representative from the computer staff. "We will have to use assembly language for a task like this," he added.

The manager really did not understand much of the conversation, but he was asked to authorize the new addition to the staff and to give his approval for developing the system. The investment for development would come from his budget. What should the manager do?

---

**TABLE 9-11**
SPSS REGRESSION Run

```
1                    16
RUN NAME             MULTIPLE REGRESSION RUN USING CARD INPUT AND RAW DATA
FILE NAME            STOCKP   DATA FOR PREDICTION OF INVESTORS INDEX
VARIABLE LIST        INVINDEX,GNP,CORPPROF,CORPDIV,YEAR
VAR LABELS           INVINDEX  INVESTORS INDEX 1949=0/
                     GNP       GROSS NATIONAL PRODUCT/
                     CORPPROF  CORPORATE PROFITS BEFORE TAXES/
                     CORPDIV   CORPORATE DIVIDENDS PAID
INPUT FORMAT         FIXED (F6.1,4F6.0)
PRINT FORMATS        INVINDEX(1) GNP TO CORPDIV(0)
N OF CASES           32
REGRESSION           VARIABLES =INVINDEX,GNP,CORPPROF,CORPDIV/
                     REGRESSION=INVINDEX WITH GNP TO CORPDIV(1)
READ INPUT DATA
    76.4    7678    269    216   1935
    99.5    8022    351    251   1936
   105.9    8820    403    250   1937
    86.7    8871    362    290   1938
    83.7    9536    541    304   1939
    70.7   10911    619    317   1940
    61.7   12486    801    273   1941
    58.7   14816    917    243   1942
    76.3   15357    882    233   1943
    76.6   15927    858    211   1944
    91.0   15552    852    195   1945
   105.8   15251    966    230   1946
    96.8   15446   1008    286   1947
   102.8   15735    908    240   1948
   100.0   16343    851    278   1949
   120.3   17471   1065    361   1950
   153.8   18547   1034    300   1951
   158.2   20027   1081    296   1952
   146.5   20794   1089    287   1953
   165.6   20186    953    282   1954
   212.7   21920   1206    321   1955
   245.9   23811   1313    340   1956
   236.0   24117   1202    364   1957
   218.8   24397   1242    371   1958
   242.6   25242   1378    388   1959
   256.9   15849   1295    397   1960
   326.1   25615   1314    436   1961
   314.4   28287   1422    470   1962
   336.0   29740   1525    511   1963
   394.0   31650   1718    583   1964
   433.1   33814   1836    629   1965
   408.5   35822   1762    655   1966
FINISH
```

Source: N. Nie et al., *Statistical Package for the Social Sciences*, 2d ed., McGraw-Hill, New York, 1975.

system is written in FORTRAN. It makes it possible to name variables for a particular study, save the variable names and data on a file, and create new variables from logical relationships among existing variables. The package features extensive data-management facilities that are complemented by a number of statistical tests, including the preparation of frequency distributions, testing for differences among populations, calculating measures of association, performing analysis of variance, and performing a series of multivariate procedures such as regression analysis and factor analysis.

Table 9-11 contains an example of an SPSS program, and Table 9-12 presents

**TABLE 9-12**
OUTPUT FROM REGRESSION

```
MULTIPLE REGRESSION RUN USING CARD INPUT AND RAW DATA                    04/ 2/74      PAGE    2
FILE   STOCKP   (CREATION DATE = 04/12/74)   DATA FOR PREDICTION OF INVESTORS INDEX
• • • • • • • • • • • • • • • • • • • • M U L T I P L E   R E G R E S S I O N • • • • • • • • • • • •   VARIABLE LIST  1
DEPENDENT VARIABLE..    INVINDEX   INVESTORS INDEX 1949=0                                             REGRESSION LIST  1

VARIABLE(S) ENTERED ON STEP NUMBER  1..   CORPDIV   CORPORATE DIVIDENDS PAID

MULTIPLE R            0.93667              ANALYSIS OF VARIANCE   DF    SUM OF SQUARES      MEAN SQUARE            F
R SQUARE             0.87735              REGRESSION            1.    339486.57326      339486.57326      214.60000
ADJUSTED R SQUARE    0.87735              RESIDUAL             30.     47458.51460        1581.95049
STANDARD ERROR      39.77374

---------------- VARIABLES IN THE EQUATION ----------------        ----------- VARIABLES NOT IN THE EQUATION -----------

VARIABLE          B        BETA     STD ERROR B      F            VARIABLE     BETA IN    PARTIAL    TOLERANCE        F

CORPDIV        0.87621    0.93667    0.05981     214.600          GNP          0.42296    0.63390    0.27549      19.481
(CONSTANT)   -119.00286                                           CORPPROF     0.33527    0.54357    0.32240      12.162

• • • • • • • • • • • • • • • • • • • • • • • • • • • • • • • • • • • • • • • • • • • • • • • • • • • • • •

VARIABLE(S) ENTERED ON STEP NUMBER  2..   GNP      GROSS NATIONAL PRODUCT

MULTIPLE R            0.96262              ANALYSIS OF VARIANCE   DF    SUM OF SQUARES      MEAN SQUARE            F
R SQUARE             0.92664              REGRESSION            2.    358556.98740      179278.49370      183.14280
ADJUSTED R SQUARE    0.92419              RESIDUAL             29.     28388.10046         978.90002
STANDARD ERROR      31.28738

---------------- VARIABLES IN THE EQUATION ----------------        ----------- VARIABLES NOT IN THE EQUATION -----------

VARIABLE          B        BETA     STD ERROR B      F            VARIABLE     BETA IN    PARTIAL    TOLERANCE        F

CORPDIV        0.53943    0.57665    0.08964      36.211          CORPPROF    -0.00946   -0.01000    0.08193       0.003
GNP            0.00620    0.42296    0.00140      19.481
(CONSTANT)   -123.08406

F-LEVEL OR TOLERANCE-LEVEL INSUFFICIENT FOR FURTHER COMPUTATION
```

```
MULTIPLE REGRESSION RUN USING CARD INPUT AND RAW DATA                    04/12/74      PAGE    3
FILE   STOCKP   (CREATION DATE = 04/12/74)   DATA FOR PREDICTION OF INVESTORS INDEX
• • • • • • • • • • • • • • • • • • • • M U L T I P L E   R E G R E S S I O N • • • • • • • • • • • •   VARIABLE LIST  1
DEPENDENT VARIABLE..    INVINDEX   INVESTORS INDEX 1949=0                                             REGRESSION LIST  1

                                            SUMMARY TABLE
VARIABLE                          MULTIPLE R   R SQUARE   RSQ CHANGE   SIMPLE R          B          BETA

CORPDIV   CORPORATE DIVIDENDS PAID   0.93667    0.87735    0.87735     0.93667      0.53943      0.57665
GNP       GROSS NATIONAL PRODUCT     0.96262    0.92664    0.04928     0.91380      0.00620      0.42296
(CONSTANT)                                                                       -123.08406
```

Source: N. Nie et al., *Statistical Package for the Social Sciences*, 2d ed., McGraw-Hill, New York, 1975.

the results of executing the program. The input program is for a multiple-regression run. The run name provides a title and the file name gives the data file a unique name. Data are envisioned as forming a matrix. The columns of the matrix represent variables such as GNP, and each row is one observation of the variables, for example, GNP for a given year. The variable list labels the different columns of data and the variable labels statement is optional input that improves the readability of the output. The input format describes how the data are placed in the input record, and the print format indicates the desired output.

There are 32 cases or observations. The regression statement invokes the procedure to compute a least squares equation using a stepwise algorithm. This

---

### SPSS AT QUAKER OATS

*Quaker Oats is very interested in the question of whether or not Americans think Chewy Granola Bars are chewy enough. To determine consumer reactions to its products, Quaker Oats conducts a great deal of market research. To analyze these data, the firm uses SPSS on a Burroughs B7900 mainframe.*

*The research laboratory receives about 800 questionnaires a week on average for three different products; each instrument contains about 20 questions. In addition to research, the personnel department uses the system to generate reports on worker productivity and to project personnel requirements.*

*Researchers also use the package to develop time-series equations to model grocery inventories. The results of this research is used to improve customer service and reduce capital devoted to inventories.*

*Computerworld*, July 9, 1984.

---

very powerful language allows the user to perform complete statistical analyses using concise statements. Consider the number of program statements required in a language such as FORTRAN to accomplish what SPSS does with a dozen statements.

Many organizations have found it useful to develop financial models of various aspects of their business. A proprietary language called EMPIRE developed by Applied Data Research helps the user to construct and execute such models. Table 9-13 is an example of the execution of an EMPIRE model of a movie theater. Table 9-14 shows a listing of the model. First the user supplies data that are not contained in the model itself, and then the report is produced. One of the most powerful features of this system is the ability to make changes; for example, the user asks for a computation and printout of profits if ticket price is raised to $6 from the $5 in the first run. A language such as EMPIRE extends the power of the computer to the end user and does not require that a professional programmer be available to assist the model builder.

The advantages of special-purpose languages should be clear from these examples. These languages are closer to the vocabulary of the user, making it more natural for a decision maker who is not a computer professional to interact with a computer. Special-purpose languages are extremely valuable to users of information systems because they provide the option of working directly with the computer without necessarily relying on a computer professional. We expect to see more of these languages as they are accepted and used increasingly in the future.

**TABLE 9-13**
EXAMPLE OF AN EMPIRE MODEL OF A MOVIE THEATER

```
 empire

------------
E M P I R E
  TRANSLATOR
    VER 2
------------


ENTER COMMAND:    execute cinema

***TRANSLATING: CINEMA

    *MODEL *

***TRANSLATION COMPLETED***

FORTRAN: CINEMA
ADRSI
LINK:    Loading
[LNKXCT CINEMA execution]

------------
E M P I R E
  EXECUTIVE
    VER 2
------------


YES... verify
THE FOLLOWING ITEMS FLAGGED "INPUT" HAVE NO VALUE SET:
EXPSAL
LAB
TPRICE
TCOST
YES... data
->expsal(cin1)2000,2400
->lab(cin1)450,550
->tprice 5.00
->tcost 3.50
->end
YES... run
YES... print from incsmt
ADJUST PAPER, THEN ENTER A CARRIAGE RETURN TO PROCEED=>
```

**TABLE 9-13**
(Continued)

CINEMA ONE AND TWO INC.
PROJECTED INCOME STATEMENT

|  | CINEMA ONE | CINEMA TWO | TOTAL BOTH CINEMAS |
|---|---|---|---|
| EXPECTED # TKTS SOLD | 2,000 | 2,400 | 4,400 |
| TICKET REVENUE | $ 10,000 | $ 12,000 | $ 22,000 |
| FIXED COST OF SALES | $ 7,000 | $ 8,400 | $ 15,400 |
| LABOR COSTS | $ 450 | $ 550 | $ 1,000 |
| GROSS PROFIT | $ 2,550 | $ 3,050 | $ 5,600 |
| INCOME TAX | | | $ 2,688 |
| PROFITS AFTER TAX | | | $ 2,912 |

YES... what is profat if tprice=6.00

PROFAT              5200.000

YES... what is profat if tcost=3.75

PROFAT              2340.000

YES... what is profat if tprice=3.85

PROFAT               280.800

YES... what is prof if tcost=2.00

PROF    (CIN1  )      5550.000
        (CIN2  )      6650.000
        (TOTAL )     12200.000

YES... what is prof if tprice=5.5

PROF    (CIN1  )      3550.000
        (CIN2  )      4250.000
        (TOTAL )      7800.000

YES... exit

***E M P I R E  -  END OF SESSION***

**TABLE 9-13**
(Continued)

```
 ty cinema.mod
00100    column section
00300    CIN1  "CINEMA/ONE"
00400    CIN2  "CINEMA/TWO"
00500    total  "TOTAL BOTH/CINEMAS"
00600    row section
00700    expsal input "EXPECTED # TKTS SOLD"
00800    salr "TICKET REVENUE"
00900    csal "FIXED COST OF SALES"
00950    lab INPUT "LABOR COSTS"
01000    prof "GROSS PROFIT"
01100    scalar section
01200    tprice input "TICKET PRICE"
01300    tcost input "COST PER TKT"
01400    trate "INCOME TAX RATE" .48
01500    inctax "INCOME TAX"
01600    profat "PROFITS AFTER TAX"
01700    rules section
01800    for col=CIN1 to CIN2 do
01900    salr=expsal(col)*tprice
02000    csal=expsal(col)*tcost
02100    prof=salr-csal-lab(col)
02200    end
02300    total=CIN1+CIN2
02400    inctax=trate*prof(total)
02500    profat=prof(total)-inctax
@
```

```
 ty incsmt.rep
00100    select CIN1:total
00200    columnwidth 15
00300    title 1 center "CINEMA ONE AND TWO INC."
00400    title 2 center "PROJECTED INCOME STATEMENT"//
00450    skip
00500    position 1
00600    print expsal
00700    skip
00800    prefix "$"
00900    print salr
01100    print csal
01150    print lab
01200    line
01300    print /,prof
01400    line
01500    print /,inctax@3,/ profat@3,/
@
```

## GOURMET COMPUTERS

*Computer systems are being adopted by fine food restaurants to help control costs. Typically these systems capture sales data at each cash register and convert the data into inventory, profitability, and productivity reports. The systems make it possible for management to keep track of the details that determine whether or not the establishment makes a profit. A computer can record each meal ordered and deduct the items consumed from inventory allowing management to determine whether all food has been accounted for properly.*

*In one system the computer compares the price of each dish with the cost of its ingredients to keep the menu prices at a group of restaurants up-to-date. The chain can react quickly and knows its costs; management feels it has already recovered the cost of the computer.*

*One Massachusetts restaurant with a $5 million annual gross put in a system for $60,000. The owners figure that the system has saved about $50,000 a year in food costs and has improved service. The server types orders into one of 16 terminals in the 500 seat dining room; drink orders print out at the bar and appetizers print at one unit in the kitchen while entrees appear on another. When the food is ready, a runner brings it to the server who now has more time to spend with the customer.*

*There are a number of packaged systems built around minicomputers and microcomputers as well as systems developed by individual restaurant owners. Some vendors claim that a restaurant with as little as $400,000 in gross sales can profit from a system.*

*Business Week,* November 3, 1980.

## PACKAGE PROGRAMS

Package programs are programs written by a vendor to be sold to multiple customers. Packages have been available since the first days of computers, but recently there has been an explosion in their sale and use.

One of the reasons is that the technology has matured. There are packages around today that are in the fourth or fifth (or more) versions; they have matured as products. The other reason that packages are gaining in popularity is the standards set by microcomputer packages. The market for personal computers is large, and a vendor knows that it will be impossible to provide extensive training to customers who purchase the package. (Micros are often programmed in Basic or Pascal, but most users work primarily with powerful packages.) Therefore, the micro package has to be "user friendly" and well documented with an easy-to-use instruction guide. Hopefully these positive features of packages for micros will influence packages for all types of computers.

While packages are certainly a type of software, we shall defer discussion of packages in greater detail until Chapter 17 where we present packages as an alternative to the traditional way of developing applications.

## MANAGEMENT PROBLEM 9-2

Sarah Nixon recently received her M.B.A. and accepted a staff position with the planning department at H & M Foundries. H & M is a large, diversified metals concern that experiences much fluctuation in demand, depending on the economy. The planning department was formed last year as an attempt by management to consider the future in making current decisions.

Sarah majored in finance in her M.B.A. program, and the idea of applying financial concepts to planning problems seemed very challenging. The head of the planning department has just asked Sarah to take the responsibility for developing a model of the firm for simulating the impact of decisions.

Clearly, such a model will require computer processing and Sarah wonders how to proceed. Should the planning department approach the information services department for help in developing a computer model? Is a computer expert needed to help program and implement the model? If so, should this individual come from the information services department, a consulting firm, or should the planning department hire its own computing staff?

Sarah has also considered contacting several firms that offer proprietary computer languages designed expressly for planners. These vendors claim that even a planner who does not have computer experience can quickly learn to write models for a computer in these simple languages.

Finally, she wonders if a spreadsheet package on a microcomputer would do the job; it certainly would be inexpensive and easy to use.

What factors should Sarah consider in making this decision? Describe the ramifications of each alternative.

## OPERATING SYSTEMS

In the first generation of computers and for many second-generation installations, the operator of the computer system had a central role in controlling its use. The operator placed each new program in the card reader and loaded an assembler on tape. The assembler translated the object program and wrote it on tape, then a loading program loaded it and began execution. For production jobs to be run repeatedly, the object program would be saved on tape or on cards and loaded before execution; it would not be assembled each time it was used.

A good operator balanced jobs that needed many tape drives with jobs that needed few or no drives, so that the large tape job could be set up while the other job computed. In the case of a poor operator, the computer might be idle for a large part of the day while tapes were loaded and unloaded.

As the above scenario indicates, operations were very inefficient. It became clear that we could use the computer itself to help make operations proceed more smoothly. The first operating systems came into widespread use during the second generation of computers and most often customers, not computer vendors, wrote the first operating systems.

## Early Systems

**Batch Monitor** The earliest operating systems were simple batch monitors (monitor, executive program, and operating systems are synonymous for our purposes) that read special control cards. These cards might include a job card containing information about the programmer and the job, for example, run-time estimate, lines to be printed, and cards to be punched. Some systems also included information for accounting, such as an account or project number. Control cards were provided to tell the operator to set up tapes or to prepare any special paper required for the printer.

The next input card for the operating system might indicate what services the user desired, such as FORTRAN compile, load, and execution. The operating system examined this card and called the FORTRAN compiler to compile the program and put it on a secondary storage device. At the end of compilation the compiler returned control to the operating system. Next the loader was called to load the program and begin its execution. At the end of the program, control again was returned to the operating system, which read the next job and continued as above.

This monitor, though simple, sequenced jobs so that an entire stack or job stream of multiple jobs could be loaded at once. As disks became more common, compilers and work space were assigned to disks so the operator did not have to mount the compiler, loader, and program object tapes. Operating systems and disk storage have drastically improved the efficiency of computer operations.

**Multiprocessing** During the second generation, at least one manufacturer offered a multiprocessing system, a computer system featuring more than one central processing unit. In reality, this system consisted of two complete computers; the smaller computer had an operating system and controlled both machines. The larger computer was a slave to the smaller machine. The small computer processed all input, and scheduled and printed all output using disks as a temporary storage area. An operating system in the large computer indicated to the control machine that it needed service—for example, when it needed a new program to process—and the control computer answered its request. This approach freed the more powerful slave computer from I/O and allowed it to concentrate on computations.

**On-Line Systems** During the second generation of computers, the need for on-line computer access for applications such as inventory control and reservations became evident. The first on-line systems featured custom-designed operating system programs to control the computer resources. Applications programs in an on-line system express the logic of the application and are called by systems programs.

The supervisor in an on-line system establishes a series of queues and schedules service for them. First, an incoming message is assembled in a communications buffer; this message may have to be converted into a different code and moved to an input queue in memory by an applications program. The operating system notes the addition of this message to the messages-to-be-processed queue.

When the central processing unit is available, the supervisor assigns it to process a queue, say, the one with our input message. An applications program called by the operating system might verify the correctness of the message (correct format, etc.), after which the message is placed in a working queue.

The supervisor calls an applications program to parse and interpret the message, during which time the message may be moved along several different working queues. The supervisor calls different applications programs to process the message further and determine a response. Finally, an output message is assembled in another queue for transmission to the terminal. The supervisor schedules the CPU to send the output message.

The demands of such an on-line system are extensive. A great deal of bookkeeping is required to enforce and monitor queue disciplines. I/O operations also involve telecommunications activities. There must be adequate fallback and recovery facilities to prevent and handle system failures; for example, messages may be in process in one of a number of queues when the

---

## MANAGEMENT PROBLEM 9-3

Ted Armstrong is president of Advanced Airlines, a small regional carrier in the southwestern United States. Ted and several fellow pilots founded the airline in the early 1950s. Although operations were precarious at first, the firm is now in the position of making a small profit on its freight and passenger operations. In addition, the line has been slowly entering the charter market through contracts for private service with oil and utility companies.

Advanced Airlines has grown to the point where it now needs an automated reservation system for passengers and freight. Since the management of the firm generally consists of pilots with little exposure to computer systems, Ted has been exploring different possibilities himself.

Two options appear feasible. First, Advanced can obtain a packaged system from a major computer manufacturer. There would be substantial effort involved in initializing the package and installing it. Advanced would also have to lease or purchase its own computer. While the economics are in question, another regional airline has indicated an interest in joining Advanced so that the two lines would be able to share the cost of the system.

The alternative is to purchase reservations services from one of the large trunk carriers that operates its own extensive reservations system. Ted has discussed this possibility and at least two trunk carriers with excess computer capacity are interested. Which option do you recommend?

---

system fails. Recovery in these systems is complex; usually all input is logged on tape and periodically all data files are dumped to tape for backup.

A typical dedicated on-line system supervisor has the following responsibilities (Martin, 1967; Yourdon, 1972):

1 Scheduling all I/O operations, error checking and corrections, etc.

2 Assembling bits from communications lines into characters, and terminal control

3 Providing an edited, checked message to applications programs

4 Controlling displays and setting up output messages

5 Scheduling all message processing

6 Allocating machine resources

7 Building and processing queues, scheduling and queuing requests for service

8 Linking all programs and subroutines together and calling various applications programs for execution, loading, and relocating applications programs in memory

9 Processing all interrupts

10 Controlling the file system

11 Initiating reliability and fault checks, running diagnostic programs, possibly reconfiguring the system to isolate malfunctioning components

12 Switching over to a backup computer when failure is diagnosed

13 Recovering from errors that caused operations to cease

**The Birth of Time Sharing** As computer systems became more heavily loaded during the first and second generation, the debugging of programs became a frustrating and time-consuming process. A programmer might be allowed only one test run a day or one run every several days. Programmers found their schedules and lives controlled by machine availability.

A group of researchers in Project MAC at MIT began to work on a solution of this problem, a solution that developed a new industry! There is a clear mismatch between the speed with which humans think and mechanically enter input or review output and the internal speeds of computers. Could we make computer users feel that they have exclusive use of their own machine by rapidly switching the computer from one user to another? One programmer's "think time" would be used by the computer for serving other programmers. Each user would share the time of the computer, especially the CPU and memory. This special case of an on-line system provides the user with a computational capability and the ability to write and execute programs.

Early time-sharing systems required specially designed operating systems; Project MAC involved a few hardware modifications to a standard computer as well (primarily to add extra core memory).

The operation of early time-sharing systems is illustrated in Figure 9-4. In this representation only one program is executing at a time because there is only one

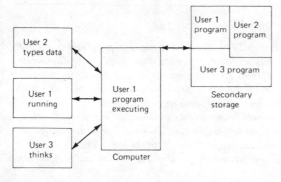

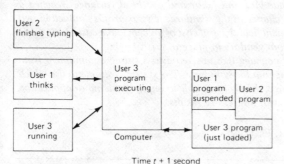

**FIGURE 9-4**
Early time-sharing processing.

central processing unit. A program executes for a short period of time until it is interrupted and "swapped" out of memory onto a secondary storage device.

Another user's program is swapped into primary memory and execution begins where it stopped when the program was previously swapped out of primary memory. In a simple round robin scheme, each user is given a maximum time slice in sequence. A program may be swapped out of primary memory even though it has used less than its time slice if it needs to send output or receive input, since these activities are handled by a data channel. The Project MAC computer could also run regular batch jobs simultaneously with time sharing; the CPU executed these tasks when not busy with time-sharing work (this is referred to as "background" processing).

### The Third Generation

By the end of the second generation, most university and job-shop computer centers were using batch monitors, and the commercial time-sharing industry was becoming established. Many business users were also using operating

---

## A MANUFACTURING PACKAGE

*Gould, Inc., a diversified electronics firm, has installed a package program to control production. The firm steadily reduced its inventory from 130 days supply to 89 days while sales volume rose threefold. The applications package runs on-line and is accessed through terminals. The system includes a bill of materials processor, inventory planning and forecasting, inventory accounting, product costing, and shop order release.*

*The system is instrumental in materials requirements planning at any level of detail. Before the system 25 percent of the dollar volume of inventory was distributed as unplanned issues and the inventory shortage report was 20 pages long. The unfavorable cost variance against standard in labor and materials was about 25 percent and profitability one year declined for the first time.*

*Today the number of unplanned issues is small and the inventory shortage report is less than 1 ½ pages. Materials are at standard and labor and overhead variances reached a favorable 50 percent necessitating a change in the standards. Pretax profits doubled in two years. Improved inventory management held the unit cost of an item to the cost of 1 ½ years earlier due to planned purchases from vendors in place of crisis buying.*

*The implementation of a major package like this requires a strong commitment from management and cooperation throughout the company. The system is simple to use which facilitates training. By using a package, the firm was able to implement a major application in a relatively short period of time with impressive results.*

*Data Processor,* September/October, 1980.

---

systems for their second-generation equipment. When the third generation of computers was announced, manufacturers had clearly embraced the idea of an operating system. The IBM 360 line could not function without such a system; the operating system handles all input/output through interrupts. In fact, there are special instructions that can be performed by the computer only when it is in "supervisory state" under the control of the operating systems. These privileged instructions are unavailable to programmers, whose jobs run in the "problem state." The operating systems also require a certain amount of core for permanently resident routines. Other parts of the operating systems are stored on disk and brought into memory as needed.

**Multisystems** In our discussion of hardware we mentioned the development of data channels to take some of the I/O burden from the CPU. However, there was still an imbalance between CPU and I/O, even with channels. In most commercial systems with intensive input/output activities, we expect to find the central processing unit idle more than 50 percent of the time, primarily because it is waiting for input/output operations.

Third-generation batch operating systems introduced the concept of multiprogramming, a process very similar to the program-swapping techniques developed for time sharing. In multiprogramming, we have more than one

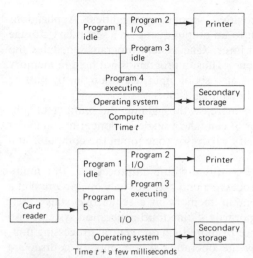

**FIGURE 9-5**
Multiprogramming.

program in a semiactive state in memory at one time; see Figure 8-5. Multiprogramming attempts to hide input/output latencies by switching the CPU to another program when it can no longer process the one on which it is working because of an I/O request. In the top half of Figure 9-5 we see a multiprogramming scheme with four programs active. Just before time t, program 2 was executing; however it needed to print several lines on a report, and the CPU assigned this activity to a data channel.

The CPU then saved the status of program 2 and looked for another program on which to work. If many multiprogramming schemes, each program has a priority and in this instance the highest priority idle program would be executed. In Figure 9-5, assume that this is program 4.

The status of program 4 is restored from its last interruption and execution begins. When the data channel has completed the present operation for program 2, it interrupts the CPU, which stops program 4, saves its status, notes the completion of I/O for program 2, and checks to see what program to start next.

Assume program 2 has high priority, and the CPU therefore restores its status and executes it. Another interrupt occurs for output, and program 4 is resumed. Program 4 terminates and program 5 is loaded: execution begins but it is soon halted for input on a second data channel. The CPU now sees that it has only two candidates for work. Programs 2 and 5 are blocked; they are unready for execution because of I/O activities. The CPU has two programs ready, 1 and 3, and it chooses to execute program 3 according to preassigned priorities. The status of the system is shown now on the bottom half of Figure 9-5. Both data channels are active, one printing output for program 2 and the other reading input cards for program 5. In addition, program 3 is executing.

Multiprogramming has also provided spooling capabilities. Applications programs actually write their output to an output queue on a secondary storage device instead of directly to the printer. One system program schedules the printer and manages the output queue. Thus, a program is not held in memory because the printer is busy. Systems also spool input, for example, by putting input in a disk input queue before beginning a job.

Multiprogramming has helped to increase throughput, the number of jobs processed per unit of time. However, it can take a single job longer to run under multiprogramming than under a unary processor (one job in the computer at a time) because of interruptions.

Multiprogramming should not be confused with multiprocessing. In a multiprogramming system, the central processing unit executes only one program at a time. Several programs are present in memory in a semiactive state; their execution has been suspended temporarily. Some third-generation systems also feature multiprocessing, the presence of more than one central processing unit. These processors are controlled by the operating system and, of course, are multiprogrammed since there is at least the potential for a program to be executing on each processor at the same time. In heavily compute-bound processing or for backup purposes, multiprocessor systems are often attractive. Several time-sharing systems, for example, employ multiprocessing.

---

**MANAGEMENT PROBLEM 9-4**

The president of Midwestern Bank is very concerned over the lack of progress on a new trust department computer system. This system is supposed to automate many of the clerical functions in the trust department. Instead of using a package, the bank decided to develop its own on-line system for use by clerks and trust officers.

However, the bank did acquire several packages to make the development of a custom-tailored on-line system easier. The bank has obtained a telecommunications control program, terminal input and output program, and database management program. However, it seems to require an inordinate amount of time to put all of the pieces together and construct the applications programs, as the computer staff calls them.

The president understands little about computer systems, but he does recognize that a tremendous investment has been made in the trust system. His computer staff complains that something known as the operating system is creating interface problems when attempts are made to install the packages. In addition, the applications programs do not work right, since the trust department keeps changing its specifications.

The president has asked you to help him understand what might be going wrong with the system. Are the excuses offered by the computer department reasonable? Is the trust department to blame for changing specifications? What action should the president take to put the project back on schedule?

---

**On-Line Systems**  During the third generation, operating systems came with more modules to facilitate the development of on-line systems, especially for supporting terminals and telecommunications processing. Systems were designed to support mixed batch processing and on-line inquiry. For example, a partition in a multiprogramming system could be devoted to an inquiry application while other partitions were devoted to batch processing. In this situation we assign the on-line partition a high priority since inquiries need to be answered quickly. Inquiries are also input/output intensive, which means they place a small burden on the CPU. Operating systems also facilitated the development of dedicated on-line systems during the third generation, for example, the airline on-line reservation package discussed earlier.

**Time Sharing**  During the third generation, Project MAC at MIT also developed a new time-sharing system called MULTICS. This system features an important innovation that influenced future computer systems. One goal of MULTICS was to provide the programmer with the appearance of a limitless memory, or a virtual memory several times larger than the actual memory. The Project MAC researchers also wanted to have pure procedures or reentrant programs. In such a program, several users execute the same program simultaneously. Each user does not need a separate copy of a reentrant compiler in memory, even though each is compiling separate programs.

In virtual memory, shown in Figure 9-6, a program and its data are broken into pages. Only the pages needed in primary memory at any one time are loaded; other pages are kept on secondary storage devices. In a demand paging scheme, a program executes in memory until it needs a page that is not in primary memory. A request for the page generates a page fault, and the supervisor locates and loads the needed page from secondary storage. In loading the page, the supervisor may replace an inactive page belonging to another program in primary memory. This entire process is transparent to the programmer, who sees a virtual memory as large as the total number of pages allowed, not the physical size of the computer's primary memory.

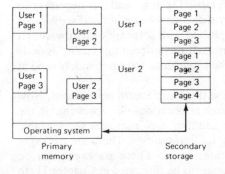

FIGURE 9-6
Paging.

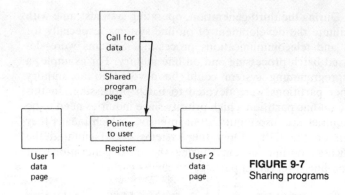

**FIGURE 9-7**
Sharing programs

Paging also facilitates the sharing of programs. Figure 9-7 illustrates one possible scheme. Both users 1 and 2 are sharing the same program. A register loaded by the operating system points to the appropriate user data page (and a similar register points to the location of execution in the shared procedure). Data are accessed indirectly through this register. By switching user pointers in the register, user 1 can execute the same copy of the program; user 1 does not need a separate copy. Only the unique parts of user 1's and user 2's programs must be kept separate, for example, their data and place in executing the program. Shared code is also important in on-line applications and for the operating system itself. When multiple messages require the same applications program, only one copy needs to be in memory; thus precious primary memory space is saved.

### Evolutionary Advances

The "third-and-a-half" generation of hardware brought improvements and modifications to operating systems. The major advance was to take virtual memory out of the exclusive domain of time sharing and include it in batch systems. To facilitate virtual memory schemes, one manufacturer added special hardware to help translate virtual addresses. Programs use addresses beyond the primary memory size of the computer in a virtual system, and it is necessary to map these addresses into physical memory space, as we saw in the discussion of time sharing. This mapping can be accomplished with software or hardware. (It should be noted that certain computer manufacturers offered this facility as early as the beginning of the 1960s. However, their machines were not widely used at the time.)

The mixing of systems continues with the third and fourth generations. Now we can have time-sharing, on-line, and batch applications all processing on the same computer system simultaneously. In addition, new packages are available to help reduce the problems of developing on-line systems. There are packages to handle inquiries and telecommunications tasks. These packages can be combined with database management systems, to be discussed in Chapter 11, to facilitate the development of tailored on-line systems. Higher-higher level languages are also becoming available.

As a summary of mainframe and minicomputer operating systems, Madnick and Donovan (1974) present a view of an operating system as a resource manager. The operating system consists of a series of managers, and each manager must accomplish the following: monitor resources; enforce policies on who, what, and how much of the resource is allocated; allocate the resource; and reclaim the resource. There are four major resource categories:

The *memory manager* keeps track of what parts of memory are in use and by whom, and what parts are free. In multiprogramming, this manager decides which process obtains what amount of memory at what point in time.

The *process manager* keeps track of the status of processes. It includes a job scheduler that chooses among jobs submitted and decides which one will be processed (it assigns resources like a CPU). The process manager must set up necessary hardware registers to allocate a CPU to a task and must reclaim the hardware at completion of the task.

The *device manager* monitors input/output resources, that is, anything connected to the computer through a data channel. It tries to schedule and allocate these resources efficiently.

The *information manager* controls the file system and its directories. Information must be protected, and this manager allocates and reclaims resources, for example, by opening and closing files.

## Microcomputer Operating Systems

The discussion above has traced the development of operating systems; the examples have been drawn primarily from mainframes. However, the vast majority of minicomputers come with time-sharing operating systems that follow the same principles described above.

Microcomputers also have operating systems, though usually they have fewer features than their mainframe counterparts. The functions of a micro-operating system are similar to any operating system: it is a manager of the computer's resources.

One of the most popular operating system works with IBM compatible personal computers and is called MS/DOS or PC/DOS. This operating system only has to be concerned with a single program executing at one time so its management tasks are easier than for a time-sharing or multiprogramming operating system.

MS/DOS actually has two layers of interest. The highest level is the command level, which is seen by users of the system. The lowest level is BIOS or basic input/output system, part of which is actually in read only memory. All input and output uses the BIOS routines so that there is no need for each application to write codes to control the lowest level of input and output to the diskettes, printer, or display.

The operating system provides a number of commands for the user. Most of the commands are concerned with managing secondary storage, the diskette drives. The user can obtain a directory of the files on a particular diskette, check to see how much room there is on a diskette, format a diskette for writing for the first time, and copy entire diskettes or individual files from one diskette to another. It is also possible to list files on the display device or printer and to delete a file that is no longer needed.

When turning on the computer for the first time, one needs to have the operating system diskette in a drive. The computer is designed to load or "boot" the operating system when it powers up. The user can also put a copy of the operating system onto most applications program diskettes and create a special file that loads the application program directly upon turning on the computer.

There are other popular operating systems for microcomputers as well, and some of these feature the ability to support more than one user working on the computer at a time. (A multiuser microcomputer's hardware also has to be designed with provision for this kind of operation.) A popular operating system that some suggest may become a standard for 16-bit and larger micros is the Unix operating system developed by Bell Laboratories and sold by AT&T.

The operating system is an integral part of today's computers; we cannot use the system without one. The operating system is the supervisor; our programs depend on it when executing on the computer.

## CONCLUSION

Software is the key to the expanded utilization of computers. As hardware becomes less expensive and more powerful, we shall continue to be constrained by the need to develop software programs for new computer applications. Programming can be a time-consuming and tedious task; however, in the space of three decades software has advanced and computer languages are becoming easier to use. There is still much to be done to remove the software bottleneck that exists in the computer field; but if users take advantage of some of the software tools that are available such as report generators, higher-higher level languages, and well-designed packages, they can accomplish a great deal.

## KEY WORDS

| | | |
|---|---|---|
| Assembler | Machine language | Privileged instruction |
| Assembly language | Mnemonic | Queues |
| Batch | Monitor | Residency |
| COBOL | MS/DOS | Shared code |
| Compiler | Multiprogramming | Source code |
| FORTRAN | Multiprocessing | Special-purpose language |
| Higher-higher level language | Object code | Spooling |
| Higher-level language | Operating system | Subroutines |
| Interrupt | On-line system | Supervisor |
| Instruction set | Packages | Translator |
| Loader | Paging | Variables |
| | Partition | Virtual memory |

## RECOMMENDED READINGS

*Byte,* McGraw-Hill, New York. (A popular microcomputer magazine including articles on operating systems.)

Madnick, S., and J. Donovan: *Operating Systems,* McGraw-Hill, New York, 1974. (A discussion of the features of modern operating systems containing many examples; the book is somewhat advanced.)

Nie, N., C. Hull, J. Jenkins, K. Steinbrunner, and D. H. Bent: *Statistical Package for the Social Sciences,* 2d ed., McGraw-Hill, New York, 1975. (This book describing the use of SPSS is one of the finest examples of system documentation extant.)

## DISCUSSION QUESTIONS

1 What changes are needed in the simple computer designed in this chapter so that an assembler can be written for it?

2 What are the advantages of machine language and assembly language?

3 Why is programming such a time-consuming task?

4 Under what circumstances, if any, should managers ever write programs?

5 What are the advantages of standardized subsets of languages such as FORTRAN and COBOL, that is, a set of statements which is compatible across all compilers?

6 Develop a checklist of the factors to consider in evaluating a packaged program.

7 What is the major appeal of packaged programs for user departments? What is the major disadvantage of these packages for the information services department?

8 Computer science researchers have developed compiler compilers, that is, programs to help generate a compiler for a language defined by the user. What potential uses of such programs exist for information systems applications?

9 What are the advantages to using subroutines or other approaches to breaking up programs into small pieces?

10 How could knowledge of computer functions aid in developing a time-sharing application to support management decision making?

11 What was the motivation behind the development of operating systems?

12 How have time-sharing techniques influenced the development of operating systems?

13 What characteristics would be desirable in a text editor for an input program on a time-sharing system? How do needs differ for a novice user and an expert? How can these conflicting needs be resolved?

14 How does virtual memory contribute to the development of programs?

15 Where can problems occur with virtual memory? Under what conditions should we expect performance of a virtual memory system to be best? Worst?

16 What is the advantage of a simple programming language such as BASIC?

17 What factors influence the choice of a programming language for an application? Why should an organization have standards for languages?

18 Documentation (flowcharts, definitions of variables, etc.) describes a program. What is the benefit of documentation?

19 How should programs be tested? What types of data should be used and who should generate the data?

20 How has increased use of direct-access files enhanced the development of operating systems?

21 How has the widespread use of operating systems affected program testing?

22 How has time sharing aided program testing? To what extent can time sharing be used for testing programs? What limits its usefulness?

23 Remote batch processing systems often feature a text editor on-line (for example, a user can enter and edit a program from the terminal, submit the job for batch runs, and examine the printed output). What advantages does this provide for program development and testing? How does it compare with time sharing for this purpose?

24 What are the major advantages of special-purpose languages? How do they extend computer usage to more individuals?

25 Operating systems usually provide utility programs, such as file copy programs and sorting programs. Under what conditions should computer installations write their own sort programs instead of using one provided by a vendor?

26 What hardware and software characteristics are responsible for the overall performance of a computer system?

27 How can the quality of software be evaluated? What standards or measures can you suggest?

28 Various goals for programs have been found to influence programmer performance—goals such as minimum number of statements, minimal use of main memory, maximum output clarity, maximum program clarity, minimum number of runs to debug, and minimum execution time. Which of these goals are incompatible? Which ones should be emphasized by management?

29 Why is conversion from second- to third-generation computers so difficult? Why was emulation offered? What is the long-range solution to this type of conversion problem?

30 Does the extensive use of packages make it more or less difficult to change computer manufacturers? On what factors does the answer to this question depend?

31 It has been suggested that through microprogramming we can develop machines with a machine language of FORTRAN or some other higher-level language. What would be the advantages and disadvantages of such a computer?

32 By a combination of hardware and software it is possible to create virtual machines; that is, one computer operating system sets up separate computers for each user. Each user than chooses an operating system and proceeds to program applications on a virtual computer. What are the uses of such a system? What are the major problems?

33 What are the disadvantages of mixed processing in which batch, time-sharing, and on-line applications run simultaneously on the same computer system?

34 What are the differences between a mainframe and microcomputer operating system?

# COMPUTER FILES

# COMPUTER FILES

## CHAPTER ISSUES

- What is a computer file?
- What does a user need to know about files?

Before we can discuss detailed systems design specifications, it is necessary to understand files and databases. Data storage and retrieval are the heart of a modern information system, and both the analyst and the user must work together to define the database.

While users do not have to understand the details of a direct-access directory, they should understand the basic difference in capabilities between direct- and sequential-access files. Methods of file storage and access probably are the major technical constraint limiting the state of the art in developing information systems today.

## FILE ELEMENTS

A file is a collection of data. A computer file is organized in some way; that is, there is some well-defined structure to the information in the file. A computer file consists of a collection of records, each of which is made up of fields. The various fields consist of groups of characters as described below.

### Data

The smallest unit of storage of interest is the character, for example, the number 9 or the letter A. We generally do not work directly with characters, but rather with groups of characters that have some intrinsic meaning, for example, Smith

| Example: | Smith, D. J. | 599 | 42 | 250 | C | G | |
|---|---|---|---|---|---|---|---|
| Field | Name | Department | Age | Salary | Occupation code | Last job code | |

**FIGURE 10-1a**
A logical record.

or 599. These groupings of characters are called "fields" and we identify them with a name; for example, Smith is an employee's surname and 599 is Smith's department number.

Groups of fields are combined to form a logical record such as the one shown in Figure 10-1a. This logical record contains all the data of interest about some entity; in this example it has all the data in the file about an individual employee.

A key to a record is some field of interest. In many files, we organize the file in order on a key. Last name is the primary key for a telephone book; that is, the telephone book is arranged in alphabetical order based on telephone subscribers' last names. We also can have secondary keys: In the case of the telephone book, the secondary key is the first name or initial. The telephone book, then, is arranged in sequence on the primary key (last name) and within the primary key is arranged in order by the secondary key (first name). Fields designated as keys are also used as a basis for retrieving information from a file. For example, an inventory part number may be the key for retrieving information about the quantity of the part on hand from a computerized inventory file.

### Storage Devices

Files of any size are usually stored on secondary storage devices. These devices are considerably cheaper than primary memory in the computer and have much greater capacity. We cannot expect to hold all the data in a file in primary memory. If we could hold these data in memory when the application is first installed, the amount of data processed for the application probably would expand over time beyond the capacity of primary memory. Therefore, most applications are designed so that any number of transactions can be processed and the files can expand in size.

Another reason for using secondary storage is that we probably do not want the data for an application to be available for computer access all the time. Secondary storage devices make it possible to store these data off-line at a reasonable cost. The off-line storage units can be mounted on a secondary storage device when we are ready to use them.

The mechanics of reading or writing data on secondary storage devices requires physical gaps between groups of characters. The number of characters actually transmitted between main computer memory and the file is called the physical record size. Between each physical record there is an interrecord gap, and we group logical records together to reduce the number of these interrecord

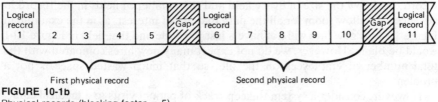

First physical record        Second physical record
**FIGURE 10-1b**
Physical records (blocking factor = 5).

gaps. For example, we might include 60 logical records in one physical record. This means that the blocking factor is 60; that is, there are 60 logical records blocked to form one physical record. See Figure 10-1b.

One reason for blocking records is to use space on the storage device more efficiently. Suppose the interrecord gap on a magnetic tape is 6/10 in. If we can record data at 1600 characters per inch, each gap could contain 960 characters if it did not have to be used as a gap. If a logical record were 500 characters long, grouping 60 together, we would have a physical record of

$$\frac{60 \text{ logical records} \times 500 \text{ characters/record}}{1600 \text{ characters/in.}}$$

$$+6/10 \text{ in. for a gap} = 19.35 \text{ in. of tape}$$

If the logical records were unblocked—that is, if the logical record were the same size as the physical record—we would have a physical record of

$$\left( \frac{500 \text{ characters}}{1600 \text{ characters/in.}} + 6/10 \text{ in. gap} \right) 60 \text{ records} = 54.74 \text{ in. of tape}$$

since there is one interrecord gap for each logical record. We would have used 35.4 in. more tape to store the 60 logical records by not blocking them.

More efficient utilization of space on the tape also means more efficient input and output operations. Since one physical record is transferred to main memory with each read (and the reverse on writing), blocking results in transfer of more information at one time and fewer read operations on the secondary storage device. The transfer rates of such devices are very fast, particularly when compared with the time required for reading. Thus, reducing interrecord gaps by blocking increases both the utilization of the storage medium and the efficiency of input and output operations.

**Record Types**

Different applications require a variety of record types and file structures. One basic distinction is between fixed- and variable-length records. In a fixed-length record, we know the size of every field and the number of fields in the record in advance. We allow room for all the data that are of interest, as in the example in Figure 10-1. A new hire will not have a last job code and that field in Figure 10-1 would be blank. However, we do not expect many new hires compared with the total number of employees on the file, so that much wasted space is not a problem.

However, consider a system to keep track of patient visits to a medical clinic, type of test conducted, and results of the test. Assume that each test result can be described by 10 to 500 characters of data except for one test that requires 2000 characters of data. The patient also can have more than one test per visit. How could we possibly set up a fixed-length record for this system? Even if there were just one test per patient we could not afford to allow for 2000 characters of data in the record when only a few of the tests would ever need that much room.

The solution to this problem is a variable-length record: the number of fields and the length of a record do not have to be specified in advance. Of course, this adds to the complexity of our programs. Under a very general scheme for variable-length records, the program has to put a code in the record to identify what is there. In this example the record would have to specify what fields are present and the size of each field. We can carry either a single code at the beginning of a record or a code that indicates the contents of each field and its length before that field. In Figure 10-2 a code that precedes the record is shown. The first number in the code, 4, gives the length of the code in characters and the rest of the code tells what variables are present and how many characters were required to record each variable.

As an alternative, often we can specify several standard formats, each of a different length. That is, to avoid having to use codes, we may be able to establish three or four different formats of varying length, for example, 100 characters, 250 characters, and 2000 characters. Each of the formats for these records could be fixed in advance, but the combination of records for the file would be of varying length. There might be two records of 500 characters followed by one of 250 characters, etc.

We can see that this type of record structure adds complexity to file design and programming, but it does save file space. In some systems we lose space on

**FIGURE 10-2**
A variable-length record code.

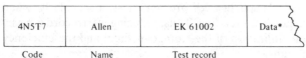

| 4N5T7 | Allen | EK 61002 | Data* |
|-------|-------|----------|-------|
| Code | Name | Test record | |

Code length = 4
First name length = 5
Test name length = 7

*Another code could be used for the data on the test or there might be a standard format in the program for the data for each type of test.

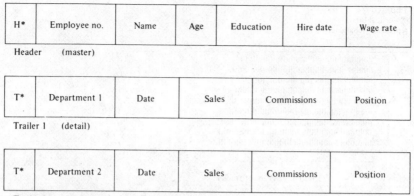

| H* | Employee no. | Name | Age | Education | Hire date | Wage rate |
|---|---|---|---|---|---|---|

Header    (master)

| T* | Department 1 | Date | Sales | Commissions | Position |
|---|---|---|---|---|---|

Trailer 1    (detail)

| T* | Department 2 | Date | Sales | Commissions | Position |
|---|---|---|---|---|---|

Trailer 2    (detail)

*Code identifying record type.

**FIGURE 10-3**
Header and trailer records of the same fixed length.

the physical record in blocking variable-length records. There may be leftover space; for example, if the physical record is 1000 characters long and the sum of the variable-length records is 950 characters, it would be possible to waste 50 characters of space in the physical record. (Some systems will break a variable-length logical record into pieces to fill two physical blocks.)

Fortunately, another alternative to fixed- and variable-length records can be used if a problem is structured so that there is a varying number of fixed-length records. As an example, consider a department store that wants to keep track of the departments where a salesperson has worked, the length of time on the job, department number, gross sales, and commissions while working in that department. In this example we have the same information for each department, but a clerk could work in several departments. One solution in designing a computer file for this information is to use header and trailer records (sometimes called master and detail records). We keep the benefits of fixed-length record processing by having header and trailer records of the same size, although it may be necessary to put the data for several departments in one trailer record. The header and trailer records are identified by a single code in Figure 10-3. There will be one header record for each employee along with a variable number of fixed-length trailer records.

## SEQUENTIAL FILES

The simplest kind of file is one in which all the records are in sequence according to some key, such as employee number, part number, etc. Many computer applications rely on sequential files and although there is a trend to other types of files, sequential files will continue to be used heavily in the future.

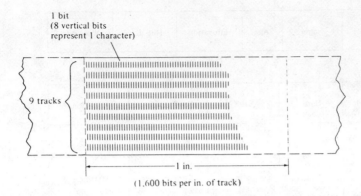

**FIGURE 10-4**
Schematic of a nine-channel tape showing capacity of 1600 bits per inch.

### Storage Media

Sequential files are most commonly associated with magnetic tape, but they can be supported on other file devices as well. In sequential files, the data are ordered on some key; for example, the telephone book is ordered on the last name, as we discussed earlier. It is also possible to have the file ordered on other keys, just as the telephone book uses a secondary key based on a subscriber's first name or initial.

A magnetic tape for computer storage is similar to the tape used on a home tape recorder. It has an underlying base that is covered with a magnetically sensitive coating. It is easiest to regard the tape as a matrix of bit positions, that is, nine rows or tracks of magnetic positions that can be either 1 or 0, stretching along the length of tape. Each character is represented by one column of bits: see Figure 10-4 (in this particular scheme eight bits are used to represent a character and one bit is used to check for errors).

The density of the tape is the number of characters that can be recorded in an inch, and is often referred to as bits per inch (which is really characters per inch). In the early days of computers, densities were quite low. In the late 1960s and early 1970s, 800 characters per inch was considered normal and 1600 characters per inch was classified as high density. Tapes are available with densities of 6250 characters per inch.

### Processing Sequential Files

Because sequential files are in a sequence (for example, numerical order) and must be kept in that sequence, much of sequential file processing involves sorting data on some key. For example, all subscribers must be sorted on their last name and first name before a telephone book can be printed. There have been numerous books and articles written on various approaches to sorting (for example, Martin, 1971). Fortunately, most computer manufacturers supply

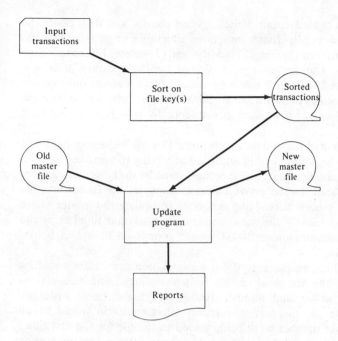

**FIGURE 10-5a**
Sequential file update schematic.

sorting packages as a part of their operating systems. These packages are very efficient and simple to use: all that is necessary is to indicate the fields, record sizes, and sort key, and to assign intermediate work areas for the sort to use.

**Updating** A schematic for updating a sequential file is shown in Figure 10-5a. Since the master file is in order, input transactions must be sorted into the same order as the file before being processed. Note that a new file is created in the update process, since it is not good practice to try to read and write from the same tape file. (In fact, how could you possibly insert a new record and keep the tape in sequence?) The old file in the sequential update provides backup. If we keep the input transactions and the old file, any errors or the accidental destruction of the new tape can easily be remedied by running the update program again and updating the old file with the transactions.

On an update there are three possible actions. First, we can modify a record; that is, we can change some part of the record read from the old file and then put it on the new file. Second, we can add a record by placing it in proper sequence on the new file. Third, we can delete a record from the old file by simply not writing it on the new file.

The logic of the sequential file update is complex because we should be able to add a record to the file, modify the new record by processing transactions against it, and delete the record, all on the same update run. (Consider someone who on the same day opens a bank account, writes several checks, and then closes the account.) This objective implies that transactions affecting a single record should be sequenced in the order of (1) add, (2) modify, and (3) delete. If there are nine types of transactions, transaction type 1 should be the creation of a new customer record, types 2 through 8 might be various other transactions that can occur, such as (in banking) deposits and withdrawals, and type 9 should be the delete. The transactions are processed in sequence by type number for each account.

The logic of a sequential file update is determined by the sequential nature of the file. The file must be maintained in sequence according to some key or keys. Incoming additions, modifications, and deletions must be in the same sequence as the file being updated. In the above banking example, the transaction file containing additions, modifications, and deletions to update the master file in the bank would be in exactly the same sequence by account number as the master file itself. Account number 10054 would appear on both files before account number 10056.

All transactions affecting the record for account number 10056 would be grouped together in the incoming group of transactions. The transactions affecting the record of account number 10056 should also be in order by transaction type. That is, the first transaction affecting 10056 would be an addition if this account number were being added to the file for the first time. Then all transactions of types 2 through 8 would appear, followed by transaction 9 if this record were to be deleted. Using this sequence for transactions, we cannot delete and add a record with the same key on the same run. For example, we are unable to close one account and assign that number to a new account on the same run, since a delete has a higher transaction number than an addition and the transactions for each master file record are in ascending order by

---

## MANAGEMENT PROBLEM 10-1

A small, special-interest magazine wishes to increase the number of issues published each year. Currently, the journal appears quarterly, but the editors desire to publish every other month. The magazine uses a computer system to print mailing labels and renewal notices. This old system is written in assembly language and allows only for the existing four issues a year. There seems to be no way to persuade the program to allow more frequent publication.

What do you think the original designer did in constructing the system to produce such inflexibility? How could the files have been designed originally to allow for more issues? Should the editors of the magazine try to modify the old system or develop a new one? What type of file design would you recommend if a new system is developed? How would the file design differ if the magazine decided to integrate the subscription system with an accounts receivable application?

---

| Old master file record number | Transaction | | | New master file |
|:---:|:---:|:---:|:---:|:---:|
| | Record | Code | Meaning | |
| 110 | 115 | 1 | Add | 110 |
| 130 | 115 | 2 | Modify | 115* |
| 150 | 130 | 2 | Modify | 130* |
| 170 | 131 | 1 | Add | 150* |
| 200 | 131 | 3 | Modify | 165 |
| | 131 | 9 | Delete | 170 |
| | 150 | 3 | Modify | 200 |
| | 165 | 1 | Add | |

*Refers to a modified record, that is, a record which has been updated by some transaction.

**FIGURE 10-5b**
Sequential file update example.

transaction number. Since the key is usually a field such as the account number or employee number, we would probably not want to reuse the deleted number immediately anyway.

An update program should be designed so that during the update, with proper authorization, it is possible to change any field in the record to correct errors. Of course, we cannot change the key field through a simple modification. Instead, if there is something wrong with a key, we delete the record with the wrong key and add a record with the correct key.

To place the transactions in the same order as the master file, we use a sort program as described at the beginning of this section. A utility sort program allows us to specify the keys and the order of the sort, either ascending or descending. Since we also want to have the transactions for each master file record in order by transaction number, we would specify a major and a minor (primary and secondary) sort key. For the above example, the major key would be account number and the minor key the transaction code. The sort program would produce as output a sorted transactions file with all transactions in the same order as the master file. Within the transactions affecting a single master file record, all transactions would be in order by transaction code.

**An Example**  The example in Figure 10-5b should help to clarify the logic of a sequential file update. The left column contains the record number of each record in the old master file. The center column contains the sorted record numbers of transactions: these transactions are sorted on record number as major sequence and transaction code as minor sequence. Finally, the right column shows the new master file.

To begin the update, the program reads an old master record, 110, and a transaction record, 115. By comparing these two numbers, the program knows that record 110 has no changes. (There is no transaction record less than 115 and since the file and transactions are in sequence, there is no transaction to modify record 110.) Record 110 is written into the new master file and the program reads the old master record 130.

Because 130 is greater than the transaction record 115, the program knows that 115 must be the addition of a new record. (Any transaction with a key that does not match a key on the master file must be an addition or an error.) A check of the transaction code verifies that it is a new record, and the new record information is held in primary memory until there are no further transactions with the new record number 115. The next transaction is read and it does apply to the new record being constructed. The new record 115 is modified (indicated by an asterisk), and the next transaction is read.

This transaction is 130, so the program knows it can write the new record 115 into the new master file. Record 130 is already in memory and so transaction 130 is used to modify it. The next transaction is read, number 131. Because 131 is greater than 130, the program is done with record 130, and it can be written into the new master file. The old master file record 150 is read next. Record 131 is an addition to the file: the next transaction modifies this new record, and the last transaction affecting record 131 deletes it. A deletion is accomplished by simply not writing the deleted record into the new master file. The next transaction, this one affecting record 150, is read and used to modify record 150.

The program reads the next transaction, which affects record 165. Now record 150 can be written into the new master file and record 170 read. The transaction for record 165 adds it to the new master file and an end-of-file mark is encountered for the incoming transactions file. Therefore, the program only needs to copy old master file records into the new master file to complete the update.

**Retrieval** Retrieval from a sequential file can be accomplished with a retrieval transaction request, and a retrieval report can be prepared during the update. If there is only one printer in the physical computer system, most operating systems allow multiple reports to be spooled for later printing, that is, to be placed on a secondary storage device and printed later. Even without this capability, one could put all the reports on a tape as the data are processed. If a report code is included on the tape, it can be sorted on the code and the different reports printed. Frequently, however, because we need complex retrieval logic that complicates the update program, or because we are using a file management package, we process retrievals in a separate run after updating the file.

One of the major disadvantages of sequential files on tape is the fact that we have to process the entire file to retrieve information. If only a few records are needed for retrieval, we still have to read the entire tape. Also, even if only a few records are changed during an update, it is necessary to update and rewrite the entire file.

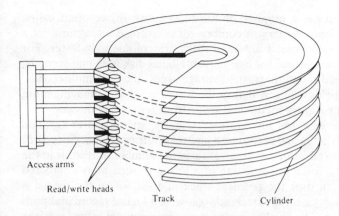

Access arms

Read/write heads

Track

Cylinder

**FIGURE 10-6**
Magnetic disk.

### DIRECT-ACCESS FILES

To overcome some of the problems above and to provide more rapid retrieval for on-line applications and more complex storage structures, direct-access files are used. These files allow more flexible file structures, but more work is required to use them.

### Storage Media

The most common device for storing direct-access files is the magnetic disk (see Figure 10-6). One type of disk consists of a series of platters mounted on a spindle. The top and bottom of each platter (except for the very top and bottom ones) are coated with a magnetic material like that on a tape. Read and write heads are fitted between the platters. By moving the heads in and out we can access any track on the rotating disk. The maximum block size or physical record size for a disk file is limited by the physical capacity of each track. If the access arms do not move, each head reads or writes on the same track of each platter. Conceptually, these tracks form a cylinder, and, when using a disk file sequentially, we write on a given track of the first platter, and then on the same track of the second platter, and so on. This minimizes the access time since the heads do not have to move.

The total access time to read or write is made up of two components, seek time and rotational-delay time. Seek time is the time used in moving the read-write heads from one position to another. Rotational delay occurs because the data we want may not be directly under the read-write heads, even though they are located over the correct track. We have to wait for the disk to revolve to the beginning of the desired data.

There are also available a number of fixed-head disk drives often called head-per-track disks. Since the largest component of average access time for a movable-head disk is seek time, fixed-head disks are considerably faster. For example, the average access time for one movable-head disk is 38 milliseconds, while, for the fixed-head counterpart, the average access time is 8 milliseconds. Recent trends in technology suggest that in the future we shall be moving more toward fixed secondary storage media and away from removable devices.

Each track on the disk has an address. Usually, manufacturer-supplied software lets us specify a file and record size and then retrieve a specific record. The records are numbered 1 through n, where n is the number of records in the file. Thus, we can treat a file as consisting of a group of separately numbered records without concern over the physical track address where the record is stored. The software associates the track address with a logical record and finds the desired record for us. The diskette drive for a microcomputer is similar to the hard disk, except the diskette is nonrigid (hence the name "floppy disk") and has just two sides. The read/write head actually touches the floppy disk when accessing the file.

## Processing Direct-Access Files

**Basics**   There is no reason why the direct-access file cannot be processed sequentially in the same manner described in the last section for tape files. In fact, in many applications we update sequentially and retrieve records by direct access.

When processing the files directly, how do we locate the record wanted? If we request a record number, the file management software will supply it for us. However, we must associate the logical record number with the information desired. For example, in an inventory application, how do we know where information on inventory part number 1432 is located? What logical record contains data on part 1432? One solution is to begin at the first record on the file and read each record until we find part 1432, but this is simply scanning the file sequentially, which has no advantage over tape processing.

To relate a key of interest (part number 1432) to a logical record on the file, a directory is used. The directory is like a map that tells us where a particular address is located in a city. The problem of finding the location of a record for a particular key is called the key-to-address transformation problem. We have the value of a field, the key (part number 1432), and we want the record number (address) where the logical record with this key is located.

**Direct**   There are three basic methods or types of directories for transforming a key to an address. The first is called the direct method and is rarely applicable. Here we let the key be the address; for example, part number 10 is stored on record 10. It is not often that an application occurs where this approach is possible. Possibly in setting up an entirely new system we could assign a part number to the inventory and use the number as a record address.

**Dictionaries** The second method for key-to-address transformation, called the dictionary approach, is probably the one used most often. A dictionary (a table in memory) relates keys to their location, for example:

| Key | Dictionary entry | Record address |
| --- | --- | --- |
| 1432 | 1432–312 | 312 |
| 4293 | 4293–137 | 137 |

We search the dictionary in primary memory (which is several orders of magnitude faster than searching the disk itself) looking for the key. The dictionary entry tells at what record that key is located. See Figure 10-7.

In the case of a very large file, the dictionary may become so big that it is stored on the disk file. Parts of the dictionary are brought into primary memory for searching. We usually try to keep dictionaries in order, so that it is not necessary to search them sequentially. A binary or some other rapid search is used to reduce search time.

In a binary search we divide the dictionary in half and compare the middle entry with the value of the key. If the key is in the bottom half of the table, then we divide the bottom half in half. A comparison of this entry and the key indicates in what quarter of the dictionary the key is located. With each successive comparison, we reduce the number of possible dictionary entries in half. By the third comparison we look at one-eighth of the dictionary. When

**FIGURE 10-7**
Dictionary lookup.

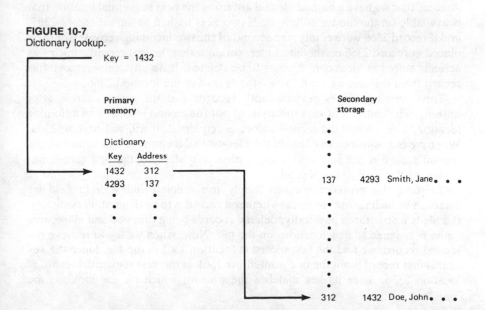

there are only a few entries left it is possible to search sequentially. Remember that the key may not be in the dictionary because there is no record with this key in the file! (For example, information may be requested on a part number that is not stocked in inventory.)

When the dictionary is in order and we use a binary search, the need to store the dictionary on disk because it is so large is no problem. The various breakpoints—the value of the key in the dictionary at the ½, ¼, ⅛ positions, and so forth—are kept in primary memory. Then, the search key is compared with these numbers and the appropriate one-eighth, say, of the dictionary is brought into memory for searching. In this way, we have formed what can be considered a hierarchical directory. That is, a limited amount of information is maintained in primary memory as a directory to a more detailed directory on the disk.

**Hashing** The final key-to-address transformation technique is randomizing, or hash coding. Here we gain access speed at the expense of storage space. Randomizing refers to performing some calculation with the key and using the result of the calculation as an address. Clearly, there is no guarantee that the computation will not result in the same address for two different keys. Such an occurrence is called a "collision," and the keys with the same address are called "synonyms." In the case of collisions, we can recalculate the address or we can look for the next open record in the file and put the data there. For this approach to work we need a file with many open locations, or eventually processing will become sequential. Experience indicates that a file 50 percent larger than the total number of records is necessary for this approach to work.

Collisions or synonyms create a problem when hashed files are modified. Assume that we have a hashed file and are using the next sequential location that is available on the file for collisions. If two keys hashed to logical record 2365, and if record 2366 were empty, the second of the two incoming records would be placed at record 2366 on the file. Later, suppose that the first record, which was actually stored at file record 2365, is to be deleted. If we physically remove this record from the file, we shall "lose" the record at file location 2366!

This situation occurs because both records had the same address after hashing. The collision of keys forced us to put the second record in an adjoining location, 2366. When the second record is requested, it will still hash to 2365. When we examine location 2365 in the file, we find it empty and assume that the second record is not in the file. Thus, physically deleting the first record has destroyed the path to the second.

To solve this problem, we can simply use a delete indicator (a field we establish in each record) to signal whether a record is to be deleted. Periodically, the file is restructured physically, deleted records being dropped and all records being reassigned to new locations on the file. Now, when we try to retrieve the second record, we find the first record at location 2365 in the file. Since the key of this first record is not the one wanted, we look at the next sequential record at location 2366. Since its key matches the one for which we are looking, the desired record has been located. Later, when the file is restructured, the first record, with the delete indicator set, would be dropped and the second record would be stored at location 2365 in the new file.

One of the most frequent computations used in randomizing is to divide the key by the largest prime number smaller than the file size in records and use the remainder as the record address. The objective of any transformation technique is to have a distribution of addresses that results in the minimum number of collisions. As an example, if a file had 1000 records the divisor would be 997. A key of 3722 would give a quotient of 3 with a remainder of 731, and 731 would become the record address for storage purposes.

## More Complex Access

So far in the discussion of direct-access files, we have talked about how to locate a unique primary key such as an inventory part number. (This key is unique because there would be only one part with a given number.) More complex structures are also possible with direct-access files. For example, we can ask questions about how many parts are needed for a particular assembly and obtain a response. Clearly, all the same things could be accomplished with tape files and sorting, but the time and processing required would be inordinate.

Consider an inventory example in which it is desired to keep track of what parts belong in what assembly. This situation is depicted in Table 10-1a, and we wish to define a file structure to answer questions such as what parts in inventory are used to build assembly number 103. To find all parts used in assembly 103 it is possible to read each record and see if the assembly field is equal to 103. In Table 10-1a we read record 1, which is used in assembly 103. Then we read records 2 and 3 without finding assembly 103. We find it again at record 4, and so on. Clearly, this process is not very efficient; there could be a hundred records between each occurrence of assembly 103.

To avoid this reading time we use a pointer, which is a piece of data whose value points to another record; in this case it points to the next record where assembly 103 is found. The inclusion of pointers in the file is shown in Table 10-1b. The pointer in record 1 points to the next occurrence of assembly 103 in record 4. Now, when looking for assembly 103, we retrieve record 1 and examine

**TABLE 10-1a**
FILE EXAMPLE

| Record no. | Part no. | Assembly | On hand | Vendor |
|------------|----------|----------|---------|---------|
| 1 | 4326 | 103 | 27 | ACME |
| 2 | 6742 | 607 | 51 | JOHNSON |
| 3 | 8137 | 12 | 100 | DAWES |
| 4 | 3218 | 103 | 13 | FRAZIER |
| 5 | 3762 | 607 | 43 | ARMOR |

**TABLE 10-1b**
FILE EXAMPLE

| Record no. | Part no. | Assembly | On hand | Vendor | Pointer |
|------------|----------|----------|---------|--------|---------|
| 1 | 4326 | 103 | 27 | ACME | 4 |
| 2 | 6742 | 607 | 51 | JOHNSON | 5 |
| 3 | 8137 | 12 | 100 | DAWES | 13 |
| 4 | 3218 | 103 | 13 | FRAZIER | 42 |
| 5 | 3762 | 607 | 43 | ARMOR | 106 |

the pointer field; it tells us that the next occurrence of assembly 103 is at record 4. We follow the chain of pointers through the file to answer the retrieval question of what parts belong in assembly 103. This type of file structure is known as a "linked list" or a "chained file."

How do we find the record of the first part in assembly 103? We could read the file sequentially, but there might be 500 or 600 records before the first part in assembly 103 is located. This problem is easily solved using a directory like the one in Table 10-1c. This directory simply points to the first part contained in assembly 103: first we retrieve this record and then follow the chain of pointers in each record through the file.

It is also possible to remove the pointers from the file and put them all in the directory, which is then called an inverted directory, as shown in Table 10-1d. If there are multiple chains, questions can be answered, without accessing the file, just by processing the directory. Suppose that the file also has a directory for vendors, with the vendor ACME located in records 1, 16, and 42. By examining the directories for part and vendor, we see that Acme supplies two parts for assembly 103, since both ACME and assembly 103 can be found in records 1 and 42. All this processing can be done with the two directories without ever accessing the file! However, the price for this added flexibility is increased programming complexity and the need to create and maintain complex directories.

How are the directories and links built in the first place? One possibility is to use the program written to create the file originally. In creating the file, a

**TABLE 10-1c**
DIRECTORY
FOR ASSEMBLIES

| Assembly | Record |
|----------|--------|
| 12 | 3 |
| 25 | 212 |
| 103 | 1 |
| 104 | 62 |
| 607 | 2 |

**TABLE 10-1d**
INVERTED
DIRECTORY FOR ASSEMBLIES

| Assembly | Record |
|----------|--------|
| 12 | 3, 13 . . . |
| 25 | 212 . . . |
| 103 | 1, 4, 42 . . . |
| 104 | 62 . . . |
| 607 | 2, 5, 106 . . . |

## MANAGEMENT PROBLEM 10-2

Scientific Laboratories, Inc. is interested in developing a new computer system to aid its researchers. Most of the members of the company are natural scientists engaged in basic research; these individuals place heavy demands on the library and support services. Currently the company uses a service bureau to develop and print a KWIC (Keyword in Context) index of articles.

This rather simple approach takes each major word in the title and alphabetizes articles on it. Thus, the same article may appear many times in the listing, once for each keyword that is major. As an example, consider a paper "The Use of PVC's and Diseases of the Lungs, Pancreas, and Liver." This article would appear five times in the KWIC index under PVC, Diseases, Lungs, Pancreas, and Liver.

The company would like to develop a more sophisticated retrieval system for the research staff. They would like to have a system that allows Boolean retrieval requests. For example, a researcher could ask for all papers that discuss PVC's and diseases of the lungs, pancreas, and liver. Such complex logic makes it possible to formulate a very specific retrieval request. The system should also be able to retrieve on journal and author's name. The library staff would provide keywords and abstracts of the papers that would be stored on-line. Copies of the articles would be available in filing cabinets in the library, and their location would be referenced by the abstract displayed on a CRT for the user.

You have been asked to sketch the basic file structures for such a system. What kind of files and keys would you choose? Show how retrieval requests would be processed.

program maintains a table in memory containing each part number. When the part number is encountered, the program places a pointer in the file to the last location in the file containing this part number and updates the pointer table. When the program is finished, the table becomes a directory and the pointers run backwards through the file.

In the example of Table 10-1a the program keeps a list of inventory part numbers in primary memory. On encountering part number 103 in record 1, the program places a 0 in the pointer field of the record and a 1 in the record address portion of the directory. Processing is done the same way for records 2 and 3 (assemblies 607 and 12). When the program encounters assembly 103 at record 4 it places the pointer from the directory (1) into the pointer field of record 4. Now, record 4 points back to record 1. Then the program updates the directory record address field to 4, and the directory points to record 4, which points to record 1. When finished, the record address field in the directory points to the most recent occurrence of assembly 103. That record points backward through succeeding records until the chain ends at record 1 with a pointer of 0. Another alternative to developing pointers in the file is to use a packaged software system. We shall discuss this topic later under database management systems.

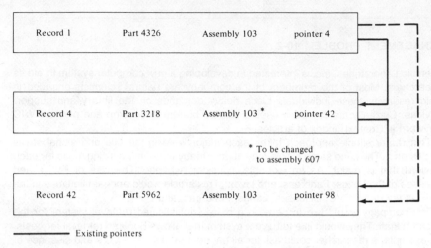

———————— Existing pointers

— — — — Desired logical relationship records 1 and 42 after change in assembly 103 for record 4

**FIGURE 10-8**
Changing chained files.

### Updating

Updating a direct-access file can be done randomly (direct) or sequentially. However, if we update on-line, then only the records that are actually changed need to be modified; it is not necessary to process the entire file. The disadvantage of this approach is that it is easy to lose an audit trail; records are changed and there is no backup copy as there is in the sequential update. To keep an old version of the file it is necessary to copy (dump) the file on some other storage medium, such as another disk file or tape.

What happens to pointers when records are added to, modified, and deleted from a direct-access file? Suppose part number 3218 in Table 10-1 is changed to assembly 607 from assembly 103. Can we just modify the assembly field in record 4? If it were not for the pointer chains running through the file, the answer to the question would be "yes." However, the modification would destroy the chain of pointers (see Figure 10-8). We could change the pointers, but in performing an update on record 4 we would have to know that the previous pointer was located at record 1.

There are three choices available. First, the program can look up assembly 103 and trace the chain of pointers through the file to find the one pointing to record 4. In this case, the program would change the pointer of record 1 from 4 to 42. Here we were lucky to find the record of interest on the first try; on the average, we would expect to follow a chain of pointers through half the file to locate the pointer immediately preceding the record to be changed.

A second alternative is to design the file with backward pointers for the assemblies; for example, a pointer from record 4 to record 1. Then, both sets of pointers have to be changed, but it is necessary only to access the three records

---

**MANAGEMENT PROBLEM 10-3**

Betty Martin, marketing manager for Interland Express Company, was amazed at the memorandum she had just received from the information services department. She had asked to have sales information for the company available for inquiry. In particular, she had wanted to know the performance for each sales representative and to retrieve information on sales by customer.

The information services department said that they had all these data, but they were not available on the right files. Betty did not understand exactly what this meant. The computer group went on to say that the data on sales were stored on a "sequential tape file"; her request would require the use of several sort programs and would produce two massive reports.

Betty knew that the company had just installed a new on-line retrieval system and asked why the data she wanted could not be made a part of that system. The information services department responded that this addition could be done but would require the design of new files and retrieval commands. The new files would be on disk and would require two directories, one on sales representatives and the other on customers.

Betty Martin was now completely perplexed. Could you explain to her the alternatives available to the computer staff in meeting her request? What are the pros and cons of each alternative? Which do you expect to be most expensive? Which is most responsive to Betty's needs?

---

that are involved for each change. This solves the problem of changing assembly 103. Here we save processing time at the cost of secondary storage and extra programming logic.

The third choice is to set a delete indicator and leave the record in the file just as we did with hash coding. In this case, we set a delete indicator at the old part number 3218 in record 4 and add a new record for part 3218 showing 607. Then we periodically restructure the file: the old file becomes input to the original file-creation program, which eliminates records with delete indicators and sets up new pointer chains and directories.

Any of these three choices solves the problem of modifying record 4 while maintaining the assembly 103 pointer chain. The last step is to modify record 4 and add assembly 607 to its chain. We can add assembly 607 to its chain simply by making the directory now point to it and letting its pointer field point to the old directory entry. That is, the directory record field for assembly 607 would now be 4 and the pointer in the new modified record 4 would be 2.

**ERROR CONTROL**

In any file operation, we should provide for some kind of backup. In a sequential or a batch system, backup is produced automatically. For an on-line system, we have to dump the files periodically if they are not updated sequentially.

Processing controls are also necessary to ensure the integrity of the file. An edit should be performed on each transaction to see if all numeric fields are filled with numeric data and to pinpoint transactions or data coding errors. It is also useful to include upper- or lower-bounds checks for reasonableness. Such a check specified by a user might be to determine if the number of items received is less than two times the number ordered. The program should keep processing but should issue notices that an error may have been made. Sometimes a record is flagged to ensure that a change is made on the next update.

For fields that are particularly crucial on the file, it may be desirable to verify all changes. For example, the program updating the file could carry a summary record at the end of the file with various totals on it. In the example used here, we could keep a total on the number of parts in inventory on a record at the end of the file. During file updating, the program would add all parts, keeping track of additions and usage. At the completion of the update, the summary record would be examined to determine if the old figure adjusted for additions and usage matches the new one.

## FILE DESIGN CONSIDERATIONS

We have discussed a large amount of technical material in this chapter on file devices and logical file structures. However, we have not described how the systems designer should decide what kind of a file structure to use. Unfortunately, file design is more of an art at this time than a science. In this section, we attempt to provide some general guidelines for file design. However, much of the structure of the files for a computer system depends on the individual application, and the designer will have to make a number of decisions from the information developed during the systems analysis steps preceding file design.

### Record Structure

The first file design decisions involve the data to be stored on the files. As the design for a new information system is developed, the requirements for information to be stored for subsequent retrieval will be specified. Related information is grouped into records, and several types of records may be in a single physical file. Record types must be defined, and so must the key fields for retrieval purposes.

Information in a file is typically updated in two ways. First, routine transactions occur that change fields in the file. For example, the receipt of a new shipment changes the balance due in an accounts-payable file and the quantity on hand in an inventory file. Other fields on the file are changed much less frequently—for example, vendors' addresses. The input for this type of change can be classified more realistically as file maintenance. In principle, it should be possible to change any field in the file with proper authorization, because errors can occur anywhere and provisions must be made to correct them. File maintenance input is usually processed by different users than in normal transaction processing, and the design of the input form and medium may differ for the two types of updates.

Having defined the basic information content of the files along with grouping of logical records, the designer approaches the problem of defining the record format. Fixed-length records are the easiest and simplest to use from a processing and programming standpoint. If there is a varying amount of fixed-length information, header and trailer records can be used. However, if the length of the record must vary, then variable-length records are necessary.

### Response versus Cost

Having defined the contents and format of the file, the analyst next examines information on the nature, volume, frequency, and response-time requirements for retrievals and updates involving the file. We must balance response-time requirements against the costs of (1) creating the database (including programming costs), (2) storing the data, (3) retrieving data, and (4) updating the data.

**Batch Files**   If there is no need for immediate inquiry or on-line updating, then batch sequential files are the cheapest to develop and maintain for most applications. In addition, these files offer good error-checking and backup features. However, even for a batch application, with seemingly no need for on-line access, direct-access files may be necessary because of processing requirements. For example, if a direct-access file structure were not used in the application of Table 10-1 to produce a bill of materials for each assembly, it would be necessary to sort the file many times and undertake very complicated processing, which might not be feasible.

**Direct-Access Files**   If processing or access response-time requirements justify the added cost, direct-access files can be selected by the designer. In the simplest case, only processing logic demands direct access, as in the example for the bill of materials processing above. For this application, it is not necessary to process retrieval requests on-line. The next level of design effort and complexity is represented by allowing on-line inquiry but updating the files in batch mode. This alternative is less costly and complex than on-line updating and offers better error control. If the only need for access is on a single key, there are simple packages available to maintain directories, for example, VSAM or virtual sequential access method.

If the information to be retrieved on-line must be up to date instantaneously —for example, in a reservations system or stolen-vehicle law-enforcement application—then on-line updating will be necessary. Of the three directory approaches discussed in this chapter, the easiest one to program is a dictionary with a linked or chained list of pointers through the file. If storage space is not a problem but speed is important, hash coding is the fastest key-to-address transformation technique. However, remember that a significant amount of extra file space must be available to realize this speed advantage. Inverted directories should be used only where there are complex retrieval requests or where presearch statistics are needed before the data file is actually accessed.

**Database Management Systems**  The acquisition of a database management system may be warranted if systems currently being designed and ones planned for the future incorporate direct-access files for any of the purposes described above. As discussed in the next chapter, these systems offer a number of advantages. Although they may require a substantial investment in capital and labor, subsequent applications should be more easily designed and implemented. There is clearly a growing trend in organizations toward the adoption of database management systems to facilitate file design for information systems.

## KEY WORDS

| | | |
|---|---|---|
| Addition | Disk | Logical records |
| Average access time | Diskette | Magnetic tape |
| Backup | Field | Modification |
| Batch processing | File | Physical record |
| Binary search | Fixed-length record | Pointer |
| Blocking factor | Floppy disk | Retrieval |
| Chained file | Hash coding | Rotational-delay time |
| Character | Header record | Secondary storage |
| Database management | Hierarchical | Seek time |
| system | Interrecord gap | Sequential file |
| Deletion | Inverted directory | Trailer record |
| Density | Key | Transactions |
| Dictionary | Key-to-address | Variable-length record |
| Direct access | transformation | VSAM |
| Directory | Linked lists | |

## RECOMMENDED READINGS

Dodd, G.: "Elements of Data Management Systems," *Computing Surveys,* vol. 1, no. 2, 1969, pp. 117–122. (An extremely well-written article describing possible file structures; read it several times to be sure you understand it.)

Martin, J.: *Computer Data Base Organization,* 2d ed., Prentice-Hall, Englewood Cliffs, N.J., 1977. (An excellent text on data files and their organization.)

Tsichritcis, D., and F. Lochovsky: *Data Models,* Prentice-Hall, Englewood Cliffs, N.J., 1982. (An advanced book about data structures.)

## DISCUSSION QUESTIONS

1 Why is a new file written during a batch update?
2 What are the advantages and disadvantages of batch updating?
3 What are the advantages and disadvantages of direct-access updating?

4 Where do users encounter computer files? Why is an understanding of their structure and operations important?

5 Compression techniques are often used to reduce file-storage requirements and input/output transfer times. Various schemes are used to compress information and eliminate redundant data. For example, we might remove blanks from a file of text and replace them with a special character and a number indicating the number of blanks that were removed. What are the advantages and disadvantages of compressing a file key along with the rest of the record for a direct-access file?

6 Is there any advantage to blocking records for direct-access retrieval?

7 What procedure do you recommend for providing file backup for an on-line system?

8 For a file of 1000-character records that contains 20,000 records, would a dictionary or hash coding be fastest for retrieval on a single key? What are the advantages and disadvantages of each type of directory?

9 Why would programming for an inverted directory be more difficult than for a dictionary and a linked-list (chained) file?

10 What are the major capabilities a database management system should offer?

11 A relatively new mass-storage device was described in this chapter that is capable of holding hundreds of millions of characters. However, access to each record on a direct basis is relatively time-consuming. In what types of applications do you think such a mass storage device might be used?

12 It has been suggested that the difficulty of updating is inversely related to the difficulty of retrieval. That is, a file structure that facilitates retrieval is likely to be very difficult to update. Do you agree with this observation? Why?

13 Why is it undesirable to have the same data stored on more than one file?

14 Database management systems stress independence between data and access programs. To what extent is this possible: that is, can a program ever be completely independent from the data it uses?

15 How does a database management system contribute to the flexibility of information systems?

16 For a mature computer installation with 50 or 100 different applications, what problems would you envision in the adoption of a database management system?

17 If a dictionary is so large that it cannot be stored in primary memory but must be placed on a disk, would you recommend that it be placed all at one location in a separate file or that the directory be interspersed with the actual data records? Why? If the directory were to be interspersed, what criteria would you use to determine where to place it relative to the data in the file? (Hint: consider the average access time for the disk, which consists of seek and rotational-delay times.)

18 Does the use of accessing techniques such as VSAM or complete database management packages mean that the analyst and programmer do not have to understand how files are structured or how the packages work? What problems can be created if the programmer and analyst are unaware of the physical and the logical structure of the data?

19 What difficulties would be created by having to add data to a file on tape, for example, to print a new piece of information on a report? What would the problem be if the information is to be retrieved on-line from a direct-access file? Would your answer differ if the added information is to be a retrieval key?

20 Can a programmer really remain ignorant of the database management system when writing applications programs that use the system? Where might a programmer run into difficulties if he or she does not understand the retrieval logic of the database management system?

21 How is it possible for the logical view of data to differ from the physical storage layout of data? (Hint: consider the discussion of direct-access files in this chapter and how those files are stored on different devices.)

22 The acquisition of a database management system is a major undertaking. It is unlikely that its first application can cost-justify the effort; instead the acquisition is amortized over a number of applications. How can the organization justify moving into a database system, given this problem?

23 Take a system that is relatively well known, like an airline reservations system. Make a list of the major transactions processed by such a system and then use it to sketch the data structures necessary to support the system.

24 Why is it such a problem for many organizations to adopt common identifiers for names that will become data in a database system? Why is it necessary to do so?

25 Can you think of an example where different users of the same data would tend to view it differently?

26 If massive amounts of computer storage become available at a low cost, will there still be the need to design secondary storage structures?

## PROBLEMS

1 Assume that you have been given the following information to be contained in a sequential tape file with fixed-length records:

| Item | Size in characters |
| --- | --- |
| Social security number | 9 |
| Last name | 15 |
| Middle initial | 4 |
| First name | 10 |
| Address line 1 | 15 |
| Address line 2 | 15 |
| Address line 3 | 10 |
| Zip code | 5 |
| Account number | 7 |
| Account balance | 10 |

The file is used by a retail store for charge-account processing.

a On what key(s) would you organize this file if it is to be updated with purchases and payments?

b Given your file organization, how would you produce a report of customers by geographic area?

c If you have a tape 2400 ft long and can record on it with a density of 1600 characters per inch, how many customers could you get on a reel, assuming a blocking factor of 1?

d What would the answer be to c with a blocking factor of 10?

**2** Given a sequential tape file, assume that it is desired to keep a record of each transaction during the year. Each customer may have 0 to an infinite number of these transactions.

    **a** What are two possible solutions for including these data?

    **b** What are the problems with each solution?

    **c** Which do you recommend?

**3** A direct-access file on a disk has been proposed for a police on-line system to locate (1) stolen vehicles and (2) cars with outstanding tickets. Officers in the field will radio inquiries to a terminal operator. The officer can inquire about (1) license plate number, (2) auto make, (3) color, or (4) make and color together. It is estimated that the proportion of inquiries will be 70, 15, 10, and 5 percent, respectively.

    **a** Describe the organization of the file and the directory for your primary key.

    **b** For the other two access keys, do you recommend a linked list or an inverted directory? Show how the file would appear under each alternative and explain the reasons behind your choice.

**4** Consider the following job-matching system that is maintained on-line. A record consists of

> Social security number
> Employee's name
> Employee's address
> Salary requirements
> Skills code
> Area

The file is used for several purposes, and it was decided to keep it on a disk in social security number order. You may assume that record addressing is relative to the beginning of the file and is independent of the physical track address.

    For one application, employer representatives call the employment office and a clerk enters their requests, which can be either by area, skills code, or some combination of the two.

    **a** How would you update this file (remember an update includes adding, deleting, and modifying records) if the skills code and area are referenced by a directory showing their initial file location and a linked list of pointers through the file? Describe how your update plan would affect subsequent inquiry file accessing.

    **b** What would your answer be to **a** if there were no points in the file and the area and skill codes were referenced through an inverted directory?

**5** A request has just been made to include two additional fields in the file in problem 4. These fields would contain a code for the employee's last two jobs.

    **a** What problems would this change create both for files and programs?

    **b** Would the change be easier with an inverted directory or a linked-list file organization?

**6** An analyst has just recommended that your company invest in the development of a financial data storage and retrieval system. The plan calls for using the system inside the company and for sales to other firms. The system will operate on-line.

    The major problem facing you is to evaluate the analyst's proposal for the file system. The use of a fully inverted directory and file—that is, inverted on every field—is recommended. The analyst feels that this file will enhance the marketability of the system, since it is difficult to anticipate all user requests.

Do you agree with the analyst? Why or why not?

The contents of the file are:

For each Fortune 500 company:

For each of the past 20 years:

Beginning stock price

Closing stock price

Average stock price

Dividends

Splits

Sales

Income

Profits

Number of shares outstanding

7 Anderson's is a chain of department stores in a large metropolitan area. There is one main department store downtown, and presently there are six suburban stores. Anderson's carries a full range of department store items from clothing to housewares to furniture. All merchandise is ordered centrally and distributed to stores from the central warehouse so that all stores carry approximately the same merchandise.

The company has a centralized computer located in their corporate offices near the main store. For customer billing and inventory, they are presently using a batch system and sequential files.

The inventory file contains fixed-length records in sequence by item number. Each record contains the following fields:

| Field | Size in characters |
| --- | --- |
| Vendor number | 10 |
| Item number | 10 |
| Department | 3 |
| Quantity on hand | 5 |
| Quantity sold | 5 |
| Quantity on order | 5 |
| Wholesale price | 7 |
| Retail price | 7 |

Anderson's keeps track only of total inventory; in other words, the "quantity on hand" field represents the total quantity of an item in all stores. Although they are considering ways to keep track of items by store, they presently do not have that capability.

The following three types of transactions may be included in an update run: (1) Orders of merchandise (remember that some items will be reorders while many items will be new merchandise never before ordered), (2) receipt of merchandise (do not worry about distribution to stores—all orders are received at the central warehouse), (3) sale of merchandise (for each item sold, part of the price ticket is sent to the central warehouse to be keypunched and entered into the system).

a Describe and illustrate with a flowchart the process for updating the inventory file. Show how the contents of the file will be changed by each transaction type.

b The company presently has a separate system for keeping information about customer credit and making it available to each sales clerk. Next to each cash register there is a small calculator-like terminal with a 10-key pad and a one-line screen for displaying a message to the sales clerk. The clerk enters the customer number from the charge plate and receives a message indicating how much above or below their credit limit the customer is or indicating that the customer cannot charge because the account is past due. The file for this system, which contains customer number, credit limit, amount due, and amount past due, is updated each night from the regular customer-billing file as part of the regular update run. What file organization would you suggest for this file with what key(s)? Justify your answer.

c Anderson does extensive mail advertising to its charge customers. Management wants a system developed that will select customers on certain criteria for selected mailings. For instance, they want to be able to select by geographical location, charge plan, age of customer, family versus single account, and credit limit. Using the customer master file (which contains all billing and address information for each charge customer) as a base, propose a file organization to accomplish this selection. Illustrate how your system works with a few records and one selection criterion.

8 General Products Corporation is a large company that produces, packages, and distributes a wide variety of grocery products nationwide. It has a customer base of about 3000 large grocery wholesalers and retail food chains. All ordering, shipping, and invoicing is coordinated through the central office. About 500 orders are received and processed per day.

The company presently uses a batch system to create customer invoices and to keep track of all payments to customer accounts. One daily processing run adds new invoices to a sequential file of outstanding invoices, while another program records all payments and removes paid invoices from the file.

a The invoice file includes, for each invoice, the following: invoice number, customer number (unique for each customer), date of order, date of invoice, total amount due, and date due. Invoice numbers are assigned in sequence as orders are processed. If the invoice file is to be stored sequentially on magnetic tape, what field or fields should be used as keys? Why? Given your choice of key, simply describe the update procedure and logic (1) to add new invoices to the file, (2) to remove paid invoices from the file.

b A separate sequential file contains detailed descriptive information about each customer, including address information, outstanding balance, outstanding overdue balance, credit limit, and other credit information. Each customer record is about 300 characters long. About 20 percent of the customers have special credit allowances for which additional information is needed, and management wants to add this information to the existing file. There are three categories of special customer credits allowances for which are needed 40, 60, and 100 additional characters, respectively. Suggest and explain a method for incorporating these data into the file.

c Because of the high volume of customer inquiries regarding their accounts and a need for better control of each account, the company wants to go to direct-access files for on-line retrieval and update of accounts receivable. Both the customer and invoice files will become direct-access files.

For direct access to the invoice file, with invoice number as the key, what would be the most efficient direct-access method? Why?

With direct access to invoice records, a customer may choose to pay on account by any of several methods; (a) by specific invoice number, (b) by oldest invoice first, (c) by most recent invoice first. Explain and illustrate, with a few sample records, how you would set up a linked list to process transaction types (b) and (c).

Explain and show diagrammatically how the linked lists would be affected when a customer paid a specific invoice (not the oldest or the most recent).

# DATABASE MANAGEMENT

# DATABASE MANAGEMENT

**CHAPTER ISSUES**

- What is the database concept?
- How do databases help a user?

In the last chapter we learned the details of how direct access files are created and accessed. The programmer must build and maintain complex directories in order to provide rapid retrieval of data; these directories create problems for updating the files as well. Consider two different applications, one to inquire about parts in inventory and another about bank balances for checking account customers. While the actual data themselves are different, each of these systems might feature a directory based on an identification number, for example, an inventory part number or a checking account number.

Why should each programmer develop separate directory and file management routines when the problems are so similar? This question led to the development of a type of systems software called a database management system. One purpose of this DBMS is to automate the directory handling and accessing tasks in developing direct-access files. We shall also see that a DBMS has many other purposes as we explore data management more in this chapter. We begin with a discussion of how different data structures can be created and then consider database management itself.

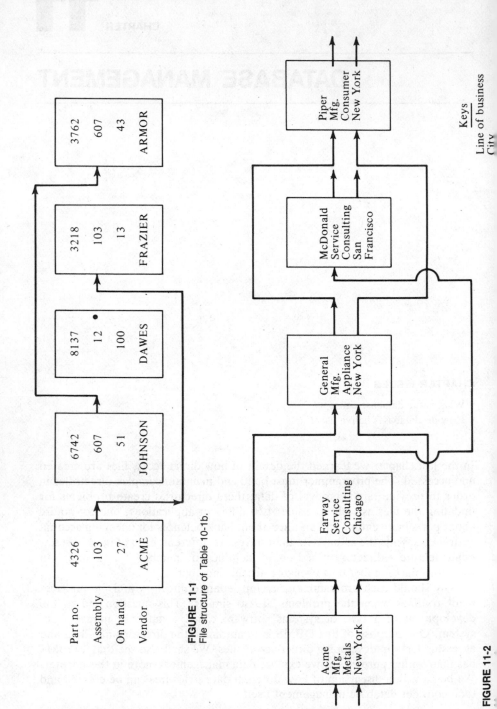

**FIGURE 11-1**
File structure of Table 10-1b.

| Part no. | 4326 | 6742 | 8137 | 3218 | 3762 |
|----------|------|------|------|------|------|
| Assembly | 103 | 607 | 12 • | 103 | 607 |
| On hand | 27 | 51 | 100 | 13 | 43 |
| Vendor | ACME | JOHNSON | DAWES | FRAZIER | ARMOR |

Keys
Line of business
City

**FIGURE 11-2**

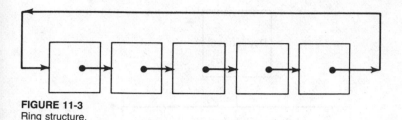

**FIGURE 11-3**
Ring structure.

## DATA STRUCTURES

Data structures are the physical and logical relationships among records in computer files. A physical data structure is simply the way data are actually found on a storage device. In a sequential file all records are located in a linear sequence; they are usually related logically according to a sequence based on some key field. On a direct-access device, the physical data structure might include some directory records at the beginning of a physical location followed by portions of the record with data.

Of more interest to the analyst are logical data structures. We can develop many different logical structures to support different types of processing applications. In fact, we have seen several logical structures earlier in the chapter but have studied these primarily from the combined view of logical and physical structuring. For example, we indicated how we would include pointers and directories in a file. A completely logical view would simply have used arrows to show the connections among different fields. In designing physical data structures, we are concerned with how to best represent the desired logical structures on physical storage devices.

We have seen a list structure earlier in Chapter 10. We can redraw that structure as shown in Figure 11-1 to emphasize the logical relationship among records. The inverted list looks almost the same from logical considerations, but the actual implementation differs since the pointers are now in the directory rather than in the actual data records. A more complex structure with two lists is shown in Figure 11-2.

A list can easily be extended to become a ring as shown in Figure 11-3. In a ring the last record in a list points back to the first record of the ring, which contains a special symbol to show that it is first. One can follow the ring to find any record, for example, the preceding record, the next record, or the first record of the ring. One can also use a ring with connections in each direction (Dodd, 1969).

Three major types of data structures are generally defined in the literature today: hierarchical, plex or network structure, and a relational file.

A hierarchical file is a case of a tree structure as shown in Figure 11-4. The tree is composed of a hierarchy of nodes: the uppermost node is called the root. With the exception of this root, every node is related to a node at a higher level called its parent. No element can have more than one parent, though it can have more than one lower-level element called children. See Martin (1977).

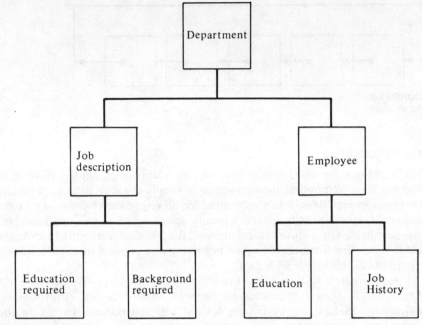

**FIGURE 11-4**
A tree or hierarchial structure.

**FIGURE 11-5**
A plex or network structure.

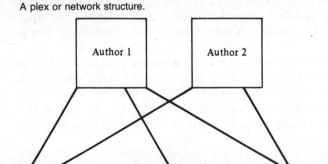

A hierarchical file is one with a tree-structure relationship between the records, for example a master detail file with two record types. Such a representation is often very convenient because much data tend to be hierarchical in nature or can easily be cast into this structure.

A network or plex structure exists when a child in a data relationship has more than one parent. An item in such a structure can be linked to any other item. (See Figure 11-5.) Martin (1977) discusses simple plex structures in which the child-to-parent mapping is simple; that is, arrows do not go in both directions. The physical data structure to support complex plex structures are far more difficult to develop than for simple structures. An examination of Figure 11-5 should show the reasons for this difficulty.

There has been much research on yet a third type of data structure called "relational." The underlying concept of a relational file system is very simple; data are organized in two-dimensional tables such as the one in Figure 11-6. Such tables are easy for a user to develop and understand. One virtue of this type of structure is that it can be described mathematically, a most difficult task for other types of data structures. The name is derived from the fact that each table represents a relation.

Since different users see different sets of data and different relationships between them, it is necessary to extract subsets of the table columns for some users and to join tables together for others to form larger tables. The mathematics provides the basis for extracting some columns from the tables and for joining various columns. This capability to manipulate relations provides a flexibility not normally available in hierarchical or plex structures.

The subject of data structures is extremely complex and a number of good references are devoted entirely to this topic. The important thing to realize is that there are many ways to represent different logical data structures. The flexibility and relatively low cost of direct-access storage make it possible to develop very complex logical data structures to support information systems. As we shall see in the next section, software exists to help implement many of these complex structures in a generalized manner.

## SYSTEMS DESIGN

It should be apparent at this point that one of the major design tasks is to determine the contents and structure of a database. The type of retrieval and reporting required by users and the availability of input determine what data have to be stored. However, it is a very complex task to specify these data, group them into records, and establish data structures for a system.

### Schema

Some of the early work on database developed the concept of an abstract schema which is the description of the logical database (we can think of this term as synonomous with "model" as used in the last section). The schema shows the

| Name | Address | Zip Code | City | Department no. |
|------|---------|----------|------|----------------|
| Smith | 16 Main | 92116 | New York | 302 |
| Jones | 37 Spencer | 07901 | Chicago | 161 |
| Morris | 19 Old Way | 83924 | New York | 302 |
| Able | 86 Fulton | 10006 | Denver | 927 |
| Charles | 19 Hunter | 11126 | Chicago | 161 |

| Name | Profession | Income |
|------|-----------|--------|
| Johnson | Bartender | 15,000 |
| Martin | Programmer | 14,000 |
| Jones | Systems Analyst | 18,000 |
| Carson | Manager | 17,000 |
| Smith | Systems Analyst | 19,000 |

| Join: | Name, | Address, | Zip Code, | Profession, | Income |
|-------|-------|----------|-----------|-------------|--------|
| | Jones | 37 Spencer, | 07901, | Systems Analyst, | 18,000 |

| Project: | City, | Department |
|----------|-------|------------|
| | New York | 302 |
| | Chicago | 161 |
| | Denver | 927 |

**FIGURE 11-6**
A relational database.

types of data and relationships among them. In database terminology, the data that are of interest are often called entities, such as student, class, major, as shown in Figure 11-7. Entities also have attributes, a student has an identification number, age, sex, and date of birth.

In this representation, we group entities into sets. In Figure 11-7 there is a set of advisors, students, majors, biographies, and classes. The sets are joined together by relationships. In the figure, an advisor is related to students by the relationship advise. This is an example of a one to n relationship; a single advisor advises n students, but each student has only one advisor. A student has one biography and there is one biography per student giving a 1 to 1 relationship. On the other hand, n students can be enrolled in m classes. Finally, n students each have one major.

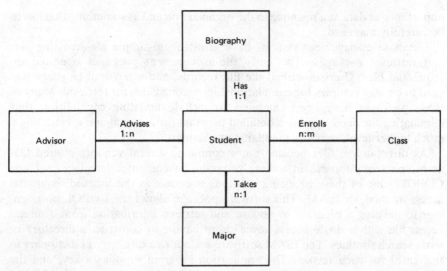

**FIGURE 11-7**
A schema.

The schema in Figure 11-7 presents an entire, simple database. However, there can be subschemas as viewed by different individuals. A professor might only care about a class list, not the major or advisor of a student. The department chairperson wants to know something about majors in the department.

Sometimes these differences are called logical views of the data. It is very likely that different users will have different logical views of data; a key task of design is to integrate these different views and create a physical database that is capable of supporting different logical views with adequate performance.

## Database Administrator

Many organizations using database software described in the next section have created a new position known as the database administrator (DBA); this individual has the responsibility for working with systems analysts and programmers to define the physical and logical views of the data to be manipulated by computers.

## DATABASE MANAGEMENT SYSTEMS

The objective of a database management system is to facilitate the creation of data structures and relieve the programmer of the problems of setting up complicated files. Database management systems have developed from a concept of the database as something distinct from the programs accessing it. In addition to easing processing, this approach has tended to highlight the importance of data as a resource in the organization and as something that has to be carefully managed.

Database management systems have grown from simple file-accessing aids and retrieval packages. The early file-management packages operated on sequential files. Users described the file records, and a retrieval language was used to express complex logical relationships among fields for retrieval. Many of these packages have been extended to include updating capabilities, thus eliminating the need to write a detailed program for retrieval and substituting a much higher-level, user-oriented language instead.

As direct-access files became more common, several vendors offered file-access packages for use in writing programs in computer languages such as COBOL. One of these accessing methods is known as the indexed sequential access method, or ISAM. This software package allows the COBOL programmer to develop a program to update and retrieve information from a direct-access file with a single access key without having to construct a directory or write search routines. The ISAM software maintains a directory (a dictionary in this case) for each record. The application program supplies a key, and the system retrieves the record. The current version of this package is called VSAM and it represents a major improvement in the system.

The software maintains overflow areas and pointers to keep the file in order sequentially. Thus, updating can be done sequentially, and retrieval can be accomplished on a direct-access basis. This type of file has been very popular because it is possible to update in batch but inquire on-line. As a file gets out of order and the overflow areas are filled, it is periodically necessary to restructure the file. Statistics are provided by the software as to when this updating is advisable. Simple access methods such as this and file-management packages have evolved into much more complex database management systems.

## Complete Database Systems

A complete database management system separates the definition of data from the programs that access it. This concept of data independence is one of the key advantages of a database management system. When programs own all the data they process, then it is quite common to have the same entity represented by different program variables in each separate program. As a result, each application stands alone and it is very difficult to answer inquiries across several applications.

The lack of data independence from traditional approaches to programming also creates a significant maintenance problem. As programs are changed to reflect changing conditions or requests from users, all the programs in a system that access the file have to be altered. At a minimum the record descriptions in the programs will have to be changed; it also may be necessary to make modifications in the programs themselves to process added data.

With a database management system (DBMS), only programs that access the actual fields altered are affected in general by a change. Programs that do not use the fields that have been altered do not usually have to be changed. As a result, we have gained some independence between the data and the programs which access those data. This kind of data independence is the essence of the database concept. Combined with the ease of access to data, data independence and other features of database management systems discussed below, we have DBMS software available which can dramatically ease the tasks of developing a computer application and maintaining it after its completion.

## Components of a DBMS

Originally the DBMS was used to refer to two very specific functions in creating a database environment. At the core of such a system is a data definition language for describing data structures and the programs that are used to build, update, and retrieve data from the database. The trend is for vendors of database management systems to create integrated tools for building and operating databases. Figure 11-8 is an overview of an integrated data dictionary, database environment. The data dictionary is used to store and define definitions of data including identifiers, location, format for storage, and other characteristics. The data dictionary can be used to retrieve the definition of data that has already been used in an application so that standards for naming can be enforced across applications (See Allen et al., 1982). Depending on the specific system, the database administrator might also store some of the description of the data structures in the dictionary, for example, entities, attributes, and relationships.

**FIGURE 11-8**
Overview of Database Management System.

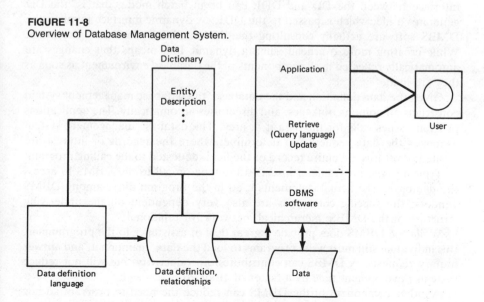

The data dictionary must have software to update itself, produce reports on its contents, and answer queries. A complete system will also tie into the data definition component of the DBMS.

The database administrator, or programmers, must use a special data-definition language with the database management system to describe the data and file structures to the system. Martin (1977) has described some of the characteristics a good data-definition language should have, which of course implies what characteristics a good database management system should include.

The language must identify various subdivisions of data, for example, items, segments, records, and files. There should be unique names for each data-item type, record type, file type, database, etc. The language should specify how data items are grouped in aggregates, records, or other subdivisions and show repeating groups of items. The language must make it possible to designate data items as keys. It is also necessary to specify how various subdivision or record types are related to make different logical structures, and it should be possible to give names to relationships among data groupings. Martin also describes additional capabilities that the language may possess, including the specification of privacy locks to prevent unauthorized reading or modifications. He also argues that the language should be concerned only with logical data description and specific addressing, indexing, or searching techniques, or the placement of data on physical storage. These topics belong to the physical definition of the files, not the logical definition.

An integrated data dictionary (DD) at the least generates a file for the data definition language which it uses to generate the schema for the DBMS. Such an interface between the DD and DDL can be in batch mode, that is, the DD generates a file, which is passed to the DDL. A dynamic interface involves the DMBS software actually consulting the DDL and DD during its execution. While creating more overhead, such a dynamic link means that changes are automatically reflected in all components of the database environment as soon as they are made.

Given the data definition and the database, the database management system constructs all pointers, linkages, and directories automatically. The applications program issues calls for the data it desires. The database management system examines the data request and determines where the records of interest are located; it returns the entire record or the field requested to the calling program.

Typically, the programmer inserts some type of call to the DBMS to access the database. The actual statements used in the program differ among DBMS vendors; the specific commands are also very dependent on the underlying structure of the DMBS: hierarchical, network, or relational.

While the DBMS does provide a great deal of assistance to the programmer, this individual still must write programs to load the data, maintain it, and answer inquiry requests. A DMBS can contribute to productivity, but will not reduce systems development time by a factor of 10 or 20.

Another component of the DBMS can reduce the need to program ad hoc

**MICROS IN A CHEMICAL PLANT**

*The Resins division of Georgia-Pacific uses a database management system and a spreadsheet package on a microcomputer to analyze quality control data. The quality control data is stored on the database management system in a plant in Painesville, Ohio.*

*The data is transmitted to a research and development center in Decatur, Georgia and to the marketing group at headquarters in Atlanta. These locations perform analyses of the data using a spreadsheet package.*

*It took about ten weeks to write the 6,000 lines of code in the database management system and set up the rather large spreadsheet. In addition, time was required to write a manual and establish telecommunications procedures. The developers estimated that it would have taken them three or four times as long to do the job on a mainframe.*

*The company has trained over 70 users in the spreadsheet package. There are other interesting applications. Chemists in one plant store the recipes for various types of plastics produced at the plant in a spreadsheet. The calculating power of the spreadsheet package is used to figure what raw ingredients have to be purchased to support production. Other managers track production targets and compare them with goals using the spreadsheet package.*

*This example illustrates the creative applications users have found for microcomputers and their powerful software packages.*

*PC Week, September 18, 1984.*

---

retrievals: the query language. The user of this language must have some knowledge of the underlying database structure (the applications programmer can conceal this structure through menus and other approaches to retrieval programs that are written as a part of an application). The query language makes it possible to formulate requests for data without the need for a program to be written. For example, a retrieval language might allow us to say:

SELECT FROM student WHERE age GT 19

Using the schema of Figure 11-7, the lowercase words above represent entities, sets, and attributes. SELECT FROM, WHERE, and GT are a part of the query language; "student" is the name of a set and "age" must be an attribute of records in the student set. The value of age is used to determine what records to retrieve, in this case records of students whose age is Greater Than 19.

**In Conclusion**

With a DBMS, it is possible to design file structures much more easily and to set up a database that can be used by a number of different applications programs. As a result the systems increase programmer productivity. These systems also

## MANAGEMENT PROBLEM 11-1

Marvin Thompson is president of Midwestern Bank and Trust. He has just returned from a bankers' convention at which the major topic was database systems. Midwestern has been studying the problem of central files for several years. The idea of a central file is to consolidate all the information about a customer of the bank. Currently, one system maintains data on loans to commercial customers, another one keeps track of demand deposits, a third keeps track of savings and certificates of deposit, and so forth.

The major advantage of central files is that they allow better service. The bank knows the total business picture of any given customer. However, as with any new system, there are disadvantages. Several representatives at the convention indicated that database management systems were not a panacea for computer problems. Because so much data were resident on expensive direct-access storage, costs were very high for central files.

Marvin wondered what major factors to consider in deciding whether or not Midwestern should move toward a central file system. If the file system is to be developed, should the bank program its own database routines or acquire a commercial database management package? What factors should it consider? Can you help Marvin structure the bank's decision problem?

---

try to avoid data redundancy; the same data are not maintained by a number of different systems, each having different files.

It can be very difficult to learn to use and install database management systems. As one can imagine, they are very complex programs and they tend to be inefficient in computer time and costly in storage. However, the importance of these costs is being reduced by the need for greater programming productivity. Machine costs are getting cheaper while human costs are getting higher.

Many organizations have achieved impressive results using database management systems. However, it is necessary to study and evaluate the systems carefully. If you do not need the most complex system, do not acquire it. Clearly, the future trend is to use database management packages to save programmer, analyst, and implementation time. There is also an insatiable demand for on-line data access by users. Currently, there are few standards and there are wide differences among the packages. It is best to look at present and planned applications and then use references supplied by the package vendor to talk with other users. Try to determine the good and bad points of each package under consideration.

### Two Examples

**A Network**   The different database management systems offer a variety of file structures, though the same file problem can usually be solved with the structure of each system. One database management system features two kinds of files, a master and a variable file. The master is accessed on some key and

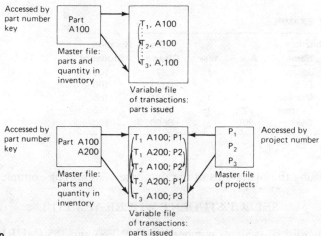

**FIGURE 11-9**
A network database example.

linked to the variable file. Within the variable file, associations among entries are linked by pointers.

Figure 11-9 shows examples of different logical file structures represented with this plex scheme. At the top of the figure we see a master file of inventory parts and their quantities in stock. This master file is linked to a variable file containing a history of usage of each part issued from the inventory.

A master file can have multiple variable files in this system. In the example of Figure 11-9, we can add another variable file to keep track of receipts of each part. It is also possible to have two master files accessing a single transaction file as shown in the bottom half of Figure 11-9. The parts and inventory master file is the same as the example in the top half of the figure. The second master file, a list of projects, is linked to all transactions that took place for a particular project. There would be two types of linkage in the variable file—one for transactions for the same part, and the other for transactions for the same project. This same logical structure could be represented by database management systems using other forms such as a hierarchical tree structure.

One major advantage is that database management systems set up all the directories and pointers automatically. The user specifies only the logical structure of the files; much of the complex programming for direct-access retrieval and updating is thus eliminated by the database management system.

**A Relational System** The system described in this section has been developed for a microcomputer and is based on the relational data model. Table 11-1 shows two relations that could be defined using this system: STUDENT and CLASS.

To begin the development of the database, the user would use the DEFINE command to describe each relation. The system helps the user define an input format on the computer's display device to enter data for each relation.

Once the data shown in Table 11-1 have been entered, the user can ask

**TABLE 11-1**
RELATIONAL EXAMPLE

| Student Relation | | | | Class Relation | |
|---|---|---|---|---|---|
| Student# | Name | Age | Year | Class# | Student# |
| 100 | Jones | 19 | 1 | B371 | 100 |
| 150 | Smith | 21 | 4 | B371 | 160 |
| 155 | Murray | 18 | 1 | B371 | 165 |
| 160 | Berman | 22 | 4 | B400 | 150 |
| 165 | Doe | 20 | 3 | B600 | 160 |

questions using the operations of the database system. For example, we could type:

SELECT STUDENT WHERE Year EQ 1

And obtain a list of students number 100 (JONES) and 155 (MURRAY).

To obtain a class list we could perform a join operation:

JOIN STUDENT CLASS MATCHING Student #

This operation would produce a new relation containing the columns (nonredundant) of the student and class relations. Student number 160 would appear in two places in the new relation, once for class B371 and once for class B600. We could print the results as a class list or just select one class and print the students enrolled in it.

## MANAGEMENT PROBLEM 11-2

Marlyn Atkins is Vice President of Human Resources for Multinational Manufacturing, Inc (MM). Her firm employs nearly 100,000 people around the world. Filling vacancies when they arise is a constant problem; preference is given to existing employees. However, it is very difficult to know that an existing employee may have the skills needed for an opening so that they can be notified to apply.

Marlyn talked to representatives of the MM computer staff and they indicated that a new, relational database management system they had acquired might help her. Currently there is a personnel system that is updated in batch mode once each month. It contains data on the employee including header records with name, education, skill, salary, and similar data. Trailer records reflect job history; the positions the employee has held in the firm.

The new database system extracts data from sequential files like the ones used in the personnel system and then builds relations which are available for inquiry through a query language that is part of the package.

Can you help Marlyn define relations and formulate a few sample inquiries to extract the kind of information she needs from the existing personnel system using the new database manager?

## CRIMINAL DATABASES

*There is a significant number of large databases containing information about stolen vehicles and criminal records. The Massachusetts system is a good example since it has upgraded its services. The Criminal Justice Information System consists of a large mainframe computer with 31 trunk lines each of which serves up to 12 agencies. The agencies are about 300 municipal police departments and other law enforcement agencies in the state. The system connects to the National Crime Information Center in Washington, the state's Registry of Motor Vehicles and the National Law Enforcement Telecommunications Systems in Phoenix.*

*Local police officers make inquiries of the system, for example, whether a person is wanted on criminal charges, whether a car has been reported stolen and whether the driver has a valid license. The system now offers 30 second or less response where in the past an answer might have taken 20 minutes. The system is available 99.6% of it scheduled up time.*

*The local police dispatcher keys a request into a terminal and the system routes the message to the appropriate agencies. The system can be used by the officer to alert up to 26,000 agencies about a wanted criminal; each of these agencies is connected to its own states' information system.*

*Computerworld,* July 16, 1984.

## CHOOSING A MODEL

The choice of a particular database management system is a complicated one. We should ask if the system is easy to use, understand, manipulate, and implement. Just as with any other package, the computer department will be interested in the quality of the computer code in the system and with its documentation.

There are advocates of all three major data models: hierarchical, network, and relational. Academically, the choice is relational because of the many features it offers. Relational data models can be analyzed formally which gives them a strong foundation and some degree of standardization across implementations.

Relational models are also favored because the retrieval and data manipulation languages tend to be easy to understand and use. Also, relational systems tend to appear simple to the user, making retrieval and manipulation easier. Thinking of data in the form of tables is conceptually more simple than complex hierarchical or plex relations.

## SUMMARY

In this chapter we have discussed data structures and database management. The simple techniques in the last chapter of using pointers and directories can be applied to the creation of quite elegant data structures. To encourage data independence and to ease accessing requirements, the industry is moving to database management systems. An integrated DBMS features a data dictionary, data definition language, database management routines themselves, and a query language. The definition of the database is one of the most important activities in the technical component of systems analysis and design; database management systems can help accomplish this task and greatly expand the power of the computer.

## KEYWORDS

| | | |
|---|---|---|
| Attribute | Entity | Query language |
| Database administrator | Hierarchical | Relation |
| Database management system | Key | Relational |
| Data definition language | List | Ring |
| Data dictionary | Logical view | Schema |
| Data independence | Network | Tree |
| Data structures | Plex | VSAM |

## RECOMMENDED READINGS

Allen, F. W., M. E. S. Loomis, M. V. Mannino: "The Integrated Dictionary/Directory System," *Computing Surveys*, vol. 14, no. 2, June 1982, pp. 245–286. (A good article on dictionaries and their role in design.)

Hawryszkiewycz, I. T.: *Database Analysis and Design*, SRA, Chicago, 1984. (A good, advanced text on database, very thorough.)

Martin, J.: *Computer Data-Base Organization*, 2 ed., Prentice-Hall, Englewood Cliffs, N.J., 1977. (A classic text.)

Tsichritzis, D., and F. Lochovsky: *Data Models*, Prentice-Hall, Englewood Cliffs, N.J., 1982. (Advanced data structures.)

## DISCUSSION QUESTIONS

1 Why do users have different logical views of their data requirements?
2 Which model, hierarchy, network, or relational do you think offers the most flexibility? Which would be easiest to explain to a user?
3 Explain the concept of data independence. Can programs and data ever be totally independent?
4 What advantages does a query language provide for the computer staff? What disadvantages for users?
5 Why do most organizations use a DBMS for specific applications rather than attempt to define a comprehensive database for all applications?
6 How does a DBMS make it easier to alter the structure of a database?
7 Does a DBMS completely isolate the user from the underlying structure of the data?
8 Why does it make sense to use a data dictionary and enforce common naming standards for data items in an organization?
9 Is a DBMS only useful for applications that run on-line as opposed to batch processing?

10  What complications are added to a database management system when distributed processing is involved?

11  What kind of security and controls are needed in a DMBS?

12  In an on-line environment, a common problem is to lock out access to a record while it is being updated. Why do you think this is necessary? What scheme can be used to lock the record?

13  Recovery from a computer failure or other interruption of a system is a major consideration for organizations. What problems do you see in recovering from such a failure when using a database management system?

14  How should one back up a database used for on-line processing?

15  How can accessing data in relational tables be speeded over a straight sequential search?

16  What evaluation criteria would you recommend be applied to a decision of what database management system to acquire?

17  Why is there a need for a database administrator in an organization using a DBMS?

18  How can the systems analyst use the facilities of a DBMS during the design process for a new system?

19  To what extent is performance (in terms of speed of access) a major consideration in database design.

20  In the schema of Figure 11-6, how would an advisor query the system to determine the major for a given student? How would the query language access the database?

21  Under what conditions is it better to program a retrieval option into a system as opposed to providing a user with a general purpose query language?

22  Are there any conditions under which it would be desirable to duplicate data in a database? If so, what are they?

23  Think of an application like student registration and design a relational database for the registrar. Then, using the same data, design the system as a hierarchical database. What are the major differences?

24  Under what conditions might an organization want to have more than one vendor's DBMS? What problems do you forsee if there are multiple database systems?

25  In the last chapter we discussed hash coding; do you see an application for hash coding in the design of a database using a DBMS?

26  There has been discussion in the literature of a special computer that would operate as a database "backend." That is, the computer would handle only operations relating to the database and would interact with a central computer. What advantages do you see for such an approach?

27  What major trends in the field make database management systems feasible?

28  What does a DBMS mean for users of systems?

29  Does a DBMS from a particular vendor mean that the organization is tied to that vendor for the forseeable future?

30  For any of the file problems in the last chapter, describe how your design would be different using a database management system.

## CHAPTER 12

# COMMUNICATIONS

## CHAPTER ISSUES

- How and why do computers communicate?
- How do communications influence information processing?

Early computers processed data in batches with intervals of days or months between runs. Devices were soon developed to transmit punched cards from one location to another over phone lines, marking the beginning of the communication of data through an existing telecommunications network. The operation took place off line; the computers involved were not directly connected to the phone lines. In addition to card punches that could send and receive, there were devices to send the contents of magnetic tapes from one location to another.

In the early 1960s the first on-line systems were developed; these computers used for airline reservations served many terminals connected through various types of communications lines. (A few years earlier the first such on-line systems had been developed for defense applications.) At about the same time, terminals were attached to computers which were used for time sharing. The major difference between on-line and time-sharing systems is that the former are dedicated to a single application. For example, an airline reservations agent can only make a reservation or inquire about the status of various flights; the agent cannot write a program from the terminal. With time sharing, the user of the terminal does usually have the ability to write programs.

The use of on-line systems has expanded rapidly; today a large proportion of new systems have some portion that is on-line such as data entry, update, and/or inquiry. At the same time, there has been an expansion in the number of alternatives available for establishing communications among computer devices. One has a choice from dial-up phone service to private networks using satellites for transmission.

In this chapter we cover the fundamentals of data communications. To develop a major communications network, specialists are required due to the complexity of the problem and the large number of alternatives. However, it behooves the user to have a basic knowledge of data communications given its importance.

## BASICS

Figure 12-1 is a high-level diagram of data communications between two computer devices; we shall expand this basic schematic further. The most familiar type of communications is probably the case in which device 1 is a terminal and device 2 is a computer of some type. The transmission line may be nothing more complex than a pair of twisted wires from the terminal to a central computer that offers time-sharing services.

### Codes

The data sent over the line is represented as some type of code, that is, the sending and receiving ends of the communications lines have to agree on how to represent symbols like the letter "a", "b", "c", etc. For telex data the Baudot code is the most common; it uses five bits for each letter. (A bit is a 0 or a 1.) The number of symbols that can be represented in binary by a code is 2 raised to the power of the number of bits, eg $2^5=32$, a fairly small number of symbols when one considers the length of the alphabet!

The most frequent code for interchanging data is called ASCII (American Standard Code for Information Interchange) which is an 7 bit code (there is an eighth bit for error checking) and thus has 128 symbols. A code used with earlier computers was BCD (Binary Coded Decimal) which is a 6 bit code. Finally, there is a code that is primarily used by one manufacturer of computers known as EBCDIC (Extended Binary Coded Decimal Interchange Code), which is an 8 bit code.

All codes, then, use sequences of 0's and 1's to represent different symbols; as an example the ASCII code for H is 1001000. On the sending end, an H is translated into 1001000 for transmission, and on the receiving end the string of

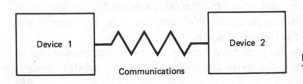

Device 1

Communications

Device 2

**FIGURE 12-1**
Telecommunications.

bits is translated back into an H. (It should be noted that computers are designed to represent data in memory in coded form. However, there is no necessary relationship between the internal coding and the codes used for transmission between computers.)

Codes often feature extra bits or characters which are used to control transmission and to detect errors. A simple transmissions scheme which sends one letter at a time might include a start and a stop bit to delimit the beginning and the end of the character for the receiving station. A basic error detection scheme is parity checking; the sending device checks to see that there is say an odd number of bits in each character; if there is an even number, the sending station makes the parity bit a 1 thus creating an odd number. Under this odd parity scheme, the receiving device also counts the bits; if there is an even number, then at least one bit has been lost in transmission. The parity scheme is rather simple; there are far more elaborate error detecting and even error correcting codes available.

### Transmission Modes

There are a number of options for transmitting data over communications lines; the most frequently used approaches are:

*Character Mode.* Data are transmitted as single characters as they are typed on a terminal. This technique is very simple and does not require complicated hardware or software.

*Block Mode.* In block mode, data are placed in a hardware memory on the sending device temporarily; the block is surrounded by appropriate characters for start and end of transmission. The data are then transmitted as a single block usually with some type of error checking sequence at the end of the block to detect errors. If there are errors, then the two nodes arrange for a retransmission of the data.

*Asynchronous Mode.* Asynchronous transmission is associated with character mode operations since the characters are sent when entered. A single bit is added to the front of each character and one or more bits at the end. These extra bits alert the receiving device to the existence of the character and delimit it.

*Synchronous Mode.* Block transmission features blocks that are of equal length and one follows another. There is no need for start and stop bits which are associated with each character in asynchronous transmission; considerable overhead is saved using block mode. The beginning of each block is identified and the sending and receiving devices must be synchronized.

### Direction

There are several ways to send data over lines. In simplex transmission the data are sent in one direction only, but this approach is rare. Using half duplex transmission, data travels in two directions, but not at the same time. Full duplex

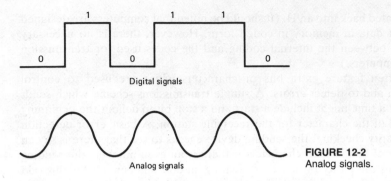

Digital signals

Analog signals

**FIGURE 12-2**
Analog signals.

is the most convenient for interactive communications; here the data are transmitted simultaneously in both directions. Note that this approach will require two lines in general since the same data path cannot carry signals in two directions at the same time.

## Signal Representation

There are two basic ways to represent signals: in analog or digital form. These signals are shown in Figure 12-2; analog signals are used because the first data transmission took place over voice telephone lines which were originally developed to carry analog signals. Since computer devices communicate in digital form, the digital signal must be placed onto an analog signal for transmission and then changed to digits at the receiving end. A modem in Figure 12-3 places the digital code on an analog signal.

Figure 12-4 shows one approach to this modulation task. In the figure we see encoding done using amplitude modulation. The analog signal is continuous and has the form of a sine wave. By using different amplitudes to represent a 0 and a 1, the digital data can be encoded for transmission over analog lines. The device that actually accomplishes this modulation is called a modem. It is possible to modulate a signal using the amplitude of the sine wave as described above, varying the frequency of the wave or changing the phase of the sine wave to encode a 0 or 1.

Due to the explosion in data transmission that has occurred over the last two decades, the phone company and private communications carriers have devel-

**FIGURE 12-3**
Modulation and demodulation.

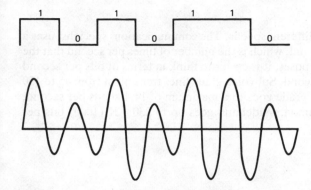

**FIGURE 12-4**
Amplitude modulation.

oped digital transmission networks. Here there is no need for a modem; the only requirement is some kind of a line interface device to connect the sending or receiving unit with the transmission line. It is also possible to send analog signals (such as voice communications) over digital lines using pulse code modulation (PCM). The analog signal is sampled at a high rate, say 8000 times per second, and converted into discrete levels for transmission. A modulator at the receiving end then reconstructs the analog signal that was transmitted.

---

### LINKING ELECTRONICS STORES

*Tandy Corporation operates some 5,500 retail stores and has 3,000 more dealer franchise outlets. The firm has sales of $2 billion per year. Retail stores and dealer sites are served from six regional warehouses.*

*Before a new computer system, order entry, inventory control and warehouse distribution were handled with a combination of batch and manual procedures. Using printed order forms completed by hand at the stores was slow, particularly since the forms were mailed to the warehouse. Once at the warehouse, staff keyed data on the orders and transmitted it to corporate headquarters. The next morning the warehouse received a printout of the invoices.*

*A new system uses a microcomputer in the store to assist management with information on what to order, how much and when to place the order to maintain optimum inventory levels. The store transmits the order to the corporate data center directly. With communications on line, the system is much more responsive than in the past.*

*The Fort Worth warehouse alone distributes 800 shipments daily with some 120,000 lines to be pulled from stock and shipped in 6,000 cartons. Combined regional value totals some 2,100 shipments of 65,000 lines in 28,000 cartons. Data describing 50 million lines and 500,000 shipments flow through the network annually.*

*Computerworld,* February 27, 1984.

---

## Speed

Transmission can occur at different speeds. The communications specialist uses a measure of speed called a baud, which is the number of times per second that the signal changes. For our purposes, it is easier to think in terms of bits per second or characters (bytes) per second. Subvoice grade lines transmit at from 45 to 150 bits per second while voice grade goes to a maximum of 14,400 bits per second, with 9600 being fairly common. Wideband goes up to 230.4 K (1000) bits per second.

## Protocols

Transmission involves protocols, which are sets of rules and procedures to control the flow of data between points. Both the sending and receiving stations need to follow the same procedures; for example, if blocks are being sent, then both stations must agree that the transmission is to be in block mode. A protocol can also increase the efficiency of transmission by reducing the amount of data that has to be sent for control purposes.

We must control:

1 Setting up a session
2 Establishing a path from node 1 to n
3 Linking the devices together
4 The hardware sending and interpreting the data

Protocols are also used to handle:

1 Detection and correction of errors
2 Formatting
3 Line control
4 Message sequencing

The International Standards Organization (ISO) has suggested a layered architecture to facilitate communications among different types of equipment. The seven logical layers are:

1 Application
2 Presentation
3 Session
4 Transport
5 Network
6 Data link
7 Physical

The highest levels should remain similar across equipment while lower levels become more dependent on the devices and manufacturers involved.

## Summary

A device sends out a code, for example ASCII letters to some type of interface which sends the message over a transmission line. For analog transmission the interface is a modem which one can use to transmit characters or blocks of data. At the receiving end, the interface unit must reconvert the code into the appropriate code for processing the transmitted data. See Figure 12-5.

## TRANSMISSION NETWORKS

### General Networks

A network connects a variety of terminals and computers together. The public, switched network is the same network used for carrying most voice traffic in the world. Here, one simply dials a number and establishes a point to point connection only when it is needed. In addition to telephone and telex, there are special private network services also providing switched connections.

Moving from the switched network, one might find a simple connection between a computer and a terminal using twisted wire pairs running directly between the two devices. One can generally directly wire for a mile or two before the loss of signal (attenuation) becomes too great and modems are needed.

A line that is used intermittently can be shared by more than one terminal. With a multidrop line the terminals each send and receive messages over the same line; a terminal identification must also be sent with the data.

Another way to reduce line costs is to have several terminals connected to a device called a multiplexer. The multiplexer combines the signals from various low-speed terminals and sends them over a higher speed line. In time division multiplexing the device samples separate incoming signals and combines them on the output line. At the receiving end the signals must be demultiplexed. With a multiplexer the speed of the output line must equal the sum of the input line speeds.

A concentrator is a hardware device that collects messages from terminals and stores them if necessary. The concentrator sends the messages over a higher speed line to the computer. However, unlike the multiplexer it can temporarily

**FIGURE 12-5**
Some communications options.

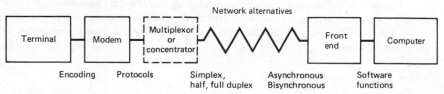

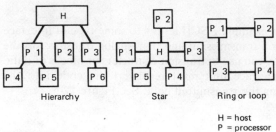

H = host
P = processor

**FIGURE 12-6**
Examples of computer-to-computer connections.

store the data so that the capacity of the high-speed line does not have to equal the sum of the capacities of the low-speed lines.

## Network Configurations

Given the various communications options, one can configure a network of computers and terminal devices in any number of ways. Figure 12-6 presents some popular options. In a hierarchical scheme, one computer controls a series

---

### 3M's NETWORK

*Minnesota Mining and Manufacturing, 3M, is the 44th largest U.S. industrial corporation with sales of $6.6 billion and 87,000 employees world-wide. The company has a long range plan to create a unified world-wide computer network.*

*There are four types of systems to be included. First there are four large mainframes which serve the highly centralized portion of the firm, some 12,000 employees in St. Paul and 10,000 others in the state.*

*The company has a few end user tools on the mainframes including SAS, a statistical analysis and graphing package. They also use Mark VI as a report generator.*

*3M also has a distributed system which consists of more than 90 minicomputers located in plants and branches nation-wide. The minis handle local processing and communicate with mainframes at headquarters. Yet another vendor's superminis, eleven in total, provide an in-house time-sharing service.*

*The company also is installing a growing number of personal computers; the information services department will support micros from three specified vendors. This company, then, illustrates the full range of computing services available today: mainframes for high volume transactions processing and large databases, distributed computers for smaller, local installations, systems devoted to time-sharing and finally a growing inventory of personal computers.*

*EDP Analyzer, October, 1983.*

of subordinate computers; an example of this approach might be a central computer controlling local grocery store computers which, in turn, control point-of-sale terminals at check out stands. The star is similar, but here a single host or central computer can communicate with each remote processor. The local computers communicate with each other through the central system.

In a ring or loop all processors can communicate with their immediate neighbors. This pattern can be extended to allow communications from any processor to any other processor. One major problem in connecting computers is the fact that they must all be able to accept data transmitted from other computers and send data to them. In theory this problem is trivial, but in practice it can be difficult to achieve satisfactory connections.

There are a large number of alternatives available in configuring a computer network and we shall need the help of a communications specialist in many situations.

## Local Area Networks

The local area network (LAN) is an important topic today; it is an approach to connecting various devices that need to communicate with each other and which are grouped closely together such as in a single building. The devices are not necessarily all computers or terminals; they may include copying machines, communicating word processors, and similar devices.

One possible scenario for the computer configuration of the coming decades is a network of various devices consisting of a number of mainframe, mini-, and microcomputers. Key to tying these diverse machines together is one or more local nets.

The usual structure of a local area network is a ring, a device that communicates with its immediate neighbors only. Another possibility is a bus in which all devices are connected to a single pathway. With either of these configurations, it is not necessary to have a central computer in charge. The LAN must, however, be able to handle the problem of more than one station trying to send data at the same time.

One solution to the contention problem is called carrier sense-multiple access with collision detection (CSMA/CD). The transmitting station sees if a channel is clear by listening for a carrier signal. If the net is busy, the station waits until it is clear and then sends a message while listening for collisions with other stations that might have started to send at the same time. If a collision is detected, the station stops sending and waits a random time interval before starting to send again.

Another alternative scheme is to use a token which is passed along the network from node to node. A station with the token can transmit; this approach is more complicated than CSMA/CD to implement, but it reduces the collision problem.

An alternative to the local network is the private branch exchange (PBX). Originally these exchanges were developed for voice communication only, for

---

**THE SEARS NETWORK**

*Sears, Roebuck & Co. plans to integrate the separate private-line data communications networks operated by its five business groups. The large network will integrate voice and data on some links.*

*The five current divisions include the merchandise group, retail and catalog sales, Allstate Insurance, Dean Witter Reynold (stock brokerage), Coldwell Banker (real estate) and Sears World Trade (international sales). The anticipated budget as five separate networks is $300 million. The purpose of the consolidation is to remove overlapping coverage, for example, in a city with one or more Sears stores, more than one Allstate office and several Dean Witter offices.*

*Between Chicago and Los Angeles the aggregate voice and data traffic require something called a T1 digital link which has a capacity of 1.54 million bits/second. This link will be subdivided into four 56K bit/sec channels with multiplexers for data. Between Seattle and Los Angeles, lower traffic demands only two 56K bit/sec digital circuits and these links will be used only for data. Local multipoint circuits will connect to the network in various cities. These links will be standard 9.6K bit/sec leased lines. The lowest level of support will be 4.8K bit/sec dial-up lines.*

*Sears is a good example of how important and costly communications has become to a modern company.*

*Computerworld*, Nov. 12, 1984.

---

example as the switchboard of a firm or university. Recognizing that most buildings already have phone lines installed, manufacturers of PBXs have developed units that handle both voice and data. The new PBXs feature digital transmission so that modems are not needed for data. Some units digitize voice at the PBX while newer systems digitize voice at the telephone instrument so that the entire operation is digital. It is possible with these devices to avoid some of the expense of cabling, though cabling may be used to connect units with a high volume of traffic between them.

We expect that many new buildings will be constructed with cables for local area networks. Other sites will make use of PBXs that can carry both voice and data, and which of these technologies will dominate is not yet certain.

### TRANSMISSION SOURCES

There is a large number of sources for communications services. We have discussed the public, switched network in which phone lines on the local level connect with AT&T Long Lines. We can also pay to lease a line or pay by the time the line is in use. The actual communications path may be through land lines, microwave communications, satellites, or some combination of the three.

Several firms offer packet switching networks. These companies lease existing lines and enhance their value (added value carriers). The customer sends a

---

**MANAGEMENT PROBLEM 12-1**

Global Manufacturing Company is considering a new computer application. The company wants to process orders in a central location, and then assign production to different plants. Each plant will operate its own production scheduling and control system; data on work in process and completed assemblies will be transmitted back to the central location that processes orders.

Global has minicomputers at each of the plants now which do routine applications like payroll and accounting. The production scheduling and control systems will be a package program running on a new computer dedicated to this application. Global has a high-level systems design for data transmission from the central computer to the plants and for the plant data to be transmitted back to central planning.

The systems staff at Global has retained you as a consultant to help them with further analysis. What kind of computer configuration seems most appropriate? What kind of transmission network do they need? What data should they collect? Prepare a plan showing the information Global must develop in order to plan this telecommunications system.

---

packet of information from a source to a destination and is likely to be charged by the number of packets rather than the distance traveled. Such a charging scheme is different from conventional charges which are usually based on time and distance.

At least ten firms offer transmission facilities. In addition, one large, high volume, transactions-oriented bank developed its own private communications network featuring a satellite transponder leased from a provider of satellite channels.

**SOFTWARE**

At some point the network must be controlled through a combination of . software and hardware logic. There are several choices as to where this logic is located:

1 Intelligent terminals
2 Concentrators
3 Front end processors
4 Computers (hosts)

Software must be used to control:

1 Network
2 Traffic flow
3 Speed conversion
4 Code conversion (e.g. terminal to internal computer code)

5 Error detection and correction
6 Formatting
7 Terminal polling

See Loomis (1983). Various equipment manufacturers provide different software packages for these purposes.

All these options must be considered by the network designer. It is important for the systems analyst to work with the communications specialist to determine where various functions are to be performed. We may want to have some data editing done at the terminal or store screen formats there to reduce the load on the host CPU and improve response times. The options available for communications networks contribute a great deal of flexibility to the systems design task.

## MICRO TO MAINFRAME LINKS

One of the most important communications issues today involves the desire of users to link their microcomputers with mainframes. The mainframe has a tremendous amount of company data; users want to extract information from this database, move it to their personal computers, and process it further with packages like spreadsheet programs.

The physical connection of the personal computer to the mainframe can be standardized. At the simplist level, the user can establish a dial-up phone connection or the microcomputer can be directly wired to a port on the mainframe. In fact, one vendor offers a version of its most popular CRT terminal with a personal computer in it as well. One can have a window addressed to personal computing and up to six windows with different tasks running in them on the mainframe. It is also possible to use a local area network to tie micros to shared peripherals like a single, hard disk drive or printer.

However, the physical communications link is only half the task. Once we have access to the mainframe, how do we extract the data needed for further processing? The information we want is likely to be stored in some kind of computer file. If it is a sequential file, then it will probably not be possible to connect to the mainframe and retrieve data any time it is convenient. A programmer who has knowledge of the mainframe application that creates the file will have to extract the data with a program.

Even if the data are on direct access files in a database management system, it still is necessary for the microcomputer user to know the query language and understand the structure of the data in order to make retrievals from the file. Here, too, it may be necessary to have special programs written to extract data and make it available to packages on the microcomputer.

Once the data are retrieved, the information has to be placed in a format on the microcomputer appropriate to the program we want to run to analyze it. What in theory looks simple, turns out to be a much more complex task than first expected!

Fortunately, vendors of database systems for mainframes are developing versions for microcomputers. The various fourth-generation languages (to be discussed later) are adding capabilities to retrieve data and place it in the appropriate format automatically for the microcomputer. The development of micro to mainframe links will be an area of continued growth and interest as personal computers continue to proliferate.

## THE FUTURE

Most experts in the field expect to see a greater integration of all communications, voice, and data. Office automation, conventional information processing, and voice communications will merge. There will be a standard series of interfaces, for example, common carriers that will interface different brands of computers and terminals so that the firm does not have to develop its own network.

The computer system of the future is likely to be a network with computers of varying capacities at different nodes. See Figure 12-7. There will be local work stations, terminals with significant logic, and built in microcomputers. Communications networks will tie all the various devices together and help to interface

**FIGURE 12-7**
A future computing complex.

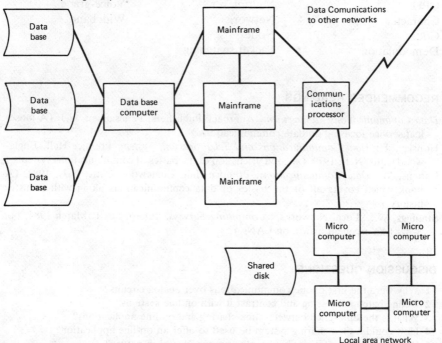

dissimilar pieces of equipment. In Figure 12-7 we have a group of interconnected mainframes for transactions processing and access to large data files. The mainframes manage a large database through a specialized database processor. A communications processor links the computer to remote workstations consisting of several microcomputers in a local area network. There is a gateway to other networks as well. All these trends will lead to an increasing availability of computation and significant opportunities for inventive computer applications.

## KEY WORDS

| | | |
|---|---|---|
| ASCII | Concentrator | Polling |
| Amplitude | Duplex | PBX |
| Analog signal | Errors | Protocol |
| Asynchronous transmission | Frequency | PCM |
| Attenuation | Full duplex | Response time |
| Baud | Half duplex | Satellite |
| Baudot code | Host | Simplex |
| Binary | Intelligent terminal | Switched network |
| Bit | Line | Synchronous |
| Block | Microwave transmission | Terminal |
| Buffer | Modulation | TDM |
| Byte | Multidrop line | Value added carrier |
| CPU | Multiplexer | Voice-grade |
| Character | Network | Wideband |
| Code | Node | |
| Demodulation | Packet switching | |

## RECOMMENDED READINGS

*Data Communications Management,* Auerback Publishers, Pennsauken, N.J. (A loose-leaf service focusing on data communications.)

Housley, T.: *Data Communications and Teleprocessing System,* Prentice-Hall, Englewood Cliffs, N.J., 1979. (A good discussion of the basics of communications systems.)

Loomis, M.: *Data Communications,* Prentice-Hall, Englewood Cliffs, N.J., 1983. (A book which covers all of the basics of data communications along with industry history.)

Stallings, W.: "Local Networks," *Computing Surveys,* vol 16, no. 1, March 1984, pp. 3–42. (An excellent article on LANs.)

## DISCUSSION QUESTIONS

1 Why were the first phone communications over analog circuits?
2 Define batch processing and contrast it with on-line systems.
3 What is the difference between time-sharing and on-line applications?
4 How could a time-sharing system be used to offer an on-line application?
5 Why are communications between computers digital in nature?

6  Why do we use an 8 bit code for transmission instead of one that is 5 or 6 bits?

7  Draw sine waves of differing amplitude, frequency, and phase.

8  For what is a protocol used in data communications?

9  What is the difference between synchronous and asynchronous transmission?

10 What is the advantage of using voice-grade lines for time sharing in a university environment?

11 Describe the steps involved in a protocol for communications between an asynchronous terminal and host time-sharing computer.

12 Describe at least one network configuration. For what applications do you think it is most suited?

13 Why are firms interested in local area networks?

14 What advantages to packet switching services offer?

15 What are the major differences between a local area network and a PBX?

16 Why would a bank develop its own entirely private communications network using satellites?

17 What function does a multiplexer serve?

18 What is the difference between a multiplexer and concentrator?

19 What are the implications of work stations replacing terminals from the standpoint of systems analysis and design?

20 Why might a local area network not have a host computer?

21 Can you think of any disadvantages of satellite communications?

22 Why is it natural to think that office automation, information processing, and data communications are all likely to come together in the future?

23 Why is a communications specialist needed to design a large network?

24 Think of a business with which you are familiar; in what ways would a network and data communications aid this firm?

25 Why does the systems designer need to have some knowledge of data communications?

BACKGROUND
  The Computer Industry
TO BUY OR NOT
  The Application
  Processing
THE SERVICES INDUSTRY
COMPARISON OF SOURCES
  Hardware
  Software
AQUISITION STRATEGY
PERFORMANCE EVALUATION
  Recommendations
  An Example
AQUISITION OF A NEW COMPUTER SYSTEM
  Mainframes and Minis
  Request for Proposals
  Recommendation
  Transition and Installation
  Other Computers
APPLICATIONS PACKAGES
  Mainframes and Minis
  Considerations and Trade-Offs
  Decision
MICROS
KEY WORDS
RECOMMENDED READINGS
DISCUSSION QUESTIONS

## CHAPTER 13

# SYSTEM ALTERNATIVES AND ACQUISITION

## CHAPTER ISSUES

- How do we select hardware and software?
- What is the difference between acquiring hardware and software for micro- versus other computers?

Users are frequently involved in the evaluation of hardware and software. The motivation for evaluation is to achieve higher performance levels from existing hardware and software or to acquire new equipment or programs. This chapter explores the problem of selecting hardware and software and suggests procedures for their acquisition.

## BACKGROUND

### The Computer Industry

In the early days of computers, manufacturers offered all the software and hardware together in one rental or purchase price. This practice was known as "bundling"; the user had no choice of what to acquire. It was very difficult for independent companies to write software and compete with manufacturers who appeared to be giving away programs free.

In response to customer pressures and possible government antitrust actions, computer manufacturers have "unbundled" and now have separate pricing for hardware and software. Software, especially applications programs, has to be rented or purchased. Separate pricing for software has created a larger marketplace but has increased the complexity of the decision process; now the user has to select among competing alternatives.

In addition to the trend toward separate pricing for software, a number of independent manufacturers (independent from the large mainframe vendors) are competing for the lucrative market for computer hardware components other than the central processing unit and the minimal primary memory that accompanies the CPU. These independent companies began by offering peripherals such as tape drives, disks, and control units for these devices. Now a number of firms offer these devices plus items such as additional primary memory for computer systems.

There are very few problems with "plug-to-plug compatible" devices; these products match the hardware and software interface of the computer manufacturer and can be substituted for the manufacturer's product directly. The manufacturer, of course, may change this interface, which makes things difficult for the independents.

The fastest growing market today is for personal computers and their software packages. Personal computers are manufactured by a number of different vendors. In addition, one can purchase one vendor's processing unit and various other components from different suppliers, components like diskette and disk drives, expanded memory, printers, and other peripherals.

Likewise, the market for packages for all types of computers—mainframe, minis, and micros—is exploding as individuals and firms try to avoid the high cost and long time required to write programs.

## TO BUY OR NOT

### The Application

Let us examine the problem of what and when to buy from the standpoint of the user organization. A user makes a request for a computer-based system; assume a systems analyst responds with a preliminary survey which is positive. Should one stop at this point and look for a package? Some in the field, particularly package vendors, would say "yes"; further analysis is a waste of time.

There are, however, several compelling reasons why there should be further work before examining packages. (We shall discuss systems analysis and design in detail in the next section.) First, a preliminary analysis of the present system should be undertaken, followed by a high-level logical design. This design includes output requirements, file contents, and input needed. Detailed file design is not required, nor do the exact formats of input and output transactions need to be specified. However, we should have a good idea of the functions of the system and some of the required features that users must have in order to work with it.

Now the design team has a plan, a benchmark specification against which to judge the various offerings from different vendors of packages and services. It is far too easy to be swayed by a convincing sales presentation; with a benchmark the design team can determine exactly what is present and what has been omitted from various systems that are already available. Now different packages can be arrayed against a custom system and estimates made of the extent to which each alternative meets user needs and desires.

Figure 13-1 shows how we might proceed. First, the problem is identified and a preliminary design document prepared for a new system. Note that at this point one is not concerned with the acquisition of hardware.

While it is premature to think about acquiring computer hardware, it is important to determine roughly what scale of hardware will be needed for the system that is being planned. Is the system capable of being run on microcomputers? Will it require a minicomputer or a large mainframe?

These questions can be answered by estimating the size of the system: how many transactions have to be processed? What are the file sizes involved? What is the volume of file activity? If the system is on-line, how many terminals are

**FIGURE 13-1**
Selection alternatives.

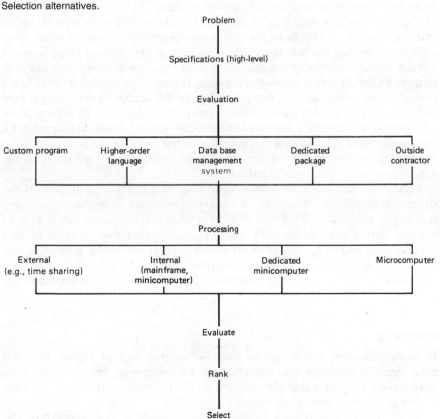

required? What is the peak volume versus the average? The answers to these questions will help narrow down the hardware alternatives, and in turn, will allow us to think more about the kind of package since packages are often written for certain sizes of operations.

Given a rough design and a feeling for the overall size of a system, alternatives such as those shown in Figure 13-1 can be explored. A common alternative is a custom system programmed to do exactly what is requested in the specifications. Of course, the specifications will have to be developed in much greater detail for programming, but this is the traditional way of developing a system.

There is also the possibility of using a fourth-generation language for development; if the firm already uses such a language it would be a good candidate. If not, the design team might want to investigate whether such a language would be a good investment for this and subsequent systems.

Similarly, we could consider a database management system if one is not already in use. This package and the associated software for querying the data and possibly generating the actual application can speed development while still providing many of the features of a custom system.

There is also the option of a dedicated package; software written by an external vendor, particularly for the application under consideration. One difficulty is finding out whether such a package exists. Several trade journals publish annual surveys of packages; there are also proprietary services that purport to list all major software packages. If your organization already has a computer one should contact representatives of the vendor to determine if they are aware of any packages for their computers. Another good source of information is trade journals in the industry, for example, banking journals for a bank application. The analyst can attend industry trade meetings to learn from other firms in the industry if they have used or considered packages in the applications area under consideration.

Finally, we can locate an outside contractor to undertake all or part of the development process. There are a variety of software consultants providing services in all phases of the life cycle. For example, we could hire a firm to actually design the system with and for us. Another possibility is to hire programmers and staff from an external firm to carry out all the steps following detailed design. Thus, a variety of external services are available either as a separate alternative or in conjunction with one of the other alternatives shown in Figure 13-1.

### Processing

In many instances, the decisions made in the top half of Figure 13-1 will determine the hardware that must be used for processing. For example, if we have chosen a package that only runs on an IBM computer, then we shall have to find IBM compatible equipment for processing.

If we are not constrained by the decisions made at first about how the problem will be solved, what are some of the processing alternatives? First, one can use an external service bureau; these organizations provide time sharing and/or batch processing. The bureaus themselves may have special packages or data available which contributes to solving our problem. More typically, we shall use some type of internal processing. For internal computing, we will usually find the options of the mainframe computer and possibly a minicomputer. Personal computers may also be an acceptable alternative for our application.

After exploring the options, the various possibilities can be compared. Each alternative should be examined on a number of criteria; then a decision can be made on the best way to proceed, considering both software and hardware processing.

## THE SERVICES INDUSTRY

We have stressed that custom development is no longer the automatic choice when a new application is being planned. There are a number of ways to obtain computer support, both in the development and operation of computing applications. In this section we discuss some of these possibilities.

**1** Computing Power. Service bureau type organizations have offered computing time and power for a number of years. While some organizations have the need for extra computing power, the steady decrease in already low hardware costs suggest that the market for raw computing power in general will shrink. Service bureaus already offer a number of custom programs and proprietary databases so that the customer can obtain a service that is not available in house.

**2** Proprietary Applications. Software houses, service bureaus (as discussed above), computer vendors, and others all offer applications dedicated to a business function like accounts receivable processing. Many of these systems have been through several major revisions, based on feedback from users. The discussion of packages in Chapter 20 points out some crucial considerations in evaluating this type of software. What is the quality of the package? How well does it suit our needs? How much are we willing to change procedures given the cost of modifications?

**3** Proprietary Databases. There is a large body of data that can be used for making various analyses and decisions; by making the data machine readable and easily available, vendors of information have created new businesses. One can purchase information on the expected trends in the economy, various statistics about companies, stock prices, and the text of legal cases, to name a few. These services can be used as an adjunct to an application or may furnish some of the needed input directly.

**4** Communications. There are a number of vendors offering communications services and equipment; see Chapter 12. Some of these services act like common carriers and provide communications networks. Other vendors offer services like electronic mail in which individuals communicate by sending messages to each other's electronic "mailboxes" in a computer file.

**MANAGEMENT PROBLEM 13-1**

Dennis Monroe is a plant manager for M&E electronics. He has just reviewed a proposal for factory management featuring microcomputers and is trying to figure out what to do. M&E has a large, central computer facility that runs factory management software for the largest plant.

Dennis' plant, however, is relatively small. The amount of information he needs about production is limited compared to the main plant which has 32 different work centers. Dennis is basically concerned with what goes into the production line and with what comes out. He must keep track of yields as well, that is, the number of good units divided by the total number produced.

The proposal is to hook together several microcomputers with a single, hard disk. Each micro will be responsible for one part of the production process and will pass information to another micro in sequence using the disk.

Dennis is a little concerned because he knows that the micro proposed, though inexpensive, is near the end of its product life cycle. He also wonders if the mainframe would be a better solution since it already has some programs which might be adapted to his plant. How would you recommend that Dennis proceed? What questions should he ask? What are the important variables in making a decision?

---

**5 Software Houses.** Software consultants or vendors (software houses) offer programming and systems design services for both batch and on-line systems, and some offer special packages as well. The software vendor may contract to manage an entire systems development effort or furnish programmers to perform work assigned by the client. The staff of the software house writes and tests batch and/or on-line programs. However, it is unusual for the average organization to have such a firm develop a time-sharing application; most organizations adopt an existing time-sharing package or users write their own programs.

A "turnkey system" is a variation on contract services made possible by the development of minicomputers. The turnkey vendor is a private contractor who provides the computer, in addition to programming, training, and installation support. The user contracts with the vendor for a complete system, and most frequently these systems involve a minicomputer. The customer owns the computer but does not have to manage a computer department or staff. Most systems are designed so that someone already employed by the customer can operate the system; computer professionals are not needed. Turnkey systems have proved very popular for small organizations that would like to take advantage of computer processing without establishing a computer department. Large organizations also use turnkey services to supplement the efforts of their own computer staff.

## MONEY, MONEY, EVERYWHERE

*Banks are rushing to install automatic teller machines or ATMs. The Bank Marketing Association estimates that there are 110 networks of ATMs so that a user can access tellers in many different locations, representing 45% of the 32,000 ATMs installed.*

*There are at least seven shared networks, the oldest of which is operating by American Express; this system links to over 1000 ATMs in 16 states. Both Mastercard and Visa are planning networks that will have between 1,000 and 3,500 terminals.*

*When these ATMs are networked, the customer has many advantages. A traveler thousands of miles from home can access a networked ATM as easily as he or she could reach the ATM down the block from home.*

*It is possible that these networks will someday form the backbone for more electronic funds transfer systems. For example, it would not take much additional development to have ATM-like terminals in various merchant locations; for example, airline ticket offices at airports would be one good candidate.*

## COMPARISON OF SOURCES

What are the advantages and disadvantages of different sources for hardware and software? We can look at the two extremes for discussion purposes: all activities are undertaken either internally or externally through an outside organization (see Table 13-1).

### Hardware

With an internal computer department, an organization has to deal with the problem of managing the computer; overhead is introduced into the organization. For this price, management gains control over its own computer operations. Data remain exclusively within organizational confines and are accessible only to employees. Processing priorities are established internally, and no other organization can preempt time from an organization with its own system. Management must provide sufficient resources to accommodate peak loads, so there can be high fixed costs for computer equipment that may not be fully utilized under this alternative. Usually, extra capacity is not provided because of the cost. Backup may be limited by the resources management is able to provide.

Organizations choosing to rely on external services have a contractual agreement with the servicing firm. There are few management responsibilities of a supervisory nature because these tasks have been delegated to an outside company. Control may be less than under the internal alternative because

TABLE 13-1
COMPARISON OF INTERNAL VERSUS EXTERNAL SERVICES

| | Internal | External |
|---|---|---|
| **Hardware** | | |
| Management | Must manage computer department | Contractual arrangement; no line management responsible except for data preparation |
| Control | Control potential high | Only through contract, influence, withholding payment |
| Security | Under own responsibility; data remains at internal location | Data in hands of external organization; other customers a threat |
| Priorities | Assigned by own employees | Determined by external management |
| Resources | Must accommodate peak loads; high fixed cost | Variable cost, pay only for what is used (beyond possible minimum charge) |
| Capacity | Limited to what is needed | Frequently more powerful equipment than could be justified by clients |
| Backup | Limited by internal resources | Usually available because of higher capacity |
| **Software** | | |
| Management | Must manage program development | Contractual arrangements, specifications on cost, time, performance |
| Staff | May have to hire experts | Expect vendors to have expertise |
| Implementation | Probably easier in terms of user reaction to internal staff | May be more difficult for "outsiders" |

litigation over contracts is costly and time-consuming. Instead, the customer seeks to influence the service organization. Many firms worry about having sensitive data in the hands of another organization, particularly when other companies have access to the same computer resources. The priority for applications is also in the hands of the organization providing services; management influences, but does not control, processing priorities. With an outside organization, the customer incurs a variable cost and pays only for the resources consumed. Frequently, the client has access to more powerful equipment than would be installed internally, since it is being shared among a number of users. Availability is less of a problem because the service bureau has high capacity to serve all its customers.

## Software

With internal software development, we must manage the development process. Internal program development often results in duplication; there may be a tendency to start from the beginning with each new system. Because there are "not-invented-here" complexes, packages are not adequately investigated. Implementation problems, however, should be minimized because internal employees deal directly with the users in the firm.

External software services are handled on a contractual basis. However, a customer may still need some individual who is familiar with computer technology to work with the contractor and monitor progress, although for the most part, clients will rely on the vendor's expertise. Implementation can be difficult for "outsiders"; however, the client may be able to take advantage of an existing package or set of routines whose cost has been amortized over a large group of users.

## ACQUISITION STRATEGY

No matter what alternative is selected, the customer has to acquire computer equipment and/or services. How do we approach this problem? There are several considerations a potential customer should have in mind. First, check a vendor's financial condition; a number of small companies have gone bankrupt in the computer industry. Even major firms have sold or discontinued their computer manufacturing activities. How likely is a vendor to be around in the future to service the product and improve it?

What kind of documentation is available, particularly for software, since modifications may be necessary? Documentation describes how the system works and how it can be used. Without it, a customer has very little information on the product purchased. What kind of vendor support is available? Does the price include installation and training by the vendor?

An extremely important research activity for a customer is to contact present users of a product to determine their level of satisfaction. How well does the product or service meet vendor claims? What problems did users have? If possible, visit users without a vendor representative to ask these questions. If it is not possible to see a product demonstrated, do not buy it. Too often, announced products are delivered years late; insist on a demonstration and attempt to evaluate the performance of the product.

Before we discuss some of the factors to be considered in the acquisition of computer systems, we shall examine techniques for evaluating system performance. Performance evaluation is important for a number of reasons, and it is likely to be a component of an acquisition decision.

## PERFORMANCE EVALUATION

A major activity in acquiring new equipment and software frequently is an evaluation of the performance of the product. We also use performance evaluation techniques with an existing system to improve its performance, either through the acquisition of additional equipment or the reduction in the amount of equipment in use. Performance is generally defined to be the response time of a system, or the volume of input it can process in a given period of time.

**Analytic Modeling** Analytic modeling involves a mathematical approach to performance evaluation and is best suited for design calculations such as the queuing analysis of an on-line system. For the average computer department, consulting help would be needed to develop such a model. Usually, analytical approaches do not model software and, therefore, do not have wide applicability to the average computer installation.

**Simulation** Simulation has been used extensively to evaluate the performance of computer systems. Simulation is not suitable for the selection of a specific piece of software such as an applications program, but simulation can include software considerations in evaluating the performance of a total computer system. Various types of simulators are available, or users can write their own using a special-purpose simulation language. (In general, this evaluation method is not advised for the typical computer department since it is a research project.)

**Benchmarks** Benchmarks represent a sample of an existing workload and do include software considerations. Any aspect of the system can be evaluated, from an entire computer system to a file management package. Strictly speaking, a benchmark is an existing job that has been recoded if necessary for the system being evaluated. The benchmark job (or jobs) is simply run on the new equipment. The use of the benchmark assumes that the existing job mix or this particular application is representative of how the product under evaluation will be used. For a thorough evaluation job with benchmarks, many different benchmarks must be developed and executed. However, benchmarks offer a high degree of flexibility and the evaluation effort can be tailored to the importance of the decision.

**Synthetic Modules** A synthetic job is coded to represent a typical function and is not restricted to being an existing job. Like a benchmark, a synthetic program is actually executed. This approach offers a great deal of flexibility; it is possible to include estimates of how the job load will change in the future. For example, certain activities such as file processing can be more highly weighted if a new database application is being planned.

It is possible to use a small group of synthetic modules to model a much larger workload by combining and weighting the different modules. As with benchmarks, the evaluator can perform a number of experiments consistent with the importance of the decision. An extensive group of synthetic modules can be developed, and scientific experiments planned for evaluation. On the other hand, a few modules and limited runs can be used to get a rough idea of performance comparisons.

**Monitoring** Monitoring is a type of performance evaluation technique different from those techniques described above; it is primarily oriented toward evaluating existing forms of hardware and software. The techniques described earlier are most useful in deciding whether to acquire something new, while monitors are often used to tune or improve the performance of an existing system. Two types of monitors are in use, but the distinction between them is blurring because they have been combined to produce a hybrid, or integrated, monitors.

A hardware monitor contains a set of probes that are attached to the component being monitored at critical points. The device collects data on elapsed time or on counts of some value, for example, the number of disk accesses. The recorded data become input to a separate batch data-reduction program. The major disadvantage of the hardware monitor is limitations on what can be measured and the fact that it is often difficult to relate the data collected to software performance.

A software monitor is a program that is embedded within or interfaced in some way with the operating system. It is called as a high-priority task every so often to collect statistics on machine status. These statistics are also generally analyzed after the end of the monitoring period. Since the software monitor has access to all operating system tables and data, it can keep track of more items than a hardware monitor. The problem with software monitors is that the measurement tool interacts with what is being measured; that is, a software monitor is a program and its execution affects the system.

Hybrid or integrated monitors use software and hardware to collect data. Often the hardware monitor is a minicomputer operating under program control.

The role of performance evaluation has changed with declining hardware costs and increasing power. We are using very fast computers to run relatively

---

**MANAGEMENT PROBLEM 13-2**

Sally Johnson has been using a spreadsheet package on her personal computer for several years. The package is supposedly integrated; it contains a database manager and word processor as well. However, Sally has found the database part a little too restrictive and is interested in a package devoted entirely to the management of data.

She has investigated three packages, each of which has different capabilities. All three claim to be based on the relational model. Each of them has a forms definition capability; users describe on the screen the input form and the system creates it for them each time they enter data. The systems also have report generators to custom-tailor reports. Finally they all have the ability to set up a file of commands so that the system acts almost like an applications generator.

Sally cannot see any major differences among these three candidates; their prices are almost the same. How can she proceed to find out which one would be best for her? What advice can you give her?

inefficient software like dedicated packages and higher order languages, because it is important to save human development time. Where does performance evaluation fit in?

First, in acquiring a package, especially one that will operate on-line, we need to be sure that the package can support the size of our application with acceptable response time. As an example, one package for use by the registrar of a university can only handle 128 terminals. If this limit cannot be changed through an upgrade to a different computer or easy changes in the software, it may be an inappropriate system for a large university. If a large installation is not available for a demonstration, then one might develop a simulated or a synthetic load to try and test the limits of what can be demonstrated to a potential buyer.

On the hardware side, if a computer is considerably faster than another for a particular task, then that speed is a factor in its favor. (See the following discussion on hardware acquisition.) Given the amount of processing power available today and the importance of packages, it is unlikely that hardware evaluation will be as important as in the past.

Monitoring, however, may become even more important as software increases in complexity and the range of design alternatives increases. For example, a monitor may show us how to better allocate or even design the files in an on-line system to improve response time. A software monitor can help us understand the behavior of a system during its development, something very helpful in looking for errors and tuning performance. We can also use monitors to improve the performance of a system, for example, to see where a code is least efficient.

Thus, performance is an issue, but not the raw speed of a computer. Rather, we must be concerned with how software and hardware work together. If there is not enough processing power, what are the alternatives? Can we improve performance through small increments in hardware or minor software changes, or is there a major cost associated with improvements? Can the system expand as our processing load increases? We shall evaluate the performance of existing systems we might consider acquiring and attempt to assess how these applications will perform in our environment. Finally, we shall be concerned with the growth path for the software and hardware.

## An Example

A cruise ship line presents an interesting example of how performance analysis can be important in the selection of a computer system. The line was investigating a software package for making cruise ship reservations. While on the surface, this reservations application sounds like any other, there are a number of important differences. One is that passengers usually want to book a particular cabin or class of cabins when making a reservation. There can also be different itineraries for the passengers in the same cabin. Thus, a package must be specifically designed for cruising.

The cruise line in this example found such a package, but was concerned about whether it could handle the volume of processing for its ships. Fortunately, the package was in use at another, noncompeting cruise line that was roughly comparable in size.

The computer vendor offered a performance evaluation tool. This tool monitored data from the actual execution of a job and used these data to develop the parameters of a queuing model of systems performance. The user of the model could ask "what if" questions to determine the impact of changing the hardware on system response time. For example, one could estimate the impact of moving to a different CPU, adding memory, and adding disk capacity.

The cruise line obtained monitored data from the firm already using the package, and used the vendor's model to analyze it. The model indicated that performance should be adequate for the cruise line and was helpful in recommending the computer configuration to acquire. In this instance a combination of evaluation techniques was important in the decision to acquire a new software and hardware package.

## ACQUISITION OF A NEW COMPUTER SYSTEM

### Mainframes and Minis

Periodically, it is necessary to upgrade a computer system either because more capacity is needed or because technical advancements have produced machines with better performance at a lower cost. The acquisition of a new computer system can be a complicated decision. In this section we describe the computer selection process and offer some suggestions of criteria to be used in the decision.

### Request for Proposals

After the need for a new system has been identified, the potential buyer will usually develop a request for bids. The request is sent to various vendors who are asked to propose equipment. The buyer should attempt to have the manufacturer do most of the work in this process. Table 13-2 shows some of the items that should be included in the request for a proposal.

All present applications should be described in detail in the proposal; we want the vendor to consider these and recommend the best equipment for the workload. Also, plans for new applications should be included. The vendor should specify what type of support will be provided and present reliability data for the equipment. We are also interested in knowing about backup: are there redundant components in the system? Can a faulty component be isolated while the system continues to run in a degraded mode? We also would like to have information about similar installations in the area.

The vendor should indicate the arrangements for demonstrations and describe how the customer can access the proposed configuration to evaluate its performance. Because moving to a new computer system is a major undertak-

TABLE 13-2
ITEMS INCLUDED IN REQUEST FOR
PROPOSAL

| | |
|---|---|
| **1** | Present applications |
| | File characteristics |
| | Input-output |
| | Volume |
| | Frequency |
| | Batch or on-line |
| **2** | Same as (1) for proposed systems |
| **3** | Vendor service |
| **4** | Reliability data |
| **5** | Backup |
| **6** | Demonstration |
| **7** | Evaluation arrangements |
| **8** | Conversion and transition |
| **9** | Descriptive material (hardware and software) |
| **10** | Price |

ing, the vendor should present a plan for the transition to the proposed system. Are there any special products or services that the vendor offers to ease the transition?

In acquiring a new system, we shall probably also ask for some descriptive material of the type shown in Table 13-3 to obtain a feeling for the type of equipment being proposed. This descriptive information includes both hardware and software capabilities. Finally, the price for the recommended system should be provided in detail, both for hardware components and software.

### Performance

The buyer should prepare for testing the proposed machine while the vendor is preparing the proposal. The typical buyer will probably want to include benchmarks and possibly synthetic modules to model the existing and planned workload. Benchmarks are also a very valuable way to indicate the difficulties that can be expected in transition. The buyer can use several existing jobs without changes to see how easy it is to run them on the new system.

### Proposal Evaluation

Meaningful criteria should be established for evaluating each proposal from the different vendors. These criteria can include items such as performance, presence of certain software, the availability of special applications packages, the ease of conversion, the response of other users currently using the equipment, etc.

Then the evaluation team should assign a weight to each criterion. It may be

TABLE 13-3
EXAMPLE OF DESCRIPTIVE PROPOSAL MATERIAL

| | |
|---|---|
| Hardware | Speed |
| CPU cycle time | Transfer rate |
| Memory cycle time and hierarchy | Tracks |
| Data path | Disks |
| Registers | Seek time |
| Type | Rotational delay time |
| Number | Average access time |
| Microprogramming features | Capacity |
| Instruction set | Removable or fixed |
| Fixed point | Bulk storage |
| Floating point | Access time |
| Decimal | Size |
| Precision | Data path |
| Interrupt structure | Input-output peripherals |
| Number | Input-output speed |
| Type | Reject rate (e.g., OCR scanners) |
| Priority | Software support |
| Memory size (each hierarchical element) | |
| Memory organization | Software |
| Data | Operating system |
| Instructions | Job and task management |
| | Multiprogramming |
| Special features | Partitions |
| Parallel operations | Size |
| Instruction look-ahead | Priority |
| Multiple processors | Overhead (time and space) |
| Data channels | Control language |
| Number | Documentation |
| Type | Utilities |
| Transfer rate | Special features |
| Control units | Compilers |
| Device assignment | Subset of language supported |
| Effect on CPU | Extensions to language |
| Storage devices | File accessing capabilities |
| Tapes | Storage requirements |
| Density | Applications programs |

possible to eliminate vendors because of one dominant failing, for example, the lack of an applications package that is critical for the evaluators. If it is not possible to eliminate vendors because of some single major failing, then a more formal evaluation procedure is necessary.

One approach that has been used is to assign an interval score to each vendor and to multiply the scores by the weights for the criteria. These weighted scores are then added to form a final weighted total. However, the results are often quite close, and the evaluation team may not have much confidence in a small numeric difference among the vendors. Another alternative is to prepare a brief scenario of how the computer department would function with each alternative system and what transitional activities would have to take place. Then the decision-making body rank-orders the scenarios and chooses the most desirable one.

### Recommendation

Most organizations formally decide on an acquisition as major as a new computer system at a high level. However, most frequently the decision is made on the basis of recommendations from the information services department manager and staff who actually undertake the evaluation. In developing a recommendation for approval, the computer department should present an executive summary of a few short pages including the reasons for the recommendation. The complete evaluation study can be available as a reference document, but the shorter summary will probably suffice for obtaining approval.

### Transition and Installation

Installing a new computer system should be treated just as a systems design project. The overriding goal is for a smooth transition; it is necessary to explain what is happening to users and to have their cooperation. A plan should be prepared showing the schedule and activities that must be undertaken to complete the changeover successfully.

### Other Computers

The purchase of a mainframe or minicomputer is fairly routine. Even when one is acquiring a computer that will be dedicated to a single software application, the decision is usually fairly easy once the package has been chosen because 1) there are usually relatively few computers for which the package is written and 2) the vendor has experience knowing what kind of computer should be used, given one's processing demands.

In the category of "other" computers, we must consider microcomputers and specialized computers. For example, there are a number of computer devices available for process control and factory automation. While this area has traditionally been the domain of the engineer, now factory computers are communicating valuable data to computers that supply information for making decisions on scheduling, raw materials, and production control, to name a few functions.

Personal computers also present a bewildering array of possibilities because of the large number of vendors. The organization is probably well-advised to develop a standard, say to support two or three specific types of personal computers and to avoid acquiring others. The staff can only develop expertise in supporting a limited number of machines. In addition, all the personal computers have the potential for needing to communicate with other computers, so that

---

**SNACK FOOD COMMUNICATIONS**

*Frito Lay, headquartered in Dallas, has 43 manufacturing plants around the U.S. and produces over a hundred snack products. The firm is also a pioneer in the use of voice mail systems. Users are able to send spoken store-and-forward messages.*

*A voice mail system differs from a phone answering machine because it allows a user to perform various sending and receiving functions. The company began with a pilot test using rented mailboxes. District managers in the vend sales division were very hard to reach; they cover two to three states and work out of their homes. Weekly status reports were very late getting to headquarters.*

*Using voice mail, on Friday mornings these district managers phoned in voice reports to their regional manager's voice mailbox. On Friday afternoon, each regional office forwarded the voice reports plus their own reports to a word processing center voice mailbox at headquarters. Monday morning a staff transcribed and distributed the reports, four days earlier than with the previous approach.*

*After another pilot study, equally successful in reducing the time delays of communications and the number of missed phone calls, the company has included voice mail as a part of its budget. Communications are improved, but there is additional cost for the system and communication lines.*

*EDP Analyzer,* August, 1983.

---

limiting the number of different computers will eventually help in arranging connection into computer networks.

Decisions for these "other" classes of computers largely depend on the function for which they are being acquired. Many personal computers have been purchased just to run spreadsheet analyses. Factory computers will be chosen for how well they perform a specific task. However, one can still apply some of the considerations for larger computers when considering other types. Specifically, expandability and compatibility along with the ability to communicate with other systems are important. Obviously, the type of software and human-machine interface are also significant, along with vendor support.

A careful analysis of the issues will help to insure that good decisions are made in the acquisition of all computer equipment. Even relatively low priced computers have implications beyond their immediate application.

## APPLICATIONS PACKAGES
### Mainframes and Minis

An applications package is a program or set of programs written for use by more than one organization. A number of these packages are for sale or rent by computer vendors and software firms.

## Considerations and Trade-Offs

The major attraction of a package today is the avoidance of developing a custom system. Custom programing is expensive and time-consuming, so when a package is available, it should be considered. Another obvious advantage of using a package is cost savings. The package developer expects to sell a number of packages to recover the investment in developing the package; the cost is thus amortized over a number of users. The cost to the developer, though, is usually higher than would be the development of a single application since the package must be more general so that it can be used by a number of customers. This increased generality makes the package larger, more complex, and often less efficient to operate than an application developed for only a single use. Some of the trade-offs, then, for a package are:

Package generality versus ease of installation and use.

Acquisition and modification cost versus the cost of developing the application within the organization.

The elapsed time to install a package versus the time to develop the application within the organization.

Operating efficiency of the package versus the alternative of a custom application within the organization.

Implementation problems of the package versus those of an application developed specifically for the needs of the organization.

The most serious problem with packages is the need for organizations to customize the programs for their unique situation. (This problem is most severe with dedicated packages like accounts receivable.) Of course, although individual organizations always claim uniqueness, often it is easy to change routine procedures to suit a package. On the other hand, there are legitimate reasons for maintaining uniqueness in the organization.

We have stressed the importance of meeting user needs and obtaining heavy user involvement in the design of systems. Many systems developed on a custom-tailored basis have failed completely or have not met their potential. It seems that packages are even less likely to succeed because they have a tendency to impose a system on a user. What can be done to lessen the implementation problem of packages?

The package vendors recognize this drawback and generally design packages to allow some custom tailoring. Two ways are often employed for providing this flexibility: the use of modules and the use of parameters. The first strategy is to provide a modular set of programs in the package; the user configures a custom applications package by selecting appropriate modules for a particular set of needs. Little or no programming is required on the part of the user since the modules are all available from the vendor. Packages also make extensive use of parameters or data values to indicate unique features for a particular user.

Often, the customizing features provided by the vendor of the package are insufficient for an organization. The less expensive packages may have to be accepted as is, but for more elaborate applications, the customer often finds it

## MANAGEMENT PROBLEM 13-2

Jack Caradine sat back in his chair and scratched his head as he muttered, "We really opened the flood gates with the ICPC two years ago. Now we can't keep up with all the user requests for packages and turnkey systems."

Jack is manager of systems development for Agrequip, a manufacturer of farm implements. Two years ago he helped one plant install a package application called ICPC for inventory control and production control. The package was an example of dedicated application: a small computer and the application were acquired specifically for the inventory and production control application.

Since that time, other users have found out about the system and have requested something similar. These requests have presented relatively few problems since Jack's staff is quite knowledgeable about the package and is now installing it at three other plants. However, what Jack is concerned about now are the requests for many different types of packages. "They start their own research with package vendors and they don't have the slightest idea of what to look for."

Jack's staff is being stretched to respond to these requests and to evaluate the packages. "Users have gotten the idea that a package is a panacea for any problem," Jack complained. "They don't realize what we have to go through to evaluate and then install a package. Every one we have put in required some modification. Sure it can be cheaper than doing it ourselves, but the cost is not just the cost of the package; it's the installation, modification, and ongoing costs of taking care of the thing. Also, we rarely find a package with all the same features we'd have put in a system designed as a custom job inside the company."

What kind of policy does Jack need? What procedures for dealing with the explosion of package activities by users would you recommend?

necessary to write custom code to modify the package. Sometimes the modifications are easy and require only the addition of some reports or the alteration of reports already in the package. Code modification can become quite extensive and may involve rewriting significant portions of the package. One organization uses the rule of thumb that a package will not be considered if it will cost more than 50 percent of the initial package cost to modify it. The important thing to remember is that the cost of a package is usually not just the purchase price; instead we must forecast and consider the cost of modifications and maintenance.

### Criteria

The information services department and a project team should agree on screening criteria for packages. Many times packages will be considered as alternatives to developing a system in-house. (The computer staff will apply these same criteria to packages considered for use primarily within the depart-

TABLE 13-4
CONSIDERATIONS IN EVALUATING
SOFTWARE PACKAGES

---

Functions included
Modifications required to package
Installation effort
User interface
Flexibility
Execution time
Changes required in existing system to use package
Vendor support
Updating of package
Documentation
Cost and terms

---

ment.) Table 13-4 lists some possible evaluation criteria for decisions on packages. The major reason for acquiring a package is the function it performs. We want to know how many desired functions are included and what effort would be required to modify the package.

It is also important to consider the user interface, that is, how difficult it is to use the package. How much information does a user have to supply? Is it simple to prepare and understand the input? Is the package flexible and can it be used if our requirements change somewhat?

The evaluation team is also concerned with how long the package requires to run and how it impacts current operations. Execution time considerations are not as important for a simple application that is run infrequently, but they can be very important for something like a database management system. Also, how does the package perform? What is the response time? We are interested in how much present procedures have to be changed to use the package.

Just as with hardware, it is necessary to evaluate vendor support and the likelihood that the vendor will remain in business. Remember that it does not take many resources to program and sell software packages. Updates and improvements for the package should be forthcoming so we are dependent on the vendor remaining in business.

With software packages, documentation is vitally important; the computer department staff may have to modify the package and will undoubtedly have to maintain it if errors occur. Guidelines for documentation were presented in Chapter 13, and these can be used to evaluate the documentation for a proposed package. Finally, we have to consider the cost; however, remember that we always underestimate how much it will cost to develop a comparable system ourselves and overestimate the cost required to modify the package!

**Decision**

In this discussion, we are interested in whether or not a package qualifies for consideration. Many of the criteria in Table 13-3 require analysis of package

## MANAGEMENT PROBLEM 13-3

The bids for a new computer system for Management Advisory Services, Inc. had just arrived. Terry Smith brought the three thick notebooks into his office and began to read. Management Advisory Services is a consulting firm that builds models and decision-support systems for its clients. The firm has used a computer since its founding 10 years ago, but the computer has always been a commercial time-sharing system. Now, it appeared that because of the extremely low cost of computer hardware, Management Advisory Services should think about acquiring its own in-house machine.

Currently the consultants with the firm have to learn a number of different systems because a variety of time-sharing service bureaus are employed. Models developed for one customer are sometimes difficult to use again; no real library of systems was being constructed, yet management realized that such a development would be necessary to ensure adequate profit margins in this competitive, service-oriented industry.

Management Advisory Services had held lengthy discussions with three vendors of time-sharing systems and had presented the needs of the firm. Now the vendors had all responded with proposed configurations and software. Terry skimmed the bids carefully and noticed immediately that the price differences among the three contenders were almost insignificant. On a more careful reading, he could not find one dominant advantage or major failing of any vendor that would have simplified the decision.

Terry sighed as he realized that a full-scale evaluation of the proposals would now be necessary. He began to make a list of the criteria that seemed important in the evaluation for Management Advisory Services. Can you help him develop the list of criteria? What should Terry do after the criteria have been agreed on by the selection committee?

---

documentation by the systems analysis staff or programmers. We also should contact present users to answer questions about vendor claims and support. Almost all these criteria are subjective, which means that several individuals should rank a package on each criteria, for example on a 1 to 7 scale. The responses can then be averaged for each criteria and a score developed for the package.

It may be desirable to divide the criteria into essential and nonessential groups. We can insist that a package get a "passing score" (established in advance) on each of the essential criteria to be considered for acquisition. Then we can examine the nonessential criteria to see if it passes enough of them to be considered.

If a package is acceptable and is the only alternative under consideration, we shall probably acquire it. However, if several packages are available, then the ones that pass the screening test can be compared using ratings or through the scenarios described in the last section. If the package under consideration is an alternative to designing an in-house system, then use the criteria established by the project team to evaluate the package in a comparison with other processing alternatives.

The users, then, help evaluate the package versus a custom-tailored application and make the decision on which would be best. If the user wishes to have the lower costs and faster development associated with the package, then he or she will have to agree that all desired features may not be present. If the decision is for a custom application, the user must recognize that costs will probably be higher than a package and that it will take longer to develop the system. The important thing is for users to make this decision themselves rather than to have it imposed on them by a superior or by the computer department. With participation, the user will understand the trade-offs and recognize the reasons for whatever choice is made.

## MICROS

Buying software for microcomputers shares some of the issues with software for mainframes and minis. We are still concerned with the user interface and user documentation. Speed of processing may also be a consideration.

For most microcomputer packages, however, modification is not an issue. These packages are too inexpensive for the vendor to make modifications for each customer. In order to protect future sales, the vendor rarely sells the source code for the program. The vendor does not encourage modifications because it does not want to support customers who make them.

Research for a micro package is also slightly different than for other types of computers. There are a number of magazines that conduct product evaluations. The potential buyer can also go to a retail computer store to look at package documentation; though it may be hard to discuss a package with a current user.

Some organizations have created internal consulting and support groups to help users with micro hardware and software acquisitions. These groups have packages to recommend and demonstrate for specific types of applications. Fortunately the cost of much micro software is low enough that one can often afford to buy and use a package for several months or a year and then switch to something else. It is worth doing research and making a careful decision, but there is nothing like trying out the software before buying it to determine if it is a good choice.

## KEY WORDS

| | | |
|---|---|---|
| Analytic models | Packages | Simulation |
| Benchmarks | Performance evaluation | Software house |
| Cycle-and-add times | Plug-to-plug compatible | Software monitor |
| Hardware monitor | equipment | Synthetic programs |
| Hybrid monitor | Remote batch | Turnkey |
| Independent manufac- | Scenarios | Unbundling |
| turer | Service bureau | |

## RECOMMENDED READINGS

*Byte* and *Popular Computing* magazines have software evaluations and comparisons. Martin, J., and L. McClure: "Buying Software Off the Rack," *Harvard Business Review,* November–December 1983, pp. 32–60. (A good guide to selection and contracting.)

## DISCUSSION QUESTIONS

1 What is wrong with the use of cycle-and-add times or instruction mixes for performance evaluation?
2 What is the major difference between monitoring and other types of performance evaluation?
3 Design a series of synthetic modules and experiments for a company that wishes to evaluate the performance of several medium-sized, multiprogrammed, general-purpose computer systems. The company has 50 percent file processing applications and 25 percent engineering applications. The rest of the work on the system is general business processing.
4 What are the problems involved in using a monitor to tune systems?
5 What are the drawbacks to analytic models and simulation studies for the average computer installation?
6 Why should a computer installation consider the use of applications packages? What are their advantages and disadvantages?
7 In what situations would you expect applications packages to be most satisfactory?
8 What would your reaction be to the development of a set of industrywide synthetic modules to be used in performance evaluation?
9 How would you characterize an existing computer workload for performance evaluation purposes? How would you include consideration for the changes in the workload that might occur in the future?
10 What performance evaluation technique would you use and why if the expected workload in the next five years will change drastically from the existing workload?
11 To what extent should different vendors than the one currently supplying your computer be included in bidding for a new system?
12 What are the advantages and disadvantages of mixed-vendor installations? (For example, the computer and main memory are from one company and the peripherals from others.)
13 What factors mitigate against the conversion to a different vendor's computer? How has the development and use of higher-level languages affected this type of conversion? What do you expect the impact of database management systems will be on conversion to a new vendor?
14 Make a list of the types of questions and information desired from a survey of other users of computer equipment under consideration for acquisition.
15 How can regular service levels be maintained during the conversion to new computer equipment? What are the dangers of acquiring new equipment?
16 What are the disadvantages of using some weighted score for ranking competing proposals for computer equipment? What advantages are presented by the use of scenarios for describing how a computer department would function under each new alternative?

17 Why is it not a good idea to be a pioneer with new equipment or software? That is, why should an installation wait before acquiring a newly developed computer system component?

18 How can a computer department avoid having to make frequent requests for additional computer capacity? What are the dangers in your strategy? How does the development of a plan for information systems activities affect this problem?

19 Most computer systems can be purchased or rented. What are the advantages and disadvantages of each alternative?

20 Why should applications packages be seriously considered as an alternative to programming and implementing a system? What are the most significant problems with these packages? How can the ease of modifying the package be determined before its acquisition?

21 Compare and contrast the major sources of software; what are the advantages and disadvantages of each?

22 Who should be involved in the decision on new computer hardware? What about software? Does the type of software make a difference?

23 What kind of packages should a computer department acquire for its own internal use?

24 Why do some programmers show a great deal of resistance to applications packages?

25 How can the vendor of an applications package make it more appealing to potential customers?

26 What are the advantages and disadvantages of running batch, on-line, and time sharing on the same computer as opposed to having specialized computers for each application?

27 For some time-sharing computers, languages and operating systems are available that were developed by users rather than the hardware vendor. What are the pros and cons of acquiring this software?

28 Some firms have used worldwide time-sharing services to install on-line systems. The user of the system does no programming; rather, the application is set up by a systems staff for the user, and the time-sharing system is used for its communications and computer power. What are the advantages and disadvantages of such systems?

29 Are there any packages that require no modifications for installation? What types of software do these packages tend to be?

30 Does the decline of hardware costs mean that less effort should be devoted to evaluation? Why or why not?

# SYSTEMS ANALYSIS AND DESIGN

One of the most exciting activities in the information systems field is the design of a new computer-based system. In this part of the book, we follow the life cycle of a system from its inception through final installation. From the considerations discussed in Part Two, on organizational issues, we recommend an approach to systems analysis and design in which users have control over the design process; the chapters in this part of the text stress the role of the manager and user in each stage of systems analysis and design. The systems analyst aids the user in making crucial decisions and performs the technical tasks necessary to develop the system.

WHAT IS A SYSTEM?
THE SYSTEMS LIFE CYCLE
RESPONSIBILITIES DURING THE LIFE CYCLE
RESOURCES FOR NEW SYSTEMS
Demands and Resources
A Resource Allocation Problem
PROBLEMS IN THE LIFE CYCLE
USER-ORIENTED DESIGN
Problems with the Conventional View
Predicted Results
Required Knowledge
Design Team
DATA COLLECTION
Observation
Interviews
Questionnaires
Comparison
DESIGN TOOLS
Flowcharts
Decision Tables
STRUCTURED DESIGN
Data Flow Diagrams
An Example
MULTIUSER VERSUS MICRO DESIGN
SUMMARY
KEY WORDS
RECOMMENDED READINGS
DISCUSSION QUESTIONS

## CHAPTER 14

# INTRODUCTION AND OVERVIEW

## CHAPTER ISSUES

- How does one develop a computer-based information system?
- What tools and techniques can be used in systems analysis and design?
- What resources should management make available for systems analysis and design?

The design of a new computer-based information system is an exciting and demanding undertaking. First, someone calls attention to a problem with existing information processing procedures. A design team assesses the benefits of using a computer to improve these procedures. Then an abstract model of present processing procedures is developed and designers create a new information processing system. The new procedures are converted into systems specifications and finally into computer programs. During the final stages of development, the system is tested and converted and becomes operational.

The design of an information system is a creative and labor-intensive task. It is creative because we are building a new set of information processing procedures just as an architect designs a new building. Systems analysis and design is a human, intellectual task. There are some portions of design that can be automated, but most of the creative aspects require human thought.

What are the roles of the user and manager in systems analysis and design? In this chapter we introduce the systems life cycle and discuss the resources available for developing new systems. We shall see that users and managers have crucial roles in all aspects of systems analysis and design.

## WHAT IS A SYSTEM?

In Chapter 4 we saw a number of examples of information systems, and in each chapter we have presented one or two applications briefs describing how a computer has been applied to an information processing problem. A system is made up of a number of interrelated components only some of which are easily seen. For example, it is difficult to characterize the actions of individuals who are involved in making decisions as a part of an information system. The flow of information and the processing of data by computer programs and/or individuals can also be obscure.

One of the major tasks in systems analysis and design is to describe systems, both existing systems and proposed new systems. Later in this chapter we shall discuss some of the tools available for preparing descriptions of systems, but for now we present an overview of a system.

Information systems can be described by four of their key components:

1 Decisions
2 Transactions and processing
3 Information and its flow
4 Individuals or functions involved

It is difficult to observe the decision process, though we can see and review the results of a decision. Transactions are usually more visible, though many current systems use computer programs, which are not easy to understand, to process transactions. In principle an observer can see information and its flows. Individuals can be observed too, but it is not always easy to figure out the information processing functions they perform.

Much of systems analysis and design, as we mentioned above, consists of developing a sufficient understanding of a system to document it. Consider the following example of a simple inventory system; we can describe it as follows:

### Decisions

1 What to reorder
2 When to reorder it
3 How much to reorder

### Transactions

1 Place an order
2 Receive merchandise
3 Withdraw goods from inventory

### Information

1 Quantity on hand for each item
2 Historical usage for each item

3 Cost of the item
4 Holding costs
5 Reorder costs
6 Interest cost (to finance inventory)

**Individuals/functions**

1 Warehouse supervisors
2 Stock clerk
3 Receiving clerks
4 Purchasing agents

Several other systems are also related to this one, including purchasing and accounts payable. The information above serves only to describe the simple inventory system. We could further document this system by going into more details, especially concerning the flow of information. We could prepare flowcharts, which we discuss at the end of this chapter to help visualize how the system works. Also we can document the various decisions in narrative form to provide a better understanding of the inventory system.

This example illustrates the difficulty of describing and defining a system. Unfortunately there is no one standard for what constitutes a system or how to document it. A number of different approaches are used, and individuals have to develop descriptive techniques that help them conceptualize a system. Most people find it easiest to start at a very high level and then work toward filling in the details. In our example above, we described the system first as being concerned with inventory. To anyone with experience in working with inventories, this description should stimulate thoughts of how inventory systems operate in general. By listing decisions, transactions, information flows, and functions, we add details to the inventory system. Further details can be added in a top-down fashion as our knowledge increases about this particular system. In the end, everyone involved in trying to learn about this system should share a common concept of the system and an understanding of the documents describing it.

## THE SYSTEMS LIFE CYCLE

A computer-based information system has a life cycle, just like a living organism or a new product. The various stages in the life cycle of a system are shown in Table 14-1. The idea for a new information system is stimulated by a need to improve information processing procedures. This need leads to the preliminary survey to determine if a system can be developed to solve these processing problems. If the results of the survey are positive, it is refined to produce a more detailed feasibility study. From the outcome of the feasibility study, a decision is made whether to proceed with the design of a system. One of the alternatives sketched in the feasibility study is chosen for development if a positive decision is made.

**TABLE 14-1**
THE SYSTEMS LIFE CYCLE

---

Inception
   Preliminary survey
Feasibility study
   Existing procedures
   Alternative systems
   Cost estimates
Systems analysis
   Details of present procedures
   Collection of data on volumes, input/output, files
Design
   Ideal system unconstrained
   Revisions to make ideal acceptable
Specifications
   Processing logic
   File design
   Input/output
   Programming requirements
   Manual procedures
Programming
Testing
   Unit tests
   Combined module tests
   Acceptance tests
Training
Conversion and installation
Operations
   Maintenance
   Enhancements

---

In systems analysis, the existing information processing procedures are documented in detail. During requirements analysis, designers attempt to learn what users expect a new system to do. One major task during this phase is to define the boundaries of the system. Does the problem just concern inventory control, or should any new system also consider the problems in purchasing when inventory has to be replenished? Data are also collected during analysis on the volume of transactions, decision points, and existing files.

The most challenging and creative part of the life cycle is the design of a new system. One approach to this task is to develop an ideal system relatively unconstrained by cost or technology; this ideal system is then refined until it becomes feasible. Detailed specifications must be prepared for the system just designed. The exact logic to be followed in processing and the contents and structure of the files must be specified. Input and output devices are selected, and the formats for I/O are developed. These requirements for processing, files, and I/O activities lead to the specification of programming requirements; these requirements can be turned over to a programming staff for coding.

In the programming stage, the actual computer programs necessary to perform the logical operations of processing are written. In some organizations this task is done by a separate group of programmers; other organizations use analyst-programmers. The same individuals who perform the systems analysis and design also code the resulting programs. Programs have to be tested carefully, first as units and then in combined modules. Usually a programming task is broken down into a series of smaller subtasks or modules; all the individual modules must operate together if the system is to work properly. During the final stages of testing, there will be some type of acceptance test in which users verify that the system works satisfactorily.

Since one purpose of the new information processing system is to change existing procedures, training is crucial. All individuals have to understand what is required by the new system. When training has been completed, it is possible to undertake conversion; it may be necessary to write special programs to convert existing files into new ones or to create files from manual records. Finally, after all these stages, the system is installed.

After the problems of installation have been resolved and the organization has adjusted to the changes created by the new system, the operational stage is begun; that is, the system now operates on a routine basis. However, this does not mean that it remains unchanged: there is a constant need for maintenance and enhancements. Maintenance is required because programs inevitably have errors that must be corrected when they appear. Because of the creative nature of design, users and the computer staff may not have communicated accurately, so that certain aspects of the system must be modified as operational experience is gained with it. As users work with the system, they will learn more about it and will develop ideas for change and enhancements. It is unreasonable to consider a computer-based information system finished; the system continues to evolve throughout its life cycle if, in fact, it is successful.

Figure 14-1 shows the resources required during each stage of the life cycle for a typical system. (The pattern of time required would be much the same.) Few resources are usually required during the inception and feasibility study. Once systems analysis is begun, more expenses will be incurred as analysts and users work on the system and its design. These stages culminate in the preparation of specifications from which programming can begin. The programming stage is intensive and requires the most resources. For a large project, the entire process of design can last two years or more, of which over a year may be required to write programs and test them. Training will occur in parallel with the later stages of programming, and finally the system will be converted and installed. After this time, the system reverts to operational status and is run on a routine basis. The resources required at this stage are steady with some increases as the system becomes older and more changes are requested.

One noticeable trend in the industry is to move more of the design process forward, that is, to spend more time in analysis and design. If a system is well specified, there are fewer changes during programming. These later changes often require major redesign of programs and files, a very costly process. The

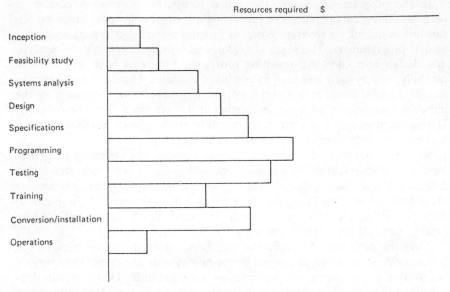

**FIGURE 14-1**
Resources required during each stage of the life cycle for a typical system.

entire systems life cycle can be compared to constructing a building. Changes are relatively inexpensive in the early conceptual stages. They become a little more expensive at the blueprint stage and exorbitant when the walls are erected. For systems, changes are much the same; in the conceptual stages of analysis and design they are reasonable. However, when programs are being written and some are complete, major design changes have the potential for creating huge time and cost overruns.

## RESPONSIBILITIES DURING THE LIFE CYCLE

Users, management, and the information services department staff interact in a number of ways during the analysis, design, and operation of information systems. In this part of the text on systems analysis and design, we shall often refer to the responsibilities of each of these groups in the development of successful systems. Because this task is so complex and demanding, it is essential that all three groups cooperate during the analysis and design process. Table 14-2 restates the stages in the systems life cycle and suggests the appropriate roles for users, management, and the information services department.

The user initiates the preliminary survey by suggesting a potential application. The information services department responds with a rough estimate of its desirability and with several alternative systems, for example, improvements to present information processing activities, a batch system, a package, or even an on-line system, each meeting some percentage of user needs. Management must

**TABLE 14-2**
RESPONSIBILITIES DURING THE SYSTEM LIFE CYCLE

| Stages | Users | Responsibilities of Management | Information services staff |
|---|---|---|---|
| Inception | Initiate study, suggest application, sketch information needs, describe existing processing procedures | Approve area for application, set objectives | Listen to requirements, respond to questions, devise alternatives, assess using rough estimates, prepare preliminary survey |
| Feasibility study | Help evaluate existing system and proposed alternatives, select alternative for design | Review feasibility, understand proposal, choose alternative | Evaluate alternatives using agreed-upon criteria |
| Systems analysis | Help describe existing system, collect and analyze data | Provide resources, attend reviews | Conduct analysis, collect data, and document findings |
| Design | Design output, input, processing logic; plan for conversion and forecast impact on users; design manual procedures; remain aware of file structures and design | Encourage user design, provide rewards, attend reviews, plan impact | Present alternatives and tradeoffs to users for their decisions |
| Specifications | Review specifications, help develop specifications for manual procedures | Understand high-level logic, key features | Combine user needs with technical requirements to develop specifications, develop technical conversion plan |
| Programming | Monitor progress | Monitor, provide buffer, extra resources | Organize programming, design modules, code programs, report progress |
| Testing | Generate test data and evaluate results | Review | Test program modules individually and in entire system |
| Training | Develop materials, conduct training sessions | Review | Aid in preparation of materials and train operations staff |
| Conversion and installation | Phase conversion, provide resources, conduct postimplementation audit | Attend user sessions, demonstrate management commitment | Coordinate conversion, perform conversion processing tasks, help in postimplementation audit |
| Operations | Provide data and utilize output, monitor system use and quality suggest modifications and enhancements | Monitor | Process data to produce output reliably, respond to enhancement requests, suggest improvements, monitor service |

approve of the basic suggestion and the idea of a new computer application in this area of the firm. Management should also participate in setting the objectives for any new system. A preliminary survey evaluates each alternative on criteria developed by a selection committee. The selection committee, with management participation, authorizes a feasibility study, possibly eliminating some alternatives suggested in the preliminary survey.

The information services department staff conducts the feasibility study with help and advice from users. Users conduct an analysis of the existing system and help the information services department evaluate various alternatives on criteria specified by the selection committee. Management reviews the feasibility of the proposed alternatives and develops an understanding of what the system will accomplish. The selection committee selects the alternative for implementation with participation and review by management. Possibly the committee chooses the alternative of no new system, in which case the application may be held in abeyance until changing conditions make it feasible.

If the decision is to proceed with the development of a new system, users and the information services department staff collaborate to analyze the existing system. Users aid by explaining existing processing procedures and providing data. The computer staff uses this information to document the existing system and help establish the boundaries of a new system. Management has a key role to play in this stage: it must provide adequate resources both for the information services department and for users. It may be necessary to hire additional staff so that users can participate or additional analysts to work on the project.

Next the design of a new system begins; we advocate that users design their own output and input and basic processing logic. The information services department acts as a catalyst, presenting alternatives for users to consider. Management encourages user design through its own attendance at review meetings. Management may provide special rewards, prizes, or other incentives to help encourage user participation in design. Management also must plan for the impact of the system on the organization at this point. Will the structure of the organization be changed? How will work groups be affected? What will specific individuals do as a result of the system? A plan for conversion, including a forecast of the impact of the system on all potential users, should be developed. A conversion plan can be started at this point and users can work on the design of any manual procedures associated with the new system.

The information services staff develops detailed specifications based on the logic and requirements specified by users; the staff also prepares a technical conversion plan. The users on the design team review the technical plans and also work on the development of specifications for manual procedures. It is vitally important at this stage for both users and managers to understand the system. Users must be familiar with the output, input, and processing logic. Management must understand the overall flow of the system and be aware of key decisions. For example, management should be aware if inventory items are to be grouped into classes and different reordering rules applied to each class. Management should help set the classification and reorder rules and understand how the logic is to work.

The user and management role during programming is one of monitoring progress. Are modern techniques being used to manage programming? Is a project schedule maintained and are resources reallocated as necessary to achieve installation on schedule? The bulk of the responsibility during this design stage rests with the information services department. The staff has to design program modules, code them, and test them both alone and in combination. Management should realize that they need to help when problems arise. The development of a computer-based system is similar to a research and development project; it is very difficult to anticipate every contingency. There will be project slippages, budget overruns, and other problems. The role of management is to provide a buffer for the project and furnish additional resources where they will help.

During testing, users should define data for test programs and an attempt should be made to generate data with errors to be sure the system will catch them. Users should carefully examine test results and evaluate the adequacy of processing. Management should also participate in the reviews of data processed by the system. Some kind of acceptance test should also be conducted by the information services department and the results evaluated by users. A parallel test of old and new procedures or pilot studies may be used for this purpose.

Training is essential for smooth conversion and installation. Users develop materials and actually conduct the training sessions. Management remains aware of the training program, attends occasional sessions to communicate support for the system, and checks that its knowledge of the system is accurate. Training can often be combined with testing; the preparation of test data serves to help train users. The information services staff aids in the preparation of materials and has the responsibility of training the operations staff.

Conversion is a crucial part of the systems life cycle and should be done in phases if possible. For example, can one department or geographic area be converted first? The information services department coordinates conversion and performs conversion procedures such as creating initial files for the new system. Users and the information services department should jointly conduct a postimplementation audit and report the results to management. How well does the system meet specifications? How good were the specifications; that is, how do users react to the system now? How do the original estimates compare with what was achieved? These data can be helpful in making estimates for future projects.

Finally, during operations, users furnish data for input and work with the output. Users and management will probably suggest enhancements and modifications to the system over time. The information services department should also look for improvements itself and respond to modifications suggested by users.

## RESOURCES FOR NEW SYSTEMS

Originally, in many organizations, the information services department had to search for new computer applications. Now, for most mature computer installa-

---

## MANAGEMENT PROBLEM 14-1

The president of Farway Manufacturing Company was pondering the firm's recent disastrous attempt to develop a computer-based system for factory-floor data collection. The company wished to improve scheduling and control over work-in-process inventories. A consultant was hired who recommended the development of a computer-based production control system.

The recommendations of the consultant were accepted and he was hired to design the system. It turned out that the consultant had designed a similar system for another manufacturing company and proposed to transfer it to Farway. This seemed like a very economical approach, so the president quickly agreed.

The consultant set about his task with zeal; within six months the necessary programming changes had been made and the system was ready to begin operation. Over one weekend, terminals were installed in all departments and on Monday morning, workers were supposed to begin using the new system to report production. The workers are paid on piece rate and are unionized.

For reasons not completely understood by the president, the system failed completely. No one provided input and the little data collected were all erroneous. What happened? Why did the systems development effort fall so miserably?

---

tions, there is more demand for services than resources available to satisfy the demand. Typically, the budget for developing new computer-based systems is only one part of the total budget for the information services department.

### Demands and Resources

What are the demands on the information services department? There are a number of responsibilities for the typical information services department:

**1** One of the first concerns is operating existing systems; that is, the information systems developed in the past must be executed on a routine basis.

**2** Maintenance also requires resources. Where many existing systems are in operation, it is necessary to make repairs and to maintain computer programs.

**3** Enhancements to existing systems are frequently requested by users; if a system is used, individuals will make suggestions for improvements. These modifications entail programming changes and sometimes even require new computer equipment.

**4** The development of a new information system requires a major commitment of resources.

Many individuals outside the information services department see only the operation of existing systems and the development of new ones. However, maintenance and enhancements require over 50 percent of the programming effort in many firms.

What are the resources available to the information services department? There are two major categories of information services resources: people and machines. Machine capabilities are necessary to develop and operate computer-based information systems. Different types of information systems require different equipment; for example, an on-line system necessitates equipment for communications and terminals. A large database application makes demands for data storage devices.

On the human side, many of the resources of the information services department are not interchangeable among jobs. We can identify a number of positions in this department:

**1** Operators are trained to operate the computer and its peripheral equipment.

**2** Clerical personnel manually process input and output; they may separate copies of reports and prepare output for distribution, and may also check input and output for accuracy.

**3** Input specialists transcribe data to machine-readable form by, for example, keying information on a CRT.

**4** Maintenance programmers repair errors in the programs that direct the computer. These individuals may also be responsible for enhancements to existing systems.

**5** Systems analysts work with users to define specifications for a new system.

**6** Applications programmers convert system specifications into the computer programs necessary to process data and produce the desired output.

**7** Systems programmers are found in large installations; they work with the control software of the computer.

**8** Managers of various functions such as operations and systems design are also employed by an information services department, if it is large enough.

**A Resource Allocation Problem**

The basic allocation problem is to match demands for services against resources (see Table 14-3). How much discretion do we have in this process? Unless some applications are to be eliminated, the information services department has to maintain equipment and needs operators, clerical personnel, control, and maintenance programmers to operate existing systems. (Some installations also need a systems programmer for this purpose.) Discretionary resources can be used for enhancements and the development of new information systems. Systems analysts, applications programmers, and necessary managers, plus machine capacity, constitute the discretionary resources available to the department.

How easily can these resources be increased? Machine capacity can be enlarged, although usually it takes many months to obtain and install new computer equipment. New personnel can, of course, be added; however, there is a limit to how rapidly new employees can be integrated into the organization

**TABLE 14-3**
DEMANDS AND RESOURCES OF THE INFORMATION SERVICES DEPARTMENT

| Demands | Resources |
| --- | --- |
| Operating existing information systems | Equipment |
| Maintenance | Human |
| Enhancements |   Operators |
| Development of new information systems |   Clerical personnel |
| |   Input specialists |
| |   Maintenance programmers |
| |   Systems analysts |
| |   Applications programmers |
| |   Systems programmers |
| |   Managers |

and become productive. Thus, in the short run, there is probably little that can be done to increase the resources devoted to the development of new systems within an organization. However, added resources can be used to purchase applications packages and/or consulting services from outside the organization. In the long run, if users are dissatisfied with the amount of resources devoted to the development of new systems, they will have to undertake efforts to increase the discretionary portion of the information services department budget.

## PROBLEMS IN THE LIFE CYCLE

It is widely recommended that the stages in the systems life cycle described in Table 14-1 be followed. However, when we have seen them followed rigorously as a checklist, usually the result has been systems that fail. What is wrong with the life cycle? Is the concept invalid? There are two major difficulties with following these stages rigidly in the development of a system. First, the stages tend to focus attention on a particular type of application, and second, they mislead analysts as to their role in the systems design process.

The first problem of the checklist is its orientation toward transactions systems and paperwork automation. Notice a complete lack of mention in the checklist of designing systems to support decision making. This approach is oriented toward tabulating operations, and the list was probably developed before the advent of modern electronic computers. Older systems were directed toward transactions processing, and the systems design stages reflect this bias. Certainly there are good reasons to develop transactions-processing information systems. However, if we have faith in the potential of information systems to improve managerial decision making, then we should focus on decisions as well as document flows in systems design.

A second problem of the checklist is even more serious. The stages suggest that a systems analyst must be in charge of the systems analysis and design activity: the analyst alone has the tools and techniques for designing the system. Any mention of users is conspicuously absent in these design steps. In Chapter 5 we discussed some of the organizational problems of systems, the fact that systems can affect power relationships and create conflict in an organization. We need to develop an entirely different role for the analyst and user to overcome these problems.

## USER-ORIENTED DESIGN

### Problems with the Conventional View

In the conventional approach to systems analysis and design described above, the analyst is a skilled leader. The analyst interviews users, collects data, and returns to the information services department to create a new system. In recognition of the fact that this approach usually does not work in systems analysis and design, numerous periodicals suggest that user participation is necessary to ensure successful systems. The writers in these journals suggest that the analyst spend more time with users, show them report formats, and so forth. However, in their viewpoint, the analyst is still clearly in charge. We label this as "pseudoparticipation"; we are consulted, but few changes are made in the system on the basis of the users' suggestions. The analyst and the information services department are still very much in charge of the project.

Instead of viewing the analyst as the designer of the system, we recommend strongly that *users should design their own systems*. Does this mean that we actually undertake some of the tasks normally carried out by the analyst? The answer is definitely "yes." Our recommended approach raises two questions: first, why should users assume this role, second, how can users do so? Our experience indicates that users are capable of responding to this approach and that successful results can be achieved (Lucas, 1974c).

There are a number of good reasons for participation and user design of systems. User involvement should not be criticized, only the way in which involvement has been attempted in the past. Real involvement requires time; users must understand the system and their recommendations have to prevail.

A more user-oriented approach to design may require deviations from the standard life cycle. Although the conceptual steps represented in the cycle may be followed, innovations will be included. For example, design is often facilitated by prototyping. A prototype is a smaller scale version of a planned feature for a new system. A good example is sales forecasting: we can code the new forecasting routine on a time-sharing system or on a personal computer and analyze past data for a limited number of products. Users will be intimately involved in this test so that they can provide feedback on the prototype and evaluate its output. When they are satisfied, the prototype can be programmed in final form with more error routines, data manipulation features, etc, that were excluded to keep the prototype simple.

## MANAGEMENT PROBLEM 14-2

As a new attempt at designing a planning system is about to begin, Robert Johnson is contemplating a previous disaster. Johnson is the director of planning for Petrochem, a diversified manufacturer of petrochemicals. The company has an ambitious acquisition program and frequently enters joint ventures with other firms.

Planning includes detailed computations of various possible outcomes from entering these ventures. The return to the company and forecasted cash flow are of particular importance to the firm. Johnson and his staff currently use calculators to make projections, and each suggested project requires a monumental clerical effort to evaluate.

Several years ago, Johnson approached the firm's information services department to ask for help. His project was rejected a number of times in favor of what he considers mundane, low-return projects, for example, putting the company telephone directory on the computer.

Finally, two years later, the information services department sent an analyst to study his problems. The analyst spent about one week in the planning department and then designed a simple batch system to automate some of the calculations. On attempting to use the system, the planning staff found that it would not perform any of the calculations needed. The staff also could not understand how to complete the input forms for the system.

After a great deal of work, Johnson persuaded the president of the company to intercede. Now, the information services department is back to try again. However, Johnson's staff wants to buy microcomputers and spreadsheet packages, and leave the information services department out of the decision.

What should Johnson do? Who is responsible for the problems at Petrochem? Is it Johnson, the information services department, users, the president, or all of them?

### Predicted Results

User participation eliminates potential difficulties of an organizational nature in systems design; it particularly helps to reduce problems created by power transfers and conflict. Users, by taking charge of the systems design activity, retain control over their information processing activities. Participation reduces the amount of power transferred from users to the information services department and the potential for conflict. Because of participation, we are not so dependent on the information services department. Knowledge gained through participating in and influencing the new system means the information services department copes with less uncertainty for users, reducing the amount of power the users surrender in developing a system. Mutual dependence is actually changed to cooperation in an effort to accomplish the common goal of developing and implementing a successful system. The user understands the system better by being in charge of it, and therefore, the amount of uncertainty associated with the project is reduced.

## A SYSTEM FOR HUMAN BLOOD MANAGEMENT

*In the United States human blood has a legal life time of 21 days from collection. During this time it can be used for transfusion to a patient of the same blood type. However, at the end of the time it must be discarded. The blood is collected from donations at regional sites, and after a series of tests it is shipped to blood banks at hospitals in the region. Blood is issued from this blood bank during its legal life time. Because some issued blood is not used it can be returned and reissued.*

*It is difficult to evaluate the performance of a regional blood system. The most common measures used are the percentage of days when extra deliveries have to be made to satisfy a hospital's demand and the outdate rate, the percentage of a hospital's supply that becomes outdated for each hospital in the region. A system has been designed to arrive at decision support mechanisms for regional blood centers. This system addresses the following inventory management questions:*

*1.  What is the minimal achievable outdate and shortage target which can be set for a region?*

*2.  What type of distribution policy is necessary to achieve these targets?*

*3.  What should the level of regional supply of blood be in order to achieve different targets?*

*This decision support system is based on a mathematical programming model. The primary objective of the model is to optimize the allocation of the regional blood resources and at the same time to observe policy constraints. The model features centralized management of blood rather than management by individual hospitals, prescheduled deliveries and a distribution system through which blood may be rotated among hospitals.*

*This decision support system was implemented in the 38 hospital region of Long Island, New York, and has been operational there for some three years. The system has been established as routine and has drastically reduced the outdating and shortage incidents in the region. Plans are being made to introduce the system in other regions in the U.S. and abroad.*

G. P. Prastacos and E. Brodheim, *Management Science*, vol. 26. no. 5, May 1980.

By performing some of the information services department tasks, user departments reduce task differences between them and the information services department and thus reduce the potential for conflict. By working together, the information services department and users develop more understanding of each other's problems, and thus help to reduce ambiguities. Heavy user participation also leads to more understanding of the jobs of information services department staff members, and vice versa, reducing job differences. Users also become more familiar with computer jargon, so that communication obstacles are reduced between the information services department and users.

How can we participate where conditions are not favorable, for example, in a single application to be used by many different individuals? Imagine a grocery

**MANAGEMENT PROBLEM 14-3**

The information services department at Madison Drugs is trying to stimulate heavy user participation in the design of information systems. A new system for financial management is in the planning stages, but problems with users seem to occupy most of the planning sessions in the department.

One of the key figures in the new system is a user named Keith Ryan. Keith has been at Madison for 20 years and is responsible for all financial transactions. The information services department chose him as the most obvious user to head the design effort. Keith is in sympathy with this selection, but says, "I don't have time to spend designing a system: I work 60 hours a week now."

The information services department recognizes the extent of Keith's efforts and devotion to the company. However, they ask why additional staff cannot be hired to remove some of the load from Keith? Keith says that he has tried to break in new people, but the demands of the job are too rigorous and they all leave.

The president of Madison wants to know why the design of this new system is taking so long. What should the manager of the information services department do? What can he suggest to the president?

---

store planning to install point-of-sales terminals for check-out operations. If a chain has several hundred or thousand checkers, all of them cannot participate in the design of the system. However, in this situation representatives of the checkers could participate in the design. These representatives can meet with their coworkers at each store as the system is implemented; any questions or problems during the design process can be explored with the checkers using these representatives as liaison agents.

There can, of course, be problems with user participation to the extent advocated here. An individual whose ideas are rejected by the group may become alienated. It may not be possible to satisfy expectations raised about future participation in, for example, operation of the system. Certainly, participation is time-consuming. We are usually already under pressure when we request a system; now it is necessary for users to additional take time to design a system. Finally, there are the dangers of pseudoparticipation. Where users do not have a real say, but only go through the motions of participation, their frustration will increase. On balance, it seems fair to say that there is too little participation at present. Whether we agree on the extent of user design or not, most organizations should be striving for more user input in the design process.

Does a user have enough knowledge and training to participate in the design of a system? In the next section we discuss the user requirements of this philosophy of systems design. They are not too severe, since the user is specifying parts of the system that are familiar; the user is certainly not programming a system.

A more serious problem with this approach is the attitude of the analyst, who may find the ideas above quite radical. Management will have to adopt the approach suggested here and influence the information services department to implement these user-design procedures. Although the analyst may perceive a diminished role at first, the more successful systems and better relationships with the users that should result from the approach will help to assuage the analyst's misgivings.

The proposed extensive involvement and influence of users is time-consuming and costly. Systems undoubtedly take longer to develop in this manner and cost more. However, we must examine the incremental costs and time of this approach and compare them with those for the conventional method of systems design. If user-controlled design results in successful systems, then a fairly small increment in cost and time should be worthwhile in view of the problems of many information systems developed under conventional procedures.

## Required Knowledge

What does the user have to know to be able to design a system? There are four components of design for which users should have elementary knowledge and extensive control:

1 Output
2 Input
3 File contents
4 Processing logic

First, users should consider the different aspects of information and decision making discussed in Chapters 2, 3, and 5. What output from a new information processing system do we desire? Working with an analyst who explains different alternatives, users develop drafts of the output, for example, a printed report or display for a CRT.

All information and output must come either directly from an input, from a file, or from computations based on input and file data. With the output defined, the contents of files and inputs can be determined. Users then design actual input methods.

Analysts may define the files by working with users. However, with no more background than Chapters 10 and 11, users should be able to make a major contribution to the definition of file contents and structure. Certainly users are in the best position to indicate the size of data items and to specify updating needs.

The response time, the degree to which data must be up to date, and the volumes of input/output activities help determine the type of system needed, for example, batch, inquiry, or on-line updating. If data do need to be up to the minute, or if various geographical locations must be coordinated as in a reservations application, an on-line updating system is necessary. If a user must be able to obtain immediate response, then at least on-line input/output for inquiry purposes must be provided.

Our final task is to specify basic processing logic. What computations does the user require to produce the desired output? How can output fields be derived? What file data are updated on a regular basis? What editing and line checks should be performed on the input?

A user who has understood and mastered the material in the text so far is in an excellent position to design input, output, processing logic, and file contents for a computer-based information system, with guidance from a computer professional.

### Design Team

To coordinate users and the information services department staff, we recommend the formation of a design team with a user as head of the team. Having a user in charge makes the user role apparent, ensures that time will be available from other users, and demonstrates a strong commitment to users on the part of the information services department. Normal job activities should be reduced for the user in charge of the design team.

In cases where there are too many individuals for all of them to be involved, liaison representatives are suggested. These people interview other users and brief them on the system as it is developed. They are responsible for soliciting participation in phases where it is meaningful.

The information services department systems designer guides the design team, teaching the tools and techniques necessary to complete the design and providing required technical advice and support, for example, by developing detailed file structures after users complete the logical file design. Systems designers monitor the project, describe the different stages, and help to schedule them. However, the actual analysis and design work is done by the users with the assistance of the analyst, rather than vice versa as in conventional systems design.

### DATA COLLECTION

What techniques are available to the design team for collecting data? As discussed earlier, the objective is to develop an understanding of key decisions and how they are supported with information. The team needs to examine decisions, the flow of information in the organization, and the types of processing undertaken.

### Observation

One technique for collecting data on a process is to observe that process. Frequently in systems analysis and design we will "walk through" a system observing crucial information flows and decision points. Then we may use one of the graphical techniques described later in this chapter to prepare documentation of our understanding of how the system functions.

Observations can also be quite structured; we may develop a rating form of some type to collect data on the frequency of inquiries, say, in a credit office. The analyst prepares a form showing the possible inquiries and then during a sample of different days and hours codes the actual inquiries.

## Interviews

The systems analyst spends a great deal of time interacting with others, particularly in interview settings. Interviews have varying degrees of structure; for a first meeting there may be no structure at all. The analyst may be getting acquainted with the user and gaining a broad understanding of the problem area.

Often, as the project progresses, more structured interviews are conducted. The analyst may wish to prepare in advance an interview schedule containing the questions to be asked and the points to be covered. The main thing is to be prepared.

One of the most common problems in interviewing is probing for the answer. The interviewer, perhaps unconsciously, encourages the interviewee to give a desired response. Often people being interviewed follow these cues and try to help the interviewer. It is very important from the standpoint of systems design to be sure that the data collected are as accurate as possible.

## Questionnaires

A questionnaire allows us to obtain data from a relatively large number of people at a reasonable cost. A questionnaire can be thought of as a structured interview form with questions designed so they can be answered without a face-to-face encounter. The design of a good questionnaire is a difficult task. Although the idea is an extension of a structured interview form, the questionnaire is, in principle, capable of being completed by the respondent alone without an interviewer being present.

Table 14-4 presents some examples of questionnaire and/or structured interview questions. (A questionnaire can also be completed in an interview setting.) The example illustrates several different types of questions. The questions with a 1-through-7 number scale assess subjective perceptions and attitudes; no real unit such as dollars, degrees, etc., measures these variables.

Another type of question is open-ended. Here we simply ask the respondent to write a short paragraph to answer our inquiry. Such a question might be, "Please indicate the four most important pieces of information that you use in your work."

As a part of our effort to determine attitudes during the design process, we may also use questionnaires and interviews. Knowing attitudes helps us prepare for how different users will respond to a new system. In fact, we could use these attitudinal ratings to include some of the least receptive people who are important potential users on a design team.

**TABLE 14-4**
SAMPLE INTERVIEW AND QUESTIONNAIRE ITEMS

Attitude Questions

Directions: Circle the number which best represents your opinion.

For example: The temperature inside today is:

Too cold _____ Too hot

1 2 3 4 5 ⑥ 7

The answer indicates that the temperature is hot.

1 My general impression of the data processing staff is that they

| are uninterested in the user | _____ 1 2 3 4 5 6 7 | are interested in the user |

| are not too competent technically | _____ 1 2 3 4 5 6 7 | are highly competent technically |

| are not too good in dealing with people | _____ 1 2 3 4 5 6 7 | are good in dealing with people |

| do low-quality work | _____ 1 2 3 4 5 6 7 | do high-quality work |

2 How do you think a computer might benefit you? (You may answer more than one.)

1 Reduce the time I spend processing papers
2 Reduce errors
3 Make my job more interesting
4 Make it easier to find information
5 Make it easier to use information
6 I don't know specifically how, but feel it would help
   Comments _____

3 What do you think the major problems with a computer would be? (You may answer more than one.)

1 It would make things more complicated
2 It would make more mistakes
3 It would be harder to use
4 It would take more of my time
5 It would lose information
6 It would make our jobs boring
7 I don't know specifically what, but feel there would be problems
   Comments _____

4 If we use a computer here, the company will not need me anymore.
   1 Strongly agree  2 Agree  3 Neutral  4 Disagree  5 Strongly disagree

Design Information

Please rate the following reports on the indicated characteristics

Inventory Status Report

| 1 | Highly accurate | _____ 1 2 3 4 5 6 7 | Highly inaccurate |

| 2 | Out of date | _____ 1 2 3 4 5 6 7 | Timely |

| 3 | Useful | _____ 1 2 3 4 5 6 7 | Useless |

Sales Analysis Report

| 4 | Highly accurate | _____ 1 2 3 4 5 6 7 | Highly inaccurate |

| 5 | Out of date | _____ 1 2 3 4 5 6 7 | Timely |

| 6 | Useful | _____ 1 2 3 4 5 6 7 | Useless |

## Comparison

Both questionnaires and interviews are important for the analyst, though interviewing will probably be used more. The advantage of the interview is that a new tangent can be followed. The respondent is not constrained by the limitations of the questions but can expand in other directions. If the question is ambiguous, the interviewer can explain what is desired. Interviews are the best technique in an unstructured setting and when it is necessary to probe issues in depth.

Questionnaires offer the advantage of being relatively inexpensive to administer to a large group of respondents. They are well suited to expanding data collection beyond the interview. For example, assume that a system is being developed that will be used by a number of sales representatives nationwide. If the firm has 500 sales representatives, it is impossible to include all of them on a design team; instead we would use representatives chosen to be typical of the types of salespersons on the force. This group might assist in developing a questionnaire for the rest of the sales force that has, until now, been uninvolved in the design. The questionnaire could explain some of the chosen tradeoffs and characteristics of the system to all potential users to obtain their input and feedback. Valuable attitudinal data could also be collected at the same time. Questionnaires are also a good way to obtain feedback in a postimplementation audit.

## DESIGN TOOLS

In the remainder of this chapter we present an overview of some of the tools that have been developed to assist the designer.

### Flowcharts

Probably the oldest graphic design aid is the flowchart. Each organization may have its own standards for flowcharting; in addition, the American National Standards Institute (ANSI) has published a standard for flowcharts.

A flowchart consists of a series of symbols and connections among them. A chart can depict a number of information processing activities ranging from a computer configuration through the detailed steps of a program. (However, flowcharting of programs at a detailed level has been declining in popularity because of the effort involved and because of failure to update flowcharts when programs change.)

Figure 14-2 contains the basic symbols in the ANSI standard. Input and output activities irrespective of media or format are represented by a parallelogram. However, specialized symbols may be used instead, for example, for a terminal. The process outline is a rectangle and is used for any kind of data processing; it is the symbol to use when no other special one is available. This symbol can stand for data transformation, movement, or logic operations.

The flowlines show the sequence among steps and the transmission of

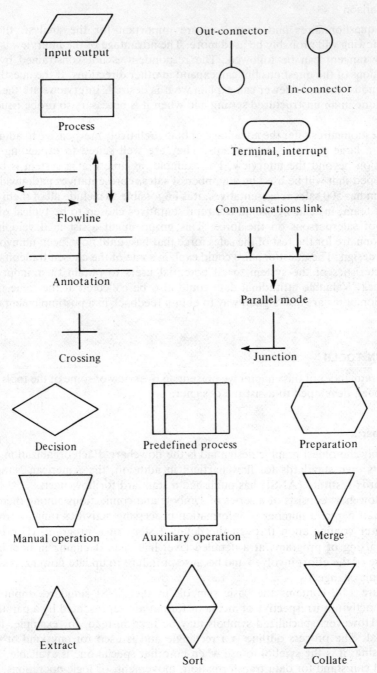

**FIGURE 14-2**
Basic and specialized symbols.

information among operations. An arrow is used to specify direction when it is not implicit in the diagram. ANSI specifies that arrows are not necessary when the flow is from top to bottom and from left to right.

An open rectangle with a dotted line connecting it to the flowchart is used to annotate the flowchart. Because charts rarely fit on a single sheet, different pieces are cross-referenced. Out-connectors are used to indicate that the flow is to be continued on another page, and an in-connector shows that another page contains the preceding processing.

An interrupt symbol shows a beginning, an end, or a break in the usual line of flow. Communications links indicate the transmission of data from one location to another.

The next set of symbols in Figure 14-2 is specialized and augments the standard processing symbols. One of the most important of these is the diamond, which represents a decision point. Multiple paths representing possible outcomes of the decision exit from this symbol.

Figure 14-3 shows some of the input/output special symbols that represent

**FIGURE 14-3**
Input/output and equipment symbols.

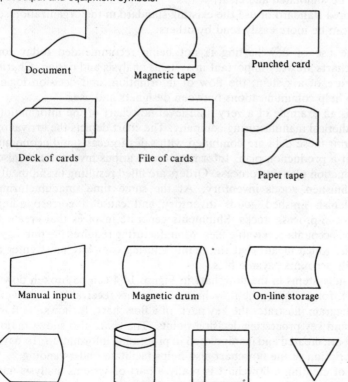

Document     Magnetic tape     Punched card

Deck of cards     File of cards     Paper tape

Manual input     Magnetic drum     On-line storage

Display     Magnetic disk     Core     Off-line storage

various types of media. This figure also contains additional symbols that can be used to represent specific computer equipment such as a disk or drum.

Given these symbols we can represent a wide variety of processes graphically. For the analyst, flowcharts of the existing system can be of great assistance in visualizing how it operates. We shall see many flowcharts of manual procedures in subsequent chapters. These charts can be used to communicate with users as well as within a design team; they also are valuable for training purposes.

Unfortunately, the many ways to combine these symbols into flowcharts can make it difficult to read and share charts among different individuals. We can offer some guidelines to facilitate the construction and the later readability of the charts (Chapin, 1976):

Use simple symbols where possible; avoid overly elaborate charts.

Try to maintain the same level of detail on the charts.

Consider using hierarchies of charts; one chart is at a high level and succeeding levels of detail are shown in charts that expand the symbols in the higher-level chart.

Develop the chart to suit the reader; if the chart is for communications with users, it should be annotated and clear.

Try to develop a standard or use the existing standard in the organization so that the charts can be more easily read by others.

Although the use of flowcharting is not being recommended today for programs, flowcharts are very important in systems analysis and design. Charts show the structure of a system, the flow of information, and decision logic. Flowcharts also help communications between designers and user.

Figure 14-4 is an example of a very high level flowchart of the information flows in a hypothetical manufacturing company. The chart depicts the arrival of orders at the firm; these data are combined with sales forecasts and economic data to arrive at a production plan. Information on various inventories is also vital to the production planning process. Orders are filled resulting in shipments that decrease finished goods inventory. At the same time, manufacturing operations replenish finished goods inventory and cause a corresponding decrease in work-in-process stocks. Shipments generate invoices that create a receivable on the accounts-receivable files. Manufacturing requires the purchase of raw materials, which means that the manufacturing company must enter a transaction on its accounts-payable files.

Each of the subsystems in the flowchart in Figure 14-4 can be broken down into more detail, for example, the flowchart of accounts receivable. However, the high-level diagram illustrates the key parts of a flowchart. It shows the flow of information and key processing/decision points. The chart also shows major files of data that are created and manipulated in processing information. To have a narrative description of the flowchart also helps facilitate understanding.

The process of creating a flowchart is really a part of systems analysis and

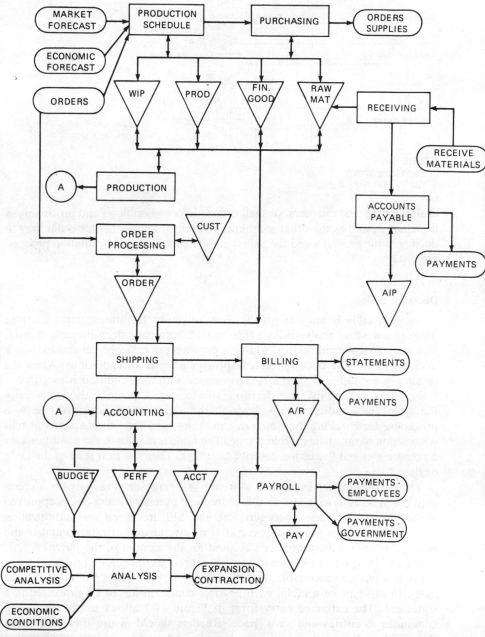

**FIGURE 14-4**
Information processing in a manufacturing firm.

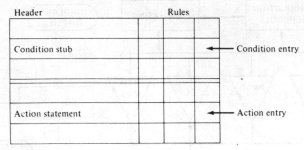

**FIGURE 14-5**
Decision table format.

design. In the next chapters we shall discuss information flows and processing; a flowchart as well as the other techniques described in this chapter is one way to document the analyst's and the users' understanding of an information processing system.

## Decision Tables

A decision table is another graphical technique to facilitate communications between users and analysts. As a side benefit, automatic decision table translators or manual algorithms exist so that a program can easily be generated from a decision table. The decision table expresses a series of conditions; when the conditions are fulfilled, then a rule associated with the condition is executed.

Figure 14-5 shows the basic decision table format. A header is used to identify the table and condition stubs describe the various conditions. A rule is a procedure for checking the different conditions, and the action statement tells what action to take when a rule is true. The table is read until the conditions for a rule are met and the action described is taken. Then the next scan of the table begins.

The decision tables in Figures 14-6 and 14-7 represent the logic for a credit card purchase authorization. In this example, a purchase under $50 is approved automatically. Purchases between $50 and $10 are given an authorization number. Finally, for purchases over $100 we give an authorization number and place a "hold" on the customer's account for the amount of the purchase.

Figures 14-6 and 14-7 illustrate two different forms of decision tables. The first figure is a limited-entry table that allows only a "yes" or a "no" entry for the rules. In this type of a table, each possible condition has to be expressed in a statement. The extended-entry form in Figure 14-7 allows us to use logical conditions as entries and save space. Readers should assure themselves that these tables adequately describe the logic for the credit card example and that the two tables are equivalent.

Decision tables have a number of advantages. First they can facilitate communications between analysts and users. In fact, users can often learn rather

| | | Rules | | |
|---|---|---|---|---|
| Credit card authorization | 1 | 2 | 3 | 4 |
| Is purchase less than $50 | Y | N | N | N |
| Is purchase between $50 and $100 | | Y | N | N |
| Is purchase over $100 | | | Y | N |
| Approve with no action | X | | | |
| Give authorization no. | | X | X | |
| Place hold on account | | | X | |
| Error | | | | X |

**FIGURE 14-6**
Limited-entry example.

easily to describe the logic of their decisions using decision tables. Decision tables are compact and express far more logic in a small location than a comparable flowchart. They are a good form of documentation that can be updated easily. Computer programs are available that translate decision tables into COBOL and FORTRAN programs automatically.

Some guidelines have been offered for table construction. First, avoid making tables too large; often several small tables are better than one. (A rule in one table can be to execute another table.) All possible rules must be presented and every rule must have an action associated with that rule. The action is to be taken if the set of conditions hold. (Tables can be action tables that consist of a single rule.)

Decision tables should be analyzed to be certain that they are complete and to avoid excessive rules, contradictions, and possible redundancies. See Fergus in Couger (1979). A table is complete if it accounts for the correct number of independent rules to cover all combinations of possible conditions. The number of rules to be accounted for is equal to the number of unique condition

**FIGURE 14-7**
Extended-entry example.

| | | Rules | |
|---|---|---|---|
| Credit card authorization | 1 | 2 | 3 |
| Is purchase p | p > $100 | $50 ≤ p ≥ $100 | 0 < p < $50 |
| Approve with no action | | | X |
| Give authorization | X | X | |
| Place hold on account | X | | |

combinations possible. This number of possible conditions is the product of the values each condition might assume.

In the example in Figure 14-7 are three conditions, each of which could be answered with two values "yes" or "no." To be complete, the table should then have $2 \times 2 \times 2$, or 8 rules. However, note that the possibilities of having two "yes" answers for a rule would be contradictory; a purchase could not be less than $50 and greater than $100 at the same time. Therefore, there is no need for rules that would have all three "yes" values.

If all the conditions in a table have the same number of values, the number or rules needed to satisfy all combinations is the number of values raised to the power of the number of conditions. Figure 14-7 has three conditions, each of which has two possible values, yielding $2^3$ or 8 possible rules. However, as mentioned above, not all possible rules will make sense, and editing is necessary.

The rules themselves must be unique and independent; they cannot contradict one another, and only one rule can apply in a given situation. It does not matter in what sequence rules are presented since only one set of conditions can be satisfied at a time.

The rules consist of relationships among the various conditions. That is, if there are three conditions in a rule—A, B, and C—then A and B and C must be true for the rule to be satisfied. Finally, if the rule is satisfied, then the logic of the table dictates that the action is to be executed (Murdick and Ross, 1975).

## STRUCTURED DESIGN

Systems analysis and design has been one of the greatest bottlenecks in the development of information processing systems. Many systems do not meet users' expectations or perform as originally envisioned. While there are a lot of reasons why something can go wrong in the development of a system, one of the most crucial activities is the actual design phase.

The flowcharts described in the previous section have been the primary tool of the designer for thirty or more years. This type of charting encourages excessive detail and does little to enhance the thought process. In an attempt to improve the design process, a number of more structured approaches have been developed.

What is structure in design? Basically, we try to take a disciplined, step-by-step approach to reduce complexity. A good example is "top down" design; this philosophy means that the designer first concentrates on an overview and then moves to successive levels of detail. If, at any step, the designer becomes confused, then he or she backs up one level to a diagram with more of an overview.

The process is very similar to the set of plans developed by an architect. When a client asks for a new building to be designed, the architect works to develop rough sketches and add detail over time. In presenting drawings to the client or even construction workers, the architect does not provide a first page with the

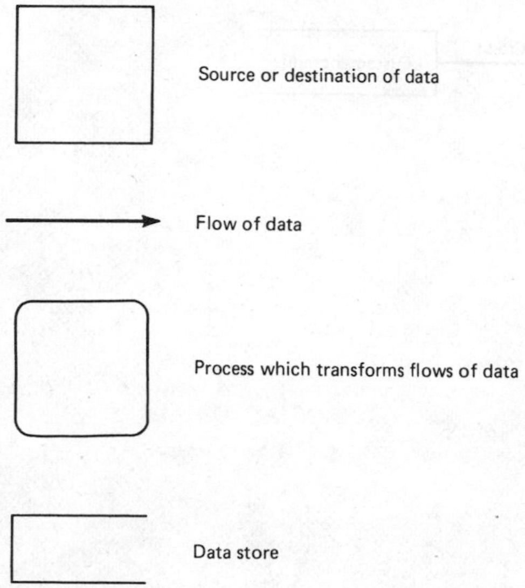

Source or destination of data

Flow of data

Process which transforms flows of data

Data store

**FIGURE 14-8**
Data flow diagram symbols.

details of the electrical wiring! Instead, usually we find the first page is a perspective of the building. The next page might be four side views followed by a page with high-level floor plan. As each page is turned we find more detail.

### Data Flow Diagrams

One of the most popular structured approaches to design is the use of data flow diagrams. See Figure 14-8. Compared to the flowcharts of the last section, the data flow diagram (DFD) is far less complex. There are only four symbols defined for the highest level of detail.

The DFD approach is more than just the symbols; it is important for the analyst to exercise discipline in preparing the charts. The recommended strategy is "top-down"; we endeavor to begin with a high level diagram and to place succeeding levels of detail on subsequent pages. In addition, as adding detail makes the drawing cluttered, the analyst should take one process or subsystem and explode its detail on a separate sheet of paper.

### An Example

Imagine that a group of entrepreneurs has decided to open a mail-order business selling software for personal computers. A customer sends in an order form and employees of the business ship software back to the customer. Figure 14-9 is a high level DFD for this firm. At this level, we see the basic flow of an order

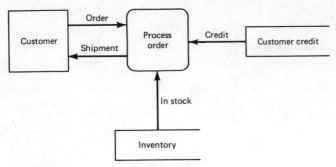

**FIGURE 14-9**
Overview of mail-order business.

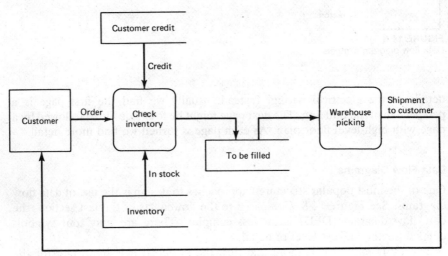

**FIGURE 14-10**
The next level of detail.

coming to the firm and a shipment going to the customer. We have to look at an inventory record and check the customer's credit.

Figure 14-10 presents the next level of detail. We see that the first action is to check the inventory to see if the software program ordered is in stock. If so, we place the order in a file marked "to be filled." The warehouse staff removes orders from this file, finds them in inventory, packages the program, and sends the shipment to the customer. If at any point, one loses track of the process, it is necessary only to back up one or two diagrams to get an overview.

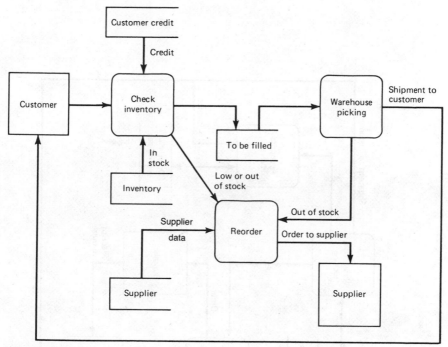

**FIGURE 14-11**
Reorder logic.

In Figure 14-11 the designer addresses the question of what to do when we are out of stock. Management has made the decision that backordering is probably not feasible; the customer will look elsewhere for the program rather than wait. However, it is important to reorder when stock is low or entirely gone. If we need more merchandise, an order must be placed with a supplier. There is also a path from warehouse picking to the reorder process in case the inventory records do not match the warehouse contents exactly. Here we would want to check the warehouse carefully and then reorder if in fact there is nothing in inventory.

Figure 14-12 adds more detail to the reorder process and includes an accounts receivable process. We see that the firm must check in merchandise when it is received from suppliers; the goods eventually are placed in inventory. Accounts receivable are important if the firm is to stay in business! We must send an invoice with the shipment of goods to the customer and create a receivables record.

It would be possible to expand Figure 14-12 further, but the diagram is beginning to get cluttered. At this point, the designer would probably take each process and treat it as a subsystem for further explosions. For example, it would be possible to treat the accounts receivable process as a subsystem and to

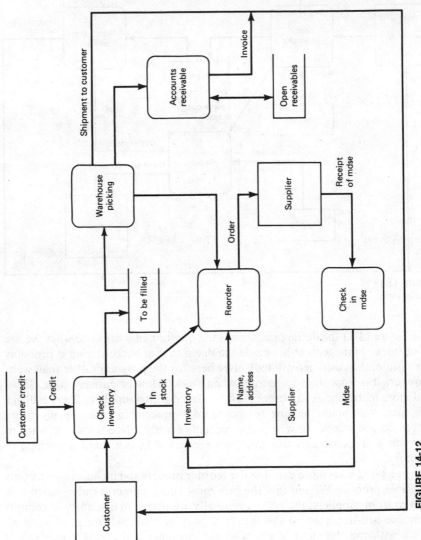

**FIGURE 14-12**
Receipt of goods and accounts receivable.

generate several pages of greater detail on how receivables are created and processed in the firm.

The DFDs and top-down approach help the analyst and the user understand the design and cope with complexity. What of the elaborate flowcharting symbols earlier? These symbols can be used to describe different hardware configurations and some kinds of manual procedures. The use of a particular set of symbols is not that important; rather, it is the concept of structuring the design and moving from lesser to greater levels of detail that contributes to the design process.

## MULTIUSER VERSUS MICRO DESIGN

It is important to distinguish between multiuser systems and single user applications when thinking about systems analysis and design. The types of systems discussed in this section of the text are largely multiuser systems used by a number of individuals in the organizations. These systems are usually developed by one group for use by another. As such, development requires input from a lot of individuals who are likely to be affected by the application.

This kind of multiuser system should be contrasted with a more personal system designed by the eventual user. Individuals frequently develop systems for their personal computers or time-sharing systems. These applications do not have the same requirements as multiuser systems, because the systems designer is the systems user. He or she does not have to worry about developing a system for others to use, nor does the system have to meet the needs of many different individuals.

Even a personal computer system we use ourselves can benefit from good design practices, but the requirements are not nearly as stringent as for a multiuser system. In these larger systems, we must worry about editing, error controls, the careful design of CRT input screens, retrieval capabilities, and file design. We must design for others as well as for ourselves, a much more complicated task!

## SUMMARY

Systems analysis and design is an activity that requires teamwork among managers, the systems staff, and users. It is a creative and exciting process that can bring about substantial change in the organization. This chapter has described the life cycle of a system, the responsibilities of various parties in developing a system, and the process of analysis and design. We have also presented some tools to assist in this process. Because a system may have a design time of two or three years and a useful life of five to seven years, the decisions that are made today will influence information processing for up to a decade. The manager and user must be involved in these decisions and see that the systems that are designed are beneficial to them and to the organization.

## KEY WORDS

| | | |
|---|---|---|
| Analysis | Estimates | Programmer |
| Analyst | Feasibility study | Programming |
| Budgets | Flowcharts | SADT |
| Conversion | Information analysis | Structured analysis |
| Data collection | Installation | Systems life cycle |
| Decision tables | Maintenance | Testing |
| Design | Operations | Training |
| Enhancements | Preliminary survey | User-controlled design |

## RECOMMENDED READINGS

Canning, R.: "The Analysis of User Needs," *EDP Analyzer,* vol. 17, no. 1, January 1979. (A good discussion of methods for defining the requirements for a new system.)

Chapin, N.: "Flowcharting with the ANSI Standard: A Tutorial," *Computing Surveys,* vol. 2, no. 2, June 1970, pp. 89–110. (A thorough discussion of flowcharting.)

Gane, C., and T. Sarson: *Structured Systems Analysis Tools and Technique,* Prentice-Hall, Englewood Cliffs, N.J., 1979. (Excellent text covering data flow diagrams and structured design.)

Lucas, H. C., Jr.: *Toward Creative Systems Design,* Columbia, New York, 1974. (A short monograph containing many more details on user-controlled system analysis and design.)

Zmud, R.: *Information Systems in Organizations,* Scott, Foresman, Glenview, Ill., 1983. (Introductory text on systems.)

## DISCUSSION QUESTIONS

1 What are the advantages of user-controlled design?

2 What are the disadvantages for the systems design staff and users of user-controlled design?

3 Would you expect user-controlled design to be more or less costly than conventional approaches?

4 What is the role of top management in managing the information services department?

5 What type of planning should be undertaken by the information services department?

6 Does a long-range information services department plan make any sense when technology is rapidly changing?

7 How should new systems development projects be charged in the organization? Should overhead, the information services department, or user department budgets absorb the cost?

8 Why have so many existing systems concentrated on information flows and transactions processing?

9 What are the problems of putting a user in charge of a design team for a new system for the information services department?

10 What are the implications of user-controlled design for the information services department? What view will have to be adopted by this department to make the recommended approach to systems design work?

11 Develop a questionnaire for obtaining data from potential users of a system on their attitudes, expectations, and thoughts for the goals of a new system.

12 The design of information systems is one of the few activities in most organizations best accomplished by a team. What possible conflicts might this create for other employees? How should the team structure be presented to reduce these problems?

13 If users design systems, will changes still be necessary after conversion when the system is in operation? Should as many changes be needed as under conventional design? Why or why not?

14 How can users be heavily involved in systems analysis and design in a large organization when there are many potential users who should be included?

15 Can top managers also participate in systems analysis and design if they will be users? Is this activity important enough for their participation?

16 How can management help a user to participate in the design of systems? What are the major factors inhibiting full participation?

17 How should the information services department budget be developed for new applications and enhancements?

18 Are there decisions in the operation of existing systems that should be influenced by users?

19 How does scarce machine capacity influence decisions on new applications?

20 To what extent can personnel resources be reallocated within the information services department to provide more flexibility in meeting demands for service?

21 Programs are available that will translate a decision table into a COBOL program that contains the logic expressed in the decision table. How would the use of such a program increase programmer productivity?

22 What are the disadvantages of flowcharts and decision tables?

23 Why do many members of the computer profession resist making changes requested in operational systems?

24 When on a cost-cutting drive, management will sometimes dictate an across-the-board budget reduction of some number, say 10 percent. Does this approach make sense for the information services department? What alternatives are available?

25 What is the most likely reason that a proposed system will be infeasible?

26 How do changes in technology, especially advances in hardware, affect the feasibility of new computer applications?

27 Where are the largest bottlenecks in the systems life cycle; that is, where are the most problems and delays probably encountered in developing a system?

28 Explain the term "bounded context," why is it important in systems analysis and design?

29 How should one choose among the different design tools and techniques discussed in this chapter?

30 Is there one design approach that is best in all situations?

31 What design approach would you choose for a system to process incoming orders for a manufacturing firm?

32 What design approach would you recommend for an interactive decision support system to be used by the treasurer of the firm to manage cash deposits?

33 What are the differences in design for a multiuser system versus a personal system on a microcomputer?

ANALYSIS OF THE EXISTING SYSTEM
SURVEY AND FEASIBILITY STUDY CONTENTS
New Systems
System Alternatives
Organizational Impact
Contents
DETERMINING FEASIBILITY AND CHOOSING AN
ALTERNATIVE
Selection Committee
Problems with Committees
Committee Responsibilities
THE SELECTION PROCESS
Decision Information
The Decision
SYSTEMS ANALYSIS
SYSTEMS DESIGN
Results
Work Responsibilities
Tradeoffs
GENERAL DESIGN CONSIDERATIONS
Output
Input
Manual Procedures
Errors
Backup
Security and Fraud
SYSTEM SPECIFICATIONS
KEY WORDS
RECOMMENDED READINGS
DISCUSSION QUESTIONS
SYSTEM DESIGN PROBLEMS

# 15

# INCEPTION THROUGH SPECIFICATIONS

## CHAPTER ISSUES

- How should the organization select alternatives for a given computer application?
- What alternatives are available for the detailed design of a system?
- How does the user trade off various design alternatives for a new system?

In this chapter we examine the first stages of the systems life cycle. We begin with the preliminary survey and the feasibility study. The output from these two studies is used to determine whether to proceed with the design of a computer-based information system and to select a single processing alternative if the system is approved. If a system is feasible, the analysis and design stages are undertaken, and the design team prepares detailed specifications.

## ANALYSIS OF THE EXISTING SYSTEM

Analysis is the study of a problem, generally done before undertaking some action to solve the problem (DeMarco, 1979). In the case of systems analysis, the first task is understand and describe existing information processing procedures in the area where a new system has been proposed. Many of the techniques recommended in the last chapter can be used to document our understanding of the present processing system, for example, flowcharts, decision tables, and some of the structured diagrams of information processing.

In many instances it will be hard to identify any organized set of procedures that represent the existing information processing system. We need to enumerate problems and determine what motivated the suggestion that a computer system might help in processing information. Whether there is a well-defined system or not, we should develop the specific information listed in Table 15-1. First, we should identify decisions that have to be made and the decision maker who is to be responsible. What are the inputs and outputs, what is the frequency of the decision, and what are the levels of cost involved?

Next, we should identify crucial information flows including the source, frequency, and volume of information. Information can be characterized according to the decision-making framework of Chapter 3. For example, we can look at the form in which data are gathered and processed, either written or verbal. If documents are involved, how many are there and what is their information content? What types of decisions are supported?

We also need to identify what processing is done to information as it flows through a system; by whom is the information processed, and what are the peak and average loads? Finally, we should estimate the current cost of information processing.

For the preliminary survey we develop very rough estimates and collect samples of documents. We may interview only a few people and use approximations. After a list of objectives for the system is developed, we use the data gathered to make a rough sketch of several alternative new systems.

The feasibility study goes into much more detail and instead of approxima-

**TABLE 15-1**
ANALYZING THE EXISTING SYSTEM

Decisions
  Decision maker
  Input
  Output
  Frequency of decision
  Level of costs

Information
  Flow
  Characteristics
  Form
  Source
  Retention

Transactions and processing
  Operations
  By whom performed
  Peak load
  Average load

Individuals/functions

tions, we actually sample the documents and develop more refined estimates. In the feasibility study, we trace the flow of information through the system and spend time with the various individuals who originate and process the data. Thus, the same framework used in the preliminary survey can be used for the feasibility study though our analysis for the feasibility study will be much more detailed.

## SURVEY AND FEASIBILITY STUDY CONTENTS

In this section we present recommendations for the contents of the preliminary survey and feasibility study. Basically, each of these documents consists of two parts: the present system and an alternative. The alternatives section actually presents several potential alternatives and evaluates them on technical, economic, and operational criteria. We must estimate technical and operational feasibility and compare costs with benefits.

### New Systems

From a technical standpoint, what is the state of the art? This analysis is related to the discussion of risk, since very few organizations should be pioneers in the development of all their new systems. Some pioneering may be desirable, but an attempt should be made to estimate exactly what is involved. Will existing technology as experienced by members of this organization be adequate for the application under consideration?

Operational feasibility addresses the question of whether or not we can run the system. Are schedules for processing realistic? Can input data actually be collected, errors corrected, and the system run on schedule? In one example an inventory system was planned in which files would be updated every 3 days. There were so many errors in the input that could not be corrected in time that the system had to move to a weekly updating schedule, reducing some of the benefits.

In examining costs versus benefits, there are a large number of factors to consider. System costs include

Development
    Computer time
    Systems analyst time
    Programmer time
    User time
Operations
    Computer costs
    Communications costs
    Operating staff costs
    Incremental user costs
    Maintenance costs

Development costs refer to the actual cost of analysis, design, and installation for the system. These costs are highly sensitive to the amount of time that must be spent to develop the system and are directly proportional to the number of analysts, programmers, and user staff involved and the length of their involvement. Computer time for testing tends to be far less expensive than the cost of staff time. Historically, the profession has done a very poor job of estimating the time required to design and install a system.

We should not forget the cost of operating a new system when assessing total costs. A new system will require the use of part of the time available on an existing computer or may necessitate an upgrade on the present system or even a new computer(s). Many modern systems involve telecommunications, which can be very costly. Incremental staff in the computer center and for users may be required to operate the system. Finally, there are the costs of routine maintenance and enhancements. No system is ever finished; "bugs" will need repairs, and users will request periodic enhancements as they work with a system.

Traditionally, benefits have been analyzed from the point of view of tangible cost savings from a computer system. Often these savings have been measured by the reduction of employees currently employed or by an estimate of the number of future employees who would have been hired without the system. (Many times savings projected in personnel have proved illusory.) Tangible savings also come from more efficient processing. For example, an inventory control system may reduce inventory balances while maintaining service levels. The firm saves the interest charges on the money previously required to finance the level of inventory needed before the computer system.

Tangible cost savings can be difficult to estimate in some cases. Emery (1974) has suggested looking at the value of perfect information as providing an upper bound on possible benefits. For example, in a forecasting application, what is the maximum benefit from having a perfect forecast of sales, that is, knowing exactly what sales will be in advance? If the cost of developing the system exceeds the maximum benefit under perfect information, then the application will undoubtedly be rejected immediately. If, however, the benefits look higher than costs, then we can make various assumptions about the impact of forecasts from the proposed system that are less than perfect.

To refine the benefits estimates, a prototype of the forecasting system could be applied using a calculator or simple computerized version of the forecast. Historical data are processed by the model to provide an estimate of the improvements the model would produce over the existing forecasting procedures.

We should not only look at tangible cost savings, but we must also consider intangibles and unquantifiable savings. This is particularly true as we move from transactions processing systems toward operational and managerial control systems where intangible benefits are more important.

The following list of benefits may prove helpful in this analysis (Kanter, 1972).

1 The ability to obtain information previously unavailable
2 The receipt of information on a more timely basis
3 Improvements in operations
4 The ability to perform calculations not possible before (for example, the simulation of production schedules)
5 Reduction in clerical activity
6 Maintenance of a competitive position
7 Improvements in decision making
8 Improvements in image, customer service, etc.
9 Contribution to corporate strategy

Emery also discusses some of the problems of quantifying the benefits from intangible savings. For example, suppose an automobile manufacturer can increase from 90 to 95 percent the probability that a dealer will have parts in stock. How can the manufacturer quantify (in dollars) the increased customer satisfaction and goodwill that results from getting his or her car repaired without having to wait for a part? Of course, where a system can be justified on the grounds of tangible savings alone, the quantification of intangible savings will not be necessary.

Although intangible savings data may not be concrete, they can be evaluated. The automobile company could survey a sample of its dealers to determine their estimates of the monetary value of reduced stockouts. Although crude, the estimate is far better than making no attempt to include this factor in the analysis of the new system. As Emery points out, if we develop only systems that show tangible savings, we may ignore many of the benefits of computer-based information systems. It is very difficult to justify a planning system or decision support aid on the basis of tangible cost savings.

Many organizations also use subjective techniques to determine whether or not a project is desirable from a cost-benefit standpoint. They argue that with intangible benefits uncertain, one still has to decide whether or not a system appears justified. These decision makers use their subjective feelings for what a reasonable cost is for the benefits provided by the system.

Regardless of the sophistication of the cost-benefit analysis, we need to develop a list of costs and benefits as a part of a feasibility study. Then agreement should be reached by all involved that the system is worth developing before proceeding.

### Systems Alternatives

**General**  One of the major activities during the survey or feasibility study will be to sketch possible alternatives for a new information processing system. Given the wide range of computer processing options available today, it is difficult not to be able to provide some computer-based assistance for a problem. The issue is not so much one of whether a system is feasible, but rather what alternative is desirable.

During a feasibility study, a design team should develop alternatives and criteria for evaluating them. For a particular situation, a user may take the least expensive and most rapidly implementable system. In another case, users may opt for a very comprehensive system to be custom programmed. The important point is as a user, insist on seeing some alternatives!

**Packages**   For many proposed systems, an applications package offers an alternative. Frequently, large amounts of money and time can be saved through the use of one of these packages, though there can be a number of drawbacks to packages. An applications package is a program or system of programs written by someone for sale. The package vendor tries to make the product very general; users supply the data parameters that apply to their situation and the package does the processing.

The major issue with the use of packages is the tradeoff between efficiency and generality. The vendor wants to make the package as general as possible so that a larger number of potential customers can use the package. However, the more general the package is, the less efficient is its processing and the more complex is the input required. The user, of course, wants the simplest input and the most efficient processing.

Generally, we overestimate the effort needed to install a package and underestimate the effort required to program the same system ourselves. In fact, most programmers prefer to design a new system than to install a package. The former activity is far more creative and challenging than working with someone else's program.

Since computer power is becoming cheaper per computation, it makes sense in many instances to acquire a package that uses computer hardware inefficiently to have an application functioning earlier. However, there can be legitimate reasons not to use packages. A set of criteria should be developed for the technical requirements a package has to meet to qualify for consideration. As a partial list of requirements consider the following:

**1** Quality and reliability. A survey of existing users should be undertaken to determine how the package has actually performed.

**2** Documentation. Can the computer department fully understand the system and is it capable of making the necessary modifications based on the documentation provided?

**3** Vendor stability and support. Will the vendor stay in business and is the vendor committed to improving the package and issuing subsequent versions of it?

**4** Compatibility with current equipment and applications. If it is necessary to spend 50 percent of the package price to modify the package, it is probably not worth it.

In summary, packages are a viable alternative, and they should be evaluated where they exist. After passing the screening requirements, packages should be considered in the same way as any other alternative and included in the survey and feasibility studies. It is still necessary to study the existing system and make estimates of technical, economic, and operational factors when an applications package is one alternative.

### Organization Impact

An attempt also should be made to estimate the impact of each alternative system on the organization. What departments and individuals will be affected by the system and what jobs will be changed? Will any existing work groups be reassigned and what will happen to any employees who are replaced by a system?

### Contents

The contents of one possible format for a survey or feasibility study are outlined in Table 15-2. The summary presents a brief overview of the reasons for the study and ranks each processing alternative (including the present system) on the criteria established by the steering committee. This summary is the primary input for decision making. Existing systems should be described according to the analysis above. Finally, each alternative is presented in detail. Here is helpful to include a scenario; that is, a short story on how the system would actually be used including management, user, and computer department activities under each alternative.

**TABLE 15-2**
OUTLINE OF PRELIMINARY SURVEY AND FEASIBILITY
STUDY CONTENTS

I Summary
  A  Goals
  B  For each alternative evaluation on standard criteria
II The existing system
  A  Problems
  B  Goals of new system
  C  Decision considerations
  D  Information flow
  E  Processing
III For each alternative proposed
  A  Overview—percentage of goals achieved, benefits
  B  Decisions
  C  Information flows
  D  Technical (files, I/O, processing)
  E  Development effort, schedule, and cost
  F  Operational aspects
  G  Impact on the organization
  H  Total costs and benefits

## DETERMINING FEASIBILITY AND CHOOSING AN ALTERNATIVE

In the early days of computer systems, the information services department usually decided what applications to undertake. As demands for services increased, problems began to develop because some user requests had to be denied. As more systems of importance to the organization developed, many information services departments felt they were placed in a difficult position if forced to choose among competing applications. The information services department is not in a position to decide whether a system is feasible or which processing alternative should be chosen if the system is to be developed.

### Selection Committee

One answer to the information systems selection problem is to convene a selection committee of users and other managers and information services department personnel. When representatives of various functional areas are included, each department is able to see why certain decisions are made. Selection of applications alternatives seems less arbitrary under these conditions. With management guidance, the committee can select applications and processing alternatives that it feels are consistent with functions currently emphasized in the organization.

---

### MANAGEMENT PROBLEM 15-1

The order processing department manager at Leisure Clothing has a serious problem. She cannot understand why the information services department is so unresponsive to her requests. The firm has an elaborate on-line order-entry system that serves the entire United States. For the past 6 months, the order processing manager has logged the requests she has made for changes to the system. The total number of requests now stands at 15 and only three of the changes have been implemented!

When the manager of the order-entry system from the information services department stopped to see her, she indicated displeasure over the lack of progress and suggested two new modifications.

The weary systems manager asked, "Do these new changes have priority over the five you suggested last week, or should we try to do those first?"

The conversation grew more heated until finally both parties were shouting at each other. What do you suppose is responsible for this conflict? What steps can each individual take to resolve the conflict? What does the department manager need to appreciate? What action should the information services department take?

---

## Problems with Committees

If the ideas expressed above are good, why have a number of organizations become dissatisfied with selection committees? First, the goals of the committees are often not clear, resulting in little direction or continuity during meetings. Frequently, the committees appear to be ratifying decisions already made by the information services department. No alternatives for a given application are suggested. Instead, the information services department presents the option of developing a complete, elaborate system or doing nothing. Almost no systems are rejected at the feasibility stage.

When decisions are made, there seems to be a failure to apply consistent

---

### GROCERY CHECKOUT

*All 88 outlets of Ralph's, a leading southern California grocery chain, use computer-based laser scanning at the checkout stand. The operation utilizes point of sales terminals that include a laser scanner, a scale, and a keyboard. Some 92% of the shelf items now carry the universal product code, a series of parallel bars which the scanner can recognize as the grocery item is passed across a window in the checkout counter. Meat and other items are hand keyed and produce items are calculated using the scale and a keyed number. As each transaction occurs, it is flashed on an electronic panel visible to customers. At the end of the checkout process, the terminal prints a receipt including a specific description of each item as well as its price.*

*Ralph's produces a series of management reports that analyze everything from dollar volume per check stand to bottle returns. The company has found that the scanning device produces improved service and shorter lines at the checkout counters. By examining the statistics on the reports, management can see the cost of an average item and know what is selling well in a particular neighborhood. Ralph's feels that it can service its customers better when it knows their buying habits and preferences.*

*With scanners the company has been able to cut down from twelve checkout stands to nine while still getting customers through the stores 20% faster than before. Chain store executives believe customers view the length of the line as second only to price when they decide where to shop. Not only the customers but the checkout clerks are enthusiastic about the scanning devices.*

*If the store's controller quits operating, an identical unit at another Ralph's can pick up the slack within 15 seconds, though the scanning process is a bit slower. In the 15 months that the system has been operating at a Pasadena store, the unit has yet to fail. Each installation's scanners and controllers cost between $175,000 and $200,000. The company, however, feels it's getting a two year payback at most stores due to increased productivity and reduced inventory loss. Even more remarkable, there have been significant sales gains in stores which the company felt had already achieved their maximum volume.*

*Data Processor, June/July 1980.*

decision criteria. Finally, in making any decision where costs and benefits are difficult to estimate, it is important to include subjective considerations. Members of committees have reported the lack of a mechanism for successfully including subjective factors in the decision process.

### Committee Responsibilities

In Chapter 6 we discussed the applications selection process and recommended that a corporate steering committee review plans for systems and set priorities for different applications areas. An applications selection committee will generally consist of lower levels of management combined with users and members of the information services staff.

As mentioned earlier, few applications are really infeasible, though certain alternatives may be infeasible or undesirable. The role of the selection committee is to choose an alternative for a given system, though that alternative may be the status quo, that is, doing nothing. This role for the committee means that there will probably be several different selection committees, each dealing with systems for different functional areas. There might also be a committee with a variety of users on it to make decisions about small projects that do not involve a major commitment of funds.

## THE SELECTION PROCESS

It is desirable to have all new systems suggested and investigated at one point in time so that all possibilities can be considered and some subset selected for implementation. Unfortunately, ideas for systems arise almost at random; some length of time is required to study the suggestions before a decision is made on whether to undertake a suggested application. The decision process recommended below, therefore, concentrates on the selection of an alternative for a single proposed application. It does not attempt to evaluate an entire portfolio of projects because we are rarely in a position to compare the entire set of proposed projects at one point in time. The commitment of resources to past projects and the characteristics of systems currently under development can be reflected in the weights assigned to the criteria described below.

### Decision Information

The approach suggested here can be used for decisions at either the preliminary survey or the feasibility study stage. The major difference between the two studies is that the feasibility study contains more data than the preliminary survey and presents more refined cost estimates.

The first task of the selection committee is to agree with the information services department on the number of alternatives for a single project and how the alternatives should be developed. As an example, suppose that one user department has proposed an inventory control system. The alternatives might

**TABLE 15-3**
SOME POTENTIAL CRITERIA FOR EVALUATING ALTERNATIVES IN PROJECT SELECTION

---

Tangible and intangible benefits
   User satisfaction
   Percentage of needs met
   Maximum potential of application
   Costs of development
   Costs of operations
Timing of costs
Timing of benefits
Impact on existing operations
Development time
Time to implement
Manpower required
   Analyst
   Programmer
   User
Probability of success
Probability of meeting estimates
New equipment required
Priority of function

---

*Source:* H. C. Lucas, Jr., and J. R. Moore, Jr.: "A Multiple-Criterion Scoring Approach to Information System Project Selection," *Infor.* vol. 14, no. 1, February 1976.

include (1) doing nothing, (2) setting up a very basic batch system, (3) purchasing a packaged program from a computer services vendor, and (4) establishing an on-line system. Each of these alternatives for an inventory control system meets some percentage of user needs at different costs. Probably three to five alternatives for each proposed application are sufficient; however, there should always be more than one alternative for a new system. The selection of the first alternative, doing nothing, is equivalent to a decision that a new system is infeasible.

The next step is for the committee to agree on a set of criteria to be used by the information services department in evaluating each alternative. Table 15-3 contains examples of possible criteria, although criteria will probably be unique for each organization. The set of criteria should be as complete as possible so that no important evaluation factors will be overlooked. However, the selection committee should avoid enumerating too many criteria, or the data collection and processing requirements for evaluation become a burden. Each criterion should be measured on a common scale, say one to seven.

There is no one correct number of criteria to use, but experience indicates that five to ten should be adequate. Criteria can be voted upon by the committee and rank-ordered for selection, or a group consensus on important criteria may be possible without the voting. It is also desirable to avoid as much overlap in the criteria as possible to avoid overweighting one factor.

Once the criteria have been determined, it is necessary to develop weights that indicate the relative importance of each criterion in arriving at the application selection decision. It is unlikely that each criterion will be regarded as equally important by all committee members, and some method will have to be used to weight the criteria for different individuals. Approaches to this process range from simple rank-ordering schemes to partial and paired comparison. The weights are of paramount importance to project selection because they reflect the priorities of the selection committee. The committee, of course, cannot expect conditions to remain constant; shifts in management policies and user needs necessitate revisions to weights over time.

## The Decision

If the recommendations above are followed, the steering committee should be in a position to review a series of alternatives for each application proposed for implementation. Each alternative should have been evaluated on the criteria established by the committee. Consider the example in Table 15-4. In this hypothetical decision problem, the steering committee is considering three alternatives: a batch inventory-control system, an applications package, and an on-line inventory system.

The first column in the table lists the criteria agreed on by the committee and the information services department, and the second column contains the weights assigned to each criterion by the committee. The remainder of the table contains the scores for each alternative as evaluated by the information services department.

There are several ways to arrive at a decision, given this information. One approach is to work toward a consensus among committee members. In this example, the applications package would probably emerge as the preferred choice because of its high rating on the important criteria of percent of user needs met, low development cost, and high probability of success. As an alternative to this qualitative approach to selecting an alternative, more formal methods are available in which historical and survey data are used to develop a single numeric score for each alternative (Lucas and Moore, 1976c).

As conditions change, the committee can modify the weights to reflect new

**TABLE 15-4**
APPLICATIONS SELECTION EXAMPLE

| Criterion | Weight | Batch system | Package | On-line system |
|---|---|---|---|---|
| Percent of user needs met | 0.35 | 60% | 75% | 90% |
| Cost of development | 0.20 | $25,000 | $12,000 | $30,000 |
| Cost of operations | 0.10 | $ 3,000 | $10,000 | $ 7,000 |
| Workers to develop | 0.15 | 3 | 1 | 3 |
| Probability of success | 0.20 | .85 | .95 | .75 |

priorities. Also, criteria can be dropped and/or added to reflect new circumstances. The major advantage of the recommended approach is the fact that it forces an objective evaluation of several alternatives for each proposed application, while providing a consistent but flexible framework for making decisions on applications.

## SYSTEMS ANALYSIS

If a system is feasible and one alternative is chosen for development, detailed systems analysis is the next stage. There are few guidelines on the depth of analysis required when the design team examines present information processing procedures. All aspects of the present processing method must be understood and documented, and the analysis should seek to identify key decisions as well as flows of data.

It is important to sample existing documents and files of data. The design team should count all types of documents and classify the information contained on them; what are both the peak and the average flows of information? What time pressure is on managers who must make key decisions in the system? Some

---

## MANAGEMENT PROBLEM 15-2

The top management of Eastern Bank and Trust practices group decision making. The highest four officers, including the chairman of the board, the president, and two executive vice presidents, meet together to make all major decisions. This committee approves the budget for the information services department and also decides on new applications.

Because of pressing business, information-systems-related decisions are often postponed from one meeting until the next. The budget director for the information services department indicated that he waited in the reception area for four meetings before his budget presentation was reached on the agenda.

The budget director's major objective is to have the information services department budget approved with as few questions as possible. The budget includes the funding for major systems development projects in the bank for the coming year. Therefore, approving the budget also involves selecting the major new applications for the coming year.

The members of the management committee are very dissatisfied with the current approach to information systems project selection decisions. They admit that no project has ever reached the feasibility study stage and been rejected. The managers indicate that they are not really making decisions, they are just ratifying the proposals of the information services department.

How can the bank solve this problem and develop a more effective project selection procedure? Why is this management committee not working well for information-systems-related decisions?

---

of these questions were asked in collecting data for the survey and feasibility studies; however, now the task is to obtain all relevant details.

The design team must also decide where to place the boundary on its studies; it is too easy to expand a simple processing problem into a huge system. What initially looks like an order-entry process turns into an accounts-receivable system and a production-control system, because eager designers expand the boundaries of the problem into other areas. In some instances, an expansive boundary may be appropriate, but a design team is well advised to take steps slowly in order to outline a manageable task.

The designers should document their understanding of present procedures with information memoranda and reports. Flowcharts and decision tables should be constructed and reviewed with users who are not on the design team. When satisfied with its understanding of the present processing procedures, in effect, the design team should hold a "walk-through" with all users involved as a final check on the analysis.

## SYSTEMS DESIGN

The most creative part of the systems life cycle is the design of new alternatives for processing. Although these ideas were sketched in the preliminary survey or feasibility study, they have to be developed in far more detail now. For example, in the last section we chose a packaged program for inventory control; (see Table 15-4). Suppose instead that the on-line system had been selected for development. The information in the feasibility study is general: the details of that system must be designed before programming can begin. What equipment is required? What are the I/O formats and file structures?

### Results

The results of this study should be complete specifications for the new system as shown in Table 15-5. Usually, we begin by specifying the desired output; that is, what does the user want from the system? Then it is necessary to determine what input is required to produce this desired output. A comparison of input and output identifies the data that must be maintained on files.

Next, we consider processing; that is, how are the input data transformed and used to modify the files? How often does a file have to be updated? How are the input and the contents of files processed to produce the desired output? Also, at this point the design team should specify manual procedures for other activities associated with the system.

For input and output files and processing, it is necessary to determine what kinds of errors are likely to occur and design procedures to locate or prevent errors. The final output of the specifications for the system should be a work plan and schedule for implementation.

**TABLE 15-5**
DETAILED SYSTEMS DESIGN SPECIFICATIONS

| | |
|---|---|
| Output | Errors |
|   Destination and use |   Design decisions |
|   Medium |   Modules |
|   Reports (samples) |   Processing |
|   Frequency | Conversion programs |
| Input |   Input |
|   Source |   Output |
|   Medium |   Errors |
|   Document (sample) |   Design decisions |
|   Fields |   Modules |
|   Estimated volume |   Processing |
| Files | Manual procedures |
|   Medium | Error control |
|   Contents |   Input error conditions |
|   Record format, field names |   Processing errors |
|   File structure (linkages, directories) |   File integrity |
|   Estimated file size |   Output errors |
|   Estimated activity |   Backup |
|   Updating frequency |   Security |
| Processing | Work plan |
|   System flow |   Program schedule, milestones |
|   Program specifications |   Time estimates |
|     Input |   Personnel required, assignments |
|     Output | |

## Work Responsibilities

At various times during the development of detailed specifications we will need to develop more data; there is no such thing as "a completed design." By this time, the design team should have developed many contacts with the rest of the organization, so returning to users for additional information should be easy.

During this stage users on the design team still have major tasks to perform and computer department representatives continue to guide design activities. For example, user team members should develop the report contents with actual users of the report. The computer department staff can then design a format for the report and draw up pro forma examples. Alternatively, users can actually draw examples of the reports they would like. Pro forma examples are reviewed thoroughly by users before programming.

Given a brief tutorial it should also be possible for users to design the input for the system and specify most of the file contents. The computer department staff certainly has to specify the details of processing and file structures, but users can supply the overall logic. Users also specify manual procedures that accompany the system. Both users and the information services department staff should think independently of possible errors and the necessary audit trails for the system. (An audit trail is a logical path by which a transaction can be traced through the computer system.)

### Tradeoffs

All during the design process, the analyst and user are making tradeoffs among the various alternatives as we have discussed in the previous chapter. With user-centered design as advocated here, the analyst does not make all decisions unilaterally. The analyst can and should narrow the choices to a reasonable number, but the user and the analyst should jointly make final selection of design alternatives.

In one of the examples described later, an incident occurs that illustrates this approach. In the design of a system to process accounts receivable on a minicomputer, a question arose as to how one could maintain an alphabetical sequence for a customer listing. Because the minicomputer had limited input/output capabilities and was slow in sorting, the analyst suggested that a numbering scheme be used to create the desired sequence.

By leaving a large number of digits between successive customers, the user could create a pseudoalphabetic listing. For example, if customer Adams were assigned number 1000, the next customer, Adamson, would be given 1010. If a new customer named Adamsen were to be added to the file, the number 1005 would be given. Over time, exact alphabetic order would not be maintained, but the results would be quite close. Certainly this process would be easier for the programmer and more efficient for computer.

The user was presented with the tradeoffs in nontechnical terms. The analyst explained the reasons for the programming choice, and the user was asked to think about how work could be done with the numbering scheme as opposed to the alternative of sorting the customer file alphabetically. The user indicated that each selling season, a large number of new customers were added to the accounts-receivable system. In addition, a large amount of work was involved in locating customers quickly on a printed report instead of one of the CRT terminals.

In this case since alphabetic sorts are the most time-consuming, the tradeoffs were between machine time and efficiency and programming ease versus user convenience. When the analyst examined the cogent reasons of the user, it became clear that the tradeoffs should be decided in favor of sorting the customers alphabetically, as the user preferred.

Although this detail is small, it could be an important one for the acceptance of the system. In the conventional approach, the analyst or programmer might have made the opposite decision unilaterally, and the results could have been disastrous. A large number of users would be inconvenienced; for them, the use of the system might constitute 40 to 60 percent of their daily activities. The out-of-sequence customer list would affect them every day in their jobs and would become a major irritant.

This one decision at a fairly late stage in the design process illustrates the kind of tradeoffs that must be made continually during design. Our philosophy of user-centered design means that the analyst eliminates grossly inappropriate alternatives and presents the user with feasible choices to consider. Together the user and the analyst determine what the important evaluation criteria are. In our example, criteria were user convenience versus machine time and programming ease. The user makes the final choice given the pros and cons of the decision alternatives. It is important to emphasize that this tradeoff activity is the essence of systems analysis and design; hundreds and even thousands of such tradeoffs will be made during each design project.

## GENERAL DESIGN CONSIDERATIONS

One approach to the design task is to develop an ideal system unconstrained by cost or technology. Then this system is refined through successive iterations until it is realistic. It is in this creative process of design that a team of designers is most important; one individual cannot hope to originate all the features of a system. It is through the synergy of the group that a new system is created.

Below we discuss guidelines for batch or on-line systems. When we discussed patterns of processing we saw that many combinations of equipment and response are possible, from centralized through distributed to decentralized systems in some combination of batch or on-line processing. These alternatives will impact the options available to the analyst. However, the discussion below can be easily applied to designs for these various patterns of processing.

### Output

The output of the computer system is the primary contact between the system and most users. The quality and usefulness of this output determine whether the system will be used, so it is essential to have the best possible output. Through much of our research on the use of information systems, we have found that users have different requirements. Some users want exception reports; they wish to be notified only if sales fall, say, five percent from last year's level. Other users may want summary information, while still others prefer complete details. To determine the different types of output desired, the design team can employ user surveys or have user members of the design team observe how other users work with information. Users should be provided with samples of reports over a period of several weeks so they can think about their contents and format.

How can designers provide output flexibility? Clearly, data have to be maintained at the lowest level of detail required for reporting purposes. There is no reason, however, why everyone must receive the same output. Summaries can be developed from detailed data for those who desire it. Designers should consider keeping a file of user preferences regarding report formats if there are

## WAREHOUSE CONTROL

*A computer that is used as a part of the point of sales scanning at Ralphs Grocery Stores also provides around the clock on-line control of four of the company's seven Los Angeles area warehouses. As soon as merchandise is received on the warehouse dock, it is entered into an on-line inventory management system via a display terminal. The system immediately assigns each pallet to a specific warehouse slot. Simultaneously a printer produces an adhesive location label giving a description of the product, number of cases, the purchase order number and where the pallet is to be stored in the warehouse. The printer also produces a summary label listing all activities relating to each purchase order including the warehouse location of each pallet received. The summary label provides both an audit trail and a document that can be forwarded to accounts payable to reconcile billing problems.*

*After each billing, the system determines which pallets need to be moved from a secondary or reserve location to a primary or picking location. Labels are printed again to direct the forklift operators. By using this method, warehouse scratches (items shown in inventory but not shipped because they cannot be located) have diminished from 14,000 to less than a 1,000 a week.*

*Data Processor,* June/July 1980.

substantial differences in requests for output. A report can then be produced according to the preferred format of each user.

Another possibility to enhance output flexibility is to employ file management packages or to develop a retrieval program that makes it easy to custom-tailor reports. The use of such packages also makes it much easier to change reports as experience with the system grows.

The design team should stress clarity in format and headings for output. One of the most frequent complaints we hear is that users cannot understand reports; it is essential to use clear, descriptive titles for different fields on a report and to avoid the use of obscure or little-known codes. If the data on a report are not obvious, a footnote should be added, explaining how the numbers were derived or referring to the appropriate documentation for an explanation. Perhaps the first page of the report should include a short description of how the computations were performed.

Another chronic complaint is that the computer systems produce too much data. Information can be made available and printed only when needed. Will an exception report do? Are data needed only infrequently? Can they be saved on a tape and printed only if necessary? If we must maintain large amounts of archival data for historical or legal purposes, it may be possible to use microfilm. The design team should also consider whether the addition of an on-line inquiry facility would eliminate the need for many printed reports.

---

## MANAGEMENT PROBLEM 15-3

Susan Friedman, the director of sales for the Trumbull department-store chain, is concerned over the complaints she has been receiving from store managers about the company's sales information system. The system has been highly successful until now; it provides information for store managers that most competitors do not have.

However, a recent survey sent to each department store in the chain indicated significant differences in how the information on the report is used. Susan has been meeting with the computer staff to review the comments from users. It seems that there are two choices: either managers can be trained to use the existing batch report produced by the system, or a more responsive output can be designed.

Susan does not like the idea of forcing the managers to use the system in a predetermined manner. She says, "The real beauty of this system is that it contains enough data to make all of the different store managers happy. They all have different ways of managing and I don't think we would be successful enforcing uniformity."

The computer staff has indicated that there are a number of possibilities for changing the output from the system, but has asked for help from Susan and the managers to determine what changes are desired.

What different output alternatives might be examined? How should they be investigated? What are the implications of each alternative for the present system, particularly for the current system, which has a sequential file structure?

---

The discussion above has referred primarily to printed output, and there are a few additional considerations that should be included in the design of on-line output. First, there should be a key on the terminal that the user can depress to obtain help. The "help" function provides an on-line set of instructions to show how to obtain information. In addition to a "help" key, there may be several levels of prompting in the system. For example, a more detailed mode of comments can be used for the novice and a terser mode for the frequent, experienced user.

Another important feature of an on-line system is adequate response time. Users who become dependent upon on-line processing are very sensitive to degraded response times; backup should therefore be provided. Users have been known to become enraged when a crucial on-line system is not functioning.

### Input

In the past few years, the trend in information systems has been toward collecting data as close to its source as possible. The objective of this philosophy is to eliminate data transcription wherever possible, for purposes of avoiding errors and reducing the time required to enter the data into the computer. The ultimate in automatic data collection, of course, is sensors attached to the input of a real-time system, such as a computer monitoring a patient in a hospital. In most commercial computer systems, a popular source-data collection technique is to use an on-line terminal.

However, there are alternatives to on-line input that are usually less costly. It may be possible to use a turnaround document in dealing with customers. For example, a bill is printed on a form and sent to a customer who returns it with payment. If the customer pays the amount due, the return card can be processed directly by a scanner. If the customer does not pay the full amount, then some kind of a keying operation is necessary to record the amount actually paid.

Scanners (OCR) can also be used for direct entry for original documents such as a sales order form. If numbers are printed carefully, the actual order form prepared by each person can be used as an input to the computer system through a scanner. In fact, the use of the scanner might actually be faster than an on-line terminal, since undoubtedly the sales personnel would have to write orders before they could key them into a terminal. By taking a few more minutes to write clearly, the order form itself is entered directly into the computer system.

It is also possible to use mark sensing for input where the user darkens a box or circle corresponding to the user's choice for input. However, optical character recognition is easier for the user to understand than mark sensing and generally is preferred except where input data are very simple. Unless there are just a few alternatives, the mark sense forms become clumsy, since a separate box or circle must be provided for each possible answer.

Batch input, unfortunately, suffers from rigidity. Since most batch input requires information in a strict format, there is also a lack of immediate feedback on errors with batch processing. Whenever possible, the design team should consider the use of existing documents for input, since these will minimize problems in understanding new and possibly more complicated forms. It is important to be sure that data to be entered can be provided legibly on the form. If a document has to be transcribed by a keying operation, it is helpful to use boxes for each character. If this is not possible, a separate well-delimited space should be provided for each character since this helps the keying operator justify the input.

For input forms intended for optical character recognition or mark sensing, it is best to work with manufacturers' representatives to determine the demands for their particular machinery. OCR has very exacting requirements for the location of information and the quality of printing on forms.

On-line interaction should be clear and polite; one should try to avoid a cumbersome input command structure and emphasize natural response. For on-line data entry, the system should provide courteous error messages and the opportunity to rekey data that are in error; messages should be polite and explain the error. It might be advisable to give no explanation unless the user types a question mark or presses some other key after receiving an error message. That way those familiar with the system can avoid tedious error messages really designed for someone with less experience.

### Manual Procedures

The systems design is not complete until we specify the manual processing procedures surrounding the computer system. What volume of activity will there be? How much time is required to perform these manual tasks? We should specify what processing the user has to perform and indicate the flow of information and the time required to complete processing. Manual input procedures are an often-overlooked part of systems design, yet poorly planned manual procedures have caused many otherwise well-designed systems to fail.

### Errors

A well-designed system handles errors; that is, it corrects them or notifies someone of the errors and continues producing valid output. It is not unusual to find more than half the instructions in a program devoted to error detection and handling, especially in an on-line system. Detection of errors in processing is the responsibility of the information services department and these problems are usually technological in nature. However, the user design team should be aware of input error possibilities and design procedures to minimize the likelihood of their occurrence and any adverse impact on the organization.

Whenever data are transcribed by some keying operation that is not on-line, they are usually key-verified to check for reporting errors. The first operator keys the data and a separate individual verifies them, using a machine that compares the keying of the original operator with the keystrokes of the verification operator. The verification process shows discrepancies that are then corrected by the operator. We assume that the data are recorded accurately on the document being keyed; however, there is nothing that guarantees accuracy.

It is not always necessary or desirable to key-verify all input fields. The use of a check digit, described below, lets the computer catch transcription errors. Some input fields such as names or descriptive information are not crucial for every application. When batch totals are used, the designer must decide whether or not it is necessary to key-verify the amount field since the computer checks it when totaling the batches on input.

We also may include a set of checks after transcription to see that data were correctly entered into the computer. For crucial fields, such as those dealing with monetary amounts, we usually employ a batch control total. A batch total is computed by keeping track of the dollar amount of a field in one batch of around 50 input documents. The batch total is entered in a batch control record that follows the documents in a batch. The computer program reading the input adds the data fields and compares them with the batch total. If the fields do not match, the program indicates an error. Batch totals provide assurances that the data, as prepared, are entered into the computer and furnish another check on the keying operation.

After checking data transformations and making sure that the data are entered, a program should perform logical checks on the source of the information. Did the originator provide correct data? For numbers that are used as keys, such as an identification number, we can use a check digit. Assume that the identification number for a part in inventory is four digits long, for example, part number 4326. During processing, we add a fifth digit to the number to serve as a check. We might compute the check digit by dividing the identification number by 11 and using the remainder as the check digit. The remainder when 4326 is divided by 11 is 3, so the number should appear in a parts catalog, in all input documents and on file as 43263. The computer programs that process the identification part number perform the same calculation; that is, a program divides 4326 by 11 is 3 and takes the remainder, checking to see that it is the same as the digit 3 in the units position.

A variety of other verification schemes also employ check digits, such as weighting each digit by a certain number. These calculations all have the same objective: to detect transposition and entry errors. Check digits are especially crucial when optical character recognition or mark sensing is used because of the possibility that the machine might make reading errors.

During the editing stage, we examine individual fields to be sure that no alphabetic characters have been placed in positions that should be all numeric. For example, if all inventory part numbers begin with the letter A or M or R, we should check to see that the first input character is one of these characters. If it is possible, we place boundaries on the input data to recognize invalid data; for example, we may be able to say that no transaction should be less than 50 cents or over $1,000,000. In a sequential update, it is likely that for many error checks we shall have to wait until the file is actually updated. The data at the edit processing stage are likely to be unsorted, and the data affecting a single master file record will not be all together.

In later stages, when sorted input is being processed, we can check the number of transactions affecting a single record to see if the amount of activity is reasonable. If there are too many transactions, there may be a problem that should be checked. For example, if usage of a part exceeds 200 percent of the prior month's usage, human intervention may be necessary to determine the reason for such abnormally high usage.

**On-Line Systems**   One of the major efforts in the design of on-line input is error detection; it is difficult to catch errors such as the transposition or transcription mistakes we discussed under batch processing. With on-line processing, transactions are frequently not entered together in a group, so that batch totals are not possible. These applications will probably make use of check digits and will also require logical checks on input. Frequently, with on-line transactions, we have access to files, therefore more complete checks can be performed on the data as they are entered. On-line input has the major advantage of providing immediate feedback on errors, however.

---

**MANAGEMENT PROBLEM 15-4**

John Washington is the manager of sales for Farway Manufacturing Company, a firm specializing in the manufacture of yard and garden supplies. The firm's products are sold in hardware stores and nurseries throughout the world by a large force of field sales representatives.

Currently, Farway is involved in the design of a new order-entry and sales-information system, and John is the user in charge of the project. The design team is in the process of choosing a method for data input and is divided over which of two alternatives would be most desirable.

One group in the firm favors optical character recognition for order entry; the sales force would be trained to print carefully when preparing order forms. The forms would be input directly to an OCR scanner connected to the firm's computer system, eliminating the need for any data transcription. Adherents of this approach point to the savings inherent in not having to transcribe order information into machine-readable form. Those opposing this alternative worry that the sales force will be uncooperative because of the changes required and the added time to print orders very carefully.

A second group that is uneasy about OCR has proposed continuing with the same, familar order form; all changes would take place at the factory and would not be noticed by the sales force. When the orders arrive at the factory, they would be grouped into batches of 50 and entered by operators using a CRT on-line to the computer. This alternative features the advantage of batch error control combined with immediate feedback as the data are entered.

John Washington is trying to determine what criteria to use in deciding between these two alternatives for input. Which alternative sounds better to you? How should John resolve this deadlock on the design team?

---

It is certainly possible to perform the same type of field checking as in batch processing, that is, checking the upper and lower bounds on the values of input numbers. Input fields can also be scanned to be sure that numeric fields do not contain alphabetic data. On-line processing generally includes inconsistency checks; if a room clerk·books two hotel reservations, then the clerk should also enter the names of two guests. In the case of extremely critical data that cannot be verified, the system should echo them back to the user and ask for confirmation.

Some systems collect data on-line, post them to a transaction file, and update the master file later in batch mode. As long as the data on the files do not have to be up to the minute, this processing strategy presents an alternative to a fully on-line updating system. It is also customary to record all input transactions on magnetic tape in an on-line system to produce an input audit trail and for backup.

The first on-line applications were developed to give individuals at different locations access to a centralized database. Generally, these were for rather simple transactions, such as making a reservation. Today, many organizations are applying on-line technology to what, in the past, would have been batch input. For example, consider an order-entry application in which the sales force sends a completed order form to the factory. In the factory, a day's receipts of orders could be placed in a batch and the number of pieces ordered added to provide a batch total.

Then an operator working on-line at a CRT enters the information from each order. First, the operator types in the customer number, and the computer retrieves and displays the customer name and address; the operator checks the computer-retrieved data against the order. If there is an error, the operator corrects the account number and continues. Each item on the order is keyed in, and the computer checks to see if the item numbers are legitimate. For example, do we make style 3245 in color 37 (blue)? Various totals are computed on the order as a further check: for example, all the items entered from the CRT can be added and the total compared with that manually computed on the order. A listing of the day's orders with a batch total should correspond to the manual batch total computed for the orders before they are entered into the system. This type of on-line input combines the advantages of batch control checking with on-line interaction.

**Output Errors** If input is correct, and processing up to the output stage has been carefully checked, we expect correct output to result. However, it may still be necessary to take certain precautions. It is likely that a report program will read data from the output of some other programs. We may want to have control totals on the different amount fields if report contents are written into an intermediate file. The report-writing program computes the same totals and checks them against the intermediate file. When the reports are actually printed, the report-printing program checks different calculations, for example, by "crossfooting" various output totals (that is, computing the same total more than one way—perhaps horizontally and vertically on a statement). We should also be alert to rounding problems, although most computer languages for information systems now feature decimal arithmetic capabilities. Some older machines that had only binary arithmetic created errors when financial statements were off by several pennies because of poor rounding procedures in programs. In one company, the inaccuracies were not appreciated by the accounting department, which lost all faith in computer processing because of this easily correctable error.

**Error Action** Many of the input and processing checks described above are designed to ensure file integrity, that is, to avoid the introduction of erroneous data or the destruction of portions of a file. This goal must be balanced against having a system that is overcontrolled, that is, a system with so many error checks that it is never able to run to completion.

For gross processing errors, such as an incorrect file, it is necessary to avoid processing until the problem can be corrected. If a series of transactions appears to be incorrect when a file is updated, the particular record in error can be skipped and an error notification issued. Alternatively, that record can be updated, but a field on the record should be used to indicate that some type of authorization for the change must be received on the next updating cycle. If control totals do not match at the end of a run, then appropriate notices have to be issued, and the operations staff has to decide whether a rerun is necessary.

### Backup

In addition to error controls during processing, we must consider the availability of backup. An audit trail is necessary; that is, there must be some way to trace transactions through a system from input to output. In an on-line system, one reason for keeping a tape of transactions is to make sure there is an audit trail. Special audit transactions may be created as a legitimate type of input for use by auditors in checking the system.

Batch updating provides automatic backup and security in the form of the old master file plus a record of transactions; we can recreate the new master file easily if anything happens to it. Usually, two versions of the master file are kept, giving rise to what is called "the grandfather-son backup strategy." For on-line systems, the contents of the file are dumped to tape, possibly several times a day. If a catastrophic failure occurs, the operator reloads the dumped files and uses the transaction-log tape to restore file changes.

Because batch computer systems also occasionally fail for hardware and software reasons, batch file updates may make use of checkpoint procedures so that a complete rerun is not necessary if an error is encountered. Some computer languages feature automatic checkpoint facilities; during a sequential update, for example, a request for a checkpoint causes the recording of all data areas and the program status on a file. In addition, information on the records that are finished processing is recorded. If the system fails for some reason, the operator can restart the program at the last checkpoint without returning to the beginning of processing.

The major problem with restarting on-line systems is that we do not know how many transactions were in process at the time of failure. Because of the time involved, we may not want to reload the dump tape, but would like to recover from a minor failure as quickly as possible. It may be feasible to ask terminal users to verify their last transactions after we update the file. Alternatively, the time of update may be a field on the file and the recovery program could identify suspected transactions which were entered, but not completely processed, at the time of the failure.

### Security and Fraud

There has been a great deal of publicity about the problems of fraud and security with computer systems. In designing a system, we have to take reasonable precautions to avoid the possibility of fraud. Independent programmers should be used for critical parts of the system, and multiple users should be involved. Procedurally, we should avoid giving authorization for sensitive changes to only one person. One of the easiest ways to develop reasonable precautions is to include an internal auditor on the design team. Security is enhanced not only by having backup files, but by storing them in separate physical locations.

## SYSTEM SPECIFICATIONS

The final design must be converted into system specifications, a task best undertaken by the staff of the information services department. The specifications must reflect the processing logic of the new system and describe the format, contents, and structure of each file in the system. Input and output must be specified in detail including the form, medium, format, and examples. The designers should explain programming requirements, and both users and the computer staff can work on the documentation of manual procedures. An example of system specifications is presented in Chapter 20 and Table 15-5 contains a list of the items that should be included in this report.

## KEY WORDS

| | | |
|---|---|---|
| Analyst | Documentation | Resource allocation |
| Alternatives | Error control | Resources |
| Backup | Exception reporting | Response time |
| Batch controls | Feasibility study | Risk |
| Check digit | Flexibility | Source data collection |
| Control totals | Input specifications | Steering committee |
| Conversion program | Manual procedures | Verification |
| Criterion | Priorities | Weight |
| Data transcription | Processing alternatives | |
| Demands | Reasonableness checks | |

## RECOMMENDED READINGS

Ackoff, R. L.: "Management Misinformation Systems," *Management Science,* vol. 14, no. 4, December 1967, pp. B140–B156. (This classic article describes a number of myths about information systems design.)

Bohl, M.: *Information Processing,* SRA, Chicago, 1984. (A good introductory text in computer systems.)

Burch, J., F. Strater, and G. Grudnitski: *Information Systems Theory and Practice,* Wiley, New York, 1983. (A good text on systems stressing design.)

Lucas, H. C., Jr., and J. R. Moore, Jr.: "A Multiple Criterion Scoring Approach to Information System Project Selection," *Infor,* vol. 14, no. 2, February 1976, pp. 1–12. (This paper describes in detail the scoring model referred to in this chapter.)

Moore, J. R., Jr., and N. R. Baker: "Computational Analysis of Scoring Models for R&D Project Selection," *Management Science,* vol. 16, no. 4, December 1969, pp.

B212–B232. (This paper presents the results of a simulation of some of the properties of scoring models; it is technical, but provides good background on this type of model compared with others.)

## DISCUSSION QUESTIONS

1 Why is the selection of an information systems project so important to an organization?

2 What are the major sources of frustrations in selecting computer applications?

3 How does the conflict model of earlier chapters apply to selection of information systems projects, if the information services department is in charge of this process and makes unilateral decisions?

4 What is source data collection? What are its advantages?

5 How would you expect an information services department to react to the idea of evaluating several different alternatives for a single system?

6 What kind of output equipment has the most pleasing user interface, in your opinion? What is the cost of more desirable equipment compared with that of a less pleasant interface?

7 Can systems design be described as a science? What is scientific about it? What characteristics make it appear to be an art?

8 What type of computer system—for example, batch or on-line—is most flexible in meeting user needs when in operation? What type is most flexible when changes are made after implementation?

9 What is the drawback for users in serving on a selection committee and/or design teams?

10 What other approaches to selection of information systems projects can you suggest?

11 Who should be on a selection committee for project selection decisions?

12 Suggest a mechanism for deciding which enhancements to existing systems should be undertaken. How does this problem differ from selecting new applications? How are the two decisions similar?

13 Why present multiple alternatives in preliminary surveys and feasibility studies?

14 How do projects already under way influence decisions on undertaking a proposed application?

15 How can one find out what applications packages might be available as a possible source of processing in a proposed system?

16 How should risk be considered in evaluating proposed applications? What are the risks in systems analysis and design? Should an organization have a portfolio of projects balanced on risk?

17 What is an audit trail in an information system? Why is such a trail of transactions necessary?

18 What are the reasons for using on-line technology if there is no need for decentralized coordination of users who access a common database?

19 Are there manual procedures with an on-line system? If so, what type? How important are they?

20 Why are some managers unsatisfied with exception reports? How can their fears be eased?

21 Are error checks more demanding for a batch system or for a system that operates on-line? What types of error checks differ for the two systems?

22 What contribution can the user make to a preliminary survey and feasibility study? How can the use of this information lead to biased recommendations?
23 How can the amount of computer output be reduced while still meeting user needs?
24 What other creative tasks are there in the organization in addition to the design of new information systems? How do they differ from this activity?
25 What are the prospects for automating systems design tasks? Where could automation be fruitfully applied in the systems life cycle?
26 Design a procedure for developing criteria and assigning them for project selection.
27 Does a system have to use the most modern technology to be successful? Why or why not? Are there disadvantages to utilizing the most up-to-date technology?

## SYSTEMS DESIGN PROBLEMS

1 One of the most common computer applications is payroll. Many organizations have custom-designed payroll systems, and a large number of service bureaus offer packages to compute an organization's payroll. The logic of the payroll process is fairly simple and is common across many organizations.

Usually a payroll master file contains data about each individual who is on the payroll. Examples of the data to be included in setting up this file for employees would be:

NAME
NUMBER OF DEPENDENTS
MARITAL STATUS
DEDUCTIONS
UNION DUES
HOSPITAL PLAN
MEDICAL PLAN
PENSION
EMPLOYEE NUMBER
WAGE RATE
SOCIAL SECURITY NUMBER

On a periodic basis, such as weekly or monthly, input must originate to trigger the computation of the payroll and the production of a check for each employee. This weekly input would have to include at a minimum:

Employee number
Regular hours worked
Overtime hours worked
Sick leave
Special deductions

Once the system is run on a periodic basis, checks should be produced along with various accumulations for different year-to-date categories. The computer program would subtract all deductions and withhold funds for tax purposes. Also included in the output would normally be a payroll register. On an annual basis, the computer system would produce W2 forms, which are summaries of earnings and taxes withheld from wages, for the IRS.

a Design the input forms to be used to place a new employee on the payroll file, and the forms to be completed weekly for each employee to be paid.

b List the file contents and approximate field sizes for the payroll master file. Do not forget to include year-to-date totals.

   **c** Draw a system flowchart for this payroll application.

   **d** Describe the modifications necessary for the system to automatically mail a check to the bank if the employee so elects, and to include a notice to the employee.

   **e** Design the file maintenance and change cards necessary to alter information about employees.

**2** Most organizations have some kind of accounts receivable, whether they are in manufacturing or in a service company. Accounts receivable was one of the first applications undertaken by many firms when computer systems were acquired. Service bureaus also offer accounts-receivable packages for sale or rent. In the early days of computers, most accounts-receivable packages were typically batch applications; today, however, there is growing interest in on-line input and payment processing.

   Consider an on-line accounts-receivable system. An accounts-receivable transaction is generated by a shipment of a product to a customer. An operator at a terminal enters the following information:

      Order number
      Shipment number
      For each shipment:
      Product code
      Quantity
      Date
      Shipping costs
      Special shipping mode
      Special discounts
      Comments

   The program accepting this input responds with the customer name and address once the order number is entered: it also prints the product descriptions, the price extension, and the total invoice cost.

   The customer receives the statement and sends in payment for one or more invoices. The next task is for an operator to enter the payments and to match them against invoices. The operator enters the invoice number, the total payment, and exceptions to indicate partial payments for items on an invoice that are not paid.

   In addition to the printed invoices, invoice register, and monthly statements, the system would provide an accounts-receivable listing, a daily cash balance, and exception reports for invoices that were partially paid or have not been paid at all. There would also be a function to allow on-line inquiry concerning payment history.

   Of course, as with any system, it is necessary to establish a new customer. The new customer information would have to include:

      The account number
      Name and address
      Credit
      Payment terms
      Normal shipping mode

   **a** Design the customer master file, the shipment and invoice files, and show any directories necessary to access these files.

   **b** Describe the overall logic of file access.

   **c** Design the screens for data input and inquiry using a CRT.

   **d** List the edits and controls that would be necessary on this system.

**3** Accounts Payable

   Accounts payable has also traditionally been a batch processing application;

however, on-line input improves the editing and the user interface with this system. To add a new vendor with whom a firm does business, it is necessary to assign a vendor number and include a name, address, and list any terms and discount that apply.

The first activity that generates an accounts payable is the issuance of a purchase order. The purchase order must contain:

Vendor number
For each item:
Item number
Item description
Quantity
Cost
Cost for the whole order, shipping costs, and special discounts

For on-line accounts payable, the system would respond with the vendor, name, and address as soon as the vendor number was entered, and would perform all the extensions of price times quantity. The output from this part of the system would be a printed purchase order. It would be also desirable to allow the purchasing department to make inquiries on a purchase order number.

The purchase order would be used as a document for receiving. The receiving department enters a purchase order number when merchandise arrives and notes any exceptions on the items, such as a particular item that was not received, or a quantity that is not what was indicated on the purchase order.

Next, the organization receives a bill from the vendor. This bill should contain the company's purchase order number and the amount owed. An individual in the accounts-payable section accesses a terminal, enters the purchase order number, and compares the bill with the original purchase order and the quantities received. On authorization for payment, the system prints a check ready for mailing to the vendor and a check register.

**a** Design the system flow for this system.

**b** Design the vendor and the open purchase order files.

**c** Design the input edits and controls for the system, and the displays for a CRT screen.

**4** Sales reporting can be a very important computer application. Often, data for sales reports come directly from shipping and/or invoicing systems in the organization. At a minimum, this application requires a customer file including a customer number, geographic code, shipment date, order number, item number, quantity shipped, and price.

From these data, it is possible to generate an output sales report. This report might be summarized by product, product type, region, or salesperson.

**a** Would you recommend that this system operate in batch or on-line mode?

**b** Design an inquiry system that would answer questions interactively concerning customers or products. Would these answers be computed on-line or would a summary file be developed?

**c** Assume that historical data are available on sales for the last 10 years. What kind of forecasting system would you design for this organization? What would be your considerations in choosing a forecasting system?

**5** The manufacturing or production function in an organization includes many activities, such as materials acquisition, production scheduling and control, work-in-process inventory control, and finished goods inventory control.

One way to start the manufacturing process is with the preparation of a bill of materials. A bill of materials lists all the components necessary to manufacture a product. Usually the input that is provided is the number of new products identified by product number and quantity. The output from this system is a list of subassemblies and the quantity required; that list contains all the parts needed to manufacture the particular product.

**a** Design the file structures for a bill-of-materials processor.

**b** Describe the logic of the explosion program.

**c** Assume the input to the bill-of-materials processor contains both the product and the date it is to be shipped to the customer. Design a system to produce a report on products that must be manufactured by a given due date.

**6** A budget is a fundamental managerial control tool in an organization. In setting up budgets, minimal input includes an account number, the type of account, a description, and where a control break is to be taken to add up the totals for a subaccount. Then for each budget cycle, input is provided on the account number, the budgeted amount of money, and the actual money spent.

The output from such a system is the budget report. It shows the account, the description, the budgeted amount, the actual amount, variance amounts, and usually percentage totals as well.

Design a master file for a budget application and describe the format of a budget report.

**7** One unusual application was suggested for a retail grocery chain. This particular organization computes what is called a markup and markdown plan each week. The markup is the general gross profit the store wishes to obtain on groceries; this markup might be 20 percent. The markdown is the amount of margin acceptable when the regular and special discount items are sold; so, for example, if a special is to be held on frozen peas, the sale on frozen peas might be 10 percent off, which is estimated to reduce the total gross profit to a level of 18 percent, which is the markdown.

In this grocery chain, pricing specialists make estimates of the sales of discount special items and the sales of all items sold at regular price. The markup goal is then compared with the estimates for the actual markup to determine if the markdown resulting from sales plan specials is acceptable.

A consultant has recommended this activity as a possible computer application. What kind of computer application does this suggest? What would be the interface between the pricing specialist and the computer? What mode of operation do you recommend?

**a** Design the files for this system.

**b** Describe the interaction between the system and the pricing specialist.

**c** Design an output report that shows the prices to be charged for items on special.

**8** General ledger is an accounting application to produce a final consolidation of all financial transactions in a company. A file must be created showing the chart of accounts for the firm. Many subsystems automatically produce entries for the general ledger, and other input comes from journal entries. Examples of input from different subsystems include payroll, vendor invoices, accounts payable, cash receipts, check writing, work in process, fixed assets, and shipments.

General ledger programs traditionally include a trial balance that is run before the final general ledger for the month. The output of the system is a detailed general ledger showing transactions against individual accounts and a consolidated ledger at the account level.

**a** Design the files necessary to produce a consolidated and a detailed general ledger.

**b** Draw a flowchart of the general ledger system showing the inputs from other systems.

**c** Design the logic for the production of financial statements (an income statement and balance sheet) from the general ledger. What alterations have to be made in the file design in **a** above to produce the financial reports?

**9** Computer technology is being applied to the retail industry, particularly to supermarket check-out operations. In these systems, some type of optical character recognition scanner reads the universal product code on items sold in the store. A minicomputer in the store contains a file with the universal produce code numbers and the current price. As the items are scanned, their price is read from the file and the entire cost of the grocery order is computed.

All during the day the computer in the store maintains a record of items sold. In the evening, the data can be transferred to a central host computer to update master records, which represent sales and, more important, inventory balances. These inventory data can then be used to restock the supermarket, so that it is not necessary for store personnel to place formal orders with the warehouse.

Such systems were designed to speed the check-out process and to ensure more rapid response for the resupply of grocery products.

**a** Design the files for the local grocery store and the files for the central host computer.

**b** Develop a backup plan that will become operative if the minicomputer in the supermarket fails.

**c** What reports could be generated from the system for the use of store management?

# PROGRAMMING THROUGH INSTALLATION

# PROGRAMMING THROUGH INSTALLATION

## CHAPTER ISSUES

- How can management monitor and aid the development of systems?
- What management actions are needed to ensure adequate training and smooth conversion to a new system?
- How does one manage systems design projects?

The next stages in the development of a new information system are programming, testing, training, conversion, and installation. Programming is a highly technical and time-consuming task, and in this chapter we suggest some modern approaches to programming to improve productivity. Careful testing and planning for installation are essential; many systems have failed because attention was not paid to these activities. What roles do the user and manager have in testing and planning for training, conversion, and installation? In this chapter we explore activities during these stages.

## PROGRAMMING

The most technical parts of computer project management and the greatest amount of uncertainty are associated with the task of writing and testing programs. In the past, we have been unable either to estimate completion times effectively or to coordinate people working on different parts of a program. In this section we present some new ideas and approaches to these tasks that should help to improve programming productivity.

For the most part we have always thought of programming as an individual task. Programmers are often detached from their coworkers, but are highly attached to the programs they write. Errors in programs are taken personally and programmers tend to be highly defensive about their programs. Weinberg (1972*a*) has suggested a new approach to programming (he calls it "egoless programming") that treats programming as a group activity rather than as an individual effort. Management must create an environment in which the programmer expects errors in the code and recognizes that help is needed to find them. Programmers in a group trade programs and look at each other's codes. Each programmer becomes better aware of the entire system and develops an understanding of how different modules fit together because of this involvement in the construction of other parts of the system. Also, more backup is provided, since several people are familiar with each module.

### Programmer Teams

One approach to improved programming is the use of a team. A chief programmer team consists of a senior chief programmer, one or more backup programmers, one to five junior programmers, and a programming secretary (Mills, 1971). The chief programmer directs the activities of the group, holding a position similar to that of a senior engineer. Programming is often viewed as a profession leading to a system analyst or management position, but one of the advantages of the team concept is that a highly paid chief programmer position can be viewed as a senior staff position in an organization. This approach presents a better career path for programmers and recognizes that skilled programming is a worthy profession in itself.

All other programmers report to the chief programmer, whose job is to design and code programs, and who will program the most critical segments of the system. This person also works with other programmers to define modules for them. The chief programmer is responsible for the management of the team as a whole, and has the opportunity to be a high-level creative programmer and, at the same time, a professional manager.

A backup programmer who is equal in ability with the chief programmer becomes totally familiar with the activities of the chief programmer and provides backup. As long as the chief programmer is able to continue to manage the project, the backup programmer serves as a research associate to help develop new ideas and program test data. A programming secretary maintains records of the project, including a complete file or library of programs, flowcharts, and program specifications. An index or directory to each part of the library is also maintained.

The entire programming team functions as a group. Various programmers follow the guidance of the chief programmer; they work on different modules and read each other's programs. Heavy use is made of the library to build, store, and retrieve information for the team. For large projects it may be necessary to have several levels of teams, with the highest level reporting to the project manager. To implement this approach management must make an extensive effort to provide an environment for and to encourage group-related activities.

### Modularization

In the early days of programming, the practice was to write a single large program to accomplish a major task, for example, the entire update of a major file. Large individual programs have proved very hard to write because of their complexity, and extremely difficult to debug and modify. Modern programming techniques call for dividing programs into modules that are reasonably small. Each module accomplishes one processing function. The modules should be written so that they are easy to understand and so that control enters at the beginning of the module and exists at the end without intervening transfers. The task of partitioning a system into modules is very difficult and not well understood today.

It is helpful to make a list of design decisions and to construct program modules around these decisions to hide them from other design decisions. (A program will usually consist of several modules.) The breakdown of programs into smaller modules makes it easier to debug and modify the system. Of course, program specifications must be developed for each module. We should list all the

---

**MANAGEMENT PROBLEM 16-1**

David Schwartz is controller of Play Toys, a manufacturer of high-quality children's toys. He has recently served as the user in charge of the development of a new integrated accounting system for the company. The specifications are complete, and the system is now being programmed by the information services department at Play Toys. David, although not managing the programming, has tried to stay in touch with progress.

He is very concerned about the problems the computer staff apparently is having with the project. There are four programmers assigned to write different portions of the system. As the computer staff manager explained it to David, there has been a great deal of frustration when the components written by each of the four programmers do not fit together. As David understands it, the programs fail to "cooperate" in the way they should.

David now has the feeling that the manager of programming for the new accounting system really is no longer in control of the project. This manager is just responding to problems and pressures. When David asks to see a schedule or tries to obtain a status report, the manager of programming is evasive and does not appear to know the answer. David feels the company needs the system very badly. If the company misses the conversion date, it may be necessary to wait an entire year because they are planning to install the new system at the beginning of the fiscal year.

What can David Schwartz do as a user to rescue the accounting project?

---

data entering from another module, the number of characters and format of any source documents to be read, and, finally, any data to be read from a file. Output for reports or output that is to be passed to another module should also be specified.

Finally, we must specify any processing to be done by the module. How are the inputs and information derived from files processed? What should the program accomplish? The processing should be described in the form of an algorithm, that is, an effective procedure for accomplishing the goals of the module. The algorithm can be expressed in English, in symbols, or in some combination of the two.

In addition to specifying the programs that will constitute the system when it is in operation, we must also define any conversion programs needed to create files or manipulate data before the installation of the system. Since these programs will be run only once for the most part, efficiency is not as important as clarity and the speed of program development.

### Top-Down Programming

Most systems are designed from the top level down; that is, a general plan is developed and refined to greater levels of detail. But systems tend to be implemented from the bottom up; that is, basic modules are written first and then integrated into subsystems.

Some evidence suggests that it may be better to reverse the implementation process (Baker, 1972; Mills, 1971). Under this top-down approach, we write the highest-level programs and test them while the next lowest level is being written. Dummy subroutine and procedure calls are used for lower-level modules that have not been written yet. Top-down programming makes the status of work clear and shows the functions that must be performed by lower-level routines. The interface between modules can be defined before the functions are actually coded. We can avoid the redesign of lower-level modules that would have been required because of some oversight discovered when lower-level modules were combined for use by a higher-level routine.

### Reviews

Design reviews in which processing is described in detail should be scheduled for different parts of the system. For example, the logic of an input error check could be presented by the programmer in charge of the module to an audience of other programming team members and perhaps a user representative from the design team. The audience notes errors and inconsistencies and makes suggestions for improvements in the module. Someone in the meeting records these comments for the person making the presentation. The purpose of these reviews is constructive; we are trying to find what has been omitted or what errors in logic are included in the design. The review is not held for employee evaluation;

the goal is to improve the product, not to criticize the speaker. Clearly, this approach requires an open and nondefensive attitude that is consistent with the environment required for "egoless" programming.

### Fourth-Generation Languages

Historically business applications have been programmed in COBOL, a higher-level language. While an improvement over assembly language, COBOL programs are still tedious to write. All the techniques described above, such as structured programming, top down design, modularization, and so on may create a 10 percent improvement in programmer productivity. However, more dramatic performance increases are needed.

A number of firms are moving away from COBOL programming and instead are using fourth-generation languages. There is no one standard for these languages as there is a COBOL standard. Some computer vendors offer the languages. Sperry has been very successful with a language called Mapper. Proprietary languages include Ramis, Nomad, Natural, and Focus.

We shall explore these languages further in Chapter 18. Basically, the languages have very high-level statements; one statement in the fourth-generation language would require many COBOL statements to accomplish the

---

**THE SEC'S ELECTRONIC FILE**

The Securities and Exchange Commission (SEC) is planning to move to a paperless system for storing the massive amount of data it keeps on U.S. companies. Some 6 million pages are filed each year by corporations. The new computerized system is called EDGAR for electronic data gathering and retrieval.

Firms will send documents like 10Ks, prospectuses, and other forms electronically via phone lines using their own computers as a source. The information will be stored by the SEC where it can be retrieved and reviewed by staff members.

The contractor for the final system will be able to sell the information in the database. Large numbers of analysts and investors make use of this information. While it is available elsewhere, often in machine-readable form, it takes a considerable period of time after filing for the information to be ready for access. EDGAR will make the data available quickly for those interested in retrieving it.

The SEC also feels that its staff will be able to make better decisions. It will be possible to retrieve and cross-reference the most recent filing with past documents in the file. It will also be possible to compare one company with similar firms which will aid in analysis.

*Business Week,* April 2, 1984.

---

same task. The languages all have some kind of data management capability as well. For example, Natural is a language designed for use with the popular ADABASE database management system.

Why use such a language? Reports from firms adopting them indicate productivity improvements of five to ten times over writing conventional COBOL programs. One investment backing firm in New York estimates that it completes five jobs for users with its fourth-generation language for each single job when it was using COBOL.

## TESTING

Users have an important role to play in testing. While programmers design a certain amount of test data, users should help develop test data for system verification. Users should not provide only average transactions, but should also generate test data with errors and data that encompass as many different conditions as possible. For example, one should try to violate rules for input by putting wrong characters in columns, such as alphabetic data where numeric data belong. These test practices ensure that programs have adequate error checking and editing features.

Next, the user should try to make illegal changes in files, for example, by updating an invalid field and using incorrect transaction codes. These errors will occur in actual operations of the system, and we should be sure that the system has been programmed to detect them so that they will not damage files and lead to incorrect output. Programs should also be tested with a high volume of transactions.

Testing also includes checking the basic logic of each program and verifying that the entire system works properly. We cannot be exhaustive in program testing because there is an overwhelming number of paths in a program. Testing individual programs involves an attempt to be sure that the most likely paths work properly. Programmers facilitate testing by coding as clearly as possible; however, we should remember the saying that no program is fully debugged. Systems should be planned so that errors are easy to find and correct. As users, we must expect to encounter occasional errors, even after installation of the system; the purpose of testing is to reduce their frequency and severity.

### Unit Testing

After the systems design, programmers write and test basic program modules. At this stage, programmers usually construct their own test data or use a program that generates these data. One problem is common to all testing: if programmers make up their own test data, only the conditions thought of in advance by the programmer will be tested. Unit testing with programmer data is necessary, of course, but it is not sufficient. Although it is important to know if the logic included in the program works properly, we are also concerned about conditions that the programmer did not include in the program. Egoless programming and team approaches help here, as they provide for input from other programmers who might think of missing logic. Structured review sessions also point out omissions. However, it is still best to have an independent source of test data for users to augment each programmer's tests. One activity for the backup programmer is to generate data for testing individual programs.

## Combined Module Testing

Modules are combined for testing after they pass individual unit tests. Top-down programming helps here, since errors frequently occur in calling sequences. Programming lower-level modules first creates major changes when we program higher-level routines and recognize an omission in a lower-level module. By carefully specifying the interface for high-level modules, programming them first, and by keeping a systems library up to date, many interface problems are avoided.

At this point in combined module testing, we also stress independent test data generation. It is important for users to be included in developing test data, because the data will be less contrived and more realistic. In one instance, management offered a prize to the user who designed the best error-detection scheme and the best processing module for the user's department's processing. The idea was to create input data that would cause another department's processing logic to fail. This "game" resulted in the development of realistic test data to run against the program logic developed in each user area.

## Testing Manual Procedures

The testing described above is concerned with programs. Another major activity occurring simultaneously with the development of programs is the design and testing of manual procedures. Manual procedures are sometimes overlooked, but they can determine the success of a system.

In one case, an airline developed an automatic seat-assignment option as part of its on-line computer reservations system. This on-line CRT-based system replaced the old approach of using cardboard cutouts of the seats torn from an outline of the plane's body. The new system was implemented at a peak holiday travel season. At one San Francisco gate, a spotlight was directed on the CRT screen at the check-in counter—a lighting effect that made it difficult to read the CRT. In addition, the device was positioned so that the agent operating the console could not stand straight; he had to bend over slightly. Long lines formed while a nontypist agent tried to assign seats and enter passenger names on the terminal. The old way of tearing off the seat stub from the cutout and handing it to the passenger was several times faster.

What happened in this example? The airline spent millions of dollars on a computer system and obviously spent no time on testing manual procedures. The design team could have employed a very simple queuing model, or even written a small simulation to test manual operations. In fact, the airline might even have programmed a simple version of the system on a time-sharing computer and actually had airline employees or real passengers simulate the boarding process.

Where there are major changes in existing manual procedures, trial testing is essential, especially with a terminal with a system that interfaces directly with customers. It is relatively easy to simulate parts of a system by developing a few input forms and having users work with these forms. However, it is important to design trial tests so they are real experiments. One company conducted a trial test, but had the entire computer department present in the small user department to answer questions and help with the test. Because of the attention and extra help, the experiment succeeded; it could not really have failed. However, when the system was introduced in the whole manufacturing plant, it was a total disaster. The experiment was not a fair or useful test because it was not representative of what would happen during actual operations.

Users are an essential component of manual procedures testing since they are the individuals who will execute these manual procedures. Can we simulate the procedures to be sure they work properly? The process of testing procedures results in users who are well-trained before conversion, since they will try the procedures before they actually have to be used.

## Acceptance Tests

Some formal procedure is generally employed to certify that a system is ready for installation; users must view the test results and "accept" the system. When feasible, a parallel test may be conducted in which the new system is run along with the old. The results of the two systems are compared to assess the validity of the new system. Parallel testing requires much extra work for users, since two systems are operated simultaneously. In the case of some systems—for example, those that are on-line—parallel operations may not be possible logically. Other approaches to acceptance testing include the development of special data by users who then validate the output of the system; such test data must be carefully developed and be as comprehensive as possible. Regardless of the approach used, some type of acceptance test is necessary before the conversion and installation of a new system.

## TRAINING

Heavy user participation in design pays dividends during training. All individuals who will be affected by a new system should receive some training. The design team develops training materials such as sample forms to be completed by users or samples of screens that will appear on a CRT. For terminal-based systems, users should have the opportunity to operate a special training version or simulated version of the new system in order to gain familiarity with it.

Several on-line systems, including the one discussed in Chapter 21, have successfully employed computer-aided instruction (CAI) to train terminal operators. CAI is a programmed learning approach in which the computer is a tutor that drills the student while recording student progress. For large systems with many operators distributed widely from a geographic standpoint, CAI may be the only economical way to provide training. The CAI programs maintain a record of progress and can be designed to let operators exercise only those functions for which they have received training.

In planning for training, all people potentially affected by the system should be considered. One approach is to predict the reaction of each individual, for example, in the form of a balance sheet (Mumford and Ward, 1968). What are the costs and benefits of the change for each affected individual? A change plan can then be customized to each individual; in some instances the design team may change the system to minimize the costs to certain users.

## CONVERSION AND INSTALLATION

Conversion is the process of preparing for the first live operation of the new system; what activities are required for the system to begin running? Usually, new files are created from either manual or existing machine-readable records. Existing procedures have to be terminated and the new ones phased into

---

## MANAGEMENT PROBLEM 16-2

The new manager of information services for a major West Coast bank is trying to improve relations with users. The bank has a history of conflict between the computer department and user departments. One approach the manager has adopted is to increase user participation in systems design. However, his own observations have confirmed those of the computer staff: users are woefully ignorant of computer systems. Furthermore, they really do not want to learn about them because of the stormy computer history of the bank.

The president of the bank has given her commitment to the project and has offered whatever resources are needed. The manager of the information services department is trying to solve the following problems:

1 How does he gain the support of department heads to encourage users to participate in training and systems design?
2 What are the most essential topics for user training?
3 What kind of courses should be offered? Who should teach them and when?
4 Who should attend the training sessions—should only those users who will be working on a system next be invited, or should there be general invitations?
5 How does he train users for microcomputers?
6 Is similiar training needed for the information services department staff?
7 How can he evaluate the results of the training program?

Can you help answer these questions and design an action plan for the manager?

---

operation. The conversion date is a target that should be well publicized in order to encourage readiness.

The major consideration in planning for conversion and installation is to proceed gradually; never convert and install a system at the peak season for the organization. It may be possible to phase in a system by department, geographic region, or on some other basis. A great deal is learned from the first unit implemented, which can be used to prepare for the next portion of the cutover. Full-scale cutover of an entire system at one point in time runs a high risk of disaster. If the system has to be installed at once because of some special requirements, then extra effort should be taken in training and users should have a chance to work on a simulated version of the system.

## DOCUMENTATION

Documentation is a term used to describe all the instructions, programs, and narratives, that is, almost anything written about the information system. Documentation serves a number of purposes. First, during systems design, it is the evolving product developed by the design team. After implementation, it is the basis for making changes to the system. The quality of documentation determines in part how much flexibility the information services department has in responding to user requests. Good documentation serves to reduce conflict between users and the information services department, since a well-documented system is easier for users to understand. Good documentation means that an adequate reference is available when problems arise, and this helps us learn how to solve problems with the system.

If a user is in charge of the design team, it is that user's responsibility to see that good documentation is developed as part of the design effort. Unfortunately, the information services department staff generally does not like to document systems; this activity is viewed as a tedious job and something that does not contribute to progress on the system. Like programming management, documentation is an activity to which time must be devoted if the system is to succeed. It is interesting to note that the new technology for programming management discussed earlier in the chapter requires far more documentation than older, more haphazard approaches. The user leader of the design team must be aware of the types of documentation needed and must work to influence the information services department to prepare it. Users on the design team can help by preparing the training and user-reference documentation for a system.

### Design Documentation

During design, the purpose of documentation is to aid in control by providing a record of what has been developed and of what has been changed. It is important to be sure that all parts of a system are considered and that those responsible for the components affected by the change are notified. What program modules and what programmers are involved if a file format or the contents of a file are altered?

Control is also the ability to retrieve past test runs and old versions of programs or files. Design documentation builds an excellent database for making future estimates of how long it will take to develop similar systems. The systems librarian should maintain a copy of all runs and progress reports so that a complete description of project activities can be found easily.

### Training Documentation

Training documentation prepares us for conversion, installation, and the eventual use of the system. Most of the information needed for training can be developed from the systems documentation discussed above. User-training documentation is used to bridge the gap between old existing procedures and those required for the new system. This documentation should be developed by user members of the design team in conjunction with other users in the organization.

We have found it best to begin training by looking at the output of a system and the input on a CRT. Output documentation should focus on key decisions and reports. Having discussed input and output, we can cover the files necessary to produce the desired output. Finally, the computer processing logic and other procedures involved are discussed. It is important to include error conditions and the remedial actions taken in training documentation.

User training should also include considerations of transitional effects, especially testing and conversion. These problems can be presented to the user group for help in developing a solution. In fact, it is best at first not to have a completely detailed plan formulated. After plans have been jointly developed for these stages, they can be documented as conversion procedures.

### Operations Documentation

The operations section of the information services department has to operate a system after it has been converted. The operations group needs information on normal operating procedures and how to respond to errors. This information is best prepared by the systems analysts and programmers, and much of it can be derived from design documentation.

### User Reference Documentation

The last type of documentation that should be developed is for user reference after the system has become operational. This information should be referred to first when we have a question or a problem. If this documentation is of sufficient quality, users can answer their own questions without having to contact the information services department, and thus the potential for conflict is reduced. There is a tremendous amount of frustration when something goes wrong with an information system and we do not understand why, or do not know how to fix it.

Fortunately, most of this material can be taken directly from other documentation, for example, the procedures parts of the training documents. This documentation should be assembled into a reference manual such as a loose-leaf binder than can be updated easily as the system evolves over time. A detailed table of contents is necessary to make this documentation easy to use as a reference. We should make available a complete discussion of the input, output, and processing logic. One of the most important components in this documentation is a list of error conditions and "fixes" (how to correct the error). It is helpful to include the names of the most knowledgeable user and the maintenance programmer who is now in charge of the system.

## POSTCONVERSION ACTIVITIES

At some point near the cutover, it is necessary to "freeze" a system temporarily as far as changes are concerned. During this critical period, all resources have to be devoted to conversion. However, the freeze in changes should be considered clearly temporary in nature; we hold changes that are suggested in abeyance until conversion is completed.

If systems are to serve us, we shall make continuing requests for changes. In fact, a responsive information services department looks for changes and suggests them to users. The fact that users are heavily involved with the design should reduce the number of modifications necessary. However, we shall make important requests for alterations as we gain experience with the system. Another reason for structured programming and good documentation is to facilitate these changes. A system is literally never finished, but as it matures, changes should become less frequent.

After the system appears to be working smoothly, it is time to examine what was accomplished and the resources required in a postimplementation audit. Now is the time for the design team to assess reactions to the system. What could be done better next time? Were the tangible savings that were forecast achieved? How do we evaluate the intangible benefits?

We should also look at the original estimates and determine if they were achieved. The accuracy of forecasts and the experience with this system provide the data from which to make estimates in the future. These data reflect what can be done by this design team in this organization. Past experience is the best source of information available for estimating the requirements for the next system for this team and organization.

## PROJECT MANAGEMENT

Unfortunately, there has been a notable lack of success in managing systems design projects. A number of problems have been reported: schedules are not met on time, systems do not meet original specifications, and there are often high cost overruns. Programming was regarded at first as a craftlike trade that did not need managing; today, the need to manage the entire development process of a system is recognized.

## Uncertainties

One of the major problems in systems analysis and design is the high level of uncertainty associated with these activities. Users are often unaware of the problems creating the need for an information system, yet they must work with the design team to develop the data for designing the system. The activities of the design team also create uncertainty for users who are asked to describe their information needs. Can users adequately explain their decision and information processing requirements?

Lack of certainty is also reflected in the development of the system itself. Is the model developed by the design team close to reality; that is, do the specifications adequately represent the needed information processing procedures? Once given the system design, programmers have to interpret the specifications and write programs. It is difficult to forecast what is involved in writing, testing, and debugging a program. There is usually uncertainty about the time required, whether or not the program will work, and whether or not it will meet specifications.

If the program and system meet specifications, then user acceptance tests are undertaken to see if the design, as represented by systems specifications, fits user needs. The task of project management is to attempt to reduce all these uncertainties, coordinate the activities of the diverse parties working on the project, and ensure that the project is completed within time and cost estimates.

## User Responsibilities

As mentioned above, users in the systems design staff can to some extent control progress through the development of specifications. Under the approach of user-controlled design, who should manage the remaining tasks? Can the user be expected to manage technical activities such as programming? Clearly the answer to this question is "no." We do not expect or advocate that users be placed in this role.

Although users do not necessarily have detailed technical knowledge, they can still monitor a project with assistance from technical staff members from the information services department. First, users can ensure that modern tools and techniques are being used by the programming staff by influencing management in the organization and the information services department. They should see that project control techniques are used and should be kept advised of critical milestones and progress. When it is clear that there are problems in maintaining the schedule, the manager should work with information services department management to see that resources are reallocated and/or new resources are added.

## MANAGEMENT PROBLEM 16-3

Jane Braun works for the information services department at National Insurance Company. This large insurance firm specializes in life and casualty insurance and has been very successful since its founding in the early 1900s. The company has a number of modern computers, although most existing applications deal with transactions processing as opposed to decision-making applications.

Jane is excited about the new system she has helped to design for National. The application is for the investment department and appears to have a significant potential for supporting some of the important decisions made by this group. Having worked on the design, Jane was chosen to manage the programming phases of the project.

Five programmers are working on the new system, four of whom seem to cooperate very well. The fifth programmer, Stan Elton, has been with National for 10 years and is considered to be an experienced programmer. Stan's past work has generally been on systems where he was the sole programmer or where he worked with one junior partner. This is his first real assignment with a larger group of programmers, and it is the first time he has not been left to his own devices for managing his own programming efforts. Computer management at National, realizing the importance of the new system, did not want to have problems with it. Therefore, they asked Jane to manage the programming part of the project.

Jane was having a great deal of trouble communicating with Stan. For every suggestion she made, Stan responded with some reason why it was not possible. Stan also refused to give estimates for when his programs would be complete. The other programmers indicated that it was difficult to coordinate with him since he preferred to work alone. What should Jane do to solve this problem with Stan?

## PROJECT SCHEDULING

To establish control over a project, it is necessary to have a schedule, milestones, data on progress, and some structure for analysis purposes. Consider the programming stage as an example; a schedule should first be estimated during the feasibility study. As systems design progresses, the schedule becomes more concrete as the magnitude of each task becomes clearer. During the feasibility study, the developers do not know how many programs are needed or how complex they are. However, by the time program specifications are completed, these requirements will be known with greater certainty.

The selection of milestones for managing programming and testing has been a difficult process. Some possibilities are:

Program modules defined
Program module flowcharted
Program module coded
Program module compiled

## THE INNKEEPER'S MICRO

*Ramada Inns has configured a micro and mainframe system to support information processing in its nationwide chain of motels. The microcomputers replaced older, dumb-terminal systems for reservations. This system is interesting because the communications program must be running constantly in the local micro so that reservations received at the central Ramada reservations site in Omaha can be downloaded at any time. Ramada programmers had to write a layer of programs to sit on top of the standard micro operating system and let it multitask, i.e., run local programs while the communications program is always available.*

*When a reservation is keyed into the system, it goes to the mainframe in Omaha. The Omaha computer looks up the phone number of the correct hotel and dials that hotel's micro to deliver the new reservation. The mainframe may batch several reservations together and send them all at one time.*

*The micro provides two advantages for the firm. First, there can be quite elaborate and "user friendly" input menus and screens given the local processing power. Second, it will be natural to develop applications for the local hotel to run for its own management purposes. The Ramada is an example of a networked transactions processing system featuring micros and mainframes all communicating with each other.*

*PC Week*, May 22, 1984.

---

Testing with programmer data
Tests with independently generated data
Tests with other modules
Tests with "live" data

One guideline is to define tasks that are estimated to take 20 to 50 hours to complete. A shorter task makes the number of tasks too large, and longer ones do not provide sufficient warning that a project is behind schedule.

We have not had great success in estimating completion times for the steps above nor in achieving them. Studies of programmer performance have shown high variances among individuals, which complicates forecasting. It is hoped that programmer teams will help to reduce some of the individual variances and make estimates more accurate.

Having defined milestones, we are faced with the problem of knowing that a milestone has been achieved; the 90-percent complete program that remains that way for a year is legend! The milestones suggested above are designed to be concrete. Also, the milestones do not reflect quality; it may be easy to write a poor program module on schedule. It is important to be sure that the milestone can be observed and evaluated. For example, a program module is defined as complete when it has passed a quality test established independently of the programmer writing the module. The manager of the project must be able to verify independently of the person reporting that the milestone has actually been achieved.

In the final analysis, we are dependent on the technical staff's cooperation in managing programming. If accurate reporting is rewarded rather than punished, then programmers should cooperate. The first step is to include programmers in management and let them see the need to keep track of a project. When milestones are not met, additional resources should be furnished in the form of assistance, a shift in workload, more teams, and so forth. In this fashion, honest reporting will be encouraged. Finally, we need a formal mechanism for analyzing the data of progress and determining where there is slack available, that is, where added resources can be obtained and where resources are in critically short supply. One useful project management technique is the "critical path" method.

The critical path method, or CPM, was developed from a military system called PERT, for Project Evaluation and Review Technique. PERT uses probability distributions to compute the most likely completion time for the major events in a project. CPM is conceptually simpler than PERT and is better suited to the development of computer systems. The critical path method breaks a project down into a series of subtasks and arranges the activities according to precedence relationships. We indicate that one task must precede another task, as a survey precedes a feasibility study. The length of time required for each task is estimated, and the various tasks are arranged in a network reflecting precedence relationships. The critical path, that is, the path through the network requiring the greatest amount of time, is identified. As tasks are completed and estimates for completion times for remaining tasks are changed, the critical path also changes. Project management can add extra resources to critical activities on the path.

The major reason CPM has not been widely used in managing programming projects is that it requires time to measure and report on progress. The approach to obtaining progress reports described above should help ameliorate some of the data collection problems. Users who are familiar with management can appreciate the need to devote resources to the management of the programming task itself. Users may have to see that time is taken to obtain estimates and update the CPM chart. Fortunately, a number of time-sharing or microcomputer packages are available that perform all the calculations and print the charts so that mechanical computations for CPM are automatic. In fact at least one CPM-based system exists specifically for computer applications project control. The system is based on the idea that tasks are assigned to individuals who must report on progress. Original estimates are updated periodically by the programming staff and the system generates a number of useful reports for the project manager. Such tools, along with the information they provide, are extremely important in project management.

It is important for management to see that systems development is managed. Project management systems, review meetings, and other approaches will help. Development is too important to be left entirely to computer professionals.

## MANAGEMENT PROBLEM 16-4

The president of American Moving and Storage has just dismissed the company's manager of information systems. The president commented, "I have finally had enough with these computer types. We have spent millions of dollars on the design of new systems, and we never seem to implement one. The trucking system was the final straw. It is over a year late and has cost us 50 percent more than the original estimates."

The president turned to his administrative vice president and said, "It's your responsibility now. From this point on, the computer department reports to you. I want things straightened out; you have 3 months."

The vice president of administrative services has no computer experience. He has been a user of some of the systems developed by the computer department and shares the president's concern over their lack of success in meeting deadlines and budgets. However, the vice president wondered what to do now. Should he try to run the department himself or hire a new manager for it?

If he takes responsibility, will the lack of any computer background hinder his ability to understand the problems of the department? What actually is responsible for all the computer difficulties at American? If he hires a new manager for the computer department, what characteristics and skills should this new employee possess?

## KEY WORDS

Automated design
Backup programmer
Changes
Chief programmer team
Combined module
  testing
Completion time
Conversion and installa-
  tion
CPM
Design aids
Documentation
Egoless programming
Fourth-generation lan-
  guage

Impact of system
Independent test data
Librarian
Milestones
Modularization
Operations documenta-
  tion
Network
Parallel testing
Participation
Postimplementation
  audit
Precedence relation
Productivity schedule
Programming goals

Review session
Structured program-
  ming
Subtasks
System library
Tasks
Top-down programming
Training documentation
Uncertainty
Unit testing
User-reference docu-
  mentation
Variance

## RECOMMENDED READINGS

Baker, F. T.: "Chief Programmer Team Management of Production Programming," *IBM Systems Journal,* vol. 11, no. 1, 1972, pp. 66–73. (An article describing the uses of a chief programmer team and many of the techniques discussed in this chapter to develop a retrieval system for the *New York Times.*)

Lucas, H. C., Jr.: *The Design, Analysis, and Implementation of Information Systems*, 3d ed., McGraw-Hill, New York, 1985. (See especially the chapter on project management.)

Mumford, E., and T. Ward: *Computers, Planning for People*, B. T. Batsford, London, 1968. (This excellent book presents suggestions for planning for the impact of a system on individuals.)

Personal computer journals for examples of project management systems for microcomputers.

Using 1-2-3, Indianapolis, Que Publishing, 1983. (A good example of a well-documented spreadsheet package for a microcomputer.)

## DISCUSSION QUESTIONS

1 What are the reasons for user participation in testing a system and planning conversion and installation?

2 What issues should be examined in a postimplementation audit?

3 Who should conduct the postimplementation audit and what should be done with the results?

4 Who should accept a system; that is, who is responsible for indicating that a system is working properly and can be considered fully converted?

5 Describe different approaches to the gradual implementation of:
   a A batch computer system
   b An on-line system

6 What are the problems and disadvantages of parallel testing?

7 After conversion, are the responsibilities of the design team ended? If not, what other tasks should the team attempt to accomplish?

8 Why is it unwise for programmers to design all their own test data?

9 Do conversion programs need to be documented carefully? Why or why not?

10 What action should a design team take if it expects sabotage or user resistance for some aspects of a new system? What is such resistance a sign of?

11 Why is it unwise to make a major change in the organization (such as departmental restructuring) concomitantly with the conversion of a new information system?

12 How does good documentation serve to reduce user conflict with the information services department and staff?

13 Why is documentation generally the weakest part of a system's design?

14 How does the presence of a systems librarian aid documentation?

15 What can be done to facilitate and encourage documentation besides employing a systems librarian? Are there any mechanical tools that will encourage documentation?

16 What is the role of documentation after a system has been converted successfully?

17 What role does documentation play in subsequent changes to a program or system?

18 How should program changes be controlled? Is it necessary to have more than one person agree on the change? Why or why not?

19 Why should test results be kept as part of the documentation of an information system?

20 Why do users need to have documentation on the data files in the system?

21 How can the computer operator use documentation to determine if an error has occurred as a result of a programming problem, a data problem, or a malfunction of the computer itself?

22 How can the design team leader influence documentation standards of the information services department? Why should agreement on documentation formats and contents be reached?

23 Why should users design the training program? How can users on the design team recognize apprehension and anticipate resistance to change? How can data gathered on this issue be evaluated to help effect a smooth implementation for everyone concerned?

24 How does the development of the chief programmer position change the career path for computer professionals? What benefits does this have for users?

25 Is programming such a craftlike trade that it defies management?

26 What motivated the development of network project management techniques such as CPM?

27 Why should users review schedules during project execution?

28 What is the precedence relationship among the major tasks in systems analysis and design?

29 In the systems life cycle, what are the points where the most serious delays are likely to occur? How do these points relate to uncertainty?

30 What advantages are there to using package programs from the standpoint of project management? What are their major disadvantages?

31 Why do programmers resist making changes in a working program after an information system has been installed? How do the techniques suggested in this chapter affect this resistance?

32 Does user management have to understand programming to be able to monitor the programming part of a project? What knowledge is required?

33 Are there any types of systems for which the user should not have any role during programming? What types? What are some of the management problems expecte: for these systems?

# 17

# ALTERNATIVES TO TRADITION

## CHAPTER ISSUES

- Is there a better way than the systems life cycle?
- What alternatives are best suited to different design situations?

There are a number of problems with the development of custom applications following the systems life cycle. First, a long period of time usually elapses before the user comprehends all the features of a system. It is very difficult to understand specifications; usually it takes a significant period of time to progress from specifications to the first tests to be seen by the user. If the user did not understand the specifications or was unable to conceptualize all the features of the system, then it might be over a year from the time that the application is first discussed until its characteristics become known through test results. In addition the development of custom systems has been associated with cost and budget overruns, particularly during programming and testing phases.

In this chapter we discuss a number of alternatives to tradition; we shall explore the following options:

Fourth-generation languages, applications generators, and nonprocedural languages
Packages
Prototyping

## GENERATORS AND NONPROCEDURAL LANGUAGES

The need to improve productivity in developing systems has led to the development of new languages for building applications. We shall define three broad categories of advanced development techniques:

**1** Report generators aid in retrieving data and producing a report. These generators are probably the first example of a nonprocedural language and were developed originally for sequential files.

**2** Query languages are languages which retrieve data from a database. The language has access to data definitions so that it can map field names entered by the user to the structure of the database. The languages provide the user with the ability to specify complex logical relationships among fields for retrieval purposes.

**3** Fourth-generation languages, applications generators, and nonprocedural languages. Fourth-generation languages are often called "nonprocedural" because the programer does not have to specify procedures in detail as with a compiler-level language. Nonprocedural languages have commands which are at a higher level than languages like COBOL. A nonprocedural language may simply interpret a series of commands entered by the programmer and do what they indicate, for example, sort records, summarize them on a field, and print a report.

Another approach is for a language processor to translate the commands into some intermediate language which then is compiled or interpreted for execution. At least one of these languages compiles machine language directly.

**4** An application generator is a complete system built around one of the nonprocedural languages and/or a database management system. The generator provides an environment for developing a complete application, from the definition of the data through all necessary procedures to update and retrieve information.

### Report Generators

Report generators provide facilities for use in extracting data from files and manipulating it. A typical language includes:

**1** Statements to define the layout of the file
**2** Statements to extract records based on logical criteria, for example SALARY GT (Greater Than) 10000
**3** The ability to compare key fields of two or more files, for example matching a summary file to a file of details
**4** Statements to manipulate the extracted data to compute new values
**5** A method for specifying the format of a report.

Some report generators also provide the ability to update files; theoretically one could develop an entire application using a report generator. See Table 17-1 for an example of a generator. Note the level at which the statements are entered; the SELECT command would require a number of lines in a compiler

**TABLE 17-1**
A REPORT GENERATOR

| File definition | | |
|---|---|---|
| F INVENT | ISFB02552025525 | |
| D ITEM | 00040005CA | 04ITEM |
| D PACK | 00170003CA | 04PACK |
| D SLOT | 01470005CA | 04SLOT |
| D SIZE | 00090008CA | 04SIZE |
| D DESC | 00200028CA | 11DESCRIPTION |
| D VENDOR | 01610004CA | 06VENDOR |
| D NETCST | 01650005CN2 | 08NET COST |
| D QUANT | 00490005CN | 13CASES ON HAND |
| D FAMILY | 01230002CA | 06FAMILY |

| Program |
|---|
| TITLE,GROCERY     PHYSICAL INVENTORY – CURRENT PRICE 'FIFO' RUN D |
| SELECT,ITEM.LT.('27000').OR.ITEM.GT.('29999') |
| CALL, GETDATE |
| NEWFLD,EXT,FLO.2, 'EXTENSION' |
| SORT,SLOT |
| COMP,DT,EXT–NETCST*QUANT |
| OPTION,STDSP–1 |
| PRINT,ITEM,SLOT,PACK,SIZE,FAMILY,DESC,VENDOR,NETCST,QUANT(S),EXT(S) |
| END |

level language. Instead, the user only has to use one word which expresses the logic clearly; we want to select records based on certain criteria. In a procedural language like COBOL a large number of statements would also be required to print the desired output report.

At first report generators were used with sequential files. They are particularly helpful in amassing data from different files, for example, an insurance company with a master record of losses on a policy basis and another file of details for each claim. Using a report generator we could sort both files into the same sequence, for example, policy number, and produce a report of each policy's total losses and a detailed history of claims.

These generators have expanded with the widespread use of direct access files and database management systems. Generators have interface routines that allow retrieval from the most popular DBMSs. The generators are sometimes called retrieval languages and are sold frequently to noninformation processing professionals, users, auditors, and others who want to develop reports quickly and do not have the time or training to use compiler-level languages. These systems can be very useful for producing a printed report of an ad hoc nature. They are very attractive to users who do not want to wait for a programmer to be assigned to produce a new report. The languages are fairly easy to use; the computer staff must provide some support in the form of consulting help and must show users files where data are stored and the formats of files.

While probably not the best approach for developing a totally new applica-

---

**MANAGEMENT PROBLEM 17-1**

Jane Rollins runs a small investment firm which manages securities for a number of corporate entities and individuals. For example, Jane has her own stocks in two entities, one as an individual investor and the other a trust established for her by a relative.

Each of the entities may own any number of different shares of stock. As shares are bought and sold, an exact record of the lot of stock, the number of shares, and the price at purchase and sale must be maintained. In addition, the bookkeepers at the firm must post all cash and stock dividends to each entity's records each time dividends are received.

All this processing is currently done on a manual basis. The staff is able to keep up, though it can take four to six weeks after quarterly dividends to finish posting. Closing the books at the end of the fiscal year and producing reports for the firm's accountants takes a great deal of time and work. Also, it is not easy to answer Jane's questions when she asks about various entities' stock holdings; for example, how much AT&T stock is managed in total across all accounts.

Jane is thinking about a computer system. However, she feels that the firm is unique, and she is not optimistic about finding a ready-made package. What advice can you give her? How should she proceed?

---

tion, the use of these report languages can provide flexibility in creating output from a system and can improve the responsiveness of the computer department in satisfying requests for new reports. To the extent that users are willing to learn how to use these languages, the user's efforts will supplement those of the computer department, in effect increasing the manpower devoted to systems work.

Report generators are very useful in extracting data from files, though they often have limited capabilities. For example, they may place restrictions on the order in which procedures are executed. However, newer versions of this type of software are far more flexible than their predecessors.

### Query Languages

Most database management systems have languages for retrieving data without writing detailed, procedural code. The statements entered by the user are interpreted by the query language processor. A typical statement for the microcomputer-based relational database management system discussed in Chapter 10 would be:

SELECT KEYWORDS WHERE TERM EQ COMPUTERS,
TECHNOLOGY

The query processor examines and interprets this line; the processor then executes the request. The user is asking for rows from a table (relation) named

"KEYWORDS" to be selected where a column in the table defined as "TERM" has an entry that is either "COMPUTERS" or "TECHNOLOGY".

The query processor first looks for the relation "KEYWORDS" in the data dictionary and checks to be sure there is a field in it named "TERM". Then it accesses the data and looks in each row for the word "COMPUTERS" or "TECHNOLOGY" in the column labeled "TERM". Records matching the request are moved to a temporary relation which becomes the result of the request. Finally, the user can print the temporary relation's values or process them further.

One important characteristic of a query language is that the user must have some knowledge of the contents and structure of the database. Data structures designed for one type of query processing can make it difficult to answer other types of queries, at least for the novice user. It is fairly simple to select rows from a table based on values in various columns; joining and matching several different relations requires a different level of knowledge and understanding.

## QBE

An interesting advanced application of a query language and a relational database system is Query By Example (QBE). "Query by Example" can be learned relatively easily and requires little data processing background. All the data are visualized as existing in a series of two-dimensional tables, that is, a table consisting of columns and rows.

To perform an operation, the user fills in an example of the solution in a blank skeleton table that is associated with an actual table. The user can input examples either of the data required or of actual data values. A series of retrieval examples will demonstrate some of the power of this particular system. The first inquiry is for a list of the names and departments of all employees in a simple personnel database (IBM 5796—PKT).

| EMP | NAME | SALARY | MGR | DEPT |
|-----|------|--------|-----|------|
|     | P.   |        |     | P.   |

In a qualified retrieval, the user requests the name, salary, manager, and department of any employee who earns less than or equal to $16,000 and works for Morgan. The P symbol asks that the data be printed.

| EMP | NAME | SALARY | MGR | DEPT |
|-----|------|--------|-----|------|
|     | P.   | P.<=16000 | P.MORGAN | P. |

A more complicated example allows one to link multiple tables together. In this example, the D1 used in the department column is an example element. It establishes a link between two or more entries in the same row or two or more rows of different tables. The same example, D1, must be used in both tables to link the tables together. This query says print the names of the employees that work in a department, D1, such that department D1 sells perfume.

| EMP | NAME | SALARY | MGR | DEPT |
|-----|------|--------|-----|------|
|     | P.   |        |     | _D1  |

| SALES | DEPARTMENT | ITEM |
|-------|------------|------|
|       | _D1        | PERFUME |

One advantage of this type of system is that the computer department can react to user needs immediately, not in several months. Also those needs can be met without writing extensive programs. The Query by Example system at one firm has cut programming requests and maintenance requirements over 30 percent and has eliminated many hard copy reports (*Data Processor*, June/July 1980).

For the most part, query languages are designed for the end-user, not for the computer professional. However, the end-user needs training and good documentation and support to become facile with query languages. Research indicates that often queries are not successful. Either the query is formulated incorrectly, or more often, the data requested are not in the database. Extensive documentation and support is needed to be sure that queries have a good chance of being answered and that user expectations are realistic about what data can be retrieved from a system.

### Applications Generators

Report generators and retrieval languages are generally used with files and applications designed without the report in question as a consideration. Query languages help users access data that are already stored in a database. Rarely with either of these tools does the user actually update the files or process transactions against them.

An applications generator is a type of fourth-generation language designed to facilitate the development of a complete application including:

1 The definition of input transactions
2 Editing transactions
3 Creation of a database

4 File updating
5 Report generation
6 Query processing

Most generators are built around database management systems since the definition and creation of a database is so critical in the systems design process.

From the standpoint of the systems life cycle, the generator attempts to reduce dramatically the time required in the programming and testing stages. This time savings in turn means users will see the results from the development of a system much more quickly than if a procedural language is used.

One should not, however, assume that the generator automates the systems design cycle; there still is a need to undertake a good systems analysis and design study. We still must have specifications before a generator can be used. A generator can help in developing specifications through prototyping, a procedure we shall discuss later in this chapter.

**Microcomputer Example**   The relational database system for personal computers actually has features that make it a type of applications generator. The database part of the system establishes relations. We could define a realtion "ARTICLES" containing the following columns:

ARTICLE#, AUTHORS, TIT'.E, JOURNAL, VOLUME, NUMBER

Another relation might be "KEYWORDS" with fields

ARTICLE#, TERM

Multiple entries for each article are possible in the "KEYWORDS" relation, e.g. computers and technology for article 85062901. Entries in the relation would then be:

85062901 COMPUTERS
85062901 TECHNOLOGY

We could create the same type of relation for "AUTHOR". We need "ARTICLE#" to link the various relations together. One approach to this number is to use the year, month, day and a sequential number for each article entered on a particular day. From that point on the user does not have to be aware of the number; it will be used internally to match relationships.

We could stop at this point and use individual commands to access the database. However, this strategy requires the user to know the structure of the database and the commands to enter data, update the files, generate queries, and produce reports.

By including a menu builder and command files, the system makes it possible

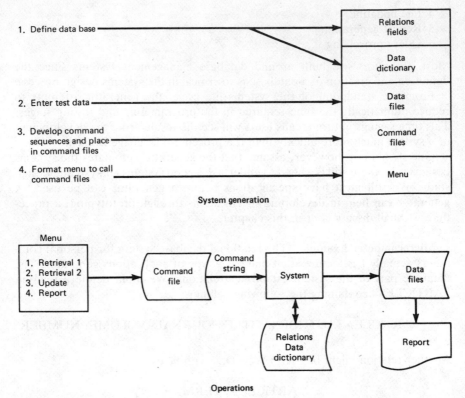

**FIGURE 17-1**
A microcomputer applications generator.

to generate applications. The menu program lets the designer construct a CRT menu, e.g.

**1** RETRIEVE ON AUTHORS
**2** RETRIEVE ON KEYWORDS
**3** UPDATE DATA

ENTER NUMBER OF CHOICE PLEASE————
The user enters a number and the system automatically invokes the appropriate command file. The designer creates the command file; it consists of a sequence of commands to carry out each function. For menu choice 1, the command file would ask for input of authors' names and then would SELECT the articles from ARTICLE where the author names in the relation in the database match the names provided on input. At the end of the command file we return to the menu display again. See Figure 17-1.

Now the user sees a fairly conventional application; he or she does not have to learn much about how the database is structured or how the command language works. The designer has generated an application without writing program code in a procedural language.

**A Mainframe Example** The same philosophy of the microcomputer example can be extended to larger mini and mainframe computers. For a larger computer, the system will be more focused on processing transactions and updating the database.

A system for mainframe computers is described by Tamir et al. (1981). This system is built around a hierarchical database management system. It includes a transactions processor which is quite sophisticated. The transaction is read from the input medium and checked for syntax as well as the validity of its data fields. The processor checks the user's authorization to update the data and then updates the database, creating whatever subsidiary transactions are required. Finally successful transactions are recorded on a journal. Applications generators of this type may interpret input commands or actually generate code like a conventional compiler or translator. The generators that produce code are sometimes called "fourth-generation languages" to indicate that source input statements are at a much higher level than those of procedural languages like COBOL.

---

**A FIFTY YARD GAIN**

*The San Diego Chargers scored three touchdowns and one long gain using a single play called the 372 F Shoot Pump. The tight end heads downfield about eight yards and then cuts to the outside while the fullback shoots to the same area to draw off the strong safety. With the safety cleared out, the quarterback fakes a pass to hold the linebacker covering the tight end; the end darts upfield to the area left open by the strong safety. Then finally the quarterback throws a pass to the tight end.*

*Sounds easy! Actually this confusing play was designed with the help of a computer. Quantel Business Computers has offered sports applications for computers for several years. The firm's systems are used by track, hockey, soccer, baseball and rugby teams as well as by U.S. and Canadian football teams.*

*The NFL teams have routinely used computers for accounting and payroll; more recent applications include analysis of potential players for the annual player draft.*

*The latest systems are those that perform game analysis. As one coach said "We can identify formations, draw pictures, define pass patterns, who caught the ball, yardage, what every receiver was doing, and how the blocking was."*

*One objective is to spot weaknesses in an opponents defense. Because there are so many players on the field and so many options, a computer is well suited to the task of game analysis.*

*Business Week, October 24, 1983.*

---

## Summary

Applications generators and nonprocedural languages offer the organization a way to reduce the time required to develop information systems: they concentrate on improving productivity in programming and testing. The reports from developers of these tools claim reductions in time for development of from five to ten times. The designer or programmer must be trained to use these systems and the organization must provide computer support. Some of the personal computer versions can be learned by a dedicated user. More capable and complex systems, however, will require the assistance of the professional computer staff.

If used well, these tools can help improve productivity. However, we still must develop specifications for the system and determine the requirements for information processing.

## PACKAGES

A package is one solution to the problems of custom systems design. We usually think of packages as software, but an increasing number of vendors sell software and the hardware on which the software is run. Thus, a package can be thought of as a problem solution that is partially or completely ready to implement. The package almost always includes computer programs and may involve hardware as well.

The use of a package can dramatically reduce the time required to install a system by saving both design time and the effort devoted to programming. There are, however, important considerations in purchasing a package. We can expect to spend far more than the cost of the package by the time it is installed, and it is unlikely that the package can be purchased one day and fully utilized the next!

### Advantages

There are a number of advantages to packages:

1 A package should require less total development time, since detailed programming specifications are not needed, nor is as much programming usually required as with a custom system.

2 In total a package should result in lower costs, though it is not always clear that lower costs result by the time one learns how to use the package and makes modifications to it.

3 We often find that a package has more functions or extra features that we might not have bothered with in a custom design.

4 If the package has been used in other locations, many of the programs included in the system have been debugged, or at least have been run successfully in an operational environment.

5 From the standpoint of user understanding of a system, a package usually

provides the opportunity to see what we are purchasing in operation before being committed to its acquisition.

### Disadvantages

While there are a lot of advantages to packages, there are some counter-arguments which raise questions about this approach:

1 A package may not include all the functions we would like to have.

2 As a result, many packages have to be modified before they are acceptable to users. Modification is difficult; it requires changes to existing code and may only be possible through the vendor. Changing existing code can be expensive and is likely to introduce errors in the system. As with any programming endeavor, modifications also take time, reducing some of the benefits expected with a package from reduced development time.

3 To avoid making major changes in a package, we may elect to change procedures in the organization. Such changes are not always easy to accomplish and can be disruptive to the firm.

4 We become critically dependent on vendor support for the software. If the vendor is not viable, we may be left with software and no way to support it, that is, to have errors corrected, receive new versions, training, etc.

5 The package may not run on the kind of computer we would like to have. The package may necessitate the purchase of hardware, and that system may not be compatible with our existing hardware or our overall plan for information processing in the organization.

### Package Design

The vendor wants to produce a general-purpose program, for example, to handle accounts-receivable processing in a large number of organizations. How can one build this generality into a system? There are four strategies:

1 Design the software with a lot of input parameters or tables; for example, an airline reservations package must have tables for city pairs between which flights operate. The input tables and parameters allow each user to tailor the system to his or her environment.

2 Provide different modules for different situations. Assume that a company is selling a registration package for universities. There must be a module that will handle grades; the vendor might have separate modules depending on the type of grades used, A through F, 100 to 0, and so on. It is unlikely that the same institution would use more than one grading scheme, so the appropriate module is included for each customer.

3 The vendor may expect the organization to change its procedures to use the package. Often it is pointed out that a small procedural change to use the

package is cheaper than the alternative of program changes. For packages that address very similar applications across companies or industries, the organization will seriously want to consider making some of these changes.

**4** Plan for custom tailoring and modifications for each customer. With this in mind, the package might be offered with a very flexible report writer so that the desired reporting formats of each customer can be developed when the package is installed. As a part of the purchase price, one vendor includes modifications to its package to print output on the preprinted forms used by its customers for invoices and statements.

Some combination or even all these approaches may be followed for any given package. Whenever a package is to be installed, the more dedicated it is to a given application, the more the input is that is required by users to describe their organization and environment.

Modifications may turn out to be the largest expense of the package, depending on how much programming is required. Some package vendors will not sell their source code; only the machine language is provided. Under these circumstances, we are totally dependent on the vendor to make any needed modifications. Are modifications that run 20 percent to 50 percent of the cost of a package justified? In one situation, the manager of a warehouse could not fill orders with the procedures included in a package. The package had to be modified. Otherwise, he could not use a procedure that had been followed for a number of years, of allocating products to preferred customers while shipping only orders that were completely filled by available stock.

Regardless of whether the vendor, an in-house programming staff, or some third party makes package modifications, there are precautions that should be taken to try and minimize future problems. One good strategy is to try to confine modifications to certain modules. All changes should be carefully documented with comments on the modified programs and external documents detailing the changes. Most packages go through continual revisions and improvements. If changes have been made and not noted, the organization will be unable to install new versions because the staff will not know what modifications to make to keep the new version compatible with custom changes in the prior version.

### Types of Packages

Packages are hard to classify; a large variety have been designed for different purposes and types of computers. See Figure 17-2. There is some debate as to what is a package and what is a language. We shall take a broad view and include a variety of candidates for classification as a package. Packages are often developed for certain types of computers, mainframes, mini or microcomputers.

**Higher-Order Languages**  These higher-order languages are also sometimes called fourth-generation languages. They can easily grow into applications generators with the addition of report generators and screen layout capabilities.

| Package type | Computer | | |
|---|---|---|---|
| | Mainframe ——————► | Minicomputer ——————► | Microcomputer |
| Higher order language/ Applications generator | Natural Focus | Inform | Focus (version for micros) |
| Systems software | DBMS Total, IMS ADABASE | RIM | Condor, DBMaster, DBase III |
| Problem-oriented languages | SPSS, SAS | SPSS, Tel-a-graf | Visicalc, Multiplan, Lotus |
| Dedicated | Accounts receivable | Garment system | Accounting |

**FIGURE 17-2**
Examples of packages.

There is a growing number of these languages for mainframe and minicomputers and at least one is available for a microcomputer.

These packages are languages; they are not dedicated to a particular application, but instead require the user to apply them to a problem. Some of the languages are designed for specific problem areas like financial modeling, but there exist a number that are really general purpose. A major advantage for the vendor is that, since the package is a language, there is little need to provide modifications for each user. Instead, the vendor concentrates on enhancing and refining the language.

**Systems Software** Software packages also exist that are designed for a specific purpose, such as a set of programs to provide database management, or programs to control the interaction of a computer with terminals. These packages can be quite general, but as an example, a database management system is usually built around one data model, hierarchical, network, or relational. These programs may also be designed for just one or a small number of computers.

**Problem-Oriented Languages** Packages in this category are like higher-order languages in many respects, but are aimed at a specific problem. A good example of this type of package is SPSS (Statistical Package for the Social Sciences) which is used by nonprogrammers to analyze data. The user does write a program, but the statements look very much like high-level commands:

```
FILE NAME       STOCK
VARIABLE LIST   INVINDEX,GNP,CORPROF,CORPDIV,YEAR
REGRESSION      VARIABLES=INVINDEX,GNP,CORPROF/
                REGRESSION=INVINDEX WITH GNP TO CORPDIV

FINISH
```

While a language, these statements are not difficult to learn and many nonprofessional programmers use this package.

The most popular package in this category is Lotus 1-2-3, a spreadsheet program for microcomputers. This package makes it possible to construct elaborate models and test their sensitivity to changes. Figure 17-3 is an example of a simple spreadsheet. A firm publishes magazines and is concerned about whether its warehouse has enough capacity to stock the magazines before they are distributed to newsstands.

The spreadsheet appears on the CRT and is referenced through numbered rows and columns designated by capital letters. The cursor (a bright light) is on location F14; the formula at F14 is shown in the window at the top. We see that F14 is calculated by adding F7 and F13. If we were to change the data value in F7, the results would automatically be reflected in cell F14.

This ability to relate rows and columns using formulas gives spreadsheet programs their power; a few data items can be changed and the results for the entire spreadsheet are shown automatically. There are many of these spreadsheet programs available, and large numbers of microcomputers have been sold just to build models like Figure 17-3.

**Dedicated Packages** The last category in Figure 17-2 contains dedicated packages, systems devoted to a particular application. This group is experiencing explosive growth as more and more installations look first to buy before programming a custom system. This kind of package presents the greatest

**FIGURE 17-3**
A spreadsheet example.

F14 (V)+F7+F13

|   | A | B | C | D | E | F | G | H |
|---|---|---|---|---|---|---|---|---|
| 1 |   |   |   |   |   |   |   |   |
| 2 |   |   |   |   | Brevis Press |   | (1000 issues) |   |
| 3 |   |   |   |   |   |   |   |   |
| 4 |   |   | Boston | N.J. | Atlanta | Chicago | Denver | L.A. |
| 5 | Sales forecast |   | 25 | 30 | 40 | 35 | 25 | 40 |
| 6 | Price/1000 issues |   | 2000 | 2000 | 2000 | 2000 | 2000 | 2000 |
| 7 | Revenue |   | 50000 | 60000 | 80000 | 70000 | 50000 | 80000 |
| 8 | % in warehouse |   | .3 | .5 | .45 | .35 | .24 | .35 |
| 9 | Warehouse required |   | 7.5 | 15 | 18 | 12.25 | 6 | 14 |
| 10 | Warehouse capacity |   | 6 | 12 | 20 | 8 | 5 | 12 |
| 11 | Variance |   | −1.5 | −3 | 2 | −4.25 | −1 | −2 |
| 12 | Cost/1000 issues |   | 2000 | 1500 | 1800 | 1600 | 1400 | 2000 |
| 13 | Overage costs |   | −3000 | −4500 | 0 | −6800 | −1400 | −4000 |
| 14 | Revenue-storage cost |   | 47000 | 55500 | 80000 | 63200 | 48600 | 76000 |
| 15 |   |   |   |   |   |   |   |   |
| 16 | Total rev |   |   |   |   |   |   | 390000 |
| 17 | Total overage |   |   |   |   |   |   | −19700 |
| 18 | Margin |   |   |   |   |   |   | 370300 |

challenge for implementation. Examples of some of these dedicated packages include systems for making airline reservations, managing production, accounting, general ledger, accounts payable, accounts receivable, bank demand deposit accounting, bank trust management, and so on.

These packages are most likely to require modifications or changes in the buyer's procedures, or both. They are not intended to be used as a language, but as an off-the-shelf substitute for a custom designed and programmed system. The fundamental tradeoff is (1) to what extent we should take the package as is or (2) pay to have the package changed or (3) change our procedures.

Packages have been around for a number of years, but three factors account for the increasing interest in this option for developing a system:

**1** The cost of programming is rising as are the risks of not completing a project on time and within budget. We now realize that specifications and features are often compromised in a custom design so that the user ends up not getting everything that was desired in the specifications.

**2** The packages themselves are getting better as many have been through several "generations" of improvements.

**3** The declining cost of hardware means that we can afford to run a package that operates inefficiently on the computer in order to save development time and cost.

---

### MANAGEMENT PROBLEM 17-2

Jack Robinson manages the computer department for Sports World Manufacturing Company, a full line manufacturer of sports equipment. He has just finished reading a proposal from one of the smaller plants for a complete inventory control and production scheduling package that runs on a small minicomputer. The minicomputer would have to be acquired as the plant has no in-house system at present.

Robinson is concerned because his department operates a large, mainframe computer that is not fully utilized. "How can I be sure that the new system will work?" he wonders. "Is the package proven? What about the money we have invested in the mainframe? Is it wise to buy another computer given the fact that we have an underutilized system now?"

Jack feels that he must respond to the plant, and he wonders what to do. He has asked your help in defining the issues. Should his staff undertake a study to evaluate the package? He could compare the package with the use of a custom system on the mainframe, or he could look for a package that had the same features that would run on the larger computer.

In addition to this request, Jack feels this is an important issue that will come up again in the future. He would like to develop a way to handle the problem when it reccurs. What is your advice?

---

**A SPEEDY TRIAL**

*Traditionally, Federal Courts have tracked their cases manually. However, the speedy trial act required a more responsive tracking system. There are 94 district or trial courts, 12 appellate courts and the Supreme Court, each with its own caseload. Each of these organizations has different needs for information; it is the Office of the Clerk in each court that is the heart of the information available.*

*A new system was recently developed for the court. The databases for each court are disjoint; they are maintained physically in separate database areas on several minicomputers located in Washington D.C. The courts access the system through a value-added telecommunications network.*

*The major database in the system is the criminal docketing database which provides information on case tracking. The records are events and represent one legally significant court transaction like a defendant being arraigned. It is possible to query the database and to determine the status of any case using the system.*

*ACM Transactions on Database Management System,*
*March, 1984.*

---

**Example**

Accounts receivable is a common business computer application. Almost all firms that sell a product or provide a service have a need to send bills to their customers. The shipment of a product or provision of a service creates a receivable, that is, an asset that represents money due from customers. It is important to keep track of receivables as this item appears on the balance sheet, and because receivables have to be managed. As payments are received they must be credited against open receivables; if payments are overdue it is important to work on collecting them.

One services and consulting firm offers a complete package for a garment manufacturer. If the manufacturer is small, it can rent terminals and run the package on the vendor's time-sharing computer. A larger customer buys the package and a computer on which to run it. While the package is quite comprehensive, we shall concentrate here on the accounts receivable portion of this dedicated application.

The package has the following functions, all of which operate on line:

1 Initialization of master files, file creation, and maintenance.

2 Daily entry of summary invoices and product returns.

3 Daily posting of cash receipts.

4 Daily sales and cash journal processing.

5 End of month aged accounts receivable reports, customer statements, and commission reports for sales representatives.

6 Information reports for credit and sales analysis.

The system contains master files about the company, division, various codes, terms, sales representatives, buying office, and customer details. Master files are supplemented by transactions files. The first of these is accounts receivable items, a file of all transactions and open receivables. An item record includes garments shipped, the quantity, and cost. A transactions file of cash receipts is also maintained with all customer checks and pointers to the invoices paid by the checks.

The last major category of files are those for posting totals. Here we find cash receipts control, a file of pointers to all open items for each customer. The customer credit file has totals owed which appears on the customer credit inquiry screen on a CRT. There is also a file of customer sales which has various totals of sales for each customer.

This package is dedicated, and all transactions are processed on-line from terminals. The software runs on a minicomputer under the control of a proprietary time-sharing operating system and database manager. If the other modules of the system are purchased, they create the open receivable in the accounts receivable file when merchandise is shipped from the warehouse. Basic information for the entire package begins at order entry when the customer's order is entered using a CRT.

When cash is received in the form of checks, a clerk working from a CRT enters the total amount and then applies the payment to open items. The clerk looks for invoices paid entirely by the check; if not obvious, then he or she must figure out what items are being paid by the check.

One firm bought the entire package including software and hardware. About 20 to 25 percent was added to the base cost of the software for modifications. In addition, the firm made some changes in the way it processes information in order to take advantage of the features of the package.

### Acquisition

Choosing a package is not an easy task. First, we have an information processing problem. If it looks as if the application is dedicated, then we should perform a systems analysis and design study. The study should be carried through to a high-level design for a new system containing outputs, the contents of files, and inputs. This design becomes a benchmark against which to evaluate various packages.

In today's environment, we should not begin to look for hardware yet. Instead, it is time for research on possible packages. There are trade journals in the computer field that rank packages and certain proprietary information firms that keep listings of packages. Another good source of information is trade journals in the industry; the garment firm above found out about the system in a garment industry trade journal. Finally, for software for microcomputers, one can visit various computer stores and look at their documentation on packages.

Evaluation of a package is difficult; it is important for users and the computer staff to understand the package in detail. We should be sure to see the package

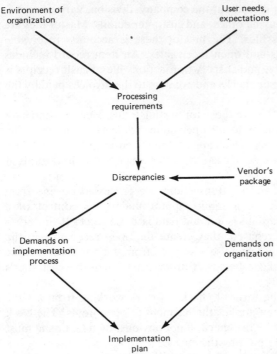

**FIGURE 17-4**
Package implementation.

work and that users understand what it will and will not do. Then estimate the extent of modifications, and determine whether the package will really work in your environment. A procedure for package purchase was discussed in more detail in Chapter 13.

Some packages are executed on the computers of the package vendor, while other are run on internal hardware. The declining cost of hardware and the advantages of internal control suggest that the trend is likely to be toward internal hardware for packages which can be operated in this manner.

## Implementation

Package implementation is not a trivial task; it may be even more difficult in certain respects than the development of a custom system. See Figure 17-4, which is a framework for package implementation. The environment of the organization, user needs, and expectations about what the system should do all combine to create processing requirements.

The package vendor offers a solution to these requirements. It is unlikely that the package will exactly match the customer's requirements, giving rise to discrepancies between the two. As an example, the customer may use eight digit part numbers while the package has provided for only six digits. During implementation, we must resolve these discrepancies, either through making changes in the organization or through special considerations in the implementation process. Finally, an implementation plan should be the result of the effort.

The vendor can help in package modification by providing flexibility in the design of the system. Using database management systems to support the package, good query languages and report generators to custom-tailor the output all help. Good documentation is very important, as is consulting help in implementation. A number of vendors also offer telephone "hot lines" to answer calls from users who have problems.

It may appear to users that they do not have to become involved, since we are purchasing a package that has already been developed. In all likelihood, users will be more involved in the development of a package, or at least more intensely involved over a shorter period of time, than with custom development. We must be sure that the requirements analysis is complete, that users in fact define processing requirements. The users also must understand in detail how the package works and think about it in their present job environment. The users must provide help in outlining the discrepancies and in deciding how they are to be resolved, through package changes or changes in company procedures. There have been just as many examples of package implementation disasters as disasters with custom systems!

### Summary

Packages are increasingly important in systems development; it is too costly to develop systems with custom programming if a package exists that will work for a given task. Remember to develop specifications on requirements at least at a high level before talking to a package vendor. It is very important to have a basis for comparing all the different packages and to avoid being swayed by features that we really do not need or want.

### PROTOTYPES

The objective of prototyping is to reduce the time needed to develop requirements for a system. The traditional design approach features an analyst who spends time with users to elicit requirements. The analyst prepares specifications which are given to the user to approve. Most users seem to have difficulty comprehending the specifications. As a result, it may not be until during testing that the user first gains an understanding of how the system will or will not work.

A prototype is a model of a system that will eventually be developed. Its purpose is to:

1 Reduce the time before the user sees something concrete from the systems design effort.
2 Provide rapid feedback from the user to the designer.
3 Help delineate requirements with fewer errors.

**4** Enhance designer and user understanding of what systems should accomplish.

**5** Bring about meaningful user involvement in systems analysis and design.

A prototype does not have to be real, for example, the architect's model of a building made from card stock is a representation of the building. Part of a system can be "dummied" using sample data, and reports can be incomplete. The prototype may become a living specification that is constantly changed as the prototype is refined. In fact, the prototype may grow into the final system without even the development of detailed specifications!

The external appearance of the prototype must be very clear. As an example, the prototype for a transactions processing system is likely to provide a fixed set of CRT screens which accept input from the user, process it, and possibly return output (Mason and Carey, 1983). The full logic of the system has not been developed yet, so there will be restrictions. However, there should be enough of a system present so that users can understand how the final version will operate.

### The Process

It is important that the prototype be developed quickly and that feedback occurs in a timely manner. The actual development process is likely to be a sequence of activities:

**1** The designer meets with the user
**2** The user describes the system
**3** The designer builds a prototype
**4** The user works with the prototype and critiques it
**5** The designer modifies the prototype or starts again
**6** Go to steps 1 or 4

Changes here should be encouraged, not discouraged! We choose the prototyping approach because a set of system specifications is usually very abstract to the user. The prototype makes the system come alive; we want users to interact with the system and make it into what they would like to have. To accomplish the objective of rapid development the designer will need to use one or more tools to develop the prototype.

**Time sharing**   One popular way to develop a model of a system or part of it is to use a time-sharing computer. Time sharing gives the designer a tool for rapid development. Using a language like BASIC or APL, a prototype can be constructed quickly for review by the user. It can also be modified rapidly as the desired features of a system become clearer.

**Personal Computer**   A personal computer can be a very effective approach to prototyping; there is no interference from other users. Many microcomputers offer special development software that is easy to use. The disadvantage is that for a large system, it is unlikely that the prototype could grow easily to the final

---

**MANAGEMENT PROBLEM 17-3**

Bob Harris is manager of systems development for Atlantic Manufacturing Company. This firm makes a variety of tools for home craftsmen and professional carpenters, mechanics, and other tradespeople.

Bob is reviewing a request from one of the plants for an integrated production scheduling and control system for shop floor control. This particular plant manufactures hand tools; the tools are relatively simple ranging from four or five parts to 50 parts in a completed tool. While the number of parts is relatively small, the volume at the plant is quite high, and scheduling is a problem because a tool can be made in a number of different ways. The plant is the classic "job shop" as opposed to an assembly line.

Harris just returned from a two-day professional seminar on prototyping, and he is eager to try this new approach to systems development. The request in front of him has raised the possibility of trying prototyping for the first time at Atlantic. Harris discussed the idea with two other analysts. They, however, are quite skeptical. "The system would be so large, that we need conventional specifications and design," one advised. The other said, "How can we build a prototype of a system this complex?"

Where do you think prototyping could be used for this suggested application?

---

application. One company, however, prototyped a personnel system using a database system or a personal computer. After deciding the final version was acceptable, the prototype was converted to run much faster on a mainframe computer.

**Software**   Above we suggested high-level languages like BASIC or APL; the designer may also want to use an applications generator to develop a prototype. The ability to produce a system quickly is a major advantage of the generator. It is quite likely that the prototype will grow here into the final application.

Another possibility is to use a simple database management system to form the foundation for a prototype. These systems make the task of developing and modifying data structures much easier than is possible with most programming languages. Retrieval commands from the DBMS may be all that is needed to develop the prototype.

Good programming and development tools are a requirement for prototyping. Remember that the prototype begins as a model; it does not have to include any of the editing and error checking of a finished system. The purpose of the exercise is to show what can be accomplished, not to demonstrate that a system is complete.

**An Example**

The firm that developed this system offers services throughout the world. The firm was investigating a change in its ownership; it is owned by its employees, but new U.S. legislation made some alterations in ownership structure potentially attractive. The vice chairman of the board asked the manager of the computer department to develop a small system to project the financial position of the firm several years in the future if the new form of ownership were adopted.

The computer department operated batch, time-sharing, and on-line systems on its computer; a database management system and various screen generators were also available. At first the computer department manager simply wrote a small program in BASIC to model the plan.

The output of the model formed one part of the recommendations made to the board of directors. After that meeting where the new plan was adopted, several managers noted the ability of the computer to forecast. One of them asked the computer department if it would be possible to forecast the benefits an employee would have several years in the future.

The industry is competitive and firms frequently hire staff from each other. Because there are a variety of stock and benefit plans, it was difficult to show an employee the total value of remaining with the company. The computer staff began to work on this problem with help from different personnel and financial managers. Various formulas were programmed and the results checked by different groups until the rules were regarded as satisfactory.

The manager of the computer department had a feeling that the system would grow, so he had the staff develop it using database management software and CRTs for data entry. The treasurer kept most of the data needed on what benefits were available to each individual, and he became very interested in the system. Computing bonuses took a long time and required heavy overtime; in general records for each employee were scattered over several files and reports were often inaccurate.

The treasurer asked that the system be made capable of maintaining all employee records and benefits. Because of the database approach and good development tools, it was fairly easy to meet his requirements. Over time, the system has evolved into a comprehensive personnel records and benefits application.

This system succeeded because it was able to grow and change over time. As users saw new features, they developed ideas for extending the application. The primary user changed to the treasurer from the president who had originally requested the projection system. The application had high visibility and senior management provided extensive input.

The use of tools was also very important in the success of this effort. High-level languages, screen formatting aids, and a database management system made it possible for the system to evolve. The ability to program a BASIC model using time sharing for the first part of the system was also crucial.

In addition to heavy user involvement, the analyst working on the application listened carefully and followed the logic defined by the users. She brought the results back to them and the managers actually debugged their own rules. By not trying to be in charge of everything, the analyst was able to develop a system with which users felt comfortable, because they understood the details of how it worked.

Not every system could be developed in this manner. In other circumstances, there might be a need for concrete specifications. However, the use of prototyping to show users what the system will do should be applicable across a wide range of settings.

Prototyping is a very effective way to improve the requirements definition phase for a system. The approach appears to be good for attracting users to the design process and obtaining their involvement and input. Done properly, it should result in systems that more closely fit user needs and which are completed more quickly with fewer operational changes required.

## SUMMARY

In this chapter we have explored some important alternatives to traditional systems analysis and design approaches. The objective of these techniques is to reduce the length of time required to follow the system's life cycle and to provide early feedback to users.

Applications generators and nonprocedural or so-called fourth-generation languages make the ISD staff more productive. Since a system can be changed easily using these techniques, it is simple to generate a preliminary system for user review. Also, reduced programming time reduces the elapsed time until users see results.

Packages have become the preferred alternative to writing systems in the last five years. Some packages we use to create a solution to a problem while others are dedicated to a particular applications area. Dedicated packages are the most difficult to implement, yet they have the potential to dramatically reduce the length of the programming stage in the life cycle.

Finally, prototyping is a technique we can use in almost any system. Instead of waiting until the design team finishes complete specifications, designers and users create a model of the system. Refinements of the model may reach a point where the prototype is a finished specification for all or a part of the system. Here, again, the user sees something concrete well before the user review stage in the traditional life cycle.

These and other innovative approaches are needed to achieve greater productivity in systems development. It may be necessary to undertake a custom programmed system. However, before accepting this recommendation, the manager should always ask, "what are the alternatives?"

## KEY WORDS

| | | |
|---|---|---|
| Accounts receivable | End user computing | Menu |
| Applications generator | Evaluation | Model |
| Database management | Expectations | Modification |
| systems | Higher-level languages | Modules |
| Dedicated package | Implementation | Nonprocedural |
| Discrepancies | Interpreter | Packages |

| | | |
|---|---|---|
| Parameters | Prototype | Support center |
| Problem-oriented languages | Query by example | System software |
| | Query language | User needs |
| Procedural | Relations | Vendor solution |
| Processing requirements | Report generators | Vendor support |

## RECOMMENDED READINGS

Martin, J.: *Applications Development Without Programmers,* Prentice-Hall, Englewood Cliffs, N.J., 1982. (A good description of a number of higher-order languages and generators.)

Martin, J., and C. McClure: "Buying Software off the Rack," Harvard Business Review, Nov.–Dec. 1983, pp. 32–60. (A good article on purchasing and contracting for packages.)

Mason, R. E. A., and T. T. Carey: "Prototyping Interactive Information Systems," *Communications of the ACM,* vol. 26, no. 5, May, 1983, pp. 347–354. (A helpful article with recommendations on prototyping.)

Naumann, J., and M. Jenkins: "Prototyping: The New Paradigm for Systems Development," *MIS Quarterly,* vol. 6, no. 3, September, 1982, pp. 29–44. (A thorough discussion of prototyping.)

Tamir, M. et al.: "DB1: A DBMS-Based Application Generator," *Proceedings of the Very Large Data Base Conference,* Glasgow, Scotland, 1981. (A description of a generator for a mainframe computer system.)

Also recommended are various language manuals for report generators, retrieval languages, and generators. For example, see articles on the systems described in Martin like NOMAD, the DATA ANALYZER, MARK V, etc.

## DISCUSSION QUESTIONS

1 What is the primary motivation behind applications generators and nonprocedural languages?
2 How does a report generator differ from a query language?
3 What are the advantages of a system like QBE? The disadvantages?
4 Should we be concerned if applications generators use the computer inefficiently? Why or why not?
5 Why are some very high-level languages called nonprocedural?
6 What distinguishes an applications generator from a query language or report generator?
7 How can it be faster for a user to write a program using a report generator than to have a professional programmer prepare the report?
8 Why must a user understand the structure of a database to use a query language?
9 If applications generators become pervasive, will there be a need for applications programmers?
10 Why have some generators grown out of database systems?
11 Is there still a place for writing custom programs in applications development?
12 What are the functions of a transactions processor in an applications generator?
13 What is the advantage of the command file in the microcomputer generator in the example on p. 383?

**14** If we see substantial numbers of computer networks in the future, what role does the database management system for personal computers have in this environment?

**15** How might an applications generator be used to help increase the users' understanding of a new system under development?

**16** Why do tools like generators seem to help improve productivity more than approaches like structured programming?

**17** How do packages reduce development time for a system? How can packages lower costs?

**18** What are all the costs associated with a package over the purchase price?

**19** Does one always get debugged programs buying a package?

**20** Why should one insist on a demonstration of a package?

**21** Why might a package not include some of the functions we want?

**22** Why do we advocate looking first not at hardware, but at the software?

**23** Why is it important to carefully control changes to a package?

**24** Under what conditions might an organizaton be willing to change its procedures to use a package?

**25** Is a large organization likely to change procedures or change a package? Why might the large firm have more need to modify a package than a small one?

**26** Why do you think a vendor of services using packages might not want to make changes in a package that it operates for a large number of firms?

**27** How does a database management package reduce one's flexibility in acquiring hardware or other software packages?

**28** Is accounts receivable likely to be the same type of application no matter what the firm? What characteristics might differ among companies?

**29** What is the user's role in determining whether or not to acquire a package?

**30** Develop an implementation strategy for the accounts-receivable example in this chapter.

**31** Why is a package a more viable alternative to a custom system today then it was 10 years ago?

**32** What are the advantages of prototyping? The disadvantages?

**33** How does a prototype for a computer system differ from an architect's model? How are they similar?

**34** Why does a prototype need to be developed quickly?

**35** How does a prototype secure more user input than conventional approaches?

**36** How have microcomputers contributed to prototyping?

**37** How does the role of the analyst differ, if at all, in prototyping versus traditional development for a custom system?

**38** How does prototyping relate to things like higher-order languages and applications generators?

**39** What are the duties of a consultant trying to support end users?

**40** Is word processing computing? How does it contribute to end user computing?

**41** Give several reasons for a policy that limits the firm to choosing microcomputers from only three different vendors.

**42** If hardware vendors are developing standard hardware interfaces, is there any need to worry about connecting equipment from dissimilar vendors into a communications network?

**43** What help does the end user need in trying to retrieve data from the files of applications that are already in operation?

## CHAPTER 18

# SUCCESSFUL IMPLEMENTATION

## CHAPTER ISSUES

- How does the organization plan systems implementation?
- How should an organization approach the relationship between the designer and user of a system?
- What is the proper manager/user role in systems analysis and design?

Managers frequently complain about the low return they receive on their organization's large investment in computer-based information systems. Many of these systems are not used to their potential or are not used at all.

- In one manufacturing company, the manager of the information services department had not distributed computer output reports for two months because he was not completely satisfied with them. Interviews with users indicated that the reports had not really been missed!
- A mining company spent several years designing a complex inventory system at its largest division. The system was finally installed and showed definite cost savings. Several years later, some managers in the company were still successfully resisting the installation of the new system in their divisions.
- A major university developed a sophisticated on-line computer system to automate a number of administrative functions. On a survey, most users expressed the desire to return to a manual system or the old batch-computer reports, because of problems with the newer system.
- Two computer systems at a major bank were supposed to calculate the

internal transfer price for borrowing and lending among branches. Each system produced a different number on its reports. Bank managers tended to doubt both figures and were afraid to rely on any of the data in the two reports because of this inconsistency.

Managers and other users of systems want to be certain that the systems work when installed. In this chapter, we explore some of the problems associated with implementation, which is basically a behavioral process. Our goal is to develop an implementation strategy that minimizes the problems of developing and operating successful information systems.

## PROBLEM AREAS

The problems described above have several sources:

1 The original design of the system
2 The interface of a system with the user
3 The process of design and implementation
4 The operation of systems

The original design of the system may have been faulty; for example, some systems do not provide the information needed by the decision maker. As we have seen, different information is required for different tasks. Other systems do not work technically; for example, there may be so many errors that no one trusts the output from the system.

The interface of the system with the user refers to the way in which we come in contact with the system, for example, through printed input forms, terminals and their associated input language, or batch reports. In one system, terminal input was so complicated that no one submitted data and the system had to be discontinued.

Implementation refers to the entire change effort associated with a new system. We design a system to improve information processing, and improvement implies that we must change existing information processing procedures. The operation of a system involves longer-term issues after a system has been designed and installed. If the operations section of the information services department does not provide good service (for example, meeting schedules for batch systems and having on-line systems available as needed), systems will not achieve their potential.

## IMPLEMENTATION

### Definition

What is implementation? In the discussion above, we stated that implementation is part of the process of designing a system and that it is also a component of organizational change. We develop a new information system to change existing information processing procedures. Implementation as we use the term should not be confused with a step in systems design. This definition, frequently used by computer professionals, is too narrow. Their definition generally refers to the last steps of systems design, which we shall refer to as conversion and installation of a new system.

Our definition stresses the long-term nature of implementation; it is a part of a process that begins with the very first idea for a system and the changes it will bring. Implementation terminates when the system has been successfully integrated with the operations of the organization. We expect most of implementation to be concerned with behavioral phenomena, since people are expected to change their information processing activities.

## Success or Failure

How do we know that we have successfully implemented a system? Researchers have not really agreed on an indicator for successful implementation. One appealing approach is a cost-benefit study. In this evaluation, one totals the costs of developing a system and compares them with the dollar benefits resulting from the system.

In theory, this sounds like a good indicator of success, but in practice it is difficult to provide meaningful estimates. Obtaining the cost side of the ratio is not too much of a problem if adequate records are kept during the development stages of the system. However, an evaluation of the benefits of a computer-based information system has eluded most analysts. How do we value the benefits of improved information processing? With transactions processing and some operational control systems, we can usually show tangible savings. For example, many transactions systems have resulted in increased productivity in processing paperwork without a proportional increase in cost. Operational control systems, such as those used to control inventories, may reduce inventory balances, saving storage and investment costs while maintaining existing service levels. For systems that aid a decision maker or provide customer service, it is much more difficult to estimate the benefits, and there are few examples of any such attempts.

In lieu of the more preferable cost-benefit analysis, we can adopt one of two indicators of successful implementation, depending on the type of system involved. For many information systems, use of the system is voluntary. A manager or other user receives a report but does not have to use the information on it or even read the report. Examples of such reports are summary data on sales for sales management, and a forecast for the marketing manager. Systems that provide on-line retrieval of information from a data bank can also often be classified as voluntary; the use of such a system is frequently at the discretion of the user. For this type of system where use is voluntary, we shall adopt high levels of use as a sign of successful implementation. We can measure use by interviews with users, through questionnaires, or in some instances by building a monitor into the system to record actual use.

For systems whose use is mandatory, such as an on-line production control system, we shall employ the user's evaluation of the system as a measure of success. For example, one can examine user satisfaction, although it will probably be necessary to measure several facets of satisfaction such as the quality of service, the timeliness and accuracy of information, and the quality of the schedule for operations. An evaluation might also include a panel of information processing experts to review the design and operation of the system. We should also note that managers might well consider a system to be successful if it accomplishes its objectives. However, to accomplish its objectives, a system must be used. We would also hope that one objective of a system would be extensive use and a high degree of user satisfaction with the system.

## RESEARCH ON IMPLEMENTATION

In recent years, the amount of research on implementation has increased dramatically. Since the implementation of computer-based information systems is similar to the implementation of operations research or management science models, we can also learn from studies of model implementation.

Most research on implementation has been an attempt to discover factors associated with success; that is, what independent variables are related to successful implementation as defined by the researchers? If there is any basis for believing a causal connection exists between independent and dependent variables, we can then develop an implementation strategy around the independent variables. For example, suppose we found in several studies using different research methodologies that top management's requesting a new system and following through with participation in its design is associated with successful implementation. If there were sufficient evidence to support this finding, we might develop an implementation strategy that emphasized top-management action.

While individual studies of implementation have addressed a number of independent variables, there is no real consensus in the field on an explanation of successful implementation or on a single implementation strategy. Table 18-1 contains a list of some of the variables in past implementation studies. The dependent variables used to measure implementation success generally can be classified as measures of usage, intended use, and/or satisfaction with a system. The independent variables fall into several classes, as shown in the table. One of the central variables in our model in Chapter 5 is the use of the system. We are concerned with factors leading to high levels of use, which we have also adopted as a measure of successful implementation. Thus, we can use the model we have already developed to help us understand the implementation process.

**TABLE 18-1**
VARIABLES ASSOCIATED WITH IMPLEMENTATION STUDIES

| Independent variables |
| --- |

Information services department
  Policies
  System design practices
  Operations policies

Involvement
  User origination of systems
  Involvement and influence
  Appreciation

Situational and personal factors
  Personality type
  Business history
  Social history
  Structural factors
  Past experience

User attitudes
  Expectations
  Interpersonal relations

Technical quality of systems
  Quality
  Model characteristics

Decision style
  Cognitive style

Management
  Actions
  Consultant/client relations
  Support
  Location of researcher
  Managerial style

User performance

| Dependent variables |
| --- |

Implementation
  Frequency of inquiries
  Reported use
  Monitored frequency of use
  User satisfaction

---

**AGRICULTURAL INFORMATION**

*Faculty members at the University of Nebraska have designed a computer network for direct use by farmers and ranchers along with agricultural specialists. There are now over a thousand users of the AGNET system. The system delivers information to clients located in 30 states and Canada.*

*There are two broad classes of system users: agricultural specialists who advise others and individuals, business and agencies making direct use of system services. Many users access the system rarely, once or twice a month or even seasonally. There are over 200 management and information programs in the library. The system is customized with respect to data for participating states. Thus, a user in Montana deals with data that are applicable to that state.*

*Examples of some of the programs include FEEDMIX which helps calculate the best ration for feed using locally available foodstuffs. PUMP is used in the classroom to teach engineering students how irrigation costs are affected by changes in application rates, altitude, or water depth. A rancher might use BEEFGROWER to estimate when a particular lot of cattle will be ready for sale and what the cost of weight gain will be. The cost of production for various crops can be calculated using CROPBUDGET and the economic value of land estimated with BUYLAND. The system also provides news items and a message service.*

*During the eruptions of Mount St. Helens, the system was used as a local communications link for the Washington State University Cooperative Extension Service. The system transmitted information to county extension agents. The Secretary of Agriculture in Washington, DC and departmental personnel used information from the areas to coordinate disaster relief programs.*

*Perspectives,* October 1980.

---

Favorable attitudes on the part of users should be extremely important in implementation; attitudes have an action component, and favorable attitudes are consistent with high levels of use and satisfaction with a system. The technical quality of systems is important; it directly affects our attitudes as users and also makes it easier to use the system physically. For example, a system with difficult input requirements or a difficult language for user input will be used less than one with a good technical design.

As we have seen in our discussion of information, personal and situational factors make a difference in an individual's approach to an information system. We can predict that the new manager will be more interested in an acquisition planning model than the 20-year veteran. Decision style is also important in determining system use; does an analytic decision maker use the same information as a heuristic one? The future use of an information system is also influenced by past experience in analyzing the information and in taking action. Successful use of information will make it more likely that a decision maker will use the system when faced with a similar problem in the future.

## AN IMPLEMENTATION STRATEGY

The research and model described in Chapter 5 suggests an implementation strategy based on our view of information systems design as a planned change in activity in the organization. We stated earlier that the reason for developing a new computer-based information system is to create change. Dissatisfaction with present processing procedures stimulates the development of a new information system. However, change can create almost insurmountable problems in the development of a system if only technical factors are considered by system designers.

What do we predict will happen as a result of the major changes undertaken during the development of a new information system? The model in Figure 5-1 helps in forecasting the results. Suppose that change is treated by a rational engineering approach. People are expected to cooperate with the design of a system because it is in their best interest to do so; we make no special efforts to ease the change process.

First, we predict that forcing change on a potential user of a system will create unfavorable attitudes; change is always difficult and threatening. If users develop negative attitudes and are afraid to cooperate with the systems design staff, the technical quality of the system will suffer because the input of users is needed to design a good system from a technical standpoint. Poor attitudes and low technical quality are likely to lead to little use of the system—a state we defined as implementation failure.

How do we avoid this type of outcome? The first step in the prevention of information system failure is to adopt an implementation strategy that recognizes systems design as a planned change activity, and stresses that successful implementation requires behavioral changes on the part of users.

Psychologists have suggested that a change approach based on user participation is most likely to be successful. A number of experiments and field studies have supported the importance of participation in making changes. Some of the reasons for the participation strategy are:

**1** Participation is ego-enhancing and builds self-esteem, which result in more favorable attitudes.

**2** Participation can be challenging and intrinsically satisfying, leading to positive attitudes.

**3** Participation usually results in more commitment to change; commitment in this case means that a system will be used more.

**4** Participating users become more knowledgeable about the change. Therefore users get to control more of the technical qualities of the system and become better trained to use it.

**5** Technical quality will be better because participants know more about the old system than the information services department staff.

**6** Users retain much of the control over their activities and should therefore have more favorable attitudes.

## MANAGEMENT PROBLEM 18-1

A major stock brokerage firm developed a sophisticated operations-research model to help customers decide what stocks to buy and when to enter and leave the market. The model is "solved" each week by a large computer system; reports are distributed regularly to brokers across the country.

In a study, each broker was found to have a slightly different way of using the recommendations. Some of the brokers call their clients who are interested in the model to give them the results. Other brokers assimilate the results and then call clients with recommendations based on the reports but do not reveal the source of their recommendations.

Some brokers do not use the system at all while other brokers use it primarily as a sales tool. That is, they show a brochure on the model to prospective customers to demonstrate the advantage of opening an account with their firm. One broker became an expert in the use of the model. However, instead of working with customers, this broker spent too much time studying the model.

How do you explain the different reactions of brokers to this model?

Base your assessment on the discussion in this chapter and on the model of information systems in the context of the organization presented in an earlier chapter. As a manager in the brokerage firm, what steps would you undertake to obtain the best results from the modeling effort?

---

How should users participate in the design of a system? Participation requires the efforts of both the information services department staff and the users. The information services department staff has to encourage participation, while users have to be willing to participate and devote considerable efforts to design work. In the past, although most information services departments have attempted to involve users, the effort frequently produced what would have to be classified as "pseudoinvolvement." To bring about the necessary involvement, a suggestion has been made that users should actually design their own systems. We shall explore this idea further in the next section.

## CREATIVE SYSTEMS DESIGN

The suggestion of having users actually design systems is aimed at solving the critical organizational behavior problems in the development and operation of computer-based information systems. This approach is based on the argument that systems design is a planned change activity in the organization. Technology is important in the development of computer-based systems, but user reactions determine the success of a system. We design systems to change and improve existing processing procedures, and this requires modifications of human behavior.

## MORTGAGES THROUGH MICROS

*First Boston Capital Group has developed a network of microcomputers to be used for mortgage origination. The system links regional mortgage providers with investors nationwide who are willing to lend money. First Boston provides firms a line of credit used to close approved loan applications locally. Then the firm buys the loans and resells them to investors.*

*Shelternet reduces the flow of paper required for obtaining a mortgage; local microcomputers transmit data to First Boston's mainframe in New York. The system also includes underwriters, loan service officers, and secondary market investors so that all interested parties are tied together. If all works as planned, it should be possible to turn around a good mortgage application in about half an hour, down from what can take weeks under manual processing systems.*

*First Boston furnishes the microcomputer with a variety of software to support the entire mortgage loan process. A preconsultation application allows users to obtain a profile based on borrower's salary and other financial information. The profile includes the ceiling price for a house and an affordable mortgage. When a particular house is located, the system calculates monthly payments including the mortgage, taxes, insurance, and other costs.*

*Finally, the system provides information on over 500 loan products available to the buyer. When the buyer selects the product, the system begins the application procedure. The applicant can always check on his or her status. The system not only speeds mortgage applications, it reduces the anxiety associated with applying for a loan.*

*PC Week*, May 29, 1984.

---

### A New Design Method

The philosophy of creative systems design has three major components:

1 User-controlled systems design
2 A definition of system quality according to user criteria
3 Special attention to the design of the interface between user and the system

The most important and radical component of the design method is user control of systems design. Why do we make this suggestion? Creative systems design places the responsibility for the design of a system with the user. The computer professional acts as a catalyst to help the user construct the system and translate it into technical specifications for computer processing. Creative design places the user in control of the design of the system.

The analyst helps direct the efforts of the user and indicates what tasks must be accomplished. For example, the first task delineated by the analyst might be the specification of output. The user is asked to think about the information it would be desirable to receive and to draw up a rough report. The analyst suggests that the user keep the report for several weeks while thinking about how it could be used. Should the information be available in inquiry form on-line? Does the information have to be updated on-line? The analyst, from knowledge of the capabilities of computer systems, presents alternatives for the user to consider.

The user might be asked to develop a method for obtaining input for the new system. The user determines the contents of forms for input after the analyst discusses alternatives such as a terminal, an optical character recognition system, or a batch-input form.

The user is then shown how the computer files are developed and the logic of computer processing. Working with the analyst, the user defines processing logic and the file structures for the system. In a similar manner, with guidance from the analyst, the user prepares plans for conversion and implementation.

The second component of creative design relates to system quality. We should evaluate the quality of information systems according to user criteria and not the criteria of the information services department and staff. In one instance, the computer department developed a new on-line system featuring the latest in communications and database management techniques. However, users were irritated because the command language was hard to use and because the system had a number of errors in it. In addition, users no longer had their old familiar reports, yet the new system was available to retrieve information for only four hours during the day! Computer professionals rated this system highly because of its technical elegance. Unfortunately, the enthusiasm of the computer staff was not shared widely by users. Instead, users were highly dissatisfied because the technology had intrigued the designers more than the needs of the user.

The interface between the user and the system is extremely important and attention to the interface is a third and final creative design component. A great deal of effort should be expended to ensure that a high-quality interface is developed. Care should be taken in determining the input and output with which the user has contact. Experimentation here is strongly recommended; users should have the opportunity to work with the new input and output forms and devices before they are made part of the system. Users should design the input or output form and choose the appropriate technology (for example, optical character recognition or on-line terminals).

### Advantages

What are the benefits of this design approach? User participation in and control over the design process has a number of payoffs for the organization. The new system is more likely to be utilized because the user, instead of the information department services staff, has psychological ownership of it. The user has invested time and ideas in the system. Because of exposure to the system during design, users will understand the system and become trained in how to use it for the conversion and installation phase.

---

**MANAGEMENT PROBLEM 18-2**

The Major Mining Company hired a consulting firm to design a new computer system for inventory control. The consultant was supposed to coordinate his efforts with the company's computer centers located in two parts of the United States. The consultant was retained because the existing workload at the company centers prevented them from developing the system and because the consulting firm had extensive technical expertise.

The computer center designated to work most closely with the consultant was extremely hostile. The standard reaction of the personnel in the center to the consultant was, "It's your system, you design it." The consultant had a rather low opinion of the staff in the computer center but knew that the staff would have to program any system designed. Therefore, the consultant tried to obtain systems analysis and programming personnel from the center. Much time was spent on this rather unproductive activity and progress on the new system was very slow.

The consultant described these problems to the vice president who had retained the firm. Although the vice president could order the computer center staff to cooperate, he knew that it was impossible to force cooperation. What can the vice president do to solve this problem? Is the problem solely at the computer center? What can the consultant do?

---

Because of their influence, users will surrender less power and less control over their activities to the information services department. Systems should have higher quality because the user is in charge. The user knows what is needed for the application, and, since the user is in control, quality will be defined according to user criteria. The user interface with the system will be appropriate because the user will have designed it.

**Disadvantages**

The method for systems design suggested above will not be easy to implement. Resistance can be expected from information services department staff members who will probably perceive a diminished role in systems design. Experience, however, should show that systems design jobs become more satisfying under this new approach because the designers' efforts will be successful. It is far more exciting to be a catalyst in the development of a successful system than to be in charge of the development of a system that fails. In addition, the technical challenge of systems design has not been removed from the duties of the information services department staff.

Resistance to these new suggestions can be expected from users too. Users may fear computer technology and question their own ability to take charge of or contribute to a systems design effort. Management support and encouragement will be necessary to help users overcome their initial fears. Once into the design process, these doubts should quickly disappear as users are caught up in the challenge and excitement of designing their own systems.

## Some Experiences

Can the user design information systems? The procedures for systems design recommended above have been used for the development of several information systems. In one instance, a feasibility study and systems design were carried out for a grass-roots labor organization. The design team consisted of union members and faculty and students from a university. The union members in general had a low level of formal education, and the design team was concerned over the impact of computer technology on the union and on its individual members. Because of hectic union organizing activities, the union staff could not devote the amount of time needed to the development of a system, although eventually several full-time union staff members began to work on the project.

To begin the analysis, the university design team interviewed members of the union staff and gathered data on existing procedures and requirements. After jointly determining that a system was feasible, the design team developed a rough design. To turn the ownership of the system over to the union, and to be sure that they were in control of the system, a day-long review meeting was held to present the draft of the system. At this meeting, the union president explained that there were many tasks to be done and that no one would be replaced by a computer. He stated that, instead, workers probably would have more interesting jobs, and he asked members to think about how the system could help the union.

The design team began its part of the meeting by stressing that the session would be successful only if at least half of the system presented was changed: the team was offering ideas and not a finished product. Elaborate flowcharts and visual aids were not used. Instead, a very simple tutorial on computer systems began the presentation. The designers spoke from rough notes and listed report contents, files, and inputs on a blackboard. The highly motivated union staff quickly grasped the relationship among reports, files, and input documents. Substantial changes to the rough system were made in front of the audience during the meeting.

Several weeks later, a follow-up meeting was held with union leaders who suggested management-oriented reports. The design team helped the union develop specifications for bids and worked on a consulting basis with the union staff that finally developed a system. The designers intentionally reduced their role as the union became more capable in the computer area. The system was successfully implemented; the level of use was high and users from the union president to clerical personnel appeared pleased with the system.

In another situation, a system was developed to support the decisions of a group of three managers. These managers had responsibility for setting production schedules in the commercial laundry products division of a major manufacturing company. The production manager wanted to minimize setups and have long product runs. The marketing manager wanted to have wide product availability at warehouses throughout the country to provide high levels of customer service. The market planning manager had to resolve differences in objectives so that the three managers could develop a feasible production plan.

---

**MANAGEMENT PROBLEM 18-3**

The Airflow Manufacturing Company has retained a consultant to help design an order-entry and accounts-receivable computer system. Airflow manufactures precision parts for the aerospace and automotive industries.

The consultant believes in the creative design techniques discussed in this chapter. As a result, she stresses the importance of extensive user involvement in the design of the system. The president of the company agrees intellectually with the consultant's advice, but recognizes there could be problems in trying to obtain the needed cooperation.

The most serious bottleneck appears to be one key employee in the office. Most of the work on processing orders and receivables is under the supervision of this one individual. There is no real second in command, even though the president tried unsuccessfully for a number of years to have an assistant trained. Several had been hired, but left during the training period because of unknown problems.

Because of the lack of an assistant and the increased information processing load created by a good business year, the president knows that obtaining help from this key supervisor will be difficult. However, the consultant, after a few days working in the firm, indicates that this individual is probably the most logical person to place in charge of the design effort.

What can the president do? Can he afford to have this key supervisor in charge of the system? If there is no alternative, what steps can the president take to be sure that the system is designed well and that normal information processing tasks are completed?

---

Because future production depended on the decision for the next month, a 12-month planning horizon was used.

In the original manual system, the managers generated possible solutions that were analyzed by clerical personnel who performed a large number of manual calculations. Upon evaluation, it was usually found that a solution had to be modified because some part of it was infeasible. More meetings and more clerical computations were required. Sometimes, almost the entire month elapsed before the next month's schedule was ready.

The research group trying to improve this decision process observed the managers at work for some 6 months. After 3 months, a rough system featuring an interactive graphics display terminal was developed. The first prototype system was shown to the market planning manager, who learned how to operate it. This manager made many suggestions for changes, which the designers incorporated into the system. Then, the market planning manager trained the production and marketing managers in the use of the system. They, too, had numerous suggestions for modifications that were incorporated into the system. Over time, the researchers modified the system for the managers in this particular decision situation. The managers were very satisfied with the system and resisted attempts by the computer department to discontinue it after the research project was officially completed.

These efforts so far have been with small groups of users who have not had complete control over design, but the techniques are promising and should be applicable to other settings. Certainly more time is required on the part of the user to participate so fully in systems design. However, the time is well spent, since a significant component of a user's activities is likely to be affected by a new computer-based information system. Given the failure of so many information systems, users must spend time on the design of systems and encourage the adoption of more participatory design techniques.

## IN CONCLUSION

When creative design was first suggested, the reasons for the approach were primarily psychological. Now there are other reasons as well: it saves time in developing systems and increases their chances of working. The need to multiply the efforts of the professional computer staff provides one incentive to have users do more. The backlog in developing computer applications is created partially by too few skilled systems analysts; users can easily assume some of these activities. In addition, there are new tools like fourth-generation languages which make it easier for users to do some of their own computing. The extremely attractive interface and software for personal computers is encouraging users to undertake information processing on their own. In the next chapter we explore this phenomenon further.

## KEY WORDS

| | | |
|---|---|---|
| Attitudes | Operations research | Quality of systems |
| Change | model | Satisfaction |
| Dependent variable | Participation | Successful implementa- |
| Failure of systems | Planned change | tion |
| Implementation | Process of design | User interface |
| Independent variable | Pseudoparticipation | |

## RECOMMENDED READINGS

Lucas, H. C., Jr.: *Implementation: The Key to Successful Information Systems,* Columbia, New York, 1981. (Presents a review of implementation literature and a new framework for approaching implementation.)

————: *Toward Creative Systems Design,* Columbia, New York, 1974. (This short monograph describes in more detail the philosophy of systems design introduced in this chapter.)

Mumford, E., and D. Henshall: *A Participative Approach to Computer Systems Design,* Associated Business Press, London, 1979. (An excellent study of participative design.)

Schultz, R., and D. Slevin: *Implementing Operations Research/Management Science,* American Elsevier, New York, 1975. (Contains the results of a conference on the implementation of OR models; many interesting studies provide insights on the implementation process.)

## DISCUSSION QUESTIONS

1 Why are favorable attitudes important for successful implementation?
2 What other definitions and measures of successful implementation can you suggest besides the ones in this chapter?
3 What are the responsibilities of users in the systems design process?
4 How do the responsibilities of managers and, say, the clerical staff differ during systems design?
5 What are the crucial differences between an operations research model and computer-based information systems from the standpoint of implementation? What are the key similarities?
6 What is the role of a consultant in helping design information systems? How does this role change under the creative systems design policies suggested in this chapter?
7 What approaches are there to evaluating the benefits of information systems?
8 How would you measure the impact of an information system on decision making?
9 How do you suppose cognitive style affects implementation? Can cognitive style act as a constraint on successful implementation?
10 How could you take cognitive style into account in designing a system?
11 What problems does user-controlled design create for users, their management, and the information services department?
12 Can user-controlled design work for a system encompassing large numbers of people, for example, a reservation system involving hundreds or thousands of agents? What strategy could be adopted in this situation?
13 How would you study the implementation process? How could such a study be used to improve implementation?
14 Why do so many information services departments resort to pseudoparticipation?
15 What are the origins of the rational engineering approach to change? Contrast this approach with more participatory techniques.
16 What are the dangers of participation? (Hint: think about raised expectations.)
17 What is the role of the information services department analyst in the design techniques discussed in this chapter?
18 As a potential or present user of information systems, how do you respond to the idea of being in charge of the design of such a system?
19 What is the key distinction between planned change and change in general?
20 Are the techniques suggested here applicable in other contexts? What situations can you suggest in which user control might be more successful than control by a group of technological experts?
21 How does the technique of creative design affect the conditions of the conflict model discussed earlier?
22 How do the change techniques suggested here relate to the power model presented earlier?
23 When does planning for successful implementation begin in designing an information system?
24 Who should suggest the development of a new information system—users or the information services department? Why?
25 Who should suggest modifications and improvement to existing systems—users or the information services department? Why?

## CHAPTER 19

# DECISION SUPPORT SYSTEMS AND END-USER COMPUTING

**CHAPTER ISSUES**

- How can users reduce the backlog of applications?
- What are the characteristics of more decision-oriented systems?

In this chapter we examine some new trends in computing. A Decision Support System (DSS) is intended to support decisions, not just process data. End-user computing means that the user actually uses a computer; he or she does not wait for a programmer or analyst to design a system or to extract data from company files.

The purpose of end-user computing is to:

1 Reduce the backlog of applications
2 Provide access to data that many users consider frozen inside applications
3 Avoid communications problems with programmers
4 Reduce delays waiting for a programmer and for a task to be completed

A Decision Support System is not end-user computing per se. This topic is included in the chapter because much of what managers do in end-user computing is to build a small DSS. The manager may not call his or her work a DSS, but the inquiries, special reports, and use of spreadsheet packages often support the user's decisions. In fact, it is widely believed that electronic spreadsheet packages are the most commonly used tools for building a DSS.

## DECISION SUPPORT SYSTEMS

One definition of a DSS is that it is a computer-based system which helps the decision maker utilize data and models to solve unstructured problems (Sprague and Carlson, 1982). This definition is rather restrictive; today if there is any level of decision making involved, the system is often called a Decision Support System. The most liberal interpretation would be that a DSS is any system that is not dedicated to transactions processing!

### Some Examples

In Chapter 21 we present several examples of DSS applications. Below are a few shorter descriptions of what one can do with this kind of application.

A major airline developed a model to help reduce fuel costs. The airline system stores data on fuel prices and availability along with storage costs and fuel capacity at each of the cities it serves. Performance parameters and the monthly itinerary are included for each of its aircraft. The system produces a list of the best fueling stations and vendors for each flight.

The system requires about fifteen minutes to produce a schedule that required a month of time to prepare manually. As a result, the airline can compute the best fueling strategy any time conditions change, several times a week if necessary. The airline calculates that it saved two cents a gallon on fuel in a month; since the planes consumed 25 million gallons of jet fuel, the savings are in the neighborhood of $500,000 per month.

A manufacturing firm was planning to install a $50 million production system at one of its plants in the Pacific Northwest. Using an ad hoc DSS, the firm investigated 32 alternative locations and decided instead to locate the new system in a southeastern plant, saving some $7 million annually in distribution costs.

A California producer of food supplements, cosmetics, and household cleaners was growing rapidly and management was making decisions based on entirely subjective criteria. The firm built a database that includes plant location, products manufactured, unit costs, production capacity, and details on 500 line items, 360 customers and 100 distribution centers.

The model in the computer calculates the impact that various delivery requirements place on transportation costs, distribution costs, and the cost of carrying inventory. For the first time, firm management is able to understand the financial impact associated with various service-level decisions according to a company spokesman. The firm expects to reduce operating costs by $850,000 a year and more importantly, to cut delivery time to customers by one-third.

Our last example is a research system, but it illustrates how powerful the technology is when the power of modeling is combined with the graphics capability of a computer system. The system, described in Sprague and Carlson (1982), is GADS (Geodata Analysis and Display System). The system was designed to help urban planners and administrators in making decisions on land use. It also has been used to help a police department realign its patrol areas.

Police officers analyzed calls for service by type, geographic area, and day and time of the week. Using the data and judgment, the officer designed a more efficient allocation of personnel to beats.

During the period in which the system was developed and evaluated, it was used for 17 specific Decision Support Systems and can be considered as a general purpose tool for building a DSS. The applications ranged from police personnel allocation and burglary analysis to school boundary formation and school closings. Urban planners used the system to evaluate growth policies. The fire department used the system for planning inspections and making plans for equipment. Finally, the system was used for computer bus route planning and determining where to locate a shopping center.

The system has four representations of data: maps, tables, scatterplots, and lists. The system has menus to aid the user in making choices and a command language. For example, there are a series of operators for displaying and manipulating maps and graphs. Other statements let the user create graphs, tables, and lists. Finally, there is an extraction language for manipulating the database.

The power from this system comes from its ability to represent data graphically. Figure 19-1 (*a* & *b*) is an example of some of the displays used by a computer vendor to plan the territories for customer engineers who repair and service computer equipment at client sites.

**FIGURE 19-1a**
Territory map for a customer engineer.

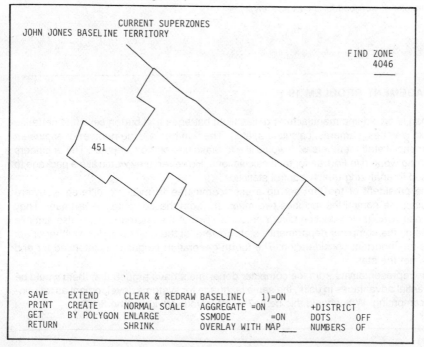

CURRENT SUPERZONES
JOHN JONES BASELINE TERRITORY

FIND ZONE
4046

451

| SAVE | EXTEND | CLEAR & REDRAW | BASELINE( 1)=ON | |
| PRINT | CREATE | NORMAL SCALE | AGGREGATE =ON | +DISTRICT |
| GET | BY POLYGON | ENLARGE | SSMODE =ON | DOTS OFF |
| RETURN | | SHRINK | OVERLAY WITH MAP___ | NUMBERS OF |

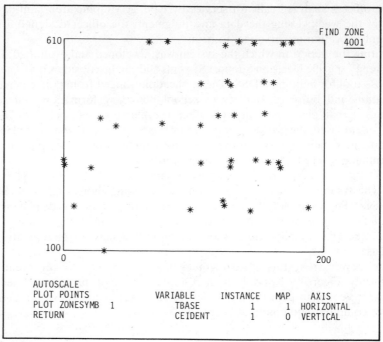

**FIGURE 19-1b**
A scatterplot of workload for a customer engineer.

## MANAGEMENT PROBLEM 19-1

Voltman is an old-line manufacturer of flashlight batteries and button cells (the batteries used in watches, cameras, calculators, etc.). The firm has a large number of engineers and financial staff members who would like to make use of the computer. The engineers have long worked in Fortran for their calculations. However, they would like a package to be used in analyzing quality control statistics.

The president of the firm set up a user committee to evaluate different software products; the committee includes two members from the computer department. They have narrowed their selection to four products. Two of these products are also suitable for use by the computer department's staff. Several of the users wonder whether or not this is an important consideration. The fourth-generation language is intended for end users, not the staff.

The representatives from the computer department have argued that there would be substantial advantages in using the same language for systems development as for end-user computing. Why should this be so? What is your advice to the firm?

**Structure**

Sprague and Carlson have developed an approach to the design and description of a DSS they call the ROMC model.

**Representation**   What is the context of the decision? Can the problem be drawn as a figure or a chart? How about representing the decision using a spreadsheet? In what context will the user interpret the output?

**Operations**   How does the user actually make the decision? For example, in Simon's terms, how does the decision maker carry out intelligence, design, and choice? Operations includes data collection, manipulation of the data, and generation of alternatives. During operations, the user modifies the alternatives and creates new ones. Finally the decision maker chooses a particular alternative.

**Memory Aids**   We need memory aids to help in representing the decision and operating on the data. Memory aids might include a database containing data from sources inside the firm or from external data acquired from outside the organization. The design of the data required for the decision is one of the key tasks in building a DSS. Memory aids may provide different views of data, say different types of graphs and tables as in GADS.

**Control**   The control system organizes all the tools and data to be used in making a decision. The control part of a DSS manages the system; it provides the user interface, control of the database, and generates various representations for the user.

How does the development of a DSS differ from traditional design?

**1** The focus is on decisions, not data flows.

**2** The construction of a DSS tends to follow an iterative or prototyping approach.

**3** Building one of these systems forces the user to become involved in the design process.

**4** The system may be designed with the help of a systems analyst or by the user alone. Most DSS built on a personal computer will be constructed by the decision maker alone.

The tools to be used to build one's own DSS will be discussed later in this chapter under end-user computing. When the information services department staff constructs a DSS, they will probably use rather traditional development tools. One requirement is generally to have some level of interaction with the system. Even in a DSS where the system is used primarily to supply data and statistical analysis, it is helpful for the user to be able to generate the statistics interactively from a terminal.

Alter (1980) has attempted to come up with a framework for classifying different types of DSS. His original framework has a number of categories which can be summarized into two main types: data-oriented and model-based DSS. A data-oriented system provides tools for the manipulation and analysis of data. Various kinds of statistical tests can be run and data can be combined in different ways for display. A model-based system generally has some kind of mathematical model of the decision being supported. For example, the model might be an operations research optimizing model or a simple model represented by a balance sheet and income statement for a firm.

Decision Support Systems offer tremendous power for managers who can generate and try many different alternatives, asking "what if" questions and seeing the results. One manager said, "I'm not being forced to take the first solution that works because it takes so long to generate an answer; using a model and a spreadsheet program on a personal computer, now I can try different alternatives and choose the one that looks best."

## EXPERT SYSTEMS

Expert systems are a type of Decision Support System, though not one that is easily developed by the user. Expert Systems represent an application from the field of Artificial Intelligence (AI). This branch of computer science is concerned with the manipulation of symbols rather than data. Early AI applications were in game playing (checkers and chess) and theorem proving. Some early researchers also tried to simulate human behavior.

Expert Systems are an example of applied Artificial Intelligence. The first systems appeared in the medical field, for example, for diagnosing illness. The idea is that the knowledge and decision-making rules of an expert are captured in a program.

Why build such a system? One purpose is to make the expertise of an individual available to others in the field. Another motivation is to capture knowledge from an expert who is likely to be unavailable in the future, for example, because of impending retirement. The Expert System can be used as a replacement or as a training device to help novices reach a high level of expertise.

One of the earliest and best known experts was developed to provide the physician with a consultant on internal medicine. See Figure 19-2 for a dialog with this system called Internist. Professor Harry Pople and Dr. Jack Meyers at the University of Pittsburgh have been developing the program and building the knowledge base. The system now covers about 80 percent of internal medicine and has knowledge of some 500 diseases and 3500 manifestations of the diseases.

Expert Systems have been developed for a variety of applications. One system at General Electric diagnoses faults in diesel locomotives. Another system is being developed to diagnose failures in computer hardware.

One of the most successful experts is in use at Digital Equipment Corporation, a manufacturer of computers. The Expert works on the problem of configuring a VAX computer. There are many different options for how a

**FIGURE 19-2**
An example of a session with INTERNIST-1.

---

Manifestations are expressed by means of precise sequences of terms in a controlled vocabulary; there are presently approximately 3500 vocabulary items that can be used to describe positive and negative findings.

```
   DISREGARDING: EXPOSURE TO RABBITS OR OTHER SMALL MAMMALS. LEG <S>
WEAKNESS BILATERAL. LEG <S> WEAKNESS PROXIMAL ONLY. PRESSURE ARTERIAL
ORTHOSTATIC HYPOTENSION. CREATININE BLOOD INCREASED. UREA NITROGEN
BLOOD 60 TO 100

   CONSIDERING: AGE 26 TO 55. SEX MALE. ANOREXIA. MYALGIA. VOMITING
RECENT. FECES LIGHT COLORED. FEVER. JAUNDICE. LIVER ENLARGED SLIGHT. SKIN
PALMAR ERYTHEMA. SKIN SPIDER ANGIOMATA. WBC 14000 TO 30000. PLATELETS
LESS THAN 50000

   RULEOUT. HEPATITIS CHRONIC ACTIVE. ALCOHOLIC HEPATITIS. HEPATIC MILIARY
TUBERCULOSIS. MICRONODAL CIRRHOSIS <LAENNECS>. HEPATITIS ACUTE VIRAL
```

At this point, INTERNIST-1 reports concerning the initial differential diagnosis that will be the focus of problem-solving attention. Three lists are displayed, labelled respectively DISREGARDING, CONSIDERING, and RULEOUT. The CONSIDERING list identifies those positive findings whose differential diagnostic tasks were combined in coming to the differential diagnostic focus, which is described by the RULEOUT list. The DISREGARDING list tells what positive findings are not consistent with the differential diagnosis as formulated and are therefore being disregarded for the moment; they will, however, be attended to in due course. The keyword RULEOUT indicates what strategy INTERNIST-1 is going to pursue relative to this task definition: in this case, as in any case when the differential list contains five or more alternatives, the program will try to find questions to ask which, if the response is negative, will serve to downgrade the score of one or more diagnoses on the list. While pursuing a RULEOUT strategy, the program limits the questions to be asked to items of information obtainable via history or physical exam.

```
   Please Enter Findings of JAUNDICE HX
   *GO
```

There are two formats used for asking questions. In the preceding line, the user is asked to provide any data that might be available within the specified category of findings. Actually, the respondent is free to enter whatever positive or negative data desired and is not constrained to the category mentioned in the query. In this case, the user chose to respond GO; this passes the initiative back to the program, which then typically follows up on the general question by asking about the specific finding of that category for which it particularly wants a YES or NO answer.

```
   JAUNDICE INTERMITTENT HX?
   NO
```

**FIGURE 19-2** (continued)

If the respondent did not have any information concerning this direct question, he could have answered N/A—meaning not available.

```
Please Enter Findings of APPETITE/WEIGHT
*GO
WEIGHT LOSS GTR THAN 10 PERCENT?
NO
```

The program asks a series of questions that have been selected in accordance with its problem-solving strategy, then repeats the scoring and partitioning of the task definition procedure.

```
    DISREGARDING: EXPOSURE TO RABBITS OR OTHER SMALL MAMMALS. LEG <S>
WEAKNESS BILATERAL. LEG <S> WEAKNESS PROXIMAL ONLY. PRESSURE ARTERIAL
ORTHOSTATIC HYPOTENSION. CREATININE BLOOD INCREASED. UREA NITROGEN
BLOOD 60 TO 100.
    CONSIDERING: AGE 26 TO 55. SEX MALE. ANOREXIA. MYALGIA. VOMITING
RECENT. FECES LIGHT COLORED. FEVER. JAUNDICE. LIVER ENLARGED SLIGHT. SKIN
PALMAR ERYTHEMA. SKIN SPIDER ANGIOMATA. WBC 14000 TO 30000. PLATELETS
LESS THAN 50000
    RULEOUT: HEPATITIS CHRONIC ACTIVE. ALCOHOLIC HEPATITIS. HEPATIC MILIARY
TUBERCULOSIS. HEPATITIS ACUTE VIRAL. INFECTIOUS MONONUCLEOSIS
```

Except for the substitution of an acute process (infectious mononucleosis) for a chronic one (micronodal cirrhosis), this differential diagnosis is not significantly changed from the initial formulation. Note that the possibility of cirrhosis has not actually been ruled out; it has merely dropped out of sight because its score has fallen below the threshold used by the task definition procedure.

```
Please Enter Findings of PAIN ABDOMEN
*GO
ABDOMEN PAIN GENERALIZED?
NO
ABDOMEN PAIN EPIGASTRIUM?
NO
ABDOMEN PAIN NON COLICKY?
NO
ABDOMEN PAIN RIGHT UPPER QUADRANT?
NO
    DISREGARDING: JAUNDICE. SKIN SPIDER ANGIOMATA. CREATININE BLOOD
INCREASED. UREA NITROGEN BLOOD 60 TO 100
    CONSIDERING: AGE 26 TO 55. EXPOSURE TO RABBITS OR OTHER SMALL
MAMMALS. SEX MALE. ANOREXIA. DIARRHEA ACUTE. MYALGIA. VOMITING RECENT.
FEVER. LEG <S> WEAKNESS BILATERAL. LEG <S> WEAKNESS PROXIMAL ONLY.
```

**FIGURE 19-2** (continued)

```
PRESSURE ARTERIAL ORTHOSTATIC HYPOTENSION. PRESSURE ARTERIAL SYSTOLIC
90 TO 110. TACHYCARDIA. WBC 14000 TO 30000. PLATELETS LESS THAN 50000
   DISCRIMINATE: LEPTOSPIROSIS SYSTEMIC. SARCOIDOSIS CHRONIC SYSTEMIC
```

The effect of the negative responses concerning abdominal pain has been to lower the scores of all of the hepatic disorders considered in the previous differential diagnosis. This time, when the partitioning algorithm is invoked the highest-ranking alternative is systemic leptospirosis; the only other diagnosis on the list capable of explaining substantially the same set of findings is systemic sarcoidosis. The keyword DISCRIMINATE indicates that the list of alternatives contains between two and four elements, the leading two of which are selected for comparative analysis. When engaged in a DISCRIMINATE mode of analysis, the program will attempt to ask questions serving to support one diagnosis at the expense of the other; more costly procedures may be called for in order to achieve this objective.

```
    Please Enter Findings of VOMITING/REGURGITATION
    *GO

    HEMATEMESIS?
    NO

    HEMOPTYSIS GROSS?
    NO

    Please Enter Findings of TEMPERATURE
    *GO

    RIGOR <S>?
    YES

    Please Enter Findings of NEUROLOGIC EXAM CRANIAL NERVE <S>
    *GO

    NERVE PARALYSIS SEVENTH CRANIAL BILATERAL?
    NO

    SPLENECTOMY HX?
    NO
```

The program is not actually interested in the answer to this question; what it wants to know is whether the spleen is enlarged. Because of the possibility of being misled by a negative answer, appropriate blocks have been created to prevent the program from asking about an increased spleen size in a patient whose spleen had been removed.

```
    Please Enter Findings of PALPATION ABDOMEN
    *GO

    SPLENOMEGALY MODERATE?
    NO

    Please Enter Findings of XRAY LUNG FIELD <S>
    *GO
```

**FIGURE 19-2** (continued)

CHEST XRAY HILAR ADENOPATHY BILATERAL?
NO

DISREGARDING: JAUNDICE. SKIN SPIDER ANGIOMATA. CREATININE BLOOD
INCREASED. UREA NITROGEN BLOOD 60 TO 100

CONSIDERING: AGE 26 TO 55. EXPOSURE TO RABBITS OR OTHER SMALL
MAMMALS. SEX MALE. ANOREXIA. DIARRHEA ACUTE. MYALGIA. VOMITING RECENT.
FEVER. LEG <S> WEAKNESS BILATERAL. LEG <S> WEAKNESS PROXIMAL ONLY.
PRESSURE ARTERIAL ORTHOSTATIC HYPOTENSION. PRESSURE ARTERIAL SYSTOLIC
90 TO 110. RIGOR <S>. TACHYCARDIA. WBC 14000 TO 30000. PLATELETS LESS
THAN 50000

PURSUING: LEPTOSPIROSIS SYSTEMIC

The questions about rigors (shaking chills) is enough to separate the scores of these
items so that now there is only one alternative left in the differential diagnosis.
Before concluding that this diagnosis is actually correct, however, the program will
now attempt to achieve a degree of separation between this diagnosis and its
nearest competitor (now below the threshold and not printed out) that is twice the
threshold value. The program invokes a PURSUING strategy, which calls for the
identification and acquisition of clinching data; at this stage, the level of question-
ing is unconstrained so the program can ask about biopsies if useful, or other
specialized procedures capable of providing pathognomonic data.

LEPTOSPIRA AGGLUTINATION POSITIVE?
YES

This finding is enough to clinch the diagnosis. However, the program proceeds to
ask additional questions that are automatically included in each consultation.

---

computer is configured; what peripherals and cables and what components are
included in the system? The system, known as R1, develops legal configurations
which engineers then check. Before the system, a technical editor spent a long
period of time to generate the configuration; now all the engineers do is check
the results of the program for correctness.

Expert systems have a knowledge base; usually they apply rules to the
knowledge to make decisions or recommendations. In the case of R1, the
knowledge base includes data on legal VAX computer configurations. The rules
are in the form: if a certain condition exists (usually a logical expression like A
and B and C and D) then take some action. See Figure 19-3 for an example of a
rule in R1.

```
PUT-UB-MODULE-6
    IF:    THE MOST CURRENT ACTIVE CONTEXT IS PUTTING UNIBUS MODULE
           IN THE BACKPLANES IN SOME BOX
    AND    IT HAS BEEN DETERMINED WHICH MODULE TO TRY TO PUT IN A
           BACKPLANE
    AND    THAT MODULE IS A MULTIPLEXER TERMINAL INTERFACE
    AND    IT HAS NOT BEEN ASSOCIATED WITH PANEL SPACE
    AND    THE TYPE AND NUMBER OF BACKPLANE SLOTS IT REQUIRES IS
           KNOWN
    AND    THERE ARE AT LEAST THAT MANY SLOTS AVAILABLE IN A
           BACKPLANE OF THE APPROPRIATE TYPE
    AND    THE CURRENT UNIBUS LOAD ON THAT BACKPLANE IS
           KNOWN
    AND    THE POSITION OF THE BACKPLANE IN THE BOX IS
           KNOWN
    THEN:  ENTER THE CONTEXT OF VERIFYING PANEL SPACE FOR A
           MULTIPLEXER
```

**FIGURE 19-3**
A rule in R1.

Analysts known as knowledge engineers build expert systems. Extracting knowledge from a decision maker or expert is not easy. We attempt to represent knowledge and decision rules using flowcharts and decision trees. Typically one would develop a very simple version of an expert and then try it on a few decisions. Then as the expert observes the system's behavior, he or she indicates where the system is wrong, and the designer adds new rules or modifies existing ones. The process is a form of prototyping and obviously the expert is heavily involved.

There is a great deal of current interest in these types of applications. It is very difficult to show a cost reduction or increases in revenues, but Expert Systems may provide an opportunity to gain an edge on the competition.

For example, the insurance industry is becoming less focused on insurance per se and more on being a financial services industry in which one product is insurance. If the insurers are to compete as financial institutions, they must make rapid decisions; customers used to instant stock and bond purchases do not expect to wait weeks for an underwriting decision on an insurance application. An expert available to agents in the field might make it possible to underwrite the policy, print it, and deliver it on the same day the applicant completes the application form.

## END-USER COMPUTING

End-user computing is a very imprecise term. Many end users have worked with computers and written programs for a number of years. Engineers frequently use languages like FORTRAN to write programs for their own needs. Some actuaries in insurance firms use FORTRAN or APL to develop their own systems.

Who is the end user? We usually define this individual as a nonprofessional in the systems field. The end user is in a different function than information systems; he or she is a user in finance, accounting, production, etc. The computer is not the primary consideration of the user, so that a full-time systems analyst working in the accounting department would not be considered an end user.

Figure 19-4 shows a possible spectrum of end-user computing. The simplest form is a user working at a terminal using a predefined menu. The system might allow the user to access a high-level command language. One retrieval system features a menu to get the user started; then he or she "programs" requests and asks for statistical analyses for the data retrieved, using high-level commands.

As we move along the spectrum we encounter query languages on mainframe computers. Here the user must have good knowledge of the database and the language. He or she enters requests in the language and possibly processes the data retrieved, as in the example above. At about the same level of user involvement in programming, we encounter the personal computer. The user works with a number of software packages, but does very little coding.

A modeling language moves us more toward programming. The user of this language actually writes a program to model the phenomenon under study.

On the personal computer side, the user moves from word processing to using a spreadsheet package. These packages present row and column coordinates which the user identifies for placing entries in each cell. The cell may contain either text or a value as discussed in Chapter 18. The value may be entered as a number or as a formula relating other cells (identified by their row and column

**FIGURE 19-4**
Spectrum of end-user computing.

| Mainframes / minicomputers | | | | |
|---|---|---|---|---|
| Terminal access | Query language | Modeling language | Generators | Procedural languages |
| Packages | Word processing | Electronic Spreadsheets | DBMS generators | Basic, Pascal |
| Personal computers | | | | |

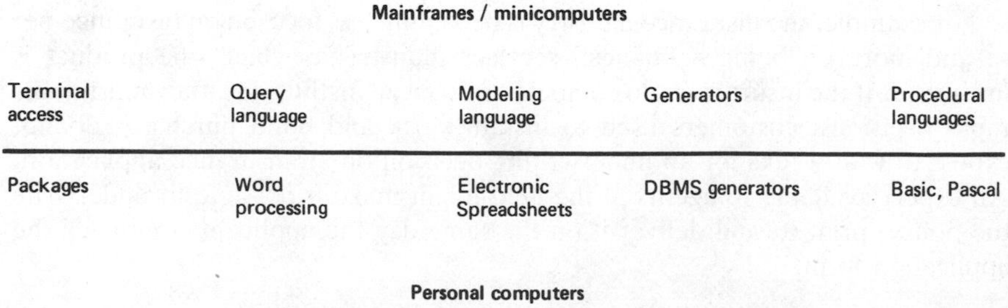

## MATERIALS REQUIREMENTS PLANNING

*In the mid 1970s Corning Glass found that it was making shipping dates only 50% of the time. With an MRP system many of the problems with meeting schedules have been eliminated.*

*First the computer sets up a master production schedule, usually on the basis of forecasts and orders that are in house already. Part of the database is a bill of material for each product manufactured; that is, a list of all components and their quantities required to produce an ordered item.*

*The MRP system uses the master production schedule and works backwards from the scheduled completion time for a product. It explodes the final product into its components and schedules the manufacture of each component (or its purchase) at an acceptable lead time. If a component takes two days to manufacture, then it must be in production at least two days before final assembly. Depending on capacity and demand, the component may be started earlier.*

*At Corning, the system has produced $6 million in savings in operations and a $20 million inventory reduction. More importantly, at a key auto supply plant, the MRP system has allowed Corning to perform better than a Japanese competitor in meeting the automaker's delivery demands.*

---

coordinates) to the one currently under consideration. Since the spreadsheet is tied together with formulas, the user can try many different alternatives by changing key numbers.

Other languages are available for special purposes as we discussed in Chapter 9, for example, SPSS for statistical analysis. The user defines the format of the data and writes a simple program to perform quite powerful statistical tests on data. There also exist a number of languages for providing output in a graphic form on a CRT or plotting device. Each of these languages contains commands at a high level:

GENERATE A PLOT
X AXIS "DOLLARS (000)"
Y AXIS "SALES" etc.

End users can also work with applications generators. The simplest generators are available using DBMS packages on personal computers. For mainframes and minicomputers there are a number of retrieval programs for sequential files and there are query languages for database systems. The retrieval systems may require the user to construct something that looks a lot like a program, but at a higher level than a compiler language.

At the extreme, end users actually write programs in a procedural language like BASIC, PASCAL, or APL. At the present time it is not clear how many users will go this far. For the next few years, we would be surprised to see significant numbers of users writing programs in these languages.

---

## MANAGEMENT PROBLEM 19-2

Nationwide Insurance, a large multiline firm, is investigating the possibility of starting a major office automation project. The firm recognizes that many of its activities revolve around information processing. While long a user of computers for basic policy processing and accounting, the firm has recently become aware of its extremely high volume of memoranda and messages transmitted primarily on paper and through the mail.

Nationwide has reviewed the literature on office automation and is trying to determine how best to apply various functions in these systems to its operations. The company operates in 25 countries around the world and in 40 of the 50 United States. The mail causes it considerable problems, and phone calls are sometimes difficult because of different time zones. Although local managers have a fair degree of autonomy, a high volume of information still flows from the field to headquarters and vice versa.

Nationwide is also concerned about its escalating travel costs. They see advantages to electronic communications but wonder about the impact of the new technology on employees and on the firm.

What features of office automation do you think would be the most suitable to Nationwide? What functions should they implement first? How would you advise the firm to approach the implementation problem for such a system? How does one evaluate the benefits and the costs? What would be required for office automation to help Nationwide?

---

### Support

End-user computing cannot be the sole responsibility of the user; there must be support. The information services staff should help in selecting whatever tools are provided for the end user. Next, the department should see that there is adequate training available in the use of the systems acquired. Finally, information services staff members should provide ongoing consulting on the use of these tools. There will be a need for consultants to help answer questions about the systems and languages with which end users are working. The ISD staff also has to help the user locate data. He or she may also need to write programs to collect data from different files, or to process these data in some way before the end user can access it.

The term "information center" has become popular for describing a support group for end users. Typically, the center is located in a suite of rooms in a user area. The information center contains terminals, microcomputers, reference manuals, and most important, consultants to work with users.

If there are microcomputers in the firm, the center makes available different computers and peripherals along with different software packages. The user can try different computers and programs in a relaxed atmosphere.

---

**MONEY MANAGEMENT, PRONTO**

*Chemical Bank in New York City is offering a service called Pronto. This system is available to Chemical customers who own a home computer and have an account of some type at the bank. Using the home computer, the user makes a connection to a Chemical mainframe via a dial-up phone line and a modem on the computer.*

*Once connected to the bank's computer, a user can make an inquiry about an account balance, transfer funds, pay bills, review statements, or keep a home budget. The bank takes care of the funds transfer for paying bills while the customer can transfer money from checking to savings accounts using the system.*

*Bill paying is one of the major features; a user can pay a bill by reviewing it on the system. For recurring bills like a mortgage or loan repayment, the system makes it possible to set up an automatic payment; the user does not have to take any action to initiate payment.*

*This system is a good example of the home use of computers; it is a precursor of the kind of systems we shall use routinely in the coming years.*

---

The consultants in the information center have a number of duties:

**1** Teaching courses about computers and software packages available
**2** Consultation on the use of packages and languages
**3** Assistance in deciding on the acquisition of computers and peripherals
**4** Help for users by extracting, merging, and reformatting data on company databases and making it available in a file for easy access by users

The philosophy of end-user computing creates a different role for both the consultant and the end user. The consultant aids the end user, answers questions, and provides help in accessing data. The end user determines the data needed and creates the program to process it.

**Policy Issues**

One policy for the information services department is to help and to support end-user computing. A more difficult problem is to control the proliferation of hardware and software. Users conducting their own research may come up with a number of different approaches. Each new system, be it hardware or software, requires the computer staff to learn how to support it. Such an effort is costly and time-consuming. Thus, the information services department may establish a policy with support from senior management that all software and hardware is purchased through and with the approval of the ISD. Then the computer staff can evaluate the systems recommended and allocate its staff to become familiar with them. The computer department can keep control so that a reasonable number of different systems is acquired.

As users acquire terminals and local computers, the information services department will have to coordinate acquisitions. Eventually, the various pieces of hardware will probably be linked in some kind of network. Compatibility among the different devices is of concern here. Again, multiple hardware vendors and different types of software place a heavy support burden on the computer staff. Coordination is vital!

The end-user is, by definition, not a systems professional. For most applications, the computer staff will allow access to data under its control, but will not allow users to change these data. The systems professional must be concerned about error checking, editing, data validation, and the protection of the integrity of the database. There is no reason to suspect that the user is necessarily aware of this aspect of systems operation. The consulting staff can raise some of these issues, particularly when local, self-contained systems are being developed by users. However, for corporate data which has been entrusted to the information service department, the computer staff will have to establish controls on data access and updating.

How far should end users go? A number of packages are available now which come close to being applications generators. Database management systems for personal computers provide facilities for setting up a menu and running an application that looks a lot like a custom programmed system.

One senior manager does not want executives writing programs; he insists that they be written by a professional programmer whose cost is far less than that of a senior executive. But what is most productive? What is a program? If a manager constructs a balance sheet using a spreadsheet package on a personal computer, is that programming? Is the use of a DBMS to define a personal application programming?

One answer is for the end user to become very facile in the use of these tools so that he or she will not spend an excessive amount of time using them. If it is possible to do so, developing one's own personal application is fast and should result in a system that meets user requirements!

### Benefits

Users have already discovered the benefits of end-user computing; they are purchasing microcomputers and packages with great enthusiasm. Other users are demanding tools that they can use to solve their own problems. To some extent, the information services department has lost the initiative. To regain it and see that the systems effort is coordinated and to avoid duplication and waste, the computer staff needs to establish a support center as described above.

End-user computing is another way to reduce the time required to develop an application. This approach provides immediate feedback; the user becomes the designer of the system. This strategy also adds to the total number of persons working to solve systems problems. By increasing the number of individuals brought to bear on the problem, we should reduce the backlog of systems work. End-user computing, then, can result in better systems and can reduce the length of time the user must wait to have an application.

## SUMMARY

In this chapter we have addressed three important topics: decision support systems, expert systems, and end-user computing. What is the connection among them? Many individuals think that the class of decision support systems encompases expert systems. Others argue that decisions support systems will become a part of the class of expert systems!

The importance of a DSS is that the system is built to support decision making, not just the processing of transactions. An expert system tries to apply the knowledge of an expert to the solution of a problem, usually a decision problem of some kind. The expert system makes the expert's knowledge more widely available.

How are DSS and expert systems related to end-user computing? End-user computing frequently involves the creation of a decision support system. The manager working at a personal computer with a spreadsheet program is building a DSS. A user accessing data with a fourth-generation language on a mainframe computer's database is frequently using the data to support his or her decisions. As yet, we do not have many expert systems, but it is possible that they will become a part of this kind of decision support, too.

## KEY WORDS

| | | |
|---|---|---|
| Control in DSS | Information center | Query language |
| Decision Support | Internist | Representation |
| System | Knowledge base | Rules |
| End user | Memory aids | Spreadsheet program |
| Expert | Operations | User interface |
| GADS | Procedural language | |
| Generators | Prototype | |

## RECOMMENDED READINGS

Alter, S.: *Decision Support Systems, Current Practices and Continuing Challenges.* Addison-Wesley, Reading, Mass., 1980. (A good survey with an interesting framework for classifying DSS.)

Feigenbaum, E., and P. McCorduck: *The Fifth Generation.* Addison-Wesley, Reading, Mass., 1983. (A discussion of the fifth-generation effort in Japan and the role of AI and Expert Systems in the fifth generation.)

Keene, P., and M. S. Scott Morton: *Decision Support Systems, An Organizational Perspective.* Addison-Wesley, Reading, Mass., 1978. (One of the first books on DSS by an early developer of these systems.)

Sprague, R., and E. Carlson: *Building Effective Decision Support Systems.* Prentice-Hall, Englewood Cliffs, N.J., 1982. (An excellent book describing the structure of a DSS and how to think about the design of one of these systems.)

## DISCUSSION QUESTIONS

1 What is a Decision Support System?
2 How do DSS differ from traditional systems?
3 How do DSS involve users in their design?
4 For what types of systems might the user need assistance in building a DSS? (Hint: consider Alter's framework.)
5 Describe an Expert System. What is the purpose of such a system?
6 How are electronic spreadsheet packages used on a microcomputer for building a DSS?
7 List several applications areas where you think an Expert System might have a payoff for a firm.
8 Why is representation important in a DSS?
9 What is a memory aid in the Sprague and Carlson model for a DSS? Why is it used?
10 Why is the user interface key in a general purpose DSS like GADS?
11 What do graphics capabilities contribute to DSS?
12 What is end-user computing?
13 What are the advantages of end-user computing? Why should we encourage it?
14 What kind of support is needed for end-user computing?
15 Should users actually write programs? Is building a DSS programming?
16 How do modern tools make a definition of programming difficult?
17 Why might a senior manager not want subordinates doing programming?
18 What is the problem with having professional programmers develop every application?
19 What is an information center?
20 How is the role of the professional systems analyst changing with new approaches such as end-user programming?
21 How does prototyping contribute to a DSS? How about to the development of an Expert System?
22 Is it possible to build a DSS around a transactions processing system?
23 What is the role of a model in a model-based DSS?
24 Why do managers want to be able to change values and run a DSS again?
25 How does knowledge engineering differ from traditional systems analysis and design?
26 What are the. major problems in using a query language?
27 What changes in software and hardware encourage end-user computing?
28 What are the major benefits of end-user computing?
29 Why should a user become skilled in using microcomputers and their software?
30 What are the major functions you see for a personal computer for a manager?

# PART FIVE

# EXAMPLES OF
# INFORMATION SYSTEMS

This part of the text integrates the material in the previous chapters through a series of examples. The first chapter in this section presents different information systems including a simple batch application, a nationwide, on-line system, a micro/mainframe application, and an electronic mail system. Chapter 21 describes four decision support systems that illustrate the use of computers to aid more sophisticated and less structured decision problems than the applications in Chapter 20. These two chapters and their examples illustrate how decision requirements, information needs, users, organizational considerations, technology, and the process of systems analysis and design combine to make computer-based information systems.

# GENERAL INFORMATION SYSTEMS

## CHAPTER ISSUES

- What systems alternatives are available for an organization?
- What kind of technology should be employed by the organization?

In this chapter we discuss three different information systems to support transactions processing and operational control decisions, and one communications system. Our purpose is to integrate material covered so far on computer technology and systems design. Our first example presents specifications for a hypothetical system, and because the system was designed for illustrative purposes, it is simple enough to be presented in some detail.

## HARDSERVE

### Background

Hardserve is a company that specializes in the wholesale distribution of merchandise to retail hardware stores.[1] Hardserve buys goods from manufacturers and stocks them in a warehouse; retail hardware stores order merchandise from Hardserve, which then ships it from inventory. If Hardserve does not have the goods requested by the retail store, the store will go elsewhere. Hardserve has usually been the first choice for retail stores trying to find an item. Because

[1]Hardserve is a subsidiary of a diversified holding company named Manhold.

of its efficient operations, it has been able to keep prices slightly lower than competitors. Naturally, the demand for goods fluctuates drastically by season. For example, tree stands are a big item just before Christmas, but there is very little demand for them in July. By the same token, lawn mowers move very rapidly during the spring, but only a few western stores need them in stock all year long.

The company recently developed an inventory-control system. This system provides better service for customers and assists in reordering and controlling inventory balances.

### Preliminary Survey

A design team was formed of users and of information services department personnel, and a steering committee judged the recommendations of a preliminary survey and feasibility study. Below we present the results of the preliminary survey.

## HARDSERVE PRELIMINARY SURVEY

### EXECUTIVE SUMMARY

For several weeks we have been conducting a preliminary survey on the advisability of developing a computerized inventory-control system. This document presents our findings for consideration by the steering committee.

### Goals

We have identified the following goals for an inventory system:

1 Reduce inventory levels while maintaining a desired level of customer service
2 Improve reorder policies
3 Improve inventory management for seasonal and slow-moving items
4 Capture sales data so purchasing can analyze trends and stock the proper merchandise

### Alternatives

We identified one package program and developed two alternatives for new systems for consideration by the steering committee. The results of our analysis are summarized below.

1 Minor improvements in the present system
  a Percentage of goals met—five percent

    **b** Tangible savings—$5000 per year
    **c** Intangible benefits*—10 percent
    **d** Time to implement—3 months
    **e** Total cost—$10,000
**2** A batch computer system with a simple economic order-quantity model
    **a** Percentage of goals met—75 percent
    **b** Tangible savings—$20,000 per year
    **c** Intangible benefits*—30 percent
    **d** Time to implement—18 months
    **e** Total cost—$50,000
**3** Computech inventory-control package
    **a** Percentage of goals met—60 percent
    **b** Tangible savings—$15,000 per year
    **c** Intangible benefits*—25 percent
    **d** Time to implement—6 months
    **e** Total cost—$55,000 ($40,000 for package, $15,000 to install and modify)
**4** An on-line inventory system
    **a** Percentage of goals met—95 percent
    **b** Tangible savings—$15,000 per year
    **c** Intangible benefits*—50 percent
    **d** Time to implement—24+ months
    **e** Total cost—$80,000

*Intangible benefits were rated on a scale of 0 to 100 percent and include consideration of such things as the user interface with the system, ease of use, improved decision making, and so forth.

## THE EXISTING SYSTEM

### Problems

The existing system is illustrated in the flowchart of Exhibit 1. At the present time we have manual processing of papers and no real inventory control. For some items we tend to overstock out of fear of running out, and for others we miss a reorder point and incur a stockout. Purchasing hears from the warehouse when a particular item has reached a reorder point marked on the bin. This reorder point is set by the warehouse manager and is based on experience. We also have no real sales forecasting because we don't know what items are moving. Accounting analyzes the physical inventory, and at the end of the year, purchasing looks at what items have sold. However, it's too late to do any good by that time.

### Goals

The goals for improvement in the system are stated in the Executive Summary.

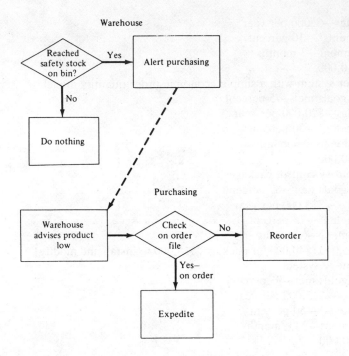

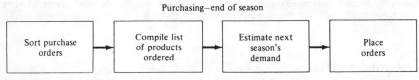

**EXHIBIT 1 OF SURVEY**

## Decision Considerations

We have identified the following crucial decisions in processing inventory:

1 What should be ordered for each new season?
2 What should be reordered during the season and when?
3 How much should be reordered each time?
4 What items should be dropped from inventory?

## Information Flows

Information processing at Hardserve is shown in Exhibit 1. The warehouse supervisor notices when the physical stock has dropped below the reorder point and prepares a report that is sent to purchasing at the end of the day. The purchasing agent either reorders the item, if it is not on order, or expedites it if

**Exhibit 2   Approximate Monthly Values**

|  | Average number of orders |
|---|---|
| January | 4,100 |
| February | 6,700 |
| March | 7,800 |
| April | 8,400 |
| May | 5,400 |
| June | 4,600 |
| July | 5,000 |
| August | 5,100 |
| September | 6,200 |
| October | 9,500 |
| November | 10,100 |
| December | 8,200 |
|  | 81,100 |

Average orders per month   6758
Maximum orders in a day   500
Average orders per day   311
Average number of items per order   5.1

an order has already been placed. At the end of the season, the purchasing department analyzes purchase orders and estimates what quantities will be needed for the next season. Decisions on the reorder amount are based on the purchasing agent's negotiations with the supplier. Approximate volumes of orders and other related data are given in Exhibit 2.

## ANALYSIS OF EACH ALTERNATIVE

### Improvements to the Present System

**Overview**   With minimal impact and cost we can make some improvements to the present system. For example, we can set up tables for economic order-quantity amounts and put better reorder points on the bins.

**Decisions and Information Flows**   These improvements would help us reorder a more economic quantity of goods each time, and we would do so at a better reorder point. However, these improvements would do little for other decisions or information processing.

**Technical**   There will be no computer processing involved in this alternative.

**Development Schedule**   A very few months would be required to implement these changes. We might use a computer program to set the economic order quantities and lot sizes, but this could be done very inexpensively on a microcomputer.

**Impact on the Organization**   There should be minimal changes and a very small impact on organizations or on jobs. The purchasing agent would have to consult a table, which would make decisions on economic order quantities more routine. However, this lets the purchasing agent shop for a better deal, for example, by looking for a better discount or lower price. Warehouse managers should be happy to have a better system of reorder points, since the current haphazard way of establishing them is of concern to the manager.

**Operational Aspects**   The only change this system needs is for purchasing to use a series of tables on the proper economic order quantities. Instead of the warehouse supervisor deciding on the reorder point, a more scientific calculation could be used.

**Costs and Benefits**   The costs in the Summary were estimated to include computer programs and printing the tables for the economic order quantity. We can use the computer for printing these tables. The benefits from this system are estimates of savings through economic ordering and reductions in the number of stockouts.

### A Batch System

**Overview**   This system would be updated once or twice a week with inputs from order processing providing data on usage. Information from the warehouse would show arrivals of merchandise. When a reorder point is nearing, the computer would notify the purchasing agent, who would place the order and notify the computer that goods were on order. Whenever desired, we could produce a usage report.

**Decisions and Information Flows**   This system would provide data for all decisions discussed in the Goals section. Information flows would be altered; the computer department would receive information from the warehouse on order processing and would send information to purchasing.

**Technical**   We would use terminals for input and reports would be printed for purchasing. We would send copies of the inventory report to accounting as well. We would probably have one file on tape with all the data on inventory.

**Development Schedule**   Development should take about 12 months, but we have allowed 18 to be safe. The system would be run on our holding company's computer and we would have a remote batch terminal here for input and output. It should be easy to manage two or three updates a week, and we could vary the number of updates depending on the season.

**Impact on Organization**   It would be necessary for us to add a data preparation and control department at Hardserve, and we would want to have a liaison here to interact with the central computer facility. We would remove the reorder notice burden from the warehouse supervisor. In interviews, the supervisors indicated that this would be a welcome change. It is a tedious and error-prone job now, and they would rather spend time supervising their employees. The purchasing agents, too, indicated that the idea of better planning and sales data would be very appealing. They now are confronted with too many emergency orders and the necessity to expedite orders all too frequently.

**Operational Aspects**   The major changes in operations have been described. Almost all departments are affected, although the changes are relatively minor. There will be a number of reports produced, and certain existing documents will have to be sent to be keyed for input into the computer system. However, there is very little additional work created for any individuals as far as manual processing is concerned.

**Costs and Benefits**   Benefit estimates were based on savings on inventory balance and a reduction in the number of stockouts. We did not really include a better service level for customers, although we think that this will be provided. Cost estimates are based upon a comparable system developed by our holding company's computer staff.

**Package Program**

**Overview**   We also looked at several package programs and selected the best one for consideration by the steering committee. This package does much the same thing as our batch system, but has some functions we don't need and lacks certain features we would like to have.

**Decisions and Information Flows**   Basically, a package program would cover the same decisions as the batch system discussed above. In fact, all the items discussed above are similar for the package except for the development schedule, costs, and benefits.

**Development Effort**   The development effort includes installing and modifying the program to produce the types of reports we would like to have. We estimate this will require less time than developing a system from scratch.

**Costs and Benefits**   The benefits of the new system would be much the same as the batch system described above. A large portion of the cost is the purchase price for the package. We would also have a small operating cost from subscribing to changes and improvements that are made in the package over time.

### An On-line System

**Overview** This alternative is the most sophisticated one presented for consideration. There would be terminals in the warehouse, receiving department, and purchasing department. Data would all be entered by the user.

**Decisions and Information Flows** We will again cover the same decisions and have basically identical information flows except that now we would not use existing documents. Instead, information would be keyed into the system by various users.

**Technical** The input and output are clearly different for this system. We would have to use direct-access files. Output would be selective, although we would probably still want to print some batch reports for a historical record.

**Development Effort** This system will take more effort to develop, even though our holding company has several on-line systems running now. Moving to on-line processing requires a more sophisticated technology, and this is reflected in the development effort.

**Operational Aspects** Operationally, the system will be easier to use and there will be far fewer documents. However, we are somewhat concerned about whether people will be able to use the terminals in the various locations. In some respects, paper processing may almost be easier since it is already familiar.

**Impact on the Organization** This system would have the greatest impact on the organization because purchasing agents, warehouse personnel, and others would use terminals directly. There is also the possibility of problems with backup and computer downtime.

**Costs and Benefits** Benefits are the highest here because data are captured at the source and are up to date when on-line. We would expect to have the same tangible savings as with the batch systems, but operating costs are somewhat higher, reducing total benefits.

## SPECIFICATIONS

After the design team completed the Hardserve preliminary survey, they submitted it to the steering committee. Members of the steering committee read the report and discussed it at length. They decided that a new system would make a positive contribution to the company, and that it should be implemented. The steering committee rejected the package system for a number of reasons[2]

---

[2]In a real situation, the committee would have seriously considered the option of the package, as it is a good way to quickly implement a system and gain experience. However, for the purposes of the example, we shall eliminate the package so we can illustrate the design of a system in detail.

and asked the design team to compare two alternatives in the feasibility study: the batch and the on-line systems. The design team spent two weeks refining the estimates in the preliminary survey. Further study convinced them that the cost and the time estimates had been too conservative. The estimates for the batch system were revised to 12 months and $80,000, while the new estimates for the on-line system were 18 months of development time and a cost of $110,000.

The steering committee examined the feasibility study and focused primarily on the percentage of the original goals met and the impact of the system on the organization. They felt that, given Hardserve's limited experience, the best approach would be to develop a batch system and implement it successfully. However, the committee did ask the design team to develop a system that could be converted easily to on-line updating in the future. Below we present the specifications developed by the design team.

In the specifications that follow, the reader should note that all parts in inventory are currently identified with a seven-digit number. The first two digits of the number are the class code for the type of item (such as lawn care) and the remaining five digits are the item number within the class. For the purposes of the computer system, a check digit will be added to this number.

**Output** The major reports from the system are shown in Table 20-1. (Normally samples of report formats would be developed by the users on the

---

## MANAGEMENT PROBLEM 20-1

Howard Atkins just became chief executive officer of Dorman's Dairies. Dorman's began as a small local dairy in the Midwest and gradually expanded to include several cities. Atkins came to Dorman's when it was acquired by a major conglomerate in the food industry.

Dorman's is fairly conservative and has no computer processing. All production, inventory, and order information is processed manually. Atkins, on the other hand, had extensive experience as a user of information systems at the parent company and felt that Dorman's profit margins could be improved substantially if the costs of information processing could be reduced. Fortunately Atkins is on good terms with the computer department at the corporate headquarters of the conglomerate so that obtaining computer time and service should be easy. In addition, Dorman can use the parent's computers until it becomes necessary to acquire its own.

Atkins is faced with two major problems. First, the employees of the dairy are not used to thinking in terms of systems. He recognizes that there will be significant problems in obtaining enthusiasm and cooperation in designing systems. The other problem is the selection of applications. What areas are most crucial? Where is the greatest potential for savings? What types of information systems should be developed? Atkins is searching for some mechanism to solve these two problems. What do you recommend?

**TABLE 20-1**
OUTPUT REPORTS

1  Inventory balance report
   Distribution: Order processing
                 Warehouse
                 Purchasing
                 Accounting
   Form:         Microfilm
   Sequence:     (1) Inventory class (first two digits of item number)
                 (2) Item number (next five digits of item number)
   Frequency:    Each update
   Contents:     Item number
                 Description
                 Units
                 Previous month's balance
                 Current month's balance
                 Current month's usage
                 Current month's receipts
                 12 months' usage
                 Reorder quantity
                 Reorder point
                 Cost
                 Physical location in warehouse
                 On-order quantity
                 Average balance
                 Leadtime

2  Reorder report
   Distribution: Purchasing
   Form:         Printed
   Sequence:     (1) Inventory class
                 (2) Item number
   Frequency:    Each update
   Contents:     Item number
                 Description
                 Units
                 Previous month's balance
                 Current month's balance
                 Current month's usage
                 12 months' usage
                 Reorder quantity
                 Reorder point
                 Cost
                 On-order quantity
                 Number of stockouts
                 Average balance
                 Expedite (if already on order)
                 Leadtime

3  Order analysis report
   Distribution: Purchasing
   Form:         Printed
   Sequence:     (1) Inventory class

**TABLE 20-1**
(Continued)

---

        (2)  Item number
             or
        (1)  By number of units ordered
             or
        (1)  By number of units ordered by class
Frequency:    As requested
Contents:     Item number
              Description
              Units
              Yearly orders
              Reorder quantity
              Reorder point
              Number of stockouts

**4**  Inventory turnover report
Distribution:  Purchasing
               Accounting
Form:          Printed (summary or detailed)
Frequency:     As requested
Sequence:      (1)  Class
               (2)  Item number
Contents:      Item number              (or class)
               Description               Description
               Units                     —
               Balance                   Balance
               12 months' usage          12 months' usage
               Reorder quantity          —
               Reorder point             —
               Cost                      Cost
               Average balance           Average balance
               Total usage               Total usage
               Average usage             Average usage
               Turnover                  Turnover

**5**  Physical inventory adjustment report
Distribution:  Accounting
Form:          Printed
Sequence:      (1)  Inventory class
               (2)  Item number
Contents:      Item number
               Description
               Units
               Previous 12 months' balance
               Current balance (book)
               Previous 12 months' usage
               Current month (usage)
               Date of physical inventory
               Adjustment quantity

---

*Note:* For size and type of fields, see file specifications.

design team for inclusion in the specifications.) Users agreed that they needed an inventory balance report to check inquiries and for historical records. However, several users confirmed that this report would be referred to infrequently. The systems design team suggested the use of microfilm with one reader each in order processing, accounting, warehousing, and purchasing.

One of the major goals of the system was to speed reorder information to purchasing on a regular basis, and the reorder report will be prepared each updating cycle to accomplish this. The recommended order quantities and the reorder point are computed in a program by a simple formula (see Buffa, 1961):

where Q = order quantity
     R = requirement or usage rate
     S = ordering cost
     i = the carrying cost as a percentage of inventory
     C = cost of an item

All these data needed to compute Q are readily available from purchasing records.

The economic order quantity is first computed when a new item is added to the inventory, or when costs change. When the balance on hand reaches the reorder point, a reorder notice is included on the order report for the item. The reorder point computation is based on the estimated usage during the lead time. To compute this point, the usage for the last month is divided by the number of days in the month. This figure is multiplied by the lead time in days to obtain the expected usage during the lead time as the reorder point. A percentage is included in the calculation to let us increase the safety stock if we experience too many stockouts. There are more sophisticated approaches to setting a reorder point and safety stock; however, this rule of thumb should be adequate for Hardserve.

The order analysis report was developed by the purchasing agents to assist in planning. The agents hope it will allow them to see trends and decide what to order during each season. Purchasing agents will override the reorder report on seasonal items; for example, they do not need to stock many lawn-care items during November. When it wants, the purchasing department can request the order-analysis report, and it will be prepared as a part of the update. The report will be produced by item number in detail or will be sorted and presented by decreasing usage. The purpose of this inventory review report is to allow analysis of items that are selling well. The report can be obtained by inventory class summarized for all the items in the class, or by individual item.

The inventory adjustment report was requested by accounting. Periodically, accounting takes physical inventory and adjusts the book inventory to reflect quantities actually in storage. (Discrepancies come from loss, damage, etc.) Not shown in Table 20-1 is a generalized retrieval report for management. In observing management, the design team found requests for inventory information were erratic. It would be very difficult to satisfy management with a formal, prescribed report. Instead, managers wanted an inquiry capability to support their decision making. At first the information services department staff members would formulate inquiries for the program; later, perhaps, managers will learn to prepare the input themselves.

**Input**  Four types of inputs in the system are shown in Table 20-2. First, customer orders come into order processing; these orders represent the demand for goods. Receipts for merchandise reflect items that have been ordered by purchasing to replenish inventory; these items arrive at the warehouse, are uncrated, and put on shelves. On-order data come from purchasing so that the reorder program will know whether something has actually been placed on

**TABLE 20-2**
INPUTS

**1**  Orders
    Source:   Current purchase order
    Medium:  Terminal (one record per item ordered)
    Fields:

| | Positions | Type |
|---|---|---|
| Customer number | 1–8 | Numeric |
| Item number | 9–17 | Numeric |
| Quantity | 18–23 | Numeric |
| Vendor number | 24–29 | Numeric |
| Price | 30–37 | Numeric (two decimal positions) |

    Estimated volume
        Average 1600 per day
        Maximum 2500 per day

**2**  Receipt of merchandise
    Source:   Warehouse copy of Hardserve purchase order
    Medium:  Terminal (one record per item ordered)
    Fields:

| | Positions | Type |
|---|---|---|
| Item number | 1–8 | Numeric |
| Quantity | 9–15 | Numeric |
| Vendor number | 16–21 | Numeric |
| Purchase order date | 22–27 | Numeric |

    Estimated volume
        Average 800 per day
        Peak 1500 per day

**3**  On order
    Source:   Purchasing department
    Medium:  Terminal (one record per item ordered)
    Fields:

| | Positions | Type |
|---|---|---|
| Item number | 1–8 | Numeric |
| Quantity | 9–15 | Numeric |

**4**  Error correction
    Source:   All users
    Medium:  Terminal
    Fields:    To be designed by update programmer

order. Error corrections come from a number of places; these corrections include file maintenance for correcting errors and for physical inventory adjustment. These data are entered by terminals to a temporary input file for later batch updating.

**Files** Table 20-3 lists the three major files in the system. First, a file is created from entering input transactions (file a in Figure 20-1). This file is the input to a sort routine that places transactions on input file b in Figure 20-1 in the same order as the master file for updating purposes. Finally, there is the master file itself (file c in Figure 20-1).

The master file for this application is placed on disk for two reasons. First, there is a plan to move to on-line inquiry in the future. Second, the president makes unusual requests for information on fairly short notice. He spends much of his time meeting with customers and vendors. With vendors, the president tries to obtain the best price possible, and in times of short supply tries to get what Hardserve has ordered. It helps him to see what types of items are purchased from a particular vendor before meeting with that vendor. The president is curious to find out both the amount and dollar volume of business that is done with the vendor firm so that he can negotiate better service. To answer his inquiries on short notice, the designers included a directory and a linked list of pointers on vendor number for up to three vendors per item. A study showed that in general, no more than two vendors were ever used for a single product.[3]

**Processing** Figure 20-1 presents the overall system flowchart. All input enters the editing program and is edited at one time. Then the input transactions are sorted to update the file. During the file update, various reports are spooled to an intermediate file and error notices are printed. The report print program uses the report file to output each report, and a special retrieval program uses the master file to produce custom-tailored output reports.

**Manual Processing** Basic manual processing operations are shown in Figure 20-2. Order entry in Figure 20-2a begins with the receipt of a customer order and the production of copies. The order is divided into warehouse locations where the different items can be found. That is, orders are divided into the regions of the warehouse where the merchandise is shelved to make picking easier. Four copies of the order are filed for the day on which they are to be filled (picked) in the warehouse.

Before that date the orders are removed from the file and sent to the warehouse. As the order is filled, the picker marks whether the full order

---

[3]This is a fairly unusual request and is included to illustrate use of directories and a linked-list file organization.

**TABLE 20-3**
FILES

---

**1** Master file
   Medium: disk
   Fields:

| | Size | Type |
|---|---|---|
| Item number (key) | 8 | Numeric |
| Description | 50 | Alphanumeric |
| Units | 5 | Alphanumeric |
| Previous month's balance | 8 | Numeric |
| Current month's balance | 8 | Numeric |
| Past 12 months' balance | 8@ = 96 | Numeric |
| Current month's usage | 6 | Numeric |
| Past 12 months' usage | 6@ = 72 | Numeric |
| Reorder quantity | 8 | Numeric |
| Usage during leadtime | 6 | Numeric |
| Most recent cost | 9 | Numeric (two decimal place: |
| On-order quantity | 8 | Numeric |
| On-order date | 6 | Numeric |
| Number of stockouts | 3 | Numeric |
| Three most recent vendors | 6@ = 18 | Numeric |
| Number of orders this year | 3@ = 9 | Numeric |
| Dollar value of orders this year | 7@ = 21 | Numeric |
| Vendor address pointers* | 6@ = 18 | Numeric |
| Leadtime (days) | 3 | Numeric |
| Delete indicator | 1 | Numeric |
| Expansion space | 20 | Numeric |

**2** Transaction file
   Medium: Disk
   Fields: see input—formats

**3** Directories (item number and vendor number)
   Medium: Disks
   Fields:   To be designed by programmer

---

*For linked-list direct-access file.

requested is shipped or not and turns in the form with the shipment. One copy of this form now goes to the information services department, and this is the only change in procedures for order processing.

The activities in placing an order are shown in Figure 20-2*b*. The purchasing agent makes out an order, but works from a computer report instead of a notice from the warehouse. Four copies of the purchase order go to the warehouse to be filed under purchase order number for receipt of the item. One copy goes to the information services department, and this is the only other change in purchasing procedures.

Receipt of the merchandise in the warehouse is shown in Figure 20-2*c*. When the item is ordered, four copies of the purchase order are placed on file in the warehouse by purchase order number. When a shipment arrives, purchase

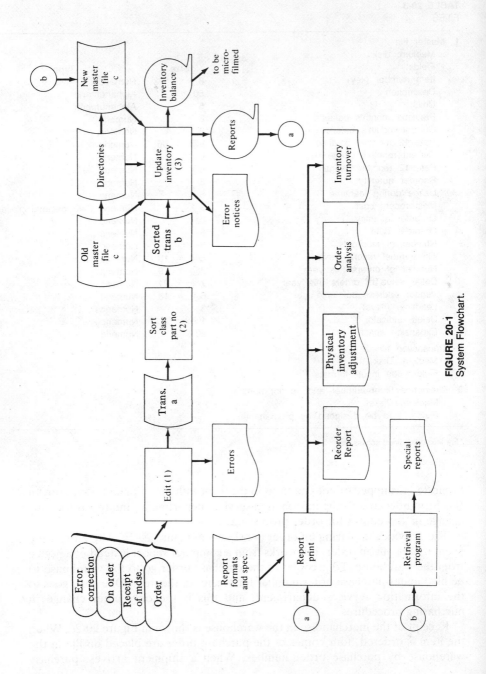

**FIGURE 20-1**
System Flowchart.

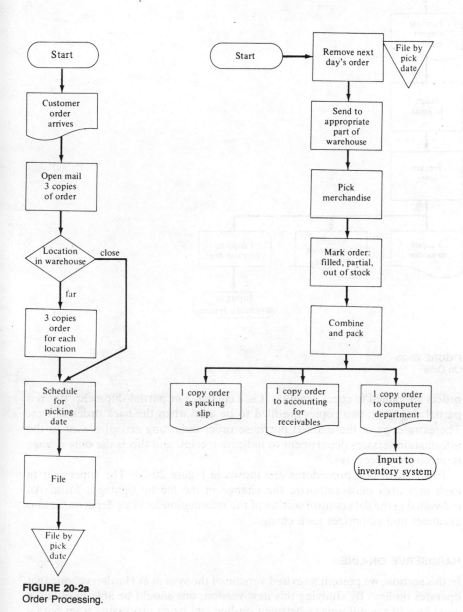

**FIGURE 20-2a**
Order Processing.

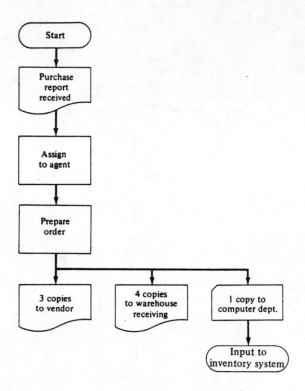

**FIGURE 20-2b**
On Order.

orders are pulled to check whether it is a complete or partial shipment. If it is a partial shipment, two copies are filed to be used when the back order arrives. The extra copy of the marked purchase order indicating arrival is sent to the information services department to indicate receipt, and this is the only change in receiving procedures.

Error correction procedures are shown in Figure 20-2*d*. The supervisor in each user area must authorize the change in the file by signing a form. An individual in the data control section of the information services department also examines and authorizes each change.

## HARDSERVE ON-LINE

In this section, we present a revised version of the system at Hardserve, one that operates on-line. By studying this new version, one should be able to obtain a good idea of the differences between on-line and batch processing from both a design and user standpoint. We think the conclusion perhaps will be that the

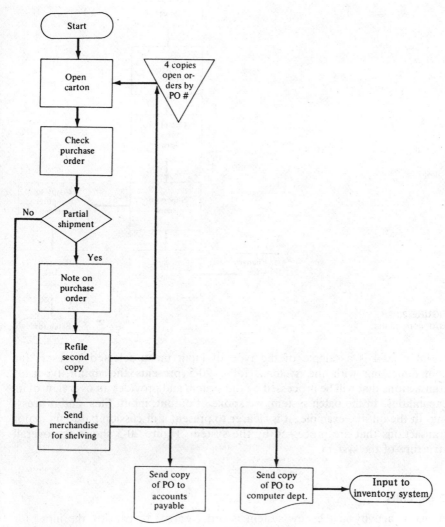

**FIGURE 20-2c**
Receipt of merchandise.

on-line version offers a substantially more pleasant user interface and processing environment at a cost of increased complexity.

The specifications that follow are preliminary; the on-line system will be changed as it is refined, and users begin to contribute more to its design. However, the specifications presented here show how an on-line system might appear, and they illustrate how radically it differs from the original batch processing version.

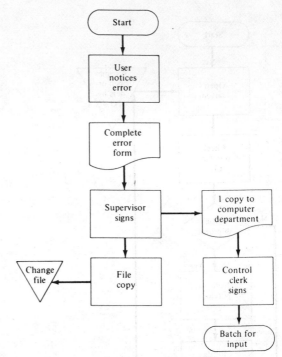

**FIGURE 20-2d**
Error corrections.

Table 20-4 is a sample of the type of input menu selected by users for communicating with the system. Table 20-5 presents the major types of transactions that will be processed by the system and provides an overview of its capabilities. In the batch system, we spoke of output, input, files, and processing. In the on-line example, it is clearer to present a discussion based on major transactions that are processed by the system. Figure 20-3 shows the overall structure of the system.

**Order Entry**

A major activity in the new system is order entry. To provide the input for processing and inventory control, we include a complete on-line order-entry capability. Table 20-6 contains the expanded data that must be keyed at the CRT as an order is being entered. To begin operations, the order-entry clerk would log on to the terminal. After entering his or her identification and password, the display shown in Table 20-4 would appear, asking for a selection of function from the menu. The clerk enters a 1, producing the screen shown in Figure 20-4. Table 20-6 shows the data that have to be entered, while Figure 20-4 is one possible screen layout for the CRT. Note that the system responds with the capital letters in the figure, and the operator fills in the blanks that are shown in italics.

The order-entry program leads the operator through each order. For example, the operator enters only the customer number. The system retrieves the

**TABLE 20-4**
SAMPLE MENU SELECTION

---

**Hardserve On-Line System**

---

DO YOU WISH TO:
1  ENTER ORDERS FROM CUSTOMERS
2  ENTER MERCHANDISE RECEIPTS
3  INDICATE AN ORDER HAS BEEN PLACED
4  INQUIRE
5  PRODUCE PICKING SLIPS
6  RECONCILE INVENTORY
7  CORRECT ERRORS, MODIFICATIONS
ENTER NUMBER OF FUNCTION DESIRED _4_

*(a)*

INQUIRY
1  INVENTORY ITEM
2  CUSTOMER ORDER (BY ORDER NUMBER, SHIP DATE DESIRED, CUSTOMER NUMBER, SEARCH-BY-DATE ORDER)
3  CUSTOMER
4  PURCHASE ORDER NUMBER
5  SHIPMENTS DUE IN
6  CUSTOMER NAME/NUMBER
7  VENDOR NAME/NUMBER
ENTER NUMBER ___

*(b)*

---

data on the name and address of the customer from the customer file, and then displays it. At this point, the operator should check that the address on the screen corresponds to the name and address on the order. If not, some type of escape facility would permit hitting a special key to renew the screen or backspacing over the customer number to erase it and retype the correct number. (The specific form of error recovery depends on the computer system and on the terminals being used. For all subsequent discussions, assume that it is possible to make these typing corrections when they are noticed by the operator.)

The operator continues to enter the items indicated. The computer program automatically performs the extensions and adds the total for the purchase order. The operator enters the total amount of the order, and the computer checks this total against its own total. If there is a discrepancy, the operator is asked to correct the order. If the order is acceptable, the operator so indicates, and a new screen is started for the next order. Another key is depressed to stop order entry.

Depending on the type of application, it might be desirable to compute a running total of all the orders entered and compare them with the total on a batch of orders obtained from an adding machine. In a very high volume operation, such an additional check might be in order to be certain that all orders are entered each day.

**TABLE 20-5**
PROCESSING LOGIC FOR MAJOR TRANSACTIONS

---

**1 Order entry from customer**
  a Key in customer number, and ship date using fill-in-blanks on formatted screen. System responds with name, address
  b For each item ordered, enter item number, vendor desired, price, and quantity. System responds with item description. See sample screen format

**2 Receipt of merchandise**
  a Display purchase order
  b Enter quantity received if different from purchase order in additional column next to ordered quantities

**3 Order placed**
  a Enter purchase order number and vendor number using fill-in-blanks on formatted screen. System responds with vendor name and address
  b Enter date due, route code, carrier, terms
  c For each item ordered, enter item number, quantity, description, price. System responds with item description
  d Key in total price of purchase order for check against system computed total

**4 Inquiry: retrieve requested data from appropriate file**
  a Inventory item: display inventory record
  b Customer order: display customer order status including customer's name, address from customer file. Option to retrieve by order number, ship date (all orders), customer number following order date
  c Customer: Display customer file record
  d Purchase order number: Display purchase order including vendor name, address from vendor file
  e Shipments due in: for date entered, display one screen at a time the purchase orders to be received on that date
  f Customer name: use first six consonants to retrieve Hardserve customer number
  g Vendor name: use first six consonants of vendor name to search directory for vendor name and display name, address, and Hardserve vendor number

**5 Produce picking slips**
  a Enter date due or customer order number for slips
  b Compare order to inventory, update inventory, modify order to show actual amount shipped

**6 Reconcile inventory**
  a Display requested customer orders
  b Enter deviations in shipping
  c Adjust inventory file, order file

---

## Receipt of Merchandise

The warehouse uses the system to check in merchandise that has been ordered. The Hardserve purchase order number should be included on the packing slip with the merchandise. From this number, the warehouse staff displays the

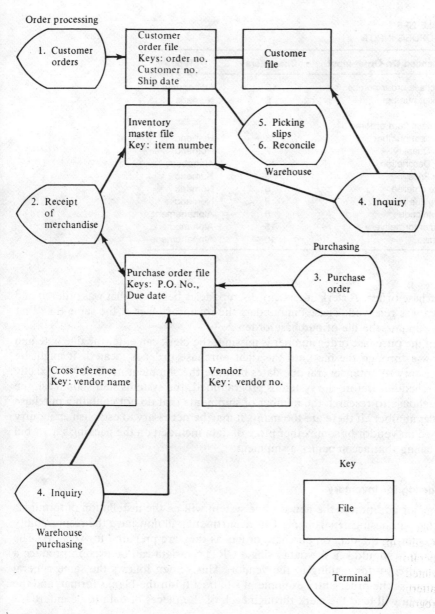

**FIGURE 20-3**
Hardserve on-line system overview.

**TABLE 20-6**
ON-ORDER INPUT

| Expanded On-Order Input | Characters | Type |
|---|---|---|
| Purchase order number | 10 | Alphanumeric |
| Vendor number | 6 | Numeric |
| | | |
| For each item ordered | | |
|     Item number | 8 | Numeric |
|     Quantity | 7 | Numeric |
|     Description | 40 | Alphabetic |
|     Price | 8 | Numeric |
| Date ordered | 6 | Numeric |
| Date due in | 6 | Numeric |
| Route code | 8 | Alphanumeric |
| Carrier for delivery | 15 | Alphanumeric |
| Terms | 10 | Alphanumeric |

purchase order. A clerk enters any discrepancies between what was ordered and what was received. These data update the inventory files at the same time that they update the file of purchase orders.[4]

If the purchase order number is missing, the clerk can enter the due date and browse through the file until the right purchase order is located. It might be necessary to enter several due dates because the shipment might not be exactly on schedule. Before the system is programmed, the systems staff should ask the warehouse to research the number of shipments that do not contain a purchase order number. If there are too many, it may be necessary to establish an inquiry based on vendor or some other piece of data included on the packing slip or bill of lading that accompanies a shipment.

### Ordering for Inventory

A major addition to the new on-line system will be the installation of terminals in the purchasing department. This department will now have the responsibility for entering the data on purchase orders as they are prepared for vendors. The operators should key the data using a CRT; the data can be used to produce a printed copy for mailing to the vendor. This screen follows the same general pattern as the order-entry example; it will be a fill-in-the-blanks format, and the program will lead the clerk through each of the pieces of data to be entered.

---

[4]The possibility of including a back-order capability is being evaluated. The design team is collecting data to determine how many back orders occur when Hardserve is out of stock, and whether goods would be received in sufficient time to fill the back order.

HARDSERVE ORDER ENTRY 4/15/81

CUSTOMER NUMBER *12345*          JONES HARDWARE
                                 75 MAIN STREET
                                 BOSTON, MASS. 02139

ORDER NUMBER  89654321          SHIP DATE 5/12/86 ACTUAL

| ITEM | DESCRIPTION | VENDOR | QUANTITY | · PRICE | EXTENSION |
|------|-------------|--------|----------|---------|-----------|
| *7777777* | SHOVEL | *672931* | *12* | 12.00 | 144.00 |
| *8888888* | HAMMER | *473612* | *24* | 5.00 | 120.00 |
|  |  |  |  |  | *264.00* |

(Computer generated messages in capital letters, User entry in italics.)

**FIGURE 20-4**
Draft customer order entry screen.

## Inquiries

One of the major advantages of an on-line system is the powerful inquiry facility it can provide. For Hardserve, there will be a number of inquiries for different groups in the firm.

**1** The warehouse and order-entry and purchasing functions will be interested in inventory balances; they need to be able to inquire on inventory-item number and obtain display of the pertinent data about the item.

**2** The system will be able to display a customer order; retrieval will be possible by order number, customer name with a link to each successive date (in case the customer phones and does not know the order number), and by ship date (primarily for the warehouse).

**3** The contents of the customer file record can be displayed.

**4** By entering the purchase order number, an operator obtains a display of the order.

**5** By entering a date, warehouse personnel can display (one at a time) the purchase orders with merchandise due on that certain date.

**6** By entering the customer's name, the system will retrieve customer names and numbers that match, based on the first six consonants of the name. The purpose of this facility is to locate a customer's number given only the customer's name.

**7** Vendor name: using the same approach as (6) above, an operator can obtain a vendor's number.

## Picking Slips

The warehouse can now call for picking slips as they are needed. The operator enters a due date or specific customer order numbers to obtain the picking slips. The system checks available inventory, produces the slip, decreases the quantity in inventory, and sorts and prints the list.

## Reconcilement

After the order has been picked, it is necessary to reconcile the picking slip with the order. Frequently, there is a discrepancy between physical inventory and book inventory. The system may suggest that something can be picked when, in fact, the item is out of stock. While filling the order, the picker crosses out the quantity ordered and writes in the quantity actually selected if there is a difference. These differences must be input to the system to maintain an accurate record of what has been shipped to the customer. At the same time, depending on company policy and control questions, the book inventory may be adjusted to reflect the stockout.

## Extensions

As with the batch example, we have tried to keep the on-line system relatively simple. A number of possible extensions would be fairly easy to implement; for example, we could provide for backordering when an item is out of stock. It would also be very easy to produce statements for customers based on the order file. However, the system sketched here provides a good basis for an on-line system for Hardserve.

## File Structures

Tables 20-7 and 20-8 contain the new and revised files for the on-line system. The first major addition is a customer order file that is also one of the most complex. There are trailer records for the actual items ordered since there will be a different number for each order. Trailers may be created through the provision of extra records between orders, with a chain to an overflow area or through a separate file of trailers that are chained to the order record and chained to each other.

This file has a directory on the Hardserve order number and another one on customer number. Since there may be several orders for the same customer, a date chain of pointers in the file connects each order for a given customer to the next most recent order. The directory to the customer points to the most recently placed order. There is also a directory and pointers on ship date for the warehouse. Figure 20-5 shows the file.

Another new file contains data on the customer. Since each order for a customer refers to the same basic information, it would be wasteful of input time

**TABLE 20-7**
HARDSERVE CUSTOMER ORDER FILE

| Customer order file (medium: disk) | | |
| --- | --- | --- |
| **Fields** | **Size** | **Type** |
| Order number | 8 | Numeric |
| Customer number | 8 | Numeric |
| Order date | 6 | Numeric |
| Order date pointer | 6 | Numeric |
| Ship date desired | 6 | Numeric |
| Ship date pointer | 6 | Numeric |
| Ship date actual | 6 | Numeric |
| **For each item ordered** | | |
| Item number | 8 | Numeric |
| Vendor desired | 6 | Numeric |
| Quantity | 7 | Numeric |
| Price | 8 | Numeric (2 decimal) |

Directory: Order number
        Customer number (note order date pointers within customer number)
        Ship date

and file space to key name, address, credit, terms, etc., for each order. Therefore we create one file, keyed on customer number, to contain all the constant information about the customer.

The next major file is the one containing purchase orders prepared by Hardserve. Like the order file, it uses trailer records to contain the data on each item included on the purchase order. The key for the file is purchase order number; also a directory and a linked list on the date the shipment is due serves to help the warehouse receiving area.

A vendor file—similar to the customer file—is needed to contain fixed information about the vendor. Because there is a frequent need to locate a vendor's number assigned by Hardserve (the vendor is unlikely to keep track of a number assigned to it by each of its customers), the system has a cross-reference file. Each time a vendor is added, this file is recreated by sorting the vendor name and number into alphabetical order, based on the name. A simple directory is constructed, based on the first six consonants of the vendor name to support inquiries to determine vendor number, given the name.

### Errors and Modifications

We have not talked about errors or modifications yet. From the discussion on the files, it should be clear that there will be a need to make changes as customer orders change, delivery dates are altered on merchandise due in, and for a

**TABLE 20-8**
OTHER NEW AND MODIFIED FILES

### Customer file (medium: disk)

| Fields | Size | Type |
|---|---|---|
| Customer number | 6 | Numeric |
| Customer name | 30 | Alphabetic |
| Customer address—line 1 | 25 | Alphabetic |
| Customer address—line 2 | 25 | Alphabetic |
| Customer address—line 3 | 25 | Alphanumeric |
| Customer address—line 4 | 25 | Alphanumeric |
| Credit rating | 4 | Alphabetic |
| Volume year-to-date | 6 | Numeric |

Directories: Customer number
First six consonants of customer name

### Purchase order file (medium: disk)

| Fields | Size | Type |
|---|---|---|
| Purchase order number (key) | 10 | Alphanumeric |
| Vendor number | 6 | Numeric |
| Date due in | 6 | Numeric |
| Due date pointer | 6 | Numeric |
| Date ordered | 6 | Numeric |
| Route code | 8 | Alphanumeric |
| Carrier for delivery | 15 | Alphanumeric |
| Terms | 10 | Alphanumeric |

### For each item ordered (trailer records)

| Fields | Size | Type |
|---|---|---|
| Item number | 8 | Numeric |
| Quantity | 7 | Numeric |
| Price | 8 | Numeric (2 decimal places) |
| Description | 40 | Alphabetic |

Directories: Purchase order number
Due date

### Vendor file (medium: disk)

| Fields | Size | Type |
|---|---|---|
| Vendor number | 6 | Numeric |
| Vendor name | 30 | Alphabetic |
| Vendor address line 1 | 25 | Alphabetic |
| Vendor address line 2 | 25 | Alphabetic |
| Vendor address line 3 | 25 | Alphanumeric |
| Vendor address line 4 | 25 | Alphanumeric |

Directory: Index sequential on vendor number

### Cross-reference file (created by sort of vendor file when new vendors added). (medium: disk)

| Fields | Size | Type |
|---|---|---|
| Vendor name | 30 | Alphabetic |
| Vendor number | 6 | Numeric |

Directory: First six consonants of vendor name

| Order no. | Customer no. | Order date | Ship date | Actual | Item Trailer Section |
|-----------|--------------|------------|-----------|--------|----------------------|
| 12345678 | 8765432 | 04 22 81 | 05 13 81 | | |
| 12345679 | 8888888 | 04 24 81 | 05 15 81 | | |
| 12345680 | 8765432 | 04 25 81 | 05 15 81 | | |
| 12345681 | 9999999 | 04 25 81 | 05 13 81 | | |

Notes:   Directory points to Customer number, then customer orders are linked by order date for customer (a link) above, ship date directory points to beginning of chain for each ship date (b links above)

**FIGURE 20-5**
Customer order file linkages (examples).

number of other reasons. These changes must be defined along with the impact on each file. A major effort will have to be devoted to this exercise because the system must be able to alter data that will change during the course of business.

## Summary

In this section we have presented a sketch of a possible on-line system for Hardserve. Comparing this system with the batch system should demonstrate the more pleasant user interface and higher levels of responsiveness of the on-line system. Now, users have instantaneous response to inquiries; much paperwork is eliminated. Errors in data entry are corrected as they are made, for the most part. The warehouse problem with merchandise due in from customers should be alleviated, and the work of the purchasing department should be simplified.

## AN ON-LINE ADMINISTRATIVE SYSTEM

International Business Machines Corporation (IBM) operates our next example of an information system. This on-line system performs many of the administrative functions of branch and regional offices and features CRT terminals. Because of the immense size and complexity of this system, we cannot present it in the same detail as the Hardserve example. However, in the remainder of this chapter we shall try to describe the system's functions and enough of its underlying technology to provide a notion of its capabilities. Much of the discussion comes from Wimbrow (1971), although this source has been updated through demonstrations and company material on the system.

### Background

IBM is a large manufacturer of business and computer equipment. Branch offices sell computer equipment, software, and education and maintain contact

---

## MANAGEMENT PROBLEM 20-2

Hardserve is developing a batch processing system for inventory control. Management has a number of good reasons for this decision, especially the desire to begin working with computers in a modest way. However, management feels that, at some point in the future, the on-line system described in this chapter will probably be justified but is unsure at what point on-line response becomes desirable.

They have asked for assistance in outlining the criteria that should be used to decide when to operate on-line. Management knows that a commitment to on-line processing will be costly and wants to be certain that there is an adequate return. Some of the important criteria in the decision to adopt on-line processing, they feel, are the volume of input and output and the need for instantaneous updating. However, management thinks there must be other factors to consider. They have asked your help to outline a decision framework for when to replace the new batch system with an on-line version.

---

with customers. Before the development of the Advanced Administrative System (AAS), IBM's order-entry system[5] was being strained by increasing sales volume and the increasing complexity of computer equipment that could be ordered by a customer.

For these reasons, AAS was initially developed to perform order entry and some 450 other logical transactions interactively. The order-entry process consists of the following steps:

1 The order is entered.
2 Validity checking takes place during entry.
3 The system assigns a delivery schedule.
4 Confirmation notices are sent to the branch office and to the customer.
5 Commission activity is generated.
6 Orders are forwarded to manufacturing.
7 Customer inventory records are created at the time of installation.
8 Billing activity is generated.

There are many opportunities for delay in this process. In the original system, before AAS, acknowledgments and delivery dates were transmitted through the mail. The validity check for an order was time-consuming when performed manually. A validity check is necessary because of the complexity of computer systems; each system usually involves a number of systems components that are interdependent. For example, certain peripherals and controllers can be used only on certain central processing units. A validity check is performed to ensure that all prerequisite devices are present on the original order and to be certain that all configurations ordered can be manufactured and operated. In the

---

[5]The reader should not be confused because the company in this example is a manufacturer of computer equipment. The system under discussion is an application of computers within the company.

original manual system, errors in orders resulted in a cyclical revision that delayed order processing further. These revisions also created inventory control and management difficulties in reconciling on-order backlogs and order totals at manufacturing plants.

Management and inventory control in the original system consisted of three files: (1) open orders, (2) installed inventory, and (3) uninstalled inventory (manufactured but not yet installed). The installed inventory file is the source of rental invoices sent to customers. The original system had difficulty coping with geographic mismatches between payment receiving centers and customer paying centers, which complicated the billing process.

All these problems were compounded in the mid-1960s when IBM planned the introduction of the 360 computer system, which dramatically increased the number of possible configurations for systems. Projections indicated that the complexity of the order-entry process and a growing volume of orders would seriously overload existing information processing procedures for order entry.

## Objective

By 1965, a study group recommended a new order system that would (1) operate interactively, that is, on-line; (2) connect branch offices, regional offices, plants, and headquarters, some 320 geographical locations requiring about 1500 terminals; and (3) operate in a conversational mode.

One important feature of the new system would be conversational, on-line interaction. A user provides one item of information at one point in time and in several minutes enters more data. The underlying computer system associates the information with each operator without exclusively dedicating itself to any one terminal. The approach is the same we observed with time-sharing and on-line systems in general. The on-line computer appears to the user as if it is maintaining a continuous and exclusive conversation with that user, although actually several hundred users are having "exclusive" conversations at the same time.

The system was originally designed to handle order-entry processing, inventory control, and accounts receivable. However, the design expanded to 16 application areas with 980 transactions, including order entry, delivery scheduling, territory assignment, payroll, commissions, publications, validation of computer group configurations, accounts receivable, customer master record, inventory of installed machines, billing, customer-student enrollment in IBM courses, and user training through computer-aided instruction (CAI).

The system has dramatically reduced the prior two to four week order-confirmation cycle. Four years after installation, IBM was processing 30 percent more transactions with 18 percent fewer people, a productivity gain of greater than 12 percent a year! The flexibility of the system is illustrated by the ability of the company to reorganize completely the assignment of clients to branch offices over a weekend.

## Special Features

One problem with a large-scale system is ensuring that only those with authorization are permitted to use it. Managers are authorized to have access, but they usually delegate this authority to operators. The manager registers employees who then receive security codes generated by the system. The manager and operator must be recognized by the system, and neither can perform functions for which they are not authorized.

The system gives the operator two attempts to enter a security code. An attempt to execute transactions for which the operator is not authorized or for which the operator is untrained brings a reminder on the first attempt from the system. If the operator makes a second attempt to enter an unauthorized transaction, or to log on with an error, or makes any other security error, the system locks the terminal. The terminal remains locked until an authorized security individual unlocks it.

The initial need to train over 5000 operators in branches throughout the country led to the inclusion of computer-aided instruction in the system. Classroom training would have been too expensive and time-consuming. Training courses are designed in a modular fashion for the overall system and for each different application. The system keeps track of operator progress and training, and an operator is not allowed to execute transactions for which he or she has not completed the appropriate CAI course.

## The System

The closest analogy to the type of system envisioned by the designers was SABRE, the first on-line airline reservation system. This second generation system was developed on a dedicated computer, using a specially coded supervisor in assembly language. Because of the progress between the second and third generations of computers in the development of operating systems, IBM utilized a more general-purpose operating system for the on-line AAS system.

Input/output devices for the system include more than 8000 terminals and low-speed printers in approximately 1300 branch office, plant, and headquarters locations. There are some 25,000 users of the system. Data are sent over medium-speed lines and concentrated by five distributed computers for transmission over high-speed lines to two central computer sites. Original system design parameters included a 5-second response to 95 percent of the input. Designers had estimated that it would be necessary to process 1.5 million inputs per 12-hour day, or an average of 50 inputs per second. By late 1980, the system was processing 1.3 million inputs per day with an average response time of five seconds.

The basic programming structure of this system is illustrated in Figure 20-6. There is an expanding number of applications, each having a group of transactions. For example, order entry consists of a number of transactions, such as

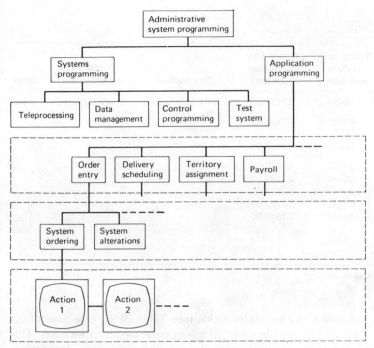

**FIGURE 20-6**
Organization of administrative system programming. *(From Wimbrow, J. H.: "A Large-Scale Interactive Administration System," 1971, courtesy IBM System Journal.)*

locating a customer record and entering a new equipment order. The lowest level consists of action programs that interact with the operator at the terminal. An example of an action program is one that lists available colors for a computer system. By 1977 there were about 10,000 applications programs in total.

The system stores action programs on secondary storage. The more heavily used programs are prefetched into main storage and remain there. Others are fetched as needed. Action programs are the applications programs; they provide all logical operations necessary to service the user at the terminal. Each message processor has a series of entry blocks that are used for entering messages from terminals, processing information, and transmitting responses back to terminals. There are fewer message and data blocks than terminals, so the system must process messages rapidly enough to prevent delays. The system assigns messages awaiting service to a queue in the teleprocessing monitor. (If the input queue becomes full, the teleprocessing monitor stops polling terminals, so the system runs out of time, but not space.) Enough capacity is provided for most actions to be processed in five seconds.

The database is structured hierarchically; an individual file will contain individual records and may also contain strings of records and groups of strings.

**TABLE 20-9**
INSTALLED MACHINE FILE

| Record key (serial number) | String key (system number) | Group key (customer number) | Description | Date of manufacture | Color |
|---|---|---|---|---|---|
| 1234 | A9421 | 27123.00 | 2401 tape unit | xx/xx/xx | Blue |
| 2345 | A9421 | 27123.00 | CPU card reader | | |
| 3456 | A9421 | 27123.00 | | | |
| 0112 | B0942 | 27123.00 | | | |
| 0479 | B0942 | 27123.00 | | | |
| 4823 | B0942 | 27123.00 | | | |
| 7894 | B0942 | 27123.00 | | | |
| 3168 | A9111 | 87941.00 | | | |
| . | . | . | | | |
| . | . | . | | | |
| . | . | . | | | |

Source: IBM Systems Journal.

A record is a series of logically related fields (see Table 20-9). One record, for example, is for a 2401 tape unit installed at a particular customer location. This record contains complete information about the unit, including description, manufacturing date, system number, serial number, color, and so forth. All fields in the record are stored contiguously in the database.

All records related to installed machines are stored in the same file, and the records in Table 20-9 constitute the installed machine file. The format and the length of the records vary widely by individual file. However, all records in a given file adhere to the same format and length. Each record has a unique key such as the serial number in Table 20-9.

Logically associated records in a file are called strings. The tape unit in Table 20-9 is associated with its control unit, CPU, and so forth, to make up a configured computer system. This system is identified by the system number (the string key in the table).

We also have associations among strings called groups. A group could be used to relate all systems (string keys) belonging to a specific customer (group key). In Table 20-9, a customer with group number 27123.00 has more than one system, each of which in turn consists of several machines. The file logic is illustrated in Figure 20-7.

Collections of identical types of records, which can possibly contain strings and groups, form files. The complete database has about 512 such files. A file may have up to three primary keys (record, string, and group) and seven secondary keys although it does not have to; for example, only two levels of association are found in the accounts-receivable file. Naturally directories connect keys to logical records in the file. Each key field has its own directory or

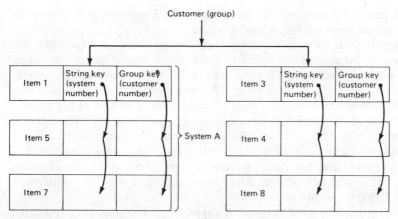

**FIGURE 20-7**
AAS file logic.

index file. For record keys there must be one entry in a directory for each record. String keys, however, take advantage of physical contiguity in the file, and pointers in the directory reference only the first record in a string. The system retrieves subsequent records in the string by reading sequentially.

The system places new data records in an overflow area allocated when the file is loaded, and modifies or creates directory records to reflect the addition. Periodically files are reorganized as retrieval time degrades because of the necessity to refer to overflow areas in the directory files. Reorganization consists of reading the old file, writing data in proper sequence in another location, and eliminating the original file. The system recreates directories to point to the new locations. The size of the database is more than 61 million data records and about 59 million directory records; there are approximately 12.2 billion characters of data in the system and over 1 billion characters of directories.

It is also necessary to provide for reconstructing the database in an on-line system in case of failure. The designers of the AAS system chose to minimize day-to-day backup costs and incur higher emergency reconstruction costs. The system also includes a trail to allow determination of what data were changed, by whom, and when. All changes to the database are journalized in the data file journal and appropriate cross-references are noted. Changes include additions, modifications, and deletions of records. The system creates journal records and logs them on to tape. This record consists of the new version of the record after a change, and the signature of the "requester" (application program name and user terminal location code).

Each record of the database has a control field to record a folio number for the last update. When a record is created, modified, or deleted, the system posts the number of the data-file journal tape currently being used by the system to the folio field in the record (each journal tape is sequentially numbered from the time the system became operational). The previous contents of the folio field associated with the record are also recorded on the journal to show where the previous journal entry for this record is located.

The journal fields forming the audit trails can also be used to recreate the files, although, because of the volume of activity, it would be impractical to begin from where the system first started. Therefore, periodically the system copies the data files to tape. Whenever a file is reorganized, the system creates an image tape containing an exact copy of the new file. The time of reorganization and the first folio number reflecting the reorganization are recorded. If files are damaged, the system processes journal tapes since the last reorganization to remove and compact records affected by the damaged file (compaction is used to eliminate duplicate updates, since only the most recent version of the record is needed). The system reloads the latest image tape and uses the transactions affecting the file to update it.

AAS is an extremely good example of a system that has grown over time; the application is almost twenty years old. Each year it is extended to include more features, and AAS becomes more vital to the operation of a firm. Given the cost of developing a system and the fact that users become dependent on vital transactions processing applications, we can expect to conduct systems analysis and design to both create new systems and to extend (without necessarily replacing) existing applications.

---

## MANAGEMENT PROBLEM 20-3

Astro Electronics is a major producer and retailer of electronic equipment, specializing in audio and television products. The firm sells to department and hi-fi stores throughout the United States. Regional offices and warehouses are in almost all major U.S. cities. Business has been expanding rapidly because of the increased level of affluence in general and the increasing consumption of audio and TV equipment by young adults.

The firm is designing a new sales information system to keep track of sales to retailers and to maintain information on the status of inventories. Because of the large amount of input and output and the need for recently updated information, the company decided to develop an on-line system.

Currently, Astro is organized on a regional basis for sales. However, management thinks that, at some time in the future, it may be necessary to organize both by region and by product line. For example, TV equipment might be handled separately from audio products.

Top management of Astro wants the design team for the new system to be sure that they do not constrain the firm's prerogatives by creating an inflexible system. They like the idea of distributed processing with regional micros. The computer department thinks the most likely problem area will be in the file structures of the new system. How can they design the files for a distributed system so that the company can easily reorganize its sales activities?

---

## SHELTERNET

First Boston Corporation offers a broad range of financial services to its customers. One of its divisions, First Boston Capital Group located in Tarrytown, New York, provides a line of credit to regional mortgage loan providers. As an example, suppose that two recent MBAs wish to purchase a house in Chicago. Needing a mortgage, the couple visits a local lending institution.

First Boston might provide the local lender with a line of credit to accept the application and commit funds. Then First Boston buys the mortgage loan from the local lender and sells the loan to so-called secondary market investors.

First Boston acts as a loan broker and helps to keep a healthy market going in secondary mortgages. Since this approach increases the total amount of funds available for mortgages, it helps home buyers and the real estate industry. How can computers facilitate this process and help First Boston gain market share?

The answer is a system based on personal computers called Shelternet. The typical subscriber to this service, of which there are about 200, is a local real estate brokerage firm that is or wants to become a mortgage provider. Shelternet links these mortgage providers with investors nationwide who are interested in loaning money for mortgages.

The typical mortgage loan application goes through a number of processing steps; it is a heavily regulated process and requires many pieces of paper. First Boston system speeds this process through microcomputers in the real estate office and a mainframe computer in New York which forms the central node of a computer-based network. Underwriters, closers, loan service personnel, and the secondary market investors described earlier can also connect to the network. It takes about half as long to complete and grant a mortgage (from application to letter of commitment) using Shelternet compared to previous, all manual processing.

First Boston developed the software to run on local personal computers; it is written almost entirely in BASIC. The micro that goes to the local lender has a variety of mortgage-origination tools to support the process of making a mortgage loan.

One set of programs is used first to enter the potential borrower's salary and financial information; the personal computer provides a profile, including the ceiling price for a house, of an affordable mortgage. Given the particulars on a specific house, e.g., the selling price, taxes, utilities, etc., the system can quickly calculate the total monthly payment at the going interest rate.

The network provides data on over 500 loan products available not just in the lender's region, but nationwide. The user chooses a product and the system begins the application procedure. If the credit report is satisfactory, the system sends a paper copy and an electronic copy of the application to an underwriter. This individual must be satisfied with the application before approving the loan. The underwriter puts a message on the system that he or she agrees to the loan.

The notice goes to the local lender and the personal computer generates a commitment letter and all closing instructions. During this entire process, all the documentation required by the federal government is generated on the micro-computer.

Basically, the personal computers in the local offices do most of the processing. They are all linked via 1200 baud modems (120 characters per second transmission) to the First Boston mainframe computer in New York; this central computer is a data collection and data storage device.

The mainframe is able to trigger a "wake up" device attached to each personal computer. At night, the mainframe instructs the microcomputer to transfer its data to the mainframe. Changes occurring that day, such as a new mortgage application or a change in status on an old application, are uploaded to the mainframe database. In a similar manner, anything that has happened to the mainframe databases during the day which might be important for the broker's region is downloaded to the personal computer. As an example, a new loan product or changes in any of the text files used to print out forms and letters would be downloaded to the personal computers.

In this manner at the start of business in the morning the local personal computers have current information on the operational status of applications and the availability of all current loan products. The First Boston mainframe begins the day with an updated status of all current mortgage applications.

Since the installation of a networked personal computer was new to many real estate brokers, First Boston has established a careful training program. Its sales staff briefly explains the system and invites potential customers to a two-day seminar on Shelternet and on becoming a mortgage-offering broker. If the customer decides to join, there is an intensive five-day training session for staff members to learn the process of handling a mortgage loan and the operation of Shelternet.

Shelternet is an excellent example of distributed processing, the power of a local microcomputer, and networking. Surely the same system could be offered on time sharing, but a micro in the office provides a great deal of flexibility. The broker substitutes a one-time purchase for hardware and software for the ongoing operating costs of time sharing. Also, if one personal computer malfunctions, only that broker is affected, not everyone on the network. If the mainframe is unavailable, the only cost is information that is slightly more out of date.

Also, the user interface with the local micro is probably a great deal more attractive than one for a centralized on-line system. Users feel in control of the processing and they are free to add other programs to the personal computer for tasks not covered by Shelternet. The system can also be used as a terminal to connect to other networks, such as one that might contain data on real estate listings and sales in the local area.

The technology provides many options; all that is required is creativity on the part of designers and users. We can have centralized, decentralized, and distributed processing. The challenge is to determine which style is best for a given application. See *PC Week,* May 29, 1984.

## ELECTRONIC MAIL

Digital Equipment Corporation (DEC) is a multinational manufacturer of computers and electronic equipment. Today the company has over 6000 active subscribers to an electronic mail system (EMS) which is used internally, not by customers.

Frequently telephone calls are incomplete because the party being called is not at his or her phone or there is a busy signal. Telephones also interrupt the individual receiving the call when often an immediate response is not needed.

The electronic mail system at DEC uses a series of computers to store and forward messages. Each subscriber has a computer account and an electronic mailbox, a file to which the mail program can write messages. Individuals are addressed by name. Users work with terminals to enter and read messages. (See the discussion of electronic mail in Chapter 4.)

The mail file is more than a repository of messages, however; it serves as an electronic filing cabinet. The user can write and edit a message, read and answer mail, forward it, file mail, and create distribution lists so that the user can send a message to several individuals by typing the name of the group. This addressing feature is very useful for project teams or for managers who wish to communicate with the staff reporting to them on a regular basis. There are also reminder or tickler files, and a user can keep a calendar on the system.

DEC has found that 63 percent of the users are managers, 23 percent individual contributors, and 14 percent secretaries. Some 62 percent of the users interact with the terminal while the remainder rely on a secretary or administrative aid to provide their messages in hard copy and enter input messages to the system.

DEC developed the system with a great deal of care. First, an experiment was conducted as a pilot project. About 40 subscribers began to use the system on a single computer node; additional users were brought into the system from various international locations to test the capacity and performance of the system. The pilot lasted almost 18 months and involved users from a broad range of positions and functions within the firm.

In general the users were happy with the speed and effectiveness of nonsimultaneous communications. The system was rated as highly effective for broadcasting information, assigning and following up on task assignments, and answering short questions. There was more timely information exchange, and the distribution of information to multiple addressees in many locations was simplified. A majority of the users felt that their personal productivity had been increased by 5 to 15 percent. The only cautionary finding was that the system appeared to reduce the amount of face-to-face contact among users.

An electronic mail system is generally not advocated for cost saving reasons; proponents claim that the benefits described above should justify the system. At DEC, the economic analysis showed that the break-even on electronic mail versus traditional methods was one additional phone call or one additional copy of a message. "For any additional copies or addresses beyond the second, EMS is significantly less costly than either the interoffice memo or the telephone call, even if the manager relied on an administrative support person to do EMS work." The costs savings do not totally pay for the system; the major justifications for it are the features of the system and improvements in productivity.

The best evaluation came from the President of DEC: "We are so used to electronic mail, and we have become so dependent upon it, that I have forgotten what life was like without it. Being able to immediately send and receive messages to approximately 6000 stations around the world is so efficient that we now can't conceive of life without electronic mail" (Crawford, 1982).

## SUMMARY

In this chapter we have reviewed in some detail systems for transactions processing, operational-control decision making, and office automation. (The AAS system is also used for managerial control purposes.) Each of these systems has inputs, files, processing, and output. The hypothetical Hardserve example is very simple and was presented in detail in both a batch and an on-line version. The AAS system is extremely complex and demonstrates some of the advantages of on-line interaction in a high-volume transactional system: there was a need to coordinate geographically decentralized activities on-line. Another major advantage of this on-line system is its ability to collect data at its source and to make immediate corrections interactively. Shelternet's microcomputers provide great flexibility in designing systems, while DEC's electronic mail system is a powerful communications tool in the organization. In the next chapter we turn to more decision-oriented information systems to illustrate further different types of applications.

## KEY WORDS

Action program
Audit trail
Computer-aided instruction (CAI)
Concentrator
Criteria
Directories
Electronic mail

Entry blocks
Economic order quantity
Feasibility study
Groups
Manual procedures
Message processing
Office automation

Packages
Preliminary survey
Records
Steering committees
Strings
Telecommunications monitor

## RECOMMENDED READINGS

Crawford, A. B.: "Corporate Electronic Mail—A Communication-Intensive Application of Information Technology," *MIS Quarterly,* vol. 16, no. 3, September 1982, pp. 1–13. (A good example of electronic mail.)

Lucas, H. C., Jr.: *The Analysis, Design, and Implementation of Information Systems,* 3d ed., McGraw-Hill, New York, 1985. (See this reference for complete details on the Hardserve system.)

Wimbrow, J. H.: "A Large Scale Interactive Administrative System," *IBM Systems Journal,* vol. 10, no. 4, 1971, pp. 260–282. (An article containing details and a description of the early IBM AAS system).

## DISCUSSION QUESTIONS

1 How would you classify the Hardserve system? What decisions are supported in each department?

2 Where should the greatest savings come from using the new system at Hardserve?

3 Develop a procedure for taking physical inventory at Hardserve. How do you enter physical inventory information into the system accurately, given the lead time between counting the items in the bin and updating the computer system?

4 How would you identify each of the different input cards and number the transactions for Hardserve?

5 How can a request for information on how much business has been done with each vendor be satisfied without using a chained direct-access file in the Hardserve example?

6 Why are so many existing forms continued in the new Hardserve system?

7 What extensions of the Hardserve system do you recommend for accounting, warehousing, and purchasing areas?

8 Is there any way to eliminate manual files of purchase orders in the warehouse and receiving station at Hardserve?

9 If the Hardserve system is placed on-line at some time, what kind of inquiries would you expect from each department? Design the files and directories to answer these questions.

10 Besides the files and directories, what other major changes will be needed to develop an on-line version of the Hardserve system?

11 Where do you anticipate the greatest behavioral problems in implementing a new system at Hardserve?

12 What conversion steps will be necessary before the new Hardserve system can begin operating?

13 Design a training program for the users of the Hardserve system.

14 What role should the members of the Hardserve steering committee play during the implementation?

15 Does it make sense for Hardserve to begin planning other applications now? Why or why not?

16 How does extensive user involvement in design prepare Hardserve for the implementation and operation of a system?

17 Why are such stringent authorization procedures necessary in a system like AAS?

18 Is a backup processor often required in on-line systems?

19 What is the purpose of a concentrator in the AAS system?

20 Why is a printer also used at branch offices in the AAS system along with CRTs?

21 Would transferring accounts among branch offices be difficult or easy in the AAS system? How would such a change be accomplished?

22 Compare and contrast AAS with an on-line airline reservation system.

23 Could a system like AAS be developed using packaged programs, for example, for telecommunications and database management? If so, why were such packages not used?

24 Why is CAI successful in training people for the use of AAS? How does this training differ, say, from training students in high school or college?

25 How can a company like Hardserve afford on-line systems? What advances in technology make this option a possibility for small firms?

26 What kinds of inquiries do you think customers would make of AAS? Are the record keys and directories sufficient to answer these requests?

27 Are there manual procedures in the AAS system? What controls do you recommend over orders and order-entry processing?

28 How could AAS backup procedures be modified to reduce the cost of recovering from damaged files? What added costs would your solution incur?

29 Why is an audit trail needed in an on-line system? What is its equivalent in a batch system, specifically in the Hardserve example?

30 How is the Hardserve system backed up in case of failure?

31 How would you estimate requirements for on-line systems equipment? What data would you collect?

32 How is conversion to an on-line system different than that for a batch system?

33 What is the purpose of the preliminary survey and feasibility studies?

34 What are the advantages from the user's standpoint of on-line systems for data entry and retrieval; what are the drawbacks?

35 Would you predict that the systems described in this chapter would upgrade or downgrade the skills required of clerical users?

36 What management information could be developed from each of the systems discussed in this chapter?

37 How does electronic mail differ from the other applications in this chapter?

38 What impact does electronic mail have on the organization?

39 What is the advantage of a local PC in Shelternet?

# DECISION SUPPORT SYSTEMS

# DECISION SUPPORT
# SYSTEMS

## CHAPTER ISSUES

- Can this organization develop and does it have a use for decision
  support systems?
- What is the proper level of sophistication and information processing
  for this organization?

In this chapter we discuss four systems that are markedly different from those in the last chapter. The first "system" is really a collection of evolving tools to support marketing decisions. The second system was developed as a research project but was soon converted into a proprietary product for commercial purposes. Various banks in the United States are currently installing revised versions of this system. The third system was recently developed to assist planning in a bank holding company, while the fourth supports an important scheduling and routing problem. All these systems exhibit the strong user-orientation required of a decision support system.

## CONNOISSEUR FOODS

Connoisseur Foods is a large, multidivisional food company whose management decided in 1969 to encourage the development of computer models and systems (Alter, 1980). As business grew, Connoisseur Foods split into separate divisions for beverages and farm products (canned goods). Later a division for frozen foods was created, and more recently, the firm has diversified into the toiletries market; they have also acquired a number of subsidiaries. Approximately three to ten major brands are in each division along with a number of minor brands and products in the prototype stage. A brand manager is generally in charge of one or two major brands or a number of minor brands. There is a marketing, production, and distribution department in each division cutting across the brand-manager structure.

The divisions enjoy different histories and personnel with different management styles. The Farm Products Division is considered to be "old line" with managers who have worked their way up through the company ranks. These managers tend to rely on their lengthy experience in the market when making major decisions. In this division, brand managers have the responsibility for many aspects of brand administration, but their superiors generally make strategic decisions and advertising allocations. The Frozen Foods Division is a study in contrasts; it has younger personnel and tends to be somewhat more aggressive and more quantitatively oriented. The division has more clearly defined lines of responsibility, and its brand managers have a greater range of decision-making responsibility.

In 1969 Connoisseur Foods and a consulting company, Business Software Corporation (BSC), began to work together. The effort began with a series of seminars at Connoisseur Foods to prepare management for some of the opportunities available from computer-based systems. During a five-year period, slow progress was made. During this period certain support tools have played an important role in some decision making, a role that is expected to expand in the future.

### Aggregate Market Response Models

Connoisseur Foods applies aggregate market response models to products where there is a reasonable database reflecting sales experience. These models are used to aid decisions about advertising, pricing, promotion, etc., and then to help monitor those decisions.

To develop a model, the decision maker has to establish reference conditions. Definitions usually come from sales and marketing activities during the recent past. One purpose of future sales and marketing decisions is to create some change in market conditions relative to the reference period. The impact of marketing decisions can be expressed by response functions.

A response multiplier curve such as the one shown in Figure 21-1 indicates that an advertising level at point $a$ will produce sales equal to .7 times the sales in the reference period. Frequently these response curves are "s-shaped" with both upper and lower limits. A curve of this shape expresses a belief that, past a certain point, additional expenditures for advertising will have no further short run impact on sales.

A model builder develops a response multiplier curve for each controllable variable so that each decision variable is a basis for estimating the impact of any given marketing plan. If a marketing plan for a product includes advertising,

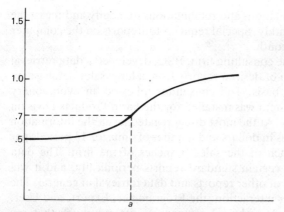

**FIGURE 21-1**
Response multiplier curve.

promotion, and prices that have multipliers from their three response curves of 1.1, .95, and 1.15, the estimated sales of the product would be 1.1 × .95 × 1.15 of the sales during the reference period.

The model building team also is likely to develop curves that reflect seasonality and sales trends. Sometimes the response curves for competitive products are incorporated into the analysis to determine their impact on the sales of Connoisseur Foods. In developing the curves, hard data on historical sales are combined with intuition and judgment.

As described above, the market response model for a product can be used to estimate the effect of various mixes of promotional activity. Such an explicit mathematical model forces the user to segment the problems into a number of smaller, more manageable parts. One's best judgment can be brought to bear without worrying at first about the interaction of the parts. Instead of relying on only one or two key variables, the decision maker can consider more effects and their interactions.

At Connoisseur Foods the models are executed interactively through a computer terminal. The analyst enters a marketing plan and the computer program prints a forecast of the results. The analyst can then evaluate variations on the plan until a satisfactory one is complete. The models are generally developed by a team, and they can be time-consuming and stressful to create. Generally one starts with a few main factors such as seasonality, sales trends, advertising, and promotions. The model can be made more sophisticated later.

**Data Retrieval**

At Connoisseur Foods, the original seminars conducted by the consultant showed that the computer-based marketing support was rather poor. Clerks performed hours of hand calculations and retabulations to modify and recast the basic sales reports printed monthly. Special requests for reports on the computer involved delays of almost a month.

To improve this situation the consulting firm, BSC, developed a data retrieval system to allow the generation of desired reports from a large sales database on a routine and on an ad hoc basis. The consultant followed an evolutionary approach; an experimental system was installed for the Farm Products Division with a plan for later expansion. At the most disaggregated level, the information in the database consists of sales in dollars and number of units for 13 periods per year for all item codes at each of the sales branches of the firm. The data retrieval system will produce certain standard reports periodically, and it will support the ad hoc generation of other reports and data retrieval in general. The system has three levels of user interaction: the Programmer, Expert, and User. The Programmer mode reveals technical features of the computer that are invisible to simpler levels. Expert mode is for the manager or analyst who wants more flexibility than the User mode; these individuals must be willing to spend more time and effort learning how to specify desired reports.

The simplest level is the User mode. Here the user initiates a report specification simply by naming the type of report needed. The system prompts with a series of questions that leads the user through the logical specification of the report. In this mode, the user only needs to know the type of report desired and the data to be included. The system assumes the responsibility for ensuring the logical completeness of the specification and for finding the data and producing the report.

The following reports can be requested in User mode:

**1 Display**   Sales of a product or product class in a given branch or region during a given period

**2 Compare**   Compare data such as the sales for a period versus sales during the same period last year; compare sales for one region versus sales for other regions

**3 Variance reports**   Forecasted versus actual sales by forecasting units

**4 Sorted listings**   Products listed in order of percentage gains or losses compared to last year

**5 Exception listing**   All products more than 15 percent below last year's sales

**6 Area test**   Evaluation of the impact of a promotional activity

Because of the size of the database for the Farm Products Division, dollar and unit sales for 400 items across 300 sales branches for 13 periods, the database will be maintained permanently on a tape. The most recent data of this 20 to 40 million number database will be on disk. A user will specify the data desired and if it is available on-line, the report will be produced immediately. If the data are on tape, the system will store the request, which will be processed by a data extraction program run during the night. The next day the data will be available to the user on a disk.

## Use of the System

The aggregate response models have been used primarily for planning and tracking; they generate estimates of sales and profits for different promotional plans for a brand. The models are also used to monitor and evaluate brand performance and the effectiveness of a marketing strategy. One of the reasons for the eventual acceptance of several brand models was their high accuracy, which is within 3 percent of actual sales. The level of use of a model is highly dependent on the brand manager and how much he or she likes to work with models.

One manager thought that the main impact of modeling efforts in the Farm Products Division was to help learn more about the business. The firm now understands more about how their most important product works in the marketplace. There were some disagreements about whether the models have had an important impact on decisions to date. There seems to be good support from top management for modeling, but less at the middle management level. For expanded use of the models by brand managers, management probably would have to give more support.

The data retrieval system, after about a year of use, requires the assistance of technical intermediaries. A brand manager decides that a report is needed and discusses it with the representative in the information services department. The firm wants to eliminate the intermediary and to adopt a mode of operation where the manager will type a request at a terminal to find out if the data are available on the disk. Assistance will be needed only for exceptional conditions rather than constantly, as it is now. It is hoped that within one year, four or five brand managers will use the system regularly without needing help from the computer staff.

There have been a number of implementation problems with the various tools. Some brand managers reason intuitively and do not like quantitative models. Top management thinks that the analytic techniques are new and that it will take time for the staff to become comfortable with them. Some of the brand managers have embraced the models, and the models are having a definite impact on the way they think about their markets. The managers report a more explicit understanding of the market process. For more details of the Connoisseur Foods decision support system, see Alter (1980).

## A PORTFOLIO SYSTEM

### Background

The system described in this section was developed as a research project and is documented in a paper by Gerrity (1971). The system has been expanded and converted into a commercial product, and more recent information for our description was developed from a study of the system. The prototype version of this portfolio management system was developed for a pension-fund management section of a major bank. The trust officer manages assets for a trust, buying

## MANAGEMENT PROBLEM 21-1

Sheila Renati joined Kaufman Brothers, an investment banking firm, after obtaining an M.B.A. from a leading business school. Sheila majored in finance and minored in information systems. At Kaufman she has enjoyed working on a number of different projects. Her most recent challenge is the design of a small decision support system for a group of managers working on client mergers and acquisitions.

This system works on a microcomputer and provides many different analyses for the managers involved. It is particularly useful in making the projections necessary to analyze a merger between two large firms. The managers remarked that the computer had allowed them to save significant amounts of time and explore many different possibilities for mergers and acquisitions. As a result, they were serving clients better and had more time to handle additional business.

Sheila worked very closely with the three key managers in the department and the system reflected their approach to decisions. She used a spreadsheet program and tailored it to the manager's problems.

A recent reorganization has resulted in one of the three key managers moving to another department; a new member of the firm has taken his place. The new merger and acquisition team is worried because its newest member has many ideas for changing the computer system. They are surprised, however, when Sheila states that she expects to make changes and that the modifications will not be too costly. What makes it possible for Sheila to respond in this manner?

---

and selling securities to maximize the objectives of the trust, such as growth in capital and maximum return. The bank receives a management fee for its efforts.

Under the conditions existing before the system was developed, managers of the portfolio had three main sources of information: (1) portfolio-related information showing the holding structure of each portfolio, (2) security-related information of historical and predictive variables for alternative investments, and (3) security prices.

The accounting group provided the portfolio information, and security data came from investment research groups. Newspapers furnished security prices. Managers received only fully priced portfolio status reports monthly from the accounting group.

The available information was fragmented and focused on individual security holdings rather than total portfolio status. Management tended to define problems in terms of single security holdings, although from a normative view, overall portfolio structure is what determines performance.

The manager's activities were carefully analyzed through observation and the administration of psychological tests. A number of problems with the current system were discovered in addition to those above.

**1** The prices on status reports were often out of date and had to be updated manually.

**2** Data were fragmented into two files, one on portfolio holdings and the other on stock history and performance data. The managers needed to see the research information juxtaposed with the account information.

**3** There was a lack of an aggregate measure of portfolio status and structure that would enable a manager to look at the distribution of the portfolio on a single dimension or to compare two variables.

**4** There was a lack of formal mechanism to compare portfolio status with goals.

**5** There were rigid report formats; for example, the holdings were listed only by industry groups. It was not possible to obtain a listing of portfolio contents, say, in order by earnings per share.

**6** Managers tended to search locally for stock buy and sell candidates. They rarely considered the entire list of 350 approved stocks for investment because of the effort involved in searching the list for stocks with certain criteria, for example, a price/earnings ratio less than 20.

**7** There was no method to consider alternatives, that is, to develop and monitor a hypothetical portfolio.

**8** In general, information sources exhibited a slow response.

### A New System

The designers tried to solve some of the problems above by providing an interactive decision system with a graphics CRT. The original system operated on an existing time-sharing computer, although present versions run as a part of a standard operating system capable of supporting mixed batch and on-line systems. Most potential users can operate this system on their own internal computer.

One version of the system currently in use has the following functions:

**1 Directory** This function provides a tabular overview of all accounts under the manager's jurisdiction. The table generated can be sorted on a number of fields, such as account identifier, market value, or fixed income performance. The manager can compare whole portfolios in a number of different ways in addition to simply listing the ones under the manager's jurisdiction.

**2 Scan** This operator allows the user to view the holdings of a particular security across a group of accounts. The manager selects the security, a sort key, and other information; a report is produced that includes the units of the security held for each account and certain data on that security, such as the percentage of the account devoted to the security.

**3 Groups** This operator produces a picture of the distribution of the holdings of an account by broad industry groups, such as consumer, petrochemical, and so forth. The display is a graphic histogram.

**4 Table** This function provides a way for the managers to design their own reports for reviewing the holdings of an account. The user types the account name and a list of the data items desired for each holding, and a report containing this information appears on the screen.

**5 Histogram**  The histogram operator allows the manager to view the distribution of any available data item for all the holdings of an account; for example, the user might want a histogram of the total market value of accounts.

**6 Scatter**  The scatter operator provides the manager with the capability of viewing the relationship between two data items associated with the securities in an account. An example of such a plot is the relationship of current price/earnings ratio against 10-year average price/earnings ratios for the holdings in the account.

**7 Summary**  The summary function displays various account summary data such as holdings, type of account, and account description.

**8 Issue**  The issue operator displays all the information pertaining to a specified issue on the list of issues approved by the bank for investment. Examples of such information include price/earnings ratio, historical price/earnings ratios, and dividends.

It is interesting to note that the designers did not take a fully normative approach. The theories of normative portfolio construction and the "efficient market hypothesis" are not included in the system. Instead, a true decision support system was developed so that the managers could use information in a manner consistent with their own decision styles.

**Results**

A monitor in the experimental version of the system showed that managers made heavy use of the graphics commands and switched back and forth among portfolios. Sessions tended to be lengthy and to generate a number of reports. Almost all the functions were used; there was no concentration on one function, for example, obtaining the status of the portfolio. Later studies of the system in full-scale operation found that the number of sessions dropped, as did the number of reports produced per session.[1] There tended to be much more of a focus on a single function by each user.

The designers of the original system felt it would provide the tools necessary for managers to change their approach to decision making. They could now focus on a single portfolio; they were not forced to look only at a single stock. The follow-up research indicated that this type of change did not occur. However, from our discussion of change and model of information systems in the organization, these results are not too surprising. The system could be used to support existing security-by-security approaches to decision making. There is no reason why a normative portfolio-centered approach should necessarily be adopted unless the individual decision maker feels that it is best. Did the managers all desire to adopt a more portfolio-centered view, or were they basically content with their current decision process?

We have said that organizational change should not be implemented through

---

[1]Charles Stabell, discussion at MIT Conference on Implementation, April 1975.

## MANAGEMENT PROBLEM 21-2

Jim Gilmore is executive vice president of Precious Metals, a firm that buys and processes rare metals such as gold and silver. Recent price fluctuations on the world market have created many problems for Precious Metals and Jim has tried to find some way to predict price changes.

He knew that some firms had been successful building computer models of various economic markets. With this in mind, he hired Management Models, a consulting firm, to investigate the possibility of building models for each of the commodities purchased by Precious Metals. The company and industry have very good data on historical prices and other economic indicators.

The modeling effort proceeded very smoothly. The resulting model produced valid results when confronted with the rapid price fluctuations of recent years. Management Models indicated that short-range forecasts should be very good, but the model should not be trusted for extrapolations past one year.

Jim Gilmore now wondered how to integrate the model into purchasing decisions. For a long time, the brokers at Precious Metals had based their decisions on intuition and experience with the market in making purchases. The new model was available on a time-sharing computer system and Gilmore wanted the brokers to use it. However, he felt sure that none of them would take advantage of it if just told that it existed. Jim wondered how to gain acceptance of this new tool.

---

information systems. Organizational and behavioral changes should be made, and then a system to support the new style can be developed. It appears in this case that the new system could be used to improve existing decision approaches or to change one's approach to decision making. Apparently there was no pressing need felt by the decision makers to change their approach, so they used the system to support existing patterns of decision making.

## A PLANNING SYSTEM

We have discussed the importance of strategic planning for a corporation. In the system discussed here, a major bank holding company known as DIB (a pseudonym), developed a pair of computer-based systems to support its planning activities. (Doyle et al., 1983).

### Background

The DIB holding company includes fifteen plus member banks located in one state along with a trust operation. In the 1970s, the company followed several strategies:

1 Acquire affiliate banks in its state
2 Expand consumer business through personal bankers, automated teller machines, and promotions

**3** Expand commercial and industrial accounts particularly by offering cash management services
**4** Expand banking operations with its over 1000 correspondent banks
**5** Expand international operations to two foreign offices
**6** Enter the agricultural lending business
**7** Open a loan office outside of the bank's major area

Bank management realized that they would need new strategies for the 1980s and beyond, and began a long-term strategic planning study. There are four objectives to the planning process:

**1** Create a strong regional image by increasing presence in certain regional markets
**2** Establish separate planning units for each market
**3** Have each unit of DIB define its own plans in the context of the overall corporate strategy
**4** Change the name of all components to a common name to build recognition among customers

## REBIS

The planners saw that detailed planning would require tremendous amounts of data and computer processing. The organization utilized two external sources for databases as a part of its planning process. These were the Federal Reserve Bank/Federal Deposit Insurance Corporation Report of Condition and Report of Income and Dividends, and the Dun and Bradstreet Commercial and Industrial Statistics database.

The federal databases contain over 500 financial variables for every insured bank in the United States, about 14,000 in total. Some 8000 of these banks are located in the region of the study. With five years of data being used, the database was about one billion characters. The D & B database consists of demographic and industrial classifications for 25,000 companies with over $10 million in revenues.

The bank believed that interstate banking would soon be permitted, and adopted a regional approach to planning. The Regional Banking Information System (REBIS) was developed to help analyze the position of DIB compared to its potential competitor banks in its target region.

After careful study, eight performance indicators were chosen for analysis in the REBIS reporting system. Data were selected over time to compute various growth statistics. This data analysis system is used to analyze competitive activity in the region and evaluate future strategies.

Reports were provided to rank banks in defined areas by size, holding company, and return on assets. See Figure 21-2. The reports showed the banks' equity, assets, net profits, return, and loans over a five-year period, along with annualized growth. The reports are used by senior management and are also furnished to individual calling officers to evaluate competition in their regions.

Regional Banking Information System

REBIS11H
05/07/82

Holding company #  Fed. Res. Dist.  SMSA  County #(FIPS code)

**1st NB Of Kaanapali**

Kaanapali, IA
0016  09  5120  053

Cert No: 05199
Bank ID: 09274037

| | As Of — 12/31/81 ($000) | 1977 Balance ($000) | Annual Change 77-78 (%) | 1978 Balance ($000) | Annual Change 78-79 (%) | 1979 Balance ($000) | Annual Change 79-80 (%) | 1980 Balance ($000) | Annual Change 80-81 (%) | 1981 Balance ($000) | Annualized Average Growth (%) |
|---|---|---|---|---|---|---|---|---|---|---|---|
| Equity Capital (1) | 213,949 | 143,802 | 7.0 | 153,937 | 9.9 | 169,198 | 10.0 | 186,060 | 10.0 | 204,628 | 9.2 |
| Total Assets (1) | 4,612,549 | 2,012,787 | 17.6 | 2,367,586 | 23.8 | 2,930,230 | 18.5 | 3,470,994 | 18.8 | 4,124,725 | 19.7 |
| Leverage (TA/EC) | 22 | 14 | | 15 | | 17 | | 19 | | 20 | |
| Net Profits | 32,609 | 17,331 | 28.1 | 22,208 | 13.3 | 25,157 | 12.6 | 28,332 | 15.1 | 32,609 | 17.3 |
| Return On Assets (%*100) | 71 | 86 | | 93 | | 85 | | 81 | | 79 | |
| Comm. and Indust. Loans (1) | 1,342,653 | 475,614 | 18.1 | 561,765 | 28.5 | 721,655 | 17.9 | 851,184 | 32.6 | 1,128,445 | 24.3 |
| Loan Loss Ratio (2:%*100) | 43 | 80 | | 6 | | 5 | | 49 | | 43 | |
| Bankers Accepts (1) (3) | 300,077 | 26,498 | 40.9 | 37,346 | 176.8 | 103,362 | 76.9 | 182,872 | 31.7 | 240,821 | 81.6 |

(1) 5 Qtrly. Average for each yr., e.g. (74Q4 + 75Q1 + 75Q2 + 75Q3 + 75Q4) / 5
(2) Net loan charge-offs/total loans
(3) Not reported for banks with total assets less than $100 million after December 1978

**FIGURE 21-2**
Sample Regional Banking Information System (REBIS) Report. (REBIS IIH) (*Courtesy* MIS Quarterly, *September 1983.*)

## The SAS/D & B System

Similar to REBIS, this data-oriented DSS was designed to identify firms with which DIB would be attempting to establish a business relationship. Senior management's analysis of these data suggested a strategy in which new marketing efforts should be directed toward middle-sized companies.

Using the D & B data, the bank identified 20,000 businesses in the region that fell into this middle category of from $5 million to $200 million in annual sales. In order to present this large volume of information, the SAS/D & B system uses map displays. See Figure 21-3. The Statistical Analysis System constructs statistical databases and plots the data on a county-by-county basis. Eventually, the system generated over 200 maps; the first use was by a planning task force to analyze specific business characteristics such as the location of businesses by type of industry.

Department heads then used the maps to plan a marketing strategy for their local areas. Thus, the system was able to support decisions at two different levels of the organization. In one year, DIB's commercial loans increased 29 percent versus an increase of only 22 percent in the bank's composite loan portfolio. It is felt, though not possible to demonstrate, that the SAS/D & B system contributed to these gains.

---

**MANAGEMENT PROBLEM 21-3**

Nancy Swanson is vice president of planning for Beauty Aid, a major manufacturer of cosmetics. The top management at Beauty Aid recently heard a presentation on planning and felt that the firm should be looking into this area. Beauty Aid has grown rapidly through its own efforts and by acquiring several smaller companies. Because of its highly profitable business and good cash position, it has been able to make acquisitions easily.

However, top management realized that business is becoming more complicated and that the next round of acquisitions will involve far larger companies than in the past. Therefore, the computational burdens of evaluating potential acquisitions and projecting conditions after the acquisition would become even more severe.

Nancy is investigating the use of computer models to help in the planning process. After conducting research on the possibilities, she has narrowed her consideration to the following alternatives:

1 Hire a group of consultants to build a model of the firm.
2 Develop the internal staff in the planning department to construct a model using a general-purpose computer language.
3 Design a model with the present planning staff using a higher-level planning language.
4 Get started on planning by using a spreadsheet package on a microcomputer.

What are the advantages and disadvantages of each alternative? What course of action do you recommend to Beauty Aid?

---

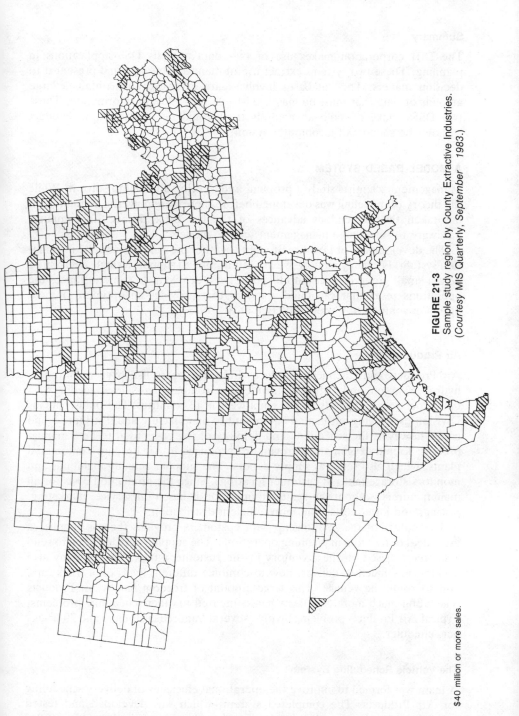

**FIGURE 21-3**
Sample study region by County Extractive Industries.
(*Courtesy MIS Quarterly, September 1983.*)

$40 million or more sales.

## Summary

The DIB corporation makes use of two data analysis DSS applications in planning. These two systems extract useful management data and present it to decision makers. The databases involved are extensive and contain a large amount of data that must be massaged to extract relevant information. These two DSSs make possible an analysis that would be impractical to conduct without the support of a computer system.

## A MODEL-BASED SYSTEM

Management scientists study a problem and develop a model to solve it. While the theory of modeling was developed before there were powerful computers, it has taken the tremendous advances of the last three decades in computer hardware to solve large management science models.

The development of DSS has brought together the modeler and the information system. For many models, we are attempting to support a single decision or help a small group of decision makers solve a problem. In some instances the operations researcher can build a model that provides an optimum or near optimum solution to a problem. (Bell et al., 1983).

### Air Products

Air Products and Chemicals produces industrial gases like oxygen, nitrogen, hydrogen, argon, and carbon monoxide. The company has sales exceeding $1.5 billion per year and nearly 19,000 employees in 13 countries. The Industrial Gas Division uses highly automated equipment to manufacture and distribute liquid gases; however, the scheduling and delivery of the gases used to be a manual process. Liquid oxygen and nitrogen are produced in Air Product's automated plants, which also serve as supply depots. The supplier actually maintains and monitors storage tanks at customer locations. Since the production costs for all manufacturers is about the same, competition is based on service, marketing, pricing, and lower costs from more efficient distribution.

The nature of the relationship with customers provides the gas supplier a great deal of freedom in planning operations. The supplier decides when to send a shipment based on the inventory in the customer's tank; the company also decides how much to deliver, how to combine different loads on a truck, and how to route the vehicle. This large amount of freedom makes Air Products scheduling much more complex when compared to other scheduling problems. Typical Air Products problems involve several hundred customers and 20 trucks per scheduler.

### The Vehicle Scheduling System

A team was formed to improve the operational efficiency of delivery scheduling for Air Products. The completed system, which was developed and tested carefully before being widely implemented, makes use of six data files:

**1** Customer file, including capacity of tanks, safety stock levels, and historical product usage

**2** Resource file containing a description of each truck in the system, capacity by state, and list of customers feasibly served by the truck

**3** Cost file including a per-mile rate for vehicle fuel and maintenance and driver pay regulations

**4** A mileage file which is a network representation of the road system of the United States

**5** Time and distance file containing the distance, travel time, and toll cost between any pair of customers computed from the mileage file

**6** The schedule file containing the schedules developed by the system

The scheduling system produces a list of trips to be performed over the next several days, including the start time, the scheduled vehicle, the quantity of product for each customer, the time at which delivery should be completed, and the length and cost of the trip. A scheduler can examine this output and make changes due to contingencies not reflected in the system.

The scheduling system solves a very large mixed integer program to near optimality using a special algorithm developed for this project. The model can contain up to 800,000 variables and 200,000 constants. The authors believe that this is one of the largest integer programs regularly solved to a state of near optimality.

This DSS contains one of the largest operations research models reported in routine use in the literature. It is an example of how the power of the computer can be used not only to compute a solution, but present it to a user through a decision support system.

### IMPLICATIONS

The systems described in this chapter differ considerably from the Hardserve, AAS, and Shelternet systems discussed earlier. The differences are not really pronounced in terms of computer technology; rather the major contrast is the type of decision supported. The immediate requirements for information in systems such as AAS necessitate instantaneous updating. In the decision support systems, most of the updating does not have to be done in real time. In these systems, it is the decision maker's need for on-line interaction that necessitates an on-line system; instant conversational response means that the decision process does not have to be interrupted to wait for the computer.

The systems dealing with transactions processing and operational control decisions in Chapter 20 become a part of the control process in the organization. They tend to embody a few decisions that are actually programmed in the procedures of the system; a certain minimal level of use is mandatory, since the systems are installed. Certainly the systems are capable of providing management with information for making decisions, but this is not the major reason the systems were developed.

On the other hand, only one system (the Scheduler) in this chapter provides routine information processing: the use of the others is almost exclusively voluntary. Three systems provide information to support decisions; they do not actually make the decisions. A number of decisions are programmed into the systems, but they are required to evaluate different alternatives and process information that is presented to and acted on by the decision maker. This type of system is risky to develop, potentially expensive, and almost impossible to justify on a cost-benefit basis. What is the value of better planning? How do we know the decision makers using these systems perform better than under previous manual systems?

Recent advances in technology make decision support systems easier to develop for even one-shot or novel decisions. Economical time-sharing systems are available, based on minicomputers that can be acquired for internal use in the company. Personal computers are used heavily for decision support, especially electronic spreadsheet packages. Low-cost graphics devices are also available to provide a variety of output alternatives.

More suitable hardware for developing decision support systems has also been accompanied by better software. There are many languages and packages available for building a microcomputer DSS. Simple time-sharing languages are available so that even a novice can program a small decision support application. Many service bureaus have packages programs that can be used alone or in combination (for example, by interfacing them through a file) to solve management decision problems. For some applications, special-purpose higher-level planning languages can be utilized. These languages are designed for the nonprofessional programmer who wants to develop a system in a language more natural than most general-purpose computer languages. As the complexity of the application increases, more elaborate packages and more computer processing power are available. Also, many organizations now have implemented database management systems, so that much of the internal data for use in management decision making already exists. Only the analysis routines and external data need to be added.

DSS are a powerful tool for management; the manager who is aware of the potential of such decision aids and knowledgeable about computers and information systems should be at a distinct advantage.

## KEY WORDS

| | | |
|---|---|---|
| Alternatives | Hypothetical portfolio | Parameters |
| Bottlenecks | Integer programming | Portfolio |
| Conflict | Interactive response | Report generator |
| Consolidation | Mathematical program- | Response functions |
| CRT |   ming | Risk analysis |
| Decision support | Multiplier | Simulation |
| Editor | Normative models | Strategic planning |
| External data | On-line updating | |
| Graphics | Optimization | |

## RECOMMENDED READING

Alter, S.: *Decision Support Systems: Current Practice and Continuing Challenges,* Addison-Wesley, Reading, Mass., 1980. (A book with several good examples of decision support systems.)

Bell, W. J. et al.: "Improving the Distribution of Industrial Gases with On-line Computerized Routing and Scheduling Optimizer." *Interfaces,* vol. 13, no. 6, December 1983, pp. 4–23.

Doyle, J. R., and J. D. Becker: "Computer Assisted Planning (CAP) at Dinero International Bank Corporation," *MIS Quarterly,* September 1983, pp. 33–46. (A good article discussing the strategy and systems at DIB.)

Gerrity, T. P.: "Design of Man-Machine Decision Systems and Application to Portfolio Management," *Sloan Management Review,* vol. 12, winter 1971, pp. 59–75. (An early DSS.)

Keen, P. G., and M. S. Scott Morton: *Decision Support Systems: An Organizational Perspective,* Addison-Wesley, Reading, Mass., 1978. (This book presents a good overview of decision support systems and the problems of developing them.)

## DISCUSSION QUESTIONS

1 Why was graphics necessary in the OPM system?

2 Does the level of technology of this early decision support system matter?

3 How would the systems design approach differ for Connoisseur's system and a batch system such as Hardserve?

4 How would a new manager react to custom-tailored systems like the market response and planning decision support system? What problems does this suggest?

5 Suppose that the decision support system helped the manager to understand problems better and the system could then be discontinued. Would such a system be a success or a failure?

6 What types of decisions are supported by each of the systems in this chapter?

7 Describe the underlying technology, for example, batch and time sharing, for each of the systems in this and in previous chapters. How does the technology compare with the types of decisions supported in the system?

8 What is the major difference between the Connoisseur system and previous manual systems? What are the advantages of the past systems from an implementation standpoint?

9 How could managers have been prepared to take a normative approach to portfolio selection before the introduction of the portfolio system described in this chapter?

10 All the interactive applications create problems for users when not working because of computer or systems problems. Why do users become so dependent on these systems? How does the batch system provide a buffer between the user on the one hand and the information services department and computer on the other?

11 What decisions have you encountered where one of these systems would have been useful?

12 How does an information system contribute to planning at DIB?

13 Is an operations research model a form of an information system?

14 How can management justify the expense of a strategic planning model that costs over a quarter of a million dollars?

15 One author has claimed that strategic planning information can come from a

company's transactions-oriented database. Does the example of a planning system in this chapter agree with this observation? What else is needed?

16 How has technology changed the cost-benefit ratio for these decision support systems since the early ones were developed in the late 1960s?

17 How might decision or cognitive style affect a manager's reactions to graphic output?

18 Why have information services departments generally not developed decision support systems? Why do they seem to concern themselves more with transactions-processing applications?

19 Why is on-line updating not always a requirement with decision support systems, while, most of the time, interactive response is necessary?

20 What software advances are needed to facilitate the development of decision support systems?

21 How can we evaluate the effectiveness of the systems in this chapter after they are installed?

22 Make a list of the types of computer systems we have discussed, from transactions through strategic planning, and describe them in terms of the benefits you would expect from each. What does your list suggest about problems with feasibility studies?

23 Why does it make sense for most organizations to develop transactions-processing systems before strategic planning applications?

24 One author has suggested that management information can never be automated. After reading about the systems in this chapter, do you agree or disagree? Has information really been automated?

25 What would be the capabilities of a general-purpose decision support system that could be used across a number of applications by different decision makers? Do you think such a system could be developed and would be advisable? What might the implementation problems be?

26 What type of system is a recent management-school graduate likely to develop, a transactions-processing or decision support system? What skills are necessary for the development of each system?

27 How would you approach the development of a personalized decision support system for a superior?

# PART SIX

# SPECIAL MANAGEMENT CONCERNS

We conclude the book with an examination of special management concerns about information systems. What are the special problems of managing information processing? What trends are expected in the future, and what do they mean for managers? The last chapter expands the boundaries of computer-based information systems beyond the organization to include society at large. What are the social implications that the manager should consider when making decisions about computer-based information systems? What is the future of information processing technology?

## CHAPTER 22

# INFORMATION SYSTEMS ISSUES FOR MANAGEMENT

## CHAPTER ISSUES

- How do we manage in a constantly changing technological environment?
- How does general management work with the manager of the information services department?
- How can management control information processing activities?

In the preceding chapters we discussed a number of organizational, technical, and systems analysis topics to prepare managers to make intelligent decisions about information systems. Having covered these background matters, we are now in a position to discuss some of the problems faced by managers in an increasingly technological business environment. How do we meet the challenges of managing all aspects of information processing in the organization?

## MANAGEMENT IN A TECHNOLOGICAL ENVIRONMENT

No matter what his or her functional area, managers today and in the future will face an increasingly technological environment. The cost of processing logic is so low, and the potential of this technology so high that the proliferation of computer devices will continue to accelerate. How will we manage under this increased level of technology? What are the management challenges?

**503**

## Top Management Considerations

One key concern of senior management is how to employ the technology strategically; how do we make this technology a part of corporate strategy? We have seen examples of how firms have gained a competitive advantage through the creative use of computing and information processing.

In order to gain this competitive edge, management must be aware of the capabilities of technology and figure out how to apply it in its own industry. The firm will have to conduct research on the technology to spot likely trends; it will also have to be aware of what other leading companies are doing. Can a model from another industry be adapted to fit ours? What are our competitors doing? How do we protect and expand our market share?

Another requirement for using technology strategically is for the firm to be able to manage information processing. There are several issues here for senior management. First, what kind of organization structure should the firm have for processing? Should we be centralized, distributed, or decentralized? In the future, many organizations are going to adopt some form of distributed processing. We expect to see less outright decentralization; instead powerful microcomputers and minis will be connected through communications to form a distributed network. The firm needs to plan for the coming computing environment so that today's decisions on hardware and software are compatible with tomorrow's needs as well.

The key problem for management in this kind of environment is to obtain the benefits of unconstrained local computer use by employees throughout the firm while maintaining control of information processing. Management should see that there are policies and plans for information processing. If there is no coordination, the eventual cost will be quite high.

Users in an uncoordinated environment are likely to purchase different hardware and software to do the same job. Worse yet, they may purchase different hardware and undertake custom programming of an application that really could be shared among several different users. Incompatibilities in equipment can also make it more difficult to share data as well as programs.

Management is then faced with a dilemma: how can we encourage creativity and still control processing for the overall benefit of the organization? Control must not be seen as the prevention of good ideas. One way a firm can provide this kind of control is through support. A company that offers a microcomputer store and consulting help will encourage users to purchase compatible products. Users are not interested in spending a great deal of time finding computers; one control is in helping them do so. Another control is to make the reasons for coordination clear so that users do not see control as arbitrary. Whatever the strategy, a key issue facing today's top management is the need to coordinate and maintain control while encouraging the creative use of information processing technology.

**Other Managers and Users**

As we move toward greater distribution of computers, functional managers in accounting, marketing, production, finance, and other areas will find themselves managing technology. Many of these individuals will not be prepared for such an assignment; they are more interested in their own specialty than in information processing. What are the issues for these functional managers?

They, too, will have to develop a structure for information processing management. The manager of a division may well have hundreds of users with their own computers and an entire, local information services department reporting to him or her. The divisional manager will need to have a structure and support groups for processing. In general, he or she will face the same problems as senior management in controlling the technology.

Functional managers will need to have a policy on the acquisition and use of microcomputers. The possible contents of such a policy are discussed later in this chapter. A major concern is the acquisition of all kinds of hardware and software. How should we select among competing applications? What approach should be taken to developing an application, custom programming, generators, or a package?

The local manager will want to see that there is support for end-user computing. This support may involve the creation of a local microcomputer store and staff, and may lead to setting up an information center to help users with fourth-generation languages.

One assignment for the technical staff will be to work with a corporate group to try creating some compatibility among software products and databases. In a network, users will want to access data at different locations, move it to their local workstation, and process it. Such a task, while easy theoretically, can be quite a challenge. The data are likely to be stored using different database management systems, each with its own query languages. Hardware and software interfaces will have to be carefully designed. In addition, users will want to access external suppliers of data through their workstations.

**Where To Process**

One of the difficult problems facing management today is where to process, that is, what criteria to apply in deciding the location of hardware and/or software. Many organizations have large mainframe computers which are capable of running a number of different applications.

Users, however, are coming to management with requests for local computers, ranging from micros to superminis, usually with a special software system they need. For example, one manufacturing organization with a large IBM mainframe computer for corporate applications has installed a Hewlett-Packard superminicomputer just for quality control in one of its plants. The investment in the HP computer is over a quarter of a million dollars, no small expenditure on

---

## MANAGEMENT PROBLEM 22-1

Roberta Hobart is president of Fashion News, a monthly magazine for the fashion industry and consumers. The company has a computer department that operates a number of systems in the areas of accounting, advertiser billing, and subscription processing. Recently, the manager of the computer department left to accept a position with another firm.

Two good candidates to become manager of the computer department are Bill McDonald and Lynn Phister. Bill is really not a computer professional. He began his career as an accountant but has been very involved in computer work. Roberta feels that he is probably quite knowledgeable except in the most technical computer areas. Lynn, on the other hand, is a true computer professional. His past jobs have included working for a computer manufacturer designing software and programming for several firms. At Fashion News, he has been manager of systems and programming. In this task, he has performed very competently, especially in solving technical problems.

Roberta feels that both men could do an adequate job. She is worried about Bill's lack of technical experience, but gives him high marks on management. The opposite evaluation applies to Lynn. He should be superb at solving technical problems, but Roberta is worried about his lack of experience as a manager, particularly in working with users.

What are the essential components of the job? Can you help Roberta make her decision? What additional information about each candidate would you like?

---

computing. In retrospect, no one in the firm is positive that the local computer was the best solution. However, the firm lacked a policy and guidelines on how to decide where to do the processing.

Some important questions that should have been asked include the following:

1 What is the payoff for the proposed application?

2 Are we doing the same thing someplace else? If so, can we utilize the same system for a new application?

3 What is the likelihood that others would want to use this type of a system? Should our planning emphasize one particular application? Or, should we take into account that there may be many users, each with his or her own version of the system?

4 What functions should be included? Does a package already exist? How long would it take to implement the system?

5 What kind of software is available?

6 How much local development would be required? Are there computer professionals available locally? If not, what consulting expertise is required?

7 What are the on-going support requirements for this application?

8 Is there a need for this system to communicate with other systems in the firm? Are data needed from other systems or locations?

By addressing these questions, management should be able to consider the alternatives for processing and decide on what makes the most sense. Given today's trends in hardware and specialized software packages, it is likely that many decisions in the future will favor local processing with some kind of communications capability.

## Managing End-User Computing

The most recent significant trend in information systems is the growth of end-user computing. Many information services departments and functional managers are not prepared for this phenomenon. Much of the emphasis of this text is on managing computing rather than reacting to unanticipated events. How does management control end-user computing?

First, management has to be convinced that this trend is a good idea. Most of us in the field think it a healthy innovation; there are not enough computer professionals to create the programs desired by users. In addition, there have been significant communications problems in the traditional approach to systems analysis and design. End-user computing helps to solve both of these problems: users have to be involved, and their efforts add to those of the computer professional.

If management wants to support end-user computing, it has to establish policies to make it work. The firm will need a policy both on technological tools and on consulting help for users. For example, a firm might choose a particular fourth-generation language, and then develop an information center to provide consulting.

A number of companies have microcomputer centers; one large communications company has a huge room with about ten different brands of personal computers placed in an attractive setting. Users are encouraged to come in and try different software packages; a staff helps them learn how to use the computer. Information centers, personal computer showrooms, and a commitment to fourth-generation languages are some examples of the things management can do to encourage end-user computing.

The greatest impediment to end-user computing is not likely to be end-users or management, but the computer professional. For over thirty years, the analyst and programmer have been in charge. Many users do not want to talk with the information services department even to get advice, because they fear the total loss of control that often happens when computer professionals take charge of a project.

Computer professionals must change if end-user computing is to be successful. The systems analyst will be less in control of every aspect of design and will become more of a consultant and a teacher. Some systems will continue to be designed with teams of users and designers. However, many others will be put together by users, with the assistance of computer professionals, we hope. Microcomputers and end-user computing are not fads; they are an important part of information processing in a firm. The computer professional must provide leadership if systems are to be successful.

## A Micro Policy

The explosion of microcomputers in organizations has forced firms to reconsider their policies toward personal computers. Early users of these devices often failed to provide guidelines for either employees or for the information services department. What are the consequences of having no control over micros?

Users tend to acquire a large number of different microcomputers from various vendors. Since each microcomputer is likely to feature different software, the same task such as spreadsheet analysis may be done by three or four different programs on as many different computers in the firm. Why is this proliferation of computers and software a problem?

First, users are unable in many cases to share data; the analysis performed on one person's computer cannot necessarily be loaded from a diskette into another computer spreadsheet package. Second, the organization is faced with the problem of supporting a large number of different computers and programs if it chooses to provide support for users. Finally, the advantage of expert advice on purchases and discounts from large purchase contracts may be lost.

A policy on microcomputers, then, must address a number of issues:

1 What hardware is approved for purchase?

2 What software is recommended for purchase?

3 Who will approve purchases, and what justification is needed from the user?

4 Which group in the organization will establish and administer blanket contracts with microcomputer vendors?

5 What is the extent to which groups like information services will support micros, e.g. through an information center, classes, and/or consulting help?

6 What kinds of applications are best served by micros?

7 What type of access will micro users have to corporate databases?

8 What assistance will be available from information services in accessing corporate data?

9 What type of communications capabilities should be supported among computers in the firm?

These issues are extremely important, as microcomputers are playing an increasing role in information processing in organizations. The firm must determine how to both support and control this phenomenon.

## The Information Services Department Manager

Many user and management problems with information services revolve around the manager of this department. Understanding this individual's position helps in developing a relationship between the information services department and users. In an insightful paper, Nolan (1973) has described the plight of managers of information services departments.

First, these managers have a wide variety of subordinates reporting to them, ranging from highly technical computer professionals to clerical personnel. Second, the department is responsible for a broad range of activities from creative systems design work to routine clerical chores. Third, the department impacts many, if not all, areas of the organization. The manager controls a large budget and is responsible for a major investment in equipment. As the department becomes larger and needs become less technical, the emphasis shifts more toward managerial problems. Unfortunately, we often find managers of information services departments with no management background, because their experience is all on the technical side of computing.

Management of the organization has tended to treat the information services department manager as a scapegoat. More seriously, top level management often views the information services department manager only as a technical specialist; they assume that the manager has no desire or ability to progress further in the organization. Given this set of attitudes, the only option open to the information services department manager is to become the manager of a larger or better department in another organization.

How should the top management of the organization respond to the information services department manager? First, top management should see the manager of the information services department as change agent, and give support to the manager's activities within the organization. Management must provide extra resources and encourage users to join design teams. Management should also consider the broad exposure that the information services department manager obtains to all other areas of the organization. Could this person be a good candidate for other managerial positions? Top management should not view the information services department manager as necessarily in a terminal position in the organization.

### The Chief Information Executive

The increased importance of information processing to the firm has led to the creation of a "chief information executive." This individual is, of course, in charge of information processing activities that use computers. However, the chief information officer is also an influential member of senior management, and is usually at least at the vice presidential level.

In addition to computer-based processing, this individual is responsible for voice and data communications and office automation. The job demands someone who can assume a role in planning, influencing other senior managers, and organizing information activities in the organization.

The issues discussed in this text are the concerns of the chief information officer; he or she must worry about strategic planning for the corporation and

---

**MANAGEMENT PROBLEM 22-2**

Cookwell is a manufacturer of cooking utensils; its products are sold in department and specialty stores throughout the world. The company has a large information services department and many computer applications in accounting, production, and sales. Historically, there have been a number of problems with computers at Cookwell. There have been five data processing managers in the last four years!

Systems seem to be late or are never implemented at all. Users in all departments are highly dissatisfied with computer services. Reports are always late and there seem to be an inordinate number of errors. The computer staff generally blames users for all the problems. Typical comments are, "The users never get us the input on time. When it does arrive, the data are wrong and we have to correct them. Then users get mad because the output is late."

Users, on the other hand, say, "The computer staff is the most arrogant group of people in this company. Whenever we ask them to do something, there is always some excuse why it cannot be done. Every new suggestion is rejected; if an application looks good, they come back with such an unrealistic cost estimate that no one will pay for it. We would be better with no computer at all."

The president of the company has avoided computer problems for as long as possible. However, things have become so serious that some action is required. Rather than fire the present manager of the department, who has been on the job only four months, the president has decided to try a new strategy. The president has hired a vice president for administration, and the computer department now reports to him. This man has no computer experience, but he is a competent general manager. What should he do to solve the computer problems?

---

how information technology can provide a competitive edge. The executive in this role must provide leadership and control over processing; it is important that planning, systems development, and operations are all undertaken successfully.

### OPERATIONAL ISSUES

Three areas of operational policy require management attention. The first is the development of a data retention policy. Although it may seem mundane, data retention is a major problem for many organizations; for example, insurance companies process thousands of pieces of paper, many with legal significance. Do they need to save the originals, copies, or even microfilm versions of these documents?

Computers generate large volumes of output in a short period of time; some of these records are vital, but which ones? The Internal Revenue Service may make certain demands on firms to supply records; generally a ruling can be obtained from the IRS as to what will be required. A more uncertain request comes from discovery procedures during litigation. What documents are available if a firm is sued? What documents are available to service a customer who needs a historical record? Legislation may also affect record retention; for example, equal opportunity laws require extensive personnel record keeping.

Many firms are using some form of microfilm to store critical data to reduce storage space requirements. Some companies have even developed computerized indices to their microfilm database so that retrieval will be relatively fast, as with bulky personnel records.

Second, management must also consider privacy, a topic of broad social concern as we shall see in the next chapter. Privacy issues include who shall have access to data, what data are actually stored, the appeal right of individuals about whom data are maintained, and the implications of potential legislative action on the firm's records. Organizations store vast amounts of data about their employees and their customers. Policy needs to be established in each of these areas to protect the firm, its employees, and its customers.

The third area of management concern is backup and security, a topic we have discussed elsewhere as well. Management must see that the essential operations of the firm can be processed; if a computer center is destroyed, could the firm remain in business? Are there adequate copies of data maintained off-site? Could the firm recover from a major catastrophe? A number of precautions should be taken in addition to the off-site storage of copies of critical records, programs, and documentation. For example, many organizations have arrangements with other firms to u₅e their computers in the case of an emergency. Few firms ever try to execute their systems in a simulated emergency on the computers that are available for backup or know whether the firm with the backup machine has adequate capacity to process information for them.

## CONTROL OF OPERATIONS

• At least twice since 1979, air defense alarms signaled the launching of Soviet missiles aimed at the United States from both land bases and submarines. The first time, officers in charge of the system suspected that something was wrong with the data, however. The missiles supposedly in flight had appeared on only one sensor and not on others. However, the defense command remained on alert status for more than five minutes, and fighter planes were sent aloft while the data were checked.

The monitors were wrong; through a human error, a connection was made between an off-line computer running a simulation exercise of the firing of land and submarine-based missiles and the on-line computer monitoring air defense at the time. Because the test tape did not simulate data from all sensors, the officers in command were suspicious. What would have happened, however, if the simulation had been complete? (No details were released on the second incident.)

• The computer operator in a medical institution forgot to remove the file protect ring on a tape that contained the only record of $500,000 in cash receipts.

He accidentally mounted the tape on the wrong drive and it was erased; past due receivables could not be identified and pursued. About the time that the reconstruction of the file was finally complete, the same accident occurred again.

• Programmers in a financial institution computed interest calculations on savings accounts as if there were 31 days in every month. In the five months it took to discover the error, over $100,000 in excess interest was paid.

• Programmers and analysts in a large mail-order house designed a "perfect" system; it would operate only if all errors were eliminated. After installation, auditors discovered that errors were occurring at the rate of almost 50 percent. The system collapsed and had to be abandoned after an investment of approximately a quarter of a million dollars. (For a discussion of these and other similar problems, see W. C. Mair et al., 1978.)

• A group of Milwaukee teenagers used a packet switching network to gain access illegally to a number of computers around the United States. They were able to find passwords and log onto the systems, in some cases damaging files.

These examples all represent the failure of control in the organization. A control system compares actual performance with some desired state. A household thermostat is an elementary control device; when the temperature in the room falls below the desired setting, the thermostat turns on the furnace to raise the temperature to the desired level.

For a control system to work, then, the organization must have a model of its desired states. Often, this model is in the form of routine procedures or generally accepted accounting practices. For problems like controlling a sales representative, standards are less clear, as is our ability to influence behavior.

All levels of control in the organization are the responsibility of management. The Foreign Corrupt Practices Act makes control a legal as well as a normal management task. This act requires that publicly held companies devise and maintain a system of internal accounting controls sufficient to provide reasonable assurances that:

**1** Transactions are executed according to management authorization.

**2** Transactions are recorded as necessary to permit the preparation of financial statements according to generally accepted accounting principles.

**3** Records of assets are compared with existing assets at reasonable intervals and that action is taken when there are differences.

Computer-based information systems have given organizations the ability to process large numbers of transactions in an efficient manner. However, these same computer-based systems create significant control problems and challenges. With thousands of transactions being processed in a short period of time, an error can spread through an immense number of transactions in minutes. Control failures can become costly; firms have been forced out of business because of their inability to control information processing activities.

There are many opportunities for errors to occur in computer-based processing. Figure 22-1 is a diagram of the most difficult case: an on-line computer

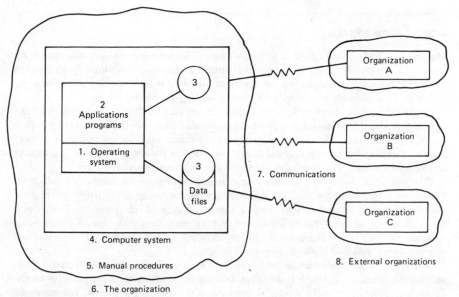

**FIGURE 22-1**
Components of an on-line system.

system with widespread access available from outside the organization. The figure highlights eight areas where the system is vulnerable.

**1** The operating system is a piece of software that controls the operations of the computer and allocates computer resources. Operating systems can and have been penetrated; they also have errors in coding just as in any other program. No one has devised a satisfactory way to check on the actions of the systems programming group that is responsible for the maintenance and any modification of the operating system.

**2** Applications programs contain the logic of individual systems operated in the organization. These programs may have errors or may be incomplete in their editing and error checking for input and processing. For an on-line system, users also are executing these programs and may in some way misuse them or create errors that the programs cannot handle.

**3** Data exist on files in the computer center; these data are often proprietary or confidential within the organization. Are the data safe from accidents? Does the system allow a user or programmer to have unauthorized access to sensitive data?

**4** The entire computer system must operate reliably if transactions are to be processed effectively. Is there adequate backup? Is the computer site physically vulnerable?

## A DAIRY FARM SYSTEM

*Managing a modern dairy farm is a complex task. The farmer must maintain records on breeding history, milk production, butterfat content, gestation and lactation cycles for each animal. Many dairy farms operate on a very small profit margin which means that these data must be accurately monitored and used in making decisions.*

*One West Virginia dairy farm uses a system sponsored by a local cooperative. A USDA official from Washington measures production one day each month for each cow; milk is sampled for analysis. The dairyman or a firm providing artificial insemination services supplies breeding information. The data are processed in Washington through a computer service firm in Utah. The user of the system receives four reports each month.*

*The individual cow record contains historical information on breeding and production. The report extrapolates the total 305 day lactation production quantity from current data. Another report groups animals into various categories such as "cows to breed," or "check for pregnancy." A third report helps the dairyman evaluate the success of the breeding program. A final report repeats some of the other information in a different format and provides other data like the average calving interval.*

*The system is used in a number of ways by the farmer. For example, the reports help in making the decision on which cows to sell because of production or breeding problems. Records of production make it possible to evaluate the breeding program. The approach has proven its value as most of the dairy farms in the U.S. employ some type of computer-based record system.*

---

5 Most computer systems have a number of associated manual procedures for the submission of input and the processing of output after it has been produced by the system. These procedures must be developed with adequate controls to ensure the accuracy and integrity of processing.

6 At a higher level than the individual user, the organization itself must be structured with control in mind. Management must take its responsibilities seriously and emphasize control.

7 On-line systems feature communications among users and systems. Communications links are subject to failure, penetration, and sabotage.

8 Many systems are also available to external users from other organizations. These individuals may make mistakes or intentionally try to misuse a computer system. Controls must protect the system from these users and the users from themselves.

## A MANAGEMENT AUDIT

Currently a great deal of effort is being devoted to developing adequate controls for organizations and their computer-based systems. The first step in this process is usually an audit of the organization's existing control system. In the remainder of this chapter we present guidelines for an audit of computer-related controls. The audit is directed toward computer center procedures, processing controls, input/output procedures, and documentation. Note that for the prototype system described above, these procedures do not adequately address the control problems with the operating system and communications lines. These two technical areas are complex, and adequate controls have not been reported in the audit and control literature. The audit procedures below do include consideration of the applications programs, data security and integrity, telecommunications, the entire computer system, manual procedures, and organizational controls in general.

### Computer Center Procedures

Table 22-1 contains a list of points raised in an audit of computer center procedures. The auditor checks an organization chart showing staffing of the center, focusing on the separation of functions between operations and control. The opportunity for fraud exists if one individual is responsible for all processing and control for a system; one classic control technique is separation of functions.

Control logs make it less likely that input or output will be lost, and logging applications in and out also makes it easier to answer questions about job status. Records of job runs and reruns are useful for making corrections and help ensure that a fraudulent run is not being disguised as an error.

Many organizations are lax in providing backup copies of crucial files and programs. It is quite possible for fire or other disasters to destroy a computer center. If backup copies of programs and files are not maintained in a safe off-site location, the organization is quite vulnerable. Its entire inventory of

**TABLE 22-1**
COMPUTER CENTER AUDIT GUIDELINES

---

Organization chart of staff and center
Separation of functions between staff; operations versus control
Separation of functions between programming and operations
Maintenance of control logs for input and output
Presence of a schedule for regular jobs
Records of jobs run, beginning, ending, errors, restarts, and reruns
File backup procedures; second copies stored in separate locations
Program backup procedures; second copies (including documentation) stored in separate
  locations
Backup arrangement for processing with another organization, including actual attempts to
  make runs
Insurance for recreating bad files, programs, payment for alternative processing
Procedures to check changes to programs
Program library and verification, for example, number of cards in deck; also logs of program
  changes
Disk and tape library controls
External labeling of files
Control of blank forms like checks

---

information systems and records vital to the functioning of the organization could be irretrievably lost. The firm should check backup procedures to be run on other systems by executing programs periodically; this practice ensures that the backup system is compatible with the organization's computer.

Programming changes should be authorized and checked to ensure that changes do not create undesired consequences and to guard against fraud. The computer center probably has a disk pack and tape library. The computer center should control access to material in the library because the library contains vital records for the organization. Finally, the organization should control blank forms such as checks. For example, control numbers should be on the checks that are recorded as the checks are used.

### Telecommunications

Computer systems are making increasing use of communications, either for remote input and output or to connect multiple computers in a network. Because the communications networks are generally outside the direct control of the organization, data security and integrity are difficult to ensure. One technique that is used is the encryption of data. Here, some type of key is used as a basis for coding data, such as following a standard algorithm. Basically a number of calculations are performed on the data to transform them to another encrypted stream of data. Without the key or the ability to execute the algorithm, the data cannot be decoded. One such algorithm has been established as a national standard and is available from at least one computer manufacturer.

Aside from encryption, communications controls revolve around error detection and correction. Hardware devices must function properly and be able to detect errors. Sometimes the errors can be corrected; if not, the device requests retransmission of the data. In applications programs all data have to be submitted. In one organization, the firm searched for a week because of a processing error; it was finally determined that the transmission of data from a remote location had been terminated before all the data had been received.

Finally, the organization also has to be concerned about the reliability and backup for the network. With many on-line systems and networks of computers, the unavailability of alternative transmission paths can seriously disrupt the operations of the organization. See Table 22-2 for telecommunications audit guidelines.

### Processing

Audit considerations in processing not only protect assets and liabilities, they also help ensure accurate processing for users. See Table 22-3. Clearly, the organization must protect files of data. For a sequential file, we check the sequence of the file during update and also confirm the sequence of incoming transactions. We check input during the update to see if transaction values are reasonable when compared with the existing contents of the file.

**TABLE 22-2**
TELECOMMUNICATIONS AUDIT
GUIDELINES

| Telecommunications |
| --- |
| Encryption |
|   Need for encoding |
|   Access to keys |
|   Algorithm employed |
| Error detection |
| Error correction |
| Retransmission |
| Reliability of network |
| Backup for network |
| Applications programs |
|   Error checking |
|   Checks on completeness of data |
|   Backup |
|   Logging of messages |

Record counts ensure that records are not accidentally lost or destroyed. A hash total is a calculation on some field: for example, the value of each item in inventory is added and carried as a control total at the end of the file. The update program computes the old totals and a new one. The computed total is checked with the total on the old master file, and a new total is written to the new master file if all figures agree.

**TABLE 22-3**
PROCESSING AUDIT GUIDELINES

| Processing |
| --- |
| Files |
|   Sequence checks |
|   Reasonableness checks on input fields |
|   Reasonableness checks on updating |
|   Record counts, hash totals to ensure integrity |
|   Trailer records with totals |
|   Error notices for unmatched transactions |
|   Use of file labels and error checking on labels for all runs |
| Checks on sequence of program execution (interprocess communication) |
| Trial balances and output checks |
| Audit trail records, especially for on-line updating |
| Ability to trace all transactions through the system |
| Backup and restart capability for long runs |
| Complete record of file changes |

Interim notices for transactions that do not match the file should be printed, because these transactions may represent an attempt to misuse the system. Most operating systems provide the capability to put machine-readable labels on a file; this information should contain as a minimum the name of the file and date created. The program should always check for the correct file to be sure that the operator has not made a mistake in mounting it.

Particularly in a batch system, a number of programs are executed in sequence. Each program should check—for example, through the use of a small communications file—that its predecessor has finished processing. Trial balances are used to develop adjustments for closing books. Output checks ensure that all output is printed and that various totals match. Audit trails make it possible to follow a flow of transactions through a system, and they are crucial to tracing an inquiry. Some long batch runs keep intermediate progress records, so that in case of failure they can be resorted at the intermediate step. Finally, all file changes should be recorded; see the discussion of the AAS system in Chapter 20 for an example of an audit trail for an on-line system.

### Input/Output Procedures

Input/output involves many procedures, and often the lack of control inherent in these operations jeopardizes computer-based processing. These procedures apply to both individual programs and systems (see Table 22-4). We should use transaction counts, batch totals, control logs, and so forth to verify that all data are received for processing. The system should be designed so that there is as much positive incentive as possible to provide data. File changes should be authorized. When data are transmitted over a distance, the receiving end should check to be sure that all data are received correctly.

When data are converted, for example from paper to magnetic medium, some technique should be used to verify conversion. This verification may take the form of a key verifier, or in other instances we can use control totals or check digits.

What action should be taken when there are errors? For many applications we continue processing, dropping the transaction in error and issuing a notice that an error has occurred. When input/output is controlled properly, a separate section, either in the information services department or a user department, proofs input and output; computer operators should not be responsible for I/O control.

We should see that someone follows up errors and checks output as well as input. Entry to the computer system should also be examined. Batch control totals are used to see that all input is entered correctly. For example, in keying, a group of 50 documents is totaled on one field manually, and a record is keyed with this total. The computer input program adds the fields and compares its total to the final total; an error represents an error either in keying or in the

**TABLE 22-4**
INPUT/OUTPUT AUDIT GUIDELINES

| Input/output procedures |
| --- |
| Manual processing |
|     Verification that all transactions have been received for processing (for example, by item counts) |
|     Incentives to provide data by source |
|     Review of proper authorization for file changes |
|     Data transmission checks |
|     Data conversion checks (for example, record counts, hash totals, control totals on card-to-tape run) |
|     Action taken if control totals do not match |
|     Proof and control function performed by other than machine operator |
|     Follow-up to see that all errors are corrected |
|     Schedule of outputs to go to users |
|     Checking of output reports |
| Machine processing |
|     Input control |
|         Batch control records, duplicate computations by computer |
|         Editing on fields (alpha or numeric) |
|         Check digits |
|         Missing data checks |
|         Prevention of duplicate processing of same input |
|     Output control |
|         Record counts on output reports |
|         Control totals |

omission of an input record. We should also edit input as processed; for example, an edit program may look for alphabetic characters in numerical fields. Check digits as described above are also useful as a check for missing data. Besides looking for missing or omitted data, we need to protect the system from processing the same input twice, which could happen if, for example, the operator loads input a second time accidentally. Output can also be checked with control totals and record counts to be sure all output is produced, especially reports placed on a temporary print file.

## Documentation

We have discussed documentation during systems design. Its importance there was in training users and providing information on how to maintain and repair the system; documentation also provides backup (see Table 22-5). The information services department should have a list of all applications and their status (discontinued, active, under development). Systems design documentation serves as a reference, or library, during the development of the system. After conversion, it is used for maintenance purposes. This library contains all

**TABLE 22-5**
DOCUMENTATION AUDIT GUIDELINES

| Documentation | |
|---|---|
| List of applications | User documentation |
| Systems design and maintenance | Output—how to interpret |
|   Table of contents | Input—how to complete and submit |
|   Feasibility study | Files |
|   Existing system | Processing procedures |
|   Specifications for new system | Errors |
|     Output | Transitional considerations |
|     Input—examples of actual forms, codes |   Testing |
|     File layout and organization |   Conversion |
|     Program modules | Operator documentation |
|     System flowchart |   System flowchart |
|     For each program |   List of programs |
|       Listing of each version |   For each program: |
|       Flowchart/decision tables |     Input and format |
|       Variable cross-reference list |     Files |
|       Module interface cross-reference |     Processing narrative |
|       Variables and identifiers (library) |     Output produced |
|     Tests |     Error conditions and action |
|       Design |     Restart |
|       Data | Distribution and processing (for example, |
|       Results |   decollating) of reports |
|   Manual procedures | Programmer responsible for system |
|     Flowcharts | User responsible for system |
|     Narrative | Cutoff for submission on input |
|     Error controls | Scheduled run time (batch) or availability |
|   Work plans |   (on-line) |
|   Progress reports | Setup requirements |
| | List of machine components used |

information about the system, including the feasibility study and specifications of the new system. We should have examples of input/output forms, file layouts, flowcharts, and decision tables. Each program should be documented in detail, including an actual listing, a flowchart, a variable list, a module list, etc. Testing records are also needed as a reference when errors occur or enhancements are made. Finally, manual procedures should be documented.

User documentation is designed to help reduce questions and simplify the use of a system. It should contain easy-to-follow instructions and examples of output and input along with descriptions of file contents. What are the major processing steps? What kinds of errors occur and how are they corrected by users?

Finally, the installation needs operator documentation to run each application. This documentation includes a system flowchart, a list of programs and their requirements (input files output), and so forth. Error conditions and operator action should be noted. What should be done with output? It is also helpful to have the names of the programmer and the user responsible for the system, along with a schedule for input cutoff and the run time for a batch system or the system availability schedule for an on-line application. Finally, the operator needs a list of the machine components used and any setup requirements for the components, for example, special forms.

### Conclusion

Adequate control and security require attention to detail, which can be hard to enforce. Periodic reviews are necessary to be certain that the organization's investment in computer-based information systems and processing equipment is protected. One firm reportedly has a group of traveling internal auditors that enter a computer center and "pull the plug" on all machines to simulate a fire or disaster. Management of the division and the information services department must then demonstrate backup procedures. Creative techniques like this may be necessary to maintain the vigilance necessary for the adequate control and security of computer processing.

### SUMMARY

In this chapter we have discussed different types of management control. At the highest level, we find management control over computing. Here, the issues deal with planning, organizing, and monitoring information processing. At this level, management establishes plans and policies; it assesses the technology and looks for ways to apply information processing creatively. Coordination across the corporation is one major control problem for senior management.

Middle-level managers in various divisions and locations share many of the same problems as top management. These local managers need to devise organization structures and management policy for information processing in the areas for which they are responsible. Both groups of managers also have to relate to information processing managers. In some corporations there will be a chief information executive to provide coordination and help local management obtain more from its investment in computing.

All levels of management are responsible for operational controls, though usually the details will be left to middle and lower management in the firm. Information processing systems process vital transactions for the firm; they must have adequate controls built into the system. The information services department must also have controls over the ongoing operation of systems.

Control at all levels is necessary for successful information processing. Senior management, users, and the information services professional all have a role in control.

## KEY WORDS

Applications programs
Audit trail
Auditor
Backup
Batch total
Check digit
• Chief information
 officer
Communications
Control logs
Documentation
Encryption

End-user computing
Errors
Hash totals
Internal auditor
Labels (internal and
 external)
Micro policy
Operating system
Operator documenta-
 tion
Postimplementation
 audit

Reasonableness checks
Record counts
Responsiveness
Schedules
Security
Sequence checks
Testing
Training
Transmission
User documentation
Verification

## RECOMMENDED READINGS

Burch, J. G., and J. L. Sardinas, Jr.: *Computer Control and Audit Systems,* Wiley, New York, 1978. (A good text on the audit and control of computers.)

Caroll, J. M.: *Computer Security,* Security World, Los Angeles, 1977. (A good reference on developing greater security for computers and systems.)

Jancura, E.: *Audit and Control of Computer Systems,* Petrocelli/Charter, New York, 1974. (A comprehensive view of auditing for computer systems.)

McFarlan, F. W.: "Management Audit of the EDP Department," *Harvard Business Review,* vol. 51, no. 3, May–June 1973, pp. 131–142. (This article contains a number of ideas on the effective operation of computer departments.)

Mair, W. C., D. W. Wood, and K. W. Davis: *Computer Control & Audit,* Institute of Internal Auditors, Wellesley, Mass., 1978. (One of the most frequently cited references on audit and control for computer systems.)

Weber, R.: *EDP Auditing: Conceptual Foundations and Practice,* McGraw-Hill, New York, 1982. (An excellent text on computer audit.)

## DISCUSSION QUESTIONS

1 What are senior management's problems in controlling information processing?

2 Why should users initiate a suggestion for an information system?

3 How can users monitor programming progress, since this is primarily a technical task and the responsibility of the information services department?

4 Describe the format and contents of good user documentation.

5 How could a system like AAS (in Chapter 20) be converted gradually?

6 Develop a conversion plan for the Hardserve example in Chapter 20.

7 How should users generate test data? What should the data include? Should users familiar with the system or those unexposed to it develop these data?

8 What is the purpose of the postimplementation audit? How should it be conducted, and what variables are important?

9 Why has the information services department manager been considered primarily a technician? What historical conditions account for this? Are there information

services department managers who are in fact not suitable for their managerial posts? What should be done about this situation?

10 Steering committees are sometimes called integrating devices. What other integrators for user and information services departments can you suggest?

11 Why does the top-level manager (to whom the information services department reports) not need a detailed knowledge of technical factors?

12 Under what conditions is an audit for a computer center's efficiency a good idea?

13 Design an audit procedure for assessing the effectiveness of computer operations.

14 How could audit requirements be taken into account during systems design?

15 What is the fundamental role of a C.P.A. in conducting an audit?

16 Can we expect to catch fraud with computer systems?

17 How can top management support end-user computing?

18 What are the duties of the chief information executive?

19 Have computer-based information systems made fraud easier? Do you think more or less can be embezzled from a computer system than from a manual system?

20 Is there any way to detect fraud if there is widespread collusion among information services department personnel and management?

21 Describe the reasons for the separation of functions among individuals processing information.

22 Of what use are control logs for input and output?

23 What kind of file backup procedures are needed in the average organization?

24 What good does a sequence check on a file do? Against what errors does it protect?

25 What is the purpose of an audit trail beyond control? How does it help users?

26 Why are manual procedures so critical to good control?

27 Can an information system be overcontrolled? What might happen under such conditions?

28 What input controls are available? Are most of these suited for both batch and on-line processing? What checks are possible with an on-line system?

29 What are the functions of different types of documentation? What problems are encountered if documentation is inadequate or nonexistent?

## CHAPTER 23

# SOCIETAL IMPLICATIONS
# AND FUTURE TRENDS

## CHAPTER ISSUES

- What are the significant societal problems created by computer-based information systems and do they apply to systems in this organization?
- What actions should management take to alleviate any potential systems problems at the societal level?
- What should be done today to take advantage of tomorrow's technology?

Computer-based information systems have an impact beyond any one organization. A user of systems may be affected by them directly as a member of an organization or indirectly as a citizen: computer-based systems can transcend the boundaries of an organization. In this chapter we discuss some of the implications of systems to become aware of the social responsibilities associated with information systems. We also look at the future of the technology to understand better how to prepare for it today.

## SOCIAL RESPONSIBILITIES

### Issues for Public Policy

There are a number of issues for public policy when considering computers and information systems. In this chapter we consider some of the most important topics for an informed manager and citizen.

**Educating for Computing** There is a definite need to educate individuals for the following roles:

**1** End users. Probably the largest group we consider will be end users, individuals in firms whose primary responsibilities are not in the computer field. These employees need to be able to use computers as a part of their work. The typical professional of the future will have some type of managerial workstation, a powerful microcomputer connected to a network. The local computer will be used to handle tasks such as word processing, spreadsheet analysis, and similar applications that do not require a larger processor. This user will have to understand something about computers, networks, and different kinds of software.

**2** Computer professionals. These individuals will work with the technology. The category includes programmers, systems analysts, computer managers, and various clerical staff members. Computer professionals must have an in-depth understanding of technology and its application. Some of these employees will work on the development of hardware and software packages; others will work applying combinations of hardware, packages, and custom programs to the problems faced by organizations.

**3** Interface personnel. Between the computer professional and the user is an interface staff. These individuals will have functional knowledge of how computers and software work, but will not have a command of all the technical details. They will have to be conversant with the kinds of problems faced by organizations and will need to understand business and management.

Our challenge is to provide education and on-the-job training for all these diverse needs. Without qualified individuals, progress in the application of computer technology will be severely retarded.

**Computers and Defense** We have mentioned the control system failures of the U.S. missile warning system. On two occasions, the system falsely indicated a Russian attack on the United States. Fortunately, according to sketchy press reports, each time military officers in charge of defense had enough evidence that the warnings were false that they did not recommend that the President order a counterattack.

These incidents are rather sobering; a catastrophic error could lead to an accidental nuclear war. The United States has been placing nuclear missiles in Western Europe, a short distance from Moscow. Currently, because of the time required for land-based missiles to reach their target, it is believed that both Russia and the United States would make a decision to counterattack through discussions among high officials.

As the time for discussions is reduced, there may be great temptation to make the decision of whether or not to launch a counterattack an automated one, that is, a decision made by computers monitoring incoming missiles and aircraft. The installation of missiles in Western Europe reduces the warning time for the Soviets from the current 20 to 30 minutes to a possible 15 minutes or less.

Many computer scientists feel that a launch-on-warning strategy in which the computer automatically evaluates the data and launches a counterattack would be very dangerous. We have already seen two errors in the U.S. system. If the Soviet Union is 10 years behind the U.S. in computer technology, is it in our interest to force the Russians into a launch-on-warning posture? Do we want to rely on U.S. or Russian technology to launch nuclear weapons automatically?

Proposals have also been made for elaborate weapons systems located in outer space; lasers are being considered to provide a fail-safe defense against missiles. Many of these weapons would require computers to control them and perform the myriad of computations needed for tracking a target. There is considerable scientific debate about both the feasibility of these weapons and their advisability in terms of nuclear strategy. As citizens, we must think about the issues of reliability and risk associated with such weapons. Do they increase the safety of U.S. citizens or increase the risk of war?

**Home Computers**   There have been both successes and failures with the use of home computers; in some instances the devices have been used for a short period of time, and then sit unused. Certainly, a large number of individuals have applications for which the computer is suited, but these are often work-related. An individual can do certain personal tasks, such as maintain budgets, keep track of a stock portfolio, and process taxes on home computers. However, there is no clear consensus at the present time whether there are in fact enough home applications for a significant market potential to exist for computers.

From an educational standpoint, all kinds of individuals need to be prepared to work with computers in their work, and possibly in their personal lives as well. There is great concern that the resources of financially better-off schools will be able to offer computer education, while poorer schools will not. If this trend occurs, will it condem a large number of students to a second-class education? Will computer literacy be a requirement to becoming an educated individual?

**The Technology Gap**   There is a serious question of whether or not computer and communications technology will accentuate the gulf that exists between the "haves" and the "have nots" both with individuals and among countries. Will those who are able to acquire computer systems or the knowledge of how to use them become the new elite? Will individuals who are not literate about computers find themselves confined to a second-class existence? It is unlikely that such extremes will evolve, but the likelihood is that significant segments of the population will become less able to deal with an economy that depends on computer-processed information.

**Home Information Services**   There are many opportunities for personal information processing services to be offered in the home, particularly through the use of two-way cable communications networks for television. One experimental system allows viewers to vote on a question through a two-way cable TV installation. Electronic banking is offered through home computers.

Other possibilities include the use of satellites to beam signals to a wide area of receivers. There are a number of current applications and experiments. One European service, which is being tested in the United States, makes a wide variety of information available on a television set equipped with a special decoding device. The viewer can access weather forecasts, plane, train, and bus schedules, up-to-the-minute news, shop-at-home, etc.

National networks have been developed through which these personal computer users can access common programs and communicate with each other through electronic mail and bulletin boards. One firm has recently made the entire contents of a newspaper available to a computer user in the home or office; the paper can be displayed on the CRT at will.

Such capabilities raise a number of policy questions. Should an information utility offering this type of service be public, private without regulation, or private with regulation? Are these uses of computers good from a broad public policy viewpoint? Is it possible that such systems would tend to create greater isolation among different groups in society? Another question concerns the basic economics of specific proposals. In addition to economics, we must consider the possibility that people are not really interested in many of the services that might be offered.

If such information and communicating capabilities are available, what will be their impact on mobility and personal habits? If these suggestions were ever implemented throughout the country, they might significantly reduce the number of occasions on which people leave their homes.

We have to be concerned about whether security and privacy can be provided effectively in such systems. Can the owner or operator of an information utility use the information for personal gain, such as conducting marketing research surveys?

Another policy question concerns having the capability for a national referendum. Is it desirable to present issues in this manner and ask for public response? Will people become tired of this invasion of privacy and lose interest in the legislative process? It is also possible that such a service would be too expensive, thus disenfranchising certain groups who are unable to afford it? Such a proposal raises the specter of sabotage or of attempts to influence the outcome of elections illegally. How easy would it be to abuse the information available for the purposes of controlling the people?

**Computers and Money** Electronic funds transfer systems have been studied extensively during the past decade and a number of systems have been proposed. To implement such a system, many of the present laws concerning credit and money would have to be rewritten. However, we do not really know the present public attitude toward electronic funds transfer. Questions of privacy are also involved here; for example, information on checks could be potentially useful to different segments of society, or such information could be used for surveillance purposes. The point of sale recorders in stores would make it possible to keep track of where a person is at the time of any transaction and thus keep a record of an individual's travels.

**Computers and Elections**   Computers have been used routinely to predict the outcome of elections and to tally votes. There have also been political candidates who have used computers widely to custom-tailor campaigns to individual areas, ethnic groups, and even individuals. Are the sophisticated computer predictions actually disenfranchising people who live on the West Coast and who will not bother to vote after computer predictions show who has won the election?

**Privacy**   Certainly one of the most widely debated topics relating to society is the issue of an individual's right to privacy. Foreign governments have suggested placing restrictions on the international flow of information. Many bills and acts have been proposed to ensure the individual's privacy. At what point does the right to privacy come in conflict with other rights? Society certainly has the need and the right to have certain kinds of information that contributes to the general welfare. Demographic information and information on income levels are vitally important in establishing national policy. However, information on wages and financial conditions is considered to be extremely sensitive by most individuals.

Certainly, current thinking is that individuals should have the right to ascertain whether information held about them is correct and to force the correction of errors. There is less agreement on the types of penalties that should be imposed for the misuse of private information maintained in some type of data bank. Other questions arise as to whether individuals should have the right to know who has requested information about them from a data bank. Some countries have become very concerned about this trend; for example, Sweden has enacted a comprehensive program to regulate the development of data banks.

A number of solutions have been proposed, and the federal government has passed legislation affecting only federal agencies. There have been suggestions to extend the federal law to the private sector. As it stands now, the legislation requires a large amount of record keeping about the pattern of access to records that contain any personal information. There are fears that the proposals for the private sector may prove extremely costly for organizations. One important issue, then, is what should be the balance between the individual's rights and the burdens and costs of protection and record keeping?

**Security**   Closely related to problems of privacy is the issue of system security. There are many possible threats to the security and integrity of a computer system, particularly on-line systems where there is widespread access by individuals external to the organization. There have been a number of well-publicized penetrations recently of various computer systems, including a major cancer research hospital on-line system. Researchers in the field are working on methods of encrypting data so that it cannot be intercepted and decoded by an unfriendly user. Such concerns are very important, given the existence of highly sensitive data on on-line databases. There are also many problems related to the prevention of system failure; individuals and organizations are dependent on many systems, and these systems must remain operational.

**Employment**  Labor leaders have been extremely concerned about the possibility of wide scale unemployment because of computers. The computer industry is one of the largest in the United States, and it has created hundreds of thousands of jobs. Naturally, the implementation of some information systems has eliminated or modified jobs, though there are few statistics to indicate the overall impact on employment.

It does appear that the continued introduction of computerized robots will reduce employment in manufacturing. The extent to which this effect will be offset by jobs building and servicing robots is unknown. However, certainly increased technology will require a higher skilled, better educated work force.

There are also implications from the implementation of information systems on the pace of technological change, job security, and the importance of retraining workers when jobs change. Has the opportunity to exercise individual initiative and has the interest of jobs been reduced or enhanced by computers?

**Liability**  Computer systems are an important part of many business operations. A few companies have already gone into bankruptcy because of errors in processing, and others have turned profitable operations into losses. It is also possible, as one recent scandal has shown, to use a computer to help perpetrate widespread fraud.

There is no way to pinpoint responsibility when a computer system fails. We have stressed that systems design is a creative task; it is possible to have errors in logic and processing that are not caught until actual operations begin. Auditing firms are particularly concerned over the use of computers to process and maintain basic information on the operations of a firm. It is a very difficult to audit computer-based systems and to be certain that controls are adequate.

**Computers and Communications**  Computing activities increasingly involve communications: on-line systems span the continent and the world. There are more networks of computers and special services offered every day. New communications companies promote alternatives for long distance communications.

With the breakup of AT&T, the communications marketplace began changing rapidly. What should public policy be under this new, deregulated environment? What will the impact be of deregulation? Who will benefit from alternative long-distance carriers? Certainly we would expect the costs of communications to change, but it is not clear whether the increased costs for local service will be enough to cause cost reductions in long distance rates.

Also, with the need for communications growing due to more on-line applications and the development of electronic mail, the total volume of communications will increase. Therefore, we would expect to pay more in total for communications, regardless of any cost reductions for individual services.

**Computers and Underdeveloped Countries**   Is it possible to use computers to help accelerate the development of preindustrialized countries? If so, how do we transfer the technical expertise required to these countries? It will be necessary to work with the leadership of such nations to develop priorities for applications and to train nationals to carry out the work. What impact will the development of systems have on other aspects of the country's economy?

**Computers and Power**   We have discussed the fact that computers can change power relationships within organizations. The same trend may occur in society as a whole. Is it possible that through the acquisition of data stored in

---

**A WELFARE SYSTEM**

*Many governmental welfare programs suffer delays in determining applicant eligibility for economic aid, and experience inconsistency in applying eligibility and benefit rules. A distributed computer system has been implemented in Wisconsin to help solve these problems and to save money for the state.*

*Local operators use on-line CRT terminals to enter applicant data; the system guides the terminal operator step-by-step through the data entry process. If the data passes the edit checks, and the host computer is currently available, a local computer transmits the application to the host. Should the host not be available, the local computer queues and stores the data that has passed the pre-edit test to be sent as soon as the host becomes available.*

*The host computer has many functions in the system. Applicant data from the local computer is posted to a daily activity base, which is used by the host to determine eligibility and benefits. The central computer has a case database which stores updated records of 100,000 AFDC\*, medical assistance, and food stamp cases. A case is a welfare unit which averages about three individuals per household.*

*The host computer first checks to determine whether the applicant is known to the system, and if he or she is currently receiving economic assistance. A complex formula is used by the system to determine aid benefits. However, this determination is completely objective. When the benefit determination is completed, the host transmits the findings back to the local computer where a sheet is printed for use by local administrators. In the evening the central computer goes off-line to process the day's activity data against the case database to update these records.*

*In even the most populous counties a determination of eligibility is generally made the same day the application is entered. The system also assists local eligibility workers in conducting scheduled reviews of welfare cases.*

\*Aid for Dependent Children

*Computer World, July 28, 1980.*

computer data banks, an organization such as a credit bureau might increase significantly the amount of power it has over citizens? Is it true that a candidate for national office who cannot afford the use of a computer may be at an insurmountable disadvantage? If there are gross imbalances in power, what can we do about it? How much responsibility does the producer of a tool have for its use?

**Complexity and Integrity**    Society in general is becoming more complex, as are batch and on-line computer systems. What is the interaction between computers and complexity? Will computers create additional complexity, or will they help us cope with the growing complexity inherent in a postindustrial, information-based economy? The answer to both questions is probably yes. We may be able to trade off some organizational and societal complexity for information systems, but these systems in turn are likely to be complex in their own right.

Consider the Connoisseur Foods system for supporting decisions in Chapter 21. Although a complex system technologically, it helped brand managers cope with the complexities of the marketplace. They seemed to understand the dynamics of the market better, having used the powerful analytical tools provided by the decision support system. However, many of the managers still felt uncomfortable with the type of decision making represented by the computer system. Some of this unease was undoubtedly from a lack of understanding of the complex technology.

**Reliability and Failure**    We have discussed some of the problems of control and system reliability. Computer-based systems are extremely complex. Although systems in the future are expected to feature more redundancy and lower failure rates, there will still be the possibility of a system failing. The results of such a systems failure range from inconvenience to catastrophe. There is a serious public concern in seeing that systems are designed and installed with adequate considerations of reliability and backup. For critical systems, there should be backup capabilities. For example, critical on-board systems in airliners have long featured redundancy, that is, several separate and independent hydraulic systems. For the most part, the computer profession has not yet approached such levels of redundancy. Some systems have extensive hardware redundancy, but very few systems have been reported where the software is independently developed and executed on separate machines to provide reliability and backup. Obviously such an approach is costly, but for certain kinds of systems envisioned in the future, such as electronic funds transfer applications, it may become necessary.

More research is needed to conduct the kind of cost-benefit analysis needed to select the proper design for reliability. The computer profession in general does not have a well-developed procedure for the analysis of the risks of various types of system failures. Without this assessment capability, it is very difficult to determine what kind of steps need to be taken to achieve acceptable levels of reliability for any given system.

**Data Flows and Trade Barriers**   In the last few years, a number of important issues have arisen around the rapid growth of the information processing industry. A large, multinational firm might wish to install common systems in several subsidiaries located in different countries. At a minimum, the firm might want to have all its subsidiaries transmit data on a periodic basis to a central computer site for reporting purposes. A midwestern bank serves all its foreign subsidiaries through a data center located in Chicago; each day transactions are transmitted from Europe to Chicago for processing to generate reports that are transmitted back to the European offices.

For the multinational and for the bank above, laws in a number of countries are threatening this type of operation. Countries with the stated purpose of controlling and protecting the personal data of their citizens are passing laws to restrict the transmission of data across their borders. One country is already limiting the ability of a bank to transmit and process data outside the country. If each country passes different legislation, it will become almost impossible to transmit data freely.

Is privacy the only reason for these governmental concerns? Many computer professionals think that other motives may be more important. First, the United States exports a considerable volume of computers and information processing equipment; foreign regulations can act as nontariff trade barriers. Third-world countries see the regulations as a way to protect the development of infant industries and as a way to prevent the domination of their economies by multinationals. Some developing countries have instituted strict regulations virtually to the extent of prohibiting the importation of certain software products. These nations do not want to become dependent on the industrialized countries.

The United States must examine all the ramifications of proposed legislation and rules governing the use of information processing technology in foreign countries. The comparative advantage that this country enjoys in exporting technology, and the fundamental ability of U.S. firms to use the technology to conduct their business are both at stake. The problem affects all of us whether directly involved in the computer industry or not.

**Harassment**   Too many times it appears we are being harassed by computers. Systems are designed to send automatically second, third, and even further overdue notices even when a customer has a legitimate complaint about a bill. Systems appear unresponsive to an individual's problems because of the need to process large volumes of information quickly. Some systems may be flexible, but require cumbersome manual procedures to update records and keep them accurate. If a clerk makes an error or omission, the computer will continue sending letters to the customer. In other situations, employees learn to rely on computer-based systems and do not provide customer service when a system is unavailable. One bank installed an on-line inquiry system for tellers cashing checks. The tellers were provided with the same hard-copy microfilm used before the on-line system for backup. However, when the new computer system was unavailable because of a malfunction, many tellers refused to cash checks and told customers to come back when the computer was working.

A Canadian survey found that 40 percent of the individuals returning questionnaires had at least one problem related to computer processing in the previous year (Stirling, 1979). Of those reporting errors, 81 percent were in billing and 8 percent in banking transactions. The largest number of errors were charges for nonexistent expenditures, inappropriate interest charges, and overcharges. Eight percent of the respondents who reported an error made no attempt to correct it, and 7 percent who tried to correct the error failed in their attempt. It took a reported average of 2.6 hours to correct an error, but 20 percent of the cases required 20 hours or more of effort to obtain satisfaction. These figures are probably good approximations for experiences in the United States as well; the picture they present is not one that inspires confidence in the way organizations respond to customer problems with computer-based systems.

### Alienation

All these problems and frustrations create the most significant social issue: widespread alienation from information systems. If the population is alienated by stories of abuses and harassment, and if people deal with poorly designed systems, clumsy interfaces, and unresponsive information services departments, the future of computer-based information systems is dim. Alienation will undoubtedly result in a lack of cooperation with systems and the failure to develop new, potentially effective applications. How can we prevent widespread alienation?

### Some Suggested Solutions

**Education**   Can we provide the general public with more education about computers and information systems? If individuals better understand computers and the problems with information systems, they are better able to cope with them. One reason for widespread participation in systems is to provide users with education and training about systems.

Education about computer-based information systems should be a part of every high-school curriculum, and certainly each college graduate should be exposed to computers. Continuing-education programs on computers should also be encouraged for citizens who want more general knowledge, as opposed to those who want to enter the computer profession. Companies can do their part by providing general education and training in the effective use of computer-based information systems.

**Technical Safeguards**   Some problems of the misuse of computer-based information systems are technical in nature. We should attempt to make systems as secure as possible to avoid penetration by the unscrupulous. Thorough testing is needed to prevent programs from accidentally disclosing sensitive data. There should be technical checks to procedures to prevent accidental entry by unauthorized individuals; for example, consider the AAS system, which locks terminals if there are two attempts at unauthorized access.

A more difficult challenge is to design a system to be secure from skilled agents, or from individuals who commit fraud through the system. Protection here may take the form of monitoring to keep track of users, or of introducing special encoding algorithms, to maintain security. Unfortunately, there is almost always some weak point in system control; for example, one could bribe an employee of the computer center.

**Controls** Some of the controls discussed in the last chapter on auditing procedures can help to prevent certain social problems from occurring. Requiring several individuals to authorize changes in programming and files and checking input carefully help to prevent problems. Controls requiring all data to be processed help solve problems such as files not being updated to reflect payments. Controls are important to the extent that they ensure accurate processing and screen out requests where access is aimed at fraud and/or mischief.

**Ombudsman** Because individuals often know so little about computer-based information systems, they are often baffled, frustrated, and alienated when confronted with computer-related problems. One device used in Europe since the eighteenth century is an independent ombudsman to whom citizens can turn for help. In the United States, there are reporters for newspapers, radio, and television who check consumer complaints and play a role similar to that of the ombudsman.

The Association for Computing Machinery, a group of computer professionals, has an information ombudsman program for citizens. However, it is not clear that the average citizen knows of the association's existence or where to turn for help. The idea of an expert who can assist citizens with grievances about computer-based information systems is excellent, although in a society as large as the United States, it may not be feasible. One alternative approach would be for each organization using computer-based information systems to have its own ombudsman. In fact, two such individuals may be necessary; one for employees, similar to a user representative suggested earlier, and one for customers or the population at large.

**Legislation** Another solution to some of the social issues, particularly privacy and abuse of power, is legislation. In 1973, Sweden enacted a law regulating personal data maintained about individuals. The act establishes a data inspection board that grants permission to keep a data bank of personal information. Sensitive data, such as a criminal conviction, can be maintained only by an agency charged by statute with keeping these records. Once permission is granted, the data inspection board issues regulations to prevent undue encroachment on privacy. Responsibility for maintaining the correct data lies with the organization maintaining the data bank, not the individual whose records are in the bank. Those organizations whose key records are in error must make corrections demanded by the individual. Damages are specified for violations of these regulations.

In 1974, a comprehensive Federal Privacy Act was passed requiring government agencies to keep elaborate records of the use of personal information. Records of inquiries by those whose records are kept must also be provided. To extend these requirements or a similar set to private-sector firms, some of the following are usually proposed in privacy legislation (Goldstein, 1975):

1 Notification of the subject about the existence of a record
2 Responding to inquiries on the contents of data and the use of records
3 Investigating complaints
4 Obtaining consent for each use of the data
5 Checking authorization for requests
6 Keeping a log of all accesses
7 Providing subject statements when disputed data are released
8 Sending corrections and/or subject statements to past recipients of information
9 Ensuring the accurate compilation of records
10 Providing additional data to give a fair picture
11 Providing a secure system

Although many of these requirements would prevent abuses of data, the regulations are potentially expensive to implement (Goldstein, 1975).

**System Design** Although undoubtedly some of the above solutions will be implemented and will help solve some of the social problems with computer-based information systems, are they really sufficient? To a large extent, many social implications are determined in the process of designing a system. By asking the appropriate questions during the design process, we can assess some of the potential problems with the impact of the system on society. For example, we can ask the following about each application:

1 Is the application a potential threat to anyone's rights? What could go wrong? For example, do the files contain rumors, hearsay information, or unevaluated reports on individuals?
2 Is there a built-in incentive against using the system? For example, does it act to police workers who must contribute the data?
3 Is it difficult for someone to use the system? That is, could an individual fill out the forms, understand the input, enter data through a terminal, or do whatever is required?
4 How many ways could someone find to defraud or penetrate the system?
5 If one wanted to misuse the data of the system, how could he or she evade the procedures that safeguard it? What could someone do to misuse the data?
6 Is the system sufficiently reliable?

The design team should encourage independent attempts to penetrate the system along the lines suggested above to verify the completeness and the viability of the design. A well-designed system is the best guarantee against harassment, abuse, privacy violations, and alienation.

## THE FUTURE OF COMPUTER-BASED INFORMATION SYSTEMS

What are the likely future trends in information processing that will affect managers and users of systems? The manager and the user should prepare to take advantage of the opportunities provided by changes in information processing technology. It has been predicted that the information processing industry will reach 1 trillion in yearly sales by 1990, making it one of the largest sectors of the economy. It is unlikely that any organization will remain untouched by this technology during the next decade. In this section, we predict some of the trends in technology and their implications for managers and users.

## HARDWARE

### Size

*New computers will be smaller, faster and have larger storage; their prices will continue to decrease.*

Very large scale integration (VLSI) will result in even more components per unit of area. One of the most promising techniques uses electron-beam lithography; electron beams expose the photo resist on a wafer. This process offers finer detail than the optical processes described earlier. As a result more complex circuits can be built far more cheaply and reliably. Currently more than 500,000 components can be fabricated and interconnected on a single chip of silicon no larger than one-tenth the size of a postage stamp. The number of components per chip should grow dramatically for at least another decade.

### Memory

*The exponential increase in the number of bits per memory chip and chip price reductions will continue.*

Another use of large scale and very large scale integration is to develop memory devices. In addition to fabricating the logic of the central processing unit, VSLI offers very fast and large computer memories at reasonable cost. A single memory chip today contains the equivalent of entire computer memory of 15 years ago.

New technology will be applied to storage devices in general, reducing costs and increasing capabilities. Several organizations are working on a type of optical disk memory in which data can be erased and rewritten. Although optical memory systems exist today, they are limited because a laser is used to inscribe data permanently for storage. Since there are few applications (aside from large information storage and retrieval systems) where data do not have to be erased and updated, this kind of storage device has not seen widespread use. Optical disk technology is emerging, and it promises to increase the capacity of disks a hundredfold and reduce the costs of data storage.

It is expected that memory in the future will be composed of a hierarchy of devices. Very large scale integration will continue the trend toward large primary memories consisting of semiconductor devices of extremely high speeds. For secondary storage there will be competition among charge-coupled devices, bubble memories, large core storage, and electromechanical devices like magnetic and optical disks. The charge-coupled and magnetic bubble memories are filling an important price-performance gap between extremely fast semiconductor memory, and slower but less expensive drum, disk, and tape memories. Fortunately, this storage hierarchy will be invisible to the user of the system. Instead, the user will see an extremely large database capability.

## Summary

The implications of hardware technology for the central processing unit and memory are that computers will become faster, larger in storage capacity, and less expensive in the future. The reduction in cost will make it possible to use computer devices in a whole range of products and systems: computers will become even more pervasive in the future than they are now.

## COMMUNICATIONS

*Advances in communications depend on regulatory changes as well as technology.*

Over the past decade the communications industry has undergone rapid change. In addition to trends toward deregulation, the entry of new carriers, and the divestiture of AT&T, entirely new types of services are now offered. For example, one company sells packet communications services; packets of data of a predefined size are sent anyplace in the United States at a flat rate per packet, independent of distance.

*New communications technologies aim at increasing the speed and reducing the costs of transmission.*

New forms of communications are being installed. One system carries voice data and video signals over underground optical cables connecting two telephone company switching offices. The underground cable consists of 24 optical fibers bound in two ribbons of 12 fibers each. The entire cable is only half an inch in diameter, yet the information capacity of each fiber is 44.7 million bits per second. (The laser light source for the fiber is turned on and off 44.7 million times per second.) A single fiber can carry 672 one-way voice signals, so that the entire cable can carry over 8000 two-way conversations. To match this capacity with copper wire would require a cable many times larger.

Both changes in the technology and in regulations should produce new opportunities for communications among machines and among individuals. However, because of continuing changes in industry regulations, cost reductions for communications are expected to be less dramatic than for computer technology.

## INPUT-OUTPUT DEVICES

*Input and output continue to be a major bottleneck in information processing, though new devices will improve the user interface with computers.*

One type of technology involves touching terminals rather than keying data. A microcomputer has been designed around this technology. The user points to the screen with his or her finger to instruct the computer on what programs to run, for example, by putting a finger on the menu choice on the screen.

Other innovative I/O devices include mice, small, hand-held "vehicles" that resemble a mouse. The user moves the mouse around on the surface of a desk; the mouse controls the movement of the cursor on the screen of a microcomputer. The user indicates the choice of a program or what action to take by pressing a button on the mouse when the cursor is touching the appropriate icon (picture symbol) on the screen.

*The use of computer graphics will increase.*

Over the last several years interest in computer graphics has increased. Basic graphics applications feature simple pictures in black and white. Charts, graphs, maps, outlines, and business forms are examples of such displays that contain a great deal of information. More complex data often can only be communicated through the availability of multiple colors. Sometimes three-dimensional figure are required, or colored maps are produced.

*Voice communication with computers will be applied in the development of information systems.*

One of the most exciting areas for communicating with computers is by voice, both for input and output. Currently some systems are able to process limited speech input for a computer. For example, one chemical company uses voice input to sort 25,000 pieces of mail arriving each day. An operator wearing a microphone headset reads the initial of the recipient's first name and the first four letters of the surname. On a small CRT the employee's name and mail zone appear, and the operator places the package in the appropriate location for delivery. According to the chemical company, the system has doubled the speed of mail processing. The operator could accomplish the same thing by keying in the characters, but both hands are occupied handling the mail because the mail is of nonstandard size and shape. The voice recognition system frees the operator's hands for the sorting job. Some vendors are selling voice recognition chips for microcomputers. However, they are for discrete, rather than continuous speech recognition.

For a computer to understand natural, continuous, fluid speech of humans, considerable knowledge about the structure of language and the context of the task must be programmed into the computer. The difficulty of devising strategies for providing this type of information has impeded the recognition of continuous speech.

At least one computer manufacturer is currently working on a continuous speech recognition system and has reported some success with it. The computer manufacturer's first application is one of automatic dictation. Envision the manager being able to dictate a letter into a microphone and have the letter appear as rapidly as the words are spoken on a CRT screen. A system like this could be tolerant of some errors that could be fixed by the manager or by a secretary. The time-consuming, rather unpleasant chore of transcribing dictation copied either manually or on some kind of recording device would be eliminated by such a system. Beyond the immediate application, a system like this would make it possible to consider the voice input of commands and questions into a computer system.

The generation of speech by computers is much further along than speech understanding. One commercially available product combines an optical character recognition device with a voice synthesizer to produce a reading machine for the blind. A book is placed flat over a glass plate, and the system converts the text into spoken words.

The difficulty in producing natural-sounding speech comes from many of the same problems that make continuous speech recognition difficult. We could store phonetic representations of all the words in the dictionary in the computer. When the machine needed to generate a sentence, it could call up the pronounciation for each word and string the words together. However, the result would be a very jerky sentence with little modulation. Therefore, attempts are made to limit the complexity and the amount of knowledge the system must have to produce speech. Phrases may be recorded and recalled for playback, or other techniques can be used to make the speech sound more realistic.

## SOFTWARE

*Advances in software will be slower than those in hardware; software will continue to be a bottleneck.*

The advances in hardware are innovative and exciting; advances in software are much more difficult to predict. The production of programs is a human intellectual task that so far has defied extensive automation. A report by the Office of Technology Assessment (1981) concluded, "The cost of information systems will be predominantly for the software, and the information industry will become increasingly labor-intensive." Their observation is still valid today.

*Users will be forced to interact more closely with computers to satisfy their information processing needs.*

If software is becoming increasingly labor-intensive, we might ask who will write programs. Many organizations spend over 50 percent of their software development budgets on the maintenance of existing applications. As more new applications enter the organization's portfolio, increasing efforts will be required for maintenance and enhancements. As a result, the number of people available to develop new systems could actually decline if the technical staff is not increased.

Unfortunately, there is a critical shortage of programmers and systems analysts, which is expected to continue over the next several decades. The question of who will write programs is a very important one. The computer revolution, to a large extent, is limited by the availability of professionals to work on software.

The shortage of personnel, the real and hidden backlog of applications, the increasing costs of maintenance, and the large number of programs requested all suggest that users will play a greater role in system development. We shall discuss the nature of this role and other alternatives to reduce the software gap below.

*There will be an expansion in the use of applications packages and outside services.*

The lack of computer professionals also suggests that more packaged applications will be used. Organizations will change their procedures, particularly small firms, to take advantage of existing program products. Companies will buy turnkey systems, systems that have been programmed for particular industries, and will adapt their procedures to them. Organizations that cannot change procedures or have unique situations may use packages but modify them heavily in attempting to save development time.

*Organizations will move rapidly toward database environments.*

The advantages of the database approach to information processing were discussed in Chapter 11. Firms often acquire a database management system for a single application, and then use it for the development of many subsequent applications. Once the system has been installed and the staff understands how to use it, database management systems can dramatically reduce the length of time required to implement a new application.

High-level application development systems have been announced. The objective is to move to an environment in which one defines the database, transactions, and their editing requirements and output while the system does the rest. Of course, it will always be necessary to specify some processing logic, but perhaps the specification will be at a high level instead of at the detailed level of conventional programming languages.

The query languages associated with database management systems are an important feature. Some of these languages are quite suitable for users in an organization. In order to access data for ad hoc inquiries, users will have to employ these languages and become familiar with the names of data in the database.

Evidence also suggests that some of the functions of a database management system will be taken over by hardware. The literature has presented examples of "database machines," computers dedicated to data processing that are used in conjunction with computers that run the applications programs.

*There will be more extensive use of prototyping in systems development.*

To assist users in visualizing a system, designers will make greater use of prototypes. That is, a simulated version of a system or a part of the system will be developed quickly and demonstrated to the user. Then the user can provide immediate feedback based on what he or she experiences. The prototype is done quickly and replaces a large, functional specification that is hard for the user to understand.

Some of the very high level languages, report generators, time-sharing systems, microcomputers, and development tools available now can be used to produce simple prototypes. Users and managers should request this approach whenever it seems feasible. Many functional areas will want to consider developing their own prototype systems rather than calling on a professional designer. For many applications, a simple prototype developed by the user may suffice for the final application after a few rounds of changes and modifications.

*There will be more end-user programming of all types.*

A central conclusion from all of the trends discussed so far is that there will be more end-user programming. End users will work with personal computers that will really be multi-purpose workstations. These workstations will include local data analysis capabilities, word processing, graphics features, and the ability to serve as a part of a larger computer network.

Users will find their personal computer workstations available with a variety of software. On a network, they will use advanced higher-level languages to retrieve data from massive databanks and analyze it locally themselves. Professional systems analysts will be employed to develop large database and transactions processing applications. They will design multi-user systems, but the individual users will probably be expected to extract and format their own reports if they wish to access the data from these systems.

*More applications will display "Artificial Intelligence."*

Artificial Intelligence (AI) refers to computer systems that exhibit some of the characteristics of human information processors. Early AI programs simulated human behavior, learned how to improve their ability to play games such as checkers, and helped diagnose medical problems.

Some of the systems attempt to store the knowledge of experts in a field and then apply it to solving a problem. Several medical diagnostic systems work in this fashion. The systems feature a knowledge base of facts and their interconnection, and an inference procedure that draws implications or conclusions after processing input to the system. There will be many more business expert systems.

Another area that employs AI techniques in *robotics*. Today, intelligent machines are performing tasks sometimes beyond the capabilities of humans. One refined robot assembles a critical, fragile part on the electron beam of a CRT. Humans frequently break the part, but the robot does not.

AI techniques are also used extensively in the speech recognition and generation systems described above. AI is moving from the laboratory into practical and useful applications. The need for decision support and diagnostic systems to aid management offers exciting opportunities for the use of AI in information systems.

## APPLICATIONS

*The number and scope of computer applications will continue to increase dramatically.*

It is difficult to predict what types of applications will be developed in the future, since they are governed by the needs of individual organizations. The technology is increasingly making various cost effective applications that might not have been considered in the past. In particular, we expect to see increasing use of systems that require large amounts of data to be available on-line. Reduced storage costs, communications costs, and more easily developed on-line systems suggest this trend.

*Computer systems will be applied to nontraditional situations such as office processing.*

The stimulus for the application of computers to office procedures comes from the relatively low investment in capital for an office worker, combined with the large percentage of the work force involved in information processing activities. It has been estimated that the average capital equipment investment for a U.S. factory worker is $25 to $50 thousand, and that the average investment for an office worker is about $2 to $3 thousand. A U.S. government study estimated that over half the work force actually processed information, rather than provided a service or a product. To improve productivity in the economy, additional capital equipment will have to be provided for the office worker, much of which will be computer-based.

Generally an office automation system includes some type of electronic mail, text editing and word processing, a calendar and/or reminder system, and some type of electronic filing of messages.

Text editing and word processing facilities improve the speed and quality with which documents can be prepared. The document is entered into a computer system using special commands that will later direct a program to format the document and print it. Changes can be made to parts of a document without having to retype the entire piece.

A calendar system helps individuals schedule appointments. A user can ask what the first hour is at which it is possible to have a meeting with a group of other individuals. As long as all participants make use of the electronic calendar, the system responds with free times for all to attend the meeting.

A reminder system operates in conjunction with an electronic mail system. The reminder system allows an individual to define a reminder (a message) to be sent at some time in the future.

One common feature of all these applications is that instead of processing data, the computer is working with text. Since the machine is not expected to understand the contents of the messages or the documents, a different type of processing and language is used for text editing and text processing than for numerical computation.

Office automation is also sometimes defined to include teleconferencing or electronic meetings. In one system, a group of individuals meets in a studio with communications equipment. The simplest machine is a type of "electronic blackboard" in which data written on a blackboard in one location appear on a television screen at a remote location. Such a system can be supplemented with video images through the use of closed circuit television. Generally, it is recommended that the individuals involved in this kind of communications process meet beforehand. The greatest success has been reported where the people all know each other reasonably well before an electronic conference is undertaken.

The purpose of this application of technology is to reduce costs and to improve communications. If travel can be reduced or eliminated through electronic means, then large savings are possible.

## THE ELECTRONIC FIRM

This preview of the future can best be summarized by thinking of an electronic firm. We expect to see the organization connected to a variety of computer networks. The most obvious nets will exist within the company, itself. These networks will connect various work groups and different geographic sites; they will be used to share data and to support office automation, particularly electronic mail.

The firm will also be connected to networks of suppliers; it will place orders directly with suppliers electronically. The supplier will send the goods and bill for them electronically. In a similar manner, after proper review, the firm will pay suppliers through electronic funds transfers; there will be no need for any paper except shipping instructions dispatched with the actual goods.

The firm will also be connected to its customers so that they can place orders in the same manner as described above. Individuals within the firm will use various networks. For example, they will connect to a database service, extract data on marketing studies, and then disconnect from the network to analyze the data locally.

In this environment, all managers will be expected to be familiar with computer technology. The purpose of this text has been to provide such familiarity, to make the reader comfortable with the technology—from hands-on personal use of a microcomputer, to systems analysis and design, to the management and control of information processing in the organization.

The future of computing rests on the efforts of individuals. If the organization and its managers are able to manage information processing effectively, then it can make a major contribution to the organization and society. The greatest impediment to the further application of computers is not the technology; it is our ability to apply and manage the technology.

## KEY WORDS

| | | |
|---|---|---|
| Alienation | Laser | Telecommunication |
| Calendar systems | Legislation | Teleconferencing |
| Control | Maintenance | Test editing |
| Decision support | Misuse of information | Transactions processing |
| Electronic mail | Ombudsman | Unstructured |
| Employment | Personal computers | Very large scale inte- |
| Fraud | Power | gration (VLSI) |
| Graphics | Privacy | Voice I/O |
| Harassment | Social impact | Word processing |
| Home services | Structured | |

## RECOMMENDED READINGS

Gilchrist, B., and A. Shenkin: "The Impact of Scanners on Employment in Supermarkets," *Communications of the ACM*, vol. 25, no. 7, 1982, pp. 441–445. (What do you think of their analysis?)

Office of Technology Assessment: "The Impact of Emerging New Computer Technologies on Public Policy," 1981. (A comprehensive survey of information processing and the policy issues it raises.)

Weil, U.: *Information Systems in the 80's,* Prentice-Hall, Englewood Cliffs, N.J., 1982. (A forecast of the future and its impact.)

## DISCUSSION QUESTIONS

1 Why is the use of a system the responsibility of the systems design team and the organization?

2 Is there any such thing as a right to privacy?

3 Does the presence of computer equipment make it easier to violate an individual's privacy?

4 Is fraud easier with a computer system than with its manual predecessor?

5 What would your response be to a proposal for a national data bank of information on citizens for purposes of social science research?

6 What kind of home computer applications would you envision that would use a television- or telephone-type terminal in private residences?

7 It has been suggested that an electronic funds transfer system could eliminate "float," that is, the use of money by a purchaser who has not yet been billed for goods or services. Would the elimination of float be desirable? How would an electronic funds transfer system affect the public?

8 In your opinion, would it be possible for a group to utilize computers to rig a nationwide election?

9 Why has computer-aided education been less successful than originally envisioned? What types of educational activities can best make use of this type of computer system? Where might computer-aided instruction be used in the design of information systems?

10 Do computers make it easier to violate an individual's right to privacy? What are the dangers of centralized government records on each citizen? What are the advantages?

11 Do employers have a responsibility to retrain workers who might be replaced by a computer system?

12 Why is the public so badly informed about the capabilities of computer systems? Do you feel most problems seen by the public are the responsibility of the computer, the manual procedures associated with the system, or the original systems design?

13 What can be done to reduce the possibility of a computer-based fraud that would cause the failure of a business?

14 How could computers and communications be used to solve some of the pressing problems of society, such as reducing the amount of energy consumed?

15 What priorities should be used by underdeveloped countries in trying to develop computer capabilities?

16 Is it possible that computer systems will become so pervasive that an elite of computer specialists will acquire dangerous amounts of power? What factors reduce the possibility of such a power shift?

17 What are the reasons for developing transaction-processing and operational-control information systems?

18 During what economic conditions would you expect the emphasis on transactions processing, as opposed to strategic planning systems, to be greatest?

19 Can strategic planning systems ever be shown to save money?

20 Why are unstructured systems risky? Under what conditions should they be developed?

21 How can an organization decide between centralized and distributed processing?

22 What management and control problems are created by distributed processing?

23 What advances in computer technology are needed to facilitate decision support systems and the development of unstructured applications?

24 Does the design of human-machine systems require a different approach than the design of transactions processing systems?

25 Why do scientists constantly try to reduce the size of computer components?

26 Why would the development of an erasable optical memory be advantageous?

27 What can be done to alleviate the labor-intensive nature of programming?

28 How can the organization identify what applications requests are best handled by users themselves?

29 What do you think the advantages of electronic mail are?

30 Can you think of problems with text editing and word processing applications? (Hint: consider the input process.)

31 Why might individuals resist the use of a calendar system?

32 What forms of resistance would you expect to see to office automation in general?

33 Why is input/output such a bottleneck in a computer system?

34 What are the implications of having greater computer power and lower costs?

35 Why is software apparently not subject to technological breakthroughs?

# GLOSSARY

**Access time**   The time required to retrieve data from secondary storage and move it to primary memory.

**Address**   The location of a character or word in computer memory. Also the location of a track or record on a random-access device.

**Algorithm**   An effective procedure for accomplishing some task. A set of repetitive steps that, when followed, terminates in a solution.

**Application package**   A program or series of programs intended for use by more than one group of users.

**Application program**   A set of instructions that embody the logic of an application. It should be distinguished from a supervisory program, which controls the operations of the computer.

**Arithmetic/logic unit**   The portion of the central processing unit that performs computations.

**Arithmetic registers**   CPU registers that actually perform arithmetic operations on data.

**ASCII**   American Standard Code for Information Interchange; a seven-bit code used frequently for asynchronous (character by character) communications.

**Assembler**   A translator that accepts assembly language as input and produces machine language as output.

**Assembly language**   A language that closely resembles machine language, although mnemonics are substituted for numeric codes in instructions and addresses. Generally, one machine-language statement is produced for each assembly-language statement during the translation process.

**Asynchronous operation**   Any operation that occurs out of phase with other operations. For example, in certain CPU's an instruction look-ahead feature, which fetches instructions before they are needed, operates asynchronously with regular instruction processing.

**Audio response**   Vocal output produced by a special device that contains prerecorded syllables or synthesizes speech.

**Audit trail**   A means for tracing data on a source document to an output such as a report, or for tracing an output to its source.

**Background program**   In a multiprogramming environment, a program that can be executed whenever the computer is not executing a program having higher priority. Contrast with foreground program.

**Backup**   Alternative procedures available for temporary or emergency use in case of system failure.

**Bandwidth**   The range of frequencies for signaling; the difference between the highest and lowest frequencies available on a channel.

**Batch computer system**   A computer system characterized by indeterminant turnaround time for output. Data and programs are collected into groups, or batches, and processed sequentially.

**Baud**   A measure of communications speed; the number of times the signal changes, which is roughly comparable to bits per second.

**Bench mark**   An existing "typical" program that is executed on a machine to evaluate machine performance.

**Bit**   A binary digit, either zero or one; the smallest unit of information storage.

**Block mode**   Synchronous transmission in which characters are sent as a block with beginning and ending delimiters.

**Blocking factor**   The number of logical records per physical record on a storage device.

**Bubble memory**   Storage constructed of tiny cylinder-shaped magnetic domains in a thin, crystalline film.

**Buffer**   An area of memory used for the temporary storage of data.

**Bus**   A path used to carry signals such as a connection between memory and the CPU in a microprocessor.

**Byte**   Generally, an eight-bit grouping that represents one character or two digits, and is operated on as a unit.

**Cache**   A small, high-speed computer memory.

**Channel**   A computer component with logic capabilities that transfers input and output from main memory to secondary memory or peripherals, and vice versa.

**Character mode**   Transmission that is serial, a character at a time.

**Check bit**   A word or a fixed-length group of characters to detect errors.

**Check digit**   A number added to a key as a result of some calculation on the key. When data are entered, the computation is performed again and compared with the check digit to ensure correct entry.

**Chip**   A small electronic device, usually made of silicon, containing a large number of electrical circuits or memory cells.

**Cognitive style**   The orientation of an individual to approach decisions in a particular way, e.g., from an analytic or heuristic view.

**Compatibility**   The extent to which one can use programs, data, and/or devices of one computer system on another without modification.

**Compiler**   A translator for high-level languages. Generally, several machine-language statements are generated for each high-level language statement.

**Computer-Aided Instruction (CAI)**   The use of an interactive computer to provide or supplement instruction on some topic.

**Concentrator**   A device with some local storage that accepts data from several low-speed lines and transmits it over a single high-speed line to a computer installation.

**Control of computer systems** Techniques to ensure the integrity and accuracy of computer processing.

**Control unit** A device that serves as an interface between channel commands and secondary storage or peripheral devices.

**Core storage** A medium of computer storage; for most second- and third-generation computers, the term is used synonymously with "primary memory."

**CPU (central processing unit)** The part of the computer that controls the interpretation and execution of instructions, the arithmetic functions, and the I/O channels; the CPU contains a number of registers.

**Critical path method (CPM)** A project scheduling and control technique focusing on the activities that contribute to the total elapsed time to completion of a project.

**CRT (cathode-ray tube)** A terminal resembling an ordinary television set that can display a large number of characters rapidly; many also have graphics capabilities.

**Cycle time** Either the time required to access information from primary storage and bring it to the CPU, or the time required to fetch, decode, and execute an instruction within the CPU itself.

**Database** A comprehensive, integrated collection of data organized to avoid duplication of data and permit easy retrieval of information.

**Database management system** Software that organizes, catalogs, stores, retrieves, and maintains data in a database.

**Data definition language** The language used with a database management system to describe the relationship among data elements.

**Data dictionary** A component of a database management system that contains names of data elements and information about them.

**Data structures** The relationship among different fields of data on secondary storage.

**Database administrator** The individual in the organization with the responsibility for the design and control of databases.

**Debugging** The task of finding and correcting mistakes in a program.

**Decision support system** A system designed to support decision makers; generally involving interactive computing and focused on one particular business problem.

**Dedicated package** A software package designed for a specific task, such as accounts receivable or payroll.

**Demodulation** The process of decoding the information from a modulated carrier wave; the reverse of modulation.

**Directory** A dictionary or an algorithm for obtaining the address of logical records on a storage device.

**Disk** A random-access magnetic device used for secondary storage in computer systems.

**Diskette** A direct-access storage medium that is flexible; read/write heads of the drive actually touch the surface of the diskette.

**Distributed processing** The dispersion and use of computers among geographically separated locations; the computers are connected by a communication network.

**Documentation** Written descriptions about a system usually with instructions on how to operate the system.

**Duplex** Data transmission in both directions simultaneously using two separate paths.

**EBCDIC** Extended binary coded decimal interchange code; an eight-bit code used by one computer manufacturer to represent characters.

**EAM (electronic accounting machine) equipment** The first devices used to manipulate punched cards. These devices had wired logic plugboards but no stored programs.

**Electronic mail** A system in which computer users have an electronic mailbox and send messages using terminals; communications occur at the convenience of the user without interruptions.

**Emulation** A technique that uses both hardware and software to execute programs written for one computer on another.

**Encryption** The coding of a data stream to prevent unauthorized access to the data.

**End-user programming** The growing trend for users of information to employ very high-level languages and other tools to access information without having a computer professional develop a program for them.

**Enhancements** The process of making changes and improvements in operations programs.

**Execute cycle** The CPU interprets an instruction and carries out the operation it signifies.

**Executive program** The control program that schedules and manages the computer's resources.

**Fetch cycle** Retrieving data or instructions from memory and moving them to the CPU.

**Field** A group of bit positions within an instruction. A subdivision of a record, consisting of a group of characters.

**Firmware** A combination of software and microprogrammed hardware used to control the operations of a particular computer.

**Fixed-length record** A record in which the length and position of each field in the record is fixed for all processing.

**Fixed point** The representation of numbers as integers with no digits to the right of the decimal point.

**Floating point** The representation of a number as a quantity times a base raised to a power; for example, the number 472 as 4.72 times $10^2$.

**Floppy** See diskette.

**Foreground program** The highest priority program in a multiprogramming environment.

**Fourth-generation language** A very high-level language that produces a number of high-level language statements for every statement in the fourth-generation language.

**Generator** A system for use by analysts and programmers to generate an application. The user works at a high level and the system produces code to execute the application.

**Graphics** Output involving figures, graphs, drawings and/or animation.

**Hardware** The physical components of the computer system.

**Hash coding** The use of a mathematical calculation on a key to generate a storage address for a direct-access file.

**Heuristic programs** Programs that are not guaranteed to arrive at an optimal or even acceptable solution; nonalgorithmic coding.

**Higher-higher level languages** User-oriented languages that have single commands that would require many lines of code in a compiler-level language.

**High-level language** A language closer to English than assembler language that, when translated, produces many machine-language instructions for each input statement.

**Identifiers** The mnemonic symbols assigned to variables in a program.

**Index** Some type of table to relate keys to addresses on a direct-access file.

**Index registers** Computer registers used to hold data for address modification, subroutine linkage, etc.

**Indicator** A piece of data used as a summary statistic, e.g., the GNP as a measure of economic activity.

**Indirect address**  An address (formed by the contents of a particular storage location) that points to another storage location, which may contain either a direct address or another indirect address.

**Information**  The interpretation of data to provide meaning by an individual; a tangible or intangible entity that reduces uncertainty about a state or event.

**Inquiry-and-post system**  A system in which inquiries are made, and data are entered and posted to a file for later updating.

**Inquiry system**  A computer system in which inquiries are processed, but updating is done in batch mode.

**Intelligent devices**  The addition of logic to a device or product, usually through the incorporation of a microcomputer.

**Interface**  The boundary between two entities that interact.

**Interpreter**  A hardware or software program that examines an instruction and executes it.

**Interrecord gap**  The physical gap that separates records on a secondary storage device.

**Interrupt**  A signal that causes the current program in the CPU to terminate execution. Depending on the nature of the interrupt, a different program may be loaded and executed.

**Instruction location counter**  A register in the CPU that points to the next instruction to be fetched for execution.

**Instruction register**  A CPU register that holds the instruction, decodes it, and then executes it.

**Instruction set**  The repertoire of instructions available on a computer.

**Iteration**  A single cycle of a repetitively executed series of steps.

**Kernel**  A series of programmed instructions that are timed from published timings and used to evaluate the performance of a specific computer or system.

**Key**  The part of a record that is used for identification and reference; for example, an employee number.

**Latency**  The time required for a mechanical storage device to begin transmitting data after a request. For a movable-head disk drive, the seek time to position the read/write heads plus the rotational delay time.

**List**  A group of logically related items that are stored with pointers to the next item on the list. Also, a series of pointers running through a storage file.

**Loader**  A program that places a translated computer program in primary memory before its execution.

**Local area network (LAN)**  A communications network connecting devices in a local area, such as one floor of a building. Used for communications and to share common devices like a printer.

**Logical record**  A collection or an association of fields on the basis of their relationship to each other.

**Machine language**  The actual string of digits the computer hardware interprets and executes.

**Magnetic core**  A small piece of magnetic material that can be used to represent a zero and a one.

**Magnetic tape unit**  A sequential storage medium that operates like a home tape recorder.

**Mainframe**  A large computer system used for multiple purposes such as batch processing, on-line applications, and time sharing.

**Maintenance**  The process of modifying operational programs to fix errors.

**Managerial-control decisions** Decisions primarily concerned with personnel and financial control; concerned with ensuring that resources are applied to achieving the goals of the organization.

**Megahertz** A measure of transmission frequencies; megacycle or millions of cycles per second.

**MICR (magnetic-ink-character recognition)** The machine reading of characters printed in magnetic ink; primarily used in check processing.

**Microcomputer** A small computer often for a single user or a small number of simultaneous users. Developed from advances in chip fabrication such that only a few chips are needed to produce an entire computer.

**Microprogramming** The combining of series of elementary hardware functions (invisible to the programmer) to make a single instruction.

**Minicomputer** A computer between the micro and mainframe; often used for a dedicated on-line application or for general time sharing.

**Mixes** The weighting of a representative series of instructions for the purpose of evaluating machine performance.

**Mnemonics** The alphabetic symbols that are used in place of numeric codes to facilitate the recognition and use of computer instructions.

**Model** A tangible or intangible representation of some physical event, entity, or process.

**MODEM (modulate and demodulate)** A device that converts digital computer signals into analog form and modulates them for transmission. Demodulation is the reverse process that occurs at the receiving point.

**Modular programming** The subdivision of a system and of programming requirements into small building blocks to reduce programming complexity and take advantage of common routines.

**Modulation** The coding of a digital signal onto an analog one, for example, by changing the amplitude of the carrier signal to represent a 0 or a 1.

**Monitor** The control program that schedules and manages the computer's resources.

**Multiplexing** The combination of several low-speed signals onto a higher speed line for communications.

**Multiplexor** A device that combines signals received from a series of low-speed lines and transmits them over a high-speed line. No storage is provided and signals must be demultiplexed on the receiving end.

**Multiprocessing** A technique for executing two or more instruction sequences simultaneously in one computer system by the use of more than one processing unit.

**Nonprogrammed decisions** Decisions that are unstructured and for which an algorithm for solution cannot be specified.

**Multiprogramming** The presence of more than one semiactive program in primary memory at the same time; by switching from program to program, the computer appears to be executing all concurrently.

**Network** A combination of communications lines tying various locations together.

**Nonprocedural** Languages in which the user tells the computer what to do, rather than exactly how to do the task. Statements are more declarative of what is to happen, than specific on the procedure to produce the desired results.

**Object language** The output of a translator, usually machine language.

**OCR (optical-character recognition)** The machine recognition of certain type styles and/or printed and handwritten characters.

**Office automation** The use of technology like word processing, electronic mail, and similar systems to improve the productivity of knowledge workers.

**Off-line** Any operation that is not directly controlled by the CPU.

**On-line system** A system that has the capability to provide direct communication between the computer and remote terminals; files are updated immediately as data are entered.

**On-line updating** Pertaining to a system in which the data entered are used to update the files immediately.

**Operating system** A control program that schedules and manages the computer's resources.

**Operational-control decisions** Day-to-day decisions concerned with the continuing operations of a company, such as inventory management.

**Overlap** The ability of the CPU to continue processing while input/output operations are underway.

**Package program** A program written for a user by multiple groups or organizations.

**Packet switched** In communications, the structuring of characters into equal-sized packets, which are sent with routing information over a network.

**Paging** The segmentation of storage into small units that are moved automatically, by hardware or software, between primary and secondary storage to give the programmer a virtual memory that is larger than primary memory.

**Parallel test** The test of a new system at the same time an existing system is in operation. The results from both systems are compared.

**Parse** The separation of an input string of symbols into its basic components.

**Peripherals** Input/output devices connected to a computer system.

**Personal computer** See microcomputer.

**Physical record** One or more logical records read into or written from main storage as a unit.

**Pointer** Data that indicate the location of a variable or record of interest.

**Power** The ability to influence behavior.

**Primary memory** The memory in which programs and data are stored and from which they are generally executed; main storage.

**Problem program** A user-written program that uses only nonprivileged instructions. It should be distinguished from a supervisory, or control, program, which may have privileged instructions.

**Problem-oriented language** A language specifically designed for one particular type of problem, such as civil-engineering computations.

**Procedural language** A language designed to facilitate the coding of algorithms to solve a problem, e.g., PL/1.

**Program** A set of instructions that directs the computer to perform a specific series of operations.

**Programmed decisions** Generally, decisions that can be made automatically by following certain rules and procedures.

**Protection** The maintenance of the integrity of information in storage by preventing unauthorized changes.

**Protocol** The set of rules or procedures for devices to communicate with each other.

**Prototype** A model of a system or a version without all the final features desired; used to provide early feedback to users.

**Pure procedure** A program in which no part of the code modifies itself. Because a reentrant program is not modified during execution, it can be used by many users.

**Query language** A language used to provide access to data stored in a database or file.

**Random Access Memory (RAM)** Memory that can be read or written under program control.

**Random access** The ability to retrieve records without serially searching a file.

**Read Only Memory (ROM)** Memory that cannot be written under program control; used to store microinstructions.

**Reasonableness checks** General range checks on data to be sure that values are within reason.

**Record, logical** A collection of related data items.

**Record, physical** One or more logical records combined to increase input/output speeds and to reduce space required for storage.

**Reentrant program** Synonymous with *pure procedure*.

**Refreshing** The regeneration of an image on a cathode-ray tube. Certain storage-tube devices eliminate the need for refreshing.

**Registers** In general, storage locations capable of holding data. In particular, index registers that can be used to modify instruction addresses, or arithmetic registers that perform calculations.

**Remote batch system** A type of computer system in which batch jobs are entered into the computer from a remote location, and the output returned to that location.

**Report generator** A program that reads information concerning items to be retrieved from a file and their required output format, processes the file to retrieve the desired records, and produces a report according to the specified format.

**Response time** The time from submission of a request until the computer responds.

**Rotational delay** On rotating secondary memory devices, the time required for a particular record to arrive under the read/write head.

**Report Program Generator (RPG)** A class of languages used to quickly prepare programs to print reports from a set of files. Can also be used to program complete applications.

**Satellite communications** The use of orbiting satellites to receive, amplify, and retransmit data to earth stations.

**Scratch file** A file on which data are stored temporarily and which is not saved.

**Secondary memory** Random-access devices such as disks and drums; programs are not executed from secondary memory devices but must be loaded into primary memory.

**Seek time** For movable-arm disks, the time required for the reading mechanism to position itself over the track desired.

**Semantics** The meaning of a programming language statement, or groups of statements.

**Semiconductor** A small component having an electrical conductivity that lies between the high conductivity of metals and the low conductivity of insulators.

**Semiconductor memory** Memory consisting of transistor devices; generally faster than core storage.

**Serial access** A sequentially organized file from which information can be retrieved only by processing through the file in order.

**Simplex** Data transmission in one direction at a time.

**Simulation** The modeling of some process that often involves the use of a computer program and probability distributions.

**Simulator** A software program that is used to execute programs written for one machine on another.

**Software** Instructions that control the physical hardware of the computer system.

**Source language** The input language to a translation process.

**Spooling** The simultaneous operation of peripherals using a disk to store output and/or input for multiple programs at the same time.

**Storage address register**  A register that holds the address of a memory location being referenced by the CPU or channel.

**Storage buffer register**  A register that holds data to be moved to or from main memory.

**Strategic-planning decisions**  Decisions of a long-term nature that deal with setting the strategy and objectives of the firm.

**Structured design**  An approach to design that attempts to provide discipline for the designers and to clarify the design itself.

**Structured programming**  A modular approach to program development that emphasizes stepwise refinement, simple control structures, and short one-entry-point/one-exit-point modules.

**Supercomputer**  Very large and fast computers designed for scientific computations.

**Supermini**  Minicomputers that are very fast and that overlap with small mainframe computers.

**Supervisor**  The control program that schedules and manages the computer's resources.

**Synchronous**  Events that are coordinated and controlled.

**Syntax**  The physical structure of a programming language or statement.

**Synthetic program**  A specially constructed program (but one that is not used for production) that is used to measure and evaluate the performance of a computer system.

**Systems programmer**  A programmer who works on the software associated with an operating or supervisory system.

**Telecommunications**  The transmission of signals over a long distance, either through private or public carriers.

**Terminals**  A device used to communicate with a central computer from a remote location, usually featuring a typewriterlike keyboard.

**Throughput**  The amount of processing done by a system in a given unit of time.

**Time sharing**  An on-line system that provides computer services (including computational capacity) to a number of users at geographically dispersed terminals.

**Top-down design**  Planning a system by looking first at the major function, then at its subfunctions, and so on, until the scope and details of the system are fully understood.

**Trade-off**  The pros and cons of different alternatives; one often is forced to trade cost savings for performance.

**Transaction**  A basic communication with a computer system, e.g., the receipt of cash from a customer.

**Transactions-processing systems**  Basic systems that process routine transactions in an organization, such as the entry of customer orders.

**Translator**  A program that accepts a source language and produces an output, or target, language that differs in some respects from the source language.

**Turnaround document**  A computer-prepared document, usually a punched card or printed report, that is sent to a customer. When returned to the sender, the document can frequently be reentered into the computer without modification.

**Turnaround time**  The length of time elapsing between the submission of input and the receipt of the output.

**Turnkey system**  A complete computer system with customer software installed for customer use.

**Unbundling**  The separation of prices for computer services and hardware.

**Uncertainty**  Lack of knowledge about a state or event.

**Variable-length records**  A record in which the number and/or length of fields may vary from other records accessed by the same program.

**Virtual machine**   The computer system as it appears to the user. The term was first used to refer to the extension of main memory to almost infinite capacity by the automatic use of secondary storage. The operating system automatically moves portions of a program that are too large for primary memory to and from secondary memory.

**Virtual memory**   Addressable space beyond physical memory that appears to the user as real; it is provided through a combination of hardware and software techniques.

**Very Large Scale Integration (VLSI)**   The production of computer chips with hundreds of thousands of components on each chip.

**Word**   A combination of bits that form a logical storage grouping. A word may be further subdivided into bytes, which can be addressed by instructions.

# BIBLIOGRAPHY

Aaron, J. D.: "Information Systems in Perspective," *Computing Surveys,* vol. 1, no. 4, December 1969, pp. 213–236.

ACM Committee on Computers and Public Policy: "A Problem List of Issues Concerning Computers and Public Policy," *Communications of the ACM,* vol. 17, no. 9, September 1974, pp. 495–503.

Ackoff, R. L.: "Management Misinformation Systems," *Management Science,* vol. 14, no. 4, December 1967, pp. B140–B156.

Allen, F. W., M. E. S. Loomis, and M. V. Manning: "The Integrated Dictionary/ Directory System," *Computing Surveys,* vol. 14, no. 2, June 1982, pp. 245–286.

Alter, S.: *Decision Support Systems: Current Practice and Continuing Challenges,* Addison-Wesley, Reading, Mass., 1980.

Anthony, R.: *Planning and Control Systems: A Framework for Analysis,* Division of Research, Graduate School and Business Administration, Harvard University, Boston, 1965.

Baker, F. T.: "Chief Programmer Team Management of Production Programming," *IBM Systems Journal,* vol. 11, no. 1, 1972, pp. 63–73.

Bartee, T. C.: *Digital Computer Fundamentals,* 4th ed., McGraw-Hill, New York, 1977.

Bauer, R. (ed.): *Social Indicators,* MIT, Cambridge, Mass., 1967.

Bell, W. J. et al.: "Improving the Distribution of Industrial Gases with On-line Computerized Routing and Scheduling Optimizer." *Interfaces,* vol. 13, no. 6, December 1983, pp. 4–23.

Blumenthal, S.: *MIS—A Framework for Planning and Development,* Prentice-Hall, Englewood Cliffs, N.J., 1969.

Bohl, M.: *Information Processing,* 4th ed., Palo Alto, SRA, 1984.

Boulden, J., and E. Buffa: "Corporate Models: On-Line, Realtime Systems," *Harvard Business Review,* vol. 48, no. 4, July–August 1970, pp. 65–83.

Burch, J. G., and J. L. Sardinas, Jr.: *Computer Control and Audit Systems,* Wiley, New York, 1978.

―――, F. Strater, and G. Grudnitski: *Information Systems Theory and Practice,* 3d ed, Wiley, New York, 1983.

Buffa, E. S.: *Modern Production Management,* Wiley, New York, 1961.

Canning, R.: "The Analysis of User Needs," *EDP Analyzer,* vol. 17, no. 1, January 1979.

Chapin, N.: "Flowcharting with the ANSI Standard: A Tutorial," *Computing Surveys,* vol. 2, no. 2, June 1970, pp. 89–110.

Cardenas, A., L. Presser, and M. Marin (eds.), *Computer Science,* Wiley-Interscience, New York, 1972.

Carroll, J. M.: *Computer Security,* Security World, Los Angeles, 1977.

Couger, J. D.: "Evaluation of Business Systems Analysis Techniques," *Computing Surveys,* vol. 6, no. 3, September 1973, pp. 167–198.

―――, and R. W. Knapp: *Systems Analysis Techniques,* New York, Wiley, 1979.

Crawford, A. B.: "Corporate Electronic Mail—A Communication-Intensive Application of Information Technology," *MIS Quarterly,* vol. 16, no. 3, September 1982, pp. 1–13.

Davis, G. B., and M. Olson: *Management Information Systems: Conceptual Foundations, Structure, and Development,* 2d ed., McGraw-Hill, New York, 1984.

Dearborn, O., and H. Simon: "Selective Perception: A Note on the Departmental Identification of Executives," *Sociometry,* vol. 21, 1958, pp. 140–144.

Dearden, S.: "MIS is a Mirage," *Harvard Business Review,* January–February 1972, pp. 90–99.

De Marco, T.: *Structured Analysis and System Specification,* Prentice-Hall, Englewood Cliffs, N.J., 1979.

Dodd, G.: "Elements of Data Management Systems," *Computing Surveys,* vol. 1, no. 7, June 1969, pp. 117–133.

Doktor, R., and W. Hamilton: "Cognitive Style and the Acceptance of Management Science Recommendations," *Management Science,* vol. 19, no. 8, April 1973, pp. 884–894.

Doyle, J. R., and J. D. Becker: "Computer Assisted Planning (CAP) at Dinero International Ban Corporation." *MIS Quarterly,* September 1983, pp. 33–46.

Edelson, B. I.: "Global Satellite Communication," *Scientific American,* February 1977, vol. 22, no. 8, pp. 58–74.

Emery, J.: "Cost/Benefit Analysis of Information Systems," in J. D. Couger and R. W. Knapp (eds.), *Systems Analysis Techniques,* Wiley, New York, 1974.

Feigenbaum, E., and P. McCorduck: *The Fifth Generation,* Addison-Wesley, Reading, Mass., 1983.

Gane, C., and T. Sarson: *Structured Systems Analysis Tools and Technique,* Prentice-Hall, Englewood Cliffs, N.J., 1979.

Gerrity, T. P.: "Design of Man-Machine Decision Systems: An Application to Portfolio Management," *Sloan Management Review,* vol. 12, no. 2, winter 1971, pp. 59–75.

Gilchrist, B., and A. Shenkin: "The Impact of Scanners on Employment in Supermarkets," *Communications of the ACM,* vol. 25, no. 7, 1982, pp. 441–445.

Goldstein, R. G.: "The Costs of Privacy," *Datamation,* October 1975, pp. 65–69.

Gorry, G. A., and M. S. Scott Morton: "A Framework for Management Information Systems," *Sloan Management Review,* vol. 13, no. 1, 1971, pp. 55–70.

Gries, D.: *Compiler Construction for Digital Computers,* Wiley, New York, 1971.

Hawryszkiewycz, I. T.: *Database Analysis and Design,* SRA, Chicago, 1984.

Hellerman, H.: *Digital Computer System Principles,* McGraw-Hill, New York, 1967.

Hennings, C. R., D. J. Hickson, J. M. Pennings, and R. E. Schneck: "Structural Conditions of Intraorganizational Power," *Administrative Science Quarterly,* vol. 19, no. 1, March 1974, pp. 22–44.

Hickson, P. J., C. R. Hennings, C. A. Lee, R. R. Schneck, and J. M. Pennings: "Strategic Contingencies Theory of Interorganizational Power," *Administrative Science Quarterly,* vol. 16, no. 2, June 1971, pp. 216–219.

Hodges, D.: "Microelectronic Memories," *Scientific American,* vol. 237, no. 3, September 1977, pp. 130–145.

Hoffman, L.: "Computers and Privacy: A Survey," *Computing Surveys,* vol. 1, no. 2, June 1969, pp. 85–104.

Housley, T.: *Data Communications and Teleprocessing Systems,* Prentice-Hall, Englewood Cliffs, N.J., 1979.

Husson, S.: *Microprogramming Principles and Practices,* Prentice-Hall, Englewood Cliffs, N.J., 1970.

IBM: *Improved Technology for Application Development—Management Overview,* IBM Corp., 1973.

Jancura, E.: *Audit and Control of Computer Systems,* Petrocelli/Charter, New York, 1974.

Johnson, R., J. Vallee, and K. Spangler: *Electronic Meetings, Technological Alternatives and Social Choices,* Addison-Wesley, Reading, Mass., 1979.

Kanter, J.: *Management-Oriented Management Information Systems,* Prentice-Hall, Englewood Cliffs, N.J., 1972.

Kantrow, A.: "The Strategy-Technology Connection," *Harvard Business Review,* July–August 1980, pp. 6–21.

Keen, P. W., and M. S. Scott Morton: *Decision Support Systems: An Organizational Perspective,* Addison-Wesley, Reading, Mass., 1978.

Kelly, J. F.: *Computerized Management Information Systems,* Macmillan, New York, 1970.

Kendall, R. C.: "Management Perspectives on Programs, Programming and Productivity," Guide Meeting, 1977.

Leavitt, H. J., and T. L. Whisler: "Management in the 1980's," *Harvard Business Review,* November–December 1958, pp. 41–48.

Lientz, B. P., E. B. Swanson, and G. E. Tompkins: "Characteristics of Application Software Maintenance," *Communications of the ACM,* vol. 21, no. 6, June 19, 1978, pp. 466–471.

Loomis, M.: *Data Communications,* Prentice-Hall, Englewood Cliffs, N.J., 1983.

Lucas, H. C., Jr.: "An Empirical Study of a Framework for Information Systems," *Decision Sciences,* vol. 5, no. 1, January 1974a, pp. 102–113.

———, K. W. Clowes, and R. B. Kaplan: "Frameworks for Information Systems," *Infor,* vol. 12, no. 3, October 1974b, pp. 245–260.

———: *Toward Creative Systems Design,* Columbia, New York, 1974c.

———: *Why Information Systems Fail,* Columbia, New York, 1975.

———: *The Implementation of Computer-Based Models,* National Association of Accountants, New York, 1976a.

———: *The Analysis, Design, and Implementation of Information Systems,* 3d ed., McGraw-Hill, New York, 1985.

———, and J. R. Moore, Jr.: "A Multiple-Criterion Scoring Approach to Information System Project Selection," *Infor,* vol. 14, no. 1, February 1976c, pp. 1–12.

————, and J. Turner: "A Top Management Policy for Information Systems," *Sloan Management Review*, Spring 1982, pp. 25–36.

————: *Implementation: The Key to Successful Information Systems*, Columbia, New York, 1981.

McFarlan, F. W.: "Management Audit of the EDP Department," *Harvard Business Review*, vol. 51, no. 3, May–June, 1973, pp. 131–142.

Madnick, S., and J. Donovan: *Operating Systems*, McGraw-Hill, New York, 1974.

Mair, W. C., D. W. Wood, and K. W. Davis: *Computer Control & Audit*, Institute of Internal Auditors, Wellesley, Mass., 1978.

Martin, J.: *The Design of Real-Time Systems*, Prentice-Hall, Englewood Cliffs, N.J., 1967.

————: *Telecommunications and The Computer*, Prentice-Hall, Englewood Cliffs, N.J., 1969.

————, and P. Norman: *The Computerized Society*, Prentice-Hall, Englewood Cliffs, N.J., 1970.

————: *Applications Development Without Programmers*, Prentice-Hall, Englewood Cliffs, N.J., 1982.

————, and L. McClure: "Buying Software Off the Rack," *Harvard Business Review*, November–December 1983, pp. 32–60.

Martin, W. A.: "Sorting," *Computing Surveys*, vol. 3, no. 4, December 1971, pp. 147–174.

Mason, R., and I. Mitroff: "A Program for Research in Management Information Systems," *Management Science*, vol. 19, no. 5, January 1973, pp. 475–487.

————, and T. T. Carey: "Prototyping Interactive Information Systems," *Communications of the ACM*, vol. 26, no. 5, May 1983, pp. 347–354.

Masterman, J.: *The Double-Cross System*, Avon, New York, 1972.

McFarlan, W., and J. McKenney: *Corporate Information Systems Management*, Richard Irwin, Homewood, Ill., 1983.

Merten, A. G., and E. H. Sibley: "Implementation of a Generalized Data Base Management System Within an Organization," *Management Informatics*, vol. 2, no. 1, February 1973, pp. 21–31.

Mills, H. D.: "Chief Programmer Team's Principles and Procedures," IBM Federal System Division, Gaithersburg, Md., 1971.

Mintzberg, H.: *The Nature of Managerial Work*, Harper & Row, New York, 1973.

Montgomery, D., and G. Urban: *Management Science in Marketing*, Prentice-Hall, Englewood Cliffs, N.J., 1969.

————: "Marketing Decision Systems: An Emerging View," *Journal of Marketing Research*, vol. 7, May 1970, pp. 226–234.

Moore, J. R., Jr., and N. R. Baker: "Computational Analysis of Scoring Models for Rand D Project Selection," *Management Science*, vol. 16, no. 4, December 1969a, pp. B212–B232.

Mumford, E., and O. Banks: *The Computer and The Clerk*, Routlege, London, 1967.

————, and T. B. Ward: *Computers: Planning for People*, B. T. Batsford, London, 1968.

Murdick, R. G., and J. E. Ross: *Information Systems for Modern Management*, 2d ed., Prentice-Hall, Englewood Cliffs, N.J., 1975.

Naumann, J., and M. Jenkins: "Prototyping: The New Paradigm for Systems Development," *MIS Quarterly*, vol. 6, no. 3, September 1982, pp. 29–44.

Nie, N., C. Hull, J. Jenkins, K. Steinbrenner, and D. H. Bent: *Statistical Package for the Social Sciences*, 2d ed., McGraw-Hill, New York, 1975.

Nolan, R. L.: "Plight of the EDP Manager," *Harvard Business Review,* vol. 51, no. 3, May–June 1973, pp. 143–152.

————: "Managing Information Systems by Committee," *Harvard Business Review,* July–August 1982, pp. 72–79.

Office of Technology Assessment, "The Impact of Emerging New Computer Technologies on Public Policy," 1981.

Olsen, R. A.: *Manufacturing Management: A Quantitative Approach,* International Textbook, Scranton, Pa., 1968.

Osborne, A.: *An Introduction to Microcomputers,* 2d ed., vol. 1, Osborne/McGraw-Hill, Berkeley, Calif., 1980.

Parsons, G: "Information Technology: A New Competitive Weapon," *Sloan Management Review,* (Fall 1983, pp. 3–14.

Pounds, W. F.: "The Process of Problem Finding," *The Industrial Management Review,* vol. 11, no. 1, fall 1969, pp. 1–20.

Rosen, R.: "Contemporary Concepts of Microprogramming and Emulation," *Computing Surveys,* vol. 1, no. 4, December 1969, pp. 197–212.

Sammet, J.: *Programming Languages: History and Fundamentals,* Prentice-Hall, Englewood Cliffs, N.J., 1969.

Sanders, D.: *Computers Today,* McGraw-Hill, New York, 1983.

Senn, J.: *Information Systems in Management,* Wadsworth, Belmont, Calif., 1978.

Schultz, R., and D. Slevin: *Implementing Operations Research/Management Science,* American Elsevier, New York, 1975.

Scott Morton, M. S.: *Management Decision Systems,* Division of Research, Graduate School of Business Administration, Harvard University, 1971.

Simon, H.: *The Shape of Automation for Men and Management,* Harper & Row, New York, 1965.

Sprague, R., and E. Carlson: *Building Effective Decision Support Systems,* Prentice-Hall, Englewood Cliffs, N.J., 1982.

Stallings, W.: "Local Networks." *Computing Surveys,* vol 16, no. 1, March 1984, pp. 3–42.

Stirling, T. D.: "Consumer Difficulties with Computerized Transactions: An Empirical Investigation," *Communications of the ACM,* vol. 22, no. 5, May 1979, pp. 283–289.

Takeuchi, H., and A. H. Schmidt: "New Promise of Computer Graphics," *Harvard Business Review,* vol. 58, no. 1, January–February 1980, pp. 122–131.

Tamir, M. et al.: "DB1: A DBMS-Based Application Generator," *Proceedings of the Very Large Data Base Conference,* Glasgow, Scotland, 1981.

Timmreck, E. M.: "Computer Selection Methodology," *Computing Surveys,* vol. 5, no. 4, December 1973, pp. 199–222.

Turn, R.: *Computers in the 1980s,* Columbia, New York, 1974.

Turner, J.: "Computers in Bank Clerical Functions: Implications for Productivity and the Quality of Working Life," unpublished doctoral dissertation, Columbia University, New York, 1980.

Tzchritzis, D., and F. Lochovsky: *Data Models,* Prentice-Hall, Englewood Cliffs, N.J., 1982.

*Using 1-2-3,* Indianapolis, Que Publishing, 1983.

Walton, R. E., and J. M. Dutton: "The Management of Interdepartmental Conflict: A Model and Review," *Administrative Science Quarterly,* vol. 14, no. 1, March 1969, pp. 73–84.

Weber, R.: *EDP Auditing: Conceptual Foundations and Practice,* McGraw-Hill, New York, 1982.

Weil, U.: *Information Systems in the 80's,* Prentice-Hall, Englewood Cliffs, N.J., 1982.

Weinberg, G. M.: *The Psychology of Computer Programming,* Van Nostrand, New York, 1972a.

Weinberg, G. M.: "The Psychology of Improved Programming Performance," *Datamation,* vol. 18, no. 11, November 1972b, pp. 82–85.

Whisler, T. L.: *Information Technology and Organizational Change,* Wadsworth, Belmont, Calif., 1970.

Wimbrow, J. H.: "A Large-Scale Interactive Administrative System," *IBM Systems Journal,* vol. 10, no. 4, 1971, pp. 260–282.

Zmud, R.: *Information Systems in Organizations,* Scott, Foresman, Glenview, Ill., 1983.

# INDEX

# INDEX